The British Empire and the First World War

The British Empire played a crucial role in the First World War, supplying hundreds of thousands of soldiers and labourers as well as a range of essential resources, from foodstuffs to minerals, mules, and munitions. In turn, many imperial territories were deeply affected by wartime phenomena, such as inflation, food shortages, combat, and the presence of large numbers of foreign troops.

This collection offers a comprehensive selection of essays illuminating the extent of the Empire's war contribution and experience, and the richness of scholarly research on the subject. Whether supporting British military operations, aiding the imperial economy, or experiencing significant wartime effects on the home front, the war had a profound impact on the colonies and their people.

The chapters in this volume were originally published in *African Identities*, *Australian Historical Studies*, *The Journal of Imperial and Commonwealth History*, *First World War Studies* or *The Round Table: The Commonwealth Journal of International Affairs*.

Ashley Jackson is Professor of Imperial and Military History at King's College London, UK, and a Visiting Fellow at Kellogg College, Oxford University, UK. He is the author of numerous books on British imperial history, including *The British Empire and the Second World War* and *The British Empire: A Very Short Introduction*.

The British Empire and the First World War

Edited by
Ashley Jackson

LONDON AND NEW YORK

First published 2016 by Routledge

2 Park Square, Milton Park, Abingdon, Oxon OX14 4RN
711 Third Avenue, New York, NY 10017, USA

Routledge is an imprint of the Taylor & Francis Group, an informa business

First issued in paperback 2017

Chapters 2, 4–7, 11, 13–16, 18, 21, 23–24 © 2016 Taylor & Francis
Chapters 3, 8, 10, 12, 19, 22, 25-26 © 2016 The Round Table Ltd.
Chapters 9, 17, 20 © Editorial Board, Australian Historical Studies

All rights reserved. No part of this book may be reprinted or reproduced or utilised in any form or by any electronic, mechanical, or other means, now known or hereafter invented, including photocopying and recording, or in any information storage or retrieval system, without permission in writing from the publishers.

Notice:
Product or corporate names may be trademarks or registered trademarks, and are used only for identification and explanation without intent to infringe.

British Library Cataloguing in Publication Data
A catalogue record for this book is available from the British Library

ISBN 13: 978-1-138-93219-7 (hbk)
ISBN 13: 978-1-138-29490-5 (pbk)

Typeset in Sabon
by RefineCatch Limited, Bungay, Suffolk

Publisher's Note
The publisher accepts responsibility for any inconsistencies that may have arisen during the conversion of this book from journal articles to book chapters, namely the possible inclusion of journal terminology.

Disclaimer
Every effort has been made to contact copyright holders for their permission to reprint material in this book. The publishers would be grateful to hear from any copyright holder who is not here acknowledged and will undertake to rectify any errors or omissions in future editions of this book.

Contents

Citation Information ix
Notes on Contributors xiii

1. Introduction
   Ashley Jackson and James E. Kitchen 1

2. The First World War as a global war
   Hew Strachan 19

3. Sir Charles Lucas and *The Empire at War*
   Ashley Jackson 31

Part I: War on Imperial Frontiers

4. South Africa and World War I
   N.G. Garson 40

5. Spoils of War: Sub-Imperial Collaboration in South West Africa and New Guinea, 1914–20
   Colin Newbury 56

6. 'Khaki crusaders': crusading rhetoric and the British Imperial soldier during the Egypt and Palestine campaigns, 1916–18
   James E. Kitchen 74

7. From defeat to victory: logistics of the campaign in Mesopotamia, 1914–1918
   Kaushik Roy 94

8. British Understandings of the Sanussiyya Sufi Order's *Jihad* against Egypt, 1915–17
   John Slight 115

9. Marching to the Beat of an Imperial Drum: Contextualising Australia's Military Effort During the First World War
   Rhys Crawley 125

CONTENTS

Part II: Home Fronts

10. Cyprus's Non-military Contribution to the Allied War Effort during World War I — 142
    Antigone Heraclidou

11. African agency and cultural initiatives in the British Imperial military and labor recruitment drives in the Gold Coast (colonial Ghana) during the First World War — 150
    Kwabena O. Akurang-Parry

12. Norman Lindsay and the 'Asianisation' of the German Soldier in Australia during the First World War — 172
    Emily Robertson

13. War Opinion in South Africa, 1914 — 193
    Bill Nasson

14. The War Munitions Supply Company of Western Australia and the Popular Movement to Manufacture Artillery Ammunition in the British Empire in the First World War — 215
    John S. Connor

15. The Expatriate Firms and the Colonial Economy of Nigeria in the First World War — 234
    Peter J. Yearwood

16. The Influence of Racial Attitudes on British Policy Towards India during the First World War — 253
    Gregory Martin

17. William Morris Hughes, Empire and Nationalism: The Legacy of the First World War — 273
    James Cotton

Part III: Soldiers and Fighting Fronts

18. 'You will not be going to this war': the rejected volunteers of the First Contingent of the Canadian Expeditionary Force — 292
    Nic Clarke

19. Dominion Cartoon Satire as Trench Culture Narratives: Complaints, Endurance and Stoicism — 315
    Jane Chapman and Dan Ellin

20. 'Accurate to the Point of Mania': Eyewitness Testimony and Memory Making in Australia's Official Paintings of the First World War — 333
    Margaret Hutchison

21. Informing the enemy: Australian prisoners and German intelligence on the Western Front, 1916–1918 — 351
    Aaron Pegram

CONTENTS

22. The Prisoner Dilemma: Britain, Germany, and the Repatriation of Indian Prisoners of War — 369
    Andrew Tait Jarboe

23. 'All in the Same Uniform'? The Participation of Black Colonial Residents in the British Armed Forces in the First World War — 379
    Jacqueline Jenkinson

24. Australian and New Zealand fathers and sons during the Great War: expanding the histories of families at war — 403
    Kathryn M. Hunter

25. Loss and Longing: Emotional Responses to West Indian Soldiers during the First World War — 419
    Richard Smith

26. Conclusion: The First World War Centenary in the UK: 'A Truly National Commemoration'? — 429
    Andrew Mycock

Index — 441

Citation Information

The following chapters were originally published in *First World War Studies*. When citing this material, please use the original page numbering for each article, as follows:

Chapter 2
The First World War as a global war
Hew Strachan
First World War Studies, volume 1, issue 1 (March 2010) pp. 3–14

Chapter 6
'Khaki crusaders': crusading rhetoric and the British Imperial soldier during the Egypt and Palestine campaigns, 1916–18
James E. Kitchen
First World War Studies, volume 1, issue 2 (October 2010) pp. 141–160

Chapter 7
From defeat to victory: logistics of the campaign in Mesopotamia, 1914–1918
Kaushik Roy
First World War Studies, volume 1, issue 1 (March 2010) pp. 35–55

Chapter 18
'You will not be going to this war': the rejected volunteers of the First Contingent of the Canadian Expeditionary Force
Nic Clarke
First World War Studies, volume 1, issue 2 (October 2010) pp. 161–183

Chapter 21
Informing the enemy: Australian prisoners and German intelligence on the Western Front, 1916–1918
Aaron Pegram
First World War Studies, volume 4, issue 2 (October 2013) pp. 167–184

Chapter 24
Australian and New Zealand fathers and sons during the Great War: expanding the histories of families at war
Kathryn M. Hunter
First World War Studies, volume 4, issue 2 (October 2013) pp. 185–200

CITATION INFORMATION

The following chapter was originally published in *African Identities*. When citing this material, please use the original page numbering for each article, as follows:

Chapter 11
African agency and cultural initiatives in the British Imperial military and labor recruitment drives in the Gold Coast (colonial Ghana) during the First World War
Kwabena O. Akurang-Parry
African Identities, volume 4, issue 2 (October 2006) pp. 213–234

The following chapters were originally published in *The Journal of Imperial and Commonwealth History*. When citing this material, please use the original page numbering for each article, as follows:

Chapter 4
South Africa and World War I
N.G. Garson
The Journal of Imperial and Commonwealth History, volume 8, issue 1 (October 1979) pp. 68–85

Chapter 5
Spoils of war: Sub-imperial collaboration in South West Africa and new Guinea, 1914–20
Colin Newbury
The Journal of Imperial and Commonwealth History, volume 16, issue 3 (May 1988) pp. 86–106

Chapter 13
War Opinion in South Africa, 1914
Bill Nasson
The Journal of Imperial and Commonwealth History, volume 23, issue 2 (May 1995) pp. 248–276

Chapter 14
The War Munitions Supply Company of Western Australia and the Popular Movement to Manufacture Artillery Ammunition in the British Empire in the First World War
John S. Connor
The Journal of Imperial and Commonwealth History, volume 39, issue 5 (December 2011) pp. 795–813

Chapter 15
The Expatriate Firms and the Colonial Economy of Nigeria in the First World War
Peter J. Yearwood
The Journal of Imperial and Commonwealth History, volume 26, issue 1 (January 1998) pp. 49–71

CITATION INFORMATION

Chapter 16
The Influence of Racial Attitudes on British Policy Towards India during the First World War
Gregory Martin
The Journal of Imperial and Commonwealth History, volume 14, issue 2 (May 1986) pp. 91–113

Chapter 23
'All in the Same Uniform'? The Participation of Black Colonial Residents in the British Armed Forces in the First World War
Jacqueline Jenkinson
The Journal of Imperial and Commonwealth History, volume 40, issue 2 (June 2012) pp. 207–230

The following chapters were originally published in *The Round Table*. When citing this material, please use the original page numbering for each article, as follows:

Chapter 3
Sir Charles Lucas and The Empire at War
Ashley Jackson
The Round Table, volume 103, issue 2 (March 2014) pp. 165–173

Chapter 8
British Understandings of the Sanussiyya Sufi Order's Jihad against Egypt
John Slight
The Round Table, volume 103, issue 2 (March 2014) pp. 233–242

Chapter 10
Cyprus's Non-military Contribution to the Allied War Effort during World War I
Antigone Heraclidou
The Round Table, volume 103, issue 2 (March 2014) pp. 193–200

Chapter 12
Norman Lindsay and the 'Asianisation' of the German Soldier in Australia during the First World War
Emily Robertson
The Round Table, volume 103, issue 2 (March 2014) pp. 211–231

Chapter 19
Dominion Cartoon Satire as Trench Culture Narratives: Complaints, Endurance and Stoicism
Jane Chapman & Dan Ellin
The Round Table, volume 103, issue 2 (March 2014) pp. 175–192

Chapter 22
The Prisoner Dilemma: Britain, Germany, and the Repatriation of Indian Prisoners of War
Andrew Tait Jarboe
The Round Table, volume 103, issue 2 (March 2014) pp. 201–210

CITATION INFORMATION

Chapter 25
Loss and Longing: Emotional Responses to West Indian Soldiers during the First World War
Richard Smith
The Round Table, volume 103, issue 2 (March 2014) pp. 243–252

Chapter 26: Conclusion
The First World War Centenary in the UK: 'A Truly National Commemoration'?
Andrew Mycock
The Round Table, volume 103, issue 2 (March 2014) pp. 153–163

The following chapters were originally published in *Australian Historical Studies*. When citing this material, please cite the original journal article, using the original page numbering for each article, as follows:

Chapter 9
Marching to the Beat of an Imperial Drum: Contextualising Australia's Military Effort During the First World War
Rhys Crawley
Australian Historical Studies, volume 46, issue 1 (March 2015) pp. 64–80

Chapter 17
William Morris Hughes, Empire and Nationalism: The Legacy of the First World War
James Cotton
Australian Historical Studies, volume 46, issue 1 (March 2015) pp. 100–118

Chapter 20
'Accurate to the Point of Mania': Eyewitness Testimony and Memory Making in Australia's Official Paintings of the First World War
Margaret Hutchison
Australian Historical Studies, volume 46, issue 1 (March 2015) pp. 27–44

For any permission-related enquiries please visit:
http://www.tandfonline.com/page/help/permissions

Notes on Contributors

Kwabena O. Akurang-Parry is a Ghanaian poet and historian, and was previously an Associate Professor of African History and World History at Shippensburg University, Pennsylvania, USA. He received his Ph.D. in African history from York University, Toronto, Canada, in 1999.

Jane Chapman is Professor of Communications at the University of Lincoln, UK, and a visiting Fellow at Wolfson College and the Centre of South Asian Studies, at the University of Cambridge, UK. She is the author of ten books and many articles and book chapters. Her most recent monographs are *Comics and the World Wars- a cultural record'* (2015) *'Comics, the Holocaust and Hiroshima'* (2015) and *Gender, Citizenship and Newspapers: Historical and Transnational Perspectives* (2013).

Nic Clarke is a Lecturer at the University of Ottawa, Canada, and the Royal Military College of Canada.

John S. Connor is a Senior Lecturer in the History Program at the University of New South Wales – Canberra, Australia. His research interests include the British Empire and the First World War, frontier and colonial warfare, and Australian and Commonwealth military history. He is the author of *Anzac and Empire: George Foster Pearce and the foundations of Australian defence* (2011).

James Cotton is Professor Emeritus at the Australian Defence Force Academy, University of New South Wales – Canberra, Australia. He is currently working on several projects including the documentary record of Australian foreign relations, 1920–1936 (in collaboration with Historical Documents, Department of Foreign Affairs and Trade), the history of the international relations discipline in Australia, and current regional relations.

Rhys Crawley is a Research Fellow in the Strategic and Defence Studies Centre at the Australian National University, Canberra, Australia. The author of *Climax at Gallipoli: The failure of the August Offensive* (2014), he researches, teaches, and writes on aspects of Australian military, logistic, security, and intelligence history.

Dan Ellin has recently been awarded his Ph.D. from the Department of History at the University of Warwick, UK. His thesis is titled 'The many behind the few: the Emotions of Erks and WAAFs of RAF Bomber Command 1939–1945'.

Noel Garson is a retired Professor of History at the University of the Witwatersrand, Johannesburg, South Africa.

NOTES ON CONTRIBUTORS

Kathryn M. Hunter is an Associate Professor in the School of History, Philosophy, Political Science and International Relations at Victoria University of Wellington, New Zealand. Her research interests include the social areas of the First World War, and gender histories in colonial societies. She is the author of *Holding on to Home: New Zealand Stories and Objects of the First World War* (with Kirstie Ross, 2014).

Margaret Hutchison is a Ph.D. candidate and Graduate Teaching Fellow at ANU College of Asia and the Pacific, Australia. Her research centres on the role of official war art in the construction of a memory of the First World War in Australia.

Ashley Jackson is Professor of Imperial and Military History at King's College London, UK, and a Visiting Fellow at Kellogg College, University of Oxford, UK. He is the author of numerous books on British imperial history, including *The British Empire and the Second World War* (2006), and *The British Empire: A Very Short Introduction* (2013).

Andrew Tait Jarboe is an Assistant Professor of Liberal Arts at Berklee College of Music, Boston, MA, USA. He is the editor of *Empires in World War I: Shifting Frontiers and Imperial Dynamics in a Global Conflict* (with Richard Fogarty, 2014).

Jacqueline Jenkinson is a Lecturer in the Department of History at the University of Stirling, UK. She is currently researching the settlement of, treatment of, and legislation regarding migrant groups to Britain in the 19th and 20th centuries.

James E. Kitchen is a Senior Lecturer in the Department of War Studies at the Royal Military Academy, Sandhurst, UK. His principal research interests are in the First World War, particularly in its global dimensions, and the campaigns fought in the Middle East. He is the author of *The British Imperial Army in the Middle East: Morale and Military Identity in the Sinai and Palestine Campaigns, 1916–18* (2014).

Antigone Heraclidou is a Lecturer at the European University Cyprus. In May 2012, she received her Ph.D. in History from the Institute of Commonwealth Studies, SAS, University of London, UK. Her thesis was entitled "Politics of Education in Colonial Cyprus, 1931–1956, with special reference to the Greek-Cypriot community".

Gregory Martin was previously affiliated with Emmanuel College, University of Cambridge, UK.

Andrew Mycock is a Senior Lecturer in Politics at the University of Huddersfield, UK. He is the author of *Post-imperial citizenship, national identity and education: Britain and post-Soviet Russia* (2014).

Bill Nasson is a Professor in the History Department at Stellenbosch University, Cape Town, South Africa. In 2011 he won the Recht Malan Prize for Best Non-Fiction for *The War in South Africa: The Anglo-Boer War 1899–1902*, which was also shortlisted for the Alan Paton Award. He specialises in the history of war and society.

Colin Newbury is an Emeritus Fellow of Linacre College, University of Oxford, UK.

NOTES ON CONTRIBUTORS

Aaron Pegram is a Ph.D. student in the Research School of Humanities and the Arts at the Australian National University, Canberra, Australia. His Ph.D. research examines the experience of 3,800 members of the Australian Imperial Force captured on the Western Front during the First World War and their subsequent imprisonment in Germany.

Emily Robertson is a Graduate Student in the School of Humanities and Social Sciences at the University of New South Wales, Sydney, Australia. Her Ph.D. research is centred on Australian propaganda during the First World War.

Kaushik Roy is Reader at the Department of History at Jadavpur University, Kolkata, India. He has been affiliated with the International Peace Research Institute (PRIO) since 2006, notably through the Centre for the Study of Civil War, and was appointed a PRIO Global Fellow in 2014. He is the author of *Frontiers, Insurgencies and Counter-Insurgencies in South Asia* (Routledge, 2015).

John Slight is a Research Fellow in the Faculty of History at the University of Cambridge, UK, based at St. John's College. He is a political and social historian whose broad research interest is the history of the Red Sea, its surrounding littorals and this area's links with the wider world since c.1850, and the relationship between British imperialism and the Muslim world, focused on Britain's 'Muslim Empire'. He is the author of *The British Empire and the Hajj, 1865–1956* (forthcoming 2015).

Richard Smith is a Senior Lecturer in the Department of Media and Communications at Goldsmith's College, University of London, UK. He has written widely on the experience of West Indian troops in both World Wars and the race and gender implications of military service in the British Empire, including *Jamaican Volunteers in the First World War: Race, Masculinity and the Development of National Consciousness* (2004, 2009).

Sir Hew Strachan is an Emeritus Fellow of All Souls College, University of Oxford, UK. His research interests include military history from the 18th century to date, including contemporary strategic studies, but with a particular interest in the First World War and in the history of the British Army. His most recent books are *Clausewitz's On War: a Biography* (2007), and *The First World War: A New Illustrated History* (2003).

Peter J. Yearwood is a Senior Lecturer in history at the University of Papua New Guinea. He has previously worked for the University of Jos, Nigeria, and is Joint Editor of *South Pacific Journal of Philosophy and Culture*.

The British Empire and the First World War: Paradoxes and New Questions

Ashley Jackson and James E. Kitchen

From start to finish, the First World War was a global and imperial conflict. The British Empire's war began and ended in Africa. The first shot of the war to be fired by a soldier under British command was that of Regimental Sergeant-Major Alhaji Grunshi of the West African Frontier Force on 12 August 1914 as Anglo-French forces set about dismantling the small German presence in Togoland.[1] Together with the invasion of Cameroon, this was a campaign that reflected both a metropolitan desire to limit Germany's ability to interdict Allied maritime supply lines and a sub-imperial and metropolitan wish to secure, and potentially expand, Entente colonial possessions. Similarly, the muddled end to Britain's First World War beyond Western Europe is exemplified by the belated surrender of Colonel Paul von Lettow-Vorbeck's forces at Abercorn in Northern Rhodesia 14 days after European armies had stopped eviscerating one another on the Western Front. From first shot until final surrender, and through the nature of its conduct, the First World War can be viewed through a variety of global and imperial lenses which challenge a more traditional Eurocentric focus.

If one views the events of 1914–18 from the standpoint of the interwar years, the First World War was, above all, a global struggle. This was a point that myriad publications in the 1920s and 1930s sought to emphasize. Between 1921 and 1926 Sir Charles Lucas, a Colonial Office civil servant, oversaw the production of a multi-volume and multi-author history of the Empire's contribution to Allied victory over the Central Powers, entitled *The Empire at War*. This wide-ranging work – the scope of which has rarely, if ever, been matched – examined every aspect of the imperial war effort, from the considerable contribution made by the 'white' Dominions, through to the efforts of smaller imperial territories, such as the participation of Jamaican troops in the battles over the Jordan Valley in 1918.[2] The achievement of Lucas's publication was in part to emphasize the truly global nature of the British imperial war effort, with campaigns fought from France to Samoa, from German South-West Africa to Archangel. It also made apparent to its readership the extent to which the whole Empire was mobilized behind the single cause of victory over Prussian militarism and the containment of the Central Powers' imperial ambitions. It did perhaps neglect to mention the militarizing and aggrandizing tendencies of the British Empire itself, but the core point remained: victory in 1918 was a product of a collective imperial endeavour.

Lucas's *The Empire at War* was one of the many *lieux de mémoire* that were created in the interwar British Empire. The book was thus a site of commemoration produced in order to recall, and establish continuity of memory with, British imperial mobilization, struggle and success in 1914–18.³ Alongside Lucas's work sat the more formal and utilitarian publication of the British official history, produced under the supervision of Brigadier-General Sir James Edmonds. Through its sheer scale and detail it stood as a testament to the battlefield challenges that had been met and largely overcome by British imperial forces. Unlike the German official history, entitled *Der Weltkrieg*, the British version, although more prosaically titled, did actually take a global perspective on the war.⁴ It devoted entire volumes to the campaigns beyond the Western Front, such as those authored by Major-General George MacMunn and Cyril Falls on the campaigns in Egypt and the Levant. Here the exploits of the Egyptian Expeditionary Force in 1916–18 offered a microcosm of the wider imperial war effort. These were campaigns that involved troops from across the Empire, including Indian infantry- and cavalrymen, Australian and New Zealand mounted troops and British West Indians. A small detachment of Rarotongan boat people was even transported from the Pacific to help the advancing army land supplies on the beaches opposite Gaza, the skill sets of colonial subjects being deployed to serve specific military needs in an imperial war. Illustrating the penetrative power of a global conflict, the extraordinary length of the British Empire's military tentacles, and the exhaustive nature of the official war histories, there was even a volume chronicling the activities of imperial forces operating in Iran throughout the war.⁵

The breadth of the imperial war effort was not only recalled in officially sanctioned publications from the imperial metropole. Throughout the interwar years a multitude of formation histories appeared recalling the specific battlefield exploits of individual battalions, regiments, divisions or expeditionary forces dispatched by a variety of Dominions and colonies. These works often told the personal stories of the men who served, what it felt like to travel far from home, to learn new military roles, and then to deploy these on the industrial battlefield. The audience for such publications was relatively small, focused on former comrades and their families and friends. Nevertheless, they still captured a specific moment in the history of the British Empire and the role that these colonial and Dominion troops had played – no matter how small – in shaping the imperial war effort.⁶

The act of commemorating the British imperial military contribution also took more solid form in bricks, mortar and stone, reflecting the general commemorative culture that developed among former combatant states in the post-war years.⁷ War memorials were, and remain, among the most prominent imperial *lieux de mémoire* of the Great War. For example, in November 1932 a statue to the men of the Australian and New Zealand Mounted Division was unveiled at Port Said in Egypt, a site of memory for Dominion troops within what was then only a pseudo-colonial state following tentative steps towards Egyptian independence in 1922. The memorial did not survive the anti-colonial fervour of 1956, being torn down by the local population in the wake of the Suez Crisis. Nonetheless, the statue of an Australian Light Horseman reaching down to help his wounded New Zealand comrade, sculpted by Web Gilbert and Bertram Mackennal, encapsulated the Dominion experience in the First World War.⁸ The conflict was a moment of shared hardship on the battlefield that saw, in this case, the Dominions coming together for the defence of the British Empire, hence the memorial's symbolic position at the gateway to the Suez Canal, the arterial hub of imperial communications.

This was one of many memorials to the sacrifices of Dominion troops that sprung up in the interwar years around the battlefields and recruiting grounds of the Empire.

In most cases the focus remained resolutely on the Western Front, with Canada eulogizing the spectacular success achieved in securing Vimy Ridge in April 1917. South Africa instead concentrated its commemorative efforts on the traumatic blood loss suffered by its 1st Brigade at Delville Wood on the Somme in July 1916. For Australia and New Zealand the focus of commemoration was also on a military disaster, the debacle at Gallipoli in 1915, and more specifically on the heroic achievements of the Anzacs when they landed on 25 April. The myth-making and complexities involved in Antipodean commemorative culture have spawned almost an entire sub-genre of First World War historiography, but have been ably summarized in the work of Jenny Macleod and Ken Inglis.[9] For Australia, in particular, remembering the First World War was not just about recalling collective imperial sacrifice, but also the supposed moment at which the modern nation was born in battle.

War memorials were erected throughout the colonial empire as well as the empire of the 'white' Dominions, commemorating either particular campaigns and battles or the service of colonial troops. These included the Stanley memorial in the Falkland Islands, commemorating Admiral Sturdee's victory over Vice Admiral Graf von Spee's cruiser squadron on 8 December 1914, as well as the service of Falklanders in the Empire's armed forces. The Basra War Memorial, moved close to Nasiriyah by the Iraqi government in 1997, bears the names of over 40,000 Commonwealth troops who died in Mesopotamia, and whose graves are unknown – testament to the sheer scale of combat activities around the world and their tragic death toll. The Colombo cenotaph in Sri Lanka, another 1920s creation, was moved inland from its prominent position on the Galle Face seafront lest it be used as a marker by Japanese warships in the following global struggle. While it is difficult to know for sure, it is likely that *every* territory of the British Empire had a war memorial erected, even those involved in a peripheral manner. Outside the parliamentary buildings in Gaborone, Botswana, for instance, a standard-issue granite and bronze memorial marks the fallen of the world wars, including a plaque for Trooper Jonas, a member of the Bechuanaland Protectorate Police, killed in a skirmish on the border with German South-West Africa in the early days of the war, a casualty thousands of miles from the Western front, but a casualty of the Empire's war nonetheless. Imperial commemoration and monument-making did not end with the interwar years. As late as 2002, Queen Elizabeth II unveiled a new memorial to the collective military service of African, Asian and Caribbean combatants in the two world wars. The Memorial Gates on Constitution Hill in London again reflect a decision to erect a monument with deliberate and significant resonances, designed to tie imperial sacrifices in the 'total wars' of the twentieth century into the contemporary identity of the former imperial metropole in a post-imperial age. Modern multicultural Britain was thus acknowledging its debt to its former colonial subjects.

These *lieux de mémoire* suggest that the British Empire has always played an integral part in the story and memory of the First World War, but what was true of the interwar years has not always been the case. After 1945 the British Empire and Dominion dimension of the First World War slipped from view. Increasingly the voices of British ex-servicemen came to dominate popular debate on the conflict, and these invariably reflected a Western European and Western Front bias. From an imperial history perspective as well, the events of 1939–45 and the ensuing three decades of frequently bloody decolonization suggested that what had occurred earlier in the twentieth century was merely a warm-up act for the main event. With the exception of Gallipoli, which retained prominence in the history of the First World War largely due to the fact that it fitted snugly into the popular Alan Clark archetype of bungling generalship, the extra-European battlefields and theatres of 1914–18 slipped from view in the second half of the twentieth century. If the British Empire was seen to be engaged in fighting in the Great War, it more often than not appeared on the cinema screen, where forays into the exotic sideshows of the conflict were slightly more common. The most notable examples of revelling in the imperial pleasure culture of 1914–18 included John Huston's *The African Queen* (1951), David Lean's *Lawrence of Arabia* (1962) and Peter Weir's *Gallipoli* (1981).

The British Empire appearing merely as an adjunct to the principal narrative of the Great War, or as a source of titillation to enliven dry story-telling, was not confined to the popular cultural productions of the post-1945 period. Many of the major historical works that appeared from the 1960s onwards similarly took a Eurocentric approach to the Great War. It was on the Western Front that the most blood was shed and that the fate of the 'great powers' was decided.[10] The British Empire's efforts in this theatre were noted, such as the role of the Dominions as the 'cutting edge' of the British Expeditionary Force (BEF) in 1918, but the complexities of the imperial contribution within and outside Europe were ignored.

As Andrew Tait Jarboe and Richard Fogarty have argued, since the beginning of the twenty-first century the global and imperial history of the First World War has enjoyed a considerable renaissance.[11] This has reflected a wider historiographical trend over the past 25 years that has seen the somewhat imprecise category of 'world history' emerge as an independent field of research.[12] The First World War was a conflict fought by empires – even Belgium, a minor European state, was a significant African colonial power – and which had significant imperial consequences, ultimately destroying the empires of the Hohenzollerns, Habsburgs, Romanovs and Ottomans, and aggrandizing the territorial holdings of Britain and France. The very fact that it was fought by global empires meant that the war produced global battlefields and global war aims. In many respects, the years 1914–18 – or the broader timespan of 1911–23, framed by the Italian invasion of Libya and the Treaty of Lausanne – were a hinge moment in world history.

Yet, as Hew Strachan has argued, and Jarboe and Fogarty reiterate, the European and global dimensions of the First World War were interlinked.[13] Europe was the managerial hub of the colonial great powers and was the economic centre of global trade; any war that affected Europe was bound to have global ramifications. This was a point that contemporaries were aware of, having been forcefully argued in the British journalist Norman Angell's *The Great Illusion* (1909), a pan-European publishing sensation which gained popular currency in the run-up to the outbreak of hostilities.[14] The economic issue mattered particularly from a British imperial perspective. London was the centre of global finance in 1914, largely due to the gold standard, and as such all states that traded with Britain or made use of its banking sector were tangentially drawn into the war. Some governments may have believed they were neutral, but the concept in 1914–18 was a relative rather than an absolute one.

Britain's entry into the war, more so than that of any other state, meant that finance and trade at a global level would be affected. The way Britain chose to wage the war also ensured that the conflict took on a globalizing and totalizing logic. From the outset the most powerful asset available to Britain was the Royal Navy, which ensured that the vast resources of the Empire could be mobilized and brought safely to Europe to conduct a major continental war. This, however, would take time, and helps explain Kitchener's assumption, when asked by the cabinet about the expected length of the war, that hostilities would continue for at least three years before such material and manpower advantages could be brought to bear. From the start the Royal Navy was also used to mount a blockade of commercial shipping to and from Germany, ensuring that global trade could not be used to the Central Powers' advantage. For neutral countries such as Holland, caught between the competing ambitions of Britain and Germany, the war years involved a constant process of negotiating their 'neutral' status in order to minimize the impact of war upon their own people and ensure the maintenance of friendly global trade links; in practice this often meant toeing the British line on whom to trade with and whom to reject. The economic dimensions of the First World War, and Britain's integral role within them, illustrate the global nature of the conflict from its start.

This volume of collected articles reflects the 'global turn' in First World War studies from the perspective of the British Empire. Paralleling similar developments in the historiography of France and its empire in 1914–18, particularly the work on French African soldiers by Richard Fogarty, Joe Lunn and Gregory Mann, Britain's war has increasingly come to be seen as part of a wider imperial discourse.[15] The First World War was a conflict that mobilized empires and their peoples, transported them around the globe to a variety of battlefields, and which strained imperial systems to breaking point and beyond; the British Empire experienced these global and imperial dynamics of war as did all the other empires engaged in the conflict. The articles that follow make clear the complexity of that British imperial experience. The history of 1914–18, as with the wider history of the Empire, must be a polyvocal story, recounting how soldiers, workers and labourers – even semi-literate or illiterate colonial subjects – experienced the conflict as much as how generals and statesmen viewed it. This was a Nigerian, West Indian or Punjabi war, as much as it was a British, French or German one.

The breadth and complexity of the history of the British Empire experience in 1914–18 raises a series of deeper questions. At the heart of the historiography that has emerged over the past quarter of a century debating the multiple imperial narratives of the Empire's Great War are a series of paradoxes. Of these, three stand out as of particular prominence. First, this was a war that witnessed mass participation and mobilization across the British Empire in the cause of the metropole. At the same time, however, 1914–18 and the immediate post-war years also saw the emergence of new and forceful challenges to British imperial rule. Second, these challenges at times rested on the emergence of powerful new national or proto-national identities within the colonies and Dominions; 1914–18 was thus a nation-making moment. In contrast, it was also a period that witnessed powerful expressions of imperial unity as the Empire came together to meet a common foe. Third, from the strategic perspective this existential threat was met in two seemingly conflicting ways, through imperial protection and expansion. British imperial military campaigns were designed at times around the principle of defence, of protecting existing key strategic communications links, territory and resources, but on other occasions, a desire to place Britain at the optimal position from which to rapaciously exploit the spoils of the defeated powers, and deny them to her allies, took over. These three paradoxes – mobilization/resistance, nation/empire and defence/expansion – in no way reflect a definitive assessment of the current historiography on the British Empire in the First World War. They do, however, help to illuminate the exciting avenues that historical debates have progressed along as historians of the British Empire have engaged with the conflict's 'global turn'.

One of the most striking features of 1914–18 was the extent to which the Empire was mobilized to provide manpower on the battlefield, labour in militarized rear areas and workers to service industrial production. For Britain, one of its principal strategic advantages was the ability to draw on its vast global territories to boost its military and material commitment to the Entente war effort. F. W. Perry's work on the recruitment of colonial and Dominion subjects to fill the range of military and labouring services required by the Empire's war effort remains the definitive account of this imperial mobilization.[16] The figures for recruitment were staggering: alongside the 4.9 million men enlisted in Britain, 1.4 million Indians, 458,000 Canadians, 8,000 Newfoundlanders, 332,000 Australians, 112,000 New Zealanders, 136,000 South Africans, 16,000 West Indians, 34,000 East Africans and 25,000 West Africans fought and laboured in aid of the Empire's campaigns.[17] But this was not all, for a host of smaller contributions flowed from colonies such as Bechuanaland, Fiji, Hong Kong, Jamaica, Mauritius, the Seychelles, and Swaziland. This vast pool of imperial manpower enabled London to commit fully to the Western Front in conjunction with the French by 1916 and increasingly to take the lead after mid-1917, but also to run a series of simultaneous subsidiary theatres around the globe. Britain could thus fight Germany in Europe while also eliminating German colonial possessions in Africa and containing the Ottoman threat to the Suez Canal and Mesopotamian oil. In a 'total war' fought on such a worldwide scale numbers mattered, and the ability to recruit on a global scale opened up strategic options for Whitehall policy-makers.

The most significant manpower role was played by the Indian Army, which provided seven separate expeditionary forces to service a variety of imperial campaigns, from the jungles of East Africa to the deserts of Mesopotamia and Palestine. In some respects this merely saw sepoys taking on the role for which they had been envisaged in pre-war imperial strategic thought; the Indian Army was in essence a fire brigade fighting the myriad smaller wars, often reflecting pre-existing colonial rivalries, which were subsumed into the wider First World War. By fighting such campaigns and by relieving British garrison battalions in key colonial outposts, such as Malta, the Indian Army freed British soldiers to serve on the Western Front. This manpower substitution role continued throughout the war, with Indians enlisted through the ramped-up recruiting drive of 1917–18 used to Indianize the campaign in Palestine in its final year. More significantly, the costly nature of European warfare, particularly the bloody opening battles of manoeuvre in France and Belgium, meant that the Indian Army was needed in autumn 1914 on the fields of Flanders to safeguard the British contribution to the Entente. The role of the Indian Corps under Lieutenant-General Sir James Willcocks in 1914–15 has been one of the most hotly contested areas of British imperial historiography on the war, with claims and counterclaims about sepoy morale and their ability to endure industrialized battle.[18] George Morton-Jack's thorough account makes clear that although the sepoys faced difficulties in adapting to the brutal character of the Western Front – as did the armies of all the major belligerents at the war's start – they coped well.[19] Ultimately, Willcocks's men played a vital role in boosting the BEF's manpower until the Territorial Force and Kitchener volunteers could form the bulk of the army by late 1915. It was only the sub-imperial ambitions of the Government of India, and principally the Viceroy Lord Hardinge, that led to the two Indian infantry divisions being shifted to Mesopotamia in early 1916.

Failure in extra-European campaigns in the first half of the war, notably at Kut and Tanga, has clouded the Indian Army's tactical and operational reputation ever since.[20] Recent work by Kaushik Roy, Andrew Syk and James Kitchen on the successful Indian campaigns to take Baghdad and defeat the Turks at Megiddo have demonstrated that by the end of the war the Indian Army was a capable component within the British Empire's combined arms military machine.[21]

What remains most striking about the large swathes of imperial recruitment during the First World War was that it was carried out on a voluntary basis, with the formations sent overseas by India, Australia and the British West Indies remaining all-volunteer organizations throughout the war. In other cases, notably New Zealand and Canada, the solution that Britain had turned to in 1916 following the heavy losses on the Western Front was also adopted: conscription. Formal extraction of servicemen from the available male population not only ensured that the numbers needed at the front could be found, but that the flow of manpower was more predictable and not subject solely to the fervour of particular recruiting drives. By the later campaigns of the war it was evident that the all-volunteer Australian Imperial Force (AIF) was, though among the best combat troops deployed by the Empire, unable to withstand the attritional strain of industrialized combat. Australian Prime Minister William Hughes had tried on two occasions – October 1916 and December 1917 – to introduce conscription through referenda, but both times had been defeated by the will of the Australian voting public.[22] As John Darwin has argued, this did not represent a rejection of a 'British' war, nor reflect a perception that Australian troops were being misused by London, but was instead an assertion of a voluntaristic ideal prevalent in white settler societies of the nineteenth and early twentieth centuries. Coupled to this was a particularly Australian fear that an open-ended commitment to the Western Front would decimate the country's white manpower, leaving it both demographically vulnerable and unable to dominate the South Pacific region.

The Australian controversies over conscription make clear the first paradox of the British Empire's Great War. The Empire may have been mobilized on a scale never before seen, but this mobilization was contested; 1914–18 was thus a moment of imperial loyalty and disloyalty, 'collaboration' and resistance. In the case of India alone there were a number of outbreaks of unrest within the army. Most notably, in February 1915 the 5th Light Infantry at Singapore mutinied, killing some of their British officers and local Europeans before fleeing into the jungle.[23] Nearly all of the mutineers were subsequently captured and 43 executed as a symbolic warning of the retribution that the colonial state would mete out to rebellious military subjects. Although seemingly linked to pan-Islamic appeals by the Ottoman Caliph, moments of unrest such as occurred at Singapore were much more closely tied to poor officer–man relations within the units concerned. Unrest was not just confined to the Indian Army. The Government of India was also deeply concerned throughout the war about domestic threats, such as the subversive campaign of the Ghadrite movement, which drew on the funds and international connections of the global Sikh diaspora.

Increasingly, the extraction of manpower came to be challenged throughout the Empire. In Africa, where large areas of the continent were aggressively scoured for porters and labourers to service the British campaigns there, resistance to recruiting could take many forms.[24] Nominally voluntary recruiting systems increasingly involved a coercive element as local recruiters put pressure on chiefs to find as many men as possible. Recruitment was far from being a moment of pan-imperial unity in which the imperial subject became part of a wider British Empire cause, as more often than not old scores were settled by chiefs against families and individuals who had previously opposed them. For the young men at the sharp end of this intensive recruiting machine, flight was often the simplest option. In some cases the challenge could be more intense, as with the millenarian uprising in Nyasaland led by the Baptist preacher John Chilembwe in 1915. Such revolts rolled together a variety of grievances that the war only intensified; extraction of manpower served to highlight the brutalities of colonial pacification and the extension of the colonial state into the everyday lives of its subjects.

The outbreaks of disloyalty and resistance to the imperial war effort were, however, most pronounced in the Dominions and, much closer to Britain, in Ireland. From very early in the war these territories began to cause problems. In late 1914 through to spring 1915 the South African campaign in German South-West Africa sparked a significant armed challenge from around 11,000 poor rural Afrikaners who longed to rewrite the imperial settlement of 1902. The revolt touched on pro-German sympathies and opposition to the Anglicized South African Union, but was ultimately crushed by the Unionist loyalists of Jan Smuts and Louis Botha. Much more significant from the perspective of London was the bloody outbreak of violence that swept Dublin in Easter 1916. Although understood by its leaders to be the latest entry in the lexicon of Irish republican martyrology rather than a realistic challenge to British rule, it was nonetheless viewed with alarm by Herbert Asquith's government. The military response under the command of General Sir John Maxwell was swift and decisive. Troops were used to restore order in Dublin in a series of bitter house-to-house battles, lasting 6 days and leaving 450 dead. The decision to execute 16 of the ringleaders ensured that the republican cause gained the martyrs it sought.[25] The Irish problem that had gnawed away at late Victorian and Edwardian politics, and was seemingly settled at the start of the war, thus returned to centre stage. By 1918 it was the spectre of conscription that drove the rise of Sinn Féin to become a mass, nationwide movement, and which would seal the inability of the British to restore order after the Great War. In this, Ireland was far from being exceptional. As John Darwin has argued, it was resistance to conscription in Ireland, Quebec and Australia that formed one of the principal problems for the British Empire during the First World War.[26] The war effort required the extraction of levels of imperial manpower that enhanced existing problems within the imperial relationship, such as those which animated the English–French divide in Canada. The voluntary ethos of much recruiting served to contain these tensions, but a 'total war' could not be fought and won without conscription. Britain had thus, in some respects, to choose between stoking the fires of anti-imperial upheaval and winning the war.

If wartime was a testing period for the British Empire then the immediate post-war years suggested even more clearly the limits of British rule. As John Gallagher argued, the period from 1918 to 1922 represented a crisis moment for the Empire.[27] Imperial resources and peoples had been stretched to breaking point by the exertions of wartime and, perhaps crucially, in many areas the colonial state had become increasingly intrusive and coercive. A series of crises swept the Empire in these years, beginning with the Egyptian Revolution of spring 1919, followed by unrest in the Punjab and the flowering of Gandhi's civil disobedience campaign of strikes and boycotts. Most significant was the outbreak of a sustained and at times militarily effective insurgency in Ireland, particularly in the south-west around Cork.[28] The seeming inability of the

British state to contain this paramilitary violence without recourse to brutal excesses – many committed by its own paramilitaries, the Black and Tans and Auxiliaries – only served to highlight the exhaustion of British rule. Alongside all these problems Britain faced a pressing need to demobilize large parts of its armed forces and to return the state to a peacetime footing. Despite the grand ambitions of imperial statesmen such as Winston Churchill, Nathaniel Curzon and Alfred Milner, the reality by 1923 was one of contradictions: Britain had won the First World War but also lost most of Ireland; the Ottoman Empire's territories had been redistributed but Turkish nationalism had humiliated British arms at Chanak; and the nascent revolutionary Bolshevik state had resisted British attempts to aid counter-revolutionary forces in its destruction. The complexities of the immediate post-war period for the Empire, having been so well examined by John Gallagher, Charles Townshend, John Darwin and Keith Jeffery in the early 1980s, are returning to prominence in the debates on the British Empire and the First World War.[29] In part this reflects a wider European historical concern with the tangled endings to the conflict and the manner in which it links into wider discourses on twentieth-century history.[30]

The 'crisis of empire' moment also highlights the second paradox of the British Empire and the First World War. 1914–18 witnessed effusive expressions, both public and private, of imperial loyalty, whether sepoys fighting for the King-Emperor or the rallying to the imperial cause in 1914 of Australians, Canadians, New Zealanders and Rhodesians. In contrast to other imperial polities, such as the Ottoman or Habsburg empires, this imperial unity did survive the strains of wartime, and would even pass through a second 'total war' before the bonds of empire were fully broken. These pan-imperial ties could be seen in the purchase of a complete motor ambulance for the Indian Corps on the Western Front by the Maharaja of Gwalior for £20,060. Even more impressively, a group of over 30 other Indian princes purchased an entire hospital ship to care for wounded sepoys, costing over £400,000.[31] The heads of the Indian princely states were keen to be engaged in supporting the British war effort, and to be seen to be doing so as good, loyal client-rulers for Delhi and London. It was in the realm of financial support that this imperial loyalty was most often demonstrated. Canada, for example, lent over $1 billion to Britain during the course of the war, as well as helping to produce a large share of the munitions expended by the BEF on the Western Front.[32] Wartime needs thus became the vehicle for arguments, such as those made by the arch-imperialist Milner, that the Empire needed to integrate further to ensure its self-sufficiency and security.

Although imperial unity and support was one product of the First World War, it was not the entire story. At the same time powerful currents pushed the Empire in a different direction, highlighting local national and racial identities in opposition to an all-embracing British imperial conception of the relationship between centre and periphery. Most notably, the blood sacrifice made by the AIF, and to a lesser extent by New Zealanders, at Gallipoli cemented a unique Antipodean sense of national identity, one that was particularly masculine and forged in battle. This wartime and post-war construction of 'Australian-ness' was aided by Charles Bean's and Ellis Ashmead-Bartlett's mythologizing of the Gallipoli experience in their journalistic dispatches.[33] The war also augmented the power of Afrikaner nationalism and its growing prominence in the South African Union, and constitutional reform in India advanced the cause of self-government. A more interesting and complex moment of national 'birth' also took place among the British territories of the Caribbean, and more specifically among the men who volunteered to serve in the British West Indies Regiment (BWIR). Their experience of a British Empire at war that viewed them as second-class combatants, only allowed to serve in labouring roles on the Western Front although permitted to kill Turks in Palestine, made clear that the King-Emperor was not always a colour-blind master. Failure to pay adequate and equal wages to BWIR men and the build-up of discontent over their racialized treatment spilled over into mutiny at Taranto in December 1918. Botched ex-serviceman settlement schemes, designed mainly to break up ex-soldier communities and distribute them around the rural backwaters of the Caribbean (in particular off-loading Jamaican problems to Cuba), ensured that these feelings of disgruntlement continued into the post-war years. Richard Smith has shown how the experience of wartime service and post-war economic problems fuelled the rise of pan-Africanism and support for national self-determination among BWIR ex-servicemen.[34]

What makes these moments of national 'birth' during the First World War all the more fascinating is the extent to which they were interwoven into the fabric of the Empire. Thus BWIR men campaigning for better pay and conditions did so by appealing to the imperial military authorities, before turning to collective disobedience. Similarly, but on a grander political scale, the statesmen that led the Dominions – William Hughes, Robert Borden, Jan Smuts and Louis Botha – complained bitterly about the British conduct of the war and the squandering of Dominion lives. They did so, however, through the means of imperial fora, such as the imperial war cabinet or conferences held in the latter half of the conflict. They tolerated an unequal relationship in the running of the war, and one that led to frequent disputes, in order to demonstrate an imperial loyalty that was expected to lead to imperial reform after the end of hostilities. The war did not settle the position of the Dominions within the British imperial system, but merely produced a stronger desire that the blood sacrifices of wartime needed to be rewarded with a greater degree of autonomy, a debate that shaped London–Dominion relations until the Statute of Westminster in 1931 made clear their self-governing status. As Timothy Winegard has argued, a similar process of working within the imperial framework was evident among the indigenous populations of the Dominions during the First World War. Here communities such as the Maori, Australian Aborigines or Canadian Indians tried hard to demonstrate their loyalty to the British Empire, principally by trying to provide manpower, in the hope that such demonstrations of loyalty would be rewarded with greater local autonomy in the future. This reciprocal relationship of loyalty and reward proved more beneficial for the settler communities within the Dominions, with indigenous peoples gaining little from the First World War.[35]

The third paradox was one that exercised political and military leaders during the First World War, as much as it has excited historical debate since. At the heart of the British imperial war effort was the thorny strategic question of whether the Empire was – or should be from the viewpoint of contemporaries – engaged in a global or a European war. As Hew Strachan has argued, a global war was not in Britain's interests, but was a benefit to Germany.[36] Any distraction of imperial resources in campaigns away from Europe meant the diminution of the military efforts that could be made on the Western Front. Hence the efforts in 1914 to destroy German wireless transmitters and to capture colonial port facilities that would allow the *Kriegsmarine* to interdict Britain's global shipping lanes, through which flowed the men and raw materials needed to bring European victory. The focus of the European and global aspects of Britain's war effort in large part reflected the personalities directing the war. Under Asquith, Europe remained the principal point of effort. Even 'sideshows' such as Gallipoli were intended more to defeat extra-European threats, in this case from the Ottoman Empire, than to allow for a new expansionist campaign to be unleashed.

The last two years of the war represented a dramatic shift in this dynamic, as Lloyd George saw the campaigns beyond the Western Front as the theatres in which Britain's global interests could best be served. Robin Prior has provided the clearest assessment of the 'Easterners' and 'Westerners' debates that wracked imperial strategic decision-making in the latter stages of the war.[37] The two approaches were not always mutually exclusive when campaigns played out on the ground. The defence of the Suez Canal, for example, was best conducted from the far eastern side of Sinai, where a small British force opposite Gaza could easily block any Turkish forays by controlling the principal communication routes, whereas a large garrison was needed to man the static defences along the east bank of the Canal. Saving imperial manpower thus, in part, motivated the decision in 1916 to expand the campaign out of Egypt and towards Palestine; imperial defence was served by imperial offence. The complex debates that shaped the conduct of operations in Palestine during 1917–18, which resulted in the capture of Jerusalem and then the occupation of much of the Levant, have been dissected by Matthew Hughes.[38] He makes it clear that imperial strategy-making during the second half of the First World War was an iterative process, with plans being reshaped and influenced both by the policy-makers at the centre and the men on the spot, both observing and making predictions about the development of the nascent British Middle Eastern empire and its future security needs.

What makes the imperial focus of Britain's war effort, as some saw it by 1917–18, particularly contradictory were the publicly avowed aims that Britain was fighting for. President Woodrow Wilson's Fourteen Points speech, promising a war fought to encourage self-determination of peoples and a peace that would not be annexationist, coupled with Bolshevik anti-imperialist rhetoric, forced the Lloyd George coalition into an uncomfortable position. Thus, at the same time as fighting a decidedly expansionist war in the Middle East and Africa, Lloyd George was also laying claim to Britain's position as a supporter of the right of national populations to determine their own destinies, particularly in the former Habsburg lands. Similarly, while defending her own empire, Britain also deliberately acted to undermine other empires, most notably that of the Ottomans through the sponsoring of the Arab nationalist cause from 1916 onwards.[39] These conflicts between imperial and national ends came to a head in the process of post-war peace making. The fudged solution of League of Nations mandates allowed Britain to expand its imperial possessions, but to do so behind the façade of a progressive policy of aiding the political development of its new subject peoples. Although, as Susan Pedersen has argued, the League of Nations Permanent Mandates Commission did offer a new source of international scrutiny for British imperial rule, the war had seemingly made the British Empire larger and safer.[40] The First World War may have been decided ultimately by the bloody battles on the Western Front, and it was there that the Empire made its greatest efforts, but it was a war with clear global and imperial ramifications.

The paradoxes briefly addressed above represent some of the more prominent themes that have emerged from the historiography of the British Empire and the First World War. These bigger debates have given rise to a series of deeper questions about the British imperial experience under the strains of 'total war' that have dominated much of the twenty-first-century discussion of 1914–18. It is these more specific areas which are reflected in this current volume and which will form much of the historical inquiry into the conflict in the years to come. In part reflecting the cultural turn that has dominated so much historical scholarship since the 1970s, historians of the British Empire are increasingly interested in how the First World War affected cross-cultural interactions, both within and outside the Empire. There is a vibrant historiography examining the relationships between sepoys and the French and English civilians they met, touching on profound questions of how race and gender roles were explored. Historians such as David Omissi and Andrew Tait Jarboe have examined the complexities of these relationships and the manner in which they influenced individual and institutional understandings of imperial and racial identities, and how these could shift over time. Prisoner of war camps were also sites where these cross-cultural and cross-imperial interactions were played out, with attempts made by the imprisoning powers to subvert existing imperial and racial identities. Daniel Steinbach has provided a fascinating account of how similar processes affected European civilians interned in Africa, where the racial hierarchies of imperial rule were momentarily reversed.[41]

War ultimately remains an activity engaged in by military formations carrying out acts of organized violence against each other. As such, the British imperial battlefields of the First World War have increasingly become sites of historiographical debate. Gallipoli has always produced a healthy body of argument that seeks to challenge the supremacy of the Western Front in the military historical canon, but it has been joined by the Mesopotamian, Palestinian and East African theatres where questions of command, leadership, logistics and morale have recently been addressed.[42] One of the key problems that the military history of the Empire in 1914–18 faces is the need to integrate tactical, operational and strategic approaches, linking the local and individual into wider debates. This integrated approach is best exemplified by Christopher Pugsley's *The Anzac Experience* (2004), although it is an exception rather than the historiographical norm.[43]

The multitude of imperial home fronts, particularly those of the colonies rather than Dominions, remain poorly served in the historiography. Tan Tai-Yong has produced a detailed study of the Punjab at war in the twentieth century, but this has not been matched by comparable accounts of other sub-imperial regions or whole colonies.[44] Issues of illiteracy and fading oral historical memory have hampered attempts to recapture particular imperial home fronts, but these problems, as the articles presented here suggest, can be overcome. Far too much of the wider historiography of the First World War is focused on the experiences of Western European peoples, with historians engaging often in cyclical debates on the existence, or not, of war cultures. More interesting and fundamental questions about how those European states managed and exploited their colonial possessions during a 'total war', and how their imperial subjects experienced that totalizing process, are frequently neglected. As Jarboe and Fogarty argue, this is an unsustainable position, as the European states that fought the First World War were imperial polities and saw themselves as such, and therefore their home fronts were intimately bound up with their empires' experiences of the war.

A similar process of broader contextualization and complication is often needed for British imperial histories of the First World War. The conflict needs to be seen through a comparative lens, setting the British colonial and Dominion experiences in contrast to those of other empires, both global, such as France, and European, such as Austria-Hungary. Robert Gerwarth and Erez Manela's *Empires at War* (2014) provides a superlative example of how such a comparative framework can be established, and highlights the new and interesting questions that emerge from taking such an approach.[45]

This volume of collected articles, taken from a selection of five Taylor & Francis journals and published between 1979 and 2015, highlights the extent to which the historiography of the British Empire in the First World War has already evolved and encompassed many of the arguments and paradoxes discussed in this introduction.[46] Numerous problems remain to be addressed and all of the articles in this volume pose challenging questions about our perceived narrative of the relationship between the war and the Empire. As with any historiography, that on the British Empire is evolving all the time, and this volume makes clear that it is, and will continue to be, particularly vibrant in the field of First World War studies.

Hew Strachan's piece demonstrates the manner in which the First World War was a truly global conflict – bigger, even, than the vast colonial empires that shaded the world map. He explains how, for example, Africa and the Mediterranean were directly linked to the wider war ambitions and strategies of the main belligerents. He shows how Germany sought to use allies and imperial possessions to pressure Britain globally, how Islamic revolution became a weapon to be channelled by competing empires, how Britain's colossal financial power brought the reverberations of war to countries all over the world, and how the war presented Japan with opportunities to advance its status in the international system and stake territorial claims in China and the Pacific.

N. G. Garson elucidates the ways in which war affected South Africa. Britain sought to use the Dominion to seize German territory, an aim that chimed with South Africa's own ambitions. Early in the war South African forces replaced British garrison troops in order to release them for service in Europe, a common practice throughout the Empire. The war exacerbated political divisions between British South Africans and Afrikaners, giving a fillip to Afrikaner nationalism that crystalized around issues such as conscription. The 1914 Boer rebellion was the first of a number of colonial rebellions that would occur in the Empire during and immediately after the war. Indicative of where power lay in the imperial relationship, the British government decided without consultation to divert 30,000 Australian and New Zealand troops, en route to the fighting fronts, to South Africa to suppress the rebellion, though in the end they were not required. In line with most parts of the Empire, the war also brought rapid economic advancement and social change, including price rises, tax hikes to fund the war effort, and urbanization. It also entrenched discriminatory practices against Africans. Addressing South Africa as well as Australia, Colin Newbury's article examines attitudes towards the capture of neighbouring German colonies when war was declared. This was not solely motivated by the British government's wish to capture strategic outposts or the Dominions' own desires for greater security in depth through extending their buffer zones in places such as New Guinea and Germany's African holdings. Australia was driven by the urge to keep Asian penetration to a minimum, and there was also an economic imperative as business circles and Dominion governments looked to expropriate German firms, sell their assets, and open up opportunities for local, British and American capital investment.

A significant proportion of the articles explore the experiences of imperial troops. James Kitchen argues that wartime and post-war crusading rhetoric associated with British forces fighting the Ottoman Empire failed to reflect the actual attitudes of the men of the Egyptian Expeditionary Force. While their mindset exhibited distinct orientalist strands, this was characterized more by 'glorified tourism' than a crusading spirit. Jane Chapman and Dan Ellin record cartoon satire among Dominion forces in the trenches, revealing how disparagement humour was an important buttress to front-line morale. Aaron Pegram examines the way in which the thousands of Australian prisoners in German hands were interrogated by German intelligence, and how in turn those men attempted to resist this. Andrew Tait Jarboe investigates a little-known episode: German attempts to reorient the allegiance of Indian Army prisoners through pan-Islamic and pan-nationalist propaganda. This met with little success, but caused anxiety for the Government of India when the former prisoners of war returned from their incarceration, requiring government monitoring. Jacqueline Jenkinson addresses the participation of black men resident in Britain who joined British forces. Regarding themselves as British, they met opposition from British people who did not view them in this way, and the seaport riots of 1919 featured white residents turning on African and Caribbean men who were accused of taking 'their' jobs. Richard Smith traces the pre-war development of West Indian fighting formations and explores wartime attitudes to, and representations of, West Indian soldiers, which reflected anxieties regarding white male efficiency. Further developing the theme of racial concerns and stereotypes influencing the experience and utility of non-white colonial forces, Gregory Martin explores racial attitudes through the example of the foundation of Indian military hospitals in Britain and the granting of King's commissions to Indian soldiers.

Another powerful theme in the selected articles is military campaigns on imperial frontiers: Kaushik Roy shows how logistics shaped the British Empire's campaign in Mesopotamia in both the pre- and post-Kut periods. He also explores the geostrategic causes of campaigns in this region: protecting Britain's oil trove and fear lest the capture of Basra threaten key sea lines of communication, and Germany's attempts, through political intrigue and 'railpolitik' (to borrow Thomas Otte's memorable expression) to press Britain at vulnerable points. John Slight describes the imperial campaign in response to the Sanussiya sufi order's jihad against Egypt, while Rhys Crawley assesses the overall significance of Australian land and maritime forces in the context of the Empire's eleven separate fighting fronts.

The colonial home front is another distinct theme in this volume. Antigone Heraclidou shows how small colonies were affected by the war and contributed to it. In the case of Cyprus, not only were thousands of men recruited into imperial formations, but the island's mules became mainstays of campaigns in Egypt, Palestine and Gallipoli, and its food and raw materials were in great demand too. The island was used extensively for rest and recuperation for imperial and Allied troops, and convalescent homes were established for soldiers recovering from sickness or wounds. Kwabena Akurang-Parry explains how men were recruited in the Gold Coast through chiefs and the agency of local intellectuals and the African press. Emily Robertson shows how the Australian public was encouraged to revile the 'Hun' through cultural representations that drew upon the established demonization of the Japanese, the Hun thus becoming Asianized as one hate figure was elided with another, the spiked *pickelhaube* helmet coming to rest upon a grossly stereotyped Asian head. Kathryn

Hunter, meanwhile, explores the relationship between Australian fathers and their soldier sons. Bill Nasson reveals the extensive range of reactions to the declaration of war among South Africa's diverse communities. While the familiar outburst of patriotism and a rush to rally to the colours characterized the response in some quarters, this was not shared by the small Russian Jewish population, poor whites, disgruntled republicans, African peasants or the Indian community represented by Gandhi, then resident in the Dominion.

John Connor shows how, in Western Australia, the empire-wide popular movement to manufacture artillery ammunition led to the formation of the War Munitions Supply Company. Peter Yearwood, meanwhile, shows how war increased the cost of imports into Nigeria while reducing the price paid for the colony's exports, particularly because the important German market was eliminated. British firms came to dominate the colonial economy, and a process of company mergers got under way that led, for example, to the formation in the immediate post-war years of Unilever. Nic Clarke records the effects of rejection on Canadian men considered unfit for military service. Often suffering from invisible ailments, some of which would not have physically debarred them from service, they experienced shame and social ostracism, while the records also reveal family members' attempts to get their sons or husbands exempted from service. Margaret Hutchison explains how official Australian war art was altered after the war as an authentic portrayal of what happened on the battlefield trumped aesthetic considerations alone. Andrew Mycock ends the volume by considering the contentious and politicized nature of British First World War centenary commemorations, relating to the participation of the British 'nations' and the former colonies.

If the British Empire's First World War is to be properly understood it also needs to be integrated into the wider history of the Empire itself in the nineteenth and twentieth centuries. In particular, the histories of the two world wars and of decolonization, and also re-colonization, cannot be set apart from one another, but are part of a grander narrative. As Jo Guldi and David Armitage have argued, taking a broader chronological perspective poses new questions and provides unforeseen insights that are often lost in a narrow focus on particular case studies.[47] The British imperial system was more than the sum of its disparate territories and peoples, and as such the history of the British Empire in the First World War needs to be contextualized both spatially and temporally, which in the process will open up new points for collaborative and comparative debates.[48] This volume, covering such a diverse range of imperial themes and avenues in relation to the First World War, represents a step towards constructing just such a broad and more inclusive total history of the British Empire in the twentieth century's first 'total war'.

Notes

1. H. Strachan, *The First World War. Volume I: To Arms* (Oxford, 2001), 495.
2. A. Jackson, 'Sir Charles Lucas and *The Empire at War*', *The Round Table*, CIII (2014), 165–173.
3. For a theoretical discussion of *lieux de mémoire* see P. Nora, 'General Introduction: Between Memory and History', in P. Nora (ed.), *Realms of Memory: Rethinking the French Past. Volume I: Conflicts and Divisions* (New York, 1992), 1–20.
4. H. Strachan, 'The First World War as a Global War', *First World War Studies*, I (2010), 5.
5. G. MacMunn and C. Falls, *Military Operations Egypt and Palestine I: From the Outbreak of the War with Germany to June 1917* (London, 1928); C. Falls, *Military Operations*

Egypt and Palestine II: From June 1917 to the End of the War (London, 1930). The Committee on Official Histories decided not to publish Brigadier-General Frederick Moreby's *Operations in Persia, 1914–1919*. Running to four volumes, the India Office objected to its publication given the 'highly secret' nature of much of the content. In 1929 the decision was revisited, and 500 copies printed for internal government use by HMSO, though the Office later destroyed 300 of these. It was finally published in 1987.

6. Antipodean examples of this regimental literature include G. H. Bourne, *Nulli Secundus: The History of the 2nd Australian Light Horse Regiment, Australian Imperial Force, August 1914–April 1919* (Tamworth, 1926); G. L. Berrie, *Under Furred Hats (6th A.L.H. Regiment)* (Sydney, 1919); C. G. Powles, *The History of the Canterbury Mounted Rifles 1914–1919* (Auckland, 1928).
7. The literature on commemoration and the memory of the First World War is vast, but a good starting point remains the superlative study by Jay Winter, *Sites of Memory, Sites of Mourning: The Great War in European Cultural History* (Cambridge, 1995). Some recent examples of interesting approaches to the issues involved in British commemoration include S. Goebel, *The Great War and Medieval Memory: War, Remembrance and Medievalism in Britain and Germany, 1914–1920* (Cambridge, 2007); A. Carden-Coyne, *Reconstructing the Body: Classicism, Modernism, and the First World War* (Oxford, 2009).
8. K. Inglis, *Sacred Places: War Memorials in the Australian Landscape* (3rd edn., Carlton, 2008), 248–249 and 357.
9. See Inglis, *Sacred Places*; J. Macleod, *Reconsidering Gallipoli* (Manchester, 2004).
10. The classic examples of side-lining the 'sideshow' theatres and the British imperial contribution in wider narratives on the First World War are A. J. P. Taylor, *The First World War: An Illustrated History* (London, 1966) and J. Keegan, *The First World War* (London, 1998). The trend, unfortunately, has continued in some twenty-first-century synoptic works, particularly those aimed at a popular audience that seems to have an insatiable appetite for all things Western Front; see G. Sheffield, *Forgotten Victory. The First World War: Myths and Realities* (London, 2001).
11. A. T. Jarboe and R. S. Fogarty, 'Introduction: An Imperial Turn in First World War Studies', in A. T. Jarboe and R. S. Fogarty (eds.), *Empires in World War I: Shifting Frontiers and Imperial Dynamics in a Global Conflict* (London, 2014), 1–20.
12. For examples of work in this field see A. G. Hopkins (ed.), *Globalization in World History* (London, 2002).
13. Strachan, 'First World War as a Global War', 6–8.
14. For a critical study of the impact of *The Great Illusion* and Norman Angell's campaigning on various aspects of international relations see M. Ceadel, *Living the Great Illusion: Sir Norman Angell, 1872–1967* (Oxford, 2009).
15. For the French imperial military experience see R. S. Fogarty, *Race and War in France: Colonial Subjects in the French Army, 1914–1918* (Baltimore, 2008); J. Lunn, *Memoirs of the Maelstrom: A Senegalese Oral History of the First World War* (Portsmouth, 1999); G. Mann, *Native Sons: West African Ex-servicemen and France in the Twentieth Century* (Durham, 2006).
16. F. W. Perry, *The Commonwealth Armies: Manpower and Organisation in Two World Wars* (Manchester, 1988).
17. Jarboe and Fogarty, 'Imperial Turn in First World War Studies', 2. The figures for African recruitment only cover those men who served in combatant roles with regiments such as the King's African Rifles. A much larger number of Africans were pressed into service as labourers and carriers. Poor record keeping means it is impossible to provide an accurate figure but current estimates suggest over one million Africans served in non-combatant roles during the First World War.
18. See J. Greenhut, 'The Imperial Reserve: The Indian Corps on the Western Front, 1914–15', *The Journal of Imperial and Commonwealth History*, XII (1983), 54–73; R. McLain, 'The Indian Corps on the Western Front: A Reconsideration', in G. Jensen and A. Wiest (eds.), *War in the Age of Technology: Myriad Faces of Armed Conflict* (New York, 2001), 167–193; G. Morton-Jack, 'The Indian Army on the Western Front, 1914–1915: A Portrait of Collaboration', *War in History*, XIII (2006), 329–362; G. Corrigan, *Sepoys in the Trenches: The Indian Corps on the Western Front, 1914–1915* (Stroud, 1999).

19. G. Morton-Jack, *The Indian Army on the Western Front: India's Expeditionary Force to France and Belgium in the First World War* (Cambridge, 2014).
20. N. Gardner, *The Siege of Kut-al-Amara: At War in Mesopotamia, 1915–1916* (Bloomington, 2014); R. Anderson, 'The Battle of Tanga, 2–5 November 1914', *War in History*, VIII (2001), 294–322.
21. K. Roy, 'From Defeat to Victory: Logistics of the Campaign in Mesopotamia, 1914–1918', *First World War Studies*, I (2010), 35–55; K. Roy (ed.), *The Indian Army in the Two World Wars* (Leiden, 2012); A. Syk, 'Command and the Mesopotamia Expeditionary Force, 1915–1918' (Oxford University, D.Phil. thesis, 2009); J. E. Kitchen, *The British Imperial Army in the Middle East: Morale and Military Identity in the Sinai and Palestine Campaigns, 1916–18* (London, 2014).
22. J. Darwin, *The Empire Project: The Rise and Fall of the British World-System, 1830–1970* (Cambridge, 2009), 305–358; S. Garton, 'The Dominions, Ireland, and India', in R. Gerwarth and E. Manela (eds.), *Empires at War: 1911–1923* (Oxford, 2014), 152–177.
23. For dissent in the Indian Army in general see D. Omissi, *The Sepoy and the Raj: The Indian Army, 1860–1940* (Manchester, 1994), 113–152.
24. B. Nasson, 'British Imperial Africa', in R. Gerwarth and E. Manela (eds.), *Empires at War: 1911–1923* (Oxford, 2014), 130–151.
25. C. Townshend, *Easter 1916: The Irish Rebellion* (London, 2005).
26. Darwin, *Empire Project*, 333–343 and 353–357.
27. J. Gallagher, 'Nationalisms and the Crisis of Empire, 1919–1922', *Modern Asian Studies*, XV (1981), 355–368.
28. C. Townshend, *The British Campaign in Ireland, 1919–1921: The Development of Political and Military Policies* (Oxford, 1975).
29. J. Darwin, *Britain, Egypt and the Middle East: Imperial Policy in the Aftermath of War, 1918–1922* (London, 1981); K. Jeffery, *The British Army and the Crisis of Empire, 1918–22* (Manchester, 1984).
30. J. Eichenberg and J. P. Newman, 'Aftershocks: Violence in Dissolving Empires After the First World War', *Contemporary European History*, XIX (2010), 183–194; R. Gerwarth and J. Horne (eds.), *War in Peace: Paramilitary Violence in Europe After the Great War* (Oxford, 2012); R. Gerwarth and J. E. Kitchen, 'Transnational Approaches to the "Crisis of Empire" After 1918: Introduction', *Journal of Modern European History*, XIII (2015), 173–182.
31. Morton-Jack, *Indian Army on the Western Front*, 286.
32. Darwin, *Empire Project*, 324–333.
33. A. Thomson, ' "Steadfast Until Death"? C. E. W. Bean and the Representation of Australian Military Manhood', *Australian Historical Studies*, XXIII (1989), 462–478; K. Fewster, 'Ellis Ashmead Bartlett and the Making of the Anzac Legend', *Journal of Australian Studies*, X (1982), 17–30.
34. R. Smith, *Jamaican Volunteers in the First World War: Race, Masculinity and the Development of National Consciousness* (Manchester, 2004); R. Smith, 'World War I and the Permanent West Indian Soldier', in A. T. Jarboe and R. S. Fogarty (eds.), *Empires in World War I: Shifting Frontiers and Imperial Dynamics in a Global Conflict* (London, 2014), 303–327; G. D. Howe, *Race, War and Nationalism: A Social History of West Indians in the First World War* (Kingston, 2002).
35. T. C. Winegard, *Indigenous Peoples of the British Dominions and the First World War* (Cambridge, 2012), 256–270.
36. Strachan, 'First World War as a Global War', 9.
37. R. Prior, *Churchill's 'World Crisis' as History* (London, 1983).
38. M. Hughes, *Allenby and British Strategy in the Middle East 1917–1919* (London, 1999).
39. K. C. Ulrichsen, *The First World War in the Middle East* (London, 2014), 149–172.
40. S. Pedersen, 'The Meaning of the Mandates System: An Argument', *Geschichte und Gesellschaft*, XXXII (2006), 560–582; E. Manela, *The Wilsonian Moment: Self-Determination and the International Origins of Anticolonial Nationalism* (Oxford 2007).
41. For prisoner of war and internment camps see R. Ahuja, 'The Corrosiveness of Comparison: Reverberations of Indian Wartime Experiences in German Prisoner of War Camps (1915–1919)', in H. Liebau, K. Bromber, K. Lange, D. Hamzah and R. Ahuja (eds.), *The World*

in World Wars: Experiences, Perceptions and Perspectives from Africa and Asia (Leiden, 2010), 131–166; D. Steinbach, 'Challenging European Colonial Supremacy: The Internment of "Enemy Aliens" in British and German East Africa During the First World War', in J. E. Kitchen, A. Miller and L. Rowe (eds.), *Other Combatants, Other Fronts: Competing Histories of the First World War* (Newcastle, 2011), 153–175. For the importance of race in the imperial history of the First World War see S. Das (ed.), *Race, Empire and First World War Writing* (Cambridge, 2011); J. H. Morrow, 'The Imperial Framework', in J. Winter (ed.), *The Cambridge History of the First World War. Volume I: Global War* (Cambridge, 2014), 405–432.

42. R. Anderson, *The Forgotten Front: The East African Campaign, 1914–1918* (Stroud, 2004); Syk, 'Command and the Mesopotamia Expeditionary Force'; A. Syk (ed.), *The Military Papers of Lieutenant General Sir Frederick Stanley Maude, 1914–1917* (Stroud, 2012); Kitchen, *British Imperial Army*; Gardner, *Siege of Kut-al-Amara*; K. C. Ulrichsen, *The Logistics and Politics of the British Campaign in the Middle East, 1914–22* (Basingstoke, 2011).
43. C. Pugsley, *The Anzac Experience: New Zealand, Australia and Empire in the First World War* (Auckland, 2004).
44. T. Tai-Yong, 'An Imperial Home-Front: Punjab and the First World War', *The Journal of Military History*, LXIV (2000), 371–410.
45. R. Gerwarth and E. Manela (eds.), *Empires at War: 1911–1923* (Oxford, 2014).
46. The journals are *African Identities, Australian Historical Studies, First World War Studies, Journal of Imperial and Commonwealth History,* and *Round Table: The Commonwealth Journal of International Affairs.*
47. J. Guldi and D. Armitage, *The History Manifesto* (Cambridge, 2014).
48. A comparative focus is at the heart of the *1914–18 Online: International Encyclopedia of the First World War* project; see J. E. Kitchen, 'Colonial Empires After the War/Decolonization', in Ute Daniel, Peter Gatrell, Oliver Janz, Heather Jones, Jennifer Keene, Alan Kramer and Bill Nasson (eds.), *1914–1918-online: International Encyclopedia of the First World War* (Berlin: Freie Universität Berlin, 2014), available at http://encyclopedia.1914-1918-online.net/article/Colonial_Empires_after_the_War-Decolonization.

The First World War as a global war

Hew Strachan

All Souls College, University of Oxford, Oxford, UK

This article discusses the widening of the First World War from a European war to a global war and what that meant for the participants. Today's politicians, who talk (albeit tautologically) of an 'increasingly globalized world', forget how already 'globalized' the world seemed in 1914, especially if you happened to live in London. The fact that the First World War was a global war was itself the product of a global order, shaped by the European great powers and held together by an embryonic economic system. The title 'the world war' was a statement about its importance, not a statement about its geographical scale. And yet the French and British official histories, unlike the German, did not use 'world war' in their titles, any more than they had used the phrase during the war itself. They preferred the title 'the Great War', and in English the war only became widely known as the First World War after 1945, in other words after there had been a Second World War. The article explores the implications of the title 'the Great War' and the idea that the war of 1914–1918 was a great European war (a name also used in Britain, especially during the war itself).

The article also examines the role of finances in the widening of the war and the global economy during a worldwide conflict. It also discusses the role of empires in the expanding war. However, the financial situation of participants, including those who entered the war at a later date, and the desire for empire were not the only factors in the creation of a global conflict. Decisions made in the interest of individual nations also had an effect on the widening of the war from a regional dispute.

The corollary of the article's argument, that the First World War was in some respects an aggregation of regional conflicts, was that the war would not simply end when the European war ended. All that was agreed on 11 November 1918 was the surrender of Germany, largely on terms which reflected the situation within Europe and specifically on the western front. Only here did the guns fell silent at 11am on that day. However, so imperative were the immediate demands of the conflict that there was scant consideration of their long-term effects. Some of the consequences of the fact that the First World War was waged as a global war remained with Europe throughout the Cold War, and others remain in the Middle East to this day.

H.M. Tomlinson was a patriot but also a pacifist, a man who reported on the war from the Western Front and in 1917 became the literary editor of *The Nation*. In 1930 his war novel, *All our Yesterdays*, was reprinted three times within a month of its publication. The book has not entered the canon of First World War literature. Tomlinson's prose is wordy and contrived. His characters, in Cyril Falls's apt criticism, 'do not live except while under the narrator's eyes and through his eyes'.[1] And yet, in his critical guide to war books, Falls called *All our Yesterdays* 'a very fine book', and according it two stars in a classification system that ranked it alongside A.P. Herbert's *The Secret Battle* and, somewhat less excusably, Ford Madox Ford's magnificent 'Tietjens tetralogy', *Parade's End*.

All our Yesterdays was designed to show how the war had cut across the lives of British lives in the first quarter of the twentieth century. The first of its five parts is entitled '1900', and the book does not reach what it calls 'War!' until the fourth. Tomlinson had been born in the east end of London, had worked as a shipping clerk, and had first found literary success with his account of a journey up the Amazon, *The Sea and the Jungle*, published in 1912. These biographical elements found their places in *All our Yesterdays*, and in Chapter 8 of Book 4 Tomlinson – as a Londoner whose living and experience of life were shaped by the City's global and maritime interests – provided a tour d'horizon of the strategic situation at the end of 1914:

> Russians were hurling Kurds from the slopes of Mount Ararat. And at Basra, that port for which Sinbad had set sail, Sikhs had arrived from the Punjab, and Gurkhas from the Himalayas; and these men, moved by the new zeal which would free us from the tyranny of obsolete and ruinous dogmas, and led by young men from English public schools, marched to dislodge Ottomans who were entrenched in the Garden of Eden. The coconut groves of New Guinea were stormed by Australians. In those days, while steaming at sunset under the snows of the Andes, British ships were sunk by their foes; who, but little later, were sunk by British warships off the Falkland Islands. Merchant vessels and their cargoes foundered in the Bay of Bengal and off the Cape of Good Hope through the explosions of torpedoes. It might have been thought that Penang, that city of light and colour with its smell of spices, would have remained inviolate, if only because it was on the Strait of Malacca, yet a German cruiser appeared there one day, scattered its anchorage with smoking wreckage, and vanished again, leaving on the waters the bodies of a number of Japanese girls, which had floated out of a sunken Russian cruiser.

There is more in the same vein, as Tomlinson employs irony to describe the mutiny of Indian troops in Singapore and the Germans' determination to hold Shantung against the Japanese. Then he concludes:

> It was already becoming clear for the first time to many onlookers that the earth was not two hemispheres as we had thought, but one simple and responsive ball, and that happenings on the shores of the Yellow Sea and elsewhere may cause disturbing noises even in Washington.[2]

Today's politicians, who talk (albeit tautologically) of an increasingly globalized world, forget how already 'globalized' the world seemed in 1914, especially if you happened to live in London. The fact that the First World War was a global war was itself the product of a global order, shaped by the European great powers and held together by an embryonic economic system. By 1930 Tomlinson's evocation of the repercussions felt in Asia and the Pacific within four months of the outbreak of a war whose epicentre lay in south-eastern Europe should, to that extent, have been a statement of the obvious. But it was not.

True, the literature of warning written before 1914, particularly works published in Germany, spoke of the coming conflict as 'the world war', *Der*

Weltkrieg.³ The policy of *Weltpolitik* or 'world policy', embraced by Germany's penultimate pre-war chancellor, Bernhard von Bülow, argued that his country's great power status was conditional on its standing in the wider world, and led the German admiralty staff to speak of world war in 1905.⁴ In Vienna, Franz Conrad von Hötzendorff, the chief of the Austro-Hungarian general staff, had an audience with the emperor, Franz Josef, in January 1913, in which he presented the annual report for 1912 of the governor of Bosnia–Herzegovina, Oskar Potiorek. Conrad took the opportunity, not for the first time, to advocate a preventive war with Serbia, but the emperor told him that he feared Russia above all and that, if there were war with Serbia, a wider conflict would follow. Franz Josef described this war as a '*Weltkrieg*'.⁵ In Berlin four months later, on 24 April 1913, Bülow's successor as chancellor, Theodor von Bethmann Hollweg, said he would do all he could to avoid war, but 'If there is a war, it will be a world war [*einen Weltkrieg*], and we must wage it on two fronts ... It will be a war for survival [*ein Existenzkampf*]'.⁶

That is really the point. The title 'the world war' was a statement about its importance, not a statement about its geographical scale. It would be a war for the very existence of the German and Austro-Hungarian empires. In each of these cases, those who spoke of the threat of world war did so for rhetorical effect, rather than in order to clarify a planning assumption. German naval officers may have anticipated a world war, but Alfred von Tirpitz, the head of the Reich's naval armaments office, built a German fleet designed overwhelmingly for operations in the North Sea. He neglected the construction of cruisers for oceanic war despite the Kaiser's wishes. When Conrad advocated war with Serbia, he was envisaging a limited war to reassert the empire's authority in the Balkans. After the crisis broke in July 1914, he was almost wilful in his disregard of the danger that a Balkan war would become a European war and a European war a world war. Finally, even Bethmann Hollweg's statement spoke only of a two-front war, a war waged simultaneously against France and Russia. He did not mention a third front, a war to the south with Italy or in the Balkans, or a war at sea, let alone war in Africa or the Far East.

After the war was over, the German official history, published by the Reichsarchiv, was called *Der Weltkrieg*, and yet its contents did not reflect the title. An account of military operations on land only, and separate from those series devoted to the war at sea and in the air, its attention to the fronts outside Europe was fleeting.⁷ There is a paradox here. The equivalent series in France and Britain have much less grandiloquent titles and yet range much further geographically. *Les Armées Françaises dans la Grande Guerre* allocated a whole volume to the war in the Cameroons. The British official history, given the overall title of the *Official History of the Great War*, devoted four volumes of its series on the land war, *Military Operations*, to Mesopotamia; one to the Cameroons; three to Egypt and Palestine; two to Gallipoli, and one (with a further volume planned but never completed) to East Africa.⁸ And yet the French and British official histories, unlike the German, did not use 'world war' in their titles, any more than they had used the phrase during the war itself. They preferred the title 'the Great War', and in English the war only became widely known as the First World War after 1945, in other words after there had been a Second World War. Admittedly Charles à Court Repington, the military correspondent of *The Times*, chose in 1920 to call his war memoirs *The First World War 1914–1918*, but his motivation (which he did not explain, but certainly included a desire to provoke) appears to have been his frustration with the peace settlement rather than a determination to reflect the global shape of the war itself. The French, even today, are as likely to call the First World War *la grande guerre* as they are to call it *la première guerre mondiale*.

Implicit in the title 'the Great War' is the idea that the war of 1914–1918 was a great European war (a name also used in Britain, especially during the war itself). Such a description carried the connotation of a civil war between civilized nations, united by Christianity and capitalism, an act of collective folly which would result in their losing their primacy in the world to the United States. According to this view, Tomlinson was wrong: the First World War did not become a world war in 1914, but in 1917, when the United States entered it and when Russia, by dint of its revolutions, left. In the same way the Second World War can be seen as a European war between 1939 and 1941, and only became a world war when Hitler invaded the Soviet Union in June 1941 and Japan attacked Pearl Harbor in December of the same year.[9] This, however, is history written with hindsight, shaped by the Cold War, and by the knowledge that the legacy of 1917 and 1941 would be a prolonged stand-off between the United States and the Soviet Union. In fact, Tomlinson was right. In 1914 Europe was the centre of the world, and as soon as Austria–Hungary's war with Serbia could no longer be limited to the Balkans it would become a world war, and not just a European one. This line of thinking produces the somewhat paradoxical notion that the ancient and doddery Franz Josef, in recognizing this danger in 1913, showed himself to be one of the more far-sighted statesmen of 1914. However, the emperor probably did not know why he was right, whereas H.M. Tomlinson did. Europe was the centre of the world in 1914 for two reasons, neither of which was necessarily of paramount consideration to the emperor or even to Austria–Hungary: the first was financial and commercial, and the second colonial and imperial.

In July 1914, 59 countries were on the gold standard. In other words, they used gold coin or backed their paper money with a set percentage of gold, and they determined a gold value for their currency and guaranteed its convertibility. During major crises, the central banks of the leading nations cooperated. In 1907, in a crisis which reminds us that the financial storm of 2009 has many more precedents than that of 1929, the Banque de France and the Reichsbank in Germany drew on their gold reserves to support the Bank of England, caught by heavy American borrowing. Both banks pushed up their interest rates to increase their gold stocks, while trying to prevent the flow of gold to the United States. What was important in the 1907 crisis was the behaviour of the Bank of England. Unlike the central banks of France and Germany, it did not build up its gold reserves, preferring to use gold rather than to hoard it. It could do that because it was the centre of the world's money and insurance markets. Its strength was its liquidity. By 1910 the United States may have held 31% of the world's gold reserves, but it still financed its trade through London. Therefore the gold standard worked because it was in reality a sterling exchange system, with the world's commerce revolving around the pound sterling. The centrality of the pound to international exchanges and to world markets made Britain's entry to the First World War of paramount importance.[10]

When Sir Edward Grey, the British foreign secretary, told the House of Commons on the afternoon of 3 August 1914 that Britain was on the brink of war, he stressed that as a commercial and maritime nation Britain would be so affected by war in Europe that it would be little worse off if it became a belligerent than if it remained a neutral. He imagined a war fought, at least from the British perspective, almost entirely at sea; he did not anticipate Britain raising a mass army for service on the continent of Europe. Britain's economic position pivoted on the City of London, the shipping industry in which Tomlinson had worked, and its balance of trade. Indeed, in the eyes of Asquith's Liberal cabinet these were the principal strengths which Britain could contribute to the Entente's war effort.

By the same token, when Britain became a belligerent, every country in the world was affected. Those who were Britain's enemies were progressively cut off from overseas trade by the naval blockade. Despite being the world's second largest industrial power by 1914, Germany could only export or import to those neutrals on its immediate borders. It was unable to access international money markets, particularly that of New York, despite strong pro-German sentiment in at least some parts of the United States.[11] Those who were Britain's allies found that their access to the same money markets, and so to the borrowing required to pay for the overseas imports which they needed to equip their war efforts, depended on Britain's international credit-worthiness, and on the sterling–dollar exchange rate. From the war's onset, Russia could not raise funds in the United States, but Britain could. By 1916 Britain had become the vehicle by which France and Italy too raised funds in America. Finally, those who remained neutral found that their wealth and trade were increasingly compromised by the war because of the power of the sterling–dollar relationship and because of the capacity of Britain to keep its shipping and insurance business active despite hostilities. Neutrality proved to be relative, not absolute.

This was particularly true of the principal neutral, the United States. The United States may have been a late entrant to the war, but from its outset in 1914 America's recovery from depression was achieved on the back of orders from the Entente powers. Britain sold treasury bonds to American private investors, using J.P. Morgan as its agents. Much of the finance so raised was then used to maintain the sterling–dollar exchange rate so as to control the prices of goods from the United States. So heavily had the private investors of the United States sunk their resources in Allied debt that on 28 November 1916 the Federal Reserve Board, temporarily dominated by pro-German and neutral sentiment, warned them that they were speculating too heavily on an Entente victory. By then, two-fifths of Britain's daily spending on the war was directed to the United States, and it was reckoned that five-sixths of British expenditure over the next six months would have to be funded by loans, mostly raised on the New York stock market. Britain was effectively spending money in the United States which was then borrowed back to be spent in the United States again. Moreover, it was doing so not only on its own account but also on those of its allies, France, Russia and Italy. The Federal Reserve Board's warning created a crisis in Allied finances that was only resolved (and even then not fully so) by the entry of the United States to the war in 1917.[12]

Britain's entry to the war in 1914 therefore meant that finance and trade were affected globally, whether a state was belligerent or not, and Britain's adoption of economic warfare only underlined this point. But the implications were also more narrowly strategic. Each of the Entente powers, Russia, France and especially Britain, were colonial powers. As a result of their entering the war, all Africa, save Ethiopia and Liberia, much of Asia, effectively all of Australasia, and parts of the Americas also found themselves at war.

For the imperial powers themselves, empire implied resources, especially of manpower. Nowhere was this more true than of France, confronted with a falling population and obsessed accordingly with pro-natalism. In the years leading up to the outbreak of war, in order to match the size of the German army, France had to call up over 80% of its adult male population, whereas its rival could keep pace by conscripting only 57%. In 1910, General Charles Mangin had proposed raising an army from French Equatorial Africa, 'la force noire', in addition to the units already formed in French North Africa and Indo-China. By the end of the war France had raised 200,000 men from West Africa alone, and 550,000 from the empire as a whole, of whom 440,000 served in Europe.[13] In 1914 Britain's biggest army was not at home but in India. While Britain prepared one expeditionary force in August, India formed four – one each for Europe, Egypt, Mesopotamia and East Africa. India raised 1.4 million soldiers during the war, of whom 1.1 million served outside the subcontinent. Furthermore, some argue that by 1917 Britain's crack fighting units in France came from the 'white' dominions of Canada, Australia, New Zealand, and – to a lesser extent – South Africa. Together they contributed 1.2 million men, of whom 900,000 served in Europe.[14] Finally, Russia raised 15 million men in the war, the largest number of any belligerent, even if that figure only represented 39% of its population of military age. To raise less than half that total, France had to take twice that percentage. While it seems reasonable to conclude that the Russian army was predominantly European in its ethnic composition, there is no reason to suggest that it was exclusively so.

In terms of resources, the Entente had the global capacity to defeat the Central Powers in short order.[15] But economic determinism is, in isolation, a poor tool for explaining battlefield outcomes. The keys to unlocking this capacity were, first, its mobilization and, second, its concentration and application to the fighting fronts where they would be most effective. Strategically, therefore, neither France nor Britain had an interest in the war becoming global. They called it the Great War, not the world war, precisely because they needed to confine its fighting to Europe. If the war was widened, then their resources would be dispersed, not concentrated; they would have to defend their colonies, not attack Germany.

The war at sea provides an obvious illustration of this point. The Royal Navy's principal battles of 1914, to which Tomlinson referred (albeit somewhat elliptically), were fought not in the North Sea, but in the south Pacific at Coronel and, decisively, in the south Atlantic, off the Falkland islands. They were designed to remove the German cruiser threat to the world's shipping lanes, and so secure Britain's ability to tap into the world's markets. Britain's conduct of the war on land reinforces the argument. On 5 August 1914 a subcommittee of the Committee of Imperial Defence met to consider what to do with British land forces both within Europe and outside it. Its aim outside Europe was denial – to close down Germany's ability to use its African and Pacific colonies as bases for offensive operations designed to widen the war, to prevent the use of their ports by German cruisers, and to break up the German global wireless network radiating out from Nauen that would coordinate the actions of those cruisers. Britain's attacks on German colonies in 1914 were not part of an imperialist design, a manifestation of a Fischer-like war aims agenda or a fulfilment of the socialists' pre-1914 expectation that, if war came, it would be a war of imperialism. If war aims fuelled the overseas campaigns that Britain fought in 1914–15, they were inspired by so-called 'sub-imperialism', the ambitions not of

Britain but of its subordinate dominions. Australia and New Zealand had eyes on New Guinea and Samoa in the south Pacific, and South Africa hoped to expand into Namibia and up to the Zambezi. Territorial concessions were the price of their loyalty to London, not of any ambitions for an even larger post-war empire entertained in Whitehall.

By the same token, the Central Powers had an interest in widening the war, precisely to draw Entente forces away from Europe. This was a particular focus for the war between Germany and Britain. In German East Africa, Paul von Lettow Vorbeck, who had arrived as the military commander at the beginning of 1914, argued in a memorandum of 15 May 1914 that, if there were war, then the fighting in East Africa should be treated not as a self-sufficient episode but made to interact with 'the great war' in Europe. Lettow's aim, in a campaign sustained throughout 1914–1918, was not colonial (indeed, his conduct of the war devastated the German colony), but military: to use East Africa as a war zone so as to divert British resources from the main theatre of operations.[16]

The most dramatic illustration of this point was Germany's alliance with the Ottoman empire. On 13 March 1914, Helmuth von Moltke the younger, chief of the Prussian general staff, wrote to Conrad, his Austro-Hungarian counterpart:

> Turkey is militarily a nonentity! The reports of our military mission sound desperate. The state of the army is ridiculed in every report. If Turkey was previously described as a sick man, now we must speak of it as a dying one. It has no life force left, and finds itself beyond saving as it enters its final agony. Our military mission is like a medical board, whose doctors stand by the death bed of an incurable invalid.[17]

That was Wilhelm II's view, too. But Britain's attitude to the July crisis changed everything. On 30 July 1914, the Kaiser announced that 'our consuls in Turkey and India ... must inflame the whole Muslim world to rebel against this hated, treacherous and ignorant nation of criminals; if we are going to shed our blood, then England must at least lose India'.[18] This demand would culminate with the declaration of Holy War by the Caliphate on 14 November 1914, summoning Muslims to rise specifically against British, French, Russian, Serb and Montenegrin rule, but not German or Austro-Hungarian.[19]

Moltke too changed his tune. What he had inherited from his predecessor as chief of the general staff, Alfred von Schlieffen, was a plan for a short campaign within Europe, but what he faced was the need to wage a long war that embraced the world. 'This war', he remarked to his adjutant, Hans von Haeften, shortly after midnight on 30–31 July 1914, 'will grow into a world war in which England will also intervene. Few can have an idea of the extent, the duration and the end of this war.'[20] He had warned the Kaiser of as much when he was identified as Schlieffen's successor almost 10 years before,[21] but now he had to do something about it. He was particularly worried about the Eastern Front, where the German army seemed too weak to prevent a Russian invasion. Both he and his predecessor had somewhat blithely assumed that their Austro-Hungarian ally would pull the main weight of the Russian army south towards Galicia, although neither of them had any faith in the capacity of the Austro-Hungarian army to do so. Accordingly, on 5 August 1914 he called for an Islamic revolution in the Caucasus. War in the Caucasus would at the very least prevent Russia from deploying units from there to the Central Powers' Eastern Front (or the Russians' Western Front), and at best might even pull Russian units from East Prussia and Galicia to the Caucasus. The alliance with Turkey was agreed by Germany on 2 August 1914 and by Austria–Hungary on 5 August. Both imagined that the Ottoman army would attack in the Caucasus so as to lure Russian troops south and east.

On 20 August 1914, Moltke added in Morocco, Tunisia, Algeria and Afghanistan; now Islamic revolution had become the means to enable Germany to attack French North Africa and to stoke war on the north-west frontier of British India. The Ottoman empire had become the land bridge by which Germany escaped its encirclement within Europe. Germany needed all its troops and munitions in Europe, and the only instruments available to it with which to implement this expanding strategy were diplomatic. Even if it could not transport an army down the Danube to Istanbul, and thence to Anatolia, Central Asia, the Middle East and North Africa, it could at least send agents and consuls. They brought promises, not only of arms but also of gold and even of national independence. Turkey apart, most local rulers were canny enough to bide their time, waiting for the promises to gain substance, and prudent enough to play one side off against another. The Entente found itself with an extra theatre of war, but it was one which militarily it was able to contain. German diplomacy had widened the war, and it threatened to widen it further.

The globalization of what had begun as a Balkan war was not just due to finance and empire, or to the Anglo–German antagonism. None of these pressures explains why Turkey fell in with Germany's plans, nor why it resisted pressure from Britain and France to stay out of the war. The Ottoman empire had just lost most of the remaining vestiges of its European territory; it was deeply in debt, and it was wracked by domestic turmoil, suffering a succession of coups and counter-coups. These were good reasons for not compounding its problems by entering a major war, and it certainly had no interest in becoming a tool of German ambitions. But such factors added to the attractions of an ally that seemed to harbour few expansionist designs within the Ottomans' own sphere of interest, and which had suddenly become ready to treat them seriously in a way that the other European powers had not. Turkey entered the First World War because its government, or, to be more exact, elements within its government, concluded that it suited Turkey's needs to do so. What Turkey's decision reflects is that, once war broke out in Europe at the end of July 1914, a whole series of regional conflicts and latent antagonisms attached themselves to the central conflict and, by doing so, widened it.

Turkey did not care about developments in France or in East Prussia, and it did not wish to be the tool of Germany's strategy for widening the war. It agreed to the alliance with the Central Powers because it needed to recover its own position and status. It regarded both the Caucasus and Egypt as falling within its own territorial orbit, as elements of the Ottoman empire. Thus there was a short-term convergence between Germany's wider aims against Russia and Britain and Turkey's nearer goals. Moreover, the Ottoman empire needed an alliance to secure its standing in the Aegean and to recover it in the Balkans. Like Austria–Hungary and Bulgaria, it wished to overthrow the verdict of the Balkan wars of 1912–1913. On this reading, an alliance with the Central Powers was a means to create a fresh Balkan bloc that would include Bulgaria and Romania and isolate Greece.

Other later entrants to the war pursued similar regional ambitions, which also piggybacked on to the original war but did not share its motivations. The universalism of the rhetoric espoused with such speed by the original belligerents, the claim that this was a war for '*Kultur*', for 'civilization', for the rights of small nations and international law, found little echo amid the more obviously self-interested and territorial motivations of those who followed. Italy entered the war in 1915 to further its local ambitions in Austro-Hungarian Slovenia; Bulgaria and Romania also aimed to expand their frontiers at the expense of their immediate neighbours when they joined the war on opposing sides in 1915 and 1916. Both Japan and Portugal responded to the outbreak of war with concerns that were specifically extra-European. Japan exploited the Anglo-Japanese alliance in August 1914 precisely to further its territorial ambitions in China and the Pacific. Its contribution to the war in Europe was confined to a naval flotilla, reluctantly deployed in 1917 to the Mediterranean. Portugal, worried that the outcome of the war would see it lose its African colonies, was anxious to fight precisely to secure them. Britain resisted this pressure until 1916, trying to contain Portugal's involvement to Angola and Mozambique, but in 1916 Portugal requisitioned the shipping of the Central Powers that had been interned in its ports in 1914, and so provoked the latter into open hostilities. These regional interests stacked up and, as they did so, so their pressures became mutually reinforcing, especially after the United States' entry, which brought in its wake allies such as China and a clutch of South American states. Their military contributions were negligible, but they, like Japan and Portugal, recognized that this war was now so big that they could better protect their interests by fighting than by not doing so. Belligerence was a passport to the peace negotiations, which seemed likely to create a new world order.

The corollary of this argument, that the First World War was in some respects an aggregation of regional conflicts, was that the war would not simply end when the European war ended. All that was agreed on 11 November 1918 was the surrender of Germany, largely on terms that reflected the situation within Europe and specifically on the Western Front. Only here did the guns fall silent at 11 am on that day. They had already done so on the Macedonian, Italian and Palestinian fronts, in a series of independent settlements with Bulgaria, Austria (but not Hungary, which did not agree terms until 13 November), and Turkey. However, other regional conflicts persisted. The collapse of four empires, those of Russia, Turkey, Austria–Hungary, and Germany, also meant that new ones emerged, including wars between the Czechs and Hungarians, the Hungarians and Romanians, and the Poles and Russians. Some reflected the resumption of older antagonisms, for example that between the Greeks and Turks. The British Chief of the Imperial General Staff, Sir Henry Wilson, wrote to Lord Esher on 14 November 1919: 'It is again pathetic to realise that one year and three days after the Armistice we have between 20 and 30 wars raging in different parts of the world'.[22]

War had bred war, and this was true in a very direct way. Some of the wars that so irked Wilson were the ongoing effects of the strategies which the Central Powers had adopted during hostilities precisely because of their desire to widen the First World War. The 3rd Afghan War of 1919 can be seen as the pay-off for the German mission to Afghanistan in 1915. The emir, Habibullah, had played a long and circumspect hand, despite pressure from his more intemperate and pro-German brother, Nasrullah. In February 1919 Nasrullah assassinated Habibullah and led his country into a war with British India. In 1922 Egypt threw off British rule, in a similarly delayed response to German agitation, which had been orchestrated in 1914 by Max von Oppenheim. And the biggest of the wars that still raged in late 1919, the Russian Civil War, could on one reading be seen as the consequence of Germany's readiness to help Lenin get back from Switzerland to Russia in 1917, precisely because of Berlin's determination to promote internal division the better to prosecute the First World War.

It has been fashionable to see the treaty of Versailles and its attendant agreements as a cause of the Second World War. This reading blames both the idealism of Woodrow Wilson and the punitive terms demanded of Germany by the Allies for the idea that the two world wars were both 'German wars', and that the years 1919–1939 can be seen as nothing other than a prolonged armistice.[23] But the peacemakers of 1919, and pre-eminently Wilson himself, were trying to make peace, not war. Their focus may have been European more than it was global, but their ambitions, as manifested in the League of Nations, possessed a universality that was global in its aspiration. Many of the fault lines that dogged the inter-war years found their origins less in the making of the peace in 1919 than in the waging of the war in 1914–1918. It was to wage war that the Entente condoned Japan's ambitions in China in 1914–1915, and it was to pursue those that Japan broke with the League of Nations and in 1937 attacked China, so beginning the Second World War. It was also to wage war that Germany sought the alliance with the Ottoman empire and so set in train the events that led Britain (also through its need to wage war) to make contradictory promises in the Middle East to the French and the Arabs. It was also the better to wage war that the generals of the Russian army colluded in the fall of the Tsar in March 1917, so in turn enabling Germany the more effectively to employ its own strategy of promoting revolution as a means to wage war. In all these cases, so imperative were the immediate demands of the conflict that there was scant consideration of their long-term effects. Some of the consequences of the fact that the First World War was waged as a global war remained with Europe throughout the Cold War, and others remain in the Middle East to this day.

Notes
1. Falls 1930, 299.
2. Tomlinson 1930, 340–1. This essay was first delivered as a lecture at a symposium held in Vienna on 7 November 2009 to mark the 90th anniversary of the foundation of the Austrian Republic, '1918–1920: der Fall der Imperien und der Traum einer besseren Welt', and I am grateful to Wolfgang Maderthaner and Lutz Musner of the Verein für Geschichte der Arbeiterbewegung for their invitation and inspiration. Since then it has had outings as a seminar paper at Victoria University Wellington and St Andrews University, and it was the keynote lecture at the 2009 conference of the International Society for First World War Studies; I am grateful for the questions and comments raised on all these occasions.
3. Clarke 1997, for examples of the genre; see also Echevarria 2007 and Dülffer 1994.
4. Herwig 1991, 281.
5. Jerabek 1991, 100.
6. Schulte 1980, 116.
7. Pöhlmann 2002; there seems little sense that the title of the series was ever seriously debated.
8. Green 2003; again, the title does not seem to have debated.
9. For this sort of thinking, see Lukacs 1977.
10. See de Cecco 1984, 115–21; Eichengreen 1992, 3–9, 29–66.
11. See Frey 1994, 327–53; Knauss 1923 remains useful, here 73–4.
12. The essential work on this is Burk 1985, 80–93; see also Nouailhat 1979, 373–82; Cooper 1976, 209–30.
13. Michel 1982, 21–4, 404.
14. War Office 1922, 363, 379–84.
15. A point that forms a key theme of Ferguson 1998, 248–318.

16. Boell 1951, 23.
17. Mühlmann 1942, 22; see also Wallach 1976.
18. Gehrke 1960, vol. 1, 1.
19. Lewis 1977.
20. Mombauer 2001, 206.
21. von Moltke 1922, 308.
22. Jeffery 1985, 133.
23. For this sort of thinking, see Bobbitt 2002; Goodspeed 1978.

References

Bobbitt, Philip. 2002. *The shield of Achilles*. London: Alfred A. Knopf.
Boell, Ludwig. 1951. *Die Operationen in Ostafrika*. Hamburg: Dachert.
Burk, Kathleen. 1985. *Britain, America and the sinews of war, 1914–1918*. Boston: Allen & Unwin.
Clarke, I.F. 1997. *The Great War with Germany, 1890–1914: fictions and fantasies of the war-to-come*. Liverpool: Liverpool University Press.
Cooper, John Milton. 1976. The power of gold reversed: American loans to Britain, 1915–1917. *Pacific Historical Review* 45, no. 1: 209–30.
de Cecco, Marcello. 1984. *The international gold standard: money and empire*. 2nd ed. London: Palgrave Macmillan.
Dülffer, Jost. 1994. Kriegserwartung und Kriegsbild in Deutschland vor 1914. In *Der erste Weltkrieg: Wirkung, Warnehmung, Analyse*, ed. Wolfgang Michalka, 778–98. Munich: Piper.
Echevarria, Antulio J. 2007. *Imagining future war: the west's technological revolution and visions of war to come, 1880–1914*. Westport, CT: Praeger.
Eichengreen, Barry. 1992. *Golden fetters: the gold standard and the Great Depression, 1919–1939*. New York: Oxford University Press.
Falls, Cyril. 1930. *War books: a critical guide*. 2nd ed. London: Peter Davies, 1989.
Ferguson, Niall. 1998. *The pity of war*. London: Allen Lane.
Frey, Marc. 1994. Deutsche Finanzinteressen an der Vereinigten Staaten und den Niederlanden im Ersten Weltkrieg. *Militärgeschichtliche Mitteilungen* 53: 327–53.
Gehrke, Ulrich. 1960. *Persien in der deutschen Orientpolitik während des Ersten Weltkrieges*. 2 vols. Stuttgart: W. Kohlhammer.
Goodspeed, D.J. 1978. *The German wars 1914–1945*. London: Orbis Books.
Green, Andrew. 2003. *Writing the Great War: Sir James Edmonds and the Official Histories 1915–1948*. London: Routledge.
Herwig, Holger. 1991. The German reaction to the Dreadnought revolution. *International History Review* 13, no. 2: 273–83.
Jeffrey, Keith, ed. 1985. *The military correspondence of Field Marshal Sir Henry Wilson 1918–1922*. London: The Bodley Head for The Army Records Society.
Jerabek, Rudolf. 1991. *Potiorek. General im Schatten von Sarajevo*. Graz: Styria.
Knauss, Robert. 1923. *Die Deutsche, Englische und Französische Kriegsfinanzierung*. Berlin: W. de Gruyter.
Lewis, Geoffrey. 1977. The Ottoman proclamation of Jihad in 1914. In *Arabic and Islamic garland: historical, educational and literary papers presented to Abdul-Latif Tibawi by colleagues, friends, and students*, ed. Abdul-Latif Tibawi, 159–65. London: The Islamic Cultural Centre.
Lukacs, John. 1977. *The last European war*. London: Routledge & Kegan Paul.
Michel, Marc. 1982. *L'appel à l'Afrique: contributions et réactions à l'effort de guerre en AOF (1914–1919)*. Paris: Publications de la Sorbonne.
Mombauer, Annika. 2001. *Helmuth von Moltke and the origins of the First World War*. Cambridge: Cambridge University Press.
Mühlmann, Carl. 1942. *Oberste Heeresleitung und Balkan im Welkrieg 1914–1918*. Berlin: Wilhelm Limpert.
Nouailhat, Yves-Henri. 1979. *France et Etats-unis août 1914–avril 1917*. Paris: Publications de la Sorbonne.
Pöhlmann, Markus. 2002. *Kriegsgeschichte und Geschichtspolitik: Der Erste Weltkrieg. Die amtliche deutsche Militärgeschichtsschreibung 1914–1956*. Paderborn: Schöningh.

Schulte, Bernd E. 1980. *Vor dem Kreigsausbruch, 1914: Deutschland, die Türkei und der Balkan*. Dusseldorf: Droste.
Tomlinson, H.M. 1930. *All our yesterdays*. London: Harper and Brothers.
von Moltke, Helmuth. 1922. *Erinnerungen-Briefe-Dokumente 1877–1916*, ed. Eliza von Moltke. Stuttgart: Der Kommende Tag.
Wallach, Jehuda. 1976. *Anatomie einer Militärhilfe: Die preussisch-deutschen Militärmissionen in der Türkei 1835–1919*. Dusseldorf: Droste.
War Office. 1922. *Statistics of the military effort of the British empire during the Great War 1914–1920*. London: HMSO.

Sir Charles Lucas and *The Empire at War*

ASHLEY JACKSON
Defence Academy of the United Kingdom, Watchfield, UK

ABSTRACT *This article gives an overview of the British Empire's participation in the First World War. The roles of Australia, Canada, India, New Zealand and South Africa are well documented but there was also a significant contribution from and impact on the smaller and more peripheral territories. These are well covered in Sir Charles Lucas's multi-volume series* The Empire at War. *Although very much of its time, written for and by an imperial elite and now neglected, it remains an invaluable record.*

Introduction

This article offers an overview of the extent of the Empire's participation in the First World War and an assessment of the only major published work on the topic, Sir Charles Lucas's *The Empire at War*. The breadth of the imperial war experience was vast. Not only were there heavy casualties among troops from Australasia, the Americas, and Asia in European and Mediterranean theatres, but military operations extended across much of Africa, the Middle East and the Pacific, affecting place as diverse as Aden, Cameroon, Darfur, Fanning Island, Namibia, Papua New Guinea, Samoa, the Sinai Peninsula, Tanzania and Tsingtao.

The war histories of the imperial 'big five'—Australia, Canada (including Newfoundland), India, New Zealand and South Africa—are well documented. India sent 938,000 men overseas, Canada 458,000, Australia 332,000, New Zealand 112,000 and South Africa 136,000 (excluding non-whites). But the large range of obscure formations recruited in the Empire's other territories were significant too. Many colonies provided forces for local defence, thereby releasing British and other imperial troops for service in the war theatres. But most colonies also sent men on active service overseas. These formations included the 900-strong Chinese Labour Corps recruited in Amoy and Singapore and sent to Basra for service in the Mesopotamia campaign. A much larger Chinese Labour Corps of 140,000 men was recruited by the British for service in France.[1] Malaya and Singapore also provided skilled Chinese artisans for work in East Africa and Mesopotamia, and the Malay Ford Van Motor Company saw service in both Mesopotamia and Persia. The Hong Kong and Singapore Mountain Battery, meanwhile, served in Egypt, Palestine and Sinai, and Ceylon sent water transport units to

Mesopotamia as well as the Ceylon Sanitary Company.[2] Fourteen Fijians were killed at Ypres fighting with the King's Royal Rifle Corps, and the 100 men of the Fiji Labour Detachment performed transport duties in Calais, Marseilles and Italy. Of the 788 Fijians who joined the forces, 131 died. These colonial subjects also served at sea or perished at sea, such as the 607 Basotho of the South African Native Labour Contingent who went down with the SS *Mendi* off the Isle of Wight in 1917, remembered in Lesotho but not remembered in Britain. The war experience of these men is as important as that of the digger, sepoy, or tommy on the Western Front.

Beyond military activities and the recruitment of soldiers, imperial territories experienced numerous war-related effects on the home front. Colonial labour for military tasks was in great demand across the Empire. Some colonies suffered the predations of battle, some performed important strategic roles as bases for warships or soldiers and as training, hospital and prisoner of war centres. In some colonies, social and political issues, such as conscription, the demand for constitutional reform and nationalist protest, led to friction. All colonial societies were shaped by the economic side effects of a global war. Demand for certain products reached unprecedented heights; markets opened or were constricted by enemy activity at sea; inflation and the cost of living rose; and food scarcity threatened. For many people on the colonial and semi-colonial peripheries, flu and famine were war's main bequests. In Calcutta, Cairo, London and the Dominion capitals politicians and proconsuls pursued imperial ambitions in order to shore up British world power. When the war ended, the British Empire expanded significantly through the incorporation of conquered territories just as Wilsonian self-determination was fostering a new, anti-imperial climate, and soldier settlement schemes tempted British ex-servicemen to begin new lives in select colonies.[3]

Men recruited from across the British Empire formed an integral part of the British order of battle in all theatres of conflict. In Western Europe, soldiers from the Dominions and India fought and killed Germans alongside their British counterparts. Behind the front lines, hundreds of thousands of colonial troops performed essential military tasks, such as carrying ammunition and digging graves. Labour corps from China, Egypt, Fiji, Mauritius, Southern Africa, the Seychelles and elsewhere were recruited. While imperial troops were an integral part of Britain's war on the Western Front—in terms of combat and essential non-combat military tasks—the further the theatre of conflict from Western Europe, the more central the role of colonial forces became. This was the case for short campaigns—for example, those against Germany's West African and Pacific colonies—and for the more protracted campaigns in East Africa and Mesopotamia.

Sir Charles Lucas

Sir Charles Westwood Lucas (1853–1931) was a Colonial Office civil servant and historian, and Principal of the Working Men's College in St Pancras, London (1912–22). He was educated at Winchester and Balliol College, Oxford, where he gained firsts in classical moderations and Literae Humaniores and won the Chancellor's Latin essay prize. He was placed first on the civil service examination list of 1877 and was appointed to the Colonial Office, serving in the West Indian Department and the Dominions Department. He was 'much in sympathy with the imperial ideologies of Joseph Chamberlain', though with the election of the Liberal government in 1906 'the prospects of Lucas's promotion as head of the Colonial Office receded'. He retired in 1911, and spent the rest of his life writing and lecturing on the British Empire, supported from 1920 by a fellowship at All Souls College, Oxford. He 'was a major advocate of the study of imperial history and geography in schools and universities', his historical works including *A Historical Geography of the British Colonies* (1908), *A History of Canada* (1909) and *Greater Rome and Greater Britain* (1912).[4]

In early 1916 the Council of the Royal Colonial Institute decided to undertake a work to be entitled 'The Empire at War', and in the autumn agreed terms for publication with Oxford University Press.[5] The project was intended to 'trace the growth of Imperial co-operation in war time prior to the late War' and 'to give side by side a complete record of the effort made in the late War by every unit of the Overseas Empire from the greatest to the smallest, and also to tell in what particular ways and to what extent the fortunes and the development of each part were affected by the War'.[6] The project received the support of relevant British government offices of state, the governments of the Dominions, and the governors in the colonial empire, Lucas acting as a contributor and general editor coordinating the efforts of others. Lucas acknowledged the aid of the Colonial Office and more specifically the 'endless trouble' taken by the colonial governors and 'those to whom they entrusted the task of preparing narratives for the purposes of the book'.[7] This meant that, for example, the entry for Cyprus was prepared 'mainly by the Colonial Government', those for Gibraltar and Malta by Lucas himself, and Ceylon by Sir Reginald Stubbs (the Colonial Secretary in Colombo), T. Reid of the Ceylon Civil Service, and A. J. Denison of the Ceylon Association in London. The entry for India was written by Sir Francis Younghusband, North Borneo's by the colonial government, and Australia's by the historian C. E. W. Bean (later author of Australia's official war history) and others. The military parts of volume two relating to Canada and Newfoundland were revised by C. T. Atkinson, Fellow of Exeter College, Oxford, and late officer in charge of the Military Branch of the Historical Section of the Committee of Imperial Defence.

Before the volumes began to appear in 1921, Lucas published a 47-page booklet, *The War and the Empire: Some Facts and Deductions*, a summary of 'suggestions for teachers when dealing with the effects of the war and the questions which it has brought into prominence'. It considered the Empire's democracies, the war's impact upon racial (in)equality, the growth of nationhood and nationalism, and the possible implications of the rapid evolution of air power for the Empire. The booklet also tackled the issue of 'militarism', and the extent to which the Empire had grown—historically and during the recent conflict—by fighting wars with other European powers and by conquering indigenous polities. Lucas believed that 'militarism has been a favourite bugbear of the labour democracy in these islands, and for this reason, before the war, the Empire was not a congenial subject to labour audiences'. But he gave such an interpretation short shrift, averring that the 'feeling among labour circles in the United Kingdom with regard to the Empire was the result of class prejudice, combined with ignorance of history. The teaching of overseas history in the schools had been inadequate'.[8] Lucas went on to deny that militarism was part of Britain's imperial make-up; although some significant territorial additions were the result of conflict—including large gains following the recent defeat of the German and Ottoman empires—'no sane human being imagines that Great Britain and the British Empire went into the war with the object of annexing more lands and subjecting more peoples'.[9] This, historians would now argue, is debatable, though it chimed with an intense post-war desire, shared by all the former belligerents, to prove that one's own nation had not caused the war or been driven to enter it by aggression or expansionism—one of the main reasons why such lengthy and meticulous official histories of the war were published by all the major powers involved.

The planed schedule of volumes for *The Empire at War* was altered when a second volume entitled *Short History of the War* was cancelled. Instead, a great deal of material was added to the other volumes. The reason for this was that when the project was conceived in early 1916, Lucas and his colleagues did not realise how long the war would last, did not anticipate the mass of material that would be gathered, and could not foresee the costs of publication. The five volumes that were eventually published covered the history of the Empire and its military resources and collaborations (volume one, *The Empire at War*), the other four adopting a regional approach (volume two, *Canada, Newfoundland, West Indies*; volume three, *Australia, New Zealand, Pacific Islands*; volume four, *Africa*; and volume five, *India, the Mediterranean, Eastern Colonies*). A donation from the Rhodes Trust allowed maps and illustrations to be included on some scale (the volumes are lavishly illustrated; volume five, for example, contains 27 maps and 40 photographs). The volumes weigh in at 508, 324, 501, 620 and 430 pages, amounting to well over 2,000 pages of text. The longest volume, interestingly, is that on Africa.

A Snapshot of the Volumes: India, The Mediterranean and The West Indies

The Empire at War is a campaign (or military) history as well as a work of colonial history. So, pages 81–288 of volume two cover 'The Canadian Forces and the War'. Pages 20–135 of volume five describe military operations in Egypt and Palestine, and pages 202–355 cover the four campaigns involving India's expeditionary forces. Volume one charted the history of the Empire's first two centuries, the beginnings of the Indian army, the South African war of 1899–1902, the late 19th and early 20th century colonial conferences and their imperial defence arrangements, and a survey of colonial defence forces. It ended with a summary of the Empire as it stood on the eve of war. To highlight the magnitude of the Indian army's wartime contribution, readers were reminded that it was not an institution intended for imperial campaigns—meaning large-scale operations beyond India and its border regions against first class military powers. Instead it was intended for internal security and the provision of a field army for operations immediately beyond India's border against an external aggressor. By the end of 1914, however, India had sent expeditionary forces comprising over 100,000 troops to East Africa, Egypt, France and Mesopotamia.[10] By the end of the war, 1,302,394 personnel had been dispatched from India's ports, together with 172,815 animals and 3,691,836 tons of supplies and stores. India had also produced 145,758 rifles, 551,000,000 rifle cartridges and 1,360,968 shells.

Though 275 pages of volume five were taken up with campaign history, the remaining 200 pages addressed the overall war experiences of individual colonies and the manner in which imperial territories contributed to the war effort beyond the supply of fighting men and material. Section one was on Gibraltar, and followed the familiar format of summarising the emergency measures taken on the outbreak of war, censorship provisions, food supply challenges, the war's impact on the colony's import and export trade and finances, and war relief fund contributions. This latter category is one of *The Empire at War*'s most useful features, capturing the array of war-related funds that the people of the colonies contributed to or initiated. Seventy-six Gibraltarian men joined British forces, but as with many other colonies, the manpower recruited to perform civilian war-related tasks was more significant. Gibraltar's Admiralty dockyard and naval establishments, for instance, employed 2,350 locals, a very large proportion of the adult male population. Like many colonies, Gibraltar had particularly valuable services to contribute to the prosecution of the war. During the conflict (and not counting minor repairs) its dockyard repaired or refitted 350 warships and repaired 80 merchant vessels. It supplied 1,655,000 tons of coal to 5,535 warships and 2,135 merchantmen. To protect its maritime assets, wartime defensive armament work included the mounting of nearly 1,000 guns, and the Rock also housed prisoner of war camps.

Further east in the Mediterranean, Malta was an important strategic asset because of its position in relation to the sea routes connecting Britain with the east and because of the scale of military operations in the region brought about by the war against the Ottoman Empire. The King's Own Malta Regiment of Militia numbered 3,393 men and formed part of the colony's garrison, as did the Royal Malta Artillery (1,032 men) and the Royal Engineers Militia (136 men). A further 800 Maltese joined the air force. In total over 15,000 Maltese served in the military in some capacity, 7,000 of them in the Maltese Labour Corps, which sent thousands of men overseas, to places such as Salonika, Italy (a mining company), and Gallipoli (stevedoring companies). A further 1,500 Maltese performed motor transport tasks for the Army Service Corps. On the naval side, 15,900 Maltese served with the Royal Navy and in its shore establishments. A total of 31,739 Maltese worked for the colonial government and British military formations, and over 100,000 Allied servicemen passed through the island during the course of the war. Maltese factories produced hand-grenades for use in the Dardanelles, though the island's most important roles were as a strategic naval base and a hospital station for Allied forces massed in the region. Military hospitals expanded rapidly; in September 1915 10,000 men were receiving treatment, and the island's bed capacity peaked at 25,000.

The third British territory in the Mediterranean was Cyprus, still formally a Turkish territory when war broke out though quickly annexed to the Crown (along with Egypt and the Sudan) when Turkey became an enemy. Cyprus exported large amounts of food, fuel and pack animals to the British expeditionary forces in the Dardanelles and Egypt. Products exported for military purposes included oats, barley, wheat, onions, chopped straw, vinegar, bran, potatoes, carobs, raisins, eggs and 40,000 goats, as well as timber and fuel. Over 13,000 Cypriots were recruited by the army as muleteers, which affected domestic food production given the absence of so many men. The Cyprus Military Police force (763 men) conducted anti-espionage work and patrolled the extensive coastline. Like the other Mediterranean colonies, Cyprus also provided camp facilities; 10,000 prisoners of war passed through a camp at Famagusta, and a camp was created at Monarga in order to train the Armenian corps for service in Palestine. Elsewhere, camps at Mount Troodos and Limassol provided accommodation for 500 convalescing servicemen.

Sustaining military operation in all theatres required large amounts of human and animal labour. The provision of human labour and transport animals, according to Lucas, was the main way in which Egypt 'cooperated' in the Empire's war effort. During the course of 1916, 10,000 Egyptians were sent to France, 8,000 to Mesopotamia, and 600 to Salonika. In 1918, 135,000 Egyptians were employed with the Egyptian Expeditionary Force alone. Of this number, 100,000 served in the Labour Corps, 23,000 worked as drivers in the Camel Transport Corps, and 6,000 worked in horse and donkey transport. Egypt maintained 40,000 camels in the field for military purposes, with an annual mortality of 30%.

Section one of volume two of *The Empire at War* was entitled 'The War Effort of the British West Indies', which documented the contribution of the extensive island empire in this region in terms of 'men, money, and munitions', the latter loosely interpreted to capture the supply of commodities such as rum, sugar, cocoa and lime-juice to British forces and the British home front. Niche products supported military production, such as the British Honduran mahogany used to manufacture propellers for airplanes and airships, and Sea Island cotton used to make aeroplane wings and balloons. Trinidad supplied oil for the Royal Navy, and the pre-war slump in agricultural prices was in most cases reversed by the war, to the extent that the value of land rose dramatically, the price of plantations in Barbados, for instance, rising from £30 to £200 per acre. 'This prosperity was not, however, shared to any great extent by the labouring classes. Wages rose, but the rise was by no means commensurate with the increase in cost of living engendered by increased prices of imported articles.'[11] In particular, shipping shortages and Germany's turn to unrestricted submarine warfare 'demonstrated forcibly' the dependence of the West Indian territories on imported foodstuffs, which led to the appointment of food commissions and food controllers, as well as measures to increase domestic production. In Barbados, for example, the Vegetable Produce Act of 1917 made it compulsory for landowners to plant a designated acreage with vegetables, corn and roots. With sea communications between Caribbean islands and Britain diminished, along with the import–export business that depended upon them, Canada and the United States were turned to as markets and a source of food and manufactured goods, and American companies began to make inroads into West Indian markets.

War also brought military activity to the region, including defensive measures given the threat of German raiders such as the *Dresden* and *Karlsruhe* and enemy landing parties, and the dispatch of troops in support of the imperial war effort. A detachment of the Royal Canadian Garrison Artillery was stationed in St Lucia from 1915 to 1918, alongside French soldiers from Martinique. Heavy guns were mounted in Barbados, St Kitts, St Vincent, the Bahamas and elsewhere, often manned by the Royal Marines Light Infantry and the Royal Marines Artillery. As a precaution against the threat of enemy submarines, the West Indies Motor Launch Flotilla was created, comprising a dozen vessels that patrolled key waterways in places such as the Gulf of Paria. Bermuda was a base for the Royal Navy's North America and West Indies Squadron, regularly visited by warships, and a coaling port and port of refuge for Allied merchant vessels.

Jamaica was second only to New Zealand in adopting compulsory military service, and was the powerhouse of West Indian military recruitment. Not only did Jamaicans recruited in their home island serve in the military, but they were also drawn from overseas communities, such as the 2,100 Jamaicans recruited from the large number of men working in the Panama Canal Zone. The West India Regiment, originally raised in the

18th century, served in the campaigns against German East and West Africa early in the war, and a new and separate British West Indies Regiment was created, the first contingent arriving in Britain in autumn 1915 for training at Seaford Camp in Sussex. Altogether, 11 battalions were raised for this formation. Elements moved to Egypt early in 1916 for training in Alexandria before deploying to the Canal Zone on defensive duties. Other battalions served in France, carrying heavy shells, in East Africa on lines of communication and in Mesopotamia (including the Honduras Contingent). British West Indies Regiment battalions also saw active service as part of the Egyptian Expeditionary Force, distinguishing themselves in the Jordan Valley in 1918 during the advance on Amman. The West Indies contributed a total of about £2 million in cash to the British government, war funds and British charities. Contributions also came in the form of specific items or monies for specific items, such as the nine military aircraft donated by the West Indian colonies and the 300 polished walking-sticks of creole hardwood sent from Trinidad and Tobago for the use of wounded men servicemen in Britain.

Assessing *The Empire at War*

The Empire at War was a significant and exhaustive work and remains, nearly a century later, the most important published work on the subject. Even if they received only a half-page entry, the smallest and most peripheral British territories appeared in the study, including the Cocos Island, Sarawak and Wei-Hai-Wei. It also covered parts of the world that were not in the Empire, such as the British communities in Japan, Latin America and North China, and the war effort of Egypt. It was very much a product of its time, a classic imperial history of the pre-Second World War era, with a frontispiece of King George V, patron of the Royal Colonial Institute, in some of the volumes, the Duke of Connaught in others, along with an image of the Cenotaph in Whitehall. Many of the illustrations depicted senior politicians, admirals and generals.

An illustration of *The Empire at War*'s tone is provided by Sir Francis Younghusband's assessment of India at the end of the war:

> It might have been expected that after a victorious war in which India had not—considering her huge population—suffered any grievous loss in manhood and had suffered little or no material loss, she would be contented, prosperous, and happy. It might have been expected further that when the British had played such a glorious part and at the close of the war stood at Baghdad and Mosul, Jerusalem and Aleppo, at the gates of Constantinople and on the banks of the Rhine, and when the whole German fleet was in their hands, the prestige of the British in India would never have stood higher or anything like so high. Yet the amazing fact is that India was less contented after the war than it was before, and British prestige was lower.[12]

Younghusband rehearsed some of the elements that might have led to this 'amazing' state of affairs. 'Why should she not herself be free' from the domination 'she' had helped fight against? The Irish rebellion of 1916 had been keenly observed, and there were plenty of elements within Indian society ready to stir up 'bad blood'. There were then the unsettling machinations of Bolsheviks, 'Mohammedans' unsettled by the

Empire's fight against the Ottoman Empire, and the novel cry of 'self-determination'. Efforts had been made to mitigate these new circumstances, Younghusband continued, including the Montagu-Chelmsford reforms, the dispatch of Indian representatives as part of the British Empire Delegation to Versailles, and the commissioning of Indian officers. Whether these measures would be enough it was far too early to say, and extremists would always 'pester for more', he lamented.

This sentiment reflected the fact that *The Empire at War* was very much an official history, produced by and for an imperial elite not yet used to questioning Britain's world role and its imperial power. It took for granted the Empire's loyalty to Britain, the beneficence of British rule, and viewed nationalism with suspicion. While acknowledging that something as large as the British Empire could not speak with a single voice, and that there were 'malcontents' within its bounds, Lucas contended that the Empire stood for 'law, liberty, and justice', and that its people preferred that pathway to that offered by the Germans.[13] The volumes were compiled in a manner that embedded the 'official' view of the Empire as evinced by British district commissioners and governors in the colonies and Colonial Office civil servants in Whitehall. The material was compiled by governors and their district commissioners, which meant that a picture of calm and loyal war service was enshrined on the ground and then passed back to London, where it was taken at face value. But none of this alters the fact that *The Empire at War* remains a unique and valuable source. Though rarely consulted and almost impossible to procure second hand—even with the wonder of online global booksellers at one's fingertips—*The Empire at War* is an invaluable and unique record of the Empire's wartime contribution.[14]

Notes

1. See Brian Fawcett (2000) 'The Chinese Labour Corps in France, 1917–1932', *Journal of the Royal Asiatic Society Hong Kong Branch*, 40, and Guoqi Xu (2011) *Strangers on the Western Front: Chinese Workers in the Great War*. Cambridge, MA: Harvard University Press, pp. 33–111.
2. See Ivor Lee and John Starling (2009) *No Labour, No Battle: Military Labour during the First World War*. Stroud: The History Press.
3. For a brief overview of the Empire and the war, see Holland (1999) and Jackson (2008) (Available online at http://britishempireatwardotorg.files.wordpress.com/2012/09/bbc-history-magazine2.pdf, accessed 11 February 2014.)
4. Butlin (2011).
5. See the chapter on the war in Trever Reese (1968) *The History of the Royal Commonwealth Society, 1858–1968*. Oxford: Oxford University Press.
6. Lucas, *The Empire at War*, volume one, p. v.
7. Butlin (2011).
8. Lucas (1919, pp. 14–15).
9. Lucas (1919, p. 18).
10. See J. Greenhut (1983) 'The Imperial Reserve: the Indian Corps on the Western Front, 1914–1915', *Journal of Imperial and Commonwealth History*, 12, pp. 54–73.
11. Lucas, *The Empire at War*, volume two, p. 328.
12. Lucas, *The Empire at War*, volume five, pp. 343–344.
13. Sentiments expressed in chapter 13 of volume two, 'The Empire at War'.
14. It is interesting to note that this exercise was not repeated during and after the Second World War; as many historians will have discovered, although Sir John Shuckburgh was commissioned to prepare a 'civil history' of the Empire-Commonwealth during the Second World War, it was never completed to the extent of its predecessor, and plans for publication were scrapped.

References

Butlin, R. (2011) Sir Charles Lucas, *Dictionary of National Biography*, online version accessed 22 February 2014.

Connelly, M. (2005) The British campaign in Aden, 1914–1918, *Journal of the Centre for First World War Studies*, 1(3), pp. 65–96.

Holland, H. (1999) The British Empire and the Great War, 1914–1918, Oxford History of the British Empire, Vol. 4, *The Twentieth Century*. Oxford: Oxford University Press.

Jackson, A. (2008) The British Empire and the First World War, *BBC History Magazine*, 9, pp. 51–96.

Jarboe, A. (2013) Soldiers of Empire: Indian Sepoys in and Beyond the Imperial Metropole during the First World War, 1914–1919, PhD Thesis, Northeastern University, Boston, MA.

Lucas, C. (1919) *The War and the Empire: Some Facts and Deductions*. London: Oxford University Press.

Lucas, C. (1921–26) *The Empire at War*, 5 Vols. London: Oxford University Press.

Morrow, J. (2004) *The Great War: An Imperial History*. London: Routledge.

Page, M. (Ed.) (1987) *Africa and the First World War*. Basingstoke: Macmillan.

South Africa and World War I

by N. G. Garson

I

The imperial and commonwealth context is a convenient one in which to assess the political impact of World War I on South Africa. In some ways the South African experience was one shared with the other dominions so that certain parallels may be drawn. In others the distinctiveness of the South African case asserted itself, suggesting points of contrast.

Like the other dominions, the Union entered World War I in August 1914 not as an ally of Great Britain but as a subordinate part of the British Empire, committed by the British declaration of war. There was no right of neutrality. All that the Union government was competent to decide was the extent of South Africa's participation: here the Union experienced with the other dominions the consequence of Britain's undivided control of foreign policy before 1914. Likewise the Union was to benefit during the war from Britain's increasing sensitivity to dominion views, itself the price of obtaining dominion co-operation in the war effort. The outcome was the emergence of the Imperial War Cabinet and the Imperial War Conference in 1917, in which South Africa played a full part, with the subsequent bonus of Smuts' individual membership of the British War Cabinet in 1918.[1] The general dominion aspiration for 'status' persisted beyond the war into the peace-making phase, with the claim of the dominions to separate signing of the peace treaty and separate membership of the League of Nations.

The build-up of a European diplomatic crisis in the years before the outbreak of the war meant not only that Britain's external concerns were primarily European, but that imperial and dominion affairs were deemed to have importance only in relation to the empire's potential contribution to a likely European war.[2] When war came, just as the dominions were dependent partners of one of the major belligerents, so geographically was each dominion's position more or less peripheral, remote from the major theatres of the war. There was a widespread belief that great world issues would be settled by the war, including the fate of western civilization itself. But everyone understood that if the war in fact settled these questions, it would be in Europe that this would be done. The typical dominion war contribution took the form of an addition to the British military and naval concentrations in Europe, which were under British command.

The war in Africa did constitute a separate theatre from that of Europe, and South Africa's involvement in the former, through the South West African and East African campaigns, admittedly made her contribution somewhat distinctive. But the African theatre was undeniably subordinate. Even when surveying their country's involvement in the African campaigns, most South Africans still perceived their situation to be that of spectators viewing the great struggle from afar. For many the effect was to make those South African political issues that were not directly related to the war in Europe seem parochial and unimportant.

Certain features of the South African participation in the war emerge from an outline of its various phases. The Union government's first response to the news of the outbreak of war was to offer to replace the troops of the imperial garrison with Union troops. The British acceptance of this offer was followed on 7 August by a request, reiterated with greater urgency two days later, that Union forces should seize the harbours of Swakopmund and Luderitzbucht, together with the interior wireless stations, in particular the long-distance station at Windhoek. While these British requests did not amount to an invitation to conquer the whole of South West Africa, that prospect was present at the outset, in the warning that any territory occupied must be left to the disposal of the imperial government at a general peace settlement after the war.

The government of Generals Botha and Smuts acceded to the request and began immediate preparations for the campaign before securing the approval of parliament in September. Parliamentary approval of the government's policy was followed by public protests in the Orange Free State against the proposal to conquer South West Africa. Already in the Transvaal the veteran General de la Rey and the commandant-general, Beyers, had become involved in plans for an armed rising, as had the Free Stater General de Wet. The initial plan fell through as a result of the death of de la Rey on 15 September, shot by a policeman who had mistaken him for a member of a local criminal gang. But on 8 October Lieutenant-Colonel 'Manie' Maritz, the commander at Upington of a Union force being used in the operation against South West Africa, went into rebellion and joined the Germans. His action was followed by the outbreak of rebellion or 'armed protest' under Beyers in the Transvaal and de Wet in the Free State. Meanwhile the government, in response to Maritz's outbreak, had proclaimed martial law over the entire Union and declared its intention of commandeering burghers to suppress any rising. Clashes between government and rebel commandos continued, until the death of Beyers and the surrender of de Wet in December 1914 virtually brought the rebellion to an end.

If the rebellion had got out of hand troops from elsewhere in the British Empire would have been sent to suppress it. The toppling of Botha and Smuts from power would have imperilled a vital imperial interest in South Africa. The colonial secretary, Harcourt, recognised this in warning the recently arrived governor-general, Lord Buxton, that 'the safety of the Union' was far more important than the conquest of South West Africa. In this telegram to Buxton on 23 October 1914 Harcourt communicated an offer from the imperial government to make 30,000 Australian and New Zealand troops available in South Africa to help suppress the rebellion.[3] These troops were already at sea *en route* to Europe. Although they were redirected to coal at Colombo instead of Mauritius, as originally planned, the offer was kept open.[4]

At the time the offer was first made the full extent of the rebellion had not become apparent. While indicating their appreciation, Botha and Smuts preferred to defer their decision until the troops had reached Mauritius, by which time they would be better placed to judge whether or not they would be needed. The Union cabinet finally rejected the offer on 9 November.[5] Beyers in the Transvaal and de Wet in the Orange

Free State had meanwhile taken the field with their rebel commandos. Obviously Botha and Smuts preferred to use only South African forces and now they also believed these to be capable of suppressing the rebellion unaided. Had events turned out differently they would certainly have supported the intervention of imperial troops.[6] Earlier the fear that imperial (possibly Indian) troops might be used instead had served to strengthen the resolve of Botha and Smuts to respond positively to the British request to the Union to undertake the conquest of South West Africa.[7] The episode of the 30,000 'Anzac' troops illustrates also the absence of control on the part of dominion governments over the forces they contributed to the imperial war effort, for the Australian and New Zealand cabinets were not consulted about the possible change of plan regarding the use of these troops. Not surprisingly the whole episode was kept secret.[8]

The suppression of the rebellion was followed by the campaign in South West Africa. This was undertaken mainly by the burgher forces commandeered to deal with the rebels and was brought to a successful conclusion in July 1915. Meanwhile ultra-British patriots had indulged in a spell of rioting, directed against allegedly German concerns and their owners, following the sinking of the *Lusitania* by a submarine in May 1915. During 1916 the Union's chief concern in the war was the East African campaign. South African troops formed the bulk of the imperial forces under the command of Smuts. Although the campaign failed in its principal object of forcing the surrender of the German forces under Lettow-Vorbeck, Smuts succeeded in establishing British control over most of the former German colony. His departure at the end of the year was accompanied by that of most of the Union troops, many of whom subsequently joined the South African contingent which had already distinguished itself at Delville Wood (part of the battle of the Somme) in July 1916 and continued to serve on the western front until the end of the war.

As far as the extent of the South African contribution to the imperial war effort is concerned, on the more obvious criteria of commitment in terms of men and money, it seems rather overshadowed by what was offered by the other dominions.[9] Part of the explanation for the difference lies in the greater involvement of the South African forces initially in southern Africa (suppressing the rebellion and conquering South West Africa) and then in East Africa, rather than in Europe. A further consideration is the fact, made abundantly clear by the outcome of the general election of October 1915, that at least half of the Afrikaner voters were opposed to any active participation by South Africa in the war. Yet whatever conclusions may be drawn as to the South African war effort in comparison with the other dominions, the expenditure of men and money was certainly great enough to exert a marked impact on the domestic political scene. New issues were raised and superimposed on the 'normal' or pre-war political process, while questions concerning the conduct of the war became a constant preoccupation of the government, serving, at least in the earlier phases of the war, to crowd out many of its pre-war problems.

One major focus of concern was the commandeering or compulsory call-up of all citizens eligible for military service. In contrast to the conscription crisis in the other dominions, the opposition to commandeering reached a climax at an early stage in the war and was closely related to the 1914 rebellion. In the initial planning of the South West African campaign, under Smuts as Minister of Defence, there was evidently no intention to confine the forces that would be used to volunteers. Then, as a concession to the doubts of F. S. Malan and two other ministers about the wisdom of sending an expedition to South West Africa, it was agreed that one of the conditions of acceding to the British request to send forces into the German colony would be that these should be volunteers only. In the event this condition was not attached to the Union's accession to the British request on 10 August 1914 and the planning of the expedition continued on the basis that volunteers would be supplementary to the other Defence Force units to be deployed. It was only as Afrikaner opposition to the proposed campaign mounted, following the death of de la Rey and the resignation of Beyers as commandant-general in mid-September, that the government gave public assurances that it would employ volunteers only. Even so, these assurances seemed to conflict with its arrangements in practice.[10]

The government's equivocation on the volunteers issue was a contributory cause of the rebellion, to the extent that many burghers joined the rebel commandos in order to resist being conscripted for service in South West Africa. In the event, the conquest of South West Africa in 1915 was undertaken mainly by commandeered forces: the forces which had been commandeered to suppress the rebellion remained in the field. The government justified its action in using such troops on the ground that the outbreak of the rebellion had changed the situation and freed it from its earlier assurances. The rebellion, after all, was a threat to the security of the state and, quite apart from commandeering, had necessitated the drastic measure of proclaiming martial law.

Contention over commandeering or conscription was a specific symptom of a more profound problem, that of the divisive effects of war. The distinguishing feature of South Africa's case in this respect was the depth of the divisions immediately opened up by the government's decision to accede to the British request to conquer South West Africa. A rift between Afrikaners and 'British-minded' South Africans was revealed that was far wider than that produced by any other issue that had arisen since the Anglo-Boer war. Since then too short a period had intervened for the achievement of Anglo-Afrikaner conciliation, let alone the united white nation that Botha and Smuts had held in prospect as a certain consequence of Union. The complication of the rebellion opened up a further great rift, this time in the ranks of Afrikaners, creating a polarity between those who were prepared to follow the lead of Botha and Smuts and those who were rebels or sympathisers. The rebellion furnished the tragic dimension of civil war, the spectacle of Afrikaner shooting Afrikaner. At the same time, this breach in Afrikaner ranks did not immediately or necessarily serve to narrow the rift dividing 'loyalist' Afrikaners from most English-speaking South Africans.

All told, these divisions in South Africa, coming as they did at an early stage in the war, determined many of the attitudes taken to the government's whole conduct of the war throughout its course. From the outset General Hertzog, the Afrikaner Nationalist leader, opposed the government's war policy by invoking his principle of 'South Africa first' and claiming that active participation was not in the Union's interest. He continued to apply this touchstone throughout the war, questioning the expediency in terms of interest of each stage of South Africa's involvement. The political aftermath of the rebellion, with its mutual recriminations about government policy before, during and after that event, similarly served to keep the original issues alive at least for the rest of the war.

Nicholas Mansergh has noted one important effect of the war on the dominions: 'The challenge and the sacrifices of war sharpened their sense of separate identities and strengthened their feeling of nationality.'[11] Along with the rest South Africa developed a pride in its own special contribution. As commonwealth statesmen Botha and Smuts played a full part in asserting the political nationality of the Union, by demanding more say in the making of imperial foreign policy and an enhanced international status for the dominions.

On the other hand, with regard to nationality, the major and distinctive development in South Africa was the fillip which the war provided to the emergence of twentieth century Afrikaner nationalism. It was not merely that the war divided Afrikaners. After the 1915 general election Hertzog could plausibly claim that his newly-created National Party already commanded the allegiance of a majority of Afrikaner voters. Whereas the dominion nationality extolled by Botha and Smuts was exclusively political, Hertzog's nationalism was rooted in Afrikaner culture and the Afrikaans language. Hertzog was its chief party political advocate but this was a movement that transcended politics and penetrated the cultural, religious and social spheres of Afrikaner life. By 1917, through its articulation of a secessionist and republican objective for the future, it was embracing an ideology that was potentially destructive to the imperial and commonwealth connection.

Well before the hardening of these nationalist attitudes, it is relevant to note that the British cabinet and the governor-general were themselves agreed that a primary imperial interest in South Africa during the war was to keep the government of General Botha in power. At times Buxton reminded the leaders of the British-oriented Unionist Party (officially the opposition but in fact committed to support Botha's war policy) of this and in effect warned them against carrying their opposition to aspects of the government's policies to the point where its survival might be endangered.[12] In quite another direction also the governor-general sought to protect a vital imperial interest in South Africa, the maintenance of the British connection. When Hertzog presented, in two addresses to Stellenbosch students in May 1917, what Buxton regarded as a dubious statement on the Union's relationship to the empire, the governor-general issued a correction in public (though without mentioning Hertzog by name). The outcome was a rebuke by the Nationalist organ in Cape Town, *De Burger*, which called into question the governor-general's political impartiality and alleged that he had intervened in the party arena.[13]

II

The war years were for South Africa a period of rapid economic advance and social change. Some pre-war trends were continued, sometimes in accelerated form, while other new trends began. The war was generally a boom period, with prices rising far more rapidly than wages. Official figures indicated a rise of 15 per cent in 'the cost of foodstuffs and other necessaries of life,' but other calculations suggest a rise in retail prices from 1914 to 1917–18 as great as 31 per cent.[14] The lag of wages relative to price rises of this order meant that the sharp increase in the cost of living, together with the remedies put forward to combat this trend, became a political issue. The financing of the war effort brought higher taxation, in the case both of the new income tax and indirect taxation. All this is linked to the eruption of strikes and other forms of labour unrest that characterised the last two years of the war as well as the immediate post-war years.

The war accelerated a process of urbanisation that affected all sections of the country's population. Population increase was fastest in the Transvaal as a result of this internal migration and within the province the focus of the urbanisation was the gold-bearing Witwatersrand. Linked to this was the growing industrialisation as applied to manufacturing industry rather than expanding mining activity. The anticipation that the war at sea would disrupt shipping and imports, rather than cause actual sinkings of merchant ships, stimulated these new manufacturing developments. Compared to an overall population increase of 1½ per cent p.a. during the war, the rise in industrial employment was of the order of 11 per cent p.a.[15] By the end of the war there were more workers employed in manufacturing industry than in mining. In the case of white workers alone the disparity was greater and the wage rates in manufacturing industry were far lower than those for white mineworkers. Yet within their own sphere, white mineworkers benefited from the war-time situation in contrast to black labour. Their wages rose steadily, the level for 1920 representing an advance of 60 per cent on that for 1914.[16] Also the 'status quo agreement', concluded in 1918 between the Chamber of Mines, representing the employers, and the mineworkers' union, gave them protection against the further movement of black workers into semi-skilled jobs.

Despite the hardening of discriminatory practices against the Africans—in mining and other industrial occupations, in the expulsions of rural squatters under the 1913 Natives Land Act (which set the Union's 'native policy' on its segregationist course)—the general African response to the outbreak of war showed loyalty to the British Empire and a willingness to support Botha's war policy. Despite rumours of German intrigue and African disaffection in the Transkei, the government experienced little difficulty in raising its Native Labour Contingents. The wider horizons experienced by the Africans serving outside the Union, which included the absence of formal racial discrimination in European countries and first hand experience of the achievements of trained African soldiers fighting for the Germans in East Africa, carried political implications. The greater radicalism of African political responses in the 1920s is usually linked to these experiences, though perhaps on rather speculative grounds.[17]

At the level of organised political associations both Coloured and African groups made formal declarations of their loyalty to the British Empire and the obligations this imposed in wartime. The African Political Organisation, an association of Coloureds under the leadership of Dr. A. Abdurahman, offered on various occasions to raise a corps for combatant service and eventually, in September 1915, a Coloured infantry corps was formed.[18] Leaders of the African organisation, the South African Native National Congress (later the African National Congress), left one of their conferences in August 1914 in order to offer Botha's government their services in the war. Although the SANNC subsequently protested against the government's refusal to arm blacks in the prosecution of the war, its loyalty to the British Empire was never in doubt. Both the SANNC and the APO objected in 1918 to the Union's proposed acquisition of South West Africa. In 1919 the SANNC sent a deputation to Britain in the vain hope of persuading the imperial government to utilise the peace conference as an opportunity to intervene and redress African grievances in the Union.[19]

More significant than the resolutions of small and not necessarily representative associations were the actual responses of black workers to wartime economic conditions. While the wages of white miners were raised in response to rising prices, those of black mineworkers remained static. This formed the background to the boycott of East Rand mine stores in February 1918 and the outbreak of various local strikes involving black mineworkers later in the year. Also in 1918 there took place an unsuccessful strike of black sanitary workers in Johannesburg in protest against the failure of their wages to rise, after those of white municipal employees had risen appreciably in response to strike action on their part.[20] But more than low wages were at issue. In these strikes the lack of educational facilities for Africans on the Witwatersrand and the enforcement of the pass laws were specifically pointed to, while mine-workers also protested against inadequate compensation for illness, disablement and death in the mines, and the industrial colour bar.[21] The cessation of hostilities brought no resolution of the problems experienced by black workers. In 1919 the strikes escalated into rioting and the SANNC, in a rare display of militancy, involved itself in a campaign against the pass laws.[22] It was on the basis of the wartime grievances of black workers that new organisations reflecting their aspirations emerged, the most notable instance being Clements Kadalie's Industrial and Commercial Workers Union (the ICU) in 1919.

The grievances and disabilities of Indians in South Africa constitute an interesting theme in the imperial context. Three distinct authorities were involved—the imperial government, the Union government and (through the viceroy and the secretary of state for India) the Indian government. The Indian Relief Act and the Smuts-Gandhi agreement provided a partial settlement of these issues in 1914. The initial effect of the war was to put the Indian question into abeyance. Serious grievances remained, such as those concerning the granting of licenses to Indian traders, the landownership rights of Indians in the Transvaal and the failure of Transvaal Indians to obtain the municipal franchise. But in the wartime situation the Union government could afford to ignore them, for the imperial government, needing the Union's support in the war, would bring no pressure to bear on Botha over the treatment of Indians. South African Indians for their part supported the war effort, actively as in the case of Indian Bearer Companies serving in East Africa and also with financial contributions.[23]

It was the contribution to the imperial war effort of India itself that brought to the fore once more the disabilities of Indians in South Africa. A resolution of the Indian National Congress in March 1917 called for an end to these disabilities and the whole question was raised at the Imperial Conference of 1917-8, where Indian delegates were present for the first time. Delegates of the government of India again raised the issue at the peace conference. But the war brought about no resolution of the problems of South African Indians. Court action brought by municipal authorities compounded Indian grievances over both the trading licences and land questions. In 1919 the government was obliged to introduce fresh legislation and in the same year local Indian initiatives led to the convening of a conference to consider Indian grievances.[24]

Wartime party and parliamentary politics in South Africa were generally of a desultory and parochial quality. Issues having a direct bearing on the outcome of the war no doubt possessed an intrinsic importance at the time. Historians on the other hand, for the very reason that these were in fact temporary wartime issues which soon vanished from the scene, have in retrospect found them of limited interest and have given them only passing notice. Two of these issues, the 'overseas pay question' and the 'wool question', deserve a brief examination. Both issues were evidently serious enough to endanger the survival of Botha's ministry and both of them cast an interesting light on the Union's wartime relationship with the imperial government.

The use of South African troops outside the Union, in Europe and in East Africa, raised the issue of how they were to be paid.[25] The Union parliament in 1915 made full financial provision for the South West African campaign but none for any other military contribution outside the Union. Botha's government was unwilling either to call a special session of a parliament that was due to expire later in the year, or to pledge further expenditure on the Union's war effort just before a general election. As a result the Union's first volunteer forces to be sent to Europe, before the end of 1915, were paid by the British government at imperial rates of pay, fully two-thirds less than if they had been paid at Union rates. In the case of the Union's contingent to East Africa, which was also being assembled in the latter part of 1915, the Union government persuaded the British government not only to finance the contingent, but to pay them at the higher Union rates. Once the outcome of the general election of October 1915 had confirmed them in office, Botha's ministry agreed that the Union would contribute the difference between the two rates of pay.

The South Africans serving in Europe thus became victims of discrimination, and in February 1916, during the parliamentary session, Botha's government found itself under attack, from its own English-speaking wing as well as the Unionist opposition, for its failure to make up the difference to the European contingent. In October 1916 the issue arose again in sharper form, given the prospect that South Africans about to leave East Africa for service in Europe would have to take a cut of two-thirds in their pay. Then in December 1916, Bonar Law, the colonial secretary, intervened and obtained his own government's undertaking to pay the South African troops in Europe at Union rates, in return for 'the expression of hope' that the Union government would in due course contribute an equivalent amount. With 'the expression of hope' converted into a general war contribution of £1 million from South Africa, the Union parliament in February 1917 accepted the compromise along the lines of Bonar Law's proposal.

Simple enough in retrospect, the problem had stimulated sharp political differences in the Union, enough for the governor general to describe the conflict over the issue as 'much the most serious political crisis that has occurred since I have been out here'.[26] The Nationalists, who interpreted South Africa's involvement in the war as a violation of Hertzog's principle of 'South Africa first', argued that since the war was being fought in the interest of the British Empire there should be no further contribution from the Union, particularly if the taxpayer was expected to provide it. The Unionists, empire-oriented in their loyalties, took the opposite line. It was not enough for the Union merely to contribute to its war effort, it should go further, as in the case of the other dominions, and meet the full costs of its contingents, including paying the troops at the higher Union rates. Clearly it was the Nationalist opposition which worried Botha, and indeed the refusal of the South African Party to commit itself to a further financial contribution to the war during the 1915 election campaign was a result of Botha's fear that such an undertaking would cause many of the party's Afrikaner voters to shift their allegiance to the Nationalists. Several S.A.P. Afrikaner stalwarts, in the cabinet and parliamentary caucus, were against a further financial contribution and some of them had made election pledges to that effect. On the other hand the British-oriented wing of the S.A.P., again both in the cabinet and caucus, shared the Unionist view of the matter. This division in his government and party explains the indecisiveness of Botha's stand and the cabinet's search for some compromise.

The opposition of most Afrikaners, whether Nationalist or S.A.P., to a further contribution, and the support for one on the part of most 'British' South Africans, whether Unionist or S.A.P., brings out the 'communal' or 'ethnic' element, over and above that of party, in the politics of the time. In February 1916 Botha warned Buxton that if the cabinet and parliament divided on Anglo-Afrikaner lines on the pay question, he would feel obliged to resign: 'Botha repeated what he said this morning that a split would mean a racial cleavage: and he would not go on under these conditions, and see his life's work wrecked; and so he had told Smartt'.[27]

Writing to Smuts, who had left to take up his command in East Africa, Botha explained his stand in parliament against a further financial contribution from the Union: '. . . only after I saw clearly that our party would otherwise break up did I make the statement'.[28] A year later, when there was a danger that parliament might not accept the final compromise, Botha again spoke of resigning.[29]

The 'wool question' arose in May 1917, when the Imperial government offered to buy the Union's wool at a price 55 per cent above the average for the year prior to the outbreak of the war, provided that the whole clip was committed, as in the case of similar arrangements with Australia and New Zealand.[30] Given the disruptive effect of the war on freight and shipping, these arrangements were certainly beneficial to Britain in ensuring supplies of raw wool at a stable price. As far as the Union was concerned, its government not only agreed to the proposal but asked that the surplus from the 1916–17 clip be included in the scheme. The imperial government acceded to this request.

Later in 1917 farmers began to object to what they understood would be the commandeering of their wool at a fixed price, whereas they had in the previous year been able to sell wool to Japan and the United States at prices up to three times higher than the pre-war price. The question then assumed a political character. Invoking the principle of 'South Africa first', the Nationalists argued that the government's acceptance of the scheme amounted to connivance in the economic exploitation of South African wool farmers in the British or imperial interest. As the opposition to the scheme among his own supporters mounted, Botha came to fear that his government would be defeated on the issue in the ensuing session of parliament early in 1918. As a result of his representations the imperial government in September 1917 agreed to operate the scheme on a purely voluntary basis. Some farmers then entered the scheme, not necessarily to demonstrate their commitment to the imperial war effort but rather because they calculated that, owing to German submarine attacks, there would be no shipping available to reach the American and Japanese markets. Under the voluntary scheme about one-third of the Union's clip was contracted to Britain.

Towards the end of 1917 freight and shipping became more freely available and the open market price of wool rose accordingly. Many farmers who had offered their wool under the British scheme now wished to be released from their obligations. Botha was placed in an awkward position. The wish to be released came from farmers who were largely his own supporters, since Nationalists would have been disinclined to enter the scheme. On the other hand, for Botha to request the imperial government to allow farmers to withdraw from the scheme was tantamount to asking that the Union government be permitted to renege on a contract previously entered into. Botha could see no other way out and on 6 January 1918 he put the request forward. The British government was quick to accept sacrificing the minor interest of cheaper wool to the major one of trying to keep Botha in power. As the colonial secretary, Walter Long, told Buxton a few weeks later: 'I do not hesitate to say that I regard his retention of the Office of Prime Minister in South Africa as of vital consequence, not only to South Africa and the Imperial connection, but to the successful prosecution of the war'.[31]

III

Apart from the party aspect, the war had a major impact on the relations between the Afrikaner and English-speaking sections of the white population. The attitudes in question covered a wide spectrum. At the one pole was the Afrikaner rebel of the Maritz type, who was avowedly seeking the restoration of the Boer republics by force, seizing the opportunity of the British involvement in a world war and calling in the aid of Germany, Britain's principal foe in that war, to achieve this. At the other extreme was the ultra-British loyalist position, the obvious expression of which in South Africa was the widespread anti-German rioting that took place following the sinking of the *Lusitania*. Similar outbreaks occurred elsewhere in the Empire and in Britain itself. In South Africa a 'British League' was later formed to agitate for the introduction of measures like the Enemy Trading Bill, which was directed against allegedly German or pro-German enterprises. While the ultra-British attitude was characteristically anti-German in expression, in its typical form it included a castigation of most Afrikaners as pro-German in their outlook.

Within fifteen months of the outbreak of the war, a considerable proportion of Afrikaners—possibly over half—were declared opponents of the government's war policy. These included former rebels, Nationalists who were not involved in the rebellion and other Afrikaners who found themselves sympathising with the rebel cause or predicament. There was also another section who, even where they continued to support Botha and Smuts, entertained definite reservations about the government's policy. These included some of the Afrikaner members of Botha's cabinet and some members of the South African Party caucus, but in both instances the doubtful members (one exception was de la Rey in the Senate) ended up by continuing to support Botha and Smuts. It seems a reasonable deduction from this that similar reservations were entertained by many S.A.P. supporters in the country, some of whom would have ceased to support the party as a result.

The main ground for this Afrikaner reluctance to support the plan to invade South West Africa was evidently distaste for aggressive action as Great Britain's ally (only twelve years after the British had destroyed the Boer republics), when the enemy was a country in which public opinion, if not the government, had been sympathetic to the Boers in their own great struggle. The presence in South-West Africa of some former Cape rebels of the Anglo-Boer war was a further complication. Were they to be called upon to fight their own kith and kin? Finally it seems reasonable to infer a reluctance on the part of some Afrikaners to commit themselves to active participation on the British side so early in the struggle when they believed in the likelihood of a German victory, or perhaps hoped for this outcome.

On the side of 'British' South Africa the great majority, whether British or South African born, were in favour of full participation in the war. The chief exception was a numerically insignificant group of socialists at the extreme wing of the labour movement. Given the typical Afrikaner attitudes already outlined, it is clear that a new rift between Afrikaners and English in general was opened up by the war. By evoking a surge of patriotism for the Empire, the war probably gave the English section greater unity than before, at least for as long as the war lasted. This was reflected in the rallying of English-speaking voting support of the Unionist and South African Parties, at Labour's expense, in the 1915 general election. On the other hand the creation of the new Afrikaner-English divide did not promote Afrikaner unity. The lasting bitterness created by the civil war element in the rebellion, together with intensified party conflict between the S.A.P. and the Nationalists, made unlikely the success of wartime moves to promote Afrikaner *hereniging* (reunion).

To support these assertions there is the testimony of Lord Buxton following his arrival in South Africa in September 1914. The theme on which Buxton dwelt, almost from the start, was the undoubted unpopularity of the South West African expedition among Afrikaners generally. Buxton's observations occur in his private notes on South African affairs and in his private correspondence, and many of them were made prior to the outbreak of the rebellion. Reviewing the position while the rebellion was still in progress, in a private telegram to the colonial secretary, Lewis Harcourt, he placed great emphasis on Botha's influence:

> A very slight change of mood in the Dutch public feeling, an accident, any hesitation on the part of General Botha, a little less activity on his part and that of other leaders in backing up his people by interviews, discussions, appeals, might, I believe, easily have caused a landslide—and then there would have been the devil to pay.

Buxton added that he did not believe that the majority of Afrikaners would have been 'disloyal': 'But the Dutch commandoes, or some of them, might easily have declined to fire on Dutchmen, their own kith and kin, for the sake of what, until a few years ago, was an alien and hostile Empire and flag.'

If this reaction had been widespread, a grave military situation would have resulted 'and the revolt would have assumed a racial character which would have required Imperial troops in large numbers to put it down . . .' (*sic*). Buxton indicated that this telegram might be shown to other members of the cabinet, adding this warning: 'but I do not want it even to be breathed here that I have not fully trusted the Dutch as a whole; such an idea would do much harm.'[32]

Two years later, Buxton could only confirm that relations between the two white sections had deteriorated as a result of the war:

> No one here knows, and no one here can tell but it will, I am afraid, take years to bring the racial position back to that which existed, *or was thought to exist*, say two years ago. On the other hand, the labour position here is far better than it was two years ago. The war has purified the Labour Party by exorcising the Syndicalists, and the Government and employers have at last come into closer relations, and far better relations, with the trades unions than they ever were before. . . .[33]

Buxton's view therefore was that while Anglo-Afrikaner 'race relations' had deteriorated, class tensions had been greatly eased.

We turn next to the impact of the war on specifically party politics. The most convenient measure of party fortunes during the war is the outcome of the general election of October 1915. This gave the S.A.P. 54 seats, the Unionists 40, the Nationalists 26 and Labour 4, with 6 Independents. On the whole the Nationalists did not do much better than most of their opponents had expected them to do, although their gains, at the expense of the S.A.P., more in rural votes generally, than seats, were very considerable. To keep these gains in limits, by avoiding the splitting of their own votes in three-cornered contests, the S.A.P. and the Unionists had concluded an informal electoral agreement which they tried unsuccessfully to keep secret. The main surprise of the election was the virtual elimination of Labour representation at the hands of the Unionists. This was a direct consequence of the war, on the one hand through a split in the Labour Party on the war issue and on the other through a rallying of 'British votes' of whatever class to the cause of empire in wartime. Overall, Botha could only console himself with the thought that the S.A.P. alone was stronger in parliament than the combined votes of Nationalists and Labour.[34]

For the S.A.P. the whole period of the war was a time of great trial. Since the party incorporated a wing of English-speaking or 'British' support, the general Anglo-Afrikaner rift opened up by the war had the effect of producing a new area of tension, or aggravating an existing one, inside the party. But the S.A.P. was also the victim of the war's effect in creating a new source of division within Afrikaner ranks. The evidence of by-elections in the period 1915 to 1918, provincial elections in 1916 and 1917 and the impressions of observers such as Buxton all suggest a steady erosion of Afrikaner support away from the S.A.P. to the Nationalist side. At the same time the loss of its overall majority in parliament and its consequently increased dependence on Unionist support for survival as a government, aggravated the effect of Anglo-Afrikaner tensions on the party. An insoluble problem for Botha was the way in which the appeal of Nationalist propaganda to his followers was strengthened by the counter-productive effect of ultra-imperialist outbursts from such quarters as the 'British League'.

In a consideration of the fortunes of Hertzog's National Party, the outstanding wartime features are the growth of the party's support and its ideological shift from Hertzog's original principles of language equality and 'South Africa first' to those of independence and republicanism. The general election of 1915 was the first effective test of relative Afrikaner support for Botha and Hertzog since the parting of the ways in 1912. It is difficult to say how far the election was simply a counting of minds made up before August 1914 or whether the war and the rebellion did indeed exert a decisive effect on the outcome. By the time he had formally established his party in the O.F.S. in July 1914, Hertzog probably already commanded the support of a majority of the Afrikaners of that province. His articulation of the aspirations of the Afrikaans cultural and language movement had already won him some support in the Cape. The influence of Botha and Smuts was too great for him to make much impression in the Transvaal, but some support had been forthcoming, again from cultural nationalists, including predikants and young lawyers. Essentially this pre-war pattern of Nationalist strength was confirmed in the 1915 election, and it seems clear that if there was taking place before the war a drift in Afrikaner allegiance away from the S.A.P. to the Nationalist camp, then the combined effect of the outbreak of war and the rebellion was an enormous acceleration of this trend. The indications are that it continued steadily throughout the war.

The rebellion gave expression to the Afrikaner aspiration to restore republicanism in South Africa, but it was not until 1917 that the goal of republican independence became a principle of the National Party. The initiative came from Tielman Roos, the Transvaal leader, who seized the opening provided by the references of the Allied leaders, Lloyd George and President Wilson, to self-determination as a cause for which the war was being fought. While Hertzog evidently regarded Roos' action as somewhat irresponsible, having been taken without regard for the proper party channels, the party's Federale Raad (Federal Council) duly endorsed the aim. Despite Hertzog's caution and reluctance, his ambiguous utterances could not conceal the novelty of the situation. The Nationalists were being committed to the pursuit of republican independence but by constitutional means. In 1919 the Nationalist deputation that Lloyd George received at Versailles carried the struggle into the post-war era.

The other two parties, Labour and Unionist, were in some ways caught in a reciprocal relationship during the war. Split over how far they should support the imperial war effort, the Labour party found many of their normal supporters—the skilled artisans and trade unionists in the British tradition—deserting the ranks at the 1915 election. The Unionists, as the pre-eminent 'British' party, were the obvious recipient for this disaffected block of voters, and their 40 seats gained in the election reflected their new strength. Yet they themselves were placed in an anomalous position by the war. They were still the 'official' opposition, but the outbreak of the war made them even less inclined to oppose General Botha than in the days of Jameson's leadership. At the outset the party leader, Sir Thomas Smartt, gave Botha an assurance of support for the duration of the war. The cause of the empire was to be placed above that of party and personal considerations, and the Unionists were frequently reminded by Buxton that the official British view was that the interest of the empire required that Botha should be kept in office. Since the Unionists themselves appreciated the force of this argument, they had little choice in the last resort to do otherwise than co-operate with Botha. The Unionist role was of a kind to breed frustration. They were an opposition party unable to oppose, and since there was no reorganisation of the S.A.P. government along coalition lines, they enjoyed neither 'place' in the sense of office, nor any effective 'say' in policy-making. Over a wide range of issues, such as the government's liability to finance the payment of South African forces at the higher 'overseas' pay rates, the Unionists functioned as a pressure-group seeking to enlarge the Union's contribution to the war. The S.A.P. Afrikaners would then object (particularly if increased expenditure was involved), whereupon the Unionist leaders would persuade their followers to withdraw their demands and so 'save' the government. The result was a loss of prestige to both parties involved.

Reference to the absence of coalition raises the last of the major themes to be discussed here, that of inter-party relations. During the war there were no party re-alignments. Some Afrikaners, generally not party activists, continued to advocate *hereniging*, though given the personal estrangement between Botha and Hertzog, to say nothing of the divisive effects of the war itself, there was little prospect for Afrikaner consolidation. More interesting is the question of why no S.A.P.-Unionist coalition could be negotiated during the war.

In the Harcourt Papers, which were then still at Stanton Harcourt, near Oxford, I discovered some years ago, a sealed envelope marked: '*Very Private*. Letter from Lord Buxton to Mr. Harcourt. Nov. 4th 1914. *L. Harcourt*. Eventualities.' Since the 'eventualities' referred to were to arise only in the event of Botha's death in action against the rebels, Harcourt never opened this letter. Enjoying a piece of good fortune that seldom comes the way of historians, I was the one to do so, some fifty years later. The essence of the letter is contained in the following extract:

> He said he had consulted Smuts, that his [Botha's] view was that, if anything happened, Smuts should be asked to succeed him; and that, in the circumstances, Smuts should endeavour to form a coalition Government, bringing in Smartt, and

> Merriman, and others of the Unionist [not named] . . . He [Botha] hoped that I should be inclined to give all the assistance I could, by way of persuasion, and otherwise, in the direction of a coalition Cabinet . . .
>
> After further discussion, he said that, in any case, if he remained P.M., he thought that after the War, which had brought about such active co-operation of parties, he should reconstruct his cabinet on coalition lines.[35]

This letter demonstrates that as early as November 1914 Botha recognised the force of the case for coalition, which he thought should be negotiated at once if he were removed from the scene or after the war if he remained in office. As events turned out Botha, both in public and in private, rejected coalition, not only for the duration of the war but also in the nine months period of peace before his death in August 1919.

Suggestions from the Unionist side for coalition were given greater cogency after the 1915 election, when Botha lost his overall majority. One of his reasons for continuing to resist such appeals was the calculation that coalition with the Unionists would destroy any prospect of Afrikaner reconciliation. To the end of his life Botha never finally surrendered the hope that the split in the ranks of Afrikaners could be healed. While he did not believe that his course of action, in respect both of the breach with Hertzog and his policy towards the war and the rebellion, could have been any different, he clearly recognised and regretted the extent to which Afrikaners had been divided by anything he had done. Botha regarded his Afrikaner following within the S.A.P., rather than the party as a whole, as the real basis of his power. A further objection to coalition was that such a step could weaken that basis by causing a stampede of S.A.P. Afrikaners across to the Nationalist side. There was also the office-holding angle to coalition. The admission of Unionists into the cabinet would necessitate the dropping of some of the present ministers and the result would be dissatisfaction in his own party.

From inter-party relations we turn to an assessment of the war's overall impact on the Union's party political life. Obviously the war raised issues that were quite outside the pre-war system of party politics. The war involved large doses of what Sir Keith Hancock called the 'hot stuff' of politics—the government found itself in short order having to suppress a rebellion, mount two campaigns in Africa and send troops to Europe. Whatever criticism is levelled at Botha's policy, the fact remains that the suppression of the rebellion was a vindication of order and stability. The newly formed state withstood not only that threat but all the 'hot stuff' of the war years and was undoubtedly strengthened by this achievement.

The war also went beyond party politics by its creation of a new divide in Anglo-Afrikaner relations. Most 'British' South Africans were imbued by a surge of patriotism which made loyalty to South Africa a component of a wider loyalty to the British Empire. Many Afrikaners totally rejected this conception, some of them even contemplating the forcible restoration of Boer republicanism with the help of Germany, the empire's enemy in the war. The result was a fresh source of division within the ranks of Afrikaners themselves. The rifts between Afrikaner and English, and between Afrikaner and Afrikaner, rested on clashing conceptions of patriotism or national attitudes. The war served to bring these issues to the front, and by comparison to play down the force of class or regional differences. Ideologically the war led to the articulation of the republican and secessionist goal. But the permanence of this change was less certain, for while this ideology was officially adhered to in the early 1920s, it was more or less abandoned in the decade 1924 to 1934

While there were no party re-alignments during the war, the way was prepared for the S.A.P.'s absorption of the Unionists in 1920. Botha and Smuts were clearly thinking along the lines of this ultimate objective as early as November 1914. When the Nationalist gains from the S.A.P. were shown to be irreversible, and when Labour recovered some of its losses to the Unionists, the interests of both the S.A.P. and the Unionists demanded the kind of arrangement that was made in 1920. In that sense, at least indirectly, the war helped to satisfy the conditions for the first major party development since the formation of the National Party.

Notes

1. N. Mansergh, *The Commonwealth Experience* (London) 1969, 165.
2. *Ibid.*, 167.
3. Harcourt Papers, 1914, Box 3. The Harcourt Papers are now in the Bodleian Library, Oxford.
4. *Ibid.*, draft telegram, 30 Oct. 1914.
5. *Ibid.*, Buxton's telegrams to Harcourt, 24 Oct. and 9 Nov. 1914.
6. As indicated by Buxton in an earlier telegram. *Ibid.*, 3 Nov. 1914.
7. S. B. Spies, 'The Outbreak of the First World War and the Botha Government', *South African Historical Journal*, No. 1. 1969, 52.
8. Harcourt Papers, 1914, Box 3, Harcourt's telegram to Buxton, 10 Nov. 1914. On the episode as a whole, see R. Keiser, "The South African Governor-General 1910–1919", D. Phil. thesis (Oxford, 1975), 271–2; W. R. Louis, *Great Britain and Germany's Lost Colonies 1914–1919* (Oxford, 1967) 51–2; and J. C. Corbett, *Naval Operations*, Vol. I (London, 1920), 331–2.
9. See Mansergh, 167–170, for the relative contributions of the dominions to the imperial war effort.
10. Spies, 50–1, 53.
11. Mansergh, 166.
12. For example, Buxton Papers, Buxton to Walter Long (colonial secretary), 23 March 1917 (copy), transmitting notes of his conversations with Botha. I am grateful to Mrs G. Clay for permission to consult the Buxton papers. See also Earl Buxton, *General Botha* (London, 1924) 241–2.
13. Keiser, *op. cit.*, 310–12; *Cape Times*, 5 and 12 May 1917, reports of Hertzog's addresses, and 11 June 1917, report of Buxton's address at Tulbagh; *De Burger*, 12 June 1917, editorial.
14. D. Hobart Houghton and J. Dagut, *Source Material on the South African Economy 1860–1970*, Vol. 2, (Cape Town, 1972) 192, 223.
15. *Ibid.*, 223.
16. Frederick A. Johnstone, *Class Race and Gold: a Study of Class Relations and Racial Discrimination in South Africa*, (London, 1976) 100.
17. P. Walshe, *The Rise of African Nationalism in South Africa* (London, 1970) 89.
18. H. J. and R. E. Simons, *Class and Colour in South Africa 1850–1950* (London, 1969) 178–9.
19. *Ibid.*, 176, 198, 214, 218; C.O. 551/111, Buxton's despatches of 29 Jan. and 15 Feb. 1919 transmitting respectively the resolutions of the APO on South West Africa and the 'memorial' of the SANNC to the king.
20. A. B. Keith, *War Government of the British Dominions* (Oxford, 1921), 328–9.
21. Keith, *op. cit.*, 329; Johnstone, *op. cit.*, 175–6.
22. Johnstone, *op. cit.*, 177–8; Simons, *op. cit.*, 213, 221–2.
23. B. Pachai, *The South African Indian Question 1860–1971* (Cape Town, 1971) 66–8, 73–5; Keith, *op. cit.*, 314–22.
24. Pachai, *op. cit.*, 75, 81, 83, 85–6.
25. On the 'overseas pay question', see Keiser, *op. cit.*, 290–301; Earl Buxton, *General Botha* (London, 1924) 246–55; Keith, *op. cit.*, 102–3.

26. Buxton Papers, Buxton to Bonar Law, 17 Feb. 1916 (typed copy).
27. *Ibid.*, notes of conversation with Botha, 13 Feb. 1916; Keiser, *op. cit.*, 295–6; Buxton, *op. cit.*, 250. Smartt was the leader of the opposition Unionists.
28. W. K. Hancock and Jean van der Poel (editors), *Selections from the Smuts Papers*, Vol. III (Cambridge, 1966), 336 (translated version). For Botha's speech in parliament, see *Debates of the House of Assembly . . . as reported in the Cape Times*, Vol. X, 1 (19 Nov. 1915–17 June 1916), pp. 71–2 (16 Feb. 1916).
29. Buxton Papers, Buxton to Walter Long (typed copy), enclosing notes of conversation with Botha on 22 Mar. 1916. See also Buxton, *op. cit.*, 254.
30. On the 'wool question', see Keiser, *op. cit.*, 302–4, Keith, *op. cit.*, 71 and Buxton, *op. cit.*, 256–61.
31. Buxton Papers, Long to Buxton, 8 Feb. 1918.
32. Harcourt Papers, Box 3, Vol. I, Buxton to Harcourt, telegram, 8 Nov. 1914.
33. Buxton Papers, Buxton to [correspondent unidentified], 3 May 1916 (draft).
34. *Ibid.*, notes on conversations with Botha in October, and telegram to Bonar-Law, 23 Oct. 1915.
35. Harcourt Papers, Box 3, Vol. I, Buxton-Harcourt Private and Personal Correspondence, Sept. 1914–Jan. 1915.

Spoils of War: Sub-Imperial Collaboration in South West Africa and New Guinea, 1914–20

by Colin Newbury

Ever since Richard Jebb discussed the nature of dominion nationalism and the imperial attachment as a developing alliance, historians have been at pains to explore the local and regional differences which gave rise to distinctive attitudes and policies in the developing nation states of the British Empire.[1] The test of the alliance in war clearly changed as well as strengthened the definition of common interests in foreign policy, defence and international trade. Whether wartime consultation, separate signatures to the peace treaties and the acquisition of colonial responsibilities moved the dominions very far towards distinctive formulation of their interests between 1919 and 1939 is open to question. In Australia, it has been argued, security was sought in a territorial buffer zone to the north in New Guinea, rather than foreign treaty systems and international organisations.[2] Much the same might be said of South Africa in the inter-war period, when the western flank of the Union was extended by the Mandate over South West Africa, and attention was turned inwards on the problems of political control in a developing multi-racial society. For both dominions foreign policy was defensive in style and heavily weighted towards the preservation of the high levels of internal investment and external trade that were part of the legacy of the First World War.

It will be argued here that something more than a territorial imperative for reasons of security emerged from Australian and South African insistence on retention of former German colonies. The short-term effects on the formulation of regional foreign policies in both dominions owed much to their appreciation of the cost of military occupation and their evaluation of the economic potential of the occupied territories. In the longer term, experience showed that neither New Guinea nor South West Africa was likely to benefit the dominions' economies, though sectional interests within the merchant and mining communities of both societies might present their case for special treatment in terms of taxation or transport as a 'national' issue. Even less than imperial Germany were the two sub-imperial powers prepared to make extensive state investments in the infrastructure of the Mandates. But other lessons were learned, especially by the Union's recently-created Department of Mines and by Australian mercantile companies, on the benefits and penalties of colonial monopoly.

The immediate focus of that experience was their treatment of German assets in the two territories in quite distinctive ways which parallel their domestic policies towards German properties and residents. The topic of dominion participation in reparations and the opportunities presented to British and American capital investment in former German colonies has been inadequately explored. Yet it was an important consequence of the Versailles settlement. And it raises questions about the direction and limits to sub-imperial collaboration within the British wartime alliance on the marginal battlefields, where the emphasis was on acquisition, rather than destruction, and even entailed a measure of co-operation with the enemy in a colonial conquest.

I

However xenophobic some colonial responses may have been to the presence of international rivals in Southern Africa or the Pacific from the early 1880s, there was little detailed planning on the eve of the war for military operations in neighbouring territories. The Commonwealth had learned to live with the fact of German New Guinea, after taking over the administration of British Papua in 1906. Australians were more nervous of Japan as an Asian power than of the outpost of a European power. Nor is there any evidence of hostility between the Union and German South West Africa which shared a long, undefended frontier at the Orange River and Bechuanaland.

Trade links between the dominions and either of the German colonies were tenuous and poorly developed in the face of German mercantile and shipping competition. There were some Afrikaner settlers in South West Africa and there was a small number of British traders and planters in New Guinea, but there was little British investment. As a major land and mining enterprise, the British-registered South West Africa Company was almost unique in a colony dominated by a dozen German companies and two-thirds of its capital was owned by Germans.[3] A team of businessmen and engineers from Kimberley made a detailed assessment of the territory's diamond industry in 1913, with a view to market co-ordination, rather than competition. And in 1914, on the initiative of the Union's Ministry of Finance, representatives of the German diamond companies agreed to participate in a production cartel together with Union mines.[4] But although the British consul, E. Muller, forwarded regular reports from Luderitzbucht to Pretoria, none of his observations could be construed as preparation for invasion. In German New Guinea, the company manager and planter, F.R. Jolly, who acted as British consul, sent no reports at all to the Foreign Office.

Once war had been declared on their behalf, the South African, Australian and New Zealand governments were invited by a joint naval and military committee of the Imperial General Staff on 5 August 1914 to attack German possessions to neutralize their wireless facilities. The Colonial Office added the phosphate islands of Angaur and Nauru to the list as a useful afterthought. It was hoped, too, the invitation would have the right 'political effect' on South Africa, where there was a serious division in Botha's Cabinet on the necessity for any participation in the war at all. The dominions were reminded, however, that it would be for the imperial government to dispose of any occupied territory at a peace settlement.[5]

The Australians and New Zealanders accepted at once. Western Samoa was occupied at the end of August; the radio on Nauru was destroyed; and a hastily equipped expeditionary force was landed on New Britain and captured the wireless station. On 17 September 1914 Acting-Governor Haber surrendered German possessions in Melanesia to Brigadier Holmes with full honours of war and an assurance of full pay for officers and officials. Many of the administrative officials agreed to serve at their posts in the central services, but most were shipped out with military personnel to Australia and to Germany. Even so, the terms were considered unduly generous by the Department of Defence in Melbourne and by the Committee of Imperial Defence in

London, where application was made for a refund from Germany through neutral channels, before any salaries were paid.[6]

Apart from a few incidents of looting and flogging, the plantation and trading economy of German New Guinea was delivered into Australian hands with a minimum of recrimination. German planters and merchants continued business in co-operation with Australian shippers, under Holmes's military administration. German labour controls were enforced, recruitment expanded, and military expeditions were used to counter resistance. The masters changed, but 'all boys and kanakas . . . were told that the situation was just the same as before'.[7]

By contrast with this easy takeover, operations against South West Africa cost considerably more blood and treasure and a near civil war. Plans for a joint military and naval offensive across the Orange River and along the coast were delayed because of a shortage of arms and lack of co-operation between the newly-created defence department and the naval commander-in-chief at the Cape, Rear-Admiral King-Hall.[8] Rifles were rushed in from the Straits Settlements and Hong Kong, and Swakopmund was bombarded and Luderitzbucht occupied by a small force in mid-September 1914. But the split between Botha's ministry and Hertzog's Nationalist opposition was compounded by the defection of senior staff officers with troops from the Free State and the Transvaal. From 12 October 1914 the Union was under martial law, and what had begun as a 'party quarrel' between Afrikaners developed into a poorly co-ordinated campaign by nearly 11,000 rebels to neutralize South Africa's war effort.

In the end, the *opstand* was put down by Afrikaners, leaving Botha and Smuts free in December 1914 to mobilize 30,000–40,000 men against Major Franke's 6,000 colonial troops and reservists. Despite differences of opinion between Botha and Governor-General Buxton over whether to encourage a revolt by the Rehoboth Bastards (they were told to keep quiet), imperial and colonial co-operation by land and sea was not in doubt from then on. The Union Jack was raised over Windhuk in May with its wireless station still intact. Before the end of Botha's northern campaign against the remnants of German forces, it was also agreed that South Africa would intern 900 officers and men 'with permanent domicile' in the Protectorate and allow 4,000 reservists to return to their farms and homes. Other men of military age and some medical and nursing personnel were repatriated through the Netherlands. According to the terms made with Acting-Governor Seitz, 9 July 1915, a message was sent to the Kaiser announcing that officers were permitted to keep their arms and horses and the reservists their rifles as a protection against former subjects. In all, the Union's campaigns cost more casualties putting down the rebellion than in capturing German territory.[9]

What the South Africans got for their efforts was a massive land area of some 332,000 square miles with a population of 228,000 Africans in a closely administered 'police zone' and the more distant Ovamboland, Okavango and Kaokoveld regions of settlement. Farmers, miners, traders and officials of European origins numbered 14,830, before repatriations in 1919. Money had been poured in by the imperial government to make good the conquest of the Herero and the Bondelswart, and about £15 million had been expended to construct ports and a railway system linking farms, mines and the administrative capital. Current revenues in the last years of German rule came principally from taxes on diamond production and export, bringing gross annual revenue including military expenditure and savings to £2 million for 1914/15.[10]

With a land area of about 90,000 square miles the New Guinea mainland and its archipelago of islands to the east presented formidable topographical obstacles to any imperial power which sought to rule an estimated population of four to five hundred thousand inhabitants. The Germans under the New Guinea Company and the imperial administration of 1900 to 1914 controlled little outside the coastal periphery. At enormous cost they had alienated over half a million acres and held about 150,000 acres in plantations, including the estates of the missions. Total agricultural and mercantile assets were valued at £5 million, serviced and protected by a small colonial state which depended on customs duties, head taxes and subsidies to make up annual budget deficits.[11]

After the partition of the northern Solomons in 1899 which concluded the Anglo-German division of Melanesia, the main attraction of German New Guinea for Australian commercial interests lay in cheaper labour costs than in surrounding British territory and in the carrying trade and agency work for companies importing and exporting through Sydney. Burns, Philp and Co. expanded their plantation investment from Papua and the Solomons into Bougainville and Buka in 1912 and 1913, setting up a subsidiary, the Choiseul Plantation Company, in the hope of both breaking into the local copra trade in competition with Nord-Deutscher Lloyd and escaping from more onerous land regulations in the British Protectorate.[12]

Consequently, when the expeditionary force led the way, Australian mercantilism was not far behind. Burns Philp dispatched their islands inspector, W.H. Lucas, in September 1914 with a cargo of supplies on the *Moresby* and instructions to co-operate with German merchants and replace their agents interned in Australia. Lucas adroitly directed the local carrying trade away from Far Eastern ports to Sydney by using his effective monopoly of transport; and in 1916 the company was accorded all agency work for German planters. In Melbourne, the attorney-general's department conceded that this advantage was not 'trading with the enemy' under Commonwealth legislation. More reluctantly, the Foreign Office, the Board of Trade and the Colonial Office recognized that the Australian company was needed to service the requirements of an occupied territory and was a 'special case' under the Trading with the Enemy (Extension of Powers) Act of 1915. They did, however, raise the question of reciprocal trade advantages for Japanese allies, something which Melbourne chose to ignore.[13] In any case, Lucas had other ends in view and began to make an inventory of companies and plantations for future confiscation. At his head office in Sydney, the company chairman, Sir James Burns, went further and framed a memorandum for the governor-general on Australia's 'natural destiny' in the Pacific and the place of Burns Philp in Melanesia as a mercantile bulwark against foreign competition.[14]

In the meantime, the military administration under Holmes and his successor, Colonel Pethebridge, pursued a policy of pragmatism and economic self-interest which reassured German civilians and encouraged reinvestment of earnings from plantations. By the terms of the capitulation existing currencies and commercial laws were recognized; the exchange rate was fixed at one shilling to the mark; the liquid assets of the German administration – amounting to no more than £25,000 – were taken over; and the local treasury performed the functions of a savings bank and transferred funds to Sydney agents, until a branch of the Commonwealth Bank was set up in 1916. Then German paper currency was withdrawn at the old rate of exchange and the silver-nickel specie of the German period continued at par with the Australian shilling, despite pressure from the Commonwealth to have it devalued. For local trade and payment of labourers' wages, the white man's coin of whatever origin kept its parity in New Guinea; and the fact that the King's head resembled that of the bearded Administrator Pethebridge only confirmed the soundness of the 'new marks'.[15]

As a result of Australian indulgence with the local plantation economy and command of the carrying trade, New Guinea imports and exports rose in value from £225,416 in 1915/16 to £1.2 million in 1919/20, nearly all of which passed through Australian ports. Copra exports doubled 1913 tonnages, though very little was processed in Australia. In practice, this monopoly of trans-shipments proved something of a bottleneck in competition with wartime shipping space for wheat. But the idea that the production of the captured territory might compensate for the high cost of administration took root in the minds of merchants, politicians and the military officials who contributed to the *Rabaul Record* which ran regular features on the attractions of tropical agriculture. Both Holmes and Pethebridge were soon convinced that the future of the territory was to become a British possession. Palm tree plantings doubled under their rule, and indentured labour increased from 17,529 in 1914 to 27,728 at the end of the military administration in 1921. German labour ordinances were consolidated and applied with the usual penal sanctions, standard wages, long contracts of two to three years, deferred pay and restriction of casual work. Employers' rights to inflict corporal punishment were, it is true, suspended at first and then tolerated for most of the military period until the formal abolition of flogging in 1919. But an open market in traded copra was curtailed for the benefit of planters and exporters; and the head tax for unemployed males was extended intermittently, but with measurable effect on recruitment and production.

The growing appreciation of the soldier-administrators and the merchant-shippers that there was a prize of war in the making was matched by efforts of the Sydney Chamber of Commerce to encourage import substitution for goods formerly imported from the Central Powers and, more extensively, by the general review of Australia's commercial destiny in the Inter-State Commission of 1916. The evidence heard was mercantilist and aimed at securing trade once in German hands. It was consistent with the predatory views of the economic conference of Allied Powers in Paris in June 1916; and much of its conclusions had been foreshadowed by William Hughes in his campaign to undermine the foundations of German overseas investment by ending the metal combines in Australia.[16] The presence of Hughes at the Paris conference confirmed the work of the commissioners in Melbourne and made it certain that the occupied colony would become a target for Australian shipping companies and would-be planters. Once it was known, too, that the cost of the military occupation of New Guinea (close on £1 million, 1914–21) was never likely to be covered by local revenues, there was an added incentive for claiming compensation.[17]

This was small beer, compared with the cost of the South West African campaign. By the middle of 1915 the Union government knew that there would be a deficit of £2 million, on top of military expenditure amounting to over £8.7 million for all operations in Africa and abroad. Almost 4,000 reservists and their families had to be resettled; and about one third of the civilian population was living off rations distributed through British and German officials. Exports had ceased to produce any taxes or exchange from abroad during the campaign, when the German administration had financed itself by overdrafts on the banks, by commandeering goods and livestock and by the issue of 'Seitz' notes which were not negotiable outside the Protectorate.

To prevent total collapse, four German banks were allowed to reopen alongside two South African banks which made advances to companies and traders. Credits of

14 million marks held for transmission to Germany were left intact by the occupying force and were used to fund the local Land Bank. The Deutsche Afrika Bank was allowed to obtain £300,000 in remittances through New York which were used by German merchants to pay for imports from the Union 'at considerably enhanced prices'.[18] They soon exhausted this source of currency and were left with marks devalued at 29 to the pound and the unacceptable 'Seitz'.

By these means the white community lived largely on capital and credit, until the export of hides, skins, wool and copper ore revived at the end of 1915. Union banks made advances against 'town and farm properties' to encourage a thriving import trade through Cape Town merchants. But without diamond exports no profits tax was received at all during the year, and a loss of revenue equivalent to £894,000 had to be made up from votes of Union departments. The Administrator, E.H.L. Gorges, expected a continuous deficit.

Reopening the mines for production was, therefore, a priority of the administration in co-operation with German personnel. One of General Botha's first proclamations prohibited casual prospecting in the Luderitzbucht fields, where there were company titles to be respected. Only white labour was employed in the repair of plant damaged during the war. After some argument with Acting-Governor Seitz, the administration managed to recover 75,000 carats of pre-war stock hidden during the evacuation of Windhuk, including a stone of 40 carats worth £5,000.

Copper, too, was encouraged by grants, but labour was in short supply. Of the 5,000 Ovambo employed on six months' contracts by mines, railways and farmers, no more than 2,000 were prepared to work for monthly wages of £1 and food paid by their former rulers. Both the Khan copper mine at Arandis and the Otavi Mine and Railway Company produced concentrates at about half their 1913 levels, but export was uncertain, because the American Smelting and Refining Works at New York made unacceptable demands for treatment charges and because the administration insisted that smelted ore should be sent to England for sale.

Apart from one diamond mine which resumed production towards the end of 1915, the local diamond industry was slow to recover. Output for 1916 amounted to no more than 12 per cent of pre-war production by weight. Parcels were sent to London, but no sales took place, and the mines remained dependent for working expenses on loans from the Union banks. For a territory which earned three-fifths of its ordinary revenue from diamond taxation, the collapse of the market was disastrous, and copper exports did little to help.

The main reason for this fiscal poverty was that the South African government and its military administration were not free to sell diamonds overseas. From January 1915 a War Trade Advisory Committee under Sir Francis Hopwood sought to stop enemy supplies of bulk and strategic commodities; and from June 1915 a special committee was set up by the Board of Trade for the War Trade Department to monitor the diamond traffic, on the advice of Alfred Mosely, a former Cape diamond merchant and confidant of Cecil Rhodes. Mosely warned that there was a clandestine export in industrial stones through Holland from the six or seven London firms specializing in this branch of the trade whom he tended to brand as suspect because of their German origins. Dutch dealers in industrial stones were 'taking them back in their pockets'.[19]

While they did not accept all of Mosely's allegations, the Board and the War Trade Department agreed that the large stocks of South West diamonds held by the London diamond syndicate should be frozen for the duration of the war, and that the export of rough stones, whether suitable for gems or for industrial purposes, had to be controlled by licence and by the establishment of an expert committee to monitor traffic to Holland. In order to enforce this control, Mosely advised that the Dutch dealers and cutters could be refused South African goods. The Board concluded that centralized control through London was the only effective way of preventing a leakage to Germany through neutral countries. Therefore, the Colonial Office was told that 'our Dominions should prohibit the export of any diamonds cut or uncut except to the United Kingdom'. Because expert advice was needed to decide which types of stones exported to the Continent were suitable for industrial purposes, the Board appointed Mosely and the leading diamond merchants, V.A. Litkie and Ludwig Breitmeyer, head of the syndicate, to monitor the trade. A conference with the War Trade Department and the Order in Council of 30 July 1915 confirmed the prohibition on the import of South West African stones and the export of rough diamonds except under licence, granted after a certificate of approval by the diamond export committee. A similar committee consisting of dealers trusted by Mosely was set up in Holland to monitor the trade from that end through the British consulate in Amsterdam.[20]

This effective stranglehold on an already centralized market was welcomed by the London diamond syndicate which had been unable to come to terms with the German *Diamanten Regie* for a regular share of South West exports and had to buy them in competition with Antwerp. Similarly, the syndicate had no contract with the Premier (Transvaal) Diamond Mining Company in which the Union government had a 60 per cent interest and which preferred to market separately through its own office in London. There was now a possibility that both sources could be brought into the system of contracts which operated for the De Beers and New Jagersfontein companies which supplied most of the world's rough gemstones.

At the outbreak of the war, moreover, there had been a glut on the market. An accumulation of some £3 million in small diamonds was divided between the Regie, an Antwerp syndicate and the London syndicate. With this accumulation frozen or restricted, a dangerous competition ended for the moment; and the syndicate readily accepted a prohibition on the sale of South West diamonds, provided this applied to the Union government as well. In February 1916, Bonar Law, as Secretary of State for Colonies, reminded the South Africans through the governor-general that no such sales could be made, so long as stocks in London were locked up.[21] News of German smuggling through Scandinavia for export to the United States and clandestine exports by members of the Defence Force in South West Africa reinforced the unwillingness of the War Trade Department to tolerate a market for South West goods which could not be distinguished from German pre-war stocks.

To explain this message in detail, Mosely toured South Africa in May 1916 warning against separate deals through Antwerp, but recommending acceptance of tenders by the London syndicate for restricted monthly deliveries of South West production to keep the mines operating. On his return, Mosely was sent to Holland to arrange for the cutting of these stones by trusted firms. And from these manufacturers, advised the Colonial Office, cut stones were to be returned to London for sale in North and South America by brokers approved by the diamond committee.[22]

After sample parcels were sent to Mosely at the end of the year, the Union government and the administrator had no choice but to accept this outlet, while pressing for a ceiling of 50,000 carats a month. On 3 March 1917, the government through the mines department reluctantly concluded its first agreement with the London diamond syndicate to deliver all monthly production from South West Africa up to 330,000 carats a year only, at a basic price of 46s 6d per carat with profit-sharing on sales. As an earnest of this contract for sales through a monopoly channel, the syndicate demanded the captured 'Seitz' diamonds as well.

A second reason for the dearth of diamond income was that the new administration did not understand the working of the Imperial Diamond Taxation Ordinance of 1912 which required a provisional and final assessment of the amount to be paid by companies at the rate of 60 per cent on sales with a return of 70 per cent of working costs. No such assessments were made for 1915 and 1916. The first assessment for tax was not made till the second half of 1917; and it was not paid over until the fiscal year 1919/20, while the companies waited on their income from sales abroad and disputed the administration's calculations.

Consequently, the administration of the captured colony made very little from its major source of income for the rest of the war. Apart from the delay in recovering taxes, there was a muddle over methods of evaluation applied in Luderitzbucht and in London which divided the South African Treasury from the Department of Mines. The department refused, moreover, to hand over the Seitz stones and reserved a right (contrary to the contract) to sell excess production elsewhere. The minister, F.S. Malan, and the South West producers considered the syndicate's commission of 10 per cent on re-sales too high. Suspicion of profiteering from rising diamond prices fed a departmental prejudice against the syndicate and strengthened the view that the Premier mine and South West companies would be sacrificed for the sake of sales of high-quality gem roughs from De Beers and New Jagersfontein in which there was a dominant share ownership by London merchants. From 1915, departmental officials led by the Government Mining Engineer, R.N. Kotze, looked approvingly at the German system of marketing through a 'control board' and seriously considered full or partial nationalization of the diamond industry in the captured territory and in the Union.[23]

II

Such forward planning raised long-term questions about the eventual fate of German assets in the colonies and elsewhere. The possibility of retaining the captured territories, voiced by Holmes at Rabaul as early as December 1914, and implicit in much of the Union's departmental minutes on South West Africa from 1916, was taken up at much higher levels, when Sir Lewis Harcourt presented a memorandum to Cabinet in March 1915 titled 'The Spoils'. For the Colonial Secretary it was 'out of the question to part with any of the territories now in the occupation of New Zealand and Australia'. South West Africa, as yet only half occupied, was also to be retained 'as part of the British Empire', unless used as a pawn to obtain Portuguese East Africa – the 'missing link' between the Cape and Cairo.[24]

Andrew Fisher, in his last year of office as Labour Prime Minister, and Hughes, who was about to replace him, would have shared this view, to keep out Japanese from the islands as much as the Germans. Fisher willingly accepted the Colonial Office ruling that the equator divided Japanese and Australian spheres of occupation in German Melanesia and Micronesia, encouraged by the sympathetic attitude of the governor-general, Munro-Ferguson, towards sub-imperial aspirations. And the governor-general, in turn, was influenced by the arguments presented by James Burns for acquisition of the plantations and a monopoly supply of bulk cargo for carriers in the Pacific – a point repeated and emphasized by the trade commission of 1916.[25]

But Hughes and the Australian attorney-general, Garran, like their counterparts, Smuts and J. de V. Roos in South Africa, were well aware that such speculation depended on the terms of the peace treaty. In the meantime, Australia enforced its advantages through war regulations to monopolize New Guinea's transit trade. And Hughes, in co-operation with Lucas who became his personal adviser on island affairs, extended mercantile contracts with German firms for a further six months from April 1918, refusing all requests from the Japanese and the Dutch to take up cargo Burns Philp could not carry. For, with an armistice in sight, there was a risk that the Germans might turn once again to other carriers operating from the Far East, before a peace treaty decided their fate. While the Prime Minister kept rivals at bay, Lucas prepared a plan in June 1919 for a commission to take stock of German assets and run them, as soon as Australia was given this authority.[26]

At the same time, quite a different scheme for buying out the Germans through an 'Anglo-Australian company' for about £2.5 million was prepared by Burns with the support of the acting Prime Minister, W.A. Watt, at the end of 1918. An even more ambitious project to float a 'British Australian Pacific Estates Company' for £5 million under the direction of Lord Inchcape, Lord Leverhulme and Burns with total control of New Guinea's copra exports, depots and shipping was forwarded to the governor-general and Lord Milner.[27]

It was, moreover, assumed that there would be a total expropriation, when Lucas and Atlee Hunt, secretary of the Home and Territories Department, wrote a majority opinion opposing amalgamation with Papua for a royal commission report at the end of 1919. This investigation into the future of New Guinea which they carried out with Lieutenant-Governor J.H.P. Murray was decisive on a number of issues. It was agreed German properties should be sold on preferential terms to Australian servicemen; and they agreed on the need for protective tariffs and subsidized shipping to safeguard Australia's carrying trade with the two territories. But Murray's argument for amalgamation was rejected, because Papua's laws and labour costs might prevail over the harsher and cheaper system continued under military rule – 'influenced by and imbued with German principles'. Any possibility of assimilation to a 'British tradition' was firmly set aside by Brigadier-General Johnston, as military administrator, in his unpublished submissions to the commissioners which emphasized the need for high head taxes and government-assisted recruitment to maintain the production and value of the plantations.[28]

The majority report confirmed the strongly-held opinions of Hughes who had argued Australia's case at the Imperial War Cabinet in December 1918 and accepted the mandate compromise in Paris in January 1919, with the full intention of applying the Australian Navigation Act of 1913 in all its restrictive clauses to New Guinea. When Hughes returned to Australia, the government decided to set up a board to manage the estates on the lines suggested by Lucas. The Peace Treaty Act passed by the Commonwealth Parliament did not come into effect, however, till 10 January 1920. Atlee Hunt urged action. Rules for liquidation were framed in March 1920; and an expropriation ordinance vested German properties in a public trustee from 1 September 1920, under the 'economic clauses' of Articles 121, 122 and 297 of the treaty. As chairman of the new expropriation board, Lucas was already busy at Rabaul impounding records and closing stores.

German civilians were repatriated. And as the board took over in the last months of 1920, the secretary to the prime minister's department, Percy Deane, doubled as custodian of expropriated properties. Thus, Hughes was able to keep a close watch on the territory's plunder, assisted by Lucas at Melbourne and the board's business manager, ex-consul F.R. Jolley at Rabaul. In accordance with Hughes's wartime promises, returned soldiers swelled the ranks of clerks, overseers, store managers and assistants hired to bring order into the confusion left by the departing Germans. To keep plantations up to strength, major recruiting drives had to be undertaken. The five German trading companies which had funded the planters had to be supported by advances through the board from the public trustee and the Commonwealth Bank for the period of the board's operations, 1920–27. After seven years of public management separate from the civil administration, the German properties were valued at £3 million and were judged ready for sale by tender. With rising copra prices and keen competition for bulking facilities, the 470 plantations, trade stations and undeveloped blocks of land fetched £3.4 million advanced by the banks and mercantile companies on behalf of themselves and 343 soldier-settlers whose tied mortgages burdened the local economy through the 1930s.

In South Africa a very different policy prevailed over the intimations of state intervention from within the mines department. Expropriation was not seriously considered, and the fate of German assets was closely bound up with the location and seizure of German-owned shares in the Union and abroad, invested in British mining companies and in German-registered companies.

From 1917, the British advisory committee on trading with the enemy took the line that capital invested by Germans in British companies in the Union or South West Africa would have to be vested in the public trustee, if located in England, or in the Union's custodian of enemy property. Any scheme to purchase enemy shares cheaply was rejected as 'premature'. But the Board of Trade conceded to Edmund Davis, the Australian-born mining engineer and chairman of the South West Africa Company, that enemy shareholders might be bought out through the *Discontogesellschaft* 'in some neutral town'.[29] The Colonial Office disapproved of this clandestine dealing, but Davis's company acted as 'manager' for the German copper mines, and the example set a precedent for other deals with mining companies as the war came to an end.

German properties seized within the Union fell under the custodian, W.H. Fowle, who reported in June 1917 on assets worth £12.2 million, including about 100 business properties, which were wound up or in the course of liquidation. As in Australia, there was considerable discretion about who was interned. Of 649 German entrepreneurs, 335 went into detention, compared with 5,400 in the Commonwealth.[30] The custodians in both dominions also took over shares and share dividends paid by German companies or by British companies to Germans. But none of this touched the status of German companies in South West Africa. And apart from the overtures made by Davis, there were no moves on their share capital, until the first relaxation of the wartime prohibition against dealing in ex-enemy shares early in 1919 in the United Kingdom.

Significantly, this was led by the purchase for Consolidated Mines Selection of all enemy shares held by the public trustee which were offered at cost to other shareholders.[31] Consolidated Mines had been formed by Dunkelsbuhler and Co. who included the Oppenheimers and W.L. Honnold of Anglo American for the management of gold interests on Far East Rand properties. Indeed, participatory rights in

Consolidated's leases had led to the formation of Anglo in 1917, as a way of finding sources of American capital for the enormous investments required for deep-level mining. In July 1919, the British Treasury formally permitted sales of ex-enemy shares by British subjects overseas which opened the way for other deals.

Unfortunately, the course of capital acquisitions in South West Africa is less easy to chart, because of the timing of negotiations with German proprietors and the decent interval allowed by the South African government, before approving the takeover of the diamond mining companies. Although a case has been made by Ernest Oppenheimer's biographers for his initiative in investing through Anglo in South West diamonds, it is more likely that the idea of outright purchase of German assets originated with his partner and ex-politician, Henry Hull, and the Cape businessman, Sir David de Villiers Graaff, who organized a trust to raise money and approached the German managers at Luderitzbucht. Oppenheimer was in Europe early in 1919 and accompanied Smuts to the Versailles conference as an observer, and he did not return to South Africa until the initial overtures had been made by Hull. He was aware, however, that both Smuts and Botha approved of the application of American capital to the problem of German assets which had not been taken over by the custodian.[32] Possibly all three – Hull, Graaff and Oppenheimer – left hurriedly for Europe together with Dr Erich Lubbert, W. Bradow and A. Stauch for the managers (only the movements of Hull are verifiable from passenger lists), arriving in early September to negotiate with German representatives in the Hague. There, the details of company titles were obtained and options were arranged for the sale of the mines for shares and cash, at the current rate of the devalued mark, without reference to any custodian and before formal acceptance of the terms of the Peace Treaty Ratification Bill and the Mandate Bill which were introduced to the Cape Assembly from 8 September.

Notice of the success of this coup reached the financial press on 6 September, when it was announced that a new 'South West Diamond Company' registered at the Cape had acquired the property rights of one of the German companies in the Luderitz area, but nothing more was said, while the Peace Treaty was being debated.[33] On 27 September, the government announced its method of disposing of enemy assets in the Union, where property of resident Germans was to be returned, the claims of allied nationals were to be paid and the balance – some £9 million – was not finally decided till 1920. None of this included South West property.

Such property was clearly not to be expropriated, while finance was being arranged for its purchase. The governor-general, Lord Buxton, toured South West Africa in 1919 and reassured German managers and workers on this point.[34] In August, South West's diamond mines were automatically included in plans for a revival of the 1914 quota agreement between the Union mines and the Germans, as part of the negotiations with the diamond syndicate, under the auspices of the minister of mines. The first full announcement of the takeover reached the press in London and South Africa on 1 November with the statement that Anglo had control of all the South West diamond companies. Reuters reported that H.C. Hull had completed the purchase at the Hague for £3.5 million paid by Anglo and other 'financial groups' for 'transference from Berlin to the Union' of the diamond fields. In the middle of the month there was a hitch over company titles to land owned by the *Deutsche Kolonial Gesellschaft* and Messrs Bredow, Lubbert, Scholz and Stauch were recalled to South Africa to fix the selling price of shares to be paid to smaller shareholders.[35]

Later evidence suggests that the deal was concluded in early September, but the formal agreement was dated 23 November for the sale of eleven German companies already held by the Hull-Graaff trust for a nominal sum of £3.5 million in shares and cash on behalf of Consolidated Diamond Mines of South West Africa Ltd., registered at the Cape later on 9 February 1920. The real price was much less (£2.8 million) because of the depreciation of the mark in 1919. By a second agreement, 24 November 1919, the obligation of the *Deutsche Kolonial Gesellschaft* to pay royalties to older proprietors which had also been acquired by the trust was transferred to the new company, and the South West Finance Corporation was set up separately from Consolidated Diamond Mines, on 13 April 1920, to administer these rights. The directors of Consolidated and the Corporation were identical and included Hull, Graaff, Bredow, Lubbert and Stauch.[36]

The whole transfer was made more mysterious than necessary by the government's evident desire to keep enemy assets in the captured colony a separate issue from its treatment of similar assets in the Union. The timing of announcements was, therefore, important. The documents released in the form of a parliamentary paper confirm that purchases were made before the formation of Consolidated Mines, but no dates of purchase were stated in Oppenheimer's letter to Malan, 31 October 1919. The purpose of the letter, in any case, was not to clarify the affair but to seek a formal assurance from the government that all titles would be recognized (though the German land registers were closed and they could not be confirmed). Permission was sought to make a cash payment to German owners overseas who had already received down payments for options from the trust. A formal letter from Administrator Gorges stated the titles were sound, although the *Kolonial Gesellschaft* concession on which all others rested was under investigation. The mines department, though not the minister, gave the deal a formal blessing in a letter from a junior official, adding for general consumption that the mines were to be worked in the interests of the Protectorate and the Union.[37]

Everything points, then, to a hasty conclusion to the transfer, before the terms of the Treaty or the Mandate had been ratified by the South African Assembly and before the method of handling ex-enemy assets through a custodian of enemy property had been formally decided. For the purpose of capitalization of Consolidated Diamonds and the amalgamation of the properties, German assets were regarded as transferred from 1 October 1919, while the capital for the venture was still being arranged through J.P. Morgan and Company on behalf of Anglo. A hurried proclamation (No. 59 of 1919) brought the territory under Union mining laws and cancelled German company concessions held from the *Kolonial Gesellschaft*, following a report in September 1919 by a 'minerals concession commission' which accepted the validity of the original land titles, though it continued to investigate the complex relations between the concessionary company and the colonial state which the government of the Mandate inherited. News of the successful flotation of Consolidated Diamonds was conveyed to government departments immediately in October, while the more formal exchange of notes between Oppenheimer and Malan on the proposed amalgamation of the German companies was safely delayed till the end of the month for release to Parliament. The essential position, as noted by Gorges in his letter of 3 November to Malan, was that although 'power is given in the Peace Treaty to eliminate German interests by expropriation and the transfer of proceeds to the Allied Reparation Commission . . . the Union Government have decided not to avail themselves of these powers in respect of property in South-West Africa'.[38]

The transfer meant that the principal prize was owned by a South African company approved by the government and the administrator, before the question of the fate of other enemy assets had to be resolved. There were considerable difficulties in the way of handling this complex spread of investments liable for seizure and accounting against reparations under Article 297 of the Peace Treaty. The British Treasury thought the dominions might 'pool' such assets, but the Colonial Office took the line that they would have to sort this out for themselves. The Union was entitled, in any case, to hand back £1,250,000 to Germans resident in South Africa at the outbreak of war and to pay claims amounting to £1 million which counted against reparations. In the Union, Smuts laid down that none of the subsequent discussion of assets would touch the titles to diamond properties 'the validity of which was recognized by the German Government'. The custodian of enemy property, W.H. Fowle, stood out against any scheme for transferring shares of companies registered in the United Kingdom and suggested that the balance of £9 millions in his hands should be held for 30 years as a forced loan, in return for government stock. In this way, Germans in South Africa and abroad whose assets had been confiscated would receive 'far more favourable treatment than Germans in any other part of the Allied world'.[39]

This plan commended itself to Smuts, who took sweeping powers under a proclamation of 27 August 1920 to call in all enemy assets in the form of shares held in South Africa or overseas which conflicted with the Board of Trade's policy of treating 'English assets' as the property of its own public trustee. The gesture did not result in any swapping of enemy shares with the dominion; and Rand mining companies were reluctant to assist in the arduous business of tracing ownership of bearer shares. But Smuts was able to announce to the Assembly in August 1920 the comprehensive search for share assets and the much milder treatment of property in the Union as a forced loan paying four per cent. In South West Africa, private property was left untouched, except for £700,000 which had accumulated in dividends from the mining companies, and these were treated in the same way as assets in the Union.[40] There were doubts in the Reparations Commission whether Article 297 could be interpreted in this way. For the Union had not treated enemy property as a South African asset acquired by war, but as a debt of the Union to its German owners: 'It would be anomalous to reckon a liability of an Allied Power to German nationals as being something to which that Power has to give credit to Germany'. But no enquiry was held, as requested by the British delegation's legal service.[41] And although 6,347 military, officials and police, plus a number of 'undesirables' were repatriated, 5,918 Germans remained in South West Africa and grew to 7,855 by immigration at the date of the 1921 census.

III

What began, then, as an imperial exercise in capturing strategic communications ended in the acquisition by expropriation or sale of the productive assets of two colonial economies. There was more to the war in Melanesia or the Namib desert than extension of territory for defence. South Africa had no need of a buffer zone. There was no threat from the Portuguese, and no claims were laid by the dominion to Tanganyika, after the East African campaign. The only danger presented by South West Africa lay in the subversion of Afrikaner loyalties within the Union among those who saw the British as traditional enemies.

In Australia's case there was an argument for regarding New Guinea and its archipelago as a frontier zone, but only if the exclusive immigration and mercantilist policies of the Commonwealth were extended north to keep out Asians as well as Germans. With an identity of interest between Australia's major Pacific carrier and a government dedicated to reviving and extending the 1913 Navigation Act there was little difficulty in formulating a chauvinistic policy to accompany Hughes' onslaught on German mineral interests in the Commonwealth and his populist promises of rewards for servicemen.

In both territories, moreover, there were strategic commodities which fell under the regulations of the British War Trade Department which aimed at cutting off German supplies of raw materials, stopping contraband through neutrals and capturing the marketing and manufacturing base for German industry which by 1916 was thought to be closely linked with German possession of colonies. Copra as a source of vegetable oil was important for the transfer of the oil-seed crushing industry into British hands, but it was not essential to Australia. War Trade Department regulations ensured that the Australian supply was not exported to the United States until 1919, in return for a less than strict interpretation of legislation against trading with the enemy and lengthy trans-shipment through Australian ports. Diamonds, too, were recognized as strategically important for wartime industry, for the first time. Under the Order in Council of July 1915, the imperfect central channel organized by the London diamond syndicate by 1913 was perfected and the South African government was forced to concede to the merchants a contract for all production from South West companies and the Premier mine. Separate sales to Antwerp or Amsterdam were stopped; and there was no cutting industry in the United States to offer an alternative outlet. Under pressure from the South African Treasury the Department of Mines accepted this contractual bottleneck with bad grace, working to extend state control on the model of the German *Regie* and to establish a cutting industry in South Africa itself.

There was, then, collaboration in the alliance at the periphery, in the shadow of much greater events and heavier sacrifices on the battlefields of Europe. Within the military administrations of the two territories there was also co-operation from German civilians who ran the plantation and trading economy in New Guinea and revived the mining industry in South West Africa. At the level of daily operations, after the flags had been changed, there was, too, a measure of common interest between Europeans as ruling minorities in Melanesia and the Namib desert. Possibly, this condition was understood more quickly by South Africans in the Defence Force than by the incoming Australians (there were fewer anti-German incidents at Windhuk than at Rabaul). But the Australians soon learned to allow the German system to work to their advantage, refusing ultimately to change its authoritarian ways by amalgamation with Papua. Evidence was collected in both territories on German colonial 'atrocities', and there was a demand for confiscation of assets, following German seizure of credit balances in Belgian banks in February 1917. But none of this was pushed very far, and labour regulations were hardly changed, where they were most severe, in New Guinea. The official history of the Australian occupation written by Seaforth Mackenzie, the advocate-general, was a most unwarlike tome.[42]

Where the two territories differed most was in the manner and style of their treatment of German residents and their properties. The method used by Australia was expulsion and state expropriation, in common with New Zealand, Samoa and the

British and French Cameroons. The plantations and trading companies were run for reparations with their titles vested ultimately in the custodian. Australian suspicions of overseas 'combines', whether British or German, and political pledges to the soldiers ensured that James Burns's scheme for buying out the Germans and establishing a grand mercantile and plantation monopoly stood no chance of acceptance. The South Africans were no less suspicious of monopolies directed from overseas. But Smuts welcomed capital investment through South African registered companies which allowed Anglo-American and Ernest Oppenheimer an opportunity to expand from gold back into diamonds. The technique of acquiring the German companies was locally inspired in the Cape Town trust set up by Hull and Graaff, though the financial backing and organisation of Consolidated Diamonds was essentially on the pattern of Anglo's entry into the Far East Rand.[43] The Germans were allowed to stay and many immigrated from 1919. The whole operation, moreover, was kept quite separate from the custodian's administration of German assets in the Union.

The question remains, then, whether the two dominions acted as 'ideal collaborators' (in Robinsonian terms), as a result of the wartime crisis acting on the imperial relationship. What the example reveals, perhaps, is that there were different levels of 'collaboration' between the imperial metropole and its allies, on the one hand, and within the captured colonies, on the other. There is an important typological distinction to be made between co-operation of newly-acquired subjects within a system of government, in order to keep it functioning with a minimum of social and economic disruption, after conquest; and, secondly, the patron and client relationship in international affairs which requires a measure of subordination to the senior partner to achieve common aims.

In its primary sense, a collaborative system was one of the oldest ploys in the imperial book, and the Germans fell into this role mainly at the level of production and services. A few senior officials were co-opted, but they were soon replaced at Rabaul and Windhuk, while civilians went about their business for the duration of the war. At the peace settlement, policies diverged: South Africa retained its German population (just as the Dutch had been retained after an earlier conquest); while the Australians turned to another imperial alternative – soldier settlement on the frontier, as a political reward and a reparation.

The dominions' relationship with the senior partner is another matter and cannot be considered as a system of imperial government, given the degree of autonomous evolution and the failure of imperial federation. The benefits arising from a degree of subordination in treaty-making or lack of extra-territorial jurisdiction lay principally in privileged access to sources of capital, the links of trade and transport within an imperial business network, and imperial defence. If the revised balance sheets of imperial funding are to be believed, the junior partners had done pretty well out of this alliance based on common laws and concepts of government, economic benefits and kinship.[44] When the chips were down and the alliance was under threat, they gave their manpower, accepting a large measure of imperial direction in three areas of wartime control: in the overall military operations which used dominions' forces in Europe and the Middle East; in Treasury restriction of dominions' borrowing to war funding rather than domestic infrastructure; and in reorganisation of commodity markets to deny, as far as possible, raw materials to the enemy.

There were limits to co-operation. They would not accept conscription, for example. And by 1918 the experience of South African and Australian wartime governments in running the Union and the Commonwealth led to quite separate policies for dealing with captured German assets outside constraints set by the British Treasury and the Board of Trade. The war, in J.C. Beaglehole's phrase, was a 'constitutional forcing ground', as well as a training ground in international relations'.[45] But compared with the more obvious advance in status derived from the Peace Conference, the dominions' handling of reparations is a topic that requires further investigation which may well reveal a more subtle shift towards autonomous management of local corporate investment and commercial law. The conflicting policies of dominions' statesmen on reparations are better understood than the actual value and distribution of the capital stock and other assets they administered under the terms of the peace treaty.

'Collaboration', then, is only useful as a theory of imperial behaviour if the costs and benefits are spelled out at the level of government after conquest and the very different level of inter-state co-operation for perceived goals. Both systems imply a measure of deference which came more easily from surrendered colonists than dominion governments.

At the time, neither example of sub-imperial expansion produced much in the way of imperial theorizing, compared with the voluminous materials on imperial participation in the Versailles Conference. The Australians followed their instincts and the recommendation 'to get rid of Germany' both as a source of mining investment in Australia and competition in the Pacific, set out by Hughes in September 1916 as a foreword to C. Brunsdon Fletcher's *The New Pacific* which stated the moral and commercial reasons for retaining German colonies.[46] However much he was opposed to the policy of a 'vengeful peace' and large indemnities, Smuts was equally resolved to hold on to what had been won and treat the territory as an integral part of the Union.[47] On the whole it was a pragmatic and businesslike imperialism derived from locally-perceived interests. New Guinea and South West Africa were not lost 'on the fields of Liège and in the blackened ruins of Louvain', but in the corridors of Melbourne and Pretoria and the boardrooms of Anglo-American and Burns Philp.[48]

Notes

1. See Neville Meaney, *A History of Australian Defence and Foreign Policy, 1901–23 Vol. 1, The Search for Security in the Pacific, 1901–14* (Sydney University Press, 1976), Ch. 1. For the notion of 'collaboration' adumbrated in an influential essay, see R.E. Robinson, 'Non-European foundations of European imperialism; sketch for a theory of collaboration', in Roger Owen and Bob Sutcliffe (eds), *Studies in the Theory of Imperialism* (London, 1972), 117–42; and for other references to collaboration in opposition to nationalism in South Africa, see R.E. Robinson, 'The Partition of Africa', in F.H. Hinsley (ed.), *The New Cambridge Modern History. Material Progress and World-Wide Problems, 1870–1898* (Cambridge, 1962), 635, 638–9. I am indebted to Mr Bernard Attard, St. Antony's College, Oxford, for comments on the Australian sections.
2. Meaney, 12.
3. Board of Trade to Colonial Office, 17 May 1917, CO 551/100.
4. Minutes and final agreement, 1914, Central Archives Depot (Pretoria), MNW 488; Gladstone to Harcourt, 7 May 1914, FO 368/1178.
5. 'Operations in British Dominions and Colonies August 1914, Secret'; 'Operations in the Union of South Africa and German South West Africa'; 'Operations against the German Possessions in New Guinea, Secret', Bodleian Library, MS Harcourt dep. 508.
6. 'Operations', 31 October 1914, ff. 210–12, MS Harcourt dep. 508.
7. W. Holmes, 'Diary of Events', 1 Nov. 1914, Mitchell Library (Sydney), W. Holmes MSS 15/1.

8. Gail-Maryse Cockram, *South West African Mandate* (Cape Town, 1976), Ch. 1.
9. South West Africa, killed and wounded: 385; rebellion, killed and wounded: 414; rebel losses: 190 killed and up to 350 wounded. 'Operations', f. 69, MS Harcourt dep. 508, Cf. *Cambridge History of the British Empire, vol. 8, South Africa, Rhodesia and the High Commission Territories* (Cambridge, 1963), 750, for different totals.
10. Department of Overseas Trade, *Report on the Conditions and Prospects of Trade in the Protectorate of South-West Africa* Cmd. 842 (London, 1920).
11. Stewart Firth, *New Guinea under the Germans* (Melbourne, 1982).
12. Choiseul Plantations files; Tetere land file, Burns, Philp and Company archives (Sydney); K. Buckley and K. Klugman, *The History of Burns Philp: The Australian Company in the South Pacific* (Sydney, 1981), 263–4.
13. 'Reports and memorandums', Burns to Lucas, 29 September 1914, Burns, Philp and Company archives; Forsayth to Hughes, 23 December 1915; Defence, minute, 17 Aug. 1916, CRS A4, Australian Archives (Canberra); FO to CO, 25 April 1915 and minutes, CO 418/14.
14. Atlee Hunt papers, memorandum, 19 Jan. 1915, National Library (Canberra).
15. S.S. Mackenzie, *The Australians at Rabaul. The Capture and Administration of the German Possessions in the Southern Pacific* (Sydney, 1927), Ch. 15.
16. Comptroller-general, memorandum, 29 March 1916; Pearce to Munro-Ferguson, 24 May 1916, Australian Archives, A. 3934 SC 30; Commonwealth Parliamentary Papers 1917–18 No. 66, *British and Australian Trade in the South Pacific*.
17. Munro-Ferguson to Harcourt, 10 March 1915, MS Harcourt dep. 479.
18. United States Consul, Zurich, 9 Sept. 1915; National Bank of South Africa to Finance, 18 Sept. 1915, Central Archives Depot TES 866 F5/951; Colonial Office Confidential Print African (South) No. 1054, 23; Cockram, *South West African Mandate*, 13–25.
19. Mosely to Board of Trade, 4 and 8 June 1915, BT 11/9 C, 18875. Alfred Mosely (1855–1917) had been a miner on the Kimberley diamond fields, a diamond dealer, a tariff reformer and member of government commissions after his return to the United Kingdom. The *Annual Register* makes no reference to his wartime function of co-ordinator of diamond policy for the Board of Trade. At his death, the export committee was run by Norman Melland, L. Breitmeyer, L. Abrahams and F.W. Green.
20. Memorandum, 'The Diamond Trade' [July 1915], BT 11/9 C. 18875; C. 26760; Mosely to British Consul, Amsterdam, 2 Sept. 1915, C. 30171/15. The Dutch committee consisted of A. Assher, H.H. Rozelaar and J. Rozelaar.
21. Bonar Law to Buxton, 9 Feb. 1916, Central Archives Depot, TES 886 F5/951.
22. Bonar Law to Buxton, 6 Sept. 1916, Central Archives Depot, MNW 432 MM 2455/18.
23. Minutes and memoranda by Sheridan, Kotze and the Mining Surveyor, A.C. Sutherland, 1915; Kotze to Malan, 8 March 1915, Central Archives Depot, TES 863 F5/90.
24. Memorandum, 'The Spoils', 25 March 1915 CAB 37/126/27.
25. 'Most Secret Japan-Australia', and Harcourt to Munro-Ferguson, 23 February, 19 March 1915, MS Harcourt dep. 495.
26. Lucas to Hunt, 5 June, 4 July 1919, National Library, 52/1625, 52/1623.
27. Burns to Munro-Ferguson, 25 Nov. 1918, National Library, 696/7032–7151.
28. Commonwealth Parliamentary Papers, 1920, *Interim and Final Reports of the Royal Commission on Late German New Guinea*, 42–3; Johnston to Ferrands, 20 Oct. 1919, National Library, 696/6664–6685.
29. BT to CO, 17 May, 19 Dec. 1917, CO 551/100.
30. *The African World*, 9 June 1917; *Cambridge History of the British Empire, vol. 7, part 1, Australia* (Cambridge, 1933), 570.
31. CO 687/82; *The African World*, 18 January 1919.
32. Cf. Anthony Hocking, *Oppenheimer and Son* (Johannesburg, 1973), 80–81, 87. No dates or sources are supplied. Hull arrived in Europe on the *Cap Polonio*, 4 Sept. 1919. Hocking is wrong in stating the mines were taken over by the Custodian of Enemy Property. The whole point of the sale was to avoid this.
33. *The African World*, 6 Sept. 1919.
34. Colonial Office Confidential Print Africa (South), 'Visit of the Governor-General to the South West Territory in October, 1919', (1920), 21.

35. *The African World*, 1 and 15 Nov. 1919; and for a later investigation of the purchase, J.H. Munnik, 'South West African Diamonds', 1927, Central Archives Depot, MNW 890 MM 1687/27.
36. Consolidated Diamond Mines, *Report of the Directors*, 1920.
37. A. 1–20, *Correspondence relating to the transfer of certain interests and concessions in the South West African Protectorate to the South West Africa Consolidated Diamond Company Limited*. And for documents omitted, Central Archives Depot, MNW 488 MM 2741/19. Receipt of this print by the Colonial Office was the first indication that such a deal had been concluded. It occasioned little comment and was not passed on to the Board of Trade. CO 551/127.
38. Gorges to Malan, 3 Nov. 1919, Central Archives Depot, MNW 488 MM 2741/19.
39. Fowle, memorandum, 29 April 1920, CO 551/126; Smuts, minute No. 371, 22 April 1920, CO 551/125.
40. *The Times*, 19 Aug. 1920; Treasury to CO, 5 Oct. 1920, CO 551/135.
41. Report by John Bradbury, 21 Sept. 1920, encl. in Treasury to CO, 5 Oct. 1920, CO 551/135.
42. Mackenzie, *The Australians at Rabaul*.
43. Cf. Duncan Innes, *Anglo American and the Rise of Modern South Africa* (Johannesburg, 1984), 98–9; Hocking, *Oppenheimer and Son*, 87–8.
44. Lance E. Davis and Robert A. Huttenback, *Mammon and the Pursuit of Empire. The Political Economy of British Imperialism, 1860–1912* (Cambridge, New York, 1986), esp. Ch. 6 on subsidies.
45. J.C. Beaglehole, 'The British Commonwealth of Nations' in David Thomson (ed.), *The New Cambridge Modern History, vol. xii, The Era of Violence* (Cambridge, 1964), 536.
46. C. Brunsdon Fletcher, *The New Pacific, British Policy and German Aims* (London, 1917).
47. W.K. Hancock, *Smuts. The Sanguine Years, 1870–1919* (Cambridge, 1963), Ch. 19 esp. 429, 498.
48. Cited in Wm. Roger Louis, *Great Britain and Germany's Lost Colonies 1914–1919* (Oxford, 1967), 9.

'Khaki crusaders': crusading rhetoric and the British Imperial soldier during the Egypt and Palestine campaigns, 1916–18

James E. Kitchen

Air Power Studies Division, King's College London at the Royal Air Force College, Cranwell, UK

Much of the historiography of the First World War in the Middle East suggests that the soldiers of the Egyptian Expeditionary Force motivated themselves by seeing the British campaign against the Ottoman Empire as a crusade against Islam. The construction of the campaign as a crusade was a product of the need for politicians to portray the Egyptian Expeditionary Force's operations to the British public as relevant to the wider course of the First World War. Inter-war memoirists and novelists also chose this topos in order to boost the sales of their works. By examining the letters and diaries of soldiers from across the British Empire, it is clear that this assumption is erroneous. A religious fringe within the British Imperial Army in Palestine did perceive the campaign in such terms, but they were only a minority. Instead most soldiers focused on the Islamic culture that they encountered in the Middle East, demonstrating that a strong vernacular orientalism was present in early twentieth-century British culture.

For many people, the campaign in the Middle East during the First World War is shrouded in myth. These tales come to the fore with descriptions of the Egyptian Expeditionary Force's (hereafter EEF) operations in late 1917 that ultimately led to the capture of Jerusalem. It is often asserted that the British success fulfilled a traditional Arabic prophecy which stated that the city would be freed from Ottoman occupation when the prophet brought the waters of the Nile to Palestine. By coincidence, General Edmund Allenby's (EEF Commander-in-Chief, June 1917 to March 1919) name sounded out in Arabic, *al-Nebi*, meant prophet (Hatton 1930, 208). This piece of historical symbolism was matched by the fact that the city fell to the British on 9 December, which in 1917 marked the Jewish festival of Hanukah: the celebration of Judas Maccabeus' liberation of Jerusalem from the Seleucids in 165 BC (ibid., 206).

Stories such as these lent a considerable amount of romanticism to the EEF's Middle Eastern campaign. This was reinforced by its association with one of the First World War's most enigmatic heroes, T.E. Lawrence. After his death in 1935, Lawrence was commemorated in terms which emphasized the historical allusions that seemed to permeate his Arabian exploits. Eric Kennington's effigy of Lawrence in St. Martin's church in Wareham, Dorset, has the recumbent figure resting his feet upon a piece of Hittite sculpture, while beside his head lie three unlabelled books. These objects refer to Lawrence's pre-war archaeological activities at Carchemish and the books that he carried with him while serving in Arabia: *La Morte d'Arthur*, *The Oxford Book of English Verse*, and *The Greek Anthology*. The effigy is also reminiscent of a fourteenth-century knight's tomb (Knowles 1991, 67). Lawrence himself, with his acute sense of history, helped to construct this mythical background to his military career, recording the possibly apocryphal story that one of his ancestors, Sir Robert Lawrence, had served in the Third Crusade (Siberry 2000, 95).

These allusions to the religious and historical context of the Middle Eastern campaign are not just the preserve of the hagiography that has arisen around Lawrence. The official history of the campaign contained many of these rhetorical flourishes. The author of the second volume, Cyril Falls, wrote a description of the surrender of Jerusalem that is interspersed with references to Judas Maccabeus (Falls 1930, 254). When it came to describing the battle of Megiddo, Falls could not resist the opportunity to launch into a lengthy discussion of the numerous armies that had fought over the same ground, including that of Pharaoh Thotmes III (ibid., 516). The massed use of cavalry by Allenby allowed these historical references to be carried even further. The advance of the 4th Cavalry Division, on 19 September 1918, seemed to demonstrate that 'warfare had recovered in this spectacle the pageantry whereof long-range weapons had robbed it' (ibid., 514). The masterful concluding chapter to the second volume of the official history pointed to the historical and religious landscape of Palestine as having a critical impact on the morale and fighting capabilities of the men of the EEF. Falls was clear that this conclusion was the product of the 'testimony of officers of all grades of seniority'.[1] No attempt was made, though, to see whether these opinions were corroborated by the other ranks that had served in the EEF.

Nevertheless, this assertion has become a sacrosanct tenet of attempts to comprehend combat motivation in the armies that fought in the Middle East during the First World War. For many historians, the EEF's campaign can be understood simply as a holy war fought in a landscape that abounded with innumerable references to the Bible and the crusades. General accounts of the war tend to dismiss the Middle-Eastern front as a sideshow until the capture of Jerusalem (Taylor 1966, 206). Even works of narrative military history that specifically focus on the Egyptian and Palestinian fronts are bedevilled by the need to place themselves in an expected historical context, as demonstrated by Anthony Bruce's lacklustre *The Last Crusade* (2002).

David Woodward's important and thorough discussion of the military experiences of British soldiers in the Middle East at times fits a similar pattern. He states that 'the idea of a crusade… resonated with many of [Allenby's] men', implying that the biblical relevance of the landscape acted as an important fillip to the men's morale.[2] John Grainger takes this concept a stage further by erroneously asserting that nearly all of the EEF's troops were at least nominally Christian and familiar with the biblical importance of Palestine. This leads him to the conclusion that 'to invade Palestine and wrest it from the grip of the Muslim Turk was to many of the British troops no more than a Christian duty' (Grainger 2006, 67). Grainger notes that many of the contemporary accounts refer to the campaign as a crusade, and thus it should be viewed as a holy war.[3] Even works of a more academic focus have succumbed to an overly reductionist interpretation of the EEF soldiers' attitudes towards combat in the Holy Land. Matthew Hughes, in his definitive examination of Allenby's command, states that religious references were clear in much of the correspondence of those involved (Hughes 1999, 13). Similarly, Michael Snape, writing about religion in the British Army during the First and Second World Wars, asserts that a neo-crusading ethos was to the fore during the campaigns against the Turks. This is a product, however, of his decision to focus solely on the views of two Roman Catholic officers as representative of the whole EEF.[4]

The only attempts to reconsider this approach have been made by non-military historians. Elizabeth Siberry's study of crusading rhetoric places the Palestine campaign in a wider frame of cultural reference, drawing from both nineteenth- and twentieth-century uses of the terminology. She, however, eventually comes to a similar conclusion to Falls, noting that crusading imagery was prevalent in many of the first-hand accounts. The majority of her sources consist of post-war published accounts of the campaign, rather than unpublished letter collections, diaries, or memoirs.[5] In contrast, Eitan Bar-Yosef's examination of how the Holy Land has been constructed and viewed in English culture since 1799, does make extensive use of a range of unpublished sources. He notes that crusading rhetoric was very much 'socially and culturally confined' to British officers. The rank and file of the EEF reverted to using a biblical vernacular culture derived from hymns, Sunday school classes, sermons, and the family Bible, in order to comprehend the war in Palestine. This approach ultimately undermined the crusading image, as it was overly imperialistic, and instead led the troops to focus on their home in England as their primary motivating factor. For this reason, he labels the men of the EEF as 'homesick crusaders' (see Bar-Yosef 2005, 247–94 and 2001, 87–109).

Bar-Yosef's interpretation is the first to consider fully the ideological roots of much of the writing on crusading connected with the Palestine campaign. This analysis, however, is still too accepting of the role religious traditions played in British society in the early twentieth century, without considering the limits of a biblical vernacular culture. Importantly, it is also limited by the fact that Bar-Yosef focuses exclusively on the experiences of British soldiers in late 1917, around the time of the capture of Jerusalem. This leaves a regional and temporal penumbra over the experiences of the EEF. Crucially Dominion troops, who made up a large part of the EEF's fighting arm, are not examined by Bar-Yosef. In addition, it is vital to consider how soldiers viewed the campaign during the failed Gaza operations in the first half of 1917, as well as during the Transjordan Raids and battle of Megiddo in 1918.

This raises the question of how the definition of the EEF's campaign as a crusade originated. The answer may lie in the desire to provide a historical context to many of the personal narratives of military service in the Middle East which were published in the inter-war period. The most absurd approach is found in the work of Major Vivian Gilbert, in his memoir *The Romance of the Last Crusade* (1923).[6] The book began with a short fictional chapter in which a first year Oxford undergraduate, Brian Gurnay, sits in the garden of Ivythorpe Manor in the summer of 1914, reading a novel on the crusades. The chapter contains an excerpt from this novel, describing Richard I refusing to look down on Jerusalem whilst the 'valiant knight' with him, Sir Brian de Gurnay, looks forward to a future last crusade that would 'wrest the Holy Places from the Infidel' (Gilbert 1923, 1). This leads the contemporary Brian Gurnay, who is clearly supposed to stand as a cipher for Gilbert, to look up to the sky and exclaim that he too would like to take part in a worthwhile crusade. This is followed by the trite dramatic device of Gurnay's mother appearing to inform him of the outbreak of the First World War (ibid., 5, 8). The book then shifts to Gilbert, who in 1914 was an actor on the New York stage, recording his return to Britain, his subsequent enlistment in the London Regiment and service with the 60th (London) Division in France, Salonica, and Palestine. Gilbert was attempting to use the crusading context to give his rather banal account of military life a degree of romantic resonance with the reading public.

During the inter-war period, it became almost a necessity to refer to the crusades in works on the EEF. A large number of personal narratives and unit histories alluded to the phenomenon in their titles, but then carried on with their formulaic military historical accounts. This can be seen in A. Briscoe-Moore's work on the New Zealand Mounted Rifles, which was subtitled *The Story of New Zealand's Crusaders* (Briscoe Moore 1920). The published exploits of a South African artillery battery was similarly entitled *Khaki Crusaders* and given a dramatic cover depicting a crusading knight offering his blessing on an artillery gun and its crew (Cooper 1919). Works of fiction based on the Palestine campaign, many of which were aimed at adolescent boys and written in the style of George Henty, also turned to crusading rhetoric to help entice in their readers. The prolific author Lieutenant-Colonel Frederick Brereton wrote a tale of two British agents trying to undermine the Turkish army around Gaza in 1917, entitled *With Allenby in Palestine: A Story of the Latest Crusade* (Brereton 1920). In a corresponding vein, Joseph Bowes produced *The Aussie Crusaders* (1920), set around the events of the Australian Light Horse charge at Beersheba, and which was presented inside a cover portraying the archetypal Australian warrior.

It is unsurprising, given the clear commercial benefits of referring to the crusades, that another notable ripping yarn about the First World War, David Lloyd George's war memoirs, got in on the act. During his discussion of the replacement of General Archibald Murray as commander of the EEF, Lloyd George described an interview with Allenby before he was sent out to Egypt. He stated that it was on this occasion that he gave the general a copy of George Adam Smith's *Historical Geography of the Holy Land* (1894). Lloyd George felt that this would be a better guide to fighting in Palestine than 'any survey to be found in the pigeon holes of the War Office' (Lloyd George 1936, Vol. 2, 1090). By 1917, Smith's work was very famous and had been produced in a number of editions, and it is unlikely that Allenby would have been unaware of it.[7] This does, though, illustrate the power that the crusading metaphor had come to exercise by the mid-1930s; it seems that even Lloyd George felt that he had to pander to the idea that the Palestine campaign could only be understood as a holy war, albeit one in which he inevitably played the decisive guiding role.

This notion of the Palestine campaign as a crusade was not simply a post-war construct. It had its origins in how the EEF's operations were seen by and presented to the British public during the First World War. In its account of Allenby's entry into Jerusalem on 11 December 1917, *The Times* made it clear that the holy city had been liberated from oppressive Turkish rule.[8] The article was keen to demonstrate how the EEF had not damaged the city at all during the operations to capture it, unlike all of its previous conquerors. Allenby was noted to have received a joyous and spontaneous welcome from the city's inhabitants. Importantly, it stressed the fact that the general had entered the city on foot, through the Jaffa Gate, in contrast to the Kaiser's visit in 1898. On that occasion a large gap had been made in the wall allowing the Kaiser to ride in on his horse, dressed in the radiant white uniform of a field marshal. *The Times* was not going to miss the opportunity of portraying one of the grandest moments of Britain's war in 1917 without the requisite pomp that it deserved. Nor for that matter was *Punch*, which commissioned their chief cartoonist, Bernard Partridge, to create a suitable image for the occasion (Bryant and Heneage 1994, 166). The result was a depiction of Richard I looking down on Jerusalem, with the caption 'My Dream Comes True' (Figure 1), printed in December 1917. This was an allusion to Edward Gibbon's claim that on being unable to capture the city in 1191 Richard had announced that 'those who are unwilling to rescue, are unworthy to view, the sepulchre of Christ!' (Gibbon 1995, Vol. 6, 642). *Punch* followed this up with a second bombastic cartoon by Partridge in September 1919, which showed Allenby dressed as a knight returning home from the crusades and being welcomed by Britannia (Figure 2).

It was Lloyd George who was, in part, responsible for this casting of the Palestine campaign as part of a historic Middle-Eastern holy war. In his summing up of the war during 1917 to the House of Commons, he drew particular attention to the unique characteristics of Allenby's victory. Lloyd George described Palestine as a 'famed land' that 'thrills with sacred memories', and noted that 'Beersheba, Hebron, Bethany, Bethlehem, the Mount of Olives are all names engraved on the heart of the world'.[9] It is unsurprising that for Lloyd George, well versed in chapel life, the EEF's success conjured up such romantic biblical images. This was not a spontaneous outpouring of joy at Allenby's success. The War Cabinet had decided on 21 November 1917 to control carefully how the story of Jerusalem's capture would be reported. No announcement of the city's fall was to be made until Lloyd George had had the opportunity to give assurances that its holy sites would be protected.[10] The War Cabinet was aware of the enormous propaganda value attached to the

Figure 1. Bernard Partridge, 'The Last Crusade', *Punch*, 19 December 1917. (Reproduced with permission of Punch Ltd., www.punch.co.uk.)

Figure 2. Bernard Partridge, 'The Return from the Crusade', *Punch*, 17 September 1919. (Reproduced with permission of Punch Ltd., www.punch.co.uk.)

liberation of the holy city, and chose to promote assiduously the success it had achieved in Palestine around the world. Allenby's entry into Jerusalem was filmed and the War Office Cinematograph Committee produced a newsreel, released in February 1918 (McKernan 1993, 169–80). The feature proved very popular wherever it was shown in Britain and subsequently travelled around the world with appropriate intertitles inserted, even including classical Hebrew for the Grand Rabbi at Salonika. The British government intended to milk Allenby's success for all that it was worth, and to keep promoting it well into 1918, with eight other films produced on the campaign.[11]

At a parochial level, the Middle-Eastern campaign was also referred to in terms of its crusading and religious elements. For example, *The Northampton Independent* produced a cartoon in April 1917, which portrayed a British Tommy shaking hands with a crusader in the Holy Land (Figure 3). The cartoon was headed 'History Repeated after Eight Centuries' and was followed by a brief article that explained the details of the medieval reference.[12] The paper pointed to the fact that the 1/5th Northamptonshires were currently serving in the Holy Land and were on the same ground that the crusader Simon de Senlis, the first Earl of Northampton, had fought on 821 years before. In Norwich, similar sentiments were expressed during a May 1917 memorial service for Major W.H. Jewson and Captain S.D. Page of the 1/4th Norfolk Regiment, killed at the second battle of Gaza. The Reverend Albert Lowe, of the Prince's Street Congregational Church, stated that the regiment was fighting 'against the Turk with a view to ridding the Holy Land of his corrupting presence'.[13] The rhetoric of the crusades was thus prevalent amongst a number of communities whose local units were serving in Palestine. It is also notable that both of these examples pre-date Allenby's entry into Jerusalem by over half a year. At this stage of

Figure 3. W. Humberrary, 'History Repeated after Eight Centuries', *The Northampton Independent*, 21 April 1917.

the campaign, the EEF had suffered two devastating defeats at Gaza and seemed highly unlikely to ever achieve the crusading goals being set for it at home.

By mid-1918, the EEF was in a much stronger position, having driven the Turks from southern Palestine and now occupying a line from Jaffa, through Jerusalem and down to the Dead Sea. This allowed British troops to be given leave in the holy city, providing *The Times*'s article writers with an opportunity to again reinforce the religious connotations of the EEF's campaign. It was noted in April 1918 that the British Army had been able to celebrate Easter in a location where English soldiers had never before prayed at Easter; the Christians of the city were now protected by the 'victorious sword of St. George'.[14] *The Times* also drew out the crusading context that surrounded those British soldiers who visited the churches of Jerusalem to pray. Thus in the Church of the Holy Sepulchre the troops could see the tomb of the Anglo-Norman knight Sir Philip Daubigny. In addition, the paper stressed the reverence that British soldiers showed to the Christian heritage of the city, with men kissing the stone that covered Christ's traditional tomb in the Holy Sepulchre.

It is unsurprising that, with such rhetoric being used by 1918, the General Secretary of the Palestine Exploration Fund, Ernest Masterman, saw this as a good opportunity to produce a book on Jerusalem's liberation, and *The Deliverance of Jerusalem* appeared before the war's end. The bulk of the work was concerned with the history of the city, but three chapters were devoted to describing the contemporary war with Turkey and the course it had taken in Palestine. Masterman's account of the EEF's advance was, like many of the works that would follow it, liberally seasoned with references to the region's biblical past. The route that was taken during the advance on Jerusalem was noted to be the same as that used by Antiochus III, who defeated Judas Maccabeus, and which was later used by Richard I (Masterman 1918, 34). By the end of the First World War, it was evident how an audience was expected to view the EEF's campaigns: these constituted a crusade, fought to liberate the Holy Land from oppressive rule, and as such should be described with frequent reference to the biblical and historic context.

It is also possible to find some examples of crusading rhetoric in the unpublished sources of EEF men and units. The most public espousal of this idea was contained in an Order of the Day issued after the third battle of Gaza in November 1917, by Major-General Steuart Hare, commander of the 54th (East Anglia) Division. In it, he praised his division's combat success, stating that:

> This gateway between Egypt and the Holy Land is one of the historic battle-grounds of the world, and the 54th Division has shown fighting qualities worthy of this scene of countless battles between Assyrians and Egyptians, Israelites and Philistines, Saracens and Crusaders.[15]

Crusading references could be brought out by the specific historic geography of the areas that units were operating in. Major F.S.A. Clarke, serving in the 1/10th Londons, noted that the crusader castle at Ras el Ain was reported by a number of the East Anglian men in the 54th Division to be haunted by armoured knights.[16] Similarly, when the Canterbury Mounted Rifles were stationed at Tel el Jemme, Sergeant H. Judge recorded in his diary that the hills were built by the crusaders in the shape of a double cross.[17]

It was not only medieval military architecture that sparked the men's interest. As would be expected, chaplains were more likely to see crusading allusions in the world around them. The Reverend W.A. Jones, serving with the 24th Royal Welch Fusiliers, as he approached Jerusalem took care to note in his diary that he was looking down on the city from Neby Samwil, where Richard I had looked upon the holy site with great reverence.[18] After visiting Jerusalem in December 1918, Private A.R. Surry, of the 1/7th Essex, wrote a 13-page letter to his parents going into great detail about the sacred locations he had visited. He proclaimed: 'I little thought that I should ever stand in the Holy Sepulchre itself and now after thirty months of one might say, crusading, that privilege has been mine'.[19] Even Allenby was capable of being entranced by the historic ambience of Palestine. He wrote to his wife in late November 1917 that the EEF was fighting its way up north 'by the road taken by Richard Coeur de Lion; and we have reached about the point at which he turned back'.[20] These references from a small cross-section of the EEF demonstrate that the use of crusading imagery was not confined to the officer élite. This runs counter to traditional interpretations of the role of chivalric ideology in the First World War.[21] Much of this analysis is overly concerned with a select group of literary luminaries, among which the rhetorical flourishes of Rupert Brooke and John Masefield stand out (Parker 1987, 227–8, 234).

The most potent example of crusading rhetoric, worthy of a modern neo-conservative, can be found in the correspondence of the Anglican Bishop in Jerusalem, Rennie MacInnes. In May 1917, he wrote to Reginald Wingate, High Commissioner for Egypt, to make the highly dubious suggestion that on conquering Palestine the British administration should take over all buildings that had once been churches and were now used as mosques. He enunciated his belief that the British government was often too eager to placate Muslim opinion, and that this could be damaging, as 'the measure designed by the Western mind to show magnanimity and tolerance, is regarded by the Eastern as a sign of weakness and fear'.[22] In a counterintuitive argument, he suggested that the Muslim population would expect

Britain to seize such buildings, and the conqueror's image would only be weakened if they were left in the hands of those who had desecrated them.

The British administration in Egypt took rapid steps to dissuade MacInnes from taking his idea further. It was suggested that the matter would have to be approved by the Archbishop of Canterbury first, and then a commission set up to look into the exact situation on the ground in any Ottoman territory acquired by Britain.[23] Wingate felt that any future military administration would attempt to alter the administrative *status quo* as little as possible in occupied areas, which would 'prove the most effective check to proposals of an impolitic nature made by ecclesiastics of various denominations'.[24] In order to close down finally MacInnes's suggestion, a staff captain from the EEF was appointed to make a feasibility study into the bishop's scheme. The report found that the suggestion had been natural enough for a bishop to make, but did not take any account of the military or political situation in Palestine. It also pointed out that the Orthodox and Catholic Churches, with their historic presence in the region, would have much more to gain than the Church of England from the proposal. The report's author felt the objections were obvious and unanswerable. He stated that 'Bishop MacInnes appears to regard our invasion of Palestine somewhat in the light of a Crusade, the success of which should place Christianity in a predominant position over Islam and other Confessions'.[25]

MacInnes represents an example of an individual whose strong Christian faith led him to see the war with Turkey as a religiously endorsed struggle. This may in part have been a product of his Episcopal position. When consecrated in this post in 1914, he was told that 'the Bishop in Jerusalem must be a missionary' (Winnington-Ingram 1917, 113). It is unsurprising to find that the ceremony was carried out by the Bishop of London, Arthur Winnington-Ingram, who rose to national fame during the First World War for his patriotic and bellicose rhetoric.

In contrast to the biblical references that peppered some accounts of service in the Middle East, it was often the case that soldiers wrote of their dislike for all things sacred. This anti-religious streak suggests that a number of EEF men would not have seen their service as part of a holy war. This attitude was partly a reflection of the disappointment that was felt when Jerusalem was finally encountered.[26] For Private C.T. Shaw, of the 60th Division's medical staff, the city struck him as 'the dirtiest and most miserable place I have ever set eyes on'.[27] For one soldier, Jerusalem seemed to be no better than an English provincial town (Lockhart 1920, 24). The men of the EEF had built up grandiose images of the city, a product of any religious education they had received, which could not be sustained by the reality. Moreover, closer inspection led to further disappointment as the local sanitation system was seen to be inadequate, leaving the famed city a dirty and stench-filled place.[28] Some soldiers even turned to the biblical vernacular tradition espoused by Bar-Yosef in order to offer satirical comment on the scene they encountered. Captain A. MacGregor, serving in the 39th (Reserve) Mountain Battery, noted that his men sang the hymn 'Jerusalem the Golden with milk and honey blessed' as a result of their experiences in the city. He informed his father that 'this is a joke because those who have been there state that for stenches of filth it knocks an Indian Bazaar hollow'.[29]

This disdain for the sacred elements of Palestine was exacerbated by contact with the Eastern churches. For the vast bulk of the EEF's soldiers, brought up in a Protestant culture, the aesthetics of the churches they visited proved a considerable shock. Complaints were made about the fact that as soon as a biblically important site had been identified it was immediately obliterated by a modern chapel adorned with lamps, images, pious inscriptions, and rich wall-hangings. It was noted by one soldier that 'to the ordinary Anglican, who is neither a pilgrim nor an iconoclast, there is something repugnant about the way in which the Holy Places have been treated by their guardians' (Lockhart 1920, 30). The taint of commercialism was also felt to be ever-present at many of these locations. One soldier was appalled that at the Church of the Holy Sepulchre, the guardian 'complacently exacts "bakshish" from the pilgrim, as if he were the proprietor of a peepshow' (ibid., 34). It was this most sacred of sites that often caused the greatest dismay amongst EEF soldiers who visited it. Second Lieutenant G.W. Gotto, in a letter to his parents, felt that he could not 'even attempt to describe to you the ghastly tawdriness of the place', adding that 'it looks more like a shop with a display of Xmas tree decorations'.[30] Much of this disgust stemmed from the deeply ingrained Protestant cultural tradition of iconophobia. Plain, simply decorated holy sites were not an integral part of Eastern Christianity, of which most EEF soldiers had little or no exposure until they arrived in Palestine.

The constant disputes between the Eastern Churches did not endear them to the men of the EEF, who expected to find Palestine a place of Christian harmony. Visits to sacred sites reinforced the internal problems that Christianity faced in the region. After seeing the Church of the Holy Sepulchre Captain H.C. Wolton, of the 1/5th Suffolks, noted that at first glance the division of the building between various denominations seemed like an act of Christian unity. He soon discovered that this was not the case, as each of the local denominations vied for the attention of pilgrims: 'what annoys one at Jerusalem is the fact that the wretched people assure you that about 20 of the main incidents of the New Testament took place in an area of about 40 square yards:- i.e. just in *their* particular part of the church'.[31] The same problem of internal Christian conflict was to be found in the Church of the Nativity, in Bethlehem. Here Captain Dening, serving on the 4th Cavalry Division's staff, lamented that 'where our Lord is reported to have been born a British guard [is] there to keep the peace, between Greeks, RCs and Armenians – it's sad that Christians fight in such places – and formerly had to be kept in order by a Muh[amme]d[an] guard'.[32] The eccentricities of the Eastern churches thus served to undermine the latent faith of many EEF soldiers. Christianity as practised in Palestine did not live up to the model that many men had constructed in their heads, derived from a received view of English Protestantism.

These anti-religious sentiments could also be expressed as explicit criticism of the crusading notion. For many, the war that they were fighting against the Turks did not seem to fit the bombastic rhetoric of holy war. In the conclusion to his narrative of the EEF's campaign, Major H.O. Lock of the Dorsetshire Regiment launched a stinging attack on such portentous notions (1919, 144–5):

> Will our campaign be passed down to history as 'The Last Crusade'? Presumably not. Throughout the campaign there was little or no religious animosity, except that the Turk extended no quarter to the Hindoo. To speak of this as a campaign of The Cross against The Crescent is untrue. The Turkish high command was controlled by Germans, so-called Christians. The British soldier fought with no less zest than when opposed to Turks. At the final battle, the Moslems, serving in our armies, by far outnumbered the Christians.

The military reality of the war in Egypt and Palestine was far removed from any notion of a crusade. As Lock makes clear the battle of Megiddo saw Christian,

European soldiers in the minority, and would be better viewed as a battle between two imperial powers using troops drawn from throughout their empires. The EEF by mid-1918 had been 'Indianized', with only one of its seven infantry divisions solely composed of British troops. It was not only at the operational level of the EEF's campaign that the holy war notion seemed to be inappropriate. The brutal fighting that took place in November and early December 1917 to drive the Turks back from Gaza and eventually secure Jerusalem did not suggest to the troops involved that they were on a crusade. Major Lord Hampton, commanding 'D' Squadron of the 1/1st Worcestershire Hussars Yeomanry, recalled that on 9 December 1917 his unit was taking up new positions in the line in appalling weather conditions, and as such 'even the news of the surrender of Jerusalem failed to lift us entirely out of our misery'.[33] As a result of the bitter combat he had witnessed, Gunner T.G. Edgerton, of 60th Division's artillery, found it hard to describe his battery as 'Christian soldiers'. He was adamant that 'the spirit of the Crusaders was conspicuous by its absence'.[34] The EEF's soldiers were aware, however, that back in Britain their exploits might well have the tinge of a holy war about them. Lieutenant Milsom recalled seeing a cartoon by Louis Raemaekers that depicted British soldiers kneeling bareheaded, seemingly at prayer, before Jerusalem, which was being pointed out to them by an officer using his sword. This did not fit the scene in his battalion, the 1/5th Shropshire Light Infantry, when they approached Jerusalem: 'the general thought seemed rather to be "So that is the —— place, is it?" The truth is that we were all dead tired, foot-sore, and very "fed-up-and-far-from-home-sort-of-feeling"'.[35]

This sentiment of exasperation at how the EEF's campaign was being misinterpreted was to the fore in Cecil Sommers's published account of his Middle-Eastern service, based on his diary. In the preface, nominally addressed to his daughter, he attempted to debunk such myths. He stated that if his daughter took an overly sentimental approach and tried to recall her father dressed as Richard I in shining armour, emblazoned with a red cross, then she would fail. It was made clear that the reminiscences of some of his comrades could also not be trusted, as the temporal distance from the events they were involved in would lead to an enchanted view being created that did not resemble the grim reality.[36] Sommers took time to attack other books on the campaign that would soon be written about it. His argument sagaciously noted that 'the atmosphere in which heroes move is so much more enthralling – and profitable – than the stale tobacco of the ordinary man' (Sommers 1919, v).

It was this desire to recall the prosaic elements of the EEF's campaign that motivated S.F. Hatton, who had served in the Middlesex Yeomanry, to produce an account of his wartime exploits in 1930. He stated in the preface to his work that he was writing deliberately against those war books such as *All Quiet on the Western Front* which he felt were too narrow in their portrayal of the conflict. The aim was to produce a human account, as Hatton felt it would have been told 'over a pipe of baccy and a pint of beer' (Hatton 1930, 14). Hatton's argument was that the high diction used by many war authors in fact distorted the historical record, stating (ibid., 13–14) that:

> The soldiers we knew and fought with were neither hysterical nor given to introspective analysis. According to several morbid modern war books, the appearance of a 'Jordan boil' on the nape of the neck would demand a soliloquy – This deep yellow canker gnawing away my flesh, my own flesh, flesh that is me – this pool of pus, three millions

of virulent micro-cocci eating away down to my very bones – perhaps even to my soul,' whereas what the British Tommy actually said was, 'Gawd, I've got another beauty'.

It is clear that both Hatton and Sommers represent a reaction against the way the EEF's campaign was being remembered in inter-war Britain. For them, this was not a glorious crusade, but a dirty, brutal, and uncomfortable war in which spiritual solace seemed a long way off.

If the men of the EEF were not crusaders, influenced by a strong Christian tradition, it is possible to see them as indulging in vernacular orientalism whilst they served in the Middle East (Bar-Yosef 2005, 31–5). A number of soldiers' accounts express a detailed and continual interest in an essential version of the Orient that stressed its exoticism, mystery, and otherness from Europe. The troops' first experience of this world was in Egypt, where they encountered the remains of its ancient civilization. Trooper R.H. Chandler's first few days in the country were spent visiting the tourist 'hot spots' around Cairo. Inevitably he made his way to the pyramids, about which he stated 'one cannot explain the sensation one experiences when looking at these world wonders for the first time'.[37] Captain E.B. Hinde, serving in one of the 54th Division's field ambulances, expressed similar sentiments when he travelled to Sabharah, a village south of Cairo littered with ancient treasures including a step pyramid, tombs, and a mausoleum for sacred bulls.[38] Later in 1916, he followed this up with a 10-day excursion down the Nile to visit Luxor and Karnak.[39] It was not just the physical remains of Egypt's past that attracted attention, but also the country's living inhabitants. The troops of the 1/5th Essex were amazed by the Zikr dance that was put on for them by 20 men of the Egyptian Labour Corps, in which they chanted incantations and swayed from side to side (Gibbons 1921, 47–8).

For many EEF troops, it was Egypt's and Palestine's Islamic culture and heritage that held the greatest fascination. Captain Wolton and his brother, both serving in the 1/5th Suffolks, were so taken by the history of the Arab peoples after visiting the Cairo Museum that they purchased Korans in the bazaar.[40] The notebook kept during his service by Quartermaster Sergeant G.E. Lee of the same battalion, illustrates a similar interest. He included a description of a holy rock he had seen, which Muslim women visited to ensure that they were 'fruitful'.[41] This was hardly one of Egypt's foremost tourist attractions, and must have been specifically sought out by Lee. It was, though, the many mosques that formed the spiritual landscape of the Middle East that created the most interest across the EEF. Among these, it was the Mosque of Omar in Jerusalem that received the highest praise. Sergeant R.D. McCormack, of the Auckland Mounted Rifles, visited the city in April 1918 and recorded that the Mosque of Omar was 'a wonderful place of worship, having a tremendous big dome, no end of bronze work and colouring and writings'.[42] Another soldier described it as 'the noblest building in Jerusalem, and after the Taj Mahal, probably the finest Mohammedan work in the world' (Lockhart 1920, 32). It was noted by one New Zealand Mounted Rifleman that the mosque's 'artistic grandeur' stood in direct contrast to the 'comparative tawdriness of the Christian Church built over the Calvary' (Briscoe Moore 1920, 136). The EEF's soldiers thus had far greater commendations to bestow on the Islamic architecture of Palestine than they did on its Christian buildings. This is an attitude that would seem to demonstrate the presence of a strong vernacular orientalism in British and Dominion culture.

A number of EEF units went further than simply observing the Islamic culture of the Middle East, and began to use it to represent their experiences. This can be seen most clearly in some of the Christmas cards that were produced by divisions or battalions for soldiers to send home to their friends and family. The 2/15th London Regiment's 1918 card, a very elaborate production containing three separate illustrations and a map, depicts a British soldier standing in front of a Palestinian village (Figure 4). The image contains no references to the Christian heritage of the region. Similarly, one of the 54th Division's 1917 Christmas cards shows a bucolic Middle Eastern coastal scene, in the centre of which is the Islamic shrine at Sheikh Ajlin, near Gaza (Figure 5).[43] The imagery could be even more explicit in its use of Islamic points of reference. The cover of the 54th Division's 1917 card (Figure 6) and the inside of the one produced in 1918 (Figure 7) both contain well-executed sketches of mosques. For those relations back in Britain who received these cards, the inference intended could not be clearer: these were not soldiers fighting a crusade in the Holy Land, but serving in a region steeped in the culture of Islam. In addition, these cards focused almost exclusively on the built environment of the Middle East, rather than the region's inhabitants. This stands in stark contrast to the profusion of highly sexualized imagery, particularly of local women and centred on ideas of the harem, that appeared in many pre-war postcards sent home by European visitors to Muslim countries (Alloula 1987).

This absorption of the Middle East's Islamic elements demonstrates that rather than seeing British and Dominion soldiers as crusaders, it would be apposite to portray them as the region's first mass tourists.[44] Indeed, some EEF men recognized this themselves. Driver Evans, of the Australian and New Zealand Mounted Division's logistical train, wrote of his service in Palestine in a letter home to his mother that he 'would not miss this for anything – in one way it is a huge tourist trip,

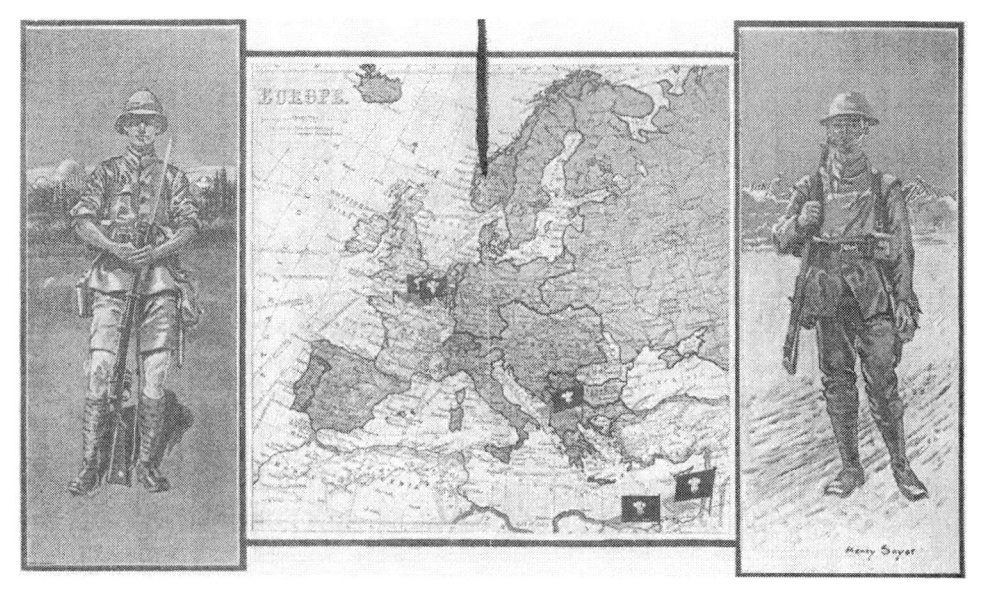

Figure 4. 2/15th London Regiment Christmas Card, 1918 (Imperial War Museum, 94/5/1, F.V. Blunt Papers).

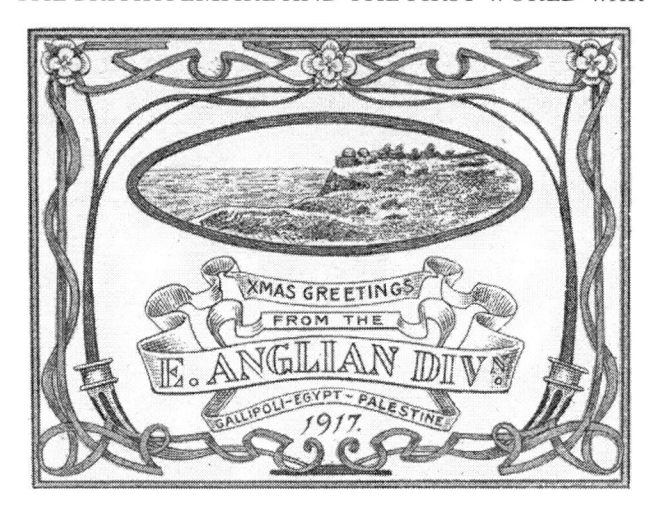

Figure 5. 54th Division Christmas Card, 1917 (Imperial War Museum, 85/4/1, C.S. Wink Papers).

Figure 6. 54th Division Christmas Card, 1917 (Imperial War Museum, 02/16/1, E.B. Hinde Papers).

we see something fresh and interesting every day'.[45] Lance-Corporal Hickman, of the 1/8th Hampshires, even went so far as to describe his travels between Gallipoli, Mudros, and Egypt as like being on a Cook's tour.[46] Major V.H. Bailey, an artillery officer with the 3rd (Lahore) Division, did not simply imagine his service in such a way; he actually set out to use his time in Egypt for a holiday. As the archetypal British tourist, he went to the Cairo Express Agency to organize his travel to Luxor and Assouan, where he was met by pre-arranged guides.[47]

A STREET IN JAFFA

Figure 7. 54th Division Christmas Card, 1918 (Norfolk Regiment Museum, Box 11, 1/4th and 1/5th Norfolk Regiment Papers).

The desire to explore the exotic landscape of Egypt and Palestine was not only pursued for the personal satisfaction of tourist soldiers; it also provided them with considerable amounts of information with which they could fill letters home. Captain MacGregor, of the 39th (Reserve) Mountain Battery, lamented in one of his missives that 'I have not succeeded in seeing anymore places of particular historical interest so I am just a bit short of "copy"'.[48] In Egypt and Palestine, where combat was often confined to clearly delineated short periods and men spent much of their time on mundane military tasks, the proximity to an abundant historical landscape allowed soldiers to write letters that would be found of interest by their friends and relatives, thus stimulating a regular correspondence.

Commanders at various levels of the army's hierarchy aided the soldiers of the EEF in this tourist process. They recognized the voracious appetite of the men for information on the Middle East. Lectures on the history of Egypt and Palestine were a regular part of many units' routines. The Australian and New Zealand Mounted Division, for example, were given addresses on the mythology of ancient Egypt and Napoleon's Middle-Eastern campaigns.[49] Local information was of critical importance to help the men enjoy their leave fully. The YMCA Anzac Hostel guide to Cairo contained a section that detailed routes to see the city's main sites in only six days, thus reducing the cost to visiting soldiers. The pamphlet contained 13 pages of descriptions of places of interest, such as the bazaars, citadel, and mosque of Sultan Hassan.[50] The hope was that these guides would facilitate the men's sightseeing.

The YMCA and military authorities were also very keen to keep visiting soldiers out of the Wazza, Cairo's notorious red light district. From 1918, information on the history of the region was provided in the EEF's educational newspaper, the *Palestine News*. Charles Pirie-Gordon, the editor, asked Mark Sykes at the Foreign Office to obtain permission to reproduce sections from various noted works on the Middle East, including the *Latin Kingdom of Jerusalem*, the *Itinerarium Regis Ricardi*, the

Caliph's Last Heritage, Baedecker's Palestine, and a work on Saladin.[51] However, it was the pamphlets written by Victor Trumper, a retired Royal Naval officer and honorary secretary of the Palestine Exploration Fund in Port Said, that had the greatest impact on the historical mindset of the EEF's soldiers. From late 1917 through to 1919 he produced four short guides to Palestine, one of which covered the south of the country, two the centre, and the last the north. The first pamphlet appeared in November 1917, just as the EEF began to advance northwards through Gaza and on to Jerusalem. In the preface, Trumper (1917) stated that the work had been written so 'that the troops in Palestine might get a more general idea as to the sites of ancient localities in the places where they are'.

The guides were largely based on George Adam Smith's *Historical Geography of the Holy Land* and the works of the Palestine Exploration Fund.[52] Each pamphlet followed the same pattern, containing descriptions of various locations based on their ancient, biblical or medieval heritage, and arranged under the current names for those sites (Trumper 1918, 6–7). Only in the first work, on Southern Palestine (1917), did Trumper include two narrative passages relating ancient Egypt and Judea's relations and then Napoleon's expedition to Syria in 1799. This was one of the rare occasions on which Trumper told soldiers anything of the region's history since the crusades. The third pamphlet, finishing his analysis of central Palestine north of Jerusalem, was published in October 1918, and it is thus the first two works that would have been extensively read by soldiers during the course of the campaign. In total, the four pamphlets sold over 20,000 copies, which must make them some of the most widely distributed educational documents amongst the men of the EEF. They proved so popular that the Nile Mission Press brought out a single volume in 1921, which ran to 124 pages, containing all of the information from the four pamphlets. Trumper expected the book to be read by Bible students and future tourists to Palestine (Trumper 1921, 5–6). The soldiers of the EEF were thus the trailblazers for individuals travelling to the region in the inter-war period.

The emphasis on tourism, much of it focused on the Middle East's Islamic heritage, and the clear existence of a vernacular orientalism among the letters, diaries, memoirs, and souvenirs of men who served in Egypt and Palestine in the First World War eradicates the notion that they were engaged in a crusade. It also serves to undermine the farrago of ideas brought to prominence in Edward Said's *Orientalism* (1978), which have exercised considerable influence on post-colonial studies.[53] The over-reliance on the high literature of nineteenth- and twentieth-century Britain in this discourse has meant that the voices of the vast bulk of society have been ignored (Bar-Yosef 2005, 61–104). The First World War represented the largest period of contact between the Orient and Occident since the crusades. Tens of thousands of British and Dominion soldiers – predominantly drawn from the working class, who would have had little opportunity to visit the Middle East before 1914 – were now exposed to its culture and heritage en masse.[54] In such circumstances, it is striking that the way in which soldiers chose to view this world demonstrated that they had imbibed a vernacular orientalist tradition. This was an idiom of cultural interaction that would persist into the British mandate period, and be most clearly expressed in the adoption of a colonial regionalism in the architectural style of the High Commissioner's residence (Fuchs and Herbert 2000). Indeed, as Timothy Mitchell has illustrated, attempts to utilize a stereotyped Middle-Eastern culture as an element of colonial rule had their origins in nineteenth-century attempts to impose control on local populations as European commerce and administration expanded into the region (Mitchell 1988, 161–79).

The experiences of EEF soldiers also suggest that it is necessary to move beyond an overly intellectual interpretation of orientalism, and instead to view it as simply expressing an interest in the history and culture of the non-Western world. It is evident that the home front construction and the post-war reconstruction of the campaign as a crusade were in opposition to the experiences and attitudes of the majority of soldiers who served in Egypt and Palestine, many of whom by mid-1918 were Muslim Indians. In contrast, the EEF soldiers' view of the campaign was best expressed in Alfred Leete's 'See the World' recruiting poster of 1919, which emphasized modern soldiering simply as glorified tourism.

Acknowledgements

I am grateful for the assistance of Martin Conway, Adrian Gregory, Robert Johnson, Harry Munt, Laura Rowe, Peter Stanley, Hew Strachan, Sam Wilson, and Rosie Young, who all commented on earlier drafts of this paper. I would also like to thank Pierre Purseigle for his help in finding visual sources to illustrate my argument. I am indebted to the Frank Denning Memorial Charity for funding my research in Australia and New Zealand. This article began life as a paper at the Military History Seminar held in All Souls College, Oxford, on 25 February 2009, and had a subsequent airing at a history seminar in the University of Exeter, on 10 February 2010. I am grateful for the comments and suggestions I received on both occasions. I would like to thank Punch Ltd., the Imperial War Museum, and the Norfolk Regiment Museum for permission to reproduce images from their archives. The analysis, opinions and conclusions expressed or implied in this article are those of the author and do not necessarily represent the views of the RAF College, the UK Ministry of Defence or any other government agency.

Notes

1. Falls 1930, 647. The correspondence between the authors of the official history and members of the EEF, compiled during the 1920s, was dominated by discussions with senior officers; the voices of the other ranks and junior officers were largely silent in the research of Falls. See National Archives (hereafter NA), CAB45/78–80, Comments and Correspondence Relating to the Compilation of the Official Histories – Egypt and Palestine.
2. Woodward 2006, 192. The dangers of publishers misrepresenting historical works in order to boost sales are illustrated by the US title of Woodward's book: *Hell in the Holy Land*. It is of note that Woodward's study is reliant almost solely on sources drawn from British archives. The multinational and multiethnic elements of the EEF are thus neglected – in particular its strong Australian, New Zealand, and Indian contingents. This also limits his ability to draw conclusions on those periods of the conflict in Egypt and Palestine when British soldiers were not at the forefront of operations, such as the battle of Romani in August 1916 or the Transjordan Raids in March–May 1918.
3. Grainger does not list the contemporary accounts that 'repeatedly' invoke this crusading rhetoric, and instead seems to be reliant on the official history for this conclusion. His bibliographical essay suggests that it is Allenby's interpretation, first set down in his reports on the campaign, that has come to dominate the historical record. Given Grainger's dubious assertions regarding the letters and diaries of EEF combatants, and a failure to adequately catalogue his unpublished sources, one can only find this conclusion to be highly suspect. See Grainger 2006, 67 and 267–8.
4. Snape 2005, 182–3. The first was educated at Ampleforth; the second served as an army chaplain, but had originally been a monk at Downside Abbey.
5. Siberry 2000, 94–7, and 1999. For a similar interpretation of crusading rhetoric, see Pendlebury 2006, 70–2.
6. See the analysis of Gilbert by Bar-Yosef (2005, 245–56); Siberry 2000, 96; Parker 1987, 228–30.
7. Smith 1919 [1894]. The work had reached 25 editions by 1931 and had sold 35,237 copies by 1942. For a full analysis of Smith's career and publications, see Butlin 1988.

8. *The Times*, 17 December 1917.
9. *Hansard*, 5th series, C (20 December 1917), 2211.
10. NA, CAB23/4, War Cabinet Minutes, 21 November 1917.
11. In some cases, the titles of the films made about the EEF's campaign indulged in crusading rhetoric: *The New Crusaders – With the British Forces in Palestine* (1918) and *With the Crusaders in the Holy Land – Allenby the Conqueror* (1918). See Low 1950, 155; McKernan 1993, 170.
12. *The Northampton Independent*, 21 April 1917.
13. Norfolk Regiment Museum (hereafter NRM), Order of Service, Memorial Service for Major W.H. Jewson and Captain S.D. Page, both of 1/4th Norfolk, Norwich, 6 May 1917.
14. *The Times*, 22 April 1918.
15. Imperial War Museum (hereafter IWM), 85/4/1, Bailey Papers, Hare, 'Order of the Day After Third Gaza', 11 November 1917.
16. Liddell Hart Centre for Military Archives (hereafter LHCMA), Clarke 1/4, Clarke, memoir, p. 21.
17. Alexander Turnbull Library, MS-Papers-4312/1, Judge, diary, 9 April 1917.
18. Museum of Army Chaplaincy Archives, Jones, diary, 9 December 1917.
19. IWM, 82/22/1, Surry, letter to parents, 26 December 1918. For further discussion of the details of this letter see Bet-El 1993.
20. Allenby, letter to Lady Allenby, 21 November 1917, in Hughes 2004, 92.
21. See Girouard 1981, 259–93; Frantzen 2004. For the role of medieval imagery in post-war memorialization culture, see Goebel 2007.
22. NA, FO882/14, Arab Bureau Papers, letter from Rennie MacInnes to Reginald Wingate, 2 May 1917.
23. NA, FO882/14, Arab Bureau Papers, letter from Rennie MacInnes to Reginald Wingate, note added by Lieutenant-Commander Hogarth, 2 May 1917.
24. NA, FO882/14, Arab Bureau Papers, letter from G.S. Symes, on behalf of Reginald Wingate, to General Clayton, 12 September 1917.
25. NA, FO882/14, Arab Bureau Papers, report by Captain R.W. Graves, 2nd Echelon, GHQ, EEF, 15 October 1917.
26. This reflected sentiments often expressed in nineteenth-century travel accounts of Palestine. See Bar-Yosef 2005, 81.
27. IWM, 81/23/1, Shaw, memoir, p. 1.
28. IWM, 81/23/1, Shaw, memoir, p. 1.
29. IWM, 05/38/2, MacGregor, letter to sister, 25 August 1918.
30. IWM, Misc 41(726), Gotto, letter to parents, 29 May 1918.
31. Suffolk Record Office (hereafter SRO), GB554/Y1/426a, Wolton, letter to parents, 7 July 1918 (Wolton's emphasis).
32. IWM, P386, Dening, diary, 25 June 1918.
33. IWM, DS/MISC/82, Hampton, memoir, p. 43.
34. IWM, 98/28/1, Edgerton, memoir, p. 1.
35. IWM, 96/48/1, Milsom, memoir, pp. 21–2.
36. Todman 2005, 187. Todman develops the idea that the mythology of the First World War has affected how veterans recalled the conflict in public.
37. Australian War Memorial (hereafter AWM), 2DRL/0817, Chandler, letter to family, 26 February 1916.
38. IWM, Con Shelf, Hinde, diary, 26 March 1916.
39. IWM, Con Shelf, Hinde, diary, 11–21 December 1916.
40. SRO, GB554/Y1/426a, Wolton, letter to parents, 27 February 1916.
41. SRO, GB554/Y1/165j, Lee, diary, p. 8.
42. Kippenberger Military Archives, 1999.2619, McCormack, diary, 6 April 1918.
43. IWM, 85/4/1, Wink, letter to Mrs Whiffen, 28 December 1917.
44. This is an approach that has been adopted to analyse the Australian Imperial Force's initial service in Egypt in 1914. See White 1990.
45. AWM, 2DRL/0015, Evans, letter to mother, 18 November 1917.
46. Hampshire Regiment Museum, M1810, Hickman, letter to wife, 6 February 1916.
47. IWM, 85/4/1, Bailey, diary, 6–13 January 1919.
48. IWM, 05/38/2, MacGregor, letter to family, 6 October 1918.
49. AWM, PR00740, Holmes, diary, 14 September 1916.
50. Anonymous, *Anzac Hostel Guide, Cairo* (Cairo, no date), pp. 18–34.

51. NA, FO395/240, Foreign Office Correspondence, telegram from Pirie-Gordon to Mark Sykes, 11 February 1918; NA, FO395/240, Foreign Office Correspondence, telegram from Pirie-Gordon to Colonel Buchan, Foreign Office, 18 March 1918.
52. Trumper 1921, 6. Trumper only acknowledged the role of Smith's work in this post-war compendium.
53. Said [1978] 2003. The work has been subject to detailed criticism since its publication, yet its academic prominence has not been diminished. See Clifford 1980; Prakash 1995; MacKenzie 1995; Macfie 2002, 73–101; Irwin 2006, 277–309. Irwin's study offers an astute and erudite survey of much of this criticism, and highlights errors of fact and inconsistencies in Said's argument. In particular, Irwin demonstrates effectively that the reliance on British and French sources, along with the exclusion of the vast body of German orientalist scholarship, led Said to produce an essentialized image of Western imperialism. This was as skewed from reality as the orientalist interpretations that Said denounced. Nevertheless, some scholars still persist in seeing this corpus of criticism as somehow demonstrating the validity of Said's approach; see Rastegar 2008. Patrick Porter's insightful analysis (2009) of the relationship between cultural studies and military affairs in both historical and contemporary contexts does, however, suggest future avenues for the exploration of Said's thesis.
54. Nineteenth- and twentieth-century tourism in the Middle East has been addressed in a number of studies; see Pemble 1987; Withey 1997, 223–62; Nasser 2007, 70–94; Brendon 1991, 120–40.

References

Alloula, M. 1987. *The colonial harem*. Manchester: Manchester University Press.

Bar-Yosef, E. 2001. The last Crusade? British propaganda and the Palestine campaign, 1917–18. *Journal of Contemporary History* 36: 87–109.

Bar-Yosef, E. 2005. *The Holy Land in English culture 1799–1917: Palestine and the question of Orientalism*. Oxford: Oxford University Press.

Bet-El, I.R. 1993. A soldier's pilgrimage: Jerusalem 1918. *Mediterranean Historical Review* 8: 218–35.

Bowes, J. 1920. *The Aussie Crusaders with Allenby in Palestine*. Oxford: Oxford University Press.

Brendon, P. 1991. *Thomas Cook: 150 years of popular tourism*. London: Secker and Warburg.

Brereton, F.S. 1920. *With Allenby in Palestine: A story of the latest Crusade*. London: Blackie and Son.

Briscoe Moore, A. 1920. *The mounted riflemen in Sinai and Palestine: The story of New Zealand's Crusaders*. Auckland: Whitcombe and Tombs.

Bruce, Anthony. 2002. *The last Crusade*. London: John Murray.

Bryant, M., and S. Heneage. 1994. *Dictionary of British cartoonists and caricaturists, 1730–1980*. Aldershot: Scholar Press.

Butlin, R. 1988. George Adam Smith and the historical geography of the Holy Land: Contents, contexts and connections. *Journal of Historical Geography* 14: 381–404.

Clifford, J. 1980. Review of E.W. Said's *Orientalism*. *History and Theory: Studies in the Philosophy of History* 19: 204–23.

Cooper, F.H. 1919. *Khaki Crusaders*. Cape Town: Central News Agency.

Falls, C. 1930. *Military operations Egypt and Palestine II: From June 1917 to the end of the war*. London: His Majesty's Stationery Office.

Frantzen, A.J. 2004. *Bloody good: Chivalry, sacrifice and the Great War*. Chicago.

Fuchs, R., and N. Herbert. 2000. Representing mandatory Palestine: Austen St. Barbe Harrison and the representational buildings of the British Mandate in Palestine, 1922–37. *Architectural History* 43: 281–333.

Gibbon, E. 1995. *The history of the decline and fall of the Roman Empire*. London: Penguin Classics.

Gibbons, T. 1921. *With the 1/5th Essex in the East*. Colchester: Benham and Company.

Gilbert, V. 1923. *The last Crusade: With Allenby to Jerusalem*. New York: William B. Feakins.

Girouard, M. 1981. *The return to Camelot: Chivalry and the English gentleman*. New Haven: Yale University Press.

Goebel, S. 2007. *The Great War and medieval memory: War, remembrance and medievalism in Britain and Germany, 1914–1940*. Cambridge: Cambridge University Press.
Grainger, J.D. 2006. *The battle for Palestine 1917*. Woodbridge: The Boydell Press.
Hatton, S.F. 1930. *The yarn of a Yeoman*. London: Hutchinson.
Hughes, M. 1999. *Allenby and British strategy in the Middle East 1917–1919*. London: Frank Cass.
Hughes, M., ed. 2004. *Allenby in Palestine: The Middle East correspondence of Field Marshal Viscount Allenby, June 1917–October 1919*. Stroud: Sutton Publishing.
Irwin, R. 2006. *For lust of knowing: The Orientalists and their enemies*. London: Allen Lane.
Knowles, R. 1991. Tale of an 'Arabian Knight': The T.E. Lawrence effigy. *Church Monuments: Journal of the Church Monuments Society* 6: 67.
Lloyd George, D. 1936. *War memoirs of David Lloyd George*. London: Nicholson and Watson.
Lock, H.O. 1919. *With the British Army in the Holy Land*. London: Robert Scott.
Lockhart, J.G. 1920. *Palestine days and nights: Sketches of the campaign in the Holy Land*. London: Robert Scott.
Low, R. 1950. *The history of the British film 1914–1918*. London: George Allen and Unwin.
Macfie, A.L. 2002. *Orientalism*. London: Longman.
MacKenzie, J.M. 1995. *Orientalism: History, theory and the arts*. Manchester: Manchester University Press.
Masterman, E.W.G. 1918. *The deliverance of Jerusalem*. London: Hodder and Stoughton.
McKernan, L. 1993. 'The supreme moment of the war': General Allenby's entry into Jerusalem. *Historical Journal of Film, Radio and Television* 13: 169–80.
Mitchell, T. 1988. *Colonising Egypt*. Cambridge: Cambridge University Press.
Nasser, N. 2007. A historiography of tourism in Cairo: A spatial perspective. In *Tourism in the Middle East*, ed. R.F. Daher, 70–94. Clevedon: Channel View Publications.
Parker, P. 1987. *The old lie: The Great War and the public-school ethos*. London: Constable.
Pemble, J. 1987. *The Mediterranean passion: Victorians and Edwardians in the south*. Oxford.
Pendlebury, A. 2006. *Portraying 'the Jew' in First World War Britain*. London: Vallentine Mitchell.
Porter, P. 2009. *Military Orientalism: Eastern war through Western eyes*. London: Hurst.
Prakash, G. 1995. Orientalism now. *History and Theory: Studies in the Philosophy of History* 34: 199–212.
Rastegar, K. 2008. Revisiting *Orientalism*. *History Today* 58: 49–51.
Said, E.W. [1978] 2003. *Orientalism*. 3rd ed. London: Penguin Books.
Siberry, E. 1999. Images of the Crusades in the nineteenth and twentieth centuries. In *The Oxford history of the Crusades*, ed. J. Riley-Smith, 363–84. Oxford: Oxford University Press.
Siberry, E. 2000. *The new Crusaders: Images of the Crusades in the nineteenth and twentieth centuries*. Aldershot: Ashgate.
Smith, G.A. [1894] 1919. *The historical geography of the Holy Land: Especially in relation to the history of Israel and of the early Church*. 20th ed. London: Hodder and Stoughton.
Snape, M. 2005. *God and the British soldier: Religion and the British Army in the First and Second World Wars*. London: Routledge.
Sommers, C. 1919. *Temporary Crusaders*. London: The Bodley Head.
Taylor, A.J.P. 1966. *The First World War: An illustrated history*. London: Penguin Books.
Todman, D. 2005. *The Great War: Myth and memory*. London: Hambleden.
Trumper, V.L. 1917. *Historical sites in southern Palestine with a brief account of Napoleon's expedition to Syria 1799*. Cairo: Nile Mission Press.
Trumper, V.L. 1918. *Historical sites in central Palestine*. Cairo: Nile Mission Press.
Trumper, V.L. 1921. *Historical sites in Palestine with a short account of Napoleon's expedition to Syria*. Cairo: Nile Mission Press.
White, R. 1990. Sun, sand and syphilis: Australian soldiers and the Orient, Egypt 1914. *Australian Cultural History* 9: 49–64.
Winnington-Ingram, A.F. 1917. *The potter and the clay*. London: Wells Gardner, Darton and Company.
Withey, L. 1997. *Grand tours and Cook's Tours: A history of leisure travel, 1750 to 1915*. London: Aurum Press.
Woodward, D.R. 2006. *Forgotten soldiers of the First World War: Lost voices from the Middle Eastern Front*. Stroud: Tempus.

From defeat to victory: logistics of the campaign in Mesopotamia, 1914–1918

Kaushik Roy

Centre for the Study of Civil War (CSCW), International Peace Research Institute, Oslo (PRIO), Norway

Britain and the Government of India embarked on the campaign in Mesopotamia for several reasons. The discovery of oil in south Persia in 1901 resulted in the formation of the Anglo-Persian Oil Company. The oil produced from this company was supplied to the Royal Navy. Germany's plan to construct a railway from Constantinople to Baghdad and Basra send tremors at London and Delhi. Germany's attempt to operate behind the façade of Turkish and Persian intrigues threatened the Anglo-Persian Oil Company's pipeline at the island of Abadan, the oilfields and the refineries. Britain was afraid that the Germans might instigate the Arab tribes to revolt. Further, capture of Basra by a hostile power would threaten Britain's sea lines of communication between Egypt and India. Logistics to a great extent had determined the texture of campaign in Mesopotamia. The logistical aspect of the Mesopotamia campaign during the Great War is yet to be studied thoroughly. The issue of supplying the British and Indian units in Mesopotamia proved crucial in shaping the course of the campaign. The first half of the paper shows how the problems of maintaining the units accelerated the disaster at Kut in April 1916. And the next section highlights the organizational restructuring of the logistical affairs which enabled the British and the Indian authorities to maintain larger number of troops with greater effectiveness from late 1916 onwards.

Britain and the Government of India embarked on the campaign in Mesopotamia for several reasons. The discovery of oil in south Persia in 1901 resulted in the formation of the Anglo-Persian Oil Company. The oil produced from this company was supplied to the Royal Navy. Germany's plan to construct a railway from Constantinople to Baghdad and Basra sent tremors to London and Delhi. Germany's attempt to operate behind the façade of Turkish and Persian intrigues threatened the Anglo-Persian Oil Company's pipeline at the island of Abadan, the oilfields and the refineries. Britain was afraid that the Germans might incite the Arab tribes to revolt. Further, capture of Basra by a hostile power would threaten Britain's sea lines of communication between Egypt and India. India not only supplied men and materials to the British war effort, but also functioned as a base for British power projection at the imperial outposts further east, such as in Singapore and Hong Kong. By August 1914, Turkey's attitude towards Great Britain became hostile. On 26 September, the Viceroy (also Governor General) of India, Lord Hardinge, was warned by London that a military expedition might have to be launched at the head of the Persian Gulf. On 16 October, Indian Expeditionary Force D (hereafter IEF D) sailed from Bombay for Bahrain. On 5 November 1914, Britain declared war on Turkey. The next day, IEF D captured the port of Fao.[1] The expedition had begun.

The initial plans were to protect the vicinity around Basra. However, weak Turkish opposition and continuous victories by the Army in India's[2] detachments encouraged both the commanders at Mesopotamia (especially the polo-playing, dashing cavalry commander Lieutenant-General John E. Nixon) and the General Head Quarter India (henceforth GHQ I) to penetrate deeper into Mesopotamia. In mid 1915, the stalemate at the Western Front, in the Egypt–Palestine sector and in Gallipoli encouraged the London government to order IEFD further north and if possible into Baghdad. A rapid advance at the cost of few casualties against the 'soft underbelly' of the Central Powers, the British policymakers hoped, would not only divert German troops from the Western Front but also boost up morale in Britain.[3] The advance, which started in late 1915 under Major-General Charles Townshend, culminated in the disaster at Kut. The Kut disaster in turn started a chain reaction that strengthened the Army in India. In late 1917, the Army in India went into an offensive in Mesopotamia, not only to regain imperial prestige but also to exact revenge on the Turks.

Logistics had to a great extent determined the texture of the campaign in Mesopotamia. The term 'logistics' is derived from the Greek word *logistike*, which means the art of supplying warfare. The logistical aspect of the Mesopotamia campaign during the Great War is yet to be studied thoroughly. The official and quasi-official histories focus on operational narrative. Brigadier-General F.J. Moberly, at the request of the Government of India (henceforth GOI), wrote the official history of the war in Mesopotamia. His duty was to exonerate the GOI from the charges levelled by the London government for inept handling of the Mesopotamia expedition till 1916. Colonel R. Evans, located at Staff College Camberley, wrote the unofficial history in 1926. He realized the importance of logistics, but blamed faulty strategy on the part of the British Empire for the debacle at Kut. In his eyes, the principal shortcoming was lack of coordination between the various parts of the empire for pooling resources to conduct a global war effectively.[4] Two modern historians, Field Marshal Lord Carver and Ron Wilcox, continue the trend of neglecting logistics in their monographs on the Mesopotamia campaign.[5] Edward J. Erickson, in his groundbreaking monograph on the Ottoman Army's military effectiveness during the First World War, asserts that logistics was never an important issue in the Mesopotamia campaign. He continues that both the Ottoman and the British authorities were paupers as far as the campaign in Mesopotamia was considered. *Materialschlacht* did not occur in Mesopotamia, unlike in France.[6] The military backgrounds of Carver and Erickson probably discourage them from analysing the logistical aspects. Most military officers-turned-historians focus on strategy, tactics and the operational level of war. Further, Carver and Wilcox have written trade books. The audience targeted by commercial publishers prefer campaign and battle studies that highlight the role of individuals and dramatize the exotic. Academic historians deal with studies of logistics. However, British-Indian military history is marginalized among both Indian and British historians. Due to the dominance of Marxism and recently postmodernism, the few studies we do have about the Army in India focus on the social and cultural aspects.[7]

The only study of logistics of the Mesopotamia campaign is an article on the Siege of Kut by Nikolas Gardner. For the debacle at Kut, he places the onus mainly on the Indian soldiers. By early February 1916, the only pack animals available at Kut were the horses and the mules. Though the British soldiers consumed them, the Indian soldiers (except the single Ghurkha battalion which consumed horseflesh) refused to incorporate them into their diet. As a result, the Indian soldiers suffered from protein deficiency. Scurvy, pneumonia and dysentery spread more rapidly among the Indian soldiers due to malnutrition. Sickness and hunger also decelerated recuperation of the wounded Indians. Due to inadequate food and spread of disease, their morale and subsequently combat effectiveness declined. Had the Indian troops consumed horse and mule flesh, writes Gardner, then the resistance at Kut could have continued for a longer period. Gardner asserts that the British officers failed to force the Indians to consume horseflesh, as this would have destroyed the fragile intricate bond that held the sahibs and the sepoys together.[8]

It is true that as regards the intensity and scope of warfare, Mesopotamia was much lower down the scale by comparison with the Western Front during the First World War. However, as this paper will show, the issue of supplying the British and Indian units in Mesopotamia proved crucial in shaping the course of the campaign. More than their Indian counterparts, the British soldiers tended to fuss about the quality of available rations. Not only did the authorities provide better rations to the British soldiers, but they were also eager to supply them more regularly and adequately with food items in comparison to the Indian troops. This was due to the imperial nature of IEF D. In the Army in India, in all matters ranging from equipment to food and clothing, British soldiers got preferential treatment vis-à-vis the Indian soldiers. The Indian soldiers cannot be blamed for not consuming horseflesh at Kut in April 1916: a military organization should cater for the cultural sensibilities and dietary habits of its soldiers. Further, the Army in India was not a national army but a quasi-mercenary force. Unlike the short service conscripts of the Western European national armies, the sepoys and sowars were long-term volunteers. Many illiterate young sons of small farmers joined the army in order to supplement their income from the farms. Further, they had no 'real' interest in fighting because neither Turks nor Germans were threatening their homes and hearths. The Muslim personnel of IEF D were particularly reluctant to fight the Turks, who were also Muslims, and the Ottoman Sultan, who was the Caliph. In addition, from 1859 onwards, the imperial authorities constructed regimental *esprit de corps* by encouraging and incorporating the traditional religious and cultural ethos of the warrior communities of South Asia.[9] So, the British officers could not summarily reject the social, cultural and religious sensibilities of their Indian soldiers.

In this essay, the term 'logistics' refers to supplying the soldiers and the animals associated with the war effort with food, medicines and other essential items and the problem of transporting these items to the battle zones. Since the Army in India was a multicultural force, the supply difficulties were exacerbated as the soldiers came from diverse social backgrounds and had different dietary habits. For instance, while the Sikhs and Muslims recruited from Punjab consumed atta (wheat flour), the Tamils and Telegu soldiers from southern India ate rice. Again, the Ghurkhas of Nepal consumed beef, but the high- and middle-caste Hindu soldiers from northern India would not touch it. And unlike the British, no community in India ate horseflesh. The demographic resources of India provided a logistical advantage to IEF D in relation to its opponent in Mesopotamia. The Army in India from 1917 onwards, unlike the Ottoman Army, had no difficulty in mobilizing adequate military manpower. In Mesopotamia, about 302,199 Indian combatants were sent from India during the four years of war. Of these, 15,652 died, 31,187 were wounded, 1444 were missing and 6735 became prisoners of war.[10] The Army in India, despite some recruiting problems, was capable of expansion even in 1918,[11] when Turkey was scraping the bottom of its manpower barrel. Further, the Army in India, unlike the Ottoman Army, did not suffer from a high desertion rate.[12] True, the consumption of shells and shots – unlike in France – was never particularly intensive in Mesopotamia. However, during 1915 and 1916, the GHQ I faced problems in supplying ammunition for the few light guns deployed in Mesopotamia. For reasons of space, supply of manpower and munitions will not be considered in this essay. Besides the actual number of soldiers and equipments that were deployed in Mesopotamia, moving the military units also proved very difficult, an issue that is highlighted in this article. Mesopotamia was indeed a difficult region for deploying and operating large bodies of troops. Edmund Candler, who was in Mesopotamia during the First World War, described it as a place 'where an army may be immobilized in the rainy season by the mud, in the spring by inundations, in the summer by heat, and in the early autumn by the sickness and exhaustion consequent upon the heat'.[13]

The first half of the paper shows how the problems of maintaining the units accelerated the disaster at Kut in April 1916. The next section highlights the organizational restructuring of the logistical affairs which enabled the British and the Indian authorities to maintain larger number of troops with greater effectiveness from late 1916 onwards. Since most of the units of the Allied side in Mesopotamia were Indians and the GOI played an important role in supplying the Mesopotamia expedition, the focus of this essay remains on the Indian units and the GOI.

The road to defeat at Kut: logistics from 5 November 1914 to 29 April 1916

On 6 November 1914, IEF D's 16th Brigade from the Army in India's 6th Pune Division[14] landed at Fao. The 16th Indian Infantry Brigade comprised of 91 British officers, 918 British other ranks, 82 Indian officers, 3,640 sepoys, 460 followers and 1,290 animals.[15] The 16th Brigade under Brigadier General W.S. Delamain had one British (2nd Dorsets) and three Indian (20th Punjabis, 104th Wellesley's Rifles and 117th Marathas) infantry battalions.[16] Lieutenant General Arthur Barrett commanded the 6th Division. He landed on 14 November with the 17th Infantry Brigade, and on 16 November defeated the Turks at Sahil or Zain. By the end of November, the 18th Infantry Brigade landed at Basra.[17] The advance continued in face of weak Turkish opposition. On 9 December 1914, Qurna was captured. By April 1915, the 12th Indian Division arrived at Mesopotamia. Nasiriya (110 miles up the Euphrates from Qurna) was captured on 25 July 1915. On 29 September 1915, Kut-Al-Amara was captured. Townshend, commanding the 6th Indian Division, advanced further and clashed with the Turks at Ctesiphon (21–24 November 1915). Townshend had about 12,000 soldiers. In November 1915, the 6th Indian Division faced four Ottoman divisions at Ctesiphon. However, on 25 November 1915, due to heavy casualties and supply difficulties, Townshend decided to retreat to Lajj. By 3 December 1915, Townshend retreated to Kut.

From 5 December 1915, the Turks started encircling Townshend's force at Kut. The Mesopotamia Command had difficulty maintaining the 6th Division, situated far north of Basra. Meanwhile, the 3rd (Lahore) and 7th (Meerut) divisions arrived at Basra from France. The logistical logjam was aggravated because these divisions had come from Marseilles, while their supply and transport and medical personnel followed later.[18] Lieutenant-General F.J. Aylmer took command over these units, which were formed as the Tigris Corps. These two divisions comprised nine Indian and three British battalions. However, the Tigris Corps failed to relieve Kut. By the beginning of 1916, the Mesopotamia Command included four divisions (48 infantry battalions).[19] As we shall see, one of the principal factors behind the surrender of Townshend's 6th Indian Infantry Division at Kut, and the failure of relief attempt by Aylmer, was the collapse of logistical support.

Soldiers had to be fed properly and regularly in order to maintain their combat effectiveness. Due to diverse cultures, the food habits of the British and Indian soldiers were also different. As mentioned earlier, even the diet of different communities of Indian soldiers varied substantially. Tables 1 and 2 show the rations that were to be provided to the British and Indian soldiers. The ration was geared to provide between 4539 calories (maximum) to 3319 calories (minimum) per day per British soldier. From the very beginning of the Mesopotamia expedition, the GOI faced problems in obtaining jam, cheese and bacon for the British soldiers. The GOI maintained a small stock of tinned meat for the British troops employed in North-West Frontier expeditions. And within India, only small amount of salted meat was locally available. These stocks were not adequate for maintaining two, and later four, divisions in Mesopotamia. As early as 15 November 1914, Hardinge requested the Secretary of State for India (Lord Crewe) to authorize the despatch of 40,000 lbs of cheese, 40,000 lbs of bacon and 60,000 lbs of jam to Bombay. From Bombay, these goods were to be shipped to Basra for the IEF D. The failure of Britain to provide these supplies forced the GOI to buy these commodities from Australia. Biscuits constituted an important part of the British troops' iron ration. Initially, the Hindu Biscuit Factory at Delhi and the Great Eastern Hotel Company at Calcutta were able to supply biscuits. Among the British troops of the 13th Division, Indian

Table 1. Daily field service ration for a British soldier.

Item	Quantity	Remarks
Bread	1 lb	At the discretion of the officer commanding on the spot, the following extra items were issued to each soldier daily: chocolate 1 oz, tinned fruit 8 oz, dry lentils 2 oz, lime juice $\frac{1}{2}$ oz, rum 4 oz
Fresh meat	1 lb	
Bacon	3 oz	
Potatoes	1 lb	
Tea	1 oz	
Sugar	$2\frac{1}{2}$ oz	
Salt	$\frac{1}{2}$ oz	
Pepper	$\frac{1}{36}$ oz	
Cheese	3 oz	
Jam	3 oz	
Tobacco	$\frac{1}{36}$ oz	Each smoker was given two match boxes weekly
Fuel	3 lb	

Source: Summary of Papers relating to Supplies (Food and Forage) (Simla: Govt. Central Branch Press, 1916), Appendix I, p. 16, Telegram no. 1551-10-Q, From General Officer Commanding Force D to Chief of General Staff, 4 May 1916 (UK Indian Office 1916, 18–9).

Table 2. Daily field ration for an Indian Soldier or an Indian follower.

Item	Quantity	Remarks
Atta	1½ lb	
Dal	4 oz	Dal is pulse
Ghee	2 oz	Ghee is clarified butter
Gur	2 oz	Instead of sugar, gur (jaggery) was provided to the Indian soldiers and followers
Tamarind	2 oz	
Potatoes	2 oz	
Dried Fruits	2 oz	
Tea	⅓ oz	
Ginger	½ oz	
Chillies	⅙ oz	
Turmeric	⅙ oz	
Garlic	⅙ oz	Compared to the British soldiers, the Indian soldiers and followers required a variety of spices
Salt	½ oz	
Tobacco	2/7 oz	
Fuel	1½ lb	Fuel refers to firewood that the Indian soldiers required for cooking their food. At the discretion of the officer commanding on the spot, the following extras were issued to each Indian soldier/follower: fresh vegetables 4 oz, limes 8 oz, rum 2 oz

Source: UK India Office 1916, 17.

biscuits were unpopular. And the Indian factories were unable to meet the rising demands of biscuits. So, the GOI turned to Egypt and Britain. And, in April 1915, orders were placed in Australia.[20]

As the tactical position of Townshend's force deteriorated, the supply situation simultaneously became critical. On 25 January and 21 February 1916, in two telegrams, the viceroy requested the Governor General (henceforth GG) of Australia to provide 500,000 and 1,000,000 lbs of preserved meat. On 11 March 1916, the GG of Australia replied that these goods will be shipped to Bombay by April of that year. On 21 February 1916, the viceroy enquired whether Australia could provide condensed milk and sterilized milk, as these two commodities were required for the hospital patients.[21] On 11 March 1916, Beauchamp Duff, the Commander in Chief of India, turned to the general officer administering Cairo, and in a telegram dated 11 March 1916 requested: 'Shall be obliged if you will dispatch following quantities of stores direct to Base Supply Officer Basra, otherwise to Embarkation Supply Officer Bombay: Biscuits 250,000 lbs, Bacon 100,000 lbs, Cheese 100,000 lbs, Condensed Milk 300,000 lbs'.[22]

Mark Harrison asserts that the relation between the British officers and the Indian soldiers was 'feudal'. The loyalty of the Indian soldiers to their British superiors was dependent on a contract that involved supplying adequate medical facilities in the field.[23] One could argue that the very failure of the British till 1916 to provide adequate medical facilities to the sepoys and sowars reduced their level of devotion to the British officers and, indirectly, their combat effectiveness in Mesopotamia. A balanced diet including fruits and vegetables was necessary for keeping the soldiers healthy. From the very beginning, the authorities failed to provide fresh fruits (except dates, which were available locally) and fresh vegetables to the IEF D. Onions and potatoes were sent from India. But, due to lack of cold storage facilities and hot weather in Mesopotamia, the potatoes were prone to rot.[24] The lack of citrus fruits and lime juice worsened the situation. By mid 1915, the Indian troops suffered from scurvy.[25] An Indian crew member of the 21st Combined Field Ambulance wrote to his friend: 'We drink river water. Wells cannot be dug here'.[26] Dysentery (due to lack of good drinking water) was the other disease to cause misery for the troops.[27] During hot weather, sand and flies contributed to the spread of disease. The medical organization failed to provide milk and ice to the Indian patients. There were even shortages of mosquito nets and sun helmets, resulting in malaria and sunstroke (especially among the British troops, who were unaccustomed to marching under a scorching sun).[28] Again, when mosquito nets did become available, the Indian troops did not like them and were not forced to use the nets.[29] Hence, a contradiction emerged between medical effectiveness of the military organization and the cultural ethos of the Indian soldiers. The adverse medical situation was aggravated by the fact that a medical organization, insufficient to meet the demands of even a single division by mid 1915, had to cater for the requirements of the entire 2nd Corps.[30] With time, the medical facilities available for the troops at Mesopotamia worsened. Before June 1915, there was only one hospital ship – the *Madras* – available for evacuating the sick and wounded from Mesopotamia and East Africa to Bombay. In July 1915, another hospital ship was provided, and one of them was allocated permanently to the Mesopotamia theatre. In March 1916, a river hospital steamer named *Bengali* was prepared in India for Mesopotamia, but it sank during the voyage to Basra.[31]

Besides food, water and medicines, there was a shortage of other essential commodities. To give an example, in January 1916, the 2nd Black Watch Regiment lacked stretchers (for removing the wounded) and blankets for the men. The 1st Battalion of the 5th Queen's Royal West Surrey Regiment, in the course of their advance from Nasiriya, suffered from shortages of tents, clothes and boots; and the men had to march and fight the Turks amidst rain, mud and cold.[32] All these factors resulted in sickness among the troops and deterioration of their morale.

Not only did the men suffer, but also the animals (see Table 3 for their dietary demands) required for the war effort. All this impacted adversely on Aylmer's relief attempt. Local grazing was not possible. West of the Euphrates, the region was an arid desert. From late 1915, the authorities failed to supply grass for the horses in adequate quantities. Even hay had to be imported from Bombay to Basra and then sent in the northern direction via pack mules, donkeys and barges. The horses' fodder was halved in December 1915, and they were given no salt ration, which in turn reduced their staying power. To give an example, in January 1916, due to a shortage of horses, the 7th Haryana Lancers had no ambulance or wagon carts.[33] In January 1916, one British officer of the 10th DCO Lancers claimed that the horses and other transport animals should be fed with oats rather than gram. However, oats were more costly than gram. India supplied both gram and oats. During September 1915, the cost of gram in India was Rs 4 per maund (1 maund = 80 pounds) and the cost of oats was Rs 7 4 Anna (16 Anna = Rs 1) per maund. The grain was collected from Bihar and Allahabad and then sent to Bombay for the onward journey to Mesopotamia.[34]

Not only did Australia and Britain fail to provide the essential commodities in the required quantities on time, but whatever goods were shipped to Basra could not

Table 3. Daily scale of rations for different types of animals.

Type of animal	Grain (lb)	Dry grass (lb)	Salt (oz)	Remarks
Australian or colonial horse and also country bred horse with the British Mounted Corps	14	14	1	The British charger was bigger and heavier compared to the silladar's horse, so the former consumed more than the latter
Arab and other small horse or horse with the Silladar Cavalry	12	12	1	Most of the Indian cavalry regiments were organized on the silladari principle. Each sowar owned his own horse and got extra money from the government for feeding and maintaining the animal. The government provided monetary compensation to the silladar (owner of the horse) when his mount died in action.
Mounted Infantry or Mounted Battery ordnance mule or Mounted Battery baggage mule or 1st class transport mule or pony	9	10	½	
Mounted Battery baggage mule or 2nd-class transport mule or pony or grass cutter pony of the Silladar	7	9	½	Each silladar maintained a syce (grass cutter) and a pony
Siege Train Artillery bullock or camel	8	20 (a)	½ (1½ oz for a camel)	If possible, bhoosa (dry straw) was issued to the camel. An extra ration of 1 lb gur was issued to the camel
Draught bullock	6	20	½	
Pack bullock or donkey	4	14	½	

Source: UK India Office 1916, 21.

be unloaded properly due to inadequate port facilities at Basra. The port of Basra is situated on the right bank of Shatt-el-Arab, 67 miles above a bar at the head of the Persian Gulf and 46 miles below Qurna, where the Tigris and one branch of the Euphrates meet to form the Shatt-el-Arab. The principal branch of the Euphrates joins the Shatt-el-Arab at Gurmat Ali, near Basra. The city of Basra, including the two suburbs (actually villages) of Ashar and Magil, had a population of 80,000. These two suburbs were close to the river and were unhealthy. The whole area, including the base of Mesopotamia Command at Basra, consisted of date palm gardens and open desert below the flood level. Only two miles of road existed, and there was no street lighting. During the rainy season, heavy traffic was impossible.

The town was subjected to regular flooding caused by strong southerly winds meeting a high river and spring tide. In November 1915, Basra was flooded, the water reaching 2′ above the mean sea level. Another disadvantage was that several creeks intersected the river frontage and made communication difficult. In addition, Basra had an inadequate supply of drinking water. There was only one well, which had previously served the Turkish barracks at Ashar.[35]

Whatever quantities were unloaded at Basra could not be rushed north for the troops of Tigris Corps, because of inadequate river transport. The three main rivers in Mesopotamia (the Euphrates, the Tigris and the Karun) were shallow, with sharp, narrow bends and concealed shoals. Between March and July, there was flood water and a steamer had to make head against a 5-knot current. During summer, the depth of the rivers fell further. In late summer and autumn, the Tigris was only 5′ deep and nothing drawing over 4′ 6″ was good for sailing.[36] From Basra to Qurna (46 miles), the Shatt-el-Arab had a varying width of 750–1800′, with a general depth of 3–6 fathoms except at low tide, when the Qurna Bar functioned as a temporary obstruction.[37] The river transport available to Mesopotamia Command was successful to meet all the demands as far as Qurna, but not to any point beyond that. In November 1914, when Barrett occupied Basra, the available river transport comprised just three steamers; among these, the *Julnar* required new engines. In addition, there were four lighters of 60 tons, one of 80 tons, two of 110 tons and 10 of 200 tons.[38]

As early as June 1915, Nixon (who took over the Mesopotamia Command on 9 April 1915) demanded four tugs with a draught of no more than 3′ 6″ and with a speed of 10 knots in slack water, with which to tow the indigenous boats. However, no such tugs were found in India. On 25 September 1915, Nixon reported to the India Office that the concentration of Townshend's force for the advance to Kut was delayed by inadequate river transport. Britain provided sporadic aid. During July–August 1915, the Admiralty sent materials for 12 shallow draught gunboats that were to be assembled at the Anglo-Persian Oil Company's works at Abadan. In October 1915, the sloop *Alert* arrived at Abadan and functioned as a naval depot.[39] During January 1916, Major H.P. Watts was in charge of the Advanced Supply Depot at Amara. All the supplies for the troops at the front had to be sent in barges towed by steamers. But, owing to shortages of river transport and increase in the quantity of stores consumed daily due to the concentration of troops needed for the relief of Kut, the Mesopotamia Command was forced to use mahailas (indigenous boats). However, these boats were able to proceed only as far as Amara, about 100 miles upstream from Basra; and their carrying capacity was in the range of 25–35 tons.[40] The Mesopotamia Command also used bellums (rowing boats) on the Shatt-el-Arab and the Euphrates, each of which could carry a load of 20 tons.[41] The Turks also lacked steamboats; they were forced to use kelleks (large skin rafts) for conveying supplies from Mosul and Jezeriyah to Baghdad.[42] During November 1915, the daily carrying capacity of the river transport available to Mesopotamia Command for transport from Basra northerly up river was 150 tons, when the actual daily requirement was 208 tons. In April 1916, while the daily carrying capacity of the river transport available rose by 250–300 tons, due to the concentration of Aylmer's force the daily requirements increased to 598 tons.[43]

On 22 March 1916, Lieutenant General Percy Lake, general officer commanding in Mesopotamia, telegraphed to the Chief of General Staff at Delhi: 'I doubt firstly whether the paralysing effect which the inadequacy and late supply of river craft has had on the operations up the Tigris is fully realized by the General Staff ... On 21 January 1916, when Aylmer fought his action at Hannah, there were 10,000 infantry and 12 guns in the country available as reinforcements, but which, owing to this cause, could not be sent up to him in time. On 8 March, the date of his last operations, I had, approximately, 12,000 infantry and 26 guns which, for similar reasons, could not be forwarded'.[44]

When the units moved away from the river banks, they were dependent on wheeled transport and on the animals for supplies. From the river banks, the supplies were carried to the units in carts. Most of these were two-wheeled, without suspension, and each was drawn by two mules. Their average speed was 2.5 miles an hour in good conditions.[45] As early as September 1915, Townshend's force was short of mules required for transporting baggage.[46] Lieutenant Colonel Dallas, Deputy Director of Supply and Transport Corps in Aylmer's relief force, noted that the wheeled transport of the 3rd and the 7th divisions could be used only when the ground was dry. Even then, four mules were required to pull a single water cart or ammunition wagon. In general, two mules could pull 10 maunds of weight in a limbered wagon; but in Mesopotamia, twice the number of mules was required because of the difficult terrain. Irrigation channels, nullahs (dried streams), bundhs (earthen embankments to conserve water for irrigation) and dusty, unsurfaced roads characterized the Mesopotamian landscape. Heavy rainfall occurred in December when the country became flooded. Overall, the lack of metalled roads in Mesopotamia meant that wagons could not be used. Sudden showers would frequently turn the sandy track into a muddy quagmire. Dallas proposed that camels and draught mules were more appropriate to such conditions. The Supply and Transport Corps was in a no-win situation. While on the one hand the Mesopotamia Command could not adequately feed the number of animals at its disposal, on the other hand it calculated that it needed more animals to keep the troops supplied. Dallas complained that a significant proportion of the animals sent from India by sea died during the voyage. He demanded a large number of North African mules and light draught horses.[47] On 31 January 1916, Dallas noted that 1,050 camels and 487 Persian mules were bought. However, the camels were undersized and weak; few could carry a load of more than four maunds.[48]

The situation at Kut worsened with time. In the words of an Indian Medical Service officer, Colonel P. Hehir, Kut was 'the most insanitary place we occupied in Mesopotamia'. There was no drainage system in Kut. Some of the streets and lanes near the banks of the river were used as urinals and latrines. Even in normal times, the town refuse was never regularly collected. The military hospital was located in the bazaar, which was densely populated and filthy.[49] On 5 December 1915, Townshend wired: 'I hope we can be relieved by a month, my rations for British troops are only [for] one month, and 55 days [for the] Indian troops. I shall have to reduce a [the] scale of rations, and commandeer all bazaar supplies'.[50] On 8 December 1915, out of 14,586 soldiers (including 3500 Indian followers) at Kut, 1,510 soldiers (including 42 Indian followers) were in the hospitals.[51]

Hehir warned on 5 February 1916: 'In the case of Indian troops the absence of dal and gur from the rations will have a detrimental effect on their condition in due course'.[52] From 6 February 1916, the troops were suffering from scurvy, and lime juice was not available. Since the Indian soldiers and followers' diet was less nutritious and had inadequate carbohydrates, the Indians were more susceptible to scurvy. More than 1,050 Indians were admitted to the hospitals for scurvy during the siege and many more were treated regimentally. On 17 February 1916, there was no milk and tea for the hospital patients. On 16 April, small pills of opium were given to the sepoys by the medical staff to stay their pangs of hunger.[53] Between 16 and 29 April, the Royal Flying Corps and the Royal Naval Air Service dropped eight tons of supplies, along with medicines and fishing nets (so that the troops could catch fish from the river for survival). However, all these measures were inadequate. On 24 April, the decision was taken to send the ship *Julnar* with 270 tons of supplies. The ship left Falahiyeh and its departure was covered by all the available pieces of artillery and machine guns in order to distract the Turks. However, the ship was discovered by the Turks, who shelled it heavily, finally capturing it at Magasis, some 8.5 miles from Kut. Now, the Mesopotamia Command had no means by which to send supplies to Townshend, and Aylmer's relief troops were unable to reach the besieged city.[54] The culmination of the Army in India's disaster occurred on 29 April 1916 when, with 2750 British and 6500 Indian soldiers, Townshend surrendered to the Turks.[55]

The above account should not give the impression that the Turks had no logistical problems. Indeed, the Mesopotamia Command was at a disadvantage, as it fought at Kut, which was at the far end of its logistical umbilical cord. By contrast, Kut was located comparatively near to the Turkish logistical nodal points. Hence, the Turks were able to concentrate a larger number of troops near Kut and were able to maintain them. Further, Aylmer's relief attempt failed due to his rigid unimaginative tactics, a problem that was not helped by low-quality drafts arriving from India.[56] In contrast, the Turkish soldiers initially under Nur-ud-din and then Khalil Pasha were able to entrench their positions with field fortifications and wait for the Army in India's detachments to attack them head-on.

The road to victory: logistics from May 1916 to 11 November 1918

In the immediate aftermath of Kut disaster, the supply situation for Mesopotamian Command was indeed gloomy. Australia could not meet all the demands of GOI due to other imperial requirements. On 26 May 1916, the GG of Australia replied that only half the amount of preserved meat demanded in the viceroy's 8 April 1916 telegram could be supplied due to other imperial demands.[57] But the supply situation was to improve – especially from August 1916 onwards, when Stanley Maude was appointed as head of the Mesopotamia Command. Compared with Nixon, Maude and his successor, Lieutenant General W.R. Marshall, gave more attention to planning and organization. However, it would be erroneous to put too much emphasis on individuals. The shock of defeat at Kut rejuvenated both the GOI and the political and military establishments in London. Further, publication of the reports of the Vincent-Bingley Commission of the GOI in 1916 and the Mesopotamia Commission (initiated by the House of Commons) in 1917 forced Britain and the GOI to realize that there was no short cut to victory. The 'sideshow' at Mesopotamia could not be waged cheaply.[58] Not only British industry, but also the emerging industries in India, were geared towards supplying the demands of IEF D.

That the GOI did not, before 1916, mobilize Indian society on a larger scale to help sustain the war effort was due to the nature of the colonial state. The British-Indian state was neither a nation-state nor a totalitarian monarchy. The colonial state was dependent on several layers of Indian intermediaries for functioning smoothly. Increasing extraction of resources from India, resulting in penetration of the bureaucratic tentacles more deeply into the levels of society, alienated the collaborating intermediaries. The Indian collaborators were wealthy landlords of north India, Punjab and the princes who ruled about one-third of British India. And the increasing burden of supplying warfare from the backward Indian economy alienated the colonial collaborators. For this very reason, the GOI did not ask for men and materials from the princely states before the Kut disaster. In April 1918, the colonial government was forced to order the princely states to increase supply of manpower and economic resources and take measures to check anti-British political propaganda in their domains.[59] In the second half of 1916, as in the latter part of 1942, the colonial state was forced to go for mass mobilization only after the British-Indian armies had suffered massive defeats. In order to placate the indigenous collaborators after the First World War, the colonial state had to choose devolution of power to the Indians (the Morley–Minto Reforms) and grant the King's Commission to the Indian recruits. In addition, under the Punjab Canal Colonies scheme land was granted, to placate serving soldiers and their families.[60] In fact, mass mobilization of Indian society from 1942 onwards strengthened anticolonial nationalism, which in turn sped up decolonization.[61]

Let us now shift our focus to the improving logistical infrastructure in Mesopotamia. By 20 May 1916, Basra was flooded. The water level reached 8′ 9½″ above mean sea level. However, the Mesopotamia Command started to develop the port facilities at Basra. The whole base area was protected with bunds (earthen embankments), the most important of which was the Shaiba Bund, which ran west from Magil to the Shaiba Ridge for about 10 miles. Its mean height was 8′ 6″. This bund was built to prevent the Euphrates from overflowing and flooding the countryside surrounding Basra. Constructed with mud and reinforced with mats and corrugated iron sheets, this bund withstood floods in 1917 and 1918. About 38 miles of road was also laid, involving the erection of several girder bridges over the creeks. The first five miles of road was made of concrete. About 80,000 gallons of water were required daily, rising to 100,000 gallons during the hot season. This was provided by eight pumping stations, each fitted with automatic chlorination system and sedimentation tanks. About 70 miles of piping were laid and storage arranged in the high-level tanks with a capacity of 320,000 gallons. From August 1916, construction of wharves (where ocean-going vessels could lie) started. The first wharf was commissioned on 3 October 1916 and the second was finished on 10 July 1917. Work on the third, fourth and fifth wharves began in August, September and November 1917, respectively. Construction of the sixth and seventh wharves started in December 1917 and January 1918. On 20 February 1918, the third, fourth and fifth wharves were completed. Since a large portion of the river frontage was swamped in the flood season, it was necessary to reclaim this area and to make them suitable for storage. The area near Magil was reclaimed by dredger and a further 800,000 square yards were reclaimed by the donkeys and light tramline haulage.[62]

Table 4 shows that the tonnage of cargo unloaded at Basra increased drastically due to development of the port facilities. The cargo unloaded at Basra during March–April 1917 was more than three times higher than during March–April 1916. Not only was the port at Basra developed, but animals, men and materials began to arrive in increasing quantities due to the unchallenged supremacy of the Royal Navy in the Indian Ocean. The presence of the German Cruiser *Emden* in the Bay of

Table 4. Cargo discharged at Basra at various dates.

Date	Tons
1916	
13 March to 12 April	43,249
13 April to 12 May	57,540
13 May to 12 June	44,325
13–30 June	22,554 (total cargo delivered in June was 30,000 tons)
July	38,916
August	44,183
September	54,256
October	50,792
November	61,214
December	81,123
1917	
January	79,085
February	93,669
March	98,073
April	94,673
May	90,504
June	73,845
July	84,559
August	109,620
September	100,136
October	108,852
November	112,503
December	104,593
1918	
January	131,838

Source: UK India Office 1918, 2.

Bengal during the latter part of 1914 somewhat decelerated the movement of troopships and other cargo vessels.[63] After that, there was no serious naval threat by the Central Powers in the Indian Ocean.

Along with developing the port of Basra, the river transport facilities were improved. Even in August 1916, the river supply transport failed to meet the demands of the Mesopotamia Command. The daily tonnage available from Basra up river in that month rose to 450 tons, but the daily requirement increased to 650 tons. However, the situation started to improve from 1917 onwards. While the daily requirement became 800 tons, in order to cater for emergencies (breakdown of steamers, sudden increase of forces), the daily tonnage capacity of the river fleet became 1200 tons.[64] By the end of 1917, the Inland Water Transport Fleet comprised 1266 vessels (including 497 barges, 365 motor boats, 339 steamers, motor barges, hospital ships and several other miscellaneous types of boat).[65] By November 1918, the number of vessels at the disposal of the Inland Transport Corps rose to 1621 craft.[66] As a point of comparison, during June 1915, Nixon had only 27 steamers and tugs.[67] Table 5 shows the increasing number of crafts and their rising carriage capacity, in the hands of Mesopotamia Command from 1917 onwards. Not only did the number of crafts rise, but their quality also improved with time. The early type of paddle steamer was designed by Messrs. Lynch and Co. to carry a cargo of 400 tons

Table 5. Crafts in use and weekly average of river traffic carried in Mesopotamia.

Period	Crafts					River traffic carried		
	Hospital ships	Steamers and tugs	Launches	Dredgers	Barges and lighters	Total including miscellaneous crafts	Personnel	Animals	Tons

Period	Hospital ships	Steamers and tugs	Launches	Dredgers	Barges and lighters	Total including miscellaneous crafts	Personnel	Animals	Tons
1916									
October							4379		5975
November							5190		9902
December							5587	433	11,787
1917									
January	5	109	222		234	570	4968	349	14,918
February	9	127	234		250	620	5248	626	17,583
March	10	144	248		280	682	7951	262	18,454
April	11	147	264		310	732	8186	797	20,755
May	17	151	302		340	810	12,691	2261	20,185
June	19	158	321		363	861	9791	1283	18,281
July	19	161	347		375	902	7761	703	18,388
August	20	163	369		392	944	9218	470	23,772
September	20	165	390		401	976	12,452	536	27,721
October	75	168	404		436	1083	14,742	710	33,546
November	77	182	415		484	1158	9475	606	36,400
December	80	189	425		521	1215	1048	1025	33,407
1918									
January	83	193	439		567	1282	7424	506	30,021
February	94	208	443		578	1323	4159	696	38,626
March	98	216	445		603	1362	5475	1120	39,672
April	96	218	470	4	645	1429	5808	790	39,055
May	96	218	482	8	653	1469	6367	695	36,473
June	97	218	485	8	660	1485	5825	535	36,712
July	97	220	490	8	662	1494	6570	468	34,735
August	97	221	497	8	745	1587	5465	366	31,556
September	97	223	507	8	750	1684	5457	393	27,670
October	97	225	517	9	746	1613	5706	385	28,660
November	97	225	524	9	747	1621	5494	632	26,921

Source: Statistical Abstract, 1914–20, 614.

at a 4′ draught. Later, the modified P-50 Class steamer was introduced. These boats were built in Glasgow at a cost of £75,000 each.

In the autumn of 1916, a metre-gauge railway connected Qurna. Qurna was developed as a port for seagoing steamers. The bar at the mouth of the old channel of the Euphrates was dredged and vessels coming from Bombay drawing 14′ were able to moor there. The stretch between Ezra's Tomb and Amara along the Tigris was 5′ deep during the summer, and the river between these two points was very narrow. Electric light was installed along this region and a system of command was established between Ezra's Tomb and the Mecheriyeh Canal for guiding the sailing vessels. Hence, the vessels were able to sail upstream even during the night.[68] In November 1918, the Inland Water Transport was under the command of Brigadier General R.H.W. Hughes, who employed 16,669 (both British and Indian) personnel. The Inland Water Transport not only ran the transport fleet but also constructed dockyards, slipways, workshops, and so on. Besides transporting men, animals, and munitions, its fleet also carried firewood for the soldiers, and bhoosa and hay for feeding the animals.[69]

In addition to the river transport, the Mesopotamia Command also constructed a rail network to push supplies for the soldiers and the animals at the front. River transport was very slow. It took a boat about 10 days to move from Basra to Falahiyeh. Transport by railways was comparatively faster.[70] From Table 6, it is clear that the number of men and animals as well as the total tonnage carried by the railways increased substantially from January 1917 onwards. After December 1916, the Shaikh Saad–Es Sinn (25 miles east of Kut) temporary railway line was constructed. The Baquba–Table Mountain railway was converted into metre gauge.[71] On 21 December 1917, the railway to Feludja was completed.[72] Before the beginning of the Mesopotamia Campaign, there was only 75 miles of railway line between Baghdad and Samara. By 9 November 1918, the Mesopotamia Command had constructed 155 miles of 4′ 8½″ gauge and 421 miles of metre gauge of rail lines. Besides the 576 miles of main railway line, the total, including sidings, came to about 800 miles of railway track, mostly constructed after mid 1916.

In addition to these figures, 200 miles of light 2′ 6″ gauge lines were also laid temporarily during various stages of military operations. A large proportion of the railway was constructed in the region subjected to flooding, and this entailed heavy earthwork and extensive bank protection activities. Two main branches of the Euphrates were bridged and the Diala river was twice crossed. In addition, irrigation canals and river 'spills' necessitated the construction of a large number of bridges and culverts.[73] Until mid 1916, there was a shortage of pontoons, so the bridges over the rivers were built with *mashhufs* – country boats made with rotten wood. Such makeshift bridges were vulnerable to the rise in water level and strong winds, and were incapable of supporting the railway lines. By 1917, these primitive bridges were replaced with pontoon bridges. Not only was the railroad developed, but the number of carriages at the disposal of the Mesopotamia Command also rose. By January 1918, there were 88 metre-gauge locomotives, 31 4′ 8.5″-gauge locomotives and 25 2′ 6″-gauge locomotives. As regards carriages and wagons, there were about 2125 metre-gauge and 346 4′ 8.5″- and 278 2′ 6″-gauge brake vans, trucks, refrigerated cars, water tanks, ambulance cars, fuel oil tanks, and so on.[74]

The railroad network of the Mesopotamia Command developed faster than that of the Turks. The Ottoman Empire, with an area of 679,360 square miles, had only 3580 miles of railroad track in 1914. The railway at the disposal of the Turkish forces

Table 6. Weekly average of traffic carried on two principal Mesopotamian railways.

	Basra-Nasirriya			Basra-Qurna-Amara		
Period	Number of personnel	Number of animals	Freight (tons)	Number of personnel	Number of animals	Freight (tons)
1916						
December	1532		4,279	74		520
1917						
January	2102	1501	4836	149		775
February	1116	3147	7168	132		253
March	1891	1902	10,527	212		464
April	6522	2118	7759	1332		770
May	3030	1597	7836	1678	458	2552
June	4464	1318	8349	1920	633	3259
July	3234	3473	8622	1950	650	2515
August	3139	1869	6534	2801	347	3301
September	2377	2647	4228	3959	98	5385
October	2842	135	5367	3991	7	7715
November	2421	126	5771	2663	24	8613
December	1615	109	4774	6443	88	6682
1918						
January	1796	130	4147	3560	74	7040
February	1438	96	4881	2320	45	10,878
March	3248	160	4147	5398	89	12,207
April	1659	83	5929	7566	145	12,499
May	1797	83	5705	4878	42	12,096
June	1728	59	5531	9118	58	8605
July	1890	74	7227	7769	44	11,697
August	2799	87	7950	5508	78	12,042
September	2772	116	8456	8285	47	14,660
October	2775	82	6301	9618	78	11,288
November	2370	36	6691	7122	70	8648

Source: Statistical Abstract, 1914–20, 616.

in Mesopotamia ran north of Baghdad 90 miles to Samarrah; beyond it was a gap of 360 miles across the desert to the railhead at Ras-el-Ain. Only in October 1918, just three weeks before the armistice, was the rail line between Constantinople and Baghdad completed.[75]

The Tata Iron and Steel work was one of the chief suppliers of rails for Mesopotamia.[76] Teakwood required for constructing the metre-gauge lines was supplied by the princely state of Mysore. The Cochin princely state provided timber worth Rs 76,000.[77] The timber (for sleepers) and coal for the railways, as well as firewood required by the soldiers and the labourers for cooking, was all brought into Mesopotamia by sea.[78] Most of the railways were constructed with Indian labourers who were trained at the Military Railway Labour Training camps of Saharanpur, Tirupattur, Gaya, Puri and Jabbalpur.[79]

For moving supplies beyond the railheads to the front where the units were actually deployed, animal transport was essential. The GOI provided most of the animals required in Mesopotamia. One source for the GOI was to buy the animals from the princely states. For instance, 167 mules, 150 cavalry horses and 35 artillery horses were bought from the Nizam of Hyderabad. The GOI's remount department also bought horses from the princely states of Rajputana.[80] In order to support the

British and Indian military units, on 31 August 1917, the Mesopotamia Command maintained 25,543 pack horses, 38,186 mules, 2952 camels and 5016 oxen. In August 1917, the Mesopotamia Command had 71,670 animals; the following year, the number of animals at its disposal rose to 88,911. On 31 August 1918, the number of animals under Mesopotamia Command amounted to 36,063 horses (including 21,414 riding horses, 13,228 light draught horses and 1076 pack horses), 44,773 mules, and 3362 donkeys.[81] Grass for the animals was supplied by the GOI's Remount Department at Aurangabad.[82]

For the easy movement of animal-drawn wagons and wheeled motor vehicles, road construction also proceeded fast. In October 1917, the Turks were on Jebel Hamrin hills; further up the Tigris, they were entrenched in front of Daur; and their left wing was at Ramadie. On the right bank of Diala river, the Turks held the line near Deli Abbas. Lieutenant General Marshall, who took over command of the IEF D on 18 November 1917, claimed that between 1 October 1917 and 31 March 1918 '[w]e built 75 bridges over the main canals – Khalis, Mansuriya, Khorassan, Mahrut, Haruniya and Ruz. Jebel Hamrin the roadless tangle of hills was pierced by a number of roads constructed by us, capable of carrying wheeled traffic'.[83] Stone suitable for road construction was not available in Mesopotamia, so was imported.[84]

Gradually, the medical infrastructure at the disposal of the Mesopotamia Command expanded. This began in May 1916, when the hospital ship *Sikkim* started evacuating the wounded from the battlefields. The men suffered from scurvy, colitis, typhoid (enteric fever), dysentery and diarrhoea. Cholera vaccine was obtained for inoculation of the affected personnel. Some attempts were made to collect ice at Amara.[85] During November 1918, the sick and convalescents numbered to 278 British officers, 47 Indian officers, 5580 British soldiers and 3740 sepoys and sowars.[86] It is interesting to note that despite the presence of larger number of Indian soldiers, the British soldiers fell ill in the hot climate of Mesopotamia in greater numbers. Nevertheless, no medical catastrophe was in the offing.

Improved logistics was one of the factors that enabled the Mesopotamia Command to go from defensive to offensive. In February 1917, Kut was recaptured and on 11 March Baghdad was taken. By 5 November 1917, Tekrit was captured.[87] On 11 November 1918, the date of armistice, Marshall, the commander in Mesopotamia, had the following units under his command: 3rd, 6th and 7th Indian Cavalry Brigades under the Tigris Front; 17th and 18th Indian Divisions under the 1st Indian Army Corps; and 14th and 15th Indian Divisions under the 3rd Indian Corps. In November 1918, the Mesopotamia Command comprised 7078 British officers, 2414 Indian officers, 83,149 British soldiers and 117,438 sepoys and sowars. In addition, there were about 115,207 Indian followers (barbers, artisans, clerks, etc) attached to the Indian units.[88] Besides the Indian followers, Indian labourers were also used for building up the military infrastructure in Mesopotamia. The non-combatants sent from India to Mesopotamia during the war numbered to 336,890 and the Mesopotamia Command was able to feed them.[89]

Conclusion

Both the Turkish forces and IEF D faced logistical problems, but at least from late 1916 onwards the latter was able to handle its logistical apparatus much better than its opponent. Despite vastly dissimilar conditions between Western Europe and Mesopotamia, the histories of logistics of warfare in these two theatres converge at some points. Dennis E. Showalter may be exaggerating when he asserts that by 1917, internal combustion engines had replaced horsepower in Mesopotamia.[90] Animals remained crucial in Mesopotamia for mobility and there cannot be any comparison with the scale of motorization in the Western Front. The British Empire failed to adequately supply both the IEF D and the British units in the Western Front during the first half of the war. If the logistical failure in Mesopotamia produced the disaster at Kut, on the Western Front, the British shell crisis during late 1914 and early 1915 was catastrophic. However, from the second half of the war, the British Empire struck back by mobilizing a large amount of resources. Martin Van Creveld, in analysing the logistics in the Western Front during First World War, argues for a revolution in logistics, citing 1916 as the turning-point because that year saw a massive increase in the production of military weapons.[91] The use of the term 'revolution' is subjective; however, the increasing supply of goods required for waging war, and the greater use of railways and improved steamers, show that the development in the logistical sphere of IEF D was both quantitative as well as qualitative.

Feeding a large number of animals and men, the latter with various foodstuffs in keeping with their cultural preference, was a daunting task that the GOI performed well from mid 1916 onwards. Praise is due to the British-Indian establishment, especially when one considers that almost everything had to be imported from outside, given that so little could be acquired locally in the waterless sandy desert and the arid regions of Mesopotamia. Both British and Indian governments took greater care in feeding and maintaining the British soldiers than the sepoys and the sowars. This was partly due to racism and partly because, compared with the Indian other ranks, the British soldiers were more vulnerable in the physical geography of Mesopotamia. The tragedy at Kut was largely the result of logistical failure; but the very expansion and consolidation of the logistical infrastructure from late 1916 onwards prevented further exploitation of their victory at Kut by the Turkish Army. Logistical support enabled Maude (who took over command from Lake in August 1916) not only to reorganize his force and go on a limited offensive, as well as allowing Marshall to proceed on the road to victory during the summer of 1918. In the final analysis, along with improved training and tactics, better logistics allowed IEF D not only to withstand the Turks, but ultimately to vanquish them.

Notes

1. Evans 1926, 2–5, 14–18.
2. The Army in India comprised the British Indian Army (sepoys and sowars with mainly British and some Indian officers; the latter were known as Viceroy's Commissioned Officers, and they were below the most junior British commissioned officers), British units stationed in India, and the military contingents from some of the princely states of the subcontinent.
3. Evans 1926, 20–31.
4. Candler 1919; Moberly 1923; Evans 1926.
5. Carver 2003; Wilcox 2006.
6. Erickson 2007, 4.
7. Roy 2006.
8. Gardner 2004.
9. For further expansion of these issues, see Roy 2008. For the contractual nature of service, see Jack 2006. Concerning the attitude of the Muslim soldiers, see Strachan 2001, 739.

10. *India's Services*, 1922, vol. 1: 23.
11. Perry 1988, 82–97.
12. Statistical Abstract, 1914–20, 625.
13. Candler 1919, vol. 2: 14–5.
14. Each Indian infantry division comprised two Indian brigades and one British brigade.
15. Wilcox 2006, 7–8.
16. Carver 2003, 11.
17. Mesopotamia Commission 1917: Appendix I, Vincent–Bingley Report, 134. Nehru Memorial Museum and Library, New Delhi.
18. Mason 1974, 431–32; Erickson 2007, 67–8; Evans 1926, 58; Carver 2003, 102; Notes from War Diaries Force D, May 1916, 8.1.1916, Part LXXII, WWI/1458/H, National Archives of India (henceforth NAI), New Delhi.
19. Erickson 2007, 91–2.
20. UK India Office 1916, 7, 12; no. 23: 23.
21. UK India Office 1916, nos. 17–18: 23.
22. UK India Office 1916, Telegram no. 43009, 11 March 1916, 22.
23. Harrison 1996, 397–8.
24. UK India Office 1916, 5.
25. Evans 1926, 36.
26. Omissi 1999, 160.
27. Mesopotamia Commission 1917: Vincent–Bingley Report, 135.
28. Mesopotamia Commission 1917, 37–8.
29. Harrison 1996, 442.
30. Evans 1926, 36.
31. Moberly 1923, vol. 1: 343.
32. Notes from the War Diaries, Force D, General Staff, Army HQ, India, June 1916, Part LXXXIV, 9, 12–3, 18, WWI/1459/H, NAI.
33. Notes from the War Diaries, Force D, General Staff, Army HQ, India, June 1916, Part LXXXIV, 9, 18, Notes from War Diaries, Force D, May 1916, 17.1.1916; Moberly 1923, vol. 1: 10.
34. Lamb 1916, United Service Institution Library, New Delhi.
35. UK India Office 1918, 1–2.
36. Candler 1919, vol. 2: 6.
37. UK India Office 1918, 4.
38. Mesopotamia Commission 1917, 44.
39. Moberly 1923, vol. 1: 341–43; Carver 1998, 105.
40. Notes from the War Diaries Force D, Part LXXII, 26.1.1916; Carver 2003, 59; Mesopotamia Commission, 44.
41. Mesopotamia Commission: Vincent–Bingley Report, 135.
42. Candler 1919, vol. 1: 129.
43. Mesopotamia Commission, 43.
44. Quoted in Mesopotamia Commission, 43.
45. Wilcox 2006, 16.
46. Carver 2003, 116.
47. Mason 1974, 432; Notes from the War Diaries Force D, Part LXXII, 27.1.1916.
48. Notes from the War Diaries Force D, Part LXXII, 31.1.1916.
49. Mesopotamia Commission, Appendix III, 169.
50. Quoted in Mesopotamia Commission, 31.
51. Mesopotamia Commission, Appendix III, 169.
52. Quoted in Mesopotamia Commission, Appendix III, 176.
53. *India's Services*, 1922, vol. 1: 27–8; Mesopotamia Commission, Appendix III, 176.
54. Despatch by Lieutenant-General P.N. Lake on the Operations of Indian Expeditionary Force D from 19 Jan.–30 April 1916, p. 11, L/MIL/17/15/108, IOR.
55. Evans 1926, 79.
56. Latter 1994; Roy 2009.
57. UK India Office 1916, no. 14: 22.
58. Majumdar 1976, 76–7.
59. Pradhan 1978, 57.

60. Martin 1986, 104; Yong 2005, 98–140.
61. Bayly 2004, 265–85.
62. UK India Office 1918, 1–2.
63. Moberly 1923, vol. 1: 91.
64. Mesopotamia Commission, 43.
65. UK India Office 1918, 21.
66. Statistical Abstract, 1914–20, 748.
67. Moberly 1923, vol. 1: 339.
68. Candler 1919, vol. 2: 6–7.
69. UK India Office 1918, 4, Appendix C.
70. Candler 1919, vol. 1, 128.
71. Statistical Abstract, 1914–20, 616; Carver 2003, 116.
72. Despatch by Lieutenant-General W.R. Marshall Commander-in-Chief of Mesopotamian Expeditionary Force on the Operations of the Mesopotamian Expeditionary Force from 1 October 1917 to 31 March 1918, p. 3, L/MIL/17/15/112, IOR.
73. Statistical Abstract, 1914–20, 758.
74. UK India Office 1918, 71, Appendices E(i) and E(ii).
75. Candler 1919, vol. 1: 44, 129; Jones 2004, 197.
76. *India's Services*, 1922, vol. 1: 38.
77. *India's Services*, 1922, vol. 2: 86, 100.
78. Wilcox 2006, 15.
79. *India's Contribution*, 1923, 89.
80. *India's Services*, 1922, vol. 2: 80, 211.
81. UK India Office, 398–99.
82. *India's Services*, 1922, vol. 2: 82.
83. Despatch by Marshall from 1 October 1917 to 31 March 1918, 1.
84. Wilcox 2006, 15.
85. Notes from War Diaries, Force D, July 1916, Part CVII, 2.5.1916–26.5.1916, WWI/1460/H, NAI.
86. Statistical Abstract, 1914–20, 104.
87. Mason 1974, 433.
88. Statistical Abstract, 1914–20, 22, 104.
89. *India's Services*, 1922, vol. 1: 24.
90. Showalter 2000, 84.
91. Van Creveld 2000, 57–72.

References

Bayly, C.A. 2004. 'The nation within': British India at war 1939–47. *Proceedings of the British Academy* 125: 265–85.

Candler, Edmund. 1919. *The long road to Baghdad*. 2 vols. London: Cassell.

Carver (Field-Marshal Lord). 1998. *Britain's army in the 20th century*. London: Pan, 1999.

Carver (Field-Marshal Lord). 2003. *The National Army Museum book of the Turkish front 1914–18: the campaigns at Gallipoli, in Mesopotamia and in Palestine*. London: Pan, 2004.

Erickson, Edward J. 2007. *Ottoman army effectiveness in World War I: a comparative study*. London and New York: Routledge.

Evans, R. (Colonel). 1926. *A brief outline of the campaign in Mesopotamia: 1914–18*. London: Sifton Praed, 1935.

Gardner, Nikolas. 2004. Sepoys and the siege of Kut-al-Amara, December 1915–April 1916. *War in History* 11, no. 3: 307–26.

Harrison, Mark. 1996. Medicine and the management of modern warfare. *History of Science* 34, no. 106, part 4: 379–410.

Harrison, Mark. 1996. Medicine and the culture of command: the case of malaria control in the British Army during the two World Wars. *Medical History* 40: 437–52.

1922. *India's services in the war*. 2 vols. Delhi: Low Price Publications, 1993.

1923. *India's contribution to the Great War*. Calcutta: Superintendent of Govt. Printing.

Jack, George Morton. 2006. The Indian Army on the Western Front, 1914–15: a portrait of collaboration. *War in History* 13, no. 3: 329–62.

Jones, Robert F. 2004. Kut. In *The Great War: perspectives on the First World War*, ed. Robert Cowley, 197–216. London: Pimlico.

Lamb, D.O.W. 1916. Oats. *Journal of the United Service Institution of India* 45, no. 202: 83–6.

Latter, Edwin. 1994. The Indian Army in Mesopotamia, 1914–18. *Journal of the Society for Army Historical Research* 72, no. 291: 160–79.

Majumdar, B.N. 1976. *History of the Army Service Corps* Vol. 3. *1914–39*. New Delhi: Sterling.

Martin, Gregory. 1986. The influence of racial attitudes on British policy towards India during the First World War. *Journal of Imperial and Commonwealth History* 14, no. 2: 91–113.

Mason, Philip. 1974. *A matter of honour: an account of the Indian Army, its officers and men.* Dehradun: EBD Educational, 1988.

Mesopotamia Commission. 1917. *Report of the Commission appointed by Act of Parliament to enquire into the Operations of War in Mesopotamia together with a separate report by Commander J. Wedgwood.* London: HMSO.

Moberly, F.J. 1923. *The campaign in Mesopotamia: 1914–18*. Vol. 1. London: HMSO.

Omissi, David, ed. 1999. *Indian voices of the Great War: soldiers' letters, 1914–18*. Houndmills, Basingstoke: Macmillan.

Perry, F.W. 1988. *The commonwealth armies: manpower and organization in two World Wars.* Manchester: Manchester University Press.

Pradhan, S.D. 1978. Indian Army and the First World War. In *India and World War I*, ed. D.C. Ellinwood and S.D. Pradhan. New Delhi: Manohar.

Roy, Kaushik. 2006. Introduction: armies, warfare and society in colonial India. In *War and society in colonial India: 1807–1945*, ed. Kaushik Roy, 1–52. New Delhi: Oxford University Press.

Roy, Kaushik. 2008. *Brown warriors of the Raj: recruitment and the mechanics of command in the Sepoy Army, 1859–1913.* New Delhi: Manohar.

Roy, Kaushik. 2009. The Army in India in Mesopotamia from 1916 to 1918: tactics, technology and logistics reconsidered. In *1917: beyond the Western Front*, ed. Ian F.W. Beckett, 132–43. Leiden: E.J. Brill.

Showalter, Dennis E. 2000. Mass warfare and the impact of technology. In *Great War, total war: combat and mobilization on the Western Front, 1914–18*, ed. Roger Chickering and Stig Forster. Cambridge: Cambridge University Press, 2005.

Strachan, Hew. 2001. *The First World War*. Vol. 1, *To arms*. Oxford: Oxford University Press.

United Kingdom India Office. 1916. Summary of papers relating to supplies (food and forage). L/MIL/17/15/120. London: British Library.

United Kingdom India Office. 1918. Mesopotamian Transport Commission Report. L/MIL/7/18588. London: British Library.

United Kingdom India Office. Statistical abstract of information regarding the armies at home and abroad 1914–20. L/MIL/17/5/2382. London: British Library.

United Kingdom India Office. Despatch by Lieutenant-General P.N. Lake on the Operations of Indian Expeditionary Force D from 19 Jan. to 30 April 1916. L/MIL/17/15/108. London: British Library.

United Kingdom India Office. Despatch by Lieutenant-General W.R. Marshall Commander-in-Chief of Mesopotamian Expeditionary Force on the Operations of the Mesopotamian Expeditionary Force from 1 October 1917 to 31 March 1918. L/MIL/17/15/112. London: British Library.

Van Creveld, Martin. 2000. World War I and the revolution in logistics. In *Great War, total war: combat and mobilization on the Western Front, 1914–18*, ed. Roger Chickering and Stig Forster. Cambridge: Cambridge University Press, 2005.

Wilcox, Ron. 2006. *Battles on the Tigris: the Mesopotamian campaign of the First World War.* Barnsley: Pen & Sword.

Yong, Tan Tai. 2005. *The garrison state: the military, government and society in colonial Punjab, 1849–1947*. New Delhi: Sage.

British Understandings of the Sanussiyya Sufi Order's *Jihad* against Egypt, 1915–17

JOHN SLIGHT
St John's College, University of Cambridge, UK

ABSTRACT *This article considers the Sanussiyya Sufi order's 1915–16 jihad on Egypt from a fresh perspective, analysing British understandings about the attack that soldiers and officials fashioned as the conflict progressed. By incorporating aspects of imperial and Islamic history and a focus on British perceptions, the article presents new directions in the study of the war in the Middle East that move beyond the concerns of older military histories. It analyses three key areas of British thinking in relation to this jihad. First, the belief that local fighters joined the campaign as a result of economic factors, chiefly the famine that swept the Western Desert from November 1915 as a result of an Anglo-Italian blockade, and that the order had little support from the local population owing to their policy of requisitioning goods. Second, the important set of perceptions that the Sanussiyya were pressured by the Ottomans to attack the British as part of their overall call for jihad against the Allied powers. Third, the divided nature of British views around the broader threat posed by the order to Egypt and the wider war effort. Finally, it examines the broader religious and ideological context of the Sanussiyya as an organised reformist Sufi order, engaged in a struggle for resistance to and survival against European imperialism—a struggle that collided with the changed strategic landscape of a region rent by conflict between the Ottoman and British empires from November 1914.*

Introduction

> Our influence in that vicinity [Sollum] has vanished, and farther east is rapidly disappearing, the Senussi soldiers are all over our part of the Western Desert.[1]

Purvis, the unlucky Coast Guard officer who sent the panicked message above, was on duty when fighters from the Sanussiyya Sufi order crossed the Egyptian border in the Western Desert on 20 November 1915. He was an inadvertent witness to the opening of a new front in what scholars have now recognised was a truly global conflict.[2] This new enemy that threatened the British protectorate in Egypt was one of the most influential Sufi orders in North Africa during this period. After its founder, Muhammad al-Senussi, returned from Mecca in 1838, preaching a reformist version of Islam, the order spread rapidly across the Sahara. French encroachment upon the Sanussiyya's area of influence from the later 19th century caused the order to react to this development militarily, couched in traditional religious terms of the 'lesser' *jihad*. When the Italians invaded Libya in 1911, the order also undertook defensive activism against this brutal assault. Given this record of militancy, the British in Egypt were concerned to maintain cordial relations with the Sanussiyya once fighting in Europe began in August 1914. This policy had wider strategic applications; it was designed to secure Egypt's western frontier to allow Britain fully to concentrate its resources on defending the Suez Canal, a vital artery for the British Empire, against Ottoman attack. In November 1915, when the Sanussiyya opened their offensive, this policy was in tatters.[3] This, then, was the moment when the military threat posed by *jihad* as a result of war with the Ottoman Empire was first confronted by the British Empire.

After the Sanussiyya moved across the Egyptian frontier and captured the coastal town of Sollum in November 1915, the British responded in force. Their campaign deployed 35,000 troops from across the British Empire against 5,000 Sanussiyya and allied Bedouin fighters. In a series of engagements in the Western Desert, the order was repeatedly defeated throughout 1916. Consequently, the majority of fighters withdrew back across the border. This left the British free to reinforce further their troops, who ejected the remaining Sanussiyya from the oasis towns in the Western Desert of Egypt, an operation that was completed by March 1917.[4] In military terms, both the Sanussiyya and Britain viewed this front as a sideshow.[5] The Sanussiyya were far more concerned with prosecuting their defensive *jihad* against Italian and French imperial expansion in North Africa. For the British, their global military priorities were first the war against Germany on the Western Front, defending the Empire as a whole from internal and external security threats, and then, in the Eastern Mediterranean theatre, the Dardanelles campaign and defending the Suez Canal against the Ottomans.

The Sanussiyya *jihad* against British Egypt has been cited in broader studies of the order, Libyan history, and the relationship between Islam and European imperialism.[6] Specific studies of the attack are, on the whole, military histories.[7] This article considers the events in the Western Desert during 1915–17 from a fresh perspective, in order to supplement existing analyses by military historians, by examining British understandings about the Sanussiyya *jihad* that soldiers and officials fashioned as the conflict progressed. In doing so, the article seeks to demonstrate how incorporating aspects of imperial and Islamic history, especially through a focus on British perceptions of the Sanussiyya which have remained understudied, can contribute new insights into future studies of the war in the Middle East that move beyond the concerns of older military histories.

Some Britons involved in this desert conflict believed that the Sanussiyya fighters were motivated primarily by economic factors—the famine that resulted from the Anglo-Italian blockade of the Western Desert from November 1915 was seen as pushing many towards fighting in a desperate bid for survival. Simultaneously, British accounts believed that the order lacked support among the local population who lived under Sanussiyya occupation because of their economic policy of requisitioning, itself a response to the blockade. Others believed that Ottoman and German intrigues, framed by the Ottoman call to *jihad* in November 1914, and resultant pressure from the Ottomans on the Sanussiyya to implement this call, were chiefly responsible for the attack. This viewpoint gave little agency to the order itself. It is generally agreed that the decision to attack Egypt by Ahmed al-Senussi, the order's leader, was heavily influenced by efforts directed from Istanbul and Berlin, but this was only part of the picture.[8] Finally, there were diverse British views around the broader threat of the Sanussiyya to British rule in Egypt and the wider war effort. These oscillated between those who thought that the order's influence in the Egyptian Western Desert and oasis towns could pose a huge threat, and those who saw the order as weak, forming only a minor and temporary danger. What British observers and participants did not discern, however, were the deeper factors motivating the order's *jihad*. Ahmed al-Senussi accepted the religious obligations of the 1914 Ottoman *jihad* proclamation within a specific context.[9] This acceptance was connected to the nature of the Sanussiyya as an organised reformist Sufi order that formed part of a wider contemporary phenomenon of Islamic revival, reform and activism, one aspect of which was a struggle for survival and resistance to European encroachment on the Muslim world. It was these impulses that collided with the radically changed political and strategic landscape created in November 1914, when the conflict spread to the Middle East.

The Western Desert under Economic Blockade

British accounts of economic conditions in the Western Desert during this event stressed that local Bedouin were forced by circumstances into the *jihad*. Sub-Lieutenant Marsh, a prisoner of the Sanussiyya for most of 1916 after his ship the SS *Tara* was torpedoed off the Libyan coast, recounted in his memoir that owing to Sanussiyya mobilisation, crops had not been planted, so the population became reliant on food imports. However, after the Sanussiyya attack the British and Italian navies instituted a blockade of the coast, along with a similar effort by the British along the western frontier.[10] The effect of the blockade was seen in stark relief by soldier Stanley George. In a letter to his mother he described 'starving' Bedouin families on his way back to Alexandria from Sollum, who entered their empty camps 'from all sides looking like scraggy moulting birds of prey ... and pick up all the half-eaten tins of bully beef and fragments of biscuits on the sand ... I do not know if these desert people joined willingly with the Sanussiyya to fight against us'.[11] In his diary, Sergeant J. M. Thomas wrote that Bedouin came in from the desert to surrender 'by the score' and were 'starving' when they did so.[12] The harsh economic reality of the war situation had rendered many Bedouin unenthusiastic adherents to the Sanussiyya *jihad*. Such measures, however, also had unintended effects. Joining the Sanussiyya was one way to provide their families with food due to the Anglo-Italian economic blockade. Moreover, it was probably accurate that Bedouin joined the Sanussiyya because they 'entertained a great veneration' for the order and believed in the struggle against the British, both of which negated material concerns such as food.[13] Ultimately, though, the food shortages caused by the Allies and Sanussiyya alike were unlikely to facilitate the order's cause among the local population.

Sanussiyya requisitioning from people living in the Western Desert's Egyptian oasis towns in 1916–17 bred a negative reaction to the order. The British were welcomed when they recaptured Siwa oasis, the last centre occupied by the Sanussiyya, in March 1917. Captain Butt, party to the entry of British forces into Siwa, wrote how 'everyone seemed to be happy that the Senussi had left, for their ways of obtaining shelter and supplies had been becoming too high handed'.[14] Captain C. H. Williams's effervescent description of the response of Siwa's population to the British—'full of gratitude for their deliverance from the tyranny of the militant Senoussi'—was apparently due to the actions of Sanussiyya fighters 'who commandeered all they wanted without the slightest scruples' whereas the British 'paid for everything most generously'.[15] The order's reputation and standing, and their extended tenure as masters of Siwa, no doubt meant they were supported by the local population, but their recourse to requisitioning probably eroded Siwan sympathy for the order's *jihad* against the British. By March 1917, the British had ejected the order from the oases of the Western Desert. The Sanussiyya presence in Siwa was a tiny remnant of the 3,000-strong force that entered the fight in November 1915.

Post-war British reports painted a devastating picture of the area affected by the Sanussiyya's *jihad* that shed further light on the ambivalence of the local population to the order's cause. One report highlighted that Tripolitania and Fezzan's population had plummeted from 650,000 to 250,000 as a result of successive conflicts between the Sanussiyya and France, Italy and then Britain. While not mentioned in the report, the conflicts also took a huge toll on human life in Cyrenaica. It went on to detail the impact of famine, emigration and the widespread destruction of property such as houses and palm gardens and herds, all of which had a hugely detrimental impact on living standards.[16] If the report is remotely accurate, it is unsurprising why most did not take up the call of *jihad*—they were too busy trying to survive the ravages of war. British awareness of this devastation contributed to an economic explanation as to why some joined the *jihad*, being forced through adverse circumstances, and why local populations welcomed the end of Sanussiyya rule, as Sanussiyya requisitioning left people hungry. This British reading of the attack ran parallel to another view, that it was part of a concerted Ottoman and German plan to attack Egypt at its weakest defensive point.

The *Jihad* as a 'Turco-German Plot'

Many British officials believed the *jihad* was largely the result of pressures exerted on the order by the Germans and Ottomans. Sudan's Governor General, Sir Reginald Wingate, corresponded extensively with Sir Gilbert Clayton, head of British intelligence in Cairo, about the Sanussiyya. In December 1914, Wingate felt sure that Enver Pasha, the Ottoman war minister, and other Ottoman officials had 'exercised a pernicious influence' on Ahmed al-Senussi's thinking, but recognised that the order's founder had been strongly anti-Ottoman, a stance reflected in his guidance to followers. Consequently, Wingate believed that Ahmed would only support the Ottomans against the British until he was 'quite certain that the Turks have had some notable successes'.[17] By March 1915, Clayton was convinced that 'German and Turkish intrigues' meant that 'no effort has been, or is being, spared to draw the Senussi into a *Jehad*'.[18] He went on to report that since the Ottomans entered the war 'strenuous efforts have been made by the Pan-Islamic party in Constantinople to induce [Ahmed al-Senussi] to proclaim a *Jehad* against England and attack Egypt'.[19] Clayton had misinterpreted Ottoman overtures to the Sanussiyya being led by a pan-Islamic faction. Instead, it was a resolutely pragmatic strategic policy, a calculation that the Ottoman attempt to seize the Suez Canal would be aided if the British were under pressure in the Western Desert from the Sanussiyya.

British intelligence reports received by Clayton reinforced his suspicions that Ottoman and German agents were active among the Sanussiyya. According to one report, Nuri, Enver Pasha's brother, along with other Ottoman officers, were in Cyrenaica, with 'probably one or two Germans', and that their 'powerful influences' were being used to persuade the Ahmed al-Senussi to attack Egypt.[20] Significantly, Clayton denied Ahmed any independence of thought or action, portraying the order's leader as out of his depth: 'he may find the situation getting beyond his control'.[21] Wingate, however, initially struck a more cautious note, believing Ahmed to be 'sitting on the fence' and that he had a 'natural aversion' to joining the Ottomans.[22] Abruptly, though, this viewpoint changed, for reasons that remain unclear. Ahmed, with 'evil Turkish spirits' at his side, was being induced to 'stir up troubles' among tribes in the Egyptian Western Desert, according to Wingate.[23] This reflected a broader, more unfounded concern that Sanussiyya involvement with the Ottomans and Germans was merely one part of a wider, connected plot by Britain's enemies 'in all parts of North Africa'.[24] In this fraught period where reliable information was a priceless—and scarce—commodity, British officials saw their enemies as a monolithic entity, stirring the forces of militant Islam against them. Clayton reported to Wingate that recently intercepted letters addressed to Muslim notables and authored by Ahmed were 'virtually a call to Jehad and Senussi describes himself as the representative of the *Khalifa* in North Africa ... a complete confirmation of our suspicions ... continually pushed by Nuri and his gang'.[25] One of these letters, rather roughly translated by British intelligence, stated:

> According to our legal books, if an enemy to the faith occupied a Moslem land and camped in its neighbourhood with the object of entering it, the *Jehad* is an incumbent duty on the native Moslems of that land ... If the natives of that land were unable alone to drive out the enemy the natives of the Moslem country adjacent to them should join in the Jehad—as all Moslems are one against non-Moslems.[26]

Despite this supposedly cast iron evidence, Wingate's interpretation of what was happening in the Sanussiyya camp changed again. He now believed that Ahmed was 'waiting to see which side is the stronger and when he is assured on the point he will come down on that side'.[27] This went somewhat against the thrust of British intelligence reports that now mostly focused on the movements of Ottoman and German officers among the Sanussiyya, thereby reinforcing British assertions that Sanussiyya policy was now directed towards serving the military strategies of the Central Powers.[28]

Once the Sanussiyya attacked Egypt, British officials continually stressed that Ottoman and German machinations were its root cause, with the order characterised as a puppet being pulled by strings in Istanbul and Berlin. Orders by General Maxwell, the officer commanding the counter-offensive, stated that the first attack by Sanussiyya fighters was undertaken without the 'knowledge and consent' of Ahmed; Sanussiyya fighters had 'mutinied at the instigation of certain Turks and Germans attached to his staff'.[29] In a letter to Ahmed, Maxwell told him that 'the influence[s] at work, headed by Nuri Bey and his German friends, appear to be working, in regard to your person'.[30] Ahmed's reply, that his only intention was 'guarding the honour of Islam ... and our influence amongst our people', showed his interpretation of the attack in a traditional religious manner, a *jihad* in defence of Islam.[31] Maxwell chose to ignore this justification, and responded that papers brought to him 'clearly prove you have allowed yourself to be influenced by Nuri Bey and his German friends'.[32] This was supported by other more dubious evidence, such as intercepted incendiary pamphlets 'evidently composed in Constantinople' exhorting Sanussiyya followers to *jihad* against Egypt, and an interrogation of a Sanussiyya messenger that resulted in the information that Ahmed 'half willingly lent himself to the Turkish plans ... his Bedouins were well bribed'.[33] These all lent credence to an increasingly rigid official view of the Sanussiyya offensive.

After the order was defeated, such understandings persisted. Negotiations were opened with Ahmed's brother Idris, who had assumed temporal leadership of the order, and a *Who's Who* of the Sanussiyya was issued to British soldiers and officials involved in the talks. Ahmed's entry described how he was 'deeply influenced by Enver Pasha during the Turco-Italian war' and 'yielded to Turco-German pressure and attacked Egypt'.[34] Such an interpretation was underlined by Ahmed's entry next to Nuri Pasha, who was, according to the pamphlet, 'constantly pushing to force Ahmed into hostilities before the former considered the time had come'.[35] General Murray, Maxwell's successor as commander in the Western Desert, echoed his predecessor's views when he reported that the attack was due to the 'vanity and cupidity of Sayed Ahmed, fostered by German and Turkish intrigue'.[36] The attack's timing during the First World War meant the British framed their understanding of this *jihad* within the parameters of this conflict, specifically within the contours of the efforts by the Ottomans and Germans to foment uprisings among Muslim populations against the Allied powers.

Broader Understandings of the Sanussiyya

The Sanussiyya's position as a reformist Sufi order that had been involved in a decades-long militant reaction to European imperialism, couched in traditional religious terms of *jihad*, means the 1915 attack should also be understood in its wider religious and ideological context, not just as a sideshow of the First World War in the Middle East. The order did not operate in a vacuum in the remote vastness of the Sahara, but was connected to the Muslim world spiritually, intellectually and commercially. It was part of a cluster of Sufi orders that had their origins in Arabia, and was an important actor in the reform and revival of the Islamic faith that spread throughout the Muslim world from the early 19th century.[37] The sophisticated organisation of the Sanussiyya polity and the military use of their *zawaya* (lodges that also served as religious, administrative and commercial centres) meant the order was well positioned to engage in defensive activism against European imperialism.[38] First the order unsuccessfully fought the French, who pushed the Sanussiyya out of central Sahara in the 1900s. Then the order engaged in a bitter struggle against the Italians who invaded the Libyan coast in October 1911. After Italy defeated Ottoman forces in Libya in 1912, the Sanussiyya, who had cooperated with the Ottomans during the conflict, continued to resist the Italian intruders. Ahmed al-Senussi viewed both struggles in strictly religious terms—as a *jihad*.[39] This resistance reflects a broader trend of Muslim leaders endowed with a religious aura and some tribal support who tried to challenge European imperialism, such as Abd al-Qadir against the French in Algeria from 1832 to 1847.[40] Despite their knowledge of the nature and history of the order, the British did not situate the *jihad* in this broader context when the Sanussiyya attacked Egypt in 1915.

British understandings of the potential and actual threat of a Sanussiyya *jihad* displayed a variety of responses to the order. These ranged from fear and apprehension to contempt, all of which were amplified by the pressures and exigencies of war, given Egypt's status as a 'front-line state' against the Ottomans and its role as a crucial supply base for the imperial war effort. Throughout 1915, British officials in London and Cairo were concerned that the order's influence on Britain's Muslim subjects in Egypt and further afield might shake the edifice of imperial rule and that this would hamper the struggle against the Central Powers. For example, Sir Henry McMahon, the British High Commissioner in Cairo, wrote to Foreign Secretary Sir Edward Grey in May 1915, arguing that 'it must be remembered that hostilities undertaken against [the Sanussiyya] by Great Britain would probably have far reaching effects on Moslem feeling, not only in Egypt and the Sudan but Arabia and possibly even in India'.[41] In Sudan, Wingate thought on similar lines: 'it is rather the politico-religious effect than the force of arms for which we must be specifically watchful'.[42] The possibility of Egypt being destabilised by the Sanussiyya because of the order's religious influence in Western Egypt was echoed by Maxwell:

> The possibility of internal disturbances was a source of greater anxiety than the external danger. This unrest was especially evident amongst the Arab population inhabiting the western edge of the cultivation-amounting in the Behera Province alone to over 120,000. The religious influence of the Senussi is great amongst these people, and their natural sympathies are inclined towards their brethren in the Western Desert.[43]

The British saw the Sanussiyya as an enemy without, capable of mobilising the potential enemy within. This ultimately stemmed from a lack of knowledge of the order's intentions towards Britain, but was exacerbated by security anxieties surrounding the Egyptian protectorate's importance to Britain during the war. From 1915, Egypt became a supply base for the British Empire's military deployments in the Dardanelles, and for later campaigns in Salonica and Palestine. The Dardanelles campaign caused British officials to worry about the Sanussiyya. Wingate wrote that due to the situation in the Dardanelles, the British were 'naturally most anxious to keep the peace with the Senussi' lest an attack by the order draw troops away from a front that was initially seen as potentially able to deliver a fatal blow to the Ottoman war effort.[44] As mentioned before, defending the Suez Canal against Ottoman attack was also seen as an important priority, given its role in connecting Britain to its territories around the Indian Ocean littoral. Any attack by the Sanussiyya from the Western Desert, then, was seen as potentially hugely disruptive to the vital function Egypt had come to play in the global war effort.

Such military and political anxieties were tempered, however, with less fearful assessments of the order's power and its intentions. Clayton believed that 'the Senussi menace is not of great importance from a military point of view'.[45] An Admiralty intelligence report from May 1915 argued that representations of the Sanussiyya as a 'world danger' were exaggerated. The order's followers were 'too much dispersed to be more than a local temporary danger' and it was doubtful 'if the strong religious feelings of the Senussi's adherents could ever weld so many different races into one whole'. Consequently, the assessment concluded that there was no 'danger from the Senussi and his followers either to Egypt or to white civilisation'.[46] While this report was wrong in its assessment of the possibility of an attack on Egypt, it was largely accurate in its assertion that the order's *jihad* against Egypt ultimately posed a fleeting danger to the wider war effort and the security of British imperial rule in Egypt. After initial setbacks when the conflict began in November 1915, the British defeated the Sanussiyya in every engagement. This bred a dismissive attitude towards the order from some in the British army. For example, Murray wrote of his 'supreme contempt' for the Sanussiyya leaders, who had 'not the remotest chance of any serious invasion of the Nile Valley, or indeed of raids worthy of that name'.[47] Nevertheless, in the final analysis, British views were more ambivalent. Despite the attack's failure, subsequent mopping-up operations and the opening of negotiations with Idris, Maxwell struck a more wary and cautious note: 'There is a danger of Idris ... utilising the present situation in order to re-organise and strengthen the Senussi forces for possible hostile action ... at some future date'.[48] This was not a solely British preoccupation—French intelligence echoed their British allies. The Allies thought it imprudent to dismiss totally the military threat posed by the order: 'Although the dream of a great Sanussiyya kingdom appears to be dissolving into anarchy it would be premature to conclude that all danger has vanished'.[49]

Conclusion

Britain's defeat of the Sanussiyya led to a decline in the order's influence in the oases of the Egyptian Western Desert. If the Ottomans, and to a lesser extent the Germans, had not applied pressure on the Sanussiyya to attack Egypt, the order would probably not have done so independently, and would have continued to focus on its ongoing *jihad* against the Italians. Britain's campaign against the Sanussiyya never came near the titanic scale of the fighting elsewhere in the region during the war, such as the campaigns in Palestine, Mesopotamia and in the Caucasus. The struggle in the Western Desert, however, was significant for its admixture of Sufi resistance to European imperialism, colonial 'pacification', and asymmetrical warfare practised by the Sanussiyya and a small coterie of Ottoman and German officers. This article has shed new light on the Sanussiyya *jihad* through analysing the variety of understandings British officials and soldiers had towards this threat from the desert. In doing so, it has underscored the fact that there remain numerous areas of the First World War's military and non-military dimensions outside Europe that demand further scholarly attention. Through their attack on Egypt, the Sanussiyya order became caught up in a global conflict that involved a hugely diverse range of actors—their followers, the nomadic and sedentary populations of the Western Desert, soldiers drawn from across the British Empire, and British officials responsible for the region's imperial security. Despite the military and intelligence demands of this conflict, however, Britain's knowledge of their foe ultimately remained limited. Among the British, the Sanussiyya continually retained a mirage-like nature—assumptions and facts about the order that seemed fixed subsequently dissolved, to be replaced by newer, equally fragile fragments of information and analysis.[50]

Notes

1. Purvis (Coast Guard Administration) to Clayton, 20 November 1915, Wingate 131/6/4, Sudan Archive, University of Durham (SAD).
2. This argument was pioneered in H. Strachan (2001) *The First World War Volume I: To Arms*. Oxford: Oxford University Press, and is summarised briefly in H. Jones (2013) 'As the centenary approaches: the regeneration of First World War historiography', *The Historical Journal*, 56(3), 857–878. See also: L. Sondhaus (2011) *World War One: The Global Revolution*. Cambridge: Cambridge University Press; J. Winter (Ed.) (2014) *Cambridge History of the First World War, Volume I: The Global War*. Cambridge: Cambridge University Press.
3. Pack, J. (forthcoming, 2017) *Britain's Informal Empire in Libya? The Anglo-Sanussi Relationship (1882–1969)*, London: Hurst and Co. and Pack, J. (2011) *British State-Building in Cyrenaica during the War Years (1941–1945)*, MSt. Thesis, University of Oxford, stress, however, that cordial relations between the British and the Sanussiyya were maintained during this conflict.
4. R. Simon (1987) *Libya between Ottomanism and Nationalism: The Ottoman Involvement in Libya during the War with Italy (1911–1919)*. Berlin: K. Schwarz. pp. 161–167, 259–278.
5. E. E. Evans-Pritchard (1949) *The Sanusi of Cyrenica*. Oxford: Oxford University Press, p. 130.
6. Simon (1987); A. A. Ahmida (1994) *The Making of Modern Libya*. Albany, NY: State University of New York Press; L. Anderson (1986) *State and Transformation in Libya and Tunisia, 1830–1980*. Princeton, NJ: Princeton University Press; Baldinetti, A. (2010) *The Origins of the Libyan Nation: Colonial Legacy, Exile and the Emergence of a New Nation-State*. Oxford: Routledge; Gazzini C.A. (2004) *Jihad in Exile: Ahmad al-Sharif al-Sanusi, 1918–1933*, MA thesis, Princeton University; Evans-Pritchard (1949); N. A. Ziadeh (1958) *Sanusiyah; A Study of a Revivalist Movement in Islam*. Leiden: Leiden University Press; C. C. Stewart (1981) 'Islam', *Cambridge History of Africa*, Vol. 7, 1905–40. Cambridge: Cambridge University Press, pp. 191–223. Sanussiyya records from this period are unfortunately no longer extant (Ziadeh, 1958, p. 101).
7. D. M. McKale (1998) *War by Revolution: Germany and Great Britain in the Middle East in the Era of World War I*. Kent, OH: Ohio University Press; McGuirk, R. (2007) *The Sanusi's Little War*. London: Arabian Publishing; Simon (1987); Strachan (2001).
8. Evans-Pritchard (1949); McKale (1998); Simon (1987); Strachan (2001); Ziadeh (1958).
9. Ambassador in Rome to Foreign Office, London, 10/3/15, FO/371/2372, The National Archives, London (TNA).
10. Memoirs of Sub-Lieutenant A. Marsh, RNR, p. 6, 97/31/1, Imperial War Museum, London (IWM).
11. Stanley George (soldier with 1st Dorset Yeomanry, Western Frontier Field Force) to his mother, Spring 1916, 97/26/1, IWM.
12. Sergeant J. M. Thomas (Welsh Regiment), diary entry 4/5/16, London, Imperial War Museum, 88/56/1, p. 2.
13. *The Sanussiyya*, by the Intelligence Division of the Admiralty War Staff, 26 May 1915, IOR/L/PS/20/G89, p. 71, India Office Records, Oriental and India Office Collections, British Library, London (OIOC).
14. M. T. Butt and A. R. Cury (1936) *Mersa Matruh: How to See It, including Siwa and the Western Desert*. Cairo: World-wide Publications, pp. 48–49.
15. Captain C. H. Williams (Pembroke Yeomanry), Desert Memories (1920), 87/22/1, p. 15, IWM.
16. *Report on Tripolitania and Fezzan*, June 1920, FO/371/3806, TNA.
17. Wingate to Clayton, 12 December 1914, Clayton 469/7/74, and Wingate to Clayton, 17 December 1914, Clayton 469/7/76, SAD. See also M. W. Daly (2007) *Darfur's Sorrow*. Cambridge: Cambridge University Press.
18. Intelligence Department, War Office, Cairo, by Clayton, 16 March 1915, Wingate 131/4/11, SAD.
19. Clayton to Wingate, 26 April 1915, Wingate 131/4/31, SAD.
20. Clayton to Wingate, 11 May 1915, Wingate 131/4/34, SAD.
21. Clayton to Wingate, 11 May 1915, Wingate 131/4/36, SAD.
22. Wingate to Clayton, 11 May 1915, Clayton 469/9/19, SAD.
23. Wingate to Fitzgerald, 28 July 1915, Wingate 131/5/4, SAD.
24. Wingate to Clayton, 29 July 1915, Wingate 131/5/8, SAD.
25. Clayton to Wingate, 20 September 1915, Wingate 131/5/15-17, SAD.
26. Ahmed al-Sanussiyya to notables of Derna, not dated, translation of papers found in house of Omar Pasha Mansur, forwarded to Wingate 9 December 1915, Wingate 131/6/73-74, SAD.

27. Wingate to Clayton, 22 November 1915, Clayton 469/10/22, SAD.
28. Intelligence Reports, 12 December 1914, FO 371/1971, 16 November 1915, FO 371/2356, and 15 December 1915, 23 December 1915, 3 January 1916, 5 March 1916, all in FO 371/2668, TNA.
29. Orders by General Maxwell, Commander-in-Chief Egypt, Cairo, 27 November 1915, Wingate 131/6/41, SAD.
30. Maxwell to Ahmed al-Sanussiyya, 3 December 1915, Wingate 131/6/47-48, SAD.
31. Ahmed al-Sanussiyya to Maxwell, 4 December 1915, Wingate 131/6/50, SAD.
32. Maxwell to Ahmed al-Sanussiyya, 3 January 1916, Wingate 131/7/5, SAD.
33. Clayton to Wingate, 12 December 1915, Wingate 131/6/84, SAD; 'Notes on a conversation with Mohamed Musa (a Senussi messenger)', not dated, Wingate 131/8/24, SAD.
34. *Senussi Who's Who*, not dated, Wingate 131/10/4, SAD.
35. Ibid.
36. Note on situation on the Western Frontier, by Major-General commanding the Western Frontier Force, 28 March 1916, Wingate 131/8/86, SAD.
37. See E. Sirreyeh (1999) *Sufis and Anti-Sufis*. Richmond: Curzon.
38. Evans-Pritchard (1949, pp. 79, 99); Ziadeh (1958, p. 119).
39. HM Ambassador in Rome to Foreign Office, 10 March 1915, FO 371/2372, TNA.
40. A concise treatment of this phenomenon is in F. Robinson (1996) *The Cambridge Illustrated History of the Islamic World*. Cambridge: Cambridge University Press, pp. 90–124.
41. McMahon to Grey, 6 May 1915, FO 371/2353/61642, TNA. This text appears to have been copied directly from a memo by Clayton, 13 April 1915, Wingate 131/4/17-18, SAD.
42. Wingate to Clayton, 9/10/15, Clayton 469/11/10, SAD. Hogarth, a scholar of the Middle East who was briefly head of the Arab Bureau in Cairo which played a seminal role in the 1916–18 Arab Revolt, concurred: "the prospect of retaliatory aggression in Sanussism [sic] is probably religious and social rather than political", Mss. Draft, *Historical Tribes of Cyrenica*, undated, GB165-0147 Hogarth, Middle East Centre Archives, St. Anthony's College, University of Oxford.
43. Lieu.-Gen. Sir John Maxwell (1916) *Operations on the Western Front [of Egypt] to 31st January 1916*, London Gazette, 3rd supplement, 21 June.
44. Clayton to Wingate, 25 August 1915, Wingate 131/5/22, SAD.
45. Memo by Clayton, 13 April 1915, Wingate 131/4/17-18, SAD.
46. *The Senussi*, by the Intelligence Division of the Admiralty War Staff, 26 May 1915, IOR/L/PS/20/G89, p. 6, Oriental and India Office Collections, British Library, London.
47. Note on situation on the Western Frontier, by Major-General commanding the Western Frontier Force, 28 March 1916, Wingate 131/8/86, SAD.
48. Murray, General Officer Commanding Egypt to High Commissioner, 6 October 1916, Wingate 131/12/18, SAD.
49. *Sanussiyya in Tripoli*, memo by French Intelligence in Tunis, 3 April 1916, Wingate 131/9/15, SAD.
50. Pack, J. (forthcoming, 2017) *Britain's Informal Empire in Libya? The Anglo-Sanussi Relationship (1882–1969)*, London: Hurst and Co. and Pack, J. (2011) *British State-Building in Cyrenaica during the War Years (1941–1945)*, MSt. Thesis, University of Oxford, hold a different interpretation to this assessment.

Marching to the Beat of an Imperial Drum: Contextualising Australia's Military Effort During the First World War

RHYS CRAWLEY

When war erupted in 1914, Britain embarked on its prewar plans of mobilising resources from its vast Empire, and created an imperial coalition which fought within a wider coalition with France, Russia and, later, the United States of America. This article examines the limited role performed by Australian naval and military forces within this wider imperial effort and assesses the extent to which Australian forces relied on British command, technology, and logistic support. It challenges common assumptions about Australia's wartime performance, including the degree to which Australian forces and commanders contributed to tactical innovation and wider planning and operational thought.

> The chronicler of the future will provide many thrilling pages of history—magnificent material for the moulding of the youthful Australian character.[1]

AUSTRALIA AND ITS MILITARY FORCES had been at war for more than two-and-a-half years when Senator George Pearce, Minister for Defence, penned the above in March 1917. During that time, ships of the Royal Australian Navy (RAN) had served around the globe as an integrated component of a British imperial navy, and Australian combat units, working as part of a British imperial army, had sustained substantial casualties—and, in the process, gained considerable fighting experience—at Gallipoli, on the Western Front, and in the Middle East. As Pearce wrote, Australian divisions on the Western Front, along with British and French formations, were cautiously pursuing the Germans as they retired, destroying everything in their path, to the newly created fortified positions known as the Hindenburg Line.[2] With newspaper headlines such as 'Enemy Still Retiring … British Occupy Sixty Villages' and 'British and French Advance', Pearce, like everyone else, would have been well aware of the wider imperial and Allied context to Australia's contribution to the war.[3]

Just as he could not foresee the terrible casualties that would be incurred over the next twelve months, or the successes that would follow as the Germans were defeated in 1918, Pearce could not predict how the 'chronicler of the future', whether politicians, generals, journalists, or historians, would 'mould' the history

---

[1] G. F. Pearce, 'Foreword: What Anzac Means', in *The All-Australian Memorial: History, Heroes and Helpers*, ed. H. B. Manderson (Melbourne: British-Australasian Publishing Service, 1917), 5.
[2] Peter Pedersen, *The ANZACS: Gallipoli to the Western Front* (Melbourne: Viking, 2007), 184–97.
[3] 'Enemy Still Retiring; 80 Miles Front Abandoned; Peronne, Nesle, and Chaulnes Fall; British Occupy Sixty Villages', *The Sydney Morning Herald*, 20 March 1917, 7; 'West Front; Cavalry in Action; British and French Advance', *The Argus*, 30 March 1917, 7.

of Australia's military effort during the First World War. He could, however, influence how the Australian effort was remembered, and he did so, perhaps unintentionally, by lending his name to publications like *The All-Australian Memorial*. Described by its editor as the 'Golden Book of the Anzacs', this 1917 publication was proudly patriotic and inward looking. The book, the editor proclaimed, 'is wholly Australian—contents, compilation and craftsmanship'.[4]

Fortunately, military historiography of the war has evolved from the 'wholly Australian' message espoused by publications like *The All-Australian Memorial*. Books such as Trevor Wilson's 1986 *The Myriad Faces of War*, and his subsequent publications with Robin Prior, have explained why the First World War unfolded as it did, and reminded readers that it was Britain, not Australia, that carried the burden of the imperial war effort in every measurable way: manpower, industrial output, resources, economics, casualties, command responsibility, and strategic direction.[5] Aspects of these themes were built upon by historians like Tim Travers, Gary Sheffield, and Dan Todman who further tested and developed them in order to both deconstruct mythology and understand what it was that led to Allied victory in 1918.[6] In addition to an increasing understanding of the complexities and the intricacies of the campaigns in which Allied formations fought, historians including Elizabeth Greenhalgh and William Philpott have emphasised the centrality of France to the outcome of the First World War, while Hew Strachan, John Morrow, Jr, and Michael Neiberg remind their readers that it was a world war, fought across the globe.[7]

This literature, while not always in agreement, is so thorough, based as it is on extensive archival research, that there is now general consensus 'that Australia played only a relatively small part in this global conflict'.[8] As the British military historian Stephen Badsey has noted, in any serious literature, Australia's war effort, military or otherwise, is always discussed in the wider

---

[4] H. B. Manderson, 'Editor's Preface', in *The All-Australian Memorial*, 9.
[5] Trevor Wilson, *The Myriad Faces of War: Britain and the Great War, 1914–1918* (Cambridge: Polity Press, 1986); Robin Prior and Trevor Wilson, *Command on the Western Front: The Military Career of Sir Henry Rawlinson, 1914–1918* (Barnsley: Pen & Sword Military Classics, 2004); Robin Prior and Trevor Wilson, *The Somme* (Sydney: University of New South Wales Press, 2006).
[6] Tim Travers, *How the War Was Won: Command and Technology in the British Army on the Western Front, 1917–1918* (Barnsley: Pen & Sword Military Classics, 2005); Tim Travers, *The Killing Ground: The British Army, the Western Front and the Emergence of Modern Warfare, 1900–1918* (London: Allen & Unwin, 1987); Gary Sheffield, *Forgotten Victory: The First World War: Myths and Realities* (London: Review, 2002); Dan Todman, *The Great War: Myth and Memory* (London: Hambledon Continuum, 2005).
[7] Elizabeth Greenhalgh, *Victory through Coalition: Britain and France during the First World War* (Cambridge: Cambridge University Press, 2005); Elizabeth Greenhalgh, *Foch in Command: The Forging of a First World War General* (Cambridge: Cambridge University Press, 2011); William Philpott, *Bloody Victory: The Sacrifice on the Somme* (London: Abacus, 2010); Hew Strachan, *The First World War* (London: Simon & Schuster, 2003); John H. Morrow, Jr, *The Great War: An Imperial History* (New York: Routledge, 2004); Michael S. Neiberg, *Fighting the Great War: A Global History* (Cambridge, MA: Harvard University Press, 2005).
[8] David Horner, *Australia's Military History for Dummies* (Brisbane: Wiley Publishing, 2010), 72. Despite the questions one may have over the quality of this series, this book is an excellent survey of Australian military history.

context of 'the British imperial experience'.[9] The importance of contextualising Australia's military effort has also made its way into the service history departments, most notably the Australian Army History Unit and Sea Power Centre–Australia, and the Australian War Memorial, all of which have hosted scholarly conferences on the First World War and disseminated their results in published conference proceedings.[10]

Frustratingly, public discourse within Australia has not evolved in line with these developments in the international scholarly literature. Popular histories, with little basis in archival research or the wider literature, continue to flood the bookshelves with accounts that fail to place their battles within a broader context of who was fighting on Australia's left and right.[11] It is not uncommon for a reader of these accounts to be left with the impression that Australia did all the fighting. Moreover, the major Anzac Day ceremonies propagate this inaccuracy by failing to look beyond Australia's contribution. In her 2013 speech at Townsville, in which the Prime Minister spoke of her gratitude for Australian service personnel, Julia Gillard, for instance, did not mention any other country.[12] Similarly, Prime Minister Tony Abbott's 2014 address in Canberra, which refreshingly spoke of the need to place Gallipoli within the broader context of operations on the Western Front, neglected to mention the important role performed by Australia's allies.[13] Abbott's choice to not pay tribute to British forces in the presence of the Duke and Duchess of Cambridge is less surprising than Foreign Minister Julie Bishop's failure to mention France, the country in which she was speaking, beyond stating that Australian troops saved Villers-Bretonneux 'in the defence of freedom'.[14]

This article examines the role undertaken by Australian naval and military forces during the First World War, contextualising that story as part of a wider, imperial effort. In so doing, it challenges some of the common assumptions about Australia's wartime performance including the level to which Australia contributed to tactical innovation; and the degree to which Australian commanders, particularly General Sir John Monash, contributed to wider planning and operational thought. It also assesses the extent to which Australian forces relied

---

[9] Stephen Badsey, 'Ninety Years on: Recent and Changing Views on the Military History of the First World War', in *1918 Year of Victory: The End of the Great War and the Shaping of History*, ed. Ashley Ekins (Auckland: Exisle Publishing, 2010), 248.
[10] The Army History Unit conference proceedings are available online. www.army.gov.au/Our-history/Army-History-Unit/Chief-of-Army-History-Conference (accessed 21 May 2014).
[11] For example, see Simon Cameron, *Lonesome Pine: The Bloody Ridge* (Sydney: Big Sky Publishing, 2013).
[12] Julia Gillard, 'Anzac Day Address', Townsville, 25 April 2013. http://pmtranscripts.dpmc.gov.au/browse.php?did=19272 (accessed 20 May 2014).
[13] The exception was his acknowledgement of the Japanese battlecruiser, *Ibuki*, which escorted the first convoy from Albany. Tony Abbott, 'Address to the Anzac Day National Ceremony, Canberra', 25 April 2014. www.pm.gov.au/media/2014-04-25/address-anzac-day-national-ceremony-canberra (accessed 21 May 2014).
[14] Julie Bishop, 'Anzac Day Dawn Service at Villers-Bretonneux', 25 April 2014. http://juliebishop.com.au/anzac-day-dawn-service-villers-bretonneux/ (accessed 21 May 2014).

on British command, technology, and logistic support, and concludes that the Australian forces made a necessarily limited contribution to victory in 1918.

An imperial commitment

Australia's reaction to the impending war in Europe was imperial from the outset. Even before the formal declaration of war, Australia's Prime Minister, Joseph Cook, had committed wholeheartedly to the security of the Empire, declaring that 'all our resources are in the Empire and for the Empire, and for the security and preservation of the Empire'.[15] Similarly, Andrew Fisher, leader of the Federal Labor Party, famously offered to defend the Empire 'to our last man and our last shilling'.[16] Such signs of loyalty did not come out of the blue; nor did they mean that Australia was entirely subservient to the 'Mother Country'. As Neville Meaney has argued, Australian politicians had previously identified a degree of Australian self-interest in their strategic planning in the early twentieth century. Working within the concept of 'Greater Britain', Australia and its leaders were both nationalists and imperialists, where Australian interests took precedence over British interests.[17]

In the years prior to the First World War this attitude had been ongoing and bipartisan. Following the 1909 Imperial Conference, Prime Minister Alfred Deakin agreed to the formation of an Australian 'fleet unit' to operate as part of an 'Imperial Pacific Fleet'.[18] With little trust in the Anglo-Japanese alliance of 1902, Deakin realised that such a move, which modernised and strengthened the imperial fleet, was in Australia's interests.[19] Similarly, he agreed in principle to bring Australia's military organisation into unity with Britain and the other Dominions, on the proviso that Australia retained control of its own forces.[20] Andrew Fisher reiterated the desire for the sovereignty of Australia's naval and military forces at the 1911 Imperial Conference—an attitude which obviously frustrated Britain's attempts to get agreement on the role of expeditionary forces and the importance of 'Imperial Unity'.[21] Nonetheless, as Keith Jeffery has concluded, the 1911 conference 'marked an especially significant stage in the development of empire-wide thinking about and planning for imperial

---

[15] Neville Meaney, 'The Problem of "Greater Britain" and Australia's Strategic Crisis 1905–1914', in *1911: Preliminary Moves*, eds Peter Dennis and Jeffrey Grey (Canberra: Big Sky Publishing, 2011), 85.
[16] Ibid.
[17] Ibid., 56–89.
[18] Keith Jeffery, 'The Imperial Conference, the Committee of Imperial Defence and the Continental Commitment', in *1911: Preliminary Moves*, eds Dennis and Grey, 24.
[19] Meaney, 66–7.
[20] Timothy Moreman, 'Lord Kitchener, the General Staff and the Army in India, 1902–14', in *The British General Staff: Reform and Innovation c. 1890–1939*, eds David French and Brian Holden Reid (London: Frank Cass, 2002), 64; Meaney, 64.
[21] 'Prime Minister's Department: Correspondence and Papers', A1108, Volume 37, National Archives of Australia (hereafter NAA), Canberra; John Connor, 'Coronation Conversations: The Dominions and Military Planning at the 1911 Imperial Conference', in *1911: Preliminary Moves*, eds Dennis and Grey, 45.

defence'.[22] The Dominions were left in no doubt of Britain's concerns about Germany, or that when war occurred (as was deemed inevitable), Britain would require assistance and support.[23]

These developments meant that in August 1914, Australia, although automatically at war, could determine the scale and nature of its effort.[24] Like India and the other Dominions—Canada, Newfoundland, New Zealand, and South Africa—Australia unhesitatingly 'rallied to the imperial war effort'.[25] The RAN was immediately placed under Admiralty control for the duration of the war.[26] Working within the restrictions of the Defence Act 1903, which excluded sending conscripts overseas, the government also began enlisting volunteers for an expeditionary force of 20,000 to be sent wherever 'desired by Home Government'.[27] The contingent's commander, Major-General William Throsby Bridges, decided to name it the Australian Imperial Force (AIF), deliberately including 'Imperial' to signify the dual nature of Australia's military effort: for the nation and the Empire.[28]

Australia's first action of the war reaffirmed the imperial nature of its commitment. Concerned about the German East Asiatic Squadron and the danger that it posed to Allied shipping, on 6 August 1914 Britain requested that Australia seize and destroy the German wireless stations used by the squadron 'as a great and urgent imperial service'.[29] A combined naval and military expeditionary force of 1,500 men was raised, equipped, and dispatched in less than two weeks.[30] The force landed near Rabaul, the capital of German New Guinea, on 11 September. 'The operation was so swift', according to David Horner, 'that it was a campaign in name only'.[31] Nonetheless, its success and similar action by the New Zealanders at Samoa removed the German wireless chain, and thereby helped secure Australia's trade routes, and protect Australia's economy.[32] The expedition to Rabaul was the only time during the war that Australia carried the full burden of effort and was responsible for its own

---

[22] Jeffery, 20.
[23] Ibid., 37–8.
[24] Connor, 'Coronation Conversations', 43.
[25] Jeffery, 39.
[26] Letter, M. L. Shepherd, Secretary, Prime Minister's Department, to Official Secretary to the Governor-General, 11 August 1914, MP1049/1, 1914/0299, NAA, Melbourne.
[27] Defence Act 1903, s. 49; Cable, Governor-General to Secretary of State for the Colonies, 3 August 1914, MP1049/1, 1914/0276, NAA, Melbourne.
[28] Peter Dennis, Jeffrey Grey, Ewan Morris, Robin Prior and Jean Bou, *The Oxford Companion to Australian Military History*, 2nd edn (Melbourne: Oxford University Press, 2008), 62.
[29] C. E. W. Bean, *Anzac to Amiens: A Shorter History of the Australian Fighting Services in the First World War* (Canberra: Australian War Memorial, 1968), 31.
[30] Ross Mallett, 'The Preparation and Deployment of the Australian Naval and Military Expeditionary Force', in *Battles Near and Far: A Century of Overseas Deployment*, eds Peter Dennis and Jeffrey Grey (Canberra: Army History Unit, 2005), 24.
[31] David Horner, 'The Evolution of Australian Higher Command Arrangements', Command paper 3/2002 (Canberra: Australian Defence College, 2005), 5.
[32] Russell Parkin, 'A Capability of First Resort: Amphibious Operations and Australian Defence Policy 1901–2001', Working Paper No. 117 (Canberra: Land Warfare Studies Centre, May 2002), 4; John Connor, 'The Capture of German New Guinea', in *Before the Anzac Dawn: A Military History of Australia to 1915*, eds Craig Stockings and John Connor (Sydney: NewSouth, 2013), 283.

logistics.[33] To place the operation in context, however, while these 1,500 men faced little resistance, millions of men were fighting across vast tracts of land in France, Belgium, Russia, the Austro-Hungarian Empire, Serbia and Africa.

The RAN at war

The role of the RAN in the First World War was undoubtedly less glamorous than the land campaigns in Gallipoli, the Western Front, and Palestine. It was also much smaller and is less well known. But as Alastair Cooper reminds us, these naval efforts were no less important.[34]

In addition to supporting the expeditionary force at Rabaul, where it suffered the loss of the submarine *AE1*, the RAN (along with Japanese and British ships) was responsible for protecting the first convoy of the AIF that left Albany on 1 November 1914. During this voyage the service scored its first victory. On 9 November HMAS *Melbourne* intercepted a 'disconnected message' indicating that the German cruiser, SMS *Emden*, was nearby. HMAS *Sydney* was sent in pursuit and, after a brief exchange of fire, defeated *Emden*.[35] The convoy continued on its journey and arrived, without incident, at Alexandria on 3 December.[36] The concerns for the safety of Australia's trade routes, however, did not ease until the Royal Navy destroyed Admiral Maximilian von Spee's squadron off the Falkland Islands on 8 December 1914. With the threat to the Pacific removed, the Admiralty recalled the RAN's largest ship, HMAS *Australia*, to 'Home Waters'. Spending most of its time escorting convoys and patrolling the North Sea, it fired only one shot in anger throughout the war. Disappointingly for its personnel, it missed out on the one major fleet action between Britain and Germany, the Battle of Jutland on 31 May and 1 June 1916, since it had been damaged in a collision with HMS *New Zealand* in April.[37]

Thereafter, confrontation with hostile ships formed a very small part of the RAN's operations.[38] Rather, its primary function was to assist the Royal Navy 'achieve and maintain naval supremacy' and control of the sea.[39] Offensively, the combined Allied fleets applied economic pressure to Germany through blockade and the capture of German merchant ships.[40] Defensively, the fleet undertook patrols in search of commerce raiders, protected trade routes, and combated the unrestricted U-boat campaign by employing a convoy system and

---

[33] Rhys Crawley, 'Sustaining Amphibious Operations in the Asia-Pacific: Logistic Lessons for Australia, 1914–2014', *Australian Defence Force Journal* 193 (March/April 2014): 31.
[34] Alastair Cooper, 'Lost at Sea: Missing out on Australia's Naval History', in *Anzac's Dirty Dozen: 12 Myths of Australian Military History*, ed. Craig Stockings (Sydney: NewSouth, 2012), 170.
[35] 'Convoy duties and the *Emden* fight', attached to memo no. 18/7871, 17 December 1918, ADM 116/1686, The National Archives, UK (hereafter TNA).
[36] David Stevens, '1914–1918: World War I', in *The Australian Centenary History of Defence*, vol. 3, *The Royal Australian Navy*, ed. David Stevens (Melbourne: Oxford University Press, 2001), 40.
[37] 'HMAS *Australia* collision with HMS *New Zealand*', MP1049/1, 1916/0133, NAA, Melbourne.
[38] Cooper, 170.
[39] David Stevens and James Goldrick, 'Victory at Sea, 1918', in *1918 Year of Victory*, ed. Ekins, 198.
[40] Ibid., 183.

conducting anti-submarine patrols. All of this was fundamental to keeping the British war economy running, and to ensuring that men and materiel could be transported to the various theatres of war.[41]

The RAN's war was therefore a 'global undertaking'.[42] Forming part of an 'Imperial Fleet', the RAN employed ships in the North Sea, Indian Ocean, Pacific, Cape, East Africa, Atlantic, West Indies, Mediterranean, Dardanelles, Sea of Marmara, Black Sea, Red Sea, China Stations, South America, North America, and Nova Scotia.[43] At its peak, the RAN numbered five thousand personnel and thirty-seven ships—most of which were commanded by Royal Navy officers—and suffered only 108 killed throughout the war.[44] Hence, although the RAN was an important component of the Imperial Fleet, its impact and influence were necessarily limited.

Apart from the sinking of the *Emden*, the most celebrated aspect of the RAN's service throughout the war was also one of its least significant. On 25 April 1915 the Australian submarine *AE2* penetrated the anti-submarine defences of the Dardanelles. Apart from harassing some enemy shipping in the Sea of Marmara, the *AE2* achieved very little before its crew was captured and the vessel scuttled on 30 April 1915. Its actions had no effect on the outcome of the Gallipoli campaign.

Gallipoli

Like the story of *AE2*, the role of the AIF at Gallipoli has often been blown out of proportion. Contrary to Australia's nationalist narrative, the Dardanelles campaign did not begin at dawn on 25 April 1915; nor was the Australian and New Zealand Army Corps (ANZAC) the first ashore. The first shots were actually fired by the Royal Navy in November 1914, and naval operations proper began in February 1915, with the combined British and French fleet—including the use of Royal Marines, who *were* the first ashore—working to destroy or silence the Ottoman coastal guns that guarded the Dardanelles and the passage to Constantinople.[45] It was only when these naval attempts failed in March 1915 that the decision to land a multinational army ashore was taken.

The Australian government was not consulted about the employment of the AIF at Gallipoli.[46] Although not diplomatically polite, this action was quite proper: the Australian government had offered the AIF for use wherever 'desired' by Britain, and it was always intended to use the AIF as a component

---

[41] Ibid., 188–9.
[42] Stevens, '1914–1918: World War I', 30.
[43] Great Britain War Office, *Statistics of the Military Effort of the British Empire during the Great War, 1914–1920* (1922; reprint, Dallington: Naval & Military Press, 1999), 770.
[44] Cooper, 170.
[45] 'Report of the committee appointed to investigate the attacks delivered on and the enemy defences of the Dardanelles Straits', series AWM 124, item 3/48, Australian War Memorial, Canberra (hereafter AWM), 22–9.
[46] Horner, 'The Evolution', 6.

of an imperial army.[47] Moreover, Bridges, as commander of the AIF, was consulted and voiced no objections. The primary objective of the 25 April landings was to secure the tip of the Gallipoli peninsula and capture the guns that had prevented the Allied navies from achieving their objectives. This task was allotted to the British 29th Division, with the 1st French Division reinforcing its right flank in the following days.[48] The ANZAC force was given the secondary objective, landing further north and cutting the Ottoman force in two, thus reducing the number of enemy troops that could be sent to defend against the main British efforts.[49] In allocating these objectives, the high command recognised that it was better to allot the main objectives to one partly experienced British division rather than two poorly trained, inexperienced and untried divisions from the antipodes.

The British carried the burden right through the Gallipoli campaign. Not only did they provide the majority of the troops and endure the majority of the casualties—thus contradicting the claim that the British had it easy and used the Australians as 'cannon fodder'— but they were responsible for the direction of the campaign.[50] Most importantly, they kept all British Empire troops fed, watered and supplied with war materials (the French were responsible for their own logistics).[51] Moreover, the naval support at Gallipoli, which was crucial to the everyday running of the campaign, was entirely a British and French endeavour. In other words, the ANZAC contingent, consisting predominantly of front-line troops and artillery, relied upon the British every day of the campaign.[52] In essence, the ANZAC forces gained experience and fought well, but they were fighting for a secondary objective in a secondary theatre.

Sinai and Palestine

Following its withdrawal from Gallipoli in December 1915, the AIF was sent to Egypt where it was reorganised before being sent to the Western Front. The majority of the light horse brigades, however, which had served without their horses at Gallipoli, were remounted and remained in the Middle East to defend Egypt and continue the war against the Ottoman Empire.[53] In March 1916 the

---

[47] Cable, Governor-General to Secretary of State for the Colonies, 3 August 1914, MP1049/1, 1914/0276, NAA, Melbourne.
[48] 'Force Order No. 1', 13 April 1915, General Headquarters, Mediterranean Expeditionary Force (hereafter GHQ MEF) war diary, AWM 4, 1/4/1 part 2, AWM.
[49] Memo, 'Instructions for GOC A& NZ Army Corps', 13 April 1915, AWM 4, 1/4/1 part 2, AWM.
[50] The 'cannon fodder' claim is one that has been made to me by many people during visits to the Gallipoli peninsula, and can still be seen in the comments sections on various internet forums. See, for instance, www.smh.com.au/federal-politics/gallipoli-was-not-churchills-great-folly-20110413-1ddzb.html (accessed 1 October 2014).
[51] Rhys Crawley, *Climax at Gallipoli: The Failure of the August Offensive* (Norman: University of Oklahoma Press, 2014).
[52] 'State of the MEF according to returns prepared by GHQ, 3rd Echelon, MEF', 31 July 1915, WO 162/69, TNA.
[53] Some light horse regiments went with the AIF to France as corps cavalry. See Jean Bou, *Light Horse: A History of Australia's Mounted Arm* (Melbourne: Cambridge University Press, 2010), 150–1.

three Australian light horse brigades were combined with the New Zealand Mounted Rifles Brigade and British horse artillery to form the Australian and New Zealand Mounted Division (more commonly known as the Anzac Mounted Division).[54] Under the command of an Australian officer, Major-General Henry (Harry) Chauvel, the Anzac Mounted Division formed part of General Sir Archibald Murray's Egyptian Expeditionary Force (EEF).[55] In addition to the light horse, Australia also committed volunteers to the Imperial Camel Corps and supplied an Australian Flying Corps squadron for work with the Royal Flying Corps.[56]

The chief concern of the EEF was to secure the Suez Canal and then expel the Ottoman armies from the Sinai peninsula.[57] From April 1916, while British engineers and the Egyptian Labour Corps constructed a railway and pipeline to transport supplies and water east into the Sinai peninsula, the Anzac Mounted Division patrolled the Sinai Desert in an attempt to stop the Ottomans from attempting another attack on the canal.[58] When a combined Ottoman, German, and Austrian force of 14,000 did attack Romani on 4 August 1916, the Anzac Mounted Division, working alongside the 52nd British Division, repulsed it.[59] The battle of Romani was 'the first large-scale victory for the light horse'.[60] It was also the last time that the Ottoman armies threatened the Suez Canal.

The allies thenceforth focused on pursuing the Ottomans and clearing them from the Sinai peninsula.[61] This task largely fell to the Desert Column, a mixed corps of two British infantry divisions, the Anzac Mounted Division, and the Imperial Camel Brigade.[62] Although the Australian light horse regiments were a key component of this corps, in October 1916 Australia and New Zealand together accounted for less than 5 per cent of the Allied troops in Egypt.[63] By January 1917 the mounted units, backed by large numbers of infantry and support troops, had defeated the Ottoman forces in the Sinai, and the Desert Column was ready to advance into Palestine.[64]

As the leading historian of the Australian light horse, Jean Bou, notes, operations in Palestine in 1917–18 were akin to those on the Western Front, with massed British artillery used to destroy Ottoman defences and suppress fire, thus opening the way for the British infantry to advance on their objectives. The

---

[54] Dennis *et al.*, *Oxford Companion*, 128.
[55] Telegram, Chief, MEDFORCE, to Chief, London, 19 March 1916, GHQ MEF war diary, AWM4, 1/4/12 part 5, AWM.
[56] 'A short history of the Desert Mounted Corps prepared by Lieut-Genl. Sir H.G. Chauvel', A1194, 33.68/15152, NAA, Canberra.
[57] Jean Bou, *Australia's Palestine Campaign* (Canberra: Army History Unit, 2010), 6.
[58] Bou, *Light Horse*, 154–5.
[59] Horner, *Australia's Military History*, 125.
[60] Bou, *Light Horse*, 157.
[61] Dennis *et al.*, *Oxford Companion*, 128.
[62] Bou, *Light Horse*, 158.
[63] Memo, 'A general review of the situation in all theatres of war, together with a comparison of the military resources of the Entente and of the Central Powers', W. R. Robertson, CIGS, October 1916, CAB 24/2/39, TNA.
[64] Horner, *Australia's Military History*, 126.

mounted troops were then used to exploit the infantry's gains.[65] Recognising the importance of exploitation, Murray added another mounted division to the Desert Column in March 1917. Commanded by a British officer, the Imperial Mounted Division included new Australian and British mounted units and British horse artillery. The formation was renamed the Australian Mounted Division in July, but despite its name it remained a mixed-nationality formation.[66]

The key to Ottoman defences in southern Palestine was Gaza, on the Mediterranean coast, but the EEF failed on two occasions, in March and April 1917, to capture this position. These failures led to a command reshuffle, which, amongst other changes, saw Chauvel promoted and given command of the Desert Column.[67] He was the first Australian to command a corps, but his force of 34,000 men, from Australia, New Zealand, Britain, and India, was further evidence of the imperial context of Australia's military effort during the war.[68]

In July 1917, when General Sir Edmund Allenby replaced Murray as Commander-in-Chief, EEF, Chauvel's corps was renamed the Desert Mounted Corps and increased to three mounted divisions. The infantry, which had formerly belonged to Chauvel's formation, was removed and incorporated into two army corps, which between them had seven infantry divisions and supporting arms.[69] According to Jean Bou, this reorganisation, which saw more resources allotted to the EEF, transformed 'an *ad hoc* colonial expeditionary force to a modern army'.[70] The Australian light horse remained an integral component of the Desert Mounted Corps, 'but its days of being the EEF's primary striking arm were over and it was a genuinely imperial all-arms force that would advance into Beersheba'.[71]

The battle of Beersheba on 31 October 1917 is the most famous of the Australian light horse actions in the Middle East.[72] What is less well recognised is that the charge by the 4th Light Horse Brigade was just one component of a wider battle, which was itself one element of a larger operation. Gaza was the main objective of these operations, but since the efforts in March and April had shown that an unassisted frontal assault by the infantry would not work, Allenby shifted his focus to Beersheba, a town on the extreme left of the Ottoman Gaza–Beersheba defensive line. By attacking Beersheba and securing its wells (which would provide water for subsequent operations), Allenby's force would then outflank the Ottomans and advance on Gaza from the rear. It was during this phase that the Desert Mounted Corps would be of most benefit, using its speed to cut off retreating Ottoman forces. All of this was part of a larger strategic plan to

---

[65] Bou, *Light Horse*, 168–9.
[66] 'A short history of the Desert Mounted Corps prepared by Lieut-Genl. Sir H.G. Chauvel', A1194, 33.68/15152, NAA, Canberra.
[67] Bou, *Light Horse*, 165.
[68] Horner, *Australia's Military History*, 129.
[69] Archibald Wavell, *The Palestine Campaigns*, 3rd edn (London: Constable, 1931), 101–2.
[70] Bou, *Light Horse*, 171.
[71] Ibid.
[72] Joan Beaumont, *Broken Nation: Australians in the Great War* (Sydney: Allen & Unwin, 2013), 368–70.

continue the advance through Palestine and into Syria.[73] The EEF was broken into three segments for the operation. The Australians, on the right, represented less than 10 per cent of the total force, or 17 per cent of the force assigned to the capture of Beersheba.[74]

One of the reasons that the attack on Beersheba succeeded was that the troops opposite Gaza, combined with the weight of artillery fire and the presence of warships in the Mediterranean Sea, had convinced the Ottomans that the main attack would take place at Gaza, not Beersheba.[75] British infantry, backed by artillery and logistic support, and enjoying air superiority thanks to the Royal Flying Corps, subsequently took Gaza on 2 November, and the EEF entered Jerusalem in December.[76] Following further reorganisation of the EEF in spring 1918, which saw Indian formations replace British ones that were sent to the Western Front, and a French mounted brigade added to Chauvel's command, the EEF enjoyed a succession of victories, culminating in the advance into Damascus and the signing of an armistice on 31 October 1918.[77]

By this stage of the war, Australia was making the largest single contribution of horsed regiments in the Desert Mounted Corps (fourteen of thirty-six). But Chauvel's formation was one of three corps and the number of Australian horsemen 'was dwarfed by the numbers of British and Indian troops who served in the EEF's two infantry corps, and its artillery regiments, air squadrons, and transport and support services'.[78] As Jean Bou concluded, 'Though the Australian contribution was sizable and important, it was neither decisive nor war winning; it was a British imperial army acting in concert with its allies that achieved victory'.[79]

The Western Front

Similarly, the Australian actions on the strategically more important Western Front did not occur in isolation. British officers at army headquarters undertook the operational planning, while the tactical attacks, which Australians did plan at corps level and below (division, brigade, and battalion), always had to align with the timings and objectives of the broader Allied strategy. This allocation of roles partly reflected the initial lack of military experience and expertise within the AIF, but mostly it was due to its size. The Australian units were too small to have strategic power, either on the battlefield or in the decision-making process. By December 1916, for example, when the last of the Australian divisions arrived on the Western Front, only five of forty-nine British Expeditionary Force (BEF) divisions were Australian. Moreover, these divisions were predominantly made

---

[73] Wavell, 103.
[74] Ibid., 112–13.
[75] Ibid., 124.
[76] Dennis *et al.*, *Oxford Companion*, 83–4; Horner, *Australia's Military History*, 130–1.
[77] Bou, *Light Horse*, 185, 188–9; Dennis *et al.*, *Oxford Companion*, 128, 407.
[78] Bou, *Australia's Palestine Campaign*, 7.
[79] Ibid., 6.

up of combat elements and therefore relied on British heavy artillery, administration, and logistics.

Australia's first major engagement after arriving in France, the battle of Fromelles (Fleurbaix) on 19 July 1916, would become known as the 'bloodiest twenty-four hours in the history of the Australian Army'.[80] The 5th Australian Division, fighting alongside the 61st British Division, suffered 5,533 casualties; both divisions failed to achieve their objectives.[81] Yet, horrific though the casualties at Fromelles were, in the words of the Australian army's historian, this was 'a small action' when compared to other battles on the Western Front.[82] Launched in support of the British offensive on the Somme, Fromelles was intended 'to prevent the enemy from moving troops southward to take part in the defence of the Somme'.[83] Despite its central place in later Australian memory of the war—which is largely due to the fact that 250 bodies of the missing were located in a mass grave and reinterred in 2010—the battle of Fromelles barely rated a mention in the diary of the British commander-in-chief, General Sir Douglas Haig.[84]

This conclusion does not, and should not, downplay the sacrifices and achievements of individual soldiers on the Western Font. Nonetheless, all of the AIF's significant engagements throughout 1916 and 1917, including Pozières, Mouquet Farm, Bullecourt, Messines, Menin Road, Polygon Wood, and Broodseinde, had a similar context to Fromelles: they were elements of a much larger Allied effort across a broad front.[85]

This was equally true of the final year of the war. When, on 21 March 1918, the Germans launched 'Operation Michael', and pushed the allies back over the Somme battlefields, Australian forces were brought in to help hold the attack, first at Dernancourt and Morlancourt. Then, on 24–25 April, Australian troops succeeded in recapturing the town of Villers-Bretonneux, thus preventing the fall of the strategically important town of Amiens. However, as Gary Sheffield has shown, it was a combined Allied effort, and the decision of the German commander General Erich Ludendorff to turn his attention to another offensive in Flanders from 7 to 29 April, that stopped the Michael offensive and allowed the allies to turn a tactical defeat into a strategic opportunity.[86] In late March 1918 the French commander General Ferdinand Foch was appointed Supreme Commander with the role of coordinating the Allied counterattack through a

---

[80] Roger Lee, *The Battle of Fromelles 1916* (Canberra: Army History Unit, 2010), 7.
[81] Jeffrey Grey, *A Military History of Australia*, 3rd edn (Melbourne: Cambridge University Press, 2008), 102.
[82] Lee, *Fromelles*, 32.
[83] Ibid., 95.
[84] Gary Sheffield and John Bourne, eds, *Douglas Haig: War Diaries and Letters 1914–1918* (London: Weidenfeld & Nicolson, 2005), 208.
[85] For more on these battles and the context in which they were fought, see Gary Sheffield, 'The Australians at Pozières: Command and Control on the Somme, 1916', in *The British General Staff*, eds French and Reid, 112–26; Robin Prior and Trevor Wilson, *Passchendaele: The Untold Story* (Melbourne: Scribe Publications, 2003).
[86] Gary Sheffield, 'Finest Hour? British Forces on the Western Front in 1918: An Overview', in *1918 Year of Victory*, ed. Ekins, 59.

series of combined offensives.[87] For the Australians, these began at the village of Le Hamel, near Villers-Bretonneux, where, on 4 July, a joint Australian and American force advanced 2,000 yards on a 7,000-yard front, proving that meticulous planning, limited objectives, and the exploitation of the new integrated weapons system of infantry, aircraft, artillery and tanks, could achieve success.[88]

When, on 8 August 1918, the battle of Amiens was launched, the main effort fell to the four corps of the BEF's Fourth Army (Australian, Canadian, III and IX British Corps) to replicate the tactics used at Le Hamel.[89] With over five hundred tanks and a mass of heavy artillery supporting it, the infantry advanced thirteen kilometres on a 16,250-metre front, inflicting 27,000 casualties on an already exhausted enemy.[90] Although 'spearheaded' by the Dominion formations, the battle of Amiens was a truly collaborative effort.[91] The Australians were supported by fourteen British artillery brigades, fifty British tanks, and enjoyed all the benefits of the BEF's airpower and logistic supremacy.[92] Moreover, although Amiens was described by General Ludendorff as 'the black day of the German Army', it was as much the efforts of the French and US forces attacking to the south, in the Chemin des Dames and Meuse–Argonne regions, that broke the power of the German armies and made their defeat in October–November 1918 possible.[93]

Command and innovation

Can it be argued, however, that the AIF made a disproportionate contribution to the Allied victory by virtue of its innovation and leadership in command? A popular narrative in Australia credits the Australian Corps and its commander, Lieutenant-General Sir John Monash, with being solely responsible for victory in 1918. His methodical planning, his grasp of tactics and technology, and his successes in 1917 and 1918, have been offered as evidence of his pre-eminence over other Allied generals. One author has described Monash as 'the outsider who won a war'.[94] Even the eminent British military historian, Sir Basil Liddell Hart, described Monash as probably having 'the greatest capacity for command

---

[87] Elizabeth Greenhalgh, 'A French Victory, 1918', in *1918: Defining Victory*, eds Peter Dennis and Jeffrey Grey (Canberra: Army History Unit, 1999), 96–7.
[88] Robin Prior, 'Stabbed in the Front: The German Defeat in 1918', in *1918 Year of Victory*, ed. Ekins, 48.
[89] Elizabeth Greenhalgh, 'Australians Broke the Hindenburg Line', in *Zombie Myths of Australian Military History*, ed. Craig Stockings (Sydney: NewSouth, 2010), 71, 76.
[90] Prior, 48.
[91] S. F. Wise, 'The Black Day of the German Army: Australians and Canadians at Amiens, August 1918', in *1918: Defining Victory*, eds Dennis and Grey, 22.
[92] Gary Sheffield, 'The Indispensable Factor: The Performance of British Troops in 1918', in *1918: Defining Victory*, eds Dennis and Grey, 80.
[93] Beaumont, 467–77.
[94] Roland Perry, *Monash: The Outsider Who Won a War: A Biography of Australia's Greatest Military Commander* (Sydney: Random House, 2004).

in modern war'.[95] Similar claims, as it happens, are made in Canada about the Canadian Corps and its commander, General Sir Arthur Currie.[96] But both, somewhat chauvinistic, claims ignore a number of influences, including the fact that the victory of 1918 was, in John Connor's words, 'a team effort'.[97]

It is true that by 1918 the Australian Corps was an elite formation, experienced in tactical planning and proficient in battle; but it provided only five of sixty BEF divisions on the Western Front—not to mention the masses of French and American divisions that fought alongside the BEF. The remaining fifty-five divisions proved to be 'the backbone of the BEF' and their 'unyielding, unremitting pressure' was, according to Gary Sheffield, just as important as the 'spearhead' formations.[98]

Monash's role also needs to be put in perspective. Despite being Australia's most senior officer on the Western Front, Monash was still only a third-tier commander. He commanded at the tactical level of war, where he was responsible for the outcome of battles, but not for the management of a campaign or strategic offensive. As Monash himself acknowledged, he was accountable for what occurred within the frontage allotted to him by his army commander.[99] Moreover, although Monash meticulously developed the plans for a number of the battles of 1918, these were based on objectives selected for him by his superiors and his plans were subject to alteration by higher headquarters.[100] Furthermore, as Monash's biographer, Geoffrey Serle, suggests, many of those who praised Monash's efforts as superior to those of his contemporaries did so with other motives—notably to add weight to their criticism of General Haig.[101]

That Monash was a successful corps commander is beyond doubt. But to what extent did his exploits influence his colleagues, and to what degree did he contribute to wider planning and operational thought within the British army? The foremost expert on Monash's military career, Peter Pedersen, concluded in 1985 that Monash's plans and his tactics were based on an approach to war that was adapted, rather than invented, from other commanders and the lessons learned from previous fighting.[102] In that sense, Monash—like his British and Canadian contemporaries—was the beneficiary of the BEF's learning culture which was ongoing throughout the war. In addition, Monash was not unique in holding pre-battle conferences to explain and debate plans and ideas with his

---

[95] Liddell Hart quoted in Geoffrey Serle, *John Monash: A Biography* (Melbourne: Melbourne University Press, 1982), 377.
[96] John Blaxland, *Strategic Cousins: Australian and Canadian Expeditionary Forces and the British and American Empires* (Montreal: McGill-Queen's University Press, 2006), 34–43; Wise, 1–32.
[97] John Connor, 'The "Superior", All-Volunteer AIF', in *Anzac's Dirty Dozen*, ed. Stockings, 48.
[98] Sheffield, 'Finest Hour', 60, 65.
[99] John Monash, *The Australian Victories in France in 1918* (Tennessee: The Imperial War Museum in association with The Battery Press, 1993), 3.
[100] Horner, 'The Evolution', 7–9.
[101] Serle, *Monash*, ch. 13.
[102] Peter Pedersen, *Monash as Military Commander* (Melbourne: Melbourne University Press, 1985), 295–6.

subordinate commanders. Monash was also just one element of the processes within the British army whereby, after a battle, brochures detailing the latest tactical developments and operational lessons were circulated amongst commanders and between formations. Finally, it needs to be appreciated that, with only 27 of the 450 generals serving in the BEF in September 1918 being Australian, and all but one of them serving in the Australian Corps, no Australian commander, even Monash, was likely to have a significant influence beyond his own locality.[103]

A similar conclusion can be reached when assessing another common belief: that the AIF was a leader in tactical innovation on the Western Front. It is beyond dispute that the Australians excelled in 1918 in the tactics of 'peaceful penetration', that is, raiding, patrolling, and intelligence-gathering in an often improvised and daring manner.[104] But the tactic—which aimed to deny no man's land to the enemy and use it for one's own purposes—had been used by the Germans, French, and British imperial armies, including the Canadian Corps, earlier in the war. In this sense, the AIF was the beneficiary of a much wider learning process that—largely due to Britain's efforts—had improved tactics, technology, training, command and staff work.[105]

Claims that the AIF won the war by itself also ignore the importance to success on the Western Front of technological developments in artillery, and the creation of integrated weapons systems in the later years of the war. Furthermore, as Ian Brown argues, logistics was the backbone of victory. Adequate supplies and a well-administered logistic system enabled the BEF to replenish its resources after the losses of March 1918 and go on the offensive in August that year. Without this system, the Allied effort would have petered out just as the Germans' had in the spring.[106]

Conclusions: a limited contribution

Between 4 August 1914 and 11 November 1918 the British Empire forces put more than 8.5 million men into the field. Of these, Australia provided the fourth largest amount (4.8 per cent) after the British Isles (66.4 per cent), India (16.8 per cent), and Canada (7.3 per cent) (see Figure 1).[107] This was a remarkable achievement for Australia; from a population of 4.9 million, 38.7 per cent of the male population aged eighteen to forty-four enlisted in the AIF.[108] Significantly,

---

[103] John Bourne, 'The BEF's Generals on 29 September 1918: An Empirical Portrait with Some British and Australian Comparisons', in *1918: Defining Victory*, eds Dennis and Grey, 100.
[104] This claim was made by C. E. W. Bean in 1942, and is repeated even today on *Wikipedia*. See http://en.wikipedia.org/wiki/Peaceful_Penetration
[105] Bourne, 'The BEF's Generals', 99; Sheffield, 'The Australians at Pozières', 124–5.
[106] Ian M. Brown, 'Feeding Victory: The Logistic Imperative behind the Hundred Days', in *1918: Defining Victory*, eds Dennis and Grey; Greenhalgh, 'Australians Broke the Hindenburg Line', 81–2.
[107] Great Britain War Office, *Statistics*, 740, 756.
[108] 'Enlistment statistics and standard, First World War'. www.awm.gov.au/encyclopedia/enlistment/ww1/ (accessed 20 May 2014).

THE BRITISH EMPIRE AND THE FIRST WORLD WAR

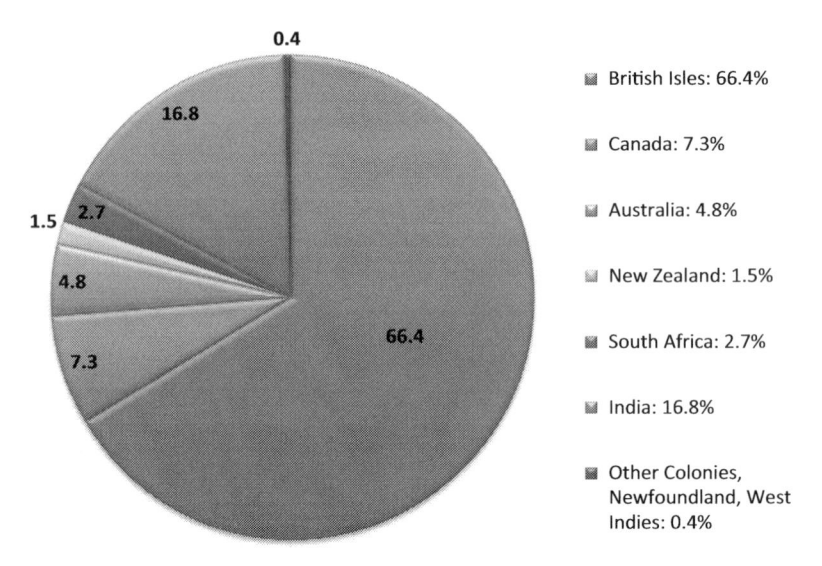

[Pie chart showing: British Isles 66.4%, Canada 7.3%, Australia 4.8%, New Zealand 1.5%, South Africa 2.7%, India 16.8%, Other Colonies, Newfoundland, West Indies 0.4%]

Figure 1. British Empire troops, 1914–18
Source: *Statistics of the Military Effort of the British Empire during the Great War, 1914–1920* (Dallington: Naval & Military Press, 1999), 740, 756.

Australia, which suffered the worst casualties as a proportion of its enlistments (New Zealand suffered more as a percentage of its population), ranked second overall in the Empire's casualties (6.8 per cent) after the British Isles

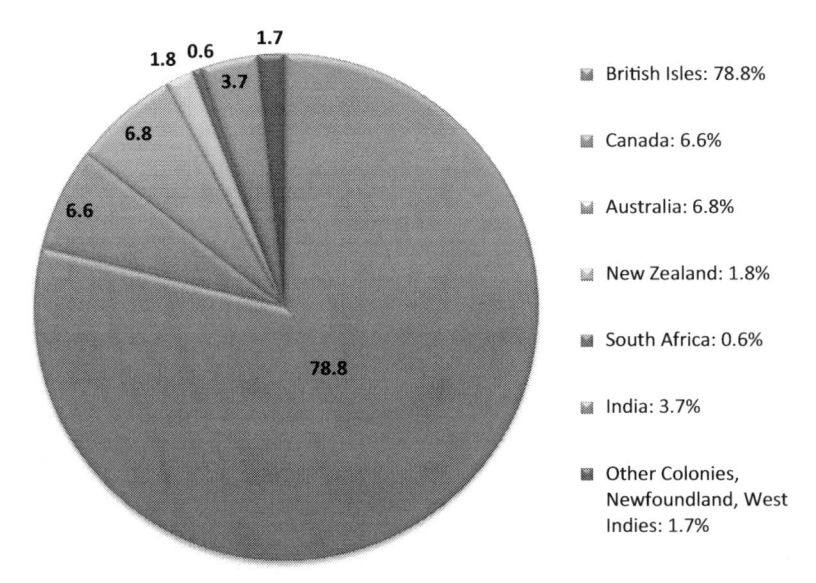

[Pie chart showing: British Isles 78.8%, Canada 6.6%, Australia 6.8%, New Zealand 1.8%, South Africa 0.6%, India 3.7%, Other Colonies, Newfoundland, West Indies 1.7%]

Figure 2. British Empire casualties, 1914–18
Source: *Statistics of the Military Effort of the British Empire during the Great War, 1914–1920* (Dallington: Naval & Military Press, 1999), 740, 756.

(78.8 per cent) (see Figure 2).[109] In the context of the wider war, however, it was total numbers—and divisions—that mattered, not the percentage of the population that fought or were killed or wounded. In terms of its overall contribution to the Empire's war effort, Australia was limited by its size and the fact that the AIF fought on only four of Britain's eleven fronts.[110]

To be sure, Australia's military performed well and the AIF deserved its status as an elite formation: by 1918 Australian soldiers were both professional and adept at fighting and killing. Yet Australia's military forces were never large enough to influence the outcome of the war by themselves, whether this be at Gallipoli, the Middle East, the Western Front, or on the world's oceans. Nor did they want to. From the outbreak of the war Australia's politicians and highest-ranking military officers realised that Australia was a very small player in a very large war. Reflecting the ideal of 'Greater Britain', the AIF and the RAN were both Australian and British, and knew that the strength of the imperial war effort was its combined weight, controlled and underpinned by Britain. It was this imperial force, with its many parts, acting in conjunction with its allies, that was ultimately victorious over Germany in 1918.

Dr Rhys Crawley
Strategic and Defence Studies Centre
Australian National University

---

[109] Great Britain War Office, *Statistics*, 756.
[110] Ibid., 739, 759–60.

Cyprus's Non-military Contribution to the Allied War Effort during World War I

ANTIGONE HERACLIDOU
Open University of Cyprus, Cyprus

ABSTRACT   *No fighting took place on Cyprus during the First World War. However, the island acquired an important role both as a source of provisions and as a recuperation home for injured soldiers. Indeed, between 1914 and 1918 the small, poor and under-developed island of Cyprus became a major provider of grain, timber, tobacco and mules while military convalescent homes on Mount Troodos were built to accommodate thousands of injured Allied soldiers. Cyprus's use for the war effort inevitably had a significant impact on the island's economy and infrastructure. During the war years the island experienced a boost in its agricultural production and an influx of money while several technical services were established to facilitate transportation and communication. By examining such themes this paper sheds important light on a critical period of Cypriot history, though one that remains largely unexplored.*

Introduction

The outbreak of the First World War was hardly felt in Cyprus. High Commissioner Sir Hamilton Goold-Adams continued to govern the island from his summer headquarters at Mount Troodos instead of rushing back to Nicosia. However, a few months later, especially after Turkey's entry into the war on 5 November 1914, things became more complicated. Although under British administration since 1878, the island nevertheless remained part of the decaying Ottoman Empire with which Britain was now at war. With the Cyprus Convention of 1878, Great Britain was engaged to join Turkey in defending the provinces of Batum, Ardahan and Kars should those be retained by Russia, and in return was assigned the occupation and administration of Cyprus.[1] Given the circumstances that now pertained, however, Cyprus could not remain under Ottoman suzerainty. The island's proximity to the Middle East placed it on the front line and enhanced its strategic value as a wartime refuelling station, so its status had to be clarified (Morgan, 2010, p. 70). On 5 November, three months following the declaration of war on Germany, Britain unilaterally annexed Cyprus, stating that 'by reason of the outbreak of war between His Majesty and His Imperial Majesty the Sultan, the Cyprus Convention was invalid'.[2]

At the same time, High Commissioner Goold-Adams, who until then had not seemed disturbed by the outbreak of war, was prompted to initiate several wartime measures. For example, on the day of Britain's declaration of war on Germany he introduced martial law and established a defence committee to deal with 'any measures of extraordinary administration' and to preserve normal conditions on the island. The Committee posted British troops to Larnaca, Limassol and Famagusta in order to requisition enemy merchant vessels docked at the ports; it introduced telegraphic censorship, imposed fixed prices on various essential foodstuffs and prohibited the export of cereal, animal feed and livestock unless the British government in Egypt made specific requests. Also, in order to prevent the export of gold and silver coins, the High Commissioner introduced the island's first paper currency and therefore paper notes were duly produced by the Government Printing Office in Nicosia.[3] However, by January 1915 it had become evident that Sir Hamilton Goold-Adams could no longer handle such a complex situation and he was instructed to take up the governorship of Queensland. He was replaced by John Eugene Clauson, a 'military high-flyer' with six years of experience at the Committee of Imperial Defence and a good knowledge of Cyprus, having previously served as the island's Chief Secretary between 1906 and 1911 (Morgan, 2010, p. 77).

Although Cyprus's strategic importance was soon to be enhanced, the island, unlike Malta where Britain had stationed its Mediterranean Fleet, remained on the periphery of strategic developments. The island's military contribution to the war effort remained limited as it was relatively far from the main theatres of land operations in Egypt, the Dardanelles and Macedonia, and had no harbour adequate for the heavier classes of warship (Georghallides, 1979, p. 88). Of course, this was also an advantage: being far from the main theatres of war meant that Cyprus was left in peace and could contribute to the war effort in other ways. And so it did. During the war Cyprus became a major provider of food and other supplies to the British army, particularly the troops stationed in Salonika and Egypt. It also accommodated hundreds of injured soldiers, prisoners of war (POWs) and refugees and facilitated British military intelligence. This article aims to shed some light on a relatively understudied part of Cypriot history by focusing on the island's contribution to the war effort.

Mules and Muleteers

Cyprus's biggest contribution to the Allies during the war was the provision of mules and muleteers. Mules were difficult to find in Britain so they had to be bought from various countries, one of them being Cyprus (Davis, 2007, pp. 34–35). Mules existed in abundance in Cyprus and Cypriots were trained and experienced muleteers, much needed by the British and Serbian armies. In March 1916 a mule depot was established in Famagusta by the Royal Army Service Corps for supplying mules to the British army fighting in Salonika. The first batch of 2,000 mules originally intended for the British army were actually supplied to the Serbian army after Britain had agreed to provide the Serbs with 4,000 mules. An Order was duly published in the *Cyprus Gazette* on 14 August 1916 announcing that anyone owning mules was subject to having them requisitioned for the military and being paid compensation. Further orders on similar lines but regarding other animals, such as horses, were published from time to time in the *Cyprus Gazette* (Davis, 2007, pp. 34–35). The need for mules was so imperative that the sale of mules by Cypriots was made compulsory and those who did not comply risked imprisonment.[4] It is estimated that by the end of the war the British army had bought 120,000 Cypriot mules (Ηλιοφώτου, 1987, p. 45).

Not just mules, however, had to be transported to the Salonika front for the Macedonian Mule Corps, but muleteers as well. In June High Commissioner Clauson informed the Colonial Office that a scheme was under consideration to raise a corps of at least 3,000 muleteers for the British army and he underlined that such a move 'offers hope of excellent results, political and also military'.[5] The need for the formation of a Cypriot mule corps was realised by the commander of British forces in Salonika at the beginning of 1916. He then asked the War Office for permission to form a mule corps in order to deal with the German–Bulgarian army at the Macedonian Front. Accordingly, the War Office sent a telegraph to the Cypriot government asking for the hiring of 3,000 muleteers (Ηλιοφώτου, 1987, p. 33). Clauson duly circulated pamphlets calling young Cypriots aged 18–35 to enlist in the Cypriot Mule Corps for service in the British army at the Macedonian front 'if they wanted to see the world'. Those enlisted would sign a one-year contract and would be remunerated with three pounds and 12 shillings per month and provided with food and clothes (Ηλιοφώτου, 1987, pp. 33–34). The pamphlet assured the men that there was no danger because this service was not of a military character and operated far from the front. To make the contract more appealing, the government offered free return to Cyprus and approximately one-and-a-half pounds per month to their families (quoted in Ηλιοφώτου, 1987, p. 43). The announcement almost certainly made things appear more attractive than they actually were. Inevitably, many Cypriots lost their life during the war either at the front or because of diseases such as malaria.

Recruitment duly began in July in Famagusta, Limassol and Paphos, and after a 15-day basic training in Famagusta at the beginning of August, 1,091 muleteers, 919 mules and 49 ponies, along with 25 interpreters were shipped to Salonika.[6] The aim of 3,000 was reached by mid-October of the same year but Clauson informed the Secretary of State that 1,000 more were urgently wanted. By the end of September 1917 approximately 5,000 muleteers returned to Cyprus because their contracts had expired while others rushed to enlist in the Greek army now that Greece had entered the war on the Allied side. Given the circumstances and the Governor's reluctance to enforce conscription, the War Office underlined the urgent need for the enlistment of 4,000 more muleteers. Therefore, new announcements were circulated and new recruitment centres operated in all towns (Ηλιοφώτου, 1987, p. 44). By January 1918, 9,208 men reached Salonika and in April of the same year the British major who was serving as commander of the Training Centre in Famagusta informed the Governor that by then 11,950 Cypriots had been recruited and that 89% of them were Greek-Cypriots and 11% Turkish-Cypriots (Ηλιοφώτου, p. 36). Between 5 July 1916 and 26 March 1919 the total number of enlisted Cypriot muleteers had reached 15,910 (Ηλιοφώτου, 1987, p. 44). This is a relatively high number given that the population of the island in 1914 was 274,108 people.[7]

Cypriots responded wholeheartedly to this call as it offered them a great opportunity to be relieved from their financial problems. Cyprus was a poor country and the largest part of the population was indebted and illiterate. This could explain why some deserted their corps with a view to being engaged by the French army for more money, something that hindered recruitment and obliged Clauson to prohibit 'persons fit for military service from leaving Cyprus'.[8] Nonetheless, Cypriot muleteers' contribution to the British army in Salonika should not be underestimated. Davis (2007, p. 36) argues that it was evident that as far as the Salonika campaign was concerned, without the Macedonian Mule Corps it would not have progressed as the army was entirely dependent on it for moving supplies and wounded soldiers. Later on, the Cypriots served in Gallipoli, Serbia, Doerani, Serres, Istanbul, Rodopi, Varna and other fronts (Λυμπουρίδης, 1999, p. 14). As a token of their appreciation, at the end of the war the Cyprus government awarded 3,000 bronze British War Medals to Cypriot muleteers who served in the British army (Λυμπουρίδης, 1999, p. 13).

Convalescent Homes, POW Camps and Military Intelligence

'Covered with fragrant pine forests', as Harry Luke described them, the Troodos Mountains offered the best environment for setting up recuperation homes for injured soldiers (Luke, 1957, p. 103). At the very beginning of the British occupation, Troodos was chosen for the establishment of a Hill Station and it actually became the only place where civilian and military establishments were united, as Nicosia was used for the civil headquarters and Polemidia for the military headquarters. Indeed, the local government very soon established an official presence at Troodos with High Commissioner Lieutenant Sir Robert Biddulph setting up a summer residence there in 1879 (Varnava, 2004, p. 7). Troodos, elevated at between 4,000 and 6,400 feet, was the best option for the exhaustively hot Cypriot summers. Indeed, during the war of 1882 in Egypt, Troodos became valuable as a base and the Mount Troodos Guards Base Hospital was established there (Varnava, 2004, p. 26). Although there was an offer of facilities early in the war, such a need emerged only after Turkey's entry into the war. As a Colonial Office official admitted: 'Things are now very different. Mount Troodos is the only cool place available in the Mediterranean and War Office might be approached with a view to installing a hospital there'.[9] It seems that Goold-Adams encouraged the establishment of convalescent homes as a form of contribution to the British war effort by the island.[10] The Colonial Office asked the War Office to lay before the Army Council the offer made by the people of Cyprus to establish a convalescent home for the wounded. H. J. Read, on behalf of the Secretary of State, noted that after the outbreak of war with Turkey, the annexation of Cyprus and the despatch of an expedition to the Dardanelles, use 'could be made of Cypriot sympathy in connection with the establishment of a hospital locally'.[11]

Throughout the first year of the war the colony was duly transformed to become a 'military convalescent depot' with the establishment of a camp capable of accommodating 500 recuperating soldiers on Mount Troodos.[12] Convalescent depots with capacity to accommodate up to 1,500 soldiers were also built in Limassol, in the village of Kyperounta, which is elevated at approximately 1,300 metres and therefore blessed with a very good climate. Troops, mostly Allied survivors of the Dardanelles campaign, who had been treated at British military hospitals in Egypt, and who were considered almost fully recovered, were transported up to the Troodos convalescent home for two weeks before being sent back to the front (Morgan, 2010, p. 78). This continued until the end of October 1915 when it was considered too cold for injured soldiers to stay there and, with the evacuation of the Allied forces from the Dardenelles, the need for hospital facilities was minimised, so troop transports to Troodos stopped and never resumed.

In 1916 Cyprus was also used for the establishment of camps for prisoners of war. In August the Commander-in-Chief of the Egyptian Expeditionary Force, Lieutenant-General Sir Archbald Murray, decided to send 3,500 Ottoman prisoners of war to Cyprus. Therefore, a vast camp capable of accommodating 6,000 prisoners was erected at Famagusta, 'admirably equipped with all accessories including several mosques' and provided 'excellent food' (Morgan, 2010, p. 89). Clauson actually believed that such a camp would have a beneficial effect on the island's Turkish-Cypriots, 'by shaking the idea of German invincibility in their slow minds and showing them British treatment of a gallant adversary' (Morgan, 2010, p. 89). The POW camp was established at Karaolos, close to Salamis, in Famagusta, and Turkish prisoners from Alexandria and other towns started arriving in Cyprus around October 1916.[13] A first group of 1,900 Turkish POWs were received on 26 November 1916. A further batch of 1,300 Turkish POWs and an additional 88 British troops arrived aboard the merchant ship *Nitonian* on 12 December 1916 and 1,900 on 26 January 1917 (Davis, 2007, p. 42). The transfer of prisoners in Famagusta had made the city more noisy, prompting a Cypriot newspaper to note that the camp, 'floodlit with electrical light', stood 'in contrast with the dark city'.[14] Although Cypriots showed the appropriate hospitality and aided the Ottoman prisoners of war, they worried that there was not enough food for the increasing population of the island and they were looking forward to the day when these refugees would leave the island.[15] In total, Cyprus accommodated 10,000 prisoners of war (Georghallides, 1979, p. 89).

In Karaolos there was also a camp that accommodated Russian refugees. It housed a few hundred refugees, mainly officers and men of the Wrangel army with their families, who were evacuated from the Crimea. They remained at the camp for more than a year and some settled in Cyprus for life. It is interesting that the sale of liquor in bottles to the Russian refugees was not permitted unless the vendors had a written order signed by the commander of the Russian refugee camp (Davis, 2007, p. 41). The Cyprus government also offered a temporary home to Cypriot repatriates as well as to Maltese and British Jewish refugees from Smyrna. Refugees were accommodated at a low cost in several inns in Larnaca until they could get a job. Additionally, in Bogazi on the Karpass Peninsula, hundreds of Armenian refugees were accommodated in camps built and financed by the French military authorities.[16] In 1916 the French had transferred from Alexandretta to Monarga, at the base of Karpass peninsula, their Légion d' Orient of Armenian volunteers (Luke, 1953, pp. 43–44).

In the same year, and more particularly after the disastrous Gallipoli campaign, Cyprus became for the first time a regional centre for espionage, owing to its proximity to Anatolia, Syria, Palestine and Egypt. At that time, British military intelligence in the Mediterranean was reorganised and the Eastern Mediterranean Special Intelligence Bureau (EMSIB) established to coordinate military and local police intelligence-gathering work. The activities of the Cyprus bureau were divided into 'A' work, 'the acquisition of information about the enemy' undertaken mainly in Asia Minor and Syria, and 'B' Work, essentially counter-espionage which involved 'safeguarding the existence of agents and their landing places in Cyprus'. 'A' work was made possible through three telegraphy stations: a British navy one in Famagusta mainly used for military intelligence communication with Ruad and occasional communication with Egypt; a British army one in Larnaca, which functioned with other stations in the Levant for secret intelligence purposes; and a French naval one in Limassol, focused on detecting enemy submarine activity. 'B' work headquarters were in Nicosia, where a team of three men worked under a zealous officer called Captain Scott, responsible for safeguarding the island's oil and fuel depots and preventing sensitive information from Egypt being passed to the enemy via Cyprus. Most of the agents recruited were refugees, desperate for work and paid only for information provided, and therefore the system inevitably leant itself to unclear and often fictional reporting. EMSIB's insistence on interfering with the administration of Clauson, whom they accused of leniency, brought their relations to logger-heads, resulting in a general overhaul of the Cyprus branch.[17] It should be noted, however, that because of intelligence activity an island-wide telephone system was established for the first time in 1917. Clauson placed the island's coastal depots under armed guard and introduced the island-wide telephone system with Famagusta at its hub, so that submarine sightings could be reported to the British naval intelligence station there and by wireless to the French patrol vessels (Morgan, 2010, p. 92).

Export of Foods, Animals and Other Products

During the war Cyprus became a major provider of food, animals and other goods, such as timber and tobacco, to the British army in the eastern Mediterranean. As Holland notes, the island may have been poor but 'unlike tiny Gibraltar and confined Malta, it had an agriculture generating an exportable surplus' (Holland, 2012, p. 171). Indeed, Cypriot products were sold in large quantities at 'record prices', enabling peasants to free themselves from debt and merchants to grow rich (Luke, 1953, p. 43).

Along with mules, donkeys and horses, among the first livestock to be provided by Cyprus were the goats that were found in excessive numbers in Cyprus and that were detrimental to the fauna of the island. Indeed, Orr (1918, p. 138) claimed in 1918 that the number of goats living on Cypriot mountains had reached 250,000, exceeding the number of people. At the end of 1914, around 1,200 goats were shipped to Malta 'for the victualing of the Indian troops'.[18] Indeed, during the war, Cyprus exported so many edible provisions that certain prohibitions on exports had to be imposed by the government in order to avoid food shortages. For example, at the end of 1916, following the export of more than 15,000 tons of potatoes, the government prohibited further exports, as potatoes were a staple for Cypriot families.[19] From 1914 until 1918 tens of thousands of goats and hundreds of thousands of eggs, along with 100,000 tons of wheat and barley, were sold every year to the Salonika and Egyptian expeditionary forces (Morgan, 2010, pp. 80–81). What is also impressive is that during the war the military authorities bought up the island's entire annual crop of carob beans, approximately 60,000 tons, to provide forage for horses and pack animals (Morgan, 2010, pp. 80–81). To give an indication of the type and quantities of products exported, between the end of 1917 and the summer of 1918 permissions were given for the exportation of: more than 1,000 tons of onions for the use of British forces in Salonika; thousands of kilos of barley; tons of macaroni for the use of the British Cypriot forces in Salonica; hundreds of tons of chopped straw and hundreds of kilos of oats; more than 200 cases of brandy; and thousands of pounds of dried figs, apricots and raisins for the canteens of the British Salonika force.[20]

In addition, to serve the increasing demand of British soldiers for cigarettes given that major providers of tobacco such as Turkey, Bulgaria and Greece were hit by the war, Cypriot farmers started for the first time to cultivate tobacco, mainly in the district of Famagusta, with great success (*Eleftheria*, 4 October 1916; Luke, 1953, pp. 43–44). For the quarter ended 31 December 1917, nine cases containing 360,000 cigarettes were exported for the use of the expeditionary force canteen in Salonika and one case containing 40,000 cigarettes for the use of the Italian Intendancy in Salonika.[21] Moreover, the island's forests were almost entirely obliterated in order to provide timber for the Allies in the Middle East. According to Colonial Office communication, timber worth over £120,000 was sold during the period of the war (Georghallides, 1979, p. 89; Morgan, 2010, p. 77).

Conclusion

During the First World War, Cyprus was not as essential as other Mediterranean British possessions to the prosecution of the war. The island was poor, agricultural, and with limited infrastructure. Its disadvantages, however, came to be regarded as advantages. The fact that the island remained at peace and that people could continue their usual agricultural activities at a time when other agricultural countries were hit by the war meant that Cyprus was a useful provider of food, animals and other essential products. Additionally, this relatively calm and peaceful atmosphere encouraged the establishment of recuperation depots and prisoner of war camps, even for Ottoman prisoners, despite the fact that almost 20% of the population of the island was Muslim. The British had managed to a great extent to win the entire population's allegiance during the war. As far as Cyprus itself was concerned, one could agree with Harry Luke that it 'did well out of it' (Luke, 1953, p. 43). Cyprus prospered during the First World War because the government bought Cypriot products at really high prices, to the benefit of both the producers and the merchants. Preparing an account of what happened in Cyprus during the year of 1916, the newspaper *Alithia* noted that the island's economic situation had improved and that because of the increase in the prices of exported goods, farmers lived such comfortable days that they would be remembered for a long time.[22] As in other countries, the aftermath of the war found Cyprus mired with financial problems, and social and political forces were set in motion that were to bring fundamental changes to the island.

Notes

1. The relevant text of the Convention can be found in Murat Metin Hakki (ed.) (2007) *The Cyprus Issue: A documented History, 1878–2007*, pp. 3–4. More information can also be found in Dwight E. Lee (1934) *Great Britain and the Cyprus Convention Policy of 1878*. Cambridge: Harvard University.
2. The Annexation Treaty can be found in Hakki (2007, pp. 5–6).
3. The National Archives, UK (TNA), CO 67/174, 11 November 1914, quoted in Morgan (2010, p. 71).
4. *Alitheia*, 12 August 1916.
5. TNA CO 67/181, Clauson to Secretary of State, 28 June 1916.
6. TNA CO 67/181, Clauson to Secretary of State, 6 August 1916.
7. *Cyprus Blue Book, 1914–15*.
8. TNA CO 67/181, Clauson to Secretary of State, 22 October 1916.
9. TNA CO 67/173, minutes, 3 June 1915, CO 67/173.
10. TNA CO 67/173, Goold-Adams to Secretary of State (telegram), 5 September 1914.
11. TNA CO 67/173, H. J. Read for the Under-Secretary of State, Draft, 5 June 1915.
12. TNA CO 67/179, 8 July 1915, quoted in Morgan (2010, p. 78).

13. *Alithia*, 21 October 1916, 28 October 1916.
14. *Alithia*, 9 December 1916.
15. *Eleftheria*, 27 March 1915.
16. *Eleftheria*, 3 February 1917.
17. Details of Military Intelligence Services in Cyprus during the War can be found in Morgan (2010, pp. 87–94) and Varnava Andrekos (2012) British Military Intelligence in Cyprus during the Great War, *War in History* (http://wih.sagepub.com), 19(3), pp. 353–378.
18. TNA CO 67/174, 24 October–2 November 1914, quoted in Morgan (2010, p. 77).
19. *Eleftheria*, 23 December 1916.
20. Secretariat Archive, Cyprus (SA), SA1: 582/1917,7 December 1917, 7 April 1917, 9 March 1918, 15 March 1918, 28 March 1918, 20 May 1918, 8 June 1918, 11 June 1918, 19 June 1918, 24 July 1918 24 July 1918.
21. SA, SA1: 582/1917, 15 January 1919.
22. *Alithia*, 6 January 1917.

References

Cyprus Blue Book: 1914–15 (1915) Nicosia: Government of Cyprus.
Davis, L. R. (2007) *Cyprus during the WWI Period*. Nicosia: Cyprus Study Circle.
Georghallides, G. S. (1979) *A Political and Administrative History of Cyprus 1918–1926*. Nicosia: Cyprus Research Centre.
Hakki Metin, M. (Ed.) (2007) *The Cyprus Issue: A Documented History, 1878–2007*. London: I.B. Tauris.
Ηλιοφώτου, Χ. (1987) *Ο Πρώτος Παγκόσμιος Πόλεμος και η Προσφορά της Κύπρου*, Λευκωσία [C. Heliophotou, The First World War and Cyprus's Contribution]. Nicosia.
Holland, R. (2012) *Blue-Water Empire: The British in the Mediterranean since 1800*. London: Allen Lane.
Luke, H. (1953) *Cities and Men: An Autobiography, Volume II: Aegean, Cyprus, Turkey, Transcaucasia & Palestine (1914–24)*. London: Geoffrey Bles.
Luke, H. (1957) *Cyprus: A Portrait and an Appreciation*. London: George G. Harrap.
Λυμπουρίδης, Α. Η (1999) Κύπρος και ο Α' Παγκόσμιος Πόλεμος: Σύντομο ιστορικό διάγραμμα της $4^{ης}$ δεκαετίας της αγγλικής κατοχής 1910–1920 [A. Lympourides, Cyprus and the First World War: A Brief Historic Diagram of the Fourth Decade of British Occupation, 1910–20]. Nicosia: O Fakos.
Morgan, T. (2010) *Sweet and Bitter Island: A history of the British in Cyprus*. London: I.B.Tauris.
Orr, C. W. J. (1918) *Cyprus under British Rule*. London: Zeno.
Varnava, A. (2012) British military intelligence in Cyprus during the Great War, *War in History*, 19(3), 353–378.
Varnava, A. (2004) Maintaining Brutishness in a setting of their own design: the Troodos Hill Station in Cyprus during the early British occupation. https://www.academia.edu/389198/Maintaining_Britishness_in_a_Setting_of_their_Own_Design_The_Troodos_Hill_Station_in_Cyprus_during_the_Early_British_Occupation, accessed December 2013.

African agency and cultural initiatives in the British Imperial military and labor recruitment drives in the Gold Coast (colonial Ghana) during the First World War

Kwabena O. Akurang-Parry

During the First World War, the Gold Coast colonial government engaged in military and labor recruitment drives in support of the British Imperial war effort. The colonial government was responsible for the policy of recruitment, the African intelligentsia championed the recruitment efforts in the form of recruiting campaigns, and the chiefs were directly responsible for the recruitment of their subjects. Overall, the subject of military and labor recruitment drives in the Gold Coast during the First World War has garnered some scholarly studies based mainly on colonial sources. The present study, based on two indigenous newspapers, namely *The Gold Coast Nation* and *The Gold Coast Leader*, contributes to the extant literature by examining the role of African agency and cultural initiatives in the Imperial recruitment drives. The first part deals with the reasons why the chiefs and the African intelligentsia became involved in the colonial state's efforts at recruitment. The second portion examines African agency and cultural initiatives in the imperial military and labor recruitment drives, while the third part discusses the results — success — of the recruitment drives. The final section looks at the problems outlined by the Gold Coast press as having posed barriers to African agency and cultural initiatives in the recruitment drives. In sum, the study shows how the colonized Africans applied aspects of indigenous worldview and ontology, including marriage and funerals, as well as aspects of the Afro-European contact, for example, the use of the Christian church as an epistemic site for the facilitation of recruitment. Overall, the study adds to our knowledge of Africa and the First World War and specifically complements Roger Thomas' study of military recruitment in the Gold Coast, showing that African agency and cultural initiatives or what he calls 'special bye-laws' did not only occur in Eastern Province, but were also applied in other parts of the Gold Coast colony, especially in the Central Province.

THE BRITISH EMPIRE AND THE FIRST WORLD WAR

Introduction

During the First World War, the European colonies in Africa participated in the war on behalf of their respective colonial powers. The British colonial government in the Gold Coast (modern Ghana) vigorously maximized human and natural resources of the Gold Coast in support of the imperial war effort. Consequently, military and labor recruitment drives took place in the Gold Coast throughout the duration of the war.[1] The colonial government and the African intelligentsia were at the forefront of the recruitment campaigns, while the chiefs were directly responsible for the actual recruitment of their subjects.[2] The colonial government was primarily responsible for the policy of recruitment. For their part, the African intelligentsia engaged in recruitment campaigns that entailed extensive public meetings and tours of duty to promote the recruitment drives. Additionally, using the local press as a political platform, they disseminated anti-German propaganda to the populace with the hope of promoting support for the British imperial war effort. Most significantly, the African intelligentsia worked in concert with the chiefs, under the auspices of the Aborigines' Rights Protection Society (ARPS), to facilitate recruitment by applying aspects of the normative culture and wordview.[3]

Overall, the subject of military and labor recruitment drives in the Gold Coast during the First World War has garnered some scholarly studies (Lucas 1920; Thomas 1975, 1983; Killingray 1978). One area that remains to be studied is how African agency and cultural capital facilitated recruitment. Roger Thomas's study of military recruitment in the Gold Coast during the First World War examines how aspects of the normative African worldview of marriage and funeral were applied successfully to recruit soldiers in Akyem Abuakwa and Krobo in the Eastern Province. However, he does not situate his conclusions in a framework of African agency and cultural initiatives (1975, pp. 66–67). Indeed, much of the history of the First World War and the Gold Coast has been constructed from colonial bureaucratic accounts that tend to overlook African perspectives and responses during the wartime (Lucas 1920; Thomas 1975, 1983; Killingray 1978). I use African agency and cultural initiatives, hidden in the folds of indigenous African newspapers, to mean the way that Africans applied multifaceted aspects of their cultural worldviews, mostly independent of colonial policy, to promote African support for the imperial war effort, especially in the area of recruitment of soldiers.

Paying particular attention to the Central Province, due to the trajectory of the extant sources, the present study examines the role of African agency and cultural initiatives in the imperial recruitment drives in the Gold Coast during the First World War. Thus it complements Thomas's study, showing that African agency and cultural initiatives or what he calls 'special bye-laws' did not only occur in Akyem Abuakwa in the Eastern Province, but were also applied in the Central Province. The first part of the present study deals with the reasons why the chiefs and the African intelligentsia became involved in the imperial and the colonial state's efforts at recruitment. The second portion examines African agency and cultural initiatives in the imperial military and labor recruitment drives, while the third part discusses the outcomes of the recruitment drives. The final section looks at the problems outlined by the Gold Coast press as having posed barriers to African agency and cultural initiatives in the recruitment drives.

On the whole, 9,890 recruits served in the Gold Coast Regiment. According to Thomas, 5,608 out of the 9,890 were recruited in the course of the war. Also, 4,908 were recruited in 1917 and 1918, and out of the total figure, 3,499 were recruited in 1917. In all, about 3,879, about 60 percent, were recruited in the Northern Territories. The total number of recruits between 1914 and 1918 was as follows: the three provinces, namely Eastern, Central, and Western supplied 926 (16 percent); Asante provided 688 (12 percent); the Northern Territories made available 3,879 (69 percent); and Togoland supplied 115 (2 percent). In fact, the peak period for Asante and the three provinces occurred in 1917. The Gold Coast regiment participated in the Togoland Campaign in August 1914, the Cameroons Campaign from September 1914 to early 1916, and the East Africa Campaign between 1914 and 1918 (Thomas 1973, pp. 59–62; Killingray 1978, pp. 46–52).

The extant literature shows that recruitment in the Northern Territories began in the early years of the war and that the chiefs in the region were directly involved in the recruitment of their subjects.[4] On the other hand, the chiefs in the three provinces only became officially involved in 1916–1917 recruitment drives (Thomas 1975, pp. 58–63). Chief Cooker of Cape Coast, speaking at a recruitment durbar in Cape Coast, the capital of the Central Province, in 1917, stated that at the beginning of the war, the colonial government did not encourage the chiefs in the three provinces to help in the recruitment drives (*The Nation*, 11 January 1917). Overall, the colonial government feared that vigorous recruitment drives in the three provinces and Asante would have adverse effects on the colonial economy because the available agricultural and mine labor needed for production in those regions would decrease.

In 1916, however, the colonial government was forced to abandon its policy of non-recruitment in Asante and the three provinces when 'riots' broke out in the eastern-most region of the Northern Territories. Aimed at the district administration, the disturbances led to the death of forty-nine people (Thomas 1975, p. 63, 1983, pp. 57–75). As a result, the colonial government was alarmed, fearing that further vigorous recruitment drives in the Northern Territories could stimulate anticolonialism in the region. Consequently, the colonial government sought to ease recruitment in the Northern Territories by focusing on the three provinces and Asante. The transformation in policy coincided with the German intensification of submarine warfare that undermined British shipping and transportation of soldiers. The situation was made worse by the Battle of the Somme between July and August 1916 that claimed the lives of about 420,000 British soldiers (Thomas 1975, p.63; Killingray 1978, pp. 48–50). Thus, in 1916–1917, the dwindling British fortunes at the European theater of the war and the need to increase the number of soldiers for the East Africa Campaign led to additional calls for recruits from the British African colonies, including the Gold

Coast. These dramatic turns of event compelled the colonial government to begin systematic recruitment drives in the three provinces and in Asante in 1916–1917.

Reasons for the chiefs and the African intelligentsia's agency in recruitment

By 1914 when the war broke out the Gold Coast colonial government had already implemented indirect rule, using chieftaincy as the mainspring of local administration (Kimble 1963, pp. 457–473). As a result the chiefs had no option of neutrality but to take part in the recruitment of their subjects. The crafting of indirect rule in the wartime is credited to Governor Hugh Clifford. He demonstrated his interest in chieftaincy as soon as he arrived in the Gold Coast in 1912. Harry Gailey, Governor Clifford's biographer, writes that Governor Clifford 'reminded all officers of their responsibility to support the chiefs and their advisers. British administrators were to consult with chiefs' (Gailey 1978, p. 279).

In a confidential dispatch in 1915 to Lewis Harcourt, the Colonial Secretary, Governor Clifford offered reasons for his reliance on chieftaincy as the nerve center of local administration:

> A few of the educated natives at Cape Coast have from time to time agitated for the recognition of elective principle, but I am convinced that the vast majority of the general public of this colony has not yet reached such an intellectual development as would enable them to exercise the franchise with wisdom and discrimination and interest of the community.
>
> (Metcalfe 1964, p. 553)

A close reading of Governor Clifford's indirect rule policy shows that his main objective was the marginalization of the African intelligentsia because of their anticolonial potential. He ostensibly considered the African intelligentsia as political parvenus who could not speak for the rest of the African population:

> a small and specialized class, whose ideas had been borrowed from the political atmosphere of Europe, without regard to local conditions in the Gold Coast, and the numbers so elected would possess no possible claim to speak for the bulk of the population.
>
> (ibid.)

Thus, Governor Clifford argued that the non-educated chiefs would be more useful to the largely illiterate population (ibid., pp. 553–554; *The Leader*, 22 July 1916).

Certain developments in the Gold Coast promoted Governor Clifford's reliance on the institution of chieftaincy. During the First World War, it became imperative for colonial officers to participate in the war, consequently, the colonial government found it convenient to rely more on the chiefs to provide support for the administration (*The Nation*, 7–14 July 1915; *The Nation*, 30 December 1915). Overall, the chiefs found favor with the colonial government for several reasons. First, the coastal chiefs had supported the British during the protracted, belligerent Anglo-Asante relationship throughout the nineteenth century. Second, the chiefs had assisted in the recruitment of labor for the gold mines at Tarkwa and Aboso. Third, support from the chiefs was further demonstrated during the First World War in the course of the Togoland Campaign of 1914 (Lucas 1920, p.13; Thomas 1975, pp. 61–62; *The Nation*, 7–14 January 1915). Finally, the authority of the chiefs had been weakened by the economic and social developments of the preceding decades (Simensen 1974, p. 42, 1975, pp. 386–389). Therefore, the chiefs were willing to use indirect rule to increase their power in order to hold sway over those challenging their authority. These explain why the chiefs became the main agents of military recruitment in the wartime. Although some chiefs resisted, they did so passively and covertly because of the fear that any overt resistance could lead to their deposition. Overall, despite the colonial government and the African intelligentsia's avid interest in promoting recruitment, the onus of actual recruitment rested with the chiefs.

Throughout the course of the war, the Gold Coast newspapers, namely *The Gold Coast Nation* and *The Gold Coast Leader*, patronized by the African intelligentsia, supported the British imperial war effort. There are several reasons for the African intelligentsia's active involvement in the imperial military and labor recruitment drives in the wartime. In September, 1914, *The Nation* published a statement by J. E. Casely Hayford, a prominent member of the African intelligentsia, who was seeking public support for subscription to the imperial war fund in Sekondi, the capital of the Western Province:

> all the people in the Gold Coast colony and Ashanti would welcome such a proposal as they had never cause to regret being under the protecting wings of this great Empire — an Empire on which the sun never set.
>
> (*The Nation*, 17 September 1914)

Similarly, the editorial of *The Leader* supported the imperial cause, stating that 'If it came to the worse tomorrow we are prepared to spill our blood for the protection of our fatherland and to maintain the flag, honor, and prestige of England' (5 September 1915). Such strong statements of support for the war made by the African intelligentsia exemplified their sense of urgency to rescue the empire from the claws of war.

Furthermore, the vigorous participation of the African intelligentsia in the recruitment drives was due to their collective fear of German colonialism. Throughout the wartime, especially during the recruitment drives of 1917, anti-German propaganda was overly demonstrated in the press accounts of the war. The fear of German imperialism was the result of German colonial rule in neighboring Togoland which was perceived as brutal. *The Nation* plaintively reported that:

> The struggle that is convulsing the whole world has a most vital interest for us. If by any unlikely chance, Germany should get the upper hand, we may be sure that in terms of settlement a small tropical country like ours would change flags, and we should experience for ourselves, the miseries that were inflicted upon our Togoland brethren.
>
> (27 May 1915)

The Gold Coast press stressed that Germany was as a hegemonic warmongering colonial power. For instance, the editorial of *The Leader* wrote in 1914 that 'Germany for a long time has been the disturbing factor in world politics. The crisis has come at last' (22 August 1914). These fears expressed about Germany were a significant factor which influenced the African intelligentsia to support the imperial war effort (ibid.; *The Leader*, 22 August 1914). Their unwavering support found more expression during the 1916–1917 colony-wide recruitment drives. In sum, more active than any group, the African intelligentsia were at the forefront of the campaigns to enlist the services of the colonial subjects for the imperial war effort.

African agency and cultural initiatives in the wartime recruitment drives

The Colonial Office appointed Colonel A. H. W. Haywood to supervise the recruitment exercise in the Gold Coast and Nigeria (Thomas 1975, pp. 64–65; Killingray 1978, pp. 48–50; *The Leader*, 20 January 1917). Acting Governor A. R. Slater placed government assistance at the disposal of Colonel Haywood, and, as well, Colonel Haywood received massive support from the African intelligentsia. Prior to the arrival of Colonel Haywood on 1 January 1917, government officials and members of the African intelligentsia had toured some parts of the Eastern Province, namely the districts of Akuapem, Koforidua, and Kibi to campaign for recruits. Also posters were released on Christmas day of 1916, appealing to people in the colony to enlist (Thomas 1975, p. 64; Killingray 1978, pp. 48–50; *The Leader*, 20 January 1917).

These efforts at recruitment were supported by *The Leader* and *The Nation*. Articles and news items published by both newspapers were generally supportive of the colonial government's recruitment drives. In fact, the press served as the African intelligentsia's campaign platform: they used both newspapers to convince the populace to enlist or contribute in other ways to the war effort. *The Nation* stated that the appeal to enlist 'should find a ready response' and that each ethnic group should form a 'company' or a battalion of soldiers (4 January 1917). In its editorial, *The Leader* enthusiastically stated under a caption, 'Gold Coast in Earnest', claiming that 'our people are now beginning to understand the nature of the call to arms, and already there are signs there is going to be full response' (24 February 1917). Although the African intelligentsia patronized the press, its message percolated to the general public through informal processes of dissemination of information between the illiterate masses and the literate group (ibid.).

Press propaganda was used to encourage people to enlist. In mid-February 1917, *The Nation* printed an apparently embellished story of a native of Cape Coast, Sergeant-Major Ahmoah, who had fought in the Cameroons Campaign and had been promoted to the rank of officer in the Gold Coast Volunteer Force by the Gold Coast colonial government. The news item noted that 'Well done Ahmoah, you have vindicated the name of your native town of Cape Coast, whose inhabitants are mighty proud of you' (*The Nation*, 27 February 1917). These words of inspiration and endearment carried the message that enlisting in the colonial army was not only an individual achievement, but also a signifier of communal responsibility and virtue. In sum, it was hoped that the publications of such elaborate accounts of warrior tradition and its consequent social mobility would attract others to enlist.

The African intelligentsia's support for the war was further demonstrated by the newspapers' glamorous allusions to contributions being made by other peoples of the British empire to the imperial war effort. *The Nation* after asking people to enlist coaxingly added that in 'Britain one man out of every five is in Khaki' — a reference to military uniform (4 January 1917). In another editorial, *The Nation* specified that India, Canada, New Zealand, and Australia had paid heed to the imperial clarion call to arms (11 January 1917). *The Leader* also quoted *The African Times and Orient Review*, edited by Duse Mohammed, that 'colored men' should take part in the war because they stood to gain in the long-term (*The Leader*, 10 March 1917).[5]

As noted, the press became a forum for anti-German campaigns, suggesting that British colonial rule was more tolerable than German colonialism. The latter was presented as militaristic, overly demanding, and cruel. Whether this was real or imagined, rumors of German atrocities in neighboring German Togoland had spread in the Gold Coast (*The Nation*, 27 May 1915). The underlying message was that the people of the Gold Coast must assist Britain in order to defeat Germany else German victory would lead to the imposition of German colonialism on the Gold Coast (ibid.). The available sources do not make clear the extent to which the spate of anti-German propaganda facilitated recruitment. However, the persistence of anti-German propaganda throughout the wartime, especially during the recruitment drives of 1914–1915 and 1916–1917, strongly suggests that it benefited recruitment.

In order to make enlistment more attractive, in January, 1917, *The Nation* published the conditions of service for the Gold Coast recruits at the rates of the West African Frontier Force (WAFF) as shown in Table 1. In addition, there were rations, pensions, and gratuities for the wounded. These were established as permanent total disablement at the rate of one-third of daily wage according to rank at the date of injury. For permanent partial injury, gratuity was as shown in Table 2.

Table 1. Conditions of service of Gold Coast recruits

Rank	*Wages*
Private.	1 shilling.
Corporal.	1 shilling and 1 pence.
Sergeant.	1 shilling and 3 pence.
Company and sergeant major	1 shilling and 6 pence

Source: *The Nation*, 4 January 1917

Table 2. Gratuity for permanent partial disablement for Gold Coast recruits in 1917

Rank	Amount in pounds sterling
Company sergeant major	10
Sergeant	8
Corporal	6
Private	4

Source: The Nation, 4 January 1917

In fact, due to the lack of data, it is difficult to compare the conditions of service in the colonial army with other sectors of employment in the Gold Coast. Conditions of service in the army were relatively unchanging, while agricultural and mine labor tended to be seasonal with fluctuating wages. According to Killingray, compared to mine or agricultural labor, the conditions of service in the colonial army were less financially rewarding (1978, pp.47–49). Hence it is likely that the publication of the conditions of service in the newspaper was geared more to the urban poor and youth than mine and agricultural laborers in the rural areas. The publication served the purpose of drawing attention to the allure of enlistment; in this regard, the urban poor and other potential recruits could use the conditions of service as an economic scale-pan to evaluate their future in the colonial army.

In order to make the efforts at recruitment successful, three public meetings were held at Cape Coast. The meetings involved several sectors of the colonial society, including colonial officials, the executive committee of the ARPS, chiefs, *asafo* companies or commoner groups,[6] leaders of ethnic and religious minorities, and local dignitaries. Also in attendance were representatives of the churches, merchants, and the colonial government (*The Leader*, 20 January 1917, 24 February 1917, 10–17 March 1917).

The first meeting was held in early January 1917, at Paptrem, a public meeting place. It was attended by Chief Sackey of Cape Coast and several of his councilors, members of the African intelligentsia, European government officials and merchants, representatives of the churches, and leaders of the Muslim community of Cape Coast. Those who spoke at the meeting included Bishop O'Rorke of the Society of the Propagation of the Gospel (SPG Mission); E. J. P. Brown, a member of the Legislative Council; and Chief Cooker of Cape Coast. Although comprehensive evidence on what transpired at the meeting is lacking, the participants addressed the benefits of recruitment and called on every district to participate in the recruitment drives. In the end, the chiefs and captains of *asafo* companies were asked to do their best to facilitate recruitment (*The Leader*, 20 January 1917).[7]

The next meeting was in February 1917, at the same venue. It was held under the chairmanship of Acting Governor Slater. Chiefs from other areas in the Central Province other than the Cape Coast district attended this meeting. They included two prominent paramount chiefs, namely Essandoh III of Nkusukum and Otu Ababio II of Abura. Nkusukum and Abura were the original Fante states whose political expansion had provided the impetus for the development of other Fante settlements. Therefore, the presence of the two eminent paramount chiefs at the meeting was an exemplification of the enthusiastic support for recruitment in Fanteland. This meeting, like the first one, vigorously called for the involvement of all sectors of society in the recruitment exercise, especially the chiefs and *asafo* companies (*The Leader*, 24 February 1917).

The first two meetings culminated into a final meeting in March 1917. In all thirty-eight indigenous rulers attended: twenty from the Central Province, sixteen from the Western Province, and two from the Eastern Province. It was agreed among participants that each chief should persuade his subjects to enlist and that further developments should be reported to the ARPS executive committee. Additionally, a decision was made that communities should contribute money and or in kind toward the imperial war effort (*The Nation*, 10–17 March 1917).

That several chiefs and dignitaries from the Central, Western and Eastern Provinces attended the final meeting affords several conclusions. First, it demonstrates the systematic organization of the recruitment efforts of the chiefs and African intelligentsia. Second, the presence of the chiefs from the three provinces shows that the 1916–1917 recruitment drives were a colony-wide affair. Third, it suggests that the people of the Gold Coast really wanted to ensure British victory in order to avert the possibility of German colonialism in the Gold Coast. Finally, it illustrates the ability of the colonial government to mobilize the human resources of the colony with minimal resistance from the chiefs and the African intelligentsia, though, as I shall demonstrate, what remained to be seen was the hostile responses of commoners.

Following the series of meetings, prominent members of the African intelligentsia embarked on tours of recruitment campaigns to further facilitate the enlistment of recruits. The African intelligentsia included Casely Hayford, Krakue Herbert, G. J. Christian, James Mercer, F. Akhurst, and J. Kwamina Awortwi, a court registrar, who acted as a secretary-interpreter for the recruitment task force (*The Leader*, 3 May 1917). In the Western Province they were joined by Mr. John Maxwell, the provincial commissioner.[8] The recruitment task force visited Dunkwa and Tarkwa districts in the Western Province. From there, they worked in the Swedru district in the Central Province, visited Kumasi and Obuasi districts in Asante, toured the Kwahu district in the Eastern Province, and finally visited Accra, the colonial capital also in the Eastern Province (ibid.; Thomas 1975, pp.70–71).

According to the editorial of *The Leader*, the recruitment task force vigorously promoted recruitment with an underlying message that youngmen should enlist in the service of the colony and the British Empire, and that communities should also assist recruits with material and moral support. In fact, the work of the recruitment task force went beyond mere recruitment. In Dunkwa, Obuasi, and Kumasi, as well as in other areas, the recruitment task force managed to douse the embers of popular resentment against recruitment. *The Leader* explained that the reason for the simmering popular resentment against recruitment was that 'people were apprehensive of coercion', in other words, they feared the probability of military conscription (3 May, 1917).

There is a paucity of evidence on how the recruitment task force influenced recruitment in the short-term. Nevertheless, the proficiency of the task force is illustrated by the fact that it was able to encourage twenty 'educated men' to enlist in Dunkwa (ibid.). Although this points to the degree of success attained by the recruitment task force, it also suggests some of the inherent weaknesses in the work of the task force and the recruitment exercise itself. That the task force was able to attract only 'educated men' suggests that the gist of their message was elitist and not wholly attractive to the illiterate masses of the agricultural communities. It also supports the argument that the wartime propaganda and the proposed remuneration for recruits that sustained the efforts at recruitment were not attractive enough to farmers: Dunkwa was an agricultural region and none of its farming population enlisted. Rather, the recruitment campaigns attracted the few local 'educated men' of Dunkwa, mostly elementary school graduates, who could not find jobs commensurate with their qualifications, therefore, found the terms of military service comparatively attractive. Thus, by the middle of April 1917, the campaign for recruits was well underway. The African intelligentsia, from the press reports, believed that the recruitment campaigns would be successful (*The Nation*, 5 May 1917). All efforts pointed to the fact that the chiefs were responsible for the enlistment of their subjects, and this was strongly supported by the colonial government.[9]

In order to make recruitment more appealing, the chiefs in conjunction with the African intelligentsia applied aspects of normative cultural order regarding marriage, funeral, and debt-payment. It was this African agency and cultural initiatives that brought success to the Cape Coast district as much as similar application of what Thomas calls 'special bye-laws' had led to successful recruitment drives in Akyem Abuakwa and Krobo (Thomas 1975, p. 67).[10] In terms of periodization and timing, it is not clear if the idea of applying aspects of the normative culture was incubated during the series of recruitment meetings held intermittently between January and March of 1917. Two interpretations may be offered as plausible explanations. First, the present evidence indicates that only the Cape Coast district in the Central Province applied aspects of the normative culture to harness recruitment. Hence, it is likely that the Cape Coast district's decision to apply aspects of normative culture to stimulate recruitment had nothing to do with the provincial and colony-wide meetings that dealt with recruitment. Second, since Nana Ofori Atta, *Okyenhene* [King of Akyem Abuakwa] passed his 'special bye-laws' in December 1916 (ibid.) it is probable that the Cape Coast Chiefs, their councilors, and the African intelligentsia, who collectively implemented similar initiatives or 'bye-laws' in 1917, borrowed from the recruitment strategies of Ofori Atta.

The chiefs and the African intelligentsia sought to assure potential recruits that their social and family life would not be jeopardized when they enlist in the colonial army. This message was carried across by using the institution of marriage, an important aspect of African rites of passage and an axis of adulthood, as a magnetic attraction to recruitment. The chiefs and the African intelligentsia sought to provide stability in the marriages of recruits. The Cape Coast traditional area proposed that anyone who 'tampered' with the wife of a recruit would be fined twenty-five pounds sterling; in the case of a betrothed wife, the fine was twelve pounds sterling (*The Nation*, 7 April 1917).[11] Undoubtedly, these policies were meant to assure recruits that their spouses would be safe from sexual harassment and intimidation during their absence. Overall, it is difficult to assess the frequency of adultery or rape of married women in the early twentieth-century Gold Coast, but the fact that these decisions were made suggests that sexual harassment and 'tampering' with other people's wives were perceived as major social problems that could impede recruitment. Also, due to the paucity of sources, it is difficult to know whether these policies were vigorously applied. Nevertheless, the fact that the policies were made public served as a social capital and may have stimulated recruitment.

The Cape Coast chiefs and the African intelligentsia made another decision that mandated the indigenous state to bear the cost of funerals on behalf of bereaved recruits. They decided that upon the death of a recruit's parent, the *oman* or state would contribute three pounds sterling and twelve shillings toward the funeral expenses. Also, a recruit would receive one pound sterling and sixteen shillings on the death of his child.[12] These incentives certainly were very significant because the Fantes, like other Akan groups, considered funeral celebrations as a significant journey on the pathways of rites of passage (Danquah 1968; Sarpong 1974). As a result, an adult was required to organize fitting funeral celebrations for his/her deceased parent that entailed costly, elaborate ritual performance. Another explanation is the presumption that a recruit's parent or child could die at a time when the recruit was on duty overseas, making it necessary for the indigenous state to bear the cost of funeral on behalf of the bereaved recruit. Here again, the available evidence fails to resolve the question of whether the policy was actually carried out or only served the purpose of attracting people to enlist.

Furthermore, the Cape Coast chiefs decided that beginning from April 1917, every widow should undergo ritual mourning. Normatively the process of ritual mourning dissociated the deceased husband's spirit from the widow. This liberated the widow from the ritually demarcated boundaries of marriage, consequently enabling her to remarry. Additionally, the Cape Coast chiefs instructed that every girl who had reached puberty age should 'make customary exhibition of herself' (*The Nation*, 7 April 1917). In other words, girls of puberty age should undergo puberty or nubility rites (Sarpong 1977) in order to prepare themselves for marital roles commensurate with their gender. Overall, puberty rites served the purpose of advertising the initiands to the public, indicating that they had reached marriageable age. In reality, the widow rituals and the puberty rites were intended to make a large pool of women of marriageable age available to prospective recruits before their departure to the East African theater of the war. Theoretically, both satisfied the collective worldview, ontology, and eschatology of the people: if a married soldier died in the course of the war, the probability that he would be assured of progeny was greater than if he had not married before going to the battlefront.

It would appear that the chiefs made the decision regarding marriage without the absolute consent of the African intelligentsia because the latter criticized the provisions that provided quasi-arranged marriages for prospective recruits (*The Nation*, 7 April 1917). It is difficult to ascertain the outcome of these decisions. Extrapolation of the evidence, however, suggests that widow rituals and puberty rites were common and may have been performed as initiated by the chiefs. What is perhaps more difficult to fathom is whether recruits capitalized on the widow rituals and puberty rites to marry. Indeed, the overriding importance is that this decision may have stimulated recruitment: at least, it was a clear demonstration that the chiefs cared about the normative ontological needs and social welfare of prospective recruits.

Additionally, the chiefs of Cape Coast made provisions specifying that as soon as a 'youngman' enlisted, his financial liabilities would cease (ibid.). Neither does the available evidence explain the process, nor does it specify which financial liabilities would cease. Also, it does not explain whether the financial liabilities were a reference to debts that existed prior to or after enlistment. However, an exegetical and comparative reading of the evidence provides some plausible conclusions (Thomas 1975, pp. 65–67; *The Nation*, 7 April 1917). First, the financial liabilities refer to personal debts, but not those of the extended family. Second, the financial liabilities did not include immovable property, for example, land. Finally, the financial liabilities refer to debts that youngmen, the targets of recruitment, had incurred prior to being recruited. Again, the evidence is tenuous because it does not clarify whether it was implemented or not, but the idea may have been certainly attractive to potential recruits.

Several Fante communities proposed financial contributions toward the upkeep of recruits and the recruitment exercise itself (*The Leader*, 26 May 1917).[13] For instance, Chief Sackey of Cape Coast and his councilors met with the inhabitants of Cape Coast and decided on a house tax to raise money to support the imperial war effort. Essentially, the money was meant not only to support the military training of recruits, but also to facilitate their military campaign in East Africa. The result, according to *The Leader*, was:

> The oman [Cape Coast people] received the message with joy and seemed to do their level best towards the success of the important work undertaken by the Regent and his councilors in conjunction with the executive committee of the ARPS.
>
> (ibid.)

The sources do not state how much money was collected. But that this decision was made at all served to lure people to enlist. It also illustrates that the people of the Cape Coast district and others supported the recruitment drives.

Apart from capitalizing on aspects of quintessential African culture and worldviews, the Christian church was also used as an ideological site for recruitment because of its preeminent position in the Central Province. Overall, church activities, including liturgical practice, were used to stimulate recruitment (*The Nation*, 21–28 April 1917). The present evidence shows that this occurred in the Cape Coast district, but it is also probable that other districts, including Winneba, Saltpond, Anomabu, and Elmina, where the church served as a powerful institution, also engaged in similar practices.

The Cape Coast recruits were invited to worship with the influential congregation of the Wesleyan or Methodist Church. *The Nation* wrote that:

> Recruits in Cape Coast with Chief Cooker have enlisted and are being drilled for East Africa attended Wesley Church under the command of their Instructor Lieutenant O'Morchoe, where Rev. J.S. Gibson, B.SC., preached a sermon based on the text: 2 Timothy, ch. 2, v. 3: 'Endure hardness as a good soldier of Jesus Christ'.
>
> (ibid.)

The fact that recruits became a part of the congregation of the elite, well-respected church indicates the recognition conferred on them by society and how the social allure of the church was used in attracting recruits. Also the worldview of the church provided spiritual nourishment for recruits. As well, the message from the pulpit, such as the above – 'Endure hardness as a good soldier of Jesus Christ' – was used to convince recruits that they were imperial martyrs who should go to war to rescue the British Empire. In sum, this entailed the use of the essences of empire, civilization, and Christianity to convince recruits, as well as potential ones, that their mission was for a good cause. In fact, it was hoped that such spiritual prescriptions would be carried over to the theater of the East Africa Campaign. Consequently, attempts were made by the newspapers through advertisements to furnish recruits bound for East Africa with a minister of religion to serve their religious needs there. Unfortunately, the advertisements proved futile: no one opted to minister to the needs of the soldiers in East Africa (*The Nation*, 2 June 1917).

Success of the recruitment campaigns: the assessment of the press

Sir Charles Lucas who participated in the Togoland campaign of 1914 and later wrote an eye-witness account of the war concluded that 'throughout the provinces' the recruitment drives 'met with a good success' (Lucas 1920, p. 15). But recent studies, based mainly on colonial government documents, have contradicted Sir Charles's observations and conclusions. Killingray, dealing generally with the Gold Coast and Asante, concludes that the recruitment drives ended in a stalemate (1978, pp. 47–52). For his part, Thomas has concluded that the recruitment campaigns registered a modicum of success only in Akyem Abuakwa and Krobo in the Eastern Province (1975, pp. 66–69).

As will be shown, the press highlighted several problems that beset the recruitment drives, however, in addition to Thomas's conclusion that the recruitment drives were successful in Akyem Abuakwa and Krobo, the press reports strongly show that the recruitment drives in the Central Province, especially the Cape Coast district, were successful. Apart from the sizeable number of men who enlisted, the population as a whole showed enthusiasm in the recruitment exercise. *The Nation* enthusiastically wrote that:

> We are pleased to report that Cape Coast has fulfilled her promise of raising hundred men. The strength of the force is now 110 men of whom 101 are Cape Coast boys, 1 from Assin Attandanso, and 8 from Assin Apinimim.
>
> (5 May 1917)

Assin Atandanso and Assin Apinimim were neighboring districts and were perhaps influenced by the overall vigorous efforts at recruitment in the Cape Coast district. Similarly, *The Leader* noted that a substantial number of Cape Coast men had enlisted, but still noted that the people of Cape Coast could have done better (12 May 1917). One week later the same newspaper reported that:

> The Cape Coast troops for the East African Campaign continue to grow in numerical strength. Scores of men from the neighboring district have been refused admission [enlistment] into the ranks of Cape Coast recruits as they fail to assign substantial reasons for not enlisting under their own Etufuhen [captains of *asafo* companies].
>
> (*The Leader*, 19 May 1917)

This implies that the Cape Coast district could have had the size of its recruits increased had it allowed people from other districts to enlist. Furthermore, it shows that there were people in neighboring districts who were willing to enlist, but faced some problems, including the social structure and exclusivity of the *asafo* companies which will be discussed in the next paragraph. While the Cape Coast district registered the greatest success in the recruitment exercise, other districts in the Central Province attained modest successes, yet the captains of *asafo* companies in such districts were blamed for failing in their recruitment bids. For example, 'Etufuhin [captains of the *asafo* companies] in Elmina, Nkusukum, Abura, Anomabu, Ekumfi, and Gomoa' were censured for not having 'done their best' to recruit their people (ibid).

As noted, the normative structure and composition of the *asafo* companies affected the recruitment exercise in the Central Province. Prospective recruits wanted to enlist by *asafo* companies, that is, they wanted to join *asafo* companies that were normatively associated with their lineage. Also, the *asafo* companies wanted to maintain their local quasi-military structures and social groupings. In fact, had these been encouraged, each town would have presented bands or 'companies' of recruits based on several *asafo* companies instead of a contingent of recruits, because each community had several *asafo* companies. It was not only the visceral yearning to enlist in one's *asafo* company that posed problems, but also recruits' intentions of enlisting in their kinship *asafo* companies with the hope of avoiding physical requirements and rigorous discipline which were crucial to military training. *The Leader,* commenting on this, emphasized that:

> We fail to see why they should not be allowed to do so [enlist by *asafo* companies] so that at the training centers the commanding officer who is best competent to decide upon physical qualifications may accept some and return others.
>
> (ibid.)

In spite of the problems associated with the *asafo* companies, the Central Province attained some significant varying successes in the recruitment drives, especially those of 1916–1917. While other districts registered modest successes, the Cape Coast district and its immediate environs attained the most significant success. For one thing, unlike in other districts, the Cape Coast chiefs were vigorously assisted by the executive committee of the ARPS in the public campaigns that preceded the recruitment drives. For another, the presence of and the interest shown by the provincial government was also instrumental in the success attained by the chiefs of Cape Coast: officials of the provincial governor's office attended the meetings, placing the enormous political weight of the provincial administration behind the work of the chiefs and the African intelligentsia (ibid.).

The press and the problems of African agency and initiatives in the recruitment drives

In general, apart from the varying successes in the Central Province, the initial optimism demonstrated by the various sectors of the colonial society proved unwarranted: in the end, the press assigned several reasons for the failure of the colony-wide recruitment drives. The editorial of *The Nation* entitled, 'The Call For Men', complained that:

> The government has been behind-hand in appealing to kings and chiefs. Very possibly the kings were not allowed to raise the bodies of troops in the beginning.
>
> (11 January 1917)

This means, as noted, that the chiefs in the three provinces and Asante were not allowed to participate in recruitment at the beginning of the war. Overall, the recruitment campaigns in the three provinces and Asante began in earnest in January 1917 and ended in April 1917. Commencing after a short notice, the populace could not be convinced overnight to enlist (ibid.).[14]

The literature on the First World War and Africa illustrates that in areas where colonial rule was harsh and overly exploitative, resistance to military recruitment occurred (Echenberg 1975). This occurred in the Sefwi district where the failure of recruitment was partly due to the harsh policies of colonial officials in the early months of 1917. *The Leader* reported that during the absence of Mr. Howard, the district commissioner, the Sefwi district 'suffer[ed] in the hands of inexperienced officials' to the extent that one official, Mr. Stratham, 'compelled debtor prisoners to work like convict prisoners'[15] and did not allow them to eat (*The Leader*, 3 March 1917). The same report stressed that inexperienced officials had deposed Kwesi Nkrumah, the paramount chief of Sefwi Bekwai, while another paramount chief, Yaw Dina, had been arrested (ibid.). Regarding the nearby district of Axim, a correspondent of *The Leader* later wrote:

> The modern Nebuchadnezzer, our Assistant District Commissioner is displaying his pranks in this district, and until there is a check of some kind on his terrorism coupled with his maladministration we would conclude Marshall [sic] law is being proclaimed in this part of the colony, or that the administration in the Western Province is gradually blending into German militarism.
>
> (*The Leader*, 11 August 1917)

The correspondent continued that the travesty of justice and high-handed fines exacted by the court of the district commissioner had alienated the local people. In all, recruitment had become a problem in the district, and 'the sooner a sergeant was sent into the area the better' (ibid.).

Another reason given by the press for the failure of the recruitment campaigns was the restricted use of firearms in the pre-war Gold Coast. The colonial government had discouraged the use of firearms before the outbreak of the First World War because of the concerns that firearms could be used to foment popular anticolonial rebellion (*The Nation*, 1 July 1917). In fact, by 1916, the colonial government had accepted the request of the French colonial authorities that lead and gunpowder should not be made available in Asante. The French believed that lead and gunpowder from Asante, especially the commercial emporium of Kumasi, were being sold in the Northern Territories, adjacent to neighboring French colonies. In sum, the French colonial authorities feared that the proliferation of firearms would enable the French colonial subjects to gain access to firearms with which they could use to strengthen popular resistance against conscription, among others. Thus, in Asante and in the Northern Territories, gunpowder and lead were controlled by the Gold Coast colonial government (*The Leader*, 5 November 1916).

Similarly the available evidence on the three provinces shows that the colonial government went to great lengths to limit the use of firearms and may have succeeded in the long-term. Speaking about recruitment in the presence of Acting Governor Slater in Cape Coast in 1917, Chief Cooker of Cape Coast bluntly explained why his subjects were reluctant to enlist:

> The fault of government in making women [effeminate] of all classes of the men in this country by exceedingly hard and fast rules in the use of firearms.
>
> (*The Leader*, 20 January 1917)

The Leader presented a better picture of the situation in 1918:

> And so we would naturally like to know whether we are to revert as far as our male population is concerned, to the old timorous, barbarous conditions of depriving the men of every means of familiarizing themselves with the use of modern arms of precision and calling upon them suddenly upon emergency, or a bolder more confident policy.
>
> (2–9 November 1918)

It is patently clear that prior to the outbreak of the war the colonial government had restricted the use of firearms. In the event of war, when men were summoned to use firearms, potential recruits were uncertain either of their own abilities to use firearms or the willingness of the colonial government to equip them for battle.

The fear of compulsory recruitment also served as barriers to enlistment (Thomas 1975, pp. 69–70). In March, 1917, writing about the problems of recruitment, *The Leader* attributed the failure of the recruitment drives in the Western Province to the inhabitants' resentment against imminent forced recruitment by the colonial government being spread through popular rumors:

> False rumor had gone abroad that compulsory service has been contemplated and color had been lent to this by reason of recent emigrations from the French coast where conscription had been resorted to.
>
> (3 March 1917)

The rumors of compulsory recruitment originated from the French Ivory Coast which shared borders with the Western Province.[16] In the Sefwi district, which was near the French Ivory Coast, the fear associated with compulsory recruitment led to a rebellion against the local colonial administration. It was only after the chief of Kwaokrom and 'the head of the youngmen' or *asafo* company had been arrested that the rebellion was quelled. It was not only in the Western Province that this occurred, but also in other parts of the colony, for example, in the Eastern Province where seasonal laborers from the French colonies worked as cocoa farm laborers (ibid.).

Apart from direct governmental policies, the press argued that the lawlessness of recruits militated against recruitment. In the Eastern Province, popular criticisms against recruits' banditry led to a spate of calls to the chiefs to either maintain law and order or abandon the recruitment of their subjects. This occurred between April and May 1917 (*The Leader*, 26 May 1917; and *The Leader*, 2 June 1917). Throughout the period of recruitment, especially in 1916–1917, recruits became a major source of communal anxieties and apprehension. For instance, a correspondent of *The Leader* wrote that misguided recruits in Akyem Abuakwa and Dwaben were harassing the inhabitants and pleaded with the commanding officer 'not to give them pass anymore' because they were making life miserable for the local inhabitants. The report noted that unruly recruits were 'extorting [from] the poor people in their villages, committing heinous crimes like adultery [rape], stealing, assault, [and] house-breaking' (19 May 1917). Eventually, the colonial government adopted stringent policies to control the intimidating and violent actions of errant recruits by subjecting them to lashes and imprisonment. Also, the colonial government stationed additional military officers in both districts to prevent further banditry (ibid.).

Another correspondent wrote that recruits in Kumasi were harassing people, especially market women, by extorting money from them and seizing their wares. The report also noted that deserting recruits had taken to the bush and were harassing outlying villages (*The Leader*, 14 July 1917). Thus, recruits' banditry and intimidation became a problem for the chiefs, the very agents of recruitment. The chiefs were called upon by their subjects to control the unruly attitudes of recruits. District commissioners also expected the chiefs to see to it that recruits in their various jurisdictions were well-behaved.

Additionally, subjects reacted against the chiefs' efforts to fulfill their recruitment obligations and quotas during the wartime. The responses of subjects ranged from passive resistance to outright rebellion. Popular resistance called into question the moral and political authority of the chiefs: why the chiefs were recruiting their subjects to fight for the very colonial government that was seen to be exploiting them. For example, the inhabitants of the Asebu district in the Central Province rebelled against Amanfi II, their paramount chief, who had dutifully sought to implement the resolutions of the final meeting on recruitment held in March, 1917, at Cape Coast. *The Leader* noted that the rebellion had become 'a source of considerable anxiety amongst the community' (23 June 1917). The same problem occurred in Anomabu, and commenting on this, *The Leader* illuminated that the 'question of recruitment for East Africa is the fundamental keynote of strain in the town' (28 July 1917). In 1917, the chiefs of Anomabu, Elmina, Nkusukum, Abura, Ekumfi, Winneba, and Gomoa, all in the Central Province, experienced popular disaffection from their subjects because of their efforts to recruit them (*The Leader*, 19 May 1917).

Overall, populist response to the chief's role as the main agent of recruitment was identified as a factor that impeded recruitment (*The Nation*, 27 April 1916). Jarle Simensen has noted in his studies of *asafo* companies in the Eastern Province that commoners came to associate wartime hardships with colonial exploitation. The *asafo* companies saw recruitment as an element in the whole bid at colonial exploitation (Simensen 1974, pp. 29–32, 1975, p.395). K. A. Busia also noted in his study of transformations in Asante chieftaincy that similar *asafo* company insurgency associated with recruitment occurred in Asante (1968, pp.107–108). The *asafo* companies, a pressure group with vested interest in the chief's role as the caretaker of his people, agitated against their chiefs' efforts at satisfying colonial policy, including military recruitment, at the expense of popular concerns. In April, 1916, speaking at Cape Coast about the problems of recruitment, Governor Clifford noted that the Central Province had experienced riots and disturbances which were the results of the resistance of the *asafo* companies (*The Nation*, 27 April 1916). In order to maintain the status and authority of the chief as the main agency of indirect rule and recruitment, the colonial government gave its political backing to the chiefs as it saw it fit. Consequently, the colonial government's disregard for popular grievances further intensified rebellions against some chiefs (Busia 1968, p.108; Simensen 1974, p.29, 1975, pp. 396–399; Akurang-Parry 2006, pp. 57–59). Thus, populist anticolonial activities posed challenges to chieftaincy, calling into question the moral authority of the chief to recruit his subjects.

Conclusion

Three groups were involved in the wartime recruitment campaigns of 1916–1917: the colonial government, the African intelligentsia, and the chiefs. I have elucidated that through the instrumentality of the African intelligentsia and the chiefs, African agency and cultural initiatives were applied to facilitate military and labor recruitments, especially in 1916–1917. Indeed, the African intelligentsia ironically showed more enthusiasm than the officials of the colonial government. Their visceral attachment to the British Empire and the popular fear of the looming German colonial menace are crucial to understanding their enthusiasm. The African intelligentsia used the press and their tours of duty to promote recruitment. It was, however, the chiefs who bore the utmost responsibility for the actual recruitment of their subjects. Several problems, including popular resistance against recruitment, rumors of conscription, and the harsh realities of colonial rule, faced the chiefs, the main recruiting agents. The chiefs, in particular, and the African intelligentsia took the initiatives to apply normative practices embedded in the worldview of the people to stimulate recruitment. It is likely that such normative practices did not occur only in Cape Coast district and Akyem Abuakwa, but were more widespread than previously thought.

Certainly, some aspects of the African agency, for example, the use of the press as a recruitment campaign platform, were the result of diffusion of innovations based on the Afro-European contact. Others, such as monetary and material contributions toward the war effort, the fostering of stability in the marriages of recruits, and the bearing of funeral expenses of bereaved recruits were undoubtedly rooted in indigenous cultures. In addition to Akyem Abuakwa and Krobo districts in the Eastern Province, stressed by Thomas as having witnessed successful recruitments, the Central Province, especially the Cape Coast district, attained considerable success because of the application of aspects of indigenous worldview, packaged to suit the needs of recruits. In the end problems inherent in the colonial situation and those of the wartime posed challenges to African agency and cultural initiatives in the colonial recruitment drives.

Kwabena O. Akurang-Parry can be contacted at the Department of History, Shippensburg University, Shippensburg, PA 17257, USA. E-mail:KAParr@ship.edu

Notes

*   Kwabena O. Akurang-Parry, a Ghanaian poet and historian, is an Associate Professor of African History and World History at Shippensburg University, Pennsylvania. He received his Ph.D. in African history from York University, Toronto, Canada, in 1999. He has published over forty articles, some of which have appeared (or are forthcoming) in *Slavery and Abolition, African Economic History, The International Journal of African Historical Studies, History in Africa, Transactions of the Historical Society of Ghana, Left History, International Journal of Regional Local Studies, Ghana Studies, African Issues, Groniek,* and the *Journal of Cultural Studies.* He is currently completing two book manuscripts: one on Slavery, Abolition, and Colonial Rule in Ghana, and the other, co-edited, on Colonialism and African Responses. Some of his poems have appeared in *The Atkinsonian, Okike, Chronicle,* and *Ufahamu.* His research foci are comparative slavery; colonial rule and African responses; and gender and labor in the Gold Coast (Ghana).

1. Military and labor recruitment drives in the wartime occurred at different times with differing results in the Northern Territories, Asante, and the three Provinces, namely Eastern, Central, and Western, therefore, wherever appropriate I have mentioned the specific region. Additionally, Gold Coast as used in this study refers to all these administrative regions.

2. For conceptual definitions of the African intelligentsia, see, for example, Kimble (1963, pp. 135–141); Lloyd (1967, pp. 125–131); Foster (1968, pp. 48–69); and McCarthy (1983, p.25) Following Foster (1968, p. 68) I use the term African intelligentsia to show that 'a considerable heterogeneity [existed] within the ... group itself'. As a group, the African intelligentsia were agents of creolization, social and economic change, cultural transmission, Euro-Christianity, and political transformation.

3. The Aborigines' Rights Protection Society (ARPS) was formed in 1897. It constituted the African intelligentsia and the chiefs. Several developments in the preceding decades, including the lack of African representation on the Legislative Council, the problem of direct taxation, and the implementation of the Native Jurisdiction Ordinance of 1883, contributed to the formation of the (ARPS). However, the main catalyst for the formation of the ARPS was the protests against the Lands Bill of 1894–97. The Lands Bill would have allowed the colonial government to take over the so-called waste or public lands. For a full historical account of the ARPS, see Kimble *A* 436–456 and 475–505; and Boahen (1975, pp. 57–66).

4. By the beginning of the First World War, the Northern Territories was being used by the colonial government as a reservoir of military and labor recruitments. See Kimble (1963, pp. 533–536).

5. Killingray (1978, p. 40) has argued that the African intelligentsia believed that the colonial government would reciprocate their contributions to the recruitment drives by offering them some latitude of political participation.

6. The *asafo* companies were originally military regiments based on lineages that defended the state in times of war. Since the colonial period, they have served as pressure groups and custodians of normative tradition and culture. See Kimble (1963, pp. 470–472). For a recent study, see Anshan (2002).

7. For an inexplicable reason, it was suggested at the meeting that in addition to Cape Coast, Accra and Kumasi would serve as military training centers for recruits. See *The Leader*, 20 January 1917.

8. The accounts of the newspapers do not mention that Acting Governor A. R. Slater accompanied the recruitment task force, but Thomas (1975, p. 70) states that he did.

9. Indeed, Governor Clifford, whose cardinal policy was the marginalization of the vociferous African intelligentsia, wanted the chiefs to be solely responsible for the recruitment exercise with minimal contribution from the African intelligentsia. See Thomas (1975, p. 82).

10. The bye-laws included the beating of gong-gong to inform the population about recruitment. Also any capable individual who persuaded anyone not to enlist in the colonial army would be arrested or would be forced to enlist, and any unfit old man who prevented anyone from enlisting would be fined £12 sterling. Furthermore, an educated man would lead each group of fifteen enlisted men. See Thomas (1975, pp. 67–68).

11. Similar bye-laws in Akyem Abuakwa mandated wives of enlisted men to swear that they had maintained their chastity while their husbands were at war. Any wife who failed to swear would be considered as having committed adultery during her husband's absence and therefore would pay the customary fee for adultery. Additionally, once a man enlisted, his wife would not be permitted to seek a divorce. Also as long as a husband remained a soldier, his wife's seducer would pay £12 sterling instead of the usual fee of £3. 12s. See Thomas (1975, p. 67).

12. In the case of Akyem Abuakwa, funeral expenses of any soldier who died was to be borne by his town. See Thomas (1975, p. 67).

13. In Akyem Abuakwa each volunteer was to be given £7 sterling by the state. See (1975, p. 67).
14. By 1917, the chiefs had to deal with the exigencies of the war and popular resentment against the colonial policy of indirect rule. Consequently, some chiefs could not be bothered by the urgency of recruitment because they had to deal with local problems, especially populist agitation, that threatened their very authority. See Akurang-Parry (2006, 51–60).
15. Debtor prisoners were those imprisoned for their inability to honor debt-payment. For a fuller account, see Akurang-Parry (2003, pp. 427–447).
16. Killingray (1978, pp. 52–53) estimates that the migrants from the French Ivory Coast numbered between 15,000 to 18,000. They fled to the Gold Coast as a form of protest migration and became farm laborers and mine workers, hence interacted with the local people. This enabled them to disseminate powerful anti-conscription ideas among the host communities.

References

Primary references: newspapers

The Gold Coast Leader, Cape Coast, 1914–1919 issues.
The Gold Coast Nation, Cape Coast, 1914–1919 issues.

Secondary references

Anshan, Li. 2002. *British Rule and Rural Protest in Southern Ghan*, Peter Lang, New York.
Akurang-Parry, Kwabena O. 2003. '"What is and what is not the law:" Imprisonment for debt and the institution of pawnship in the Gold Coast, 1821–1899', in *Pawnship, Slavery, and Colonialism in Africa*, eds Paul E. Lovejoy and Toyin Falola, Africa World Press, Trenton.
Akurang-Parry, Kwabena O. 2006. '"Disrespect and contempt for our natural rulers": the African intelligentsia and the effects of British indirect rule on indigenous rulers in the Gold Coast', *The International Journal of Regional and Local Studies*, series 2, vol. 2, pp. 43–65.
Boahen, Adu. 1975. *Ghana: Evolution and Change in the Nineteenth and Twentieth Centuries*, Longman, London.
Busia, K. A. 1968. *The Position of the Chief in the Modern Political System of* Ashanti, Frank Cass, London.
Danquah, J. B. 1968. *Akan Doctrine of God*, Frank Cass, London.
Echenberg, Myron J. 1975. 'Paying the blood tax: military conscription in French West Africa, 1914–1918', *Canadian Journal of African Studies*, vol. 9, no. 2, pp. 171–192.
Foster, Philip. 1968. *Education and Social Change in Ghana*, University of Chicago Press, Chicago.
Gailey, Harry. 1978. 'Sir Hugh Clifford', in *African Proconsuls: European Governors in Africa*, eds L. H. Gann and Peter Duignan, The Free Press, New York, pp. 266–274.
Killingray, David. 1978. 'Repercussions of World War I in the Gold Coast', *Journal of African History*, vol. 19, no. 1, pp. 39–59.
Kimble, David. 1963. *A Political History of the Gold Coast*, Oxford: University Press, London.
Lloyd, P. C. 1967. *Africa in Social Change*, Penguin, New York.
Lucas, Sir Charles. 1920. *The Gold Coast and the War*, Oxford University Press, London.
McCarthy, Mary. 1983. *Social Change and the Growth of British Power in the Gold Coast*, University Press of America, Lanham.
Metcalfe, G. E. (ed.). 1964. *Great Britain and Ghana: Documents on Ghana* History, T. Nelson, London.

Sarpong, Peter. 1974. *Ghana in Retrospect: Some Aspects of Ghanaian Culture*, Ghana Publishing Corporation, Tema.

Sarpong, Peter. 1977. *Girls Nubility Rites in Ashanti*, Ghana Publishing Corporation, Tema.

Simensen, Jarle. 1974. 'Rural mass action in the context of anti-colonial protest: the Asafo movement of Akim Abuakwa', *Canadian Journal of African Studies*, vol. 8, no. 1, pp. 25–42.

Simensen, Jarle. 1975. 'The Asafo of Kwahu, Ghana: a mass movement for local government reform under colonial government', *International Journal for African Historical Studies*, vol. 8, no. 3, pp. 383–406.

Thomas, Roger. 1975. 'Military recruitment in the Gold Coast during the First World War', *Cahier D'Etudes Africaines*, vol. 15, no. 1, pp. 57–83.

Thomas, Roger. 1983. 'The 1916 Bongo Riots and their background: aspects of colonial administration and African response in eastern upper Ghana', *Journal of African History*, vol. 24, no. 1, pp. 57–75.

Norman Lindsay and the 'Asianisation' of the German Soldier in Australia during the First World War

EMILY ROBERTSON
University of New South Wales, Canberra, Australia

ABSTRACT *From the beginning of the First World War, atrocity stories about German depredations against Belgian civilians circulated throughout the Allied world. Caricatures of German soldiers rapidly degenerated into depictions of monstrous 'Huns' who were subhuman beasts, prone to acts of rapine and banditry. The most prominent producer of 'Hun' cartoons in Australia was artist Norman Lindsay, who published extensively throughout the war. Through an analysis of the antecedents of Lindsay's monstrous 'Hun', this article will demonstrate that the rapid creation of the 'Hun' in Australia was made possible by the pre-existing racial caricatures of non-European people that were popular during this period. Chinese and Japanese people who were excluded from Australia by the White Australia policy were the previous targets of Norman Lindsay's racial caricatures; as stories of German atrocities filtered into Australia, Lindsay transferred traits of Asians on to the German 'Hun', thus transforming him into the enemy 'Other'. These traits were products of British imperial propaganda, and part of an ideology that asserted it was the job of the white man to civilise the barbaric coloured man. By 'Asianising' the German, Lindsay used a well understood language of racial caricature to reduce the German to the status of a barbarian. Race was therefore one of the central paradigms through which Australian propaganda operated.*

Introduction

During the First World War, cartoonists throughout the English-speaking world responded to Allied allegations of German atrocities by depicting the German soldier as a monstrous ogre and labelling him a 'Hun' (Gullace, 2010, pp. 61–62). The 'Hun' became a prominent symbol of the enemy's capacity for rapacious violence and was widely depicted in both government and non-government propaganda. While the simian German soldier was unique to the First World War, the racial tropes projected on to him were not. Indeed, he was an amalgam of pre-existing imagery that had been created during the 19th century as British imperialists applied scientific notions of race to colonised people throughout the globe (Robertson, 2010). The Australian transformation of the German from racially similar Aryan to monstrous 'Other' is an excellent example of how this process occurred, and clearly demonstrates that race played a central role in the Allied construction of the 'Hun'. Through an examination of the war art of Australian artist Norman Lindsay (1879–1969), this article will establish the importance of race to the creation of the 'Hun' in three ways. First, Lindsay's 'Hun' was closely modelled on anti-Asian and anti-African British imperial atrocity propaganda that long preceded the Great War. Thus, popular tropes from 'atrocious' rebellions such as the Indian Mutiny were recycled for use in 1914. Second, racial stereotyping reflected the particular culture that produced it—in this case, Lindsay's work was the product of a uniquely Australian brand of racism that pilloried the Chinese and Japanese. Third, Lindsay's racial stereotyping, although uniquely Australian, nonetheless drew upon deeply held British beliefs about the nature of imperialism, being that white civilisation waged a war against black barbarism: by 'Asianising' the German, Lindsay therefore removed his status as a white man, and enfolded him in a pre-existing and powerful imperial narrative about the 'Just War' against coloured savagery.

Lindsay produced the most enduring and notorious examples of the 'Hun' in Australia, first in the weekly Sydney magazine *The Bulletin*, and then later in the federal government's 1918 recruiting campaign. To transform the culturally and racially similar German into the 'Other', Lindsay pillaged his existing lexicon of racist caricatures of Asians, which in turn had been inspired by British imperial cartoons produced by magazines such as *Punch*: in essence, Lindsay 'Asianised' the German soldier by projecting a number of specific traits (i.e. immorality and cruelty) on to him (Holden, 1995, p. 114).

'Asianisation' has been used in this article to describe the process of 'Othering' the German because it best describes the direct nature of Lindsay's transformation of the German soldier. While 'Oriental' tropes were projected on to Chinese and Japanese people in Australia in the early 20th century, the term 'Orientalisation' does not fully encapsulate the specific type of racial stereotyping that was prevalent in Australia at the time (Lake and Reynolds, 2008, p. 34). The influx of Chinese into Australia had, following the discovery of gold in the 1850s, provided propagandists with the first template of how to respond to a threat to the self-defined national identity of a White Australia. This was achieved through the imposition of a number of base characteristics on Asians, which will be explored later in the article.

Bigotry

Norman Lindsay's abominable bogeyman was powered not only by imperial racism, but also by a brand of bigotry that was particular to Australia. Throughout the course of the First World War, *The Bulletin*'s motto was, 'Australia for the White Man'; in support of this, in its pages Lindsay frequently caricatured the various races who were deemed to threaten Australian interests or Australia's racial purity (primarily subcontinental Indians, Japanese and Chinese people). Of his work for *The Bulletin*, art historian Bernard Smith wrote, 'More than any other artist, he gave visual definition to the *Bulletin*'s editorial policy, particularly its nationalism and racism' (Smith, 1986).

Although Australian culture received many of its racial cues from Britain, Australian racial fears far exceeded those that existed in Britain, and were directed at particular races. Australia had federated in 1901 and was strongly committed to the White Australia policy.

This did not entirely please the British government, as it excluded or discriminated against non-European citizens of the Empire and thus undermined much of the self-congratulatory rhetoric of racial equality that was a feature of late 19th century imperialism (Huttenback, 1976, pp. 140–141, 280–281). While the Colonial Office in Britain supported Australia's steps to limit the number of non-European people in Australia, it was concerned that, as Joseph Chamberlain, Secretary of State for the Colonies, wrote to Sir John Forrest, Australian Minister of Defence for the Commonwealth, '… we, as Imperialists, must take care not to make invidious distinctions between the different races who live under the British flag' (Chamberlain Papers, 1901, quoted in Huttenback, 1976). However, Chamberlain sought compromise by introducing a dictation test, which had the advantage of excluding coloured people without embarrassing other countries by 'naming categories of prohibited immigrants and their countries of origin' (Chubb and Russell, 1998, p. 112).

The bureaucracy of racial exclusion, however, was not far below the surface. In 1906, Customs Officers in Australia were provided with intricate instructions as to what races to allow into Australia—anyone who was 'coloured' or 'half-caste' and not of pure European descent would not be allowed into the country (Day, 2000, p. 41). Despite the strong reservations of the British government towards the White Australia policy, it was whiteness that often connected the colonies and Dominions, not citizenship (Grenville, p. 36).[1] Australian nationalist Alfred Deakin encapsulated this paradigm when he asserted that it was the white citizens of the Empire who controlled it and gave it 'authority, force and weight', not the coloured citizens (Huttenback, 1976, p. 284).

By the early 20th century, Asians, in particular the Japanese, had come to be feared as a military threat and 'Oriental despotism, Oriental splendour, cruelty, sensuality', in Edward Said's words, was projected on to them (Said, 2003/1978, p. 4). Cartoonists adumbrated these fears, manifesting them in black and white line drawings. In 1914, Livingston Hopkins produced a cover for *The Bulletin* that used tropes of power and tyranny which would later be projected on to the 'Hun'. A Japanese man, perhaps the Emperor, sits atop his throne, with the foolish Uncle Sam (the United States had briefly lifted a ban on Asian immigrants) bowing obsequiously to him (Figure 1).

A Norman Lindsay cover, also from *The Bulletin*, depicts a menacing Japanese character, again possibly the Emperor, pouring a threatening looking Australia-shaped ink stain across the homework of Australia, represented by an innocent sleeping boy (Figure 2).

These stereotypes provided the foundation for Norman Lindsay's 'Asianised' German soldier. Demonstrating the flexible nature of racial stereotyping, the despotism and megalomania (all tropes taken from popular clichés about Indians and Middle Easterners), that were projected on to the Japanese by *The Bulletin* were swiftly reapplied to the newly Asianised German, or 'Hun', by visual propagandists throughout Australia. [2]Symbols were quickly recycled to suit the new racial threat—in *Must it Come to This?*, B. E. Pike takes the sinister shadow of the shape of Australia cast by the ink of the Japanese tyrant in Lindsay's cartoon, and transposes it on to a globe of the world. The shadow itself becomes that of the German Emperor, reaching out to take over the planet (Figure 3).

This scenario is even more powerfully recycled in Norman Lindsay's '?', otherwise known as 'German Monster' (Figure 4).

Lindsay's poster of the bloodied hands of the Hun mauling the globe fuses the atavistic, monstrous ape-hybrid that he used against the Japanese, with the German. Thus, the

THE BRITISH EMPIRE AND THE FIRST WORLD WAR

Figure 1. Livingston Hopkins or 'Hop', 'Et Tu, Sammy', *The Bulletin*, 19 February 1914. Copyright H.A. and C. Glad.

'Oriental despot' is repackaged, a familiar ogre projected on to a new threat; as Lindsay's transposition of traits of the 'Other' on to the Anglo-German soldier establishes, concepts of race within the British Empire were not static—indeed, they were surprisingly elastic and subject to alteration according to circumstance and need (Horne, 2004, p. 43).[3]

Underlying these caricatures in which moral white and black are clearly delineated is the monstrous hybrid, half-man, half-beast, the product of wicked miscegenation. These

Figure 2. Norman Lindsay, 'Sleeping at his Homework', *The Bulletin*, 19 January 1911. Copyright H.A. and C. Glad.

fears eventually gave rise to a series of Australian racial hybrids who were the progenitors of Lindsay's Hun. In 1909, Livingston Hopkins, or 'Hop', who was one of *The Bulletin*'s premier illustrators, produced an image for the cover of *The Bulletin* entitled 'The Gradual Development of Bull: J. Bull has annexed another 15,000 miles filled with niggers' (Figure 5).

The fear that proponents of the White Australia policy had of being racially eradicated by the non-white population of the Empire is very clear in this image.[4] Hop portrays Bull as a helpless victim of reverse evolution, his eyes bulging in surprise as he slides further and further down the Chain of Being until the black back of the Aboriginal is all that can be seen; John Bull's identity has been successfully eradicated by the

Figure 3. B. E. Pike, 'Must it come to this?' Printer and publisher unknown, chromolithograph on paper, c.1914–18, collection of the Australian War.

logic of miscegenation. Hop's dramatic caricatures satirise scientific drawings by isolating each figure within a separate rectangle, as though they are specimens, causing the viewer to linger on each state of racial 'decay'.

Hop's use of race was typical of illustrations in *The Bulletin*, a proud proponent of the White Australia policy which delighted in presenting a variety of derogatory racial images every week. Long before the Great War, when the Japanese were posing a threat to the security of the Empire, Norman used a murderous gorilla-man to reveal the inner spirit of the Japanese, who were frequently described in *The Bulletin* as subhuman (Figure 6).

Figure 4. Norman Lindsay, '?', 1918, Commonwealth Government of Australia, collection of the AWM.

Symbolic Representation

In a 1907 illustration, Lindsay depicts cute little monkeys dancing on stage, distracting the woman from the huge gorilla rearing up behind her, a proto-King Kong, preparing to ravage the symbolic representation of a virginal Australia. Lindsay uses stark contrast and a claustrophobic, flattened perspective to etch out a sense of horror and power in the beast. These early images provided Lindsay with a powerful visual vocabulary for

THE GRADUAL DEVELOPMENT OF BULL.

J. Bull has annexed another 18,000 square miles filled with niggers.

(1) There was a white Bull once. (2) Then he became light brown, and bought a turban. (3) He grew still more brown, and acquired a big sash and a curved sword. (4) His brownness increased, and he acquired petticoats and funny shoes. (5) Gradually he became so brown that he was practically black, and he undressed himself again and wore a loin-cloth. (6) And in the end he will ended so many niggers that he will be quite black, and the last scene will be an aboriginal Bull roasting his 'possum over a small fire.

Figure 5. Livingston Hopkins or 'Hop', 'The Gradual Development of Bull', *The Bulletin*, 18 March 1909.

his bestial, atavistic German, who resembled a gorilla crossed with Satan, an Asian-European menace. Much of the work that Lindsay produced for the war as frontispieces for *The Bulletin* were supremely masterful in conveying horror and despair, using line and contrast to wrest emotion and moral indignation out of each illustration.

The balancing act performed by Australian artists and propagandists between Empire and nation, racial bigotry and multiracial acceptance, and the contrasting use of the cultural or racial hybrid served to provide flexible interpretations of identity for Australians as they endured the destruction of a generation of men. In Australia, racial stereotypes that dominated the start of the century altered as the threat of war loomed. The

Figure 6. Norman Lindsay, 'The Monkey and the Other Monkey', *The Bulletin*, 11 June 1907. Copyright H.A. and C. Glad.

German's decline in morals and appearance in Lindsay's *Bulletin* cartoons reflected the alteration in attitude towards Germans that was propagated in the print media. While the annexation of New Guinea by Germany had caused uproar in Australia in 1884, relations between Germans and Australians within Australia were reasonably cordial by the early 20th century (Thompson, 2000, p. 7). Despite the growing economic threat to the British Empire presented by Germany, Australia had a friendly trade relationship with Germany, and the people themselves were perceived by many Australians as a group to be admired (Williams, 1999, p. 13). *The Bulletin*, which frequently prescribed which races could, or could not, be trusted by white Australians, praised the Germans in no uncertain terms: 'There is no fear that helmeted frown, with its brushed-up moustache is going to Teutonize or Prussianize the world ... It is the brown-yellow grin in a smooth, slant-eyed face that we must watch' (*The Bulletin*, 21 August 1913, p. 13). Yet by 1915, the German had become 'The Chinaman of Europe' (*The Bulletin*, 11 July 1915, p. 6).

Much as Lindsay's German 'Hun' was unique in that it was based upon racial caricatures of Asians, his use of race in his war art in and of itself was not singular. Indeed, Lindsay's Germanic archetype was very much in keeping with those portrayed in other Allied nations, where they too endowed the German with an 'alien' and simian appearance (Baker, 1990, p. 29). Thus, historian Nicoletta Gullace's assertion that Australia's peculiar racial anxieties had made Norman Lindsay's monstrous Hun particularly racialised in comparison with other Allied creations should be approached with caution (Gullace, 2010, p. 73). For example, British propagandist Horatio Bottomley described the German as 'an unnatural beast' and 'a human abortion' that required extermination (Symons, 1955, p. 166).

Caricature

British traditions of racial caricature for the development of the 'Hun' were in fact central to the development of the Australian version of the 'Hun'. From the mid-19th century, these racial caricatures were used to isolate and dehumanise unstable elements in the British Empire—and this did not apply just to Africans and Asians. As L. Perry Curtis demonstrated in his ground-breaking book *Apes and Angels, the Irishman in Victorian Literature*, white men who threatened the stability of the Empire were akin to the uncivilised Africans and Asians, and were therefore often depicted as the apelike 'Other'. In 1881, for example, *Punch* published a John Tenniel cartoon in which a dynamite and gun-wielding Irishman is depicted as a black man. By placing him on a dais with other waxworks of weapon-wielding coloured 'problems', Tenniel removed his status as a fellow Caucasian, thereby justifying a number of actions against the Irish that would have been considered unacceptable actions against the white English race (Curtis, 1997, p. 24) (Figure 7).

Many years later, Norman Lindsay affected a similar act of racial exchange upon the German.[5] In a 1917 cartoon he drew a number of lower 'specimens' of evolution, such as the Cave Dweller, the Cannibal Islander, and the Gorilla, which are all on display in an ethnographic museum. The ethnographer has updated his collection: the German has been placed at the very end (Figure 8).

This type of scientific sleight of hand was central to the act of turning the German into the 'barbaric' other, and the German was 'tarred' with a variety of different racial

Figure 7. John Tenniel, 'Time's Waxworks', *Punch*, 31 December 1881.

slurs in Australian publications. In a *Bulletin* editorial, it was argued that the German was outside the civilised ken of the average white man, or Aryan. More damningly, the German was described as the 'Chinaman of Europe':

> ... the modern German is proved out of place in the Aryan family. He is as much so as the Chinaman ... the German is a savage among pacifists. Europe, after centuries of struggle, shook itself clear of feudalism. Its impetus bore Germany along with it. Germanism's doctrine of unreasoning obedience is a recrudescence. It is a reversion to a type which is no longer regarded as civilised ... All students of China are agreed as to the incomprehensibility of the Chinese character, and none of them profess to even guess whether the ineradicable Chinese patriotism is really patriotism at all or merely detestation of the foreigner. Whatever the explanation, the Chinaman of Europe possesses this quality in the same measure as the Chinaman of Asia, whom we have long since ceased to regard as a desirable immigrant. (*The Bulletin*, 22 July 1915, p. 6)

The language of race, physiognomy and morality that had been crafted in Europe in the 18th century contributed to the casual culture of racial superiority in England that became the ultimate propaganda tool to justify British colonial expansion. Alongside this language came symbols, powerful visual clues that were repeatedly recycled and crafted into stereotypes of race that spoke of degradation, bestiality, hybridism and godlessness. Another antecedent of Norman Lindsay's monstrous hybrid Germans began with 'scientists' of physiognomy in the late 18th century, who compared black people with apes (Bindman, 2002, pp. 203–206). This was quickly parlayed into popular caricature, as despised races or groups of people were drawn as ape-like (Curtis, 1997,

Figure 8. Norman Lindsay, 'Reprisals', *The Bulletin*, 19 July 1917.
Copyright H.A. and C. Glad.

p. xx). These symbols were often produced by private concerns for public consumption, demonstrating (at least in the eyes of the producers of propaganda) that tropes of black and Asian racial inferiority were popular within the Empire during the 19th century.

As much as Australia had its peculiar racial obsessions, race was in fact a weapon on both sides in First World War propaganda: Germany decried the use of coloured people in the British armed forces, and grotesque and strange crimes were ascribed to Indian soldiers by German propaganda. Gurkhas and Sikhs were purported to be cannibals 'who liked to sneak across the lines, stealthily cut the throats of the enemy and drink the blood' (Read, 1941, pp. 136–137). Given the incipient bigotry within Australia about Indians, who served alongside Australian troops, it was vital to portray Germans as being more prone to infanticide, cannibalism and devil-worshiping than British Indian soldiers were alleged to be.

To achieve this, the German soldier was cast down with the animals and Satan. He went from inhabiting the highest part of the 'Aryan' racial tree to the lowest of soils. Yet it was not just the simple requirement to make the enemy a hated figure which resulted in the German soldier's racialisation. The creation of the Hun was also part of a much larger and more general series of atrocity propaganda campaigns that took place across the English-speaking Allied nations, from Ireland to the United States.[6] In this significant genre of First World War propaganda, the alleged atrocities committed by German soldiers against Belgian women and children were produced by propagandists in order to enhance the 'Just War' defence that was developed early in the war by the British (French, 1986, p. 22).[7]

This 'Just War' defence was extremely reliant upon traditions of racial caricature.[8] For the Australian public, the invasion of Belgium and the attacks on Belgian civilians were deemed to be attacks of inexcusable barbarism. Thus, any man who did such a thing was no longer human—he was, in effect, a man who had lost contact with his Christian God. In the scenario of 'Just War' that became the main staple of atrocity propaganda, the Australian army was morally obliged to intervene, because innocent women and children were being threatened by men who had lost their humanity.

Dehumanisation

As John Horne and Alan Kramer observed, atrocity propaganda from this period went 'beyond the categorisation of war crimes' by dehumanising 'the enemy as part of wartime cultural mobilisation' (Horne and Kramer, 2001, p. 4). The German soldiers' previously impeccable racial profile, which was highly important in the racially obsessed Empire, was deeply problematic. In seeking to establish the notion of a 'Just War' against the Germans, the Allies therefore painted the German in the darkest moral hue —literally.

What did it mean, then, in the early 20th century, to have lost one's humanity? During this period, to lose one's humanity was to lose one's 'whiteness'. Being white carried with it a series of positive moral attributes, but most particularly, it embodied civilisation; as Kipling's poem *The White Man's Burden* suggested, barbarism was the domain of the black and Asian man, and it was the onerous job of the white man to attempt to civilise him and his country (Porter, p. 2).[9] Conversely, if a white man assumed the behaviour of a black man, he had crossed into the realm of a savage. In essence, this is what the German soldier was considered to have done in Belgium—through his atrocious actions he had literally devolved into a monstrous hybrid beast.

Propaganda such as Norman Lindsay's and Rudyard Kipling's was the mechanism that transmitted, refined and continuously reinvigorated white paternalism alongside images of barbaric Asians and Africans. Their work drew upon an enormous body of unofficial imperial propaganda in which race was a central feature: advertising, fiction and illustrated children's books created a nexus of stereotypes in which the white man's civilising mission was expressed in everything from soap advertisements (in which the blackness of savagery could be partially washed away to reveal whiteness) to stories of battles in which the white man triumphed over the barbaric coloured man. Repeated tales of military exploits in which the foe was a savage coloured person reinforced ideas of racial superiority (Hollingworth, 1993, chapter 3 and p. 163; McClintock, 2007, pp. 509–510). These stories (both pictorial and textual) drew upon the phobias and triumphs that haunted the Empire from the middle of the 19th century. While many genres provided jolly imperial tales of clean battle, the darker side was expressed through the medium of atrocity propaganda.

The Black Hole of Calcutta (1757), but more particularly the Indian Mutiny (1857), were landmark stories which became the fabric of Britain's 'Other', and provided the template for much of the atrocity propaganda that was used in the First World War.[10] There is a trajectory from depictions of violence against women and children, committed by insane Asian tyrants and sepoys, to the German soldiers presented as malformed monsters, torturers and 'Oriental' despots. These were the subtle anchors of war propaganda, the source of irrational fears that gave energy and inspiration to the creation of the 'Hun' who, like the Indian, was a monster, a torturer and a tyrant. The legendary atrocities of the Mutiny dominated the white, colonial imagination, even during the First World War.[11] In 1915, British historian J. H. Little linked the First World War effort to the Black Hole, writing that the story 'presents to the British nation a band of heroes not unworthy to rank with those who turned at bay in the retreat from Mons, with those who held the trenches at Ypres or those who stormed the bloodstained heights of Gallipoli' (Dalley, 2006, p. 12).[12]

The fascination with the Black Hole and the Mutiny was due both to the British education system, which covered these events in history classes, and to the children's book market of the late 19th century, which also covered these events extensively (Castle, 1996, pp. 12–22). The Mutiny was an exceedingly popular story, and one of its main sources of fascination was the massacre of women and children by Indian sepoys at Cawnpore. 'No single incident in the history of British India so hardened the hearts of minds of the English toward their Indian subjects as did the Mutiny of 1857', writes Kathryn Castle. Nana Sahib, who ordered the execution at Cawnpore, was described in British publications as a 'monster' and a 'fiend in human shape' (Castle, 1996, pp. 20–22). The remarkably similar language employed in describing monstrous Indians and the monstrous Germans was due in part to the expediency involved in transferring Asian traits on to the German. Propaganda needed to be produced quickly, and there was already a rich lode about Indian barbarity to be mined and readapted.

In the retelling of both Indian and German atrocity tales, there was a fine line between the gutter press, which published lurid tales of crimes against women, and more sober accounts of atrocities. In the lower brow publications, however, a morbid fascination is evident, and the excitement of the reader is anticipated. An 1895 publication about the Indian Mutiny describes the incidents as 'thrilling' (Miles and Pattle, 1895, p. 5). Nineteen years later, William Le Queux, a tabloid author, wrote 'one cannot read a single page of this awful record ... without being thrilled with the horror of the unspeakable acts of civilized troops, who, at the behest of their Kaiser ... have become simply the Huns of Attila' (Le Queux, 1914, pp. 6–9). It is evident that some readers found the recounting of these atrocity tales 'thrilling', as in a form of entertainment. The repetition of images and stories of women being degraded was not merely a product of mass-literacy and cheap publishing. An image from the 1860s of an event during the Mutiny, of bare-breasted women shackled to trees, is an early example of the use of women being debased by the 'Other' to stir up indignation (and perhaps a 'thrill') in the reader (Figure 9).[13]

Just as cruelty against women and children is the focus of Mutiny stories, so too is it the main focus of First World War atrocity propaganda. As Nicoletta F. Gullace observed, 'graphic images of violence against women and children permeated British public discourse' (Gullace, 1997, p. 714). Norman Lindsay consciously engages in the Mutiny tradition of atrocity propaganda, with an image of a werewolf wearing a German helmet, slavering over a screaming woman (Figure 10).

In many of Norman Lindsay's works, man–animal hybrids, half-dog, or half-gorilla, stalk the pages, stamping on helpless women. They become conflated with the devil himself, who in Lindsay's war art is the personification of masculine sexual violence. While the majority of Lindsay's war art was published in *The Bulletin*, Lindsay's atrocity propaganda for the government was even more arresting.[14] In 1918, he contributed all of the illustrations for the six posters, five pamphlets, a film, and variety of newspaper advertisements that together formed the federal government's 'Recruiting Kit'. The existence of this comprehensive and sophisticated 'Recruiting Kit' was due to

Figure 9. Detail of 'Massacre of English Officers and their wives at Jhansi', in *The History of the Indian Mutiny*, steel engraved images. London Printing and Publishing Country, London, p. 186.

THE BRITISH EMPIRE AND THE FIRST WORLD WAR

THE WEREWOLF OF EUROPE.

And again some do speak of werewolves, men turned to beasts that do ravage frighted women and babes, and how they recover their shape and wits, or t neighbors do make an end of them with a silver bullet, which alone hath power over the demon.—*The Anatomy of Demons (1591).*

Figure 10. Norman Lindsay, 'The Werewolf of Europe', *The Bulletin*, 10 June 1915. Copyright H.A. and C. Glad.

Australia's need for voluntary enlistments.[15] Whereas Britain eventually relied upon conscripts, the Australian electorate rejected conscription in two referendums and the military was forced instead to persuade, cajole and emotionally blackmail eligible men into joining (Douglas, p. 585).

Enhanced by the addition of colour and an unremitting focus on barbarism against women and children, the pamphlets depict surreal cruelties such as babies being speared on the spur of a giant jackboot that has descended from the sky (Figure 11).

The 'Recruiting Kit' was an unprecedented federal propaganda campaign, and utilised direct advertising techniques in the form of lavishly illustrated pamphlets that were mailed out to eligible men. The use of gender and race was unremitting. In the first pamphlet, a drawing by Lindsay depicts the 'masculine' German power grinding the peaceful 'female' Belgium under his jackboot. Her face is twisted sideways, her eyes half-closed in unwilling submission, her hands bound; Lindsay has repeated his now established tradition of creating sexually alluring women, and manacled her (Figure 12).

It is an unsettling image, perhaps intended to be erotically charged as much of Norman Lindsay's other non-war art certainly was. Regardless of the erotic undertones of the image, however, Lindsay is using a motif from the British past: like Tenniel's *Punch* cartoon 'The British Lion's Vengeance on the Bengal Tiger', which depicts an Indian tiger mauling a helpless naked woman and child, Lindsay's image is ultimately aligning the German 'Other' with masculine depravity, and calling upon Australians to play the same role the British lion did—to defend and protect the innocent (Figure 13).

The 'Recruiting Kit' employed multiple tactics and mediums to project on to the German all that was previously projected on to the coloured person in Australia. A transcript of the subtitles and description of the images of the film in the Kit describes the German monster's 'hideous progress' in ghoulish detail:

Today the German Monster threatens the world with bloodshed, slavery and death [subtitle]

Figure 11. Norman Lindsay, Detail: *The Military Situation/Australia's Deadly Peril*, Commonwealth of Australia, 1918, collection of the AWM.

Figure 12. Norman Lindsay, Detail: *Our Reason For Entering the War*, Commonwealth Government of Australia, 1918, courtesy of the AWM.

Figure 13. John Tenniel, 'The British Lion's Vengeance on the Bengal Tiger', *Punch*, 22 August 1857.

The Monster then turns round, spies the globe, representing the world, and grabs it. He disappears, except for his hands, which squeeze the globe. They become drenched with blood, and blood drops from the globe ...

'The orgie [*sic*] of the monster continues: a banquet of blood on the high seas: the slaughter of innocents.' [subtitle]

The Monster then emerges from the sea: he sees the 'Lusitania' approaching, and submerges: as the ship goes by, he comes up and smashes it with his fist. He drags the women and children (reproduced from Mr. Lindsay's cartoon) down with him, and gloats over their dead bodies at the bottom of the sea.

'Gorged with blood, the Monster emerges from the sea and wreaks his vengeance on the Church, the home, the woman and the child.'[16]

Preparatory essays available in the Australian Archives provide enlightening reading about how the government employees who eventually oversaw Lindsay's 'Recruiting Kit' conceived of race. In the 'Paper on the derivation and meaning of the German word "Kultur"', the author presents a somewhat mangled version of history, calling Genghis Khan a Mogul Emperor (this was not the case, although his descendent Babar founded the Mogul dynasty centuries later). Nonetheless, he illuminates the thought processes that led to Germans being called 'Huns', after Attila the Hun. He claims that the conquests of 'Chingiz' [Genghis Khan] eventually led to the settlement of Brandenburg by Tartars. Following this, he draws a racial line in the sand between Anglo-Saxons and 'true' Prussians:

> The Tartars who originally settled down in Brandenburg are the ancestors of the true Prussians, and there is a remarkable similarity between the statements made by Kublai Khan and the present Kaiser. When Kublai Khan had nearly finished his conquests he said 'As there is only one God in Heaven there shall only be one King on earth', which is not very greatly different from the statement made by the German Emperor as follows—'All of you shall have only one Will and that is my Will. There is only one Law and that is my Law.'

Despite the lack of historical accuracy in this essay, the author demonstrates the logic of racial branding by depicting the Kaiser as an 'Oriental' despot, anti-democratic and bent on binding his people to slavery. Although unpublished, this manuscript provides important insights into the thinking of those who produced propaganda for the Australian public and illustrates the centrality of pre-existing racial stereotypes in the creation of the 'Hun' (The National Archives of Australia, c.1917).

Conclusion

As the subject of race was inherent to the development of propaganda in the Empire and Australia, it is not surprising that hated 'Asian' tropes were repackaged to be deployed against a new enemy. Norman Lindsay's work reflected a society that very quickly sought to explain and condemn morally questionable behaviour through the lens of race. The vital hate present in Lindsay's war art resonated because it successfully relocated existing racial stereotypes. In doing so, his work helped to bring the imputed moral issues of the war 'home' to a group of people who were geographically divorced from the immediate brutality of the conflict.

Notes

1. As Grenville observed, 'The division of the empire was largely on racial lines'. By 1909, all of the nations where 'white people predominated' had received a degree of independence through self-government. This was not the case with nations such as India.
2. For further descriptions on Indian 'Oriental types', see Shompa Lahiri (2000) *Indians in Britain: Anglo-Indian Encounters, Race and Identity, 1880–1930*. London: Frank Cass. For further insight into the 'Oriental tyrant' from the Far East see William Beckford (1786) *The History of the Caliph Vathek*, http://www.gutenberg.org/files/2060/2060-h/2060-h.htm. In one scene this early fictional 'Oriental tyrant' murders 50 innocent children so that a black 'Indian' demon will offer him entry to an alternative realm.
3. It is interesting to note here that concepts of racial difference were equally elastic among non-whites. Horne notes that in the United States of America, just before the First World War, 'Japan was the nation most admired by African Americans'. The Japanese were seen as a 'black people' who could successfully threaten white hegemony. See also: Ruth Craggs (2013) Book review, 'Memories of Empire Volume I: the White Man's World', *The Round Table*, 102(4), p. 391. 'Whiteness was never stable, nor was it exported to the colonies from Britain as a distinct idea and identity; rather, it was constructed, maintained, and sometimes contested in relation to colonial rule.'

4. The text beneath the image reads: '(1) There was a white Bull once. (2) Then he became light brown, and bought a turban. (3) He grew still more brown, and acquired a big sash and a curved sword. (4) His brownness increased, and he acquired petticoats and funny shoes. (5) Gradually he became so brown that he was practically black, and he undressed himself again and wore a loin-cloth. (6) And in the end he will annex so many niggers that he will be quite black, and the last scene will be an aboriginal Bull roasting his 'possum over a small fire.'
5. It should be pointed out here that Lindsay's similar use of tropes to that of John Tenniel's is hardly surprising. Lindsay was partly taught by his brother Lionel, who in turn taught himself to draw from the pages of *Punch*. See Holden (1995, p. 114) and Smith (http://adb.anu.edu.au/biography/lindsay-norman-alfred7757/text12457).
6. Atrocity propaganda was also produced by other countries, i.e. France, but as it was not widely disseminated in the English-speaking countries, it will not be included in this article.
7. This defence was framed thus: *Prussian* militarism needed to be crushed so that the *rights of small nations* such as Belgium could be protected.
8. For a detailed account of the role played by Allied atrocity propaganda *during* the war, see: Gullace, N. (1997) and R. Harris (1993) 'The "child of the barbarian": rape, race and nationalism in France during the First World War, *Past & Present*, no. 141, pp. 170–206.
9. See also Rudyard Kipling's poem 'The White Man's Burden', reproduced in C. Brooks and P. Faulkner (Eds.) (1996) *The White Man's Burdens: An Anthology of British Poetry of the Empire*. Exeter: University of Exeter Press.
10. The Black Hole of Calcutta was a small cell in which a large number of British and Indian soldiers and civilians were held overnight following the defeat of the forces by the Bengali ruler. Prisoners were alleged to have died of suffocation, dehydration and trampling.
11. The facts of the event remain extremely elusive—even the identity of the people who died is contested, as is the number of people who died. It was, and remains, a contentious event.
12. J. H. Little (1915) The Back Hole - the question of Holwell's veracity, *Bengal Past and Present*, 11, p. 76.
13. 'Massacre of English Officers and their wives at Jhansi', in *The History of the Indian Mutiny*, steel engraved images. London Printing and Publishing Country, London, p. 186.
14. For a comprehensive survey of Lindsay's *Bulletin* work during the war, see: Peter Fullerton (1983) *Norman Lindsay War Cartoons, 1914–1918*. Melbourne: Melbourne University Press.
15. The title for the Kit at the State Library of Victoria, which holds the Kit with the original cardboard folder, is *General Plan of Campaign for Reinforcing the Australian Imperial Force*. This is the same title mentioned in the catalogue database at the National Gallery of Australia. However, 'Recruiting Kit' is a term used in Roger Butler's book, which was mentioned in the introduction and this chapter, and as it is succinct and descriptive, I feel it is the ideal title.
16. *Animated Cartoon of German Monster for Picture Theatres to be Released in Midst of Campaign*, Recruiting Kit, State Library of Victoria. To see the film, go to Poppy de Souza, 'Curator's clip description', *Cartoons of the Moment—Today the German Monster Threatens the World*, http://aso.gov.au/titles/newsreels/german-monster-threatens/clip1/, accessed 20 January 2010.

References

Animated Cartoon of German Monster for Picture Theatres to be Released in Midst of Campaign, Recruiting Kit, National Film and Sound Archive.

Baker, S. (1990) Describing images of the national self: popular accounts of the reconstruction of pictorial identity in the First World War poster, *Oxford Art Journal*, 13(2), pp. 24–30.

Bindman, D. (2002) *Ape to Apollo, Aesthetics and the Idea of Race in the 18th Century*. London: Reaktion Books.

Castle, K. (1996) *Britannia's Children: Reading Colonialism through Children's Books and Magazines*. Manchester, NH: Manchester University Press.

Chamberlain Papers (1901) JC/141/1/17, private, Chamberlain to Sir John Forrest, 13 November 1901 (quoted in Huttenback, 1976).

Chubb, P. and Russell, R. (1998) *One Destiny! The Federation Story—How Australia Became a Nation*. Ringwood: Penguin Books.

Curtis, L. P. (1997) *Apes and Angels: the Irishman in Victorian Literature*, revised edn. Washington, DC and London: Smithsonian Institution Press.

Day, D. (2000) The 'White Australia', in C. Bridge and B. Attard (Eds.), *Between Empire and Nation, Australia's External Relations from Federation to the Second World War*. Melbourne: Australian Scholarly Publishing.

Douglas, R. (1970) Voluntary Enlistment in the First World War and the Work of the Parliamentary Recruiting Committee, *The Journal of Modern History*, 42(4).

French, D. (1986) *British Strategy and War Aims*. London: Allen and Unwin.

Grenville, J. A. S. (2005) *A History of the World from the 20 to the 21st century*. (London: Routledge).

Gullace, N. F. (1997) Sexual violence and family honor: British propaganda and international law during the First World War, *American Historical Review*, 102(3), 714–747.

Gullace, N. F. (2010) Barbaric anti-modernism: representations of the 'Hun' in Britain, North America, Australia, and beyond, in P. James (Ed.), *Picture This: World War I Posters and Visual Culture*. Lincoln: University of Nebraska Press.

Holden, R. A. (1995) A plague of Lindsays, in U. Prunster (Ed.), *The Legendary Lindsays*. Sydney: Beagle Press and the Art Gallery of New South Wales.

Hollingworth, J. M. (1993) The call of Empire being the Study of the Imperial Indoctrination of Australian School Children in the period 1890–1910, PhD Thesis, La Trobe University, Melbourne.

Horne, G. (2004) *Race War! White Supremacy and the Japanese Attack on the British Empire*. New York, NY: New York University Press.

Horne, J. and Kramer, A. (2001) *German Atrocities 1914: A History of Denial*. London: Yale University Press.

Huttenback, R. A. (1976) *Racism and Empire, White Settlers and Coloured Immigrants in the British Self-governing Colonies, 1830–1910*. Ithaca: Cornell University Press.

Lake, M. and Reynolds, H. (2008) *Drawing the Global Colour Line: White Men's Countries and the Question of Racial Equality*. Melbourne: Melbourne University Press.

Le Queux, W. (1914) *German Atrocities: A Record of Shameless Deeds*. London: G. Newnes.

McClintock, A. (2007) Soft-soaping Empire: commodity racism and imperial advertising, in N. Mirzoeff (Ed.), *The Visual Culture Reader*, 2nd edn. London: Routledge.

Miles, A. H. and Pattle, A. J. (1895) *52 Stories of the Indian Mutiny*. London: Hutchison.

Porter, B. (1968) *Critics of Empire: British Radical attitudes to colonialism in Africa 1895–1914*. (Basingstoke: Palgrave Macmillan).

Read, J. M. (1941) *Atrocity Propaganda: 1914–1918*. New Haven, CT: Yale University Press.

Robertson, E. (2010) The Hybrid Heroes and Monstrous Hybrids of Norman and Lionel Lindsay: Art, Propaganda and Race in the British Empire and Australia from 1880–1918, MA Thesis, Australian National University.

Said, E. (2003/1978) *Orientalism*. London: Penguin.

Smith, B., Lindsay, Norman Alfred (1879–1969), *Australian Dictionary of Biography*, National Centre of Biography, Australian National University, http://adb.anu.edu.au/biography/lindsay-norman-alfred7757/text12457, accessed 28 July 2013.

Symons, J. (1955) *Horatio Bottomley*. London: Cresset Press.

The National Archives of Australia, Paper on the derivation and meaning of the German word 'Kultur', c.1917, unpublished manuscript, AWM 25 317/2.

Thompson, R. C. (2000) in C. Bridge and B. Attard (Eds.), *Between Empire and Nation, Australia's External Relations from Federation to the Second World War*. Melbourne: Australian Scholarly Publishing.

Williams, J. F. (1999) *Anzacs, the Media, and the Great War*. Kensington, NSW: UNSW Press.

War Opinion in South Africa, 1914

Bill Nasson

One point on which historians have generally long been agreed is the depth and scale of war enthusiasm at the outbreak of the First World War in 1914. Not only did populations in belligerent European countries like Germany and France want war; popular opinion in British white settler dominions easily echoed the pro-war mood of the great metropolitan crowds around Whitehall in the early days of the August crisis. Whether in New South Wales, Australia, Natal, South Africa, or British Columbia, Canada, imperial subjects supported entry into a major European conflict with a mixture of enthusiasm, innocence and naivety. 'Australians', according to Bill Gammage, 'hailed England's declaration of war on Germany with the most complete and enthusiastic harmony in their history.'[1] 'Naive and conditioned by military training and imperialistic schooling', New Zealand youths, in the view of Paul Baker, 'welcomed war and seemed keen to fight it'.[2] Even in a rather less obviously unified South Africa, W.K. Hancock cites the tough attitude of Arthur Gillett, Quaker, liberal, and Johannesburg banker; while wrinkling his nose at hysterical jingoism, his belief was 'fight we must . . . get trained for the day that may come'.[3]

More recently, however, a newly emerging scholarly literature on the impact of war in 1914 suggests that the commonplace popular images of early Great War enthusiasm are essentially misconceived. Indeed, the very notion of a tide of war enthusiasm is now beginning to be seen as one of the classic myths or clichés of histories of the twentieth century. For Britain itself, no less, it has now been argued that the rolling waves of volunteers of August and September 1914 did not join through ignorance of the ugly realities of war. Instead, acutely aware of the miseries of Belgium and northern France, they enlisted to stave off the costs of defeat.[4] From the outset, Australians, equally, did not fall over themselves to embrace the war. While a gritty resolve to fight certainly materialised, that determination lay not just in empire patriotism, but no less strongly in such factors as growing unemployment, social deprivation, and rising xenophobia around invented domestic German or Turkish enemies.[5]

South African circumstances provide a particularly illuminating context upon which to bring to bear such reappraising historical perspectives. For war sentiment and war opinion here probably divided more ways than in any other settler colonies of the Empire. This was partly because responses to intervention in an imperialist war were formed in the lingering shadow of an earlier, anti-imperialist war at the turn of the century, when a great many settlers had displayed little loyalty and less love for Britain. And it was partly because, instead of an idiom of national mood, there existed a formidable morass of varying popular beliefs and allegiances. While there is no doubting the very great degree to which the Union as a whole was caught up in the war crisis, reaction to the conflict in Europe was rooted in a fairly fractured civil society. On one side, there were differences of rank, culture, and political station between white English-speakers, loyal Anglo-Afrikaners, and a morose rump of ordinary Afrikaners. On another, there were the complications of racial constituencies: whites, Africans, Coloureds and Indians. Even further, the pendulum of class and national loyalties between middle and professional classes, and workers, artisans and peasants, swung wide. Finally, there were the complex intersections of strong and diverse regional political cultures and rivalries between, say, Natal and the Orange Free State; and, within these, self-conscious urban and rural understandings of the world of the Union, between a white city squirearchy and farmers on the infertile margins, whose wants continued to outrun their resources. In sum, whatever the weight of recent Union expectation of a shared national consciousness, fused with imperial loyalty, South Africa was some way short of the dominion coherence of New Zealand or Australia. What this would mean for its 1914 war mood, as the present study will attempt to show, is that in the popular turmoil at the outbreak of hostilities, South African experience was both different from, and yet, in some respects, similar to, the reactions of other 'white dominions' implicated in Britain's war effort.

For a whiff of early South African war enthusiasm, quickly tempered by foreboding, we need go no further than the *South African College Magazine*, chronicle of Cape Town's well-to-do grammar school equivalent of Melbourne's Scotch College. In September 1914, it greeted hostilities in Europe as a welcome after-dinner satisfaction, crowing that, 'the blaze of war has put to shame the pale splutterings of individual and party interests'. War fixation was helping to knit together new levels of national consciousness and national integration, which were being swept along 'by gusts of fellow feeling'.[6] As a comment on white school patriotism in Edwardian South Africa, this breathless passage could have come just as naturally from the Australian *Melburnian* or the *New Zealand School Journal*.[7] Yet, what is strikingly different is just how swiftly the *South African College Magazine* shed its celebration of settler war unity. A mere two months later, it alerted dormitories to 'danger in the air. There are traitors in our midst, and enemies on our border.'[8] And, by the beginning of 1915, there was growing anxiety that the Union's political fissures were showing 'our weakness as a nation to the world'.[9]

The obvious perspective opened by these sentiments is the unexpectedly unhingeing impact of the opening of the Great War upon some of the assumed nation and empire certainties in South Africa. Unlike New Zealand, where in August 1914 there existed 'no separate declaration of war, no debates in Parliament',[10] and no real public dissension to speak of, the Union's white dominion pieties embodied little more than half the truth. War support for Britain was from the outset to be derided by the anti-British feeling of Afrikaner republican interests, for whom nation and empire were not two agreeable sides of the same historical coin, but profoundly different currencies. Naturally, these conflicting currents in white politics will be familiar to historians of early twentieth-century South Africa. At the same time, the spread of conflicting popular passions and beliefs aroused by the Union's war intervention in 1914 may be a little less familiar, if only because there are few historical syntheses of South African society and Great War experience.[11] One significance of the ferment of 1914 is not only that it shows that there was much more to war attitudes than a simple polarity between support for, and opposition to, pro-war Union government decisions. It is also highly revealing of the degree to which South Africa's many constituencies of public opinion aspired to international attachments.

To convey some sense of an atmosphere thick with war talk or talk of war, this argument will develop in four thematic stages: examining, first, the red, white and blue strands of pro-war, reflexively English empire loyalism; then considering 'major segmentation and sectional breaking away'[12] within smouldering rural Afrikaner society; and then paying some attention to vigorously diverging pro-war, anti-intervention and pacifist trends in organized white labour politics. Concluding thoughts will reflect upon the gulf between mobilized war opinion and war-related kinds of popular commotion within the broad mass of black and white society, beyond any formal political arena. It is here that we encounter responses and allegiances which neatly fit James Hinton's evocative notion that agitation against war mobilization has always rested as much in visions as in protests.[13] First, some essential perspectives should be sketched.

I

Immediately before war, some conditions in the Union of South Africa were sufficiently similar to other industrializing parts of the Empire to make the more conventional differences loom small. As in 'Wobblies' Australia or on the strike-bound wharves of New Zealand (or, for that matter, in Triple Alliance Britain itself), 1913–14 was a time of unprecedented political antagonisms among working classes and other disaffected social strata. Here, the pre-war unrest assumed divergent forms in localities of differing historical experience and political importance. A general strike in January 1914 by white miners and railway workers so alarmed the grey eminences of the Rand Club that they turned their Imperial Light Horse expertise upon 'The Labour Problem', establishing a Volunteer Force to save Johannesburg capitalism from the threat of syndicalism. The spate of white labour troubles coursed into July, with Union government and English press growing edgy about the danger of militancy spreading to African miners on the Witwatersrand gold fields.[14] Pre-war black unrest saw strikes by African and Indian miners, anti-pass protests by African women in the Orange Free State, the launch of Gandhi's *Satyagraha* campaign, and pained agitation against the 1913 Natives' Land Act, marshalled by the newly-formed South African Native National Congress (SANNC). Yet, much of this constellation of unrest had more or less peaked by August, and the crisis was certainly not a factor which in any way impeded or complicated South Africa's entry into war as a British dominion.

Naturally, that entry was not without other kinds of difficulty. On the one hand, Prime Minister Louis Botha and close cabinet cronies like Jan Smuts, both 'old Boer generals' rather prone to 'English sickness',[15] embraced intervention both as imperial duty and as a canny means of advancing national sovereignty and regional sub-imperial ambitions.[16] Elsewhere in parliament, however, the newly-constituted National Party was disdainful of British requirements. General J.B.M. Hertzog's Nationalist Afrikaners asserted the priority of a more autonomous South African interest: one, moreover, which translated into insistent opposition to 'South African forces being used in the service of the British Empire in a war which was not considered to be South Africa's war, only twelve years after the Anglo–Boer War'.[17] At their first Transvaal Congress in August, Nationalists attacked South African Party and Anglophone Unionist Party support for the war and, as declared neutralists, dissociated themselves from military participation, particularly any anticipated move against German South West Africa (GSWA).[18] In a further gloss on its hardening opposition, the National Party suggested that involvement would undermine not just the economic development essential to the maintenance of white supremacy, but that external military distractions might jeopardize that very supremacy itself. 'What would be the position', asked the MP for Rustenberg, 'if the able-bodied men went to war and a native rising took place?'[19] In this, at least, it is likely that a pistol-packing Piet Grobler spoke for a wide range of opinion on both sides of the early anti-war/pro-war divide.

The South African Party government's own war declaration on 8 September was accompanied by English press outrage against Hertzogite neutrality, and the Nationalist view that ministers were acting not as ministers of the Union but as agents of Great Britain. While the *Cape Times* grudgingly conceded 'a Dutch South African's view on independence', it barked that 'it is better to be a dependent of Britain who gives every privilege, the same as her own sons and daughters, more than any other nation in the world. It should be every British Subject's privilege to fight for that liberty, not to endanger the defences of the country and the integrity of the Empire'.[20] Responding to Hertzog's assertion that calls for war loyalty were diverting attention away from pressing domestic issues, such as Afrikaner social distress in the countryside, the *Pretoria Friend* bluntly declared, 'civilization is in danger and Hertzog is thinking about the poor condition of cattle in the Orange Free State. Britain has drawn a righteous sword for liberty. Hertzog thinks it is still too early to decide if the allies are right'.[21] These and other English newspapers made a great deal of this: of the fact that the parliamentary intransigence of Hertzogism was a blemish upon the ideal of national war unity.

Obviously, although leading white political formations were divided over war entry, nothing remotely compared with a 1914–15 Italian 'intervention crisis' to shake the Union. Quite apart from Botha and Smuts's political appreciation that South Africa could not be a neutral British dominion, and that it was already effectively at war with Germany on the expiry of Asquith's ultimatum on 4 August, Union authorities seemed to have no great difficulty in winning a general level of support for war. Without much bidding from their politicians, middle-class and lower middle-class sectors of English and loyal Anglo-Afrikaner society rallied behind Union intervention, driven by a mix of nation and empire conviction, and a seasoning of colonial jingoist enthusiasms. Early in August, rowdy urban crowds were pressing against newspaper offices for war reports, chorusing the national anthem, and carrying extravagant pro-war resolutions at meetings and rallies. Typical of these was Cape Town's 'The Call', strongly supported by students, which crowed, 'it does not need General Botha's emphatic [war] declaration . . . to provide assurance that the South African nation, with Canada, Australia and New Zealand, will range herself without hesitation or reservation by the side of the united nations of Britain and Ireland'.[22] Presumably, Irish history cannot have been too widely studied at the University of Cape Town.

A pro-war thread ran through a great many institutional contexts and also through other, more amorphous, areas of localized opinion. It was present in the public burning or shredding of the 8 September issue of the Hertzogite *Het Volk* which had concluded, 'England declared war on Germany for no other reason than self-interest',[23] by belligerent and rowdy students in Cape Town and Durban. It was present in the

Tricolour flown by scores of Cape municipalities which scrambled to host the French and Belgium Consuls, an enthusiasm undimmed by the odd dissenting newspaper correspondent who pointed out that the latter diplomat represented a country responsible for the Congo atrocities.[24] It was present in the playing of Belgian and Russian anthems by municipal orchestras, and in the singing of the *Marseillaise* by Anglican cathedral choirs. It was present in the clamour for local Austro-Hungarians and Germans who were listed German military reservists to be restrained in concentration camps, like one established on land obligingly donated by the Witwatersrand Agricultural Society.[25] It was present in scattered, mostly English-speaking rifle associations, chambers of small manufacturing capitalists, sports groups, retail federations and farmer associations which offered volunteer service, money and supplies for the war effort.

War enthusiasm was also present in the loyalist Afrikaner civic virtue of small towns like 'Patriotic Riversdale' or 'Patriotic Porterville' in which Mayors variously denounced German militarism and pledged 'services in any suitable capacity for the Union Government and the Great Empire of which the Union forms no inconsiderable part'.[26] It was present in the grounds of white schools, which dutiful teachers turned into public collection posts for war funds, and sometimes into stalls for the sale of war badges, to raise money and identify patriots. It was present in artisan and tradesman bodies, such as the Society of Automobile Mechanics of South Africa, which immediately volunteered 'members for mechanised transport and the aviation section of the Defence Force'.[27] It was present in the constructed wives and mothers framework of middle class women's voluntary social organization, whose members turned towards baking for Belgium and 'knitting warm garments for the Mother Country'.[28] And it also found an absentee kind of imperial base, in the displaced nationalist response by 'Rand Australians', 'Transvaal New Zealanders', and 'Cape Irish' to form military contingents for the Union, to say nothing of the Natal 'Sons of England At Harrismith' volunteers, and the Lancashire and Yorkshire Association's provision of 'Rosebuds' to emulate recent sterling service in the 1906–8 Bambatha Rebellion.[29] For the men of these bodies, blooded in the South African War or other colonial warfare, the prospect of a proper European war evidently proved a compelling attraction.

Predictably, given what one scholar has termed the encrusted 'imperialistic façade'[30] of English-speaking churches, pulpits were quick to condemn Prussian militarism and to support Union intervention 'in order', to quote a Transvaal Anglican Bishop, 'that the cause of right may prevail'.[31] Other clergy likened neutrality or pacifism to atheism, driven by a stiff white feather belief that volunteering for service was not a choice but a sacrifical obligation. But not every altar fell whole-heartedly into line. Some coteries of Quakers and a few Nonconformist churchman declared for peace. And there was even Anglican dissent. Shortly after Botha's war declaration, a vocal fringe of pacifists pushed an uncomfortable Natal Anglican Synod into a resolution which 'expressed no opinion as to the rights and wrongs of this present struggle', and termed 'the existence of a state of war between Christian nations ... contrary to the teaching of Christ, a hindrance towards universal brotherhood, and the cause of enormous suffering by the masses of mankind'.[32]

Somewhat surprisingly, such anti-war expression seemed not to be part of Afrikaanse Nederduitse Gereformeerde Kerk (NGK) opinion at this stage, although the loyalist national unity of Afrikaner *predikanten* would pretty soon crumble. However, in August, certainly, NGK worthies avoided controversy; indeed, they were by and large resolutely committed to the Union's war position. *Dominees* of *ordentlike* (respectable) middling congregations in rural districts and towns, like Christiaan Malherbe of Villiersdorp in the Cape, made no bones about it being 'the duty of Dutch Reformed boys to do their duty to the King and country'.[33]

Such attitudes were music to the ears of South African Party and Unionist Party elites, who saw in them a commendable understanding of how war service could also serve the cause of white South African nationhood. If Union in 1910 had established a colonial nation by title, the consequences of 1914 might now endow it with the popular patriotism to knit together a common English and Afrikaner allegiance to Union and empire. In propagandizing instincts shared with some in New Zealand, Australia and Canada, middle-class opinion-formers in the major cities regarded investment in war not merely as act of imperial duty, but equally as service in the manly cause of forging national identity and purpose.

August, therefore, heralded a rush of editorials announcing that 'Dutch and English were all Britons', who would 'now speak as one nation', as the 'tendency of the war will be to draw the two white nations closer', around a dominant British, modernizing character.[34] The present war would repair the damage left by the Boer War, declared the *Rand Daily Mail*.[35] The *Natal Witness*, no less one for grand reflection, concluded that 'this war . . . will bring the white races closer together than they have ever been in the past, and it will and must bind them together for all future times'.[36] This rhetoric received probably its most ardent expression in Edwardian South Africa's cluster of private and state collegiate boys' schools, its sylvan 'little England on the veld',[37] which by September had common rooms purring over early rates of army enlistment.[38] Here, the conceit of Englishness was such a cultural purchasing point that gentlemanly Dutch–Afrikaner boarders (the Maasdorps or the Immelmans) were as hopelessly English in their patriotic heartiness as were Scots–Afrikaners (the Campbells or the Andersons).

It was precisely this 1914 world of the pre-Union 'old' schools, like Highbury, Hilton, or Selborne, with their benches of Romano–Rhodes tradition, which responded most keenly to Smuts's initial call for two volunteer divisions for defence; it was a short jump from cadets at the *South African College School* to export service in 'Springbok', 'Scotchies' or 'Jock's Brigade' volunteer troops.[39] Appropriately, it is the *South African College Magazine* which again provides a revealing voice, with English/Dutch columns urging 'Springboks' to 'remember, it is not for England you are fighting, but for the British Empire . . . and in fighting for it, you are fighting for South Africa. Young South Africa has gone to the battlefields, and . . . will come back a nation.' Later, some of those who rather fancied themselves as Britain's European Elect in Africa, were to be discomfited to run into startled Belgian and French civilians who apparently 'thought South Africans should be black men'.[40]

The SANNC would not have found such a notion incongruous. When war news first reached a special meeting on the 1913 land issue at Bloemfontein, delegates at once resolved to 'hang up native grievances against the South African Parliament till a better time', to mount 'a patriotic demonstration', and to 'tender the authorities every assistance'.[41] While a deputation hastened to assure the Botha administration of unwavering black support for any Union war effort, SANNC members involved in a forlorn Land Act protest campaign in London were 'longing to catch the first steamer back to South Africa to join their countrymen and proceed to the front', according to Congress Secretary, Solomon Plaatje.[42] One of the more bellicose was Walter

Rubusana of the Cape South African Native Congress who, in October, offered to raise 5,000 African infantry under his own leadership. They would be available to the government for a GSWA offensive.[43] Complementing the tributary patriotism of the Christian African nationalist intelligentsia, a fair scattering of chiefs and headmen in various rural localities rallied to the war, often as a groping opportunity for a renewal of authority. Under the approving eye of local magistrates, solemn 'chiefs and people' assemblies despatched dutiful resolutions and addresses to 'His Majesty and General Botha', 'King and Union', and to the British Governor General, Lord Buxton. Allegiance was carefully ordered in this adoring idiom: empire first, Union second.

Other dignified expressions included donations by rural elders from the Ciskei and Transkei to civic war relief funds in towns like East London and Port Elizabeth, and regular pickings for the nationally prominent Prince of Wales' Fund.[44] Further pro-war impetus came from other swelling local initiatives, orchestrated by committees of small businessmen, property agents, lawyers and the like. These included direct war contribution approaches to Smuts by the organized commercial merchant elite of the Transvaal British Indian Association and the Cape British Indian Union; the banding together of a (Cape) 'Malay Ambulance Corps' which also sought arms in view of 'Turks who respect not the home of the sick';[45] and fund raising concerts staged by Coloured tradesmen. Then there were flurries of support from rural classes which had little to do with beliefs in patriotic duty. From tough northern and north-western Cape districts like Gordonia came calls to 'be in' from impoverished Baster pastoralists, seeking chiefly to revive their good fortune of recent well-paid British Army service in the South African War.

To turn to Coloured political organization, and its principal embodiment, the Cape-based African People's Organisation (APO), is in many ways to mirror the black loyalist 'mainstream' reflected by the SANNC, with which the APO had contact. Here, too, there was a lively swirl of pro-war demonstrations, petitions, and resolutions. According to one authority, the entire 'content and editorial policy' of the APO newspaper became 'completely dominated by the First World War'.[46] With the APO distributing its own attestation forms in its August newspaper issues, urban and rural branches mobilized to raise 5,000 volunteers for an active service Coloured Cape Corps, which leaders like Abdullah Abdurahman and A.H. Gool lined up for the Union authorities. By mid-September, the APO Volunteer Corps had mustered 10,000 men, already fortified by chocolate supplies from a Cape Corps Comforts Committee. A confident Abdurahman tendered war service as a firm political investment, suggesting that 'by offering to bear our share of the responsibilities', Coloured citizens would prove themselves 'not less worthy than any other sons of the British Empire'.[47] Here, news of a respectable Indian troop turnout ('no one will appreciate this more than the Indians themselves')[48] was hailed for its exemplary symbolism. Further vindication was provided by eager comparisons with Irish Home Rule restraint; claiming a natural affinity with Ulster loyalists, the APO constituency was likewise inclined, 'to leave local grievances in abeyance and rally to Country and Empire'.[49] Behaving for all the world as if he were the personal emissary of Sir Edward Grey, Abdurahman spent the early war months lecturing audiences against any equivocation towards the British cause, for 'if the British Empire fell, they would all go with it'.[50]

Behind fine speeches, it is also clear that local war sensitivities played some role in shaping the belligerence of APO war opinion. Many rural APO branches, for example, were greatly concerned by the captive position of hundreds of migrant 'Cape Boy' workers in GSWA, and calls to support the war effort were sometimes linked to petitioning for specific Union military intervention across the border to liberate Coloured labourers from German control. Yet, even such potent support for soldiering was subject to a fluctuating but persistent undertow of anxiety about the war becoming an economic or social burden. As early as August and September, the APO began to be troubled by the possible impact of the war upon rural employment and living conditions, over shrinking supplies to licensed urban Coloured hawkers, and profiteering by white dealers at their expense. Its executive also called for food price controls, and war welfare subsidies to aid 'distressed Coloured citizens'.[51]

Such observations draw attention to the fact that the backing of arms in 1914 took place within a broad front of political concerns and understandings. For instance, for conservative, petitioning black interests such as the SANNC or APO, what the war challenge mainly signified was not irrational pleasure at contributing towards Union derring-do. What war excitement regenerated, in essence, were political claims of full citizenship on the segregationist state, and what it provided was a concentrated means of mobilizing and binding respectable class followings. Following their despondency at the racially discriminatory terms of Union in 1910, black political leadership perceived the outbreak of war as a buoyant opportunity. In fact, European hostilities broke out at the very moment that the feeble programme of the APO was coming under challenge from a more assertive, radical wing in Coloured politics. As Gavin Lewis has remarked of rank and file APO reaction to August war news, 'with relief, they and their leaders fell upon it, as a possible solution to their foundering strategies'.[52]

For SANNC President, John Dube, as much as for APO leadership, the war produced a number of popular aversions around which to define good patriotic conduct. For both bodies, their position was set against the treachery of Afrikaner 'slave' states, 'totally unworthy of the generous way in which the Imperial Government treated them in 1902', deplorable white labour sectarianism, and regrettable parliamentary party dissensions.[53] In other allusions, Afrikaners were excoriated for their associations with, and regard for, GSWA, unlike black identification with their 'native Union',[54] questions were asked about the loyalty of German settlers, and Slavs in Cape Town and Johannesburg were singled out for suspicion of being pro-Austrian. Although annoyed by Botha's initial reluctance to countenance a Cape Corps service because of the racist terms of the 1912 Union Defence Force Act, this did little to temper the enthusiasm of the APO elite for the expected dividend to be earned through the educative example of volunteer service for the Allies. In this sense, educated blacks in South Africa marched in step with loyal, Westernized, urban Maoris, also keen as mustard to demonstrate not only the worth of their citizenship but to show why its substance ought to be enlarged.[55]

Given the identification of a pro-war response as a clearing ground for the incorporationist desires of a predominantly urban elite, black war patriotism acquired a distinctively constitutionalist idiom. Papers such as *Ilange lase Natal* and *Tsala ea Batho* began to dream of a moral expansion of citizenship rights, in which spontaneous service and sacrifice would be rewarded by improved political and social prospects, thereby advancing the claims of Congress leadership to African inclusion in the body of the Union. Similarly, for *Izwi la Kiti*, the coming of war lit a freehold path to a more accommodating citizenship, through becoming 'part of the Defence Forces of the Empire and Union, whose interests are theirs in common with the white people'.[56] Africans were honourable: their due now was absorption into the larger organic unities of civilized nation and empire.

At the same time, the war was not a complete distraction from unpleasant political or social realities. Indeed, an acceptance of these provided the base for a transcending altruism. Thus, for the APO's Gool, 'however great and manifold' were 'the coloured people's grievances', at 'a time like this . . . the real relations of the rulers and the ruled came out'.[57] Similar thoughts stirred the minds of SANNC intelligentsia: Africans were 'not patriotic because of good treatment', nor were they needing to be 'willing militarists' to 'pledge allegiance to the Empire'.[58] In this context, the selflessness of a Cape Corps initiative was all the greater for APO rumbling that whatever 'British liberty means in the abstract, few of us can honestly say that we love it much in practice'.[59]

Black leadership strata also believed that mobilization conditions might provide personal opportunities to invoke ties of faith and clientage with Union officials and government departments. On the part of industrious APO intellectuals such as Abe Desmore, for instance, there was expectation of greater patronage, and official recognition of a consultative role in calling up Coloured assets.[60] War needs also encouraged absurdly inflated individual claims about capacities to command and deliver a mass African contribution. Such promises, in the hope of running up political credit, applied not just to would-be Kitcheners like Rubusana, but to wily traditional paramounts, notably the Pedi chief, Sekhukhune II.

Finally, the black intelligentsia as a whole drew quite deeply upon intoxicating currents of thought which implied that one consequence for Britain of a victorious European war would be to make liberalism and welfare a more vigorous objective of empire development. From this, subject native groups should surely benefit: were the Zulu of Natal not akin to the South Slavs? Credulous SANNC representatives fell upon the evangelizing, democratic language of British war propaganda. For, in terms of reformist imperial policy towards the Union, a fight for the rights of oppressed nationalities surely spoke for itself: the abolition of racial disabilities, a wider franchise, tenure and trade, these were the democratic benefits which mattered. Such expectations were overlaid by the soothing murmurings of slippery Union politicians, like Minister of Native Affairs, F.S. Malan, who in August welcomed the SANNC war stand as 'very wise', and 'likely to impress Parliament to consider their cause sympathetically'.[61]

II

The Afrikaner republican response to war was not one to earn much government sympathy. Here, the novelty of the outbreak of hostilities was that it abruptly unsettled the post-1910 consolidation of Union through the accommodationist compromise of an independent British–Dutch component of empire. For a start, developments in other pale parts of that empire seemed to confirm the more visceral of Afrikaner separatist instincts. In Ireland, elements within the Irish Republican Brotherhood were denouncing nationalist John Redmond's backsliding acquiescence in a British Army enlistment drive.[62] Attentive commentators in the Afrikaner press held up Redmond as un-Irish, a salutary model of dishonourable behaviour.[63] Across the Atlantic, Henri Bourassa, tempestuous luminary of the Quebec 'autonomists', carried anti-imperialist enthusiasms beyond mere French-Canadian opposition to a national Canadian war effort. Building on shared republican sympathies with Hertzog's National Party, Bourassa despatched letters and copies of speeches to the Nationalist leader in the latter months of 1914, in order to encourage radical Afrikaners to rally against war entry and to assert anti-British interests.[64] Such diatribes, relayed in papers like *De Zuid Afrikaan* and *Ons Land*, had a telling effect upon disaffected segments of the middle class Afrikaner intelligentsia, for whom French–Canadian notions that German atrocities in Belgium were more than matched by those of the British in South Africa, had plenty of meaning and relevance.

Equally, an articulated republican vocabulary, and an awareness of its wider imperial dimension, was by no means the sole force behind Afrikaner opposition to Union war policy. Indeed, whatever role it played was for the most part peripheral in a good many local rural circumstances. Much forthright anti-war sentiment came, for example, from disgruntled Cape ostrich farmers, already pinched by a feather market collapse which had commenced the previous year. Similar opposition was voiced by producers in (deciduous) Fruitgrowers' Associations, who feared export losses. Wool and wheat farming communities expressed dismay at disruption, forecasting civilian war casualties in the shape of poor whites who would be made more poor. And, in the northern Cape by October, commercial farmers were becoming deeply disturbed by a war which, by closing diamond diggings and inflating food prices, was turning workless and ill-fed African workers loose into the countryside, endangering social authority over them.[65]

Other outbursts were more palpably part of an emerging, unfocused republican spleen, or of simple alienation from the state. They were most marked in marginal rural society, where many were still semi-literate or illiterate, and where fragments of war information were often digested through a lining of rumour and eccentric interpretation. At Ladybrand in the Orange Free State, for example, a group of railway workers was interned in December for appealing to local Afrikaners to billet invading German troops in their homes.[66] On the Cape West coast, some fishermen looked to befriend German submarines by renaming their boats, Bismarck and Kaiser Wilhelm.[67] Elsewhere, Rifle Association and Civilian Training Association property was maliciously damaged. In several Western Cape towns, loose brawling occurred as Afrikaner youths who tried to run up the old Boer *Vierkleur* were attacked by 'red, white and blue' coloured 'patriots'. Other incidents saw Transvaal landowners threatening to evict *bywoners* who complied with Active Citizen Force enlistment orders, and prominent Western Cape wheat farmers stalking out of church concerts when the national anthem was played.[68] Generally, resistance by burghers eligible for military service was extremely common: only a bare fraction of Afrikaners set out for volunteer enlistment centres in cities like Potchefstroom in the Orange Free State.[69]

Any summary picture of the early stage of war would amply confirm Noel Garson's observation in the 1970s that, by 1917, more than half South Africa's Afrikaner population was explicitly opposed to Union war policy.[70] Seminal to that position was the deep sense of nationalist anger that the Union, instead of at least remaining neutral, had been inserted so readily into the imperial war effort. What then further incensed men like Hertzog and Tielman Roos was Botha's brisk agreement in August to a request from Lewis Harcourt, the British Colonial Secretary, for Union forces to invade GSWA. Hertzog's fledgling National Party, its initial uncertain reach now dramatically extended by hardening war positions, growled that any seizure of neighbouring territory would run counter to 'Christian' and Afrikaner 'People's' traditions. It would also amount to treachery against a distinguished and cultured European state which had been solicitous towards Boer republicanism in its recent struggle against British imperialist greed. While Union generals like Beyers and de Wet were not particularly squeamish when it came to firing upon Afrikaner strikers, they insisted that 'Afrikaner blood should not be shed . . . in an imperialistic war between Germany and Britain'.[71] Lower down, local Orange Free State commandants explained their reluctance to attack GSWA by the presence there of their own countrymen. These included Cape rebel *bittereinders* (diehards) who, on the run at the end of the South African War, had simply reconstituted themselves across the Orange River as a new colonizing yeomanry. Such touchiness about GSWA was not only emotional. After 1902, some Afrikaner farmers had begun to diversify into its pastoral economy.

Some years before the outbreak of the First World War, Hertzog had been interviewed by a German journalist from *Tagliche Rundschau*. In outspoken comments, he predicted that the ideal of a 'general South African Republic' would be realized 'as soon as Britain was involved in a large war with a continental power'.[72] Predictably, the National Party leader was now repeatedly pilloried in the ultra-empire English press as a war traitor or German agent (likely to mastermind the poisoning of the Union's water wells), or a leader wilfully ignorant of the value of civilization. Too much the blustering politician, Hertzog remained far too prudent to cross into perilous extra-parliamentary rebellion against the Union. But a fair crop of other Afrikaner notables, with 'a more Sinn Fein outlook on the world',[73] were more politically and militarily impetuous. As a jittery Smuts put it in September, it was these hard malcontents who were contributing to 'a threatening climate of revolution or civil war'.[74]

So far as Afrikaner nationalist politics and 1914 are concerned, overriding all other disruptions was the issue of the 1914 Rebellion. From the moment several high-ranking officers resigned their Union Defence Force Commissions in protest against Botha's war policy, some form of anti-imperial military adventurism probably looked all but inevitable. One dissident General, the dreamy South African War veteran, J.H. de la Rey, took to meditating 'aloud if it were not, after all, God's will that the Boers should oppose Britain rather than wage war on her behalf'.[75] Along with a laager of subordinate commandants, Koos de la Rey was known to have been influenced by the venerable 'Siener' ('Visionary'), Niklaas ('Oom Klasie') van Rensburg, whose apocalyptic visions of British military disasters had gripped failing Boer commandos at the turn of the century. Now, once again, in August 1914, van Rensburg's Old Testament amalgam of blood spots on clouds, rivers of fire, and scriptural texts, encouraged converts to identify an escalating crisis for British power. This hell-fire construct promised the imminent collapse of empire, thereby opening the way to redeem the broken republican rights of 1899.

More broadly, protean republican objectives were also sustained by a sharp tinge of 'siener' persuasions within primitive, separatist, 'Dopper' NGK sects in the Orange Free State and Transvaal.[76] Their essential characteristic was not neutralism or pacifist belief. The need of the moment was opposition to the Union's war direction, not to the idea of war itself. For the crisis was something to be welcomed, appearing to offer an opportunity both to resolve the tension between blocked republicanism and imperial domination, and to vindicate Afrikaner *volk* sufferings of the Great Trek and Anglo-Boer War. Through political agitation fused with overheated prophecy and Covenant preaching, contemporary memory of the embattled 1899–1902 period now became tailored around the disaffections of 1914. With popular support running strongest in the classically poor harvest or bad debt regions of the north-eastern Orange Free State, Western Transvaal, and north-western Cape, an Afrikaner burgher rebellion broke out in October. For its northern leadership, Generals de Wet, de la Rey and Kemp, officers who had hastily slipped their Union Defence Force commissions, there were two settler nations within the same country. They declared the Union an imperial abomination, Botha and Smuts its miserable traitors, and proclaimed 'Independence' and the installation of a 'Provisional Republican Government' to be within reach.[77] Meanwhile, in the northern Cape, fellow-conspirator Lieutenant-General S.G. 'Manie' Maritz also gave Smuts a fright. Ordered to move against German positions on the GSWA frontier, he instead unsportingly disarmed and ran off his English-speaking troops, and then decamped with over 1,000 followers to throw in his lot with the German colonial authorities.

To crush the rising, Botha declared martial law. Demonstrating good political sense and confidence to worried Whitehall sympathizers, the Union government declined a British offer of New Zealand and Australian troop assistance; it had even less reason to accept anti-rebel coloured volunteers eagerly mustered by the APO. Commandeering 32,000 largely loyalist Afrikaner soldiers of the Union Defence Force, government forces broke the insurrection of some 11,500 burghers by December 1914. With rural Afrikaner society in rebel areas badly mauled and divided, the last flicker of rebellion petered out early in January 1915. Alas, equestrian Generals de Wet and Beyers had discovered to their cost that mounted commando exertions were no match for motorized vehicles, nor van Rensburg prophecies a substitute for adequate field intelligence.

A conciliatory Botha and Smuts settled for clemency towards the rebels. Only one officer, Kommandant Josef 'Jopie' Fourie, who had absent-mindedly forgotten to resign his Union commission before joining the rising, was executed for treason. By 1915 he was being fully assimilated as one of the more celestial of Afrikaner nationalist martyrs, sanctified by the pudgy D.F. Malan of the NGK to meet a growing magpie passion for republican icons. In general, the Rebellion experience encouraged dispersed nationalist forces to congeal around Hertzog's National Party, hardening into 'a post-rebellion world with a new Afrikaans political geography'.[78] That geography swiftly acquired some jagged features. Nationalist gatherings called to protest against possible conscription into 'Springbokken' infantry brigades were broken up by loyalist rowdies, and an assembled NGK came under great strain, remaining intact, but only precariously so. At a special conference in January 1915, pro-rebel and anti-rebel church sympathies ensured that proceedings were both complicated and delicate. To address this dilemma, NGK spiritual authority declared itself equivocal over the issue of the Rebellion being treason, and uncertain of whether or not the war declaration against Germany represented God's word. Such fuzzy religious positions on the merits of the war would probably bear useful comparison with the attitudes of Irish Roman Catholic clergy at this time.[79]

Away from the caution of a high NGK mood, at local rural church level there was often mistrust or enmity. For some Cape churches, rebel members were in disgrace for having brought shame upon law-abiding Afrikaner Christian communities. Elsewhere, numerous and fervent nationalist congregations split in northern districts like Rietfontein, with militant, separatist pro-rebel sects defining themselves not so much as opponents of Godless War as opponents of British Mammon.[80] Republican growling did not end there. Early 1915 brought marches by Afrikaner women to demand amnesty for 1914 rebels, and the founding of a Helpmekaarbeweging (Co-Operative Movement), to provide welfare and pay off their debts.[81]

An increasingly resonant nationalism was unquestionably a critical factor in the 1914 Afrikaner Rebellion. This was encapsulated most sharply by those at its head, a cohort of rural Afrikaner notables who were aggrieved over power lost during 1899–1902, haunted by antique Boer Republican purities, and for whom the measure of political audacity was the soldier's rulebook. Thus, at this level, August 1914 and the September advance on GSWA provided the essential 'signal ... for an Afrikaner rebellion against the dominant role of British imperialism in South Africa's political economy'.[82] Yet, attention should also be directed towards recent evidence and argument which suggest that it was more than demands for republican freedom and national independence which propelled so many seething Afrikaners into rebellion. By the 1910s, deepening class differentiation, wasting drought, and intensifying levels of regional and local agrarian landlessness had thrown up a despairing, debt-ridden substratum of marginal, poor white farmers and *bywoners*. They had little love for a Union government short on sweeteners. For this mass of poor burghers, armed rebellion therefore had intrinsic appeal – to acquire booty, and to secure possible title to land as a hedge against encroaching urban proletarianization.[83]

Moreover, many of these thin rebels were imbued with tingling messianic or millenarial incentives, as roving fundamentalist NGK 'Doppers' peddled the notion that they would be revitalizing their race and helping to secure the just heritage of the Afrikaner *volk*; above all, victorious rebellion would put an end to war and armies, topple the ruling capitalist interest of gold and maize money, and compose a 'promised kingdom on earth',[84] endowing dispossessed Afrikaners with a prosperous and peaceful new millennium. Rebellion, therefore, came to reflect an element of class polarization. And, in the manner in which it was commonly perceived by middle class urban loyalists, as representing unschooled primitive Calvinists or 'Dutch pro-Germans ... the uneducated class ... never much credit to the country, even in the ZAR',[85] it further embittered Unionist-Nationalist relations.[86] Beyond their ranks, a pacifist or two blamed war intervention for producing rebellion within an orderly and peaceful society. It is certainly true that an agrarian rising would not necessarily have occurred had the Great War not broken out.

III

Obviously, a vast difference existed between nationalist and white labour opposition to the Union's war declaration. What organized pacifist radicalism existed lay principally within the internal evolution of the white labour movement, which had taken shape roughly between the end of the nineteenth century and the outbreak of world war. A socialist leadership, initially dominated by immigrant British and Australian labour aristocracies, had by 1910 established an independent South African Labour Party (SALP). In 1913, this party affiliated to the Second International, and enthusiastically endorsed the Anti-War Manifesto of its Basle Conference. Labour anti-militarism was strengthened by the bruising 1913–14 experience of white workers being trampled by soldiers' boots, as urban labour radicals and a Rural Propaganda Committee began to nudge some Afrikaner workers, still 'more inclined to be republican than proletarian revolutionaries',[87] into Party affiliation.

This gradual consolidation was to be much changed by the advent of war. For a brief phase, anti-militarist and internationalist propositions held. On 2 August, before Britain's war declaration, the SALP Administrative Council condemned a looming conflict 'which can only benefit international armaments manufacturers' rings', and enjoined 'workers of the world to organise and refrain from participating in this unjust war'.[88] Associated anti-war resolutions were adopted by other small bodies of socialist opinion, including the Social Democratic Federation, Social Democratic Party, and the South African Industrial Federation. Some of these linked war motives to international 'European money power', and 'great European financiers', in ways strikingly similar to parallel Australian labour populism.[89] And such impulses were carried into the heart of the labour machine itself. It is notable that in carrying anti-war resolutions at party conferences in December 1914 and January 1915, the SALP appeared to be distinguishing itself from the war attitudes of Australian Labour or the New Zealand Social Democratic Party, and equally from those of European Socialist and Labour parties.

But the public atmosphere surrounding British entry into war had already persuaded leading SALP conservatives of the need to present a more flag-waving response to their largely English-speaking constituency of industrial workers. Most of these responded to the outbreak of war with the same instincts as most other English settlers. Trade union lodges shed pre-war 'anti-all war except class war' resolutions in favour of national interest; at the same time, jingoist party branches began to deck out 'Labour Legions', ready for combat. SALP leader, F.H.P. Creswell, was instrumental in turning the party's *The Worker* into a shrill voice for a growing pro-war faction, insisting that 'the need to see the war through was imperative by the necessities of Empire'.[90] A Major in the Rand Rifle Corps, as well as an experienced athlete of the Labour Right, Creswell used the former leadership bauble to carry several lesser Labour leaders with him into volunteer military service. By October, allied socialist organization, like the Industrial Federation, had also overturned anti-war positions. Earlier, in the special September parliamentary session, the SALP more or less fused with the war parties, and backed the GSWA expedition. Only one Labour MP abstained.[91]

As in Britain and elsewhere, division over the war issue produced an early, decisive breach within Labour ranks. Dissociating themselves from Labour war belligerence, pacifists such as Colin Wade and S.P. Bunting formed the War on War League during September, a determined minority movement which drew into its camp Bill Andrews, Chairman of Labour's Administrative Council, and also the Party Secretary, David Ivon Jones, a Welsh immigrant version of Karl Liebknecht. Drawing inspiration from a recent visit to South Africa by the leading British syndicalist, Tom Mann, who in Cape Town had assailed 'war-mongering' by 'financiers and capitalists',[92] the League resolved to resist 'this, or any other war at all times'. Declaring that workers 'had no quarrel with Germans or Austrians', it pledged itself to remedy 'Labour militarist excesses'.[93] In its first issue, the League's *War on War Gazette* called for the reinstatement of anti-war socialist internationalism, and also warned SALP nationalists of the dire electoral consequences of a pro-war stand. 'Flaunting the Union Jack', commented the *Gazette*, would do little to commend Labour virtues to 'the Dutch vote', a crucial working class constituency not comprised of 'British chauvinists'.[94] The prophetic truth of this would later be borne out by the results of the 1915 election, in which the white worker base of the SALP cracked and crumbled.

Again, as in Britain, Labour division was never so deep as to choke off completely continuing inner dialogue between pro-war and anti-war socialists. Indeed, the persuasions of radical pacifists even ensured that for a few months the War on War League would continue to have an impact upon the SALP as a whole. In a fiery struggle for political initiative, socialist pacifism exerted just sufficient influence at key local branch and regional levels to mobilize anti-war majorities at two party conferences. Moreover, when carried into several Cape farming areas, 'pacifist patriotism' also began to attract a trickle of unemployed Afrikaners in ostrich and fruit industries,[95] whose economic grievances opened their ears to radical denunciation of the war as a means by which capitalists could exploit workers who were having to make ever greater sacrifices. And, although the *War on War Gazette* was suppressed by wartime press censorship in November 1914, a beleaguered anti-war movement then sought other ways of registering its dissent, including the germination of a South African Peace and Arbitration Society, and a 'Martyr for Peace' commemoration of French Socialist leader, Jean Jaurès.[96]

The *Lusitania* episode and the forthcoming general election were to be ultimately decisive in entrenching the command of Labour's pro-war wing in the latter half of 1915. In August, a party special conference resoundingly endorsed 'support of the Imperial Government whole-heartedly in the prosecution of the war',[97] and prescribed a mandatory loyalty pledge. Following expulsions and resignations, marginalized League socialists flaked away to form, first, an International League of the SALP and, thereafter, an International Socialist League, grounded in 'native principles' of anti-militarism and proletarian internationalism. In the end, League diehards ended up honourable, but eclipsed; argument that 'Labour ceases to be Labour in South Africa once it declares war on Germany'[98] cut little ice with most white workers, and its disparaging tone can anyway hardly have boosted the anti-militarist cause. Moreover, while the eventual rejection of the job colour bar by League radicals towards the end of 1915 may have gone down well with urban black political leadership, the Abdurahmans and Dubes were appalled by the militancy of anti-British imperialism and class war socialism.

IV

Across South Africa as a whole, the intensity of political energies such as these, and the influence and pressure they exerted, meant that large combinations of people were stirred to define their positions in relation to war in 1914, taking particular care to create identities which declared for or against Union engagement. While there is no doubting the rapid spread of opinion in favour of the war, this should not necessarily be taken to signal straightforward euphoria or unqualified empire patriotism. For whole sectors of popular life remained hesitant, cautious, or sceptical in war outlook. Even within the loyalist African intelligentsia, there was some circumspection in August and September. For educationist D.D.T. Jabavu, war had been caused by a crisis of pacific European culture and institutions, not merely by a crisis of its balance of power. As he commented wryly, 'the Bantu were taken by surprise that the European nations who led in education and Christianity should find no other means than the sword . . . to settle their diplomatic differences'.[99] For its part, *Imvo Zabantsundu* criticized Germans for allowing themselves to be led astray by aggressive and militaristic leaders, and called upon belligerents to turn to ploughshares. And, while disliking the radical socialist ethos of Labour anti-militarism, the paper nevertheless applauded the local peace movement's 'struggle against Armageddon'.[100] Middle-class Africans had grasped the colonial message of civilized Christian enlightenment only too well.

Elsewhere, certainly, there was rough dominion empire chauvinism, with anti-German feeling dissolving into ever cruder Hun stereotypes. However, the meaning of popular crowd patriotism in large cities is, if not ambiguous, then at least complex. A standard piece of evidence for loyalist war dementia in the early stages of the conflict is the strength of anti-German rioting in the Union. True enough, Lusitania-inspired rioting occurred in May 1915, in which 'Huns' were beaten up by vengeful Navy bluejackets, and white and Coloured bar room hangers-on; this was accompanied by the destruction of shops identified as being German-owned or suspected of looking German, which meant some premises with Jewish names fell foul of crowd animosities.[101] Cape Town and Johannesburg rioters did not consider the war irrelevant: but, being mostly poor and mostly unemployed, their apparent pro-war violence can also be seen as an expression of standing grievances against European 'outsiders' or 'foreigners', now perceived to be war profiteering. In this sense, the war conduct of some groups of South Africans was not unlike that of the war passions of some groups of Australians in 1914 and early 1915: 'the product', to quote Robert Dare, of 'prolonged deprivation'.[102]

At another end of the anti-German scale was the pugnacious British League, confected by a section of the English mercantile elite in cities like Durban and Cape Town. Pressing for the internment or deportation of Germans and the confiscation of their business property, its zeal helped to secure a punitive 1915 Enemy Trading Bill which helpfully lined the pockets of some smaller English capitalists. One more Wolf barred from the market was one more opening for a Smith or a Jones. To this picture, those Benthamite barracks, the pick of South Africa's boys' schools, added a cultural chorus, imagining new curricula based on 'Craftics', 'Kaiserology' or 'Prussianism' as a consequence of any German conquest. F.Z.S. Peregrino's *South African Spectator* held up German colonial power as 'hell rule' which, if left to spread, would consign the Union's blacks to unprecedented 'slavery, oppression and cruelty'.[103] Seemingly convinced of this, APO branch convenors in Cape rural districts like Calvinia called for the issuing of arms to coloured men in the north-west, during an October panic over a rumoured German invasion from GSWA. Naturally, proliferating hostilities did not grow solely out of some inherent Union 'jingo' spirit. They were nourished by growing Allied propaganda in August and September 1914 about German atrocities in Alsace or Austrian atrocities against Serbs, and by the Union's own English press tendency to play anti-German sentiment as something more or less inseparable from anti-Afrikaner nationalist sentiment.

Even so, contrasting signals came from within popular opinion. Most prominent, obviously, were what amounted to first principle, Afrikaner, republican solidarities with Germany and its neighbouring colonial interest. Beyond this, in shadings within poorer rural Afrikaner society, there were wisps of a bloody-minded truculence. Expectation of a German victory, or wishful hope of one, led sullen workers to make trouble by directing 'seditious', 'disloyal', or 'treasonous' mutterings at local government officials. This led to a monotonous routine of fines, internment, or hard labour punishment in scores of remote municipalities. It was all rather alarming to Smuts. While he could confidently call South Africans to war in Johannesburg or Cape Town, here he had to act differently. One act was to maintain welfare provision for impoverished German families in country areas, so as not to inflame the feelings of sympathetic Afrikaner host communities. Even in the pro-war English press, ethnic attitudes towards Germans were not consistently hostile. While resounding enthusiasm greeted Botha's GSWA invasion, the benefits of its success were seen to be the absorption of commercially-minded Germans, 'orderly and most industrious settlers', into the Union.[104]

Within rural African experience, German sentiment also varied, depending on a myriad of local, social, or other circumstances. For instance, Rhenish, Moravian and Lutheran mission posts remained calm, their teaching authority undisturbed. Indeed, for none other than Solomon Plaatje, who had grown up on a Berlin Missionary Society station, there was disappointment that the outbreak of war had prevented him from undertaking a sentimental trip to its headquarters.[105] More quixotically, Chief Mhlolo Mvuso Matanzima Mtirara of the Transkei made an emotional contribution to German acceptance by naming a 1915 newborn son, Kaiser.[106]

At another level, as Albert Grundlingh has pointed out, people living in more isolated, quiescent rural districts felt the irrelevance of the war to colonial subjects. This was not simple apathy or political inertness: a distant European war had no tangible meaning for Africans' welfare, and observant chiefs, by turns fatalistic or disdainful, had no desire that it acquire one. Equally, in a more edgy urban development, loose collections of black mineworkers and male domestic servants, who associated English masters with wage reductions rather than human rights, were sufficiently brazen to sneer at empire prospects, and wish on German advance. War promised disruption, and that meant a potential opening for black workers to push through to elbow room and a measure of dignity. Similarly, for some Natal peasant groupings, the overriding radical meaning of the war lay in what it might do for land shortage. A spread of Zulu communities who relished the thought of Britain getting its comeuppance were effectively pro-German. In fact, some watchful coastal inhabitants were ready to welcome any German incursion, in anticipation that land appropriated by English settlers might then be restored to them.[107]

Furthermore, regions as diverse as the Witwatersrand and the Transkeian Territories displayed a shuffling but immediately visible millenarian temper. To bad seed which had been sown earlier, such as catastrophic drought and cattle loss, were added sudden wartime price inflation by white traders, wool market slump, looming shortages, and other threats to already collapsing black rural incomes. With news of Germany's drive into Belgium and France filtering back, and with the sight of garrisons being hastily withdrawn from Transkeian districts for GSWA service, late-1914 was a singularly appropriate moment for a journey of millennial hope. The keenest passengers were those in the reserves who, having become estranged from neighbours and the colonial authorities, needed new forms of collaboration or alliance to prosper once again. For some Transkeian factions, therefore, Germans and German opposition to 'the English' became, in the words of William Beinart and Colin Bundy, 'a kind of metaphor of resistance',[108] cultivating local visions of a transcendent freedom from colonial domination, with Westphalian cavalry presumably aiding Bhaca tribesmen to sweep loyalist rivals into the sea.

Other creeping chiliastic peasant responses to the onset of war included some fleeting affinity with the Afrikaner Rebellion as a redemptive revolt of small farmers against alien authority. Towards the end of 1914, disaffection in East Griqualand spilled over into armed 'moral economy' protest by pastoralists against cattle regulations and imperious local administration. Striking, too, was the appearance of little nests of prophets in parts of rural Natal and the Transvaal, whose emotional somatics were suffused with an elemental grasp of the war as the path to regaining a utopian African independence. However ephemeral their magnetism, or innocuous their actual mobilizing effects, such millennial therapeutics remain suggestive of one stark response to the arrival of war: that for those who felt most powerless to control adverse circumstances, enlarged war imagination was pulled into, and became part of, popular yearnings for social change. Here, such visions rubbed alongside those of Afrikaner 'Sieners' and 'Doppers'. Marginal men who did not share Union war aims, they moved restlessly in adjacent rural worlds. Coming to terms with the war was ultimately to come to terms with the unpalatable facts of South African colonization.

In October 1914, the Eastern Cape *Christian Express* described South Africa, 'pitted with the democracies of England, France and Belgium against the tyrannies of Prussia', wholly committed to 'a war not of our seeking'. 'The nation', continued the *Express*, 'never before went to war with such a clear and common conscience.'[109] In reality, however, there was no universal urge towards war, for editorial opinion was not necessarily public opinion. For a broad mass of communities and individuals not readily incorporated in formal movements or 'modern' ideologies, Union patriotism and pro-war attitudes never took the hold that it did within larger concentrations of Englishness and empire unionism. For imperial patriotic South Africa, the events of August 1914 and their immediate aftermath were perhaps almost as much historic millstone as historic milestone. War brought rifts, not national unity, for it provided an occasion for the discharge of particularist beliefs, loyalties and identities, grounded in contradictory political and social cross currents. It is not hard to see why many had an interest in, and enthusiasm for, Union intervention; nor, also, why imperial transmutation had firm limits.

For the real formation of a popular war temper in South Africa in 1914 was simply a manifestation of the ferment within Union society. That ferment carried the imprint of alienated sub-groups, black peasants, poor whites, disgruntled republicans, South African's equivalent of New Zealand's Waikato Maori[110] who knew enough about suffering in imperial wars to want at all costs to evade another. But what most distinguished South Africa from its sister white dominions was the richness and variety of its 1914 faint-hearts and disloyals. Not only did these include South African Russian Jews who had no stomach for supporting a British war effort which meant backing the very Tsarist regime which had persecuted them.[111] They included Mohandas Gandhi. Although he had left the country in July 1914, in a November letter he urged his Indian and white associates in the Union against any support of, or participation in, the growing war.[112] For this departed South African resident, even to nurse the wounded was to nurse the war. In this response, Gandhi added his own distinctive piece to South Africa's very divided reaction to the great imperial call to war of 1914.

University of Cape Town

Notes

This article is a revised and expanded version of a paper presented at a July 1994 symposium on 'Les Entrées en Guerre de 1914/The descent into War in 1914', Historial de la Grande Guerre, Péronne-Somme, France. I should like to thank colleagues of the Historial for helpful comments, particularly Jay Winter and Annette Becker. Grateful acknowledgement is also due to the Historical Studies Division of the Research School of Social Sciences in the Australian National University where I completed this piece as a Visiting Fellow at the end of 1994.

1. B. Gammage, *The Broken Years: Australian Soldiers in the Great War* (Harmondsworth, 1985), 4.
2. P. Baker, *King and Country Call: New Zealanders. Conscription and the Great War* (Christchurch, 1988), 15.
3. W.K. Hancock, *Smuts, Vol. I: The Sanguine Years, 1870–1919* (Cambridge, 1962), 377.
4. A. Gregory, 'British Public Opinion and the Descent into War', unpublished symposium paper, 'Les Entrées en Guerre de 1914', Centre de Recherche, Historial de la Grande Guerre, Péronne-Somme, July 1994.
5. R. Dare, ' "Bells and Bands": Australian Responses to the Outbreak of the Great War', unpublished symposium paper, 'Les Entrées en Guerre de 1914'.
6. *South African College Magazine*, 15, 3 (1914), I.
7. For which, see E.P. Malone, 'The New Zealand School Journal and Imperial Ideology', *New Zealand Journal of History*, 7, 2 (1973), 13–17; C. McGeorge, 'Race, Empire and the Maori in the New Zealand primary school curriculum, 1880–1940', in J.A. Mangan (ed.), *The Imperial Curriculum: Racial Images and Education in the British Colonial Experience* (London, 1993), 71.
8. *South African College Magazine*, 15, 4 (1914), 1.
9. Ibid., 16, 2 (1915), 5.
10. Baker, *King and Country Call*, 19.
11. Excluding a handful of specialized works dealing with South Africa's military experience, and very fleeting overviews in general histories, there is really only S.E. Katzenellenbogen, 'Southern Africa and the War of 1914–18', in M.R.D. Foot (ed.), *War and Society* (London, 1973), 107–21; N.G. Garson, 'South Africa and World War 1', *Journal of Imperial and Commonwealth History*, 8, 1 (1979), 68–85; also, tentatively, Nasson, 'A Great Divide: Popular Responses to the Great War in South Africa', *War and Society*, 12, 1 (1994), 47–64.
12. D. Schreuder, 'Colonial Nationalism and Tribal Nationalism: Making the White South African State, 1899–1910', in J. Eddy and D. Schreuder (eds), *The Rise of Colonial Nationalism* (Sydney, 1988), 220.
13. J. Hinton, *Protests and Visions: Peace Politics in Twentieth-Century Britain* (1989), viii.
14. *Cape Times*, 10 July 1914; *Weekly Telegraph*, 15 July 1914; A. Grundlingh, *Fighting Their Own War: South African Blacks and the First World War* (Johannesburg, 1987), 6–7.
15. G. Schutte, 'Afrikaner Historiography and the Decline of Apartheid: Ethnic Self-Reconstruction in Times of Crisis', in E. Tonkin (ed.), *History and Ethnicity* (London, 1989), 223–24.
16. See, for example, R. Hyam, *The Failure of South African Expansion 1908–1948* (London, 1972), 23–46; P.R. Warhurst, 'Smuts and Africa: A study in sub-imperialism', *South African Historical Journal*, 16 (1984), 82–100; P.J. Yearwood, 'Great Britain and the Repartition of Africa 1914–19', *Journal of Imperial and Commonwealth History*, 18, 3 (1990), 320.
17. S.B. Spies, 'The Outbreak of the First World War and the Botha Government', *South African Historical Journal*, 1 (1969), 52.
18. *De Burger*, 18 August 1914; T.R.H. Davenport, *South Africa: A Modern History* (London, 1991 edn.), 233.
19. *Union House of Assembly Debates*, 10 Sept. 1914, col.82.
20. *Cape Times*, 12 Sept. 1914.
21. *Pretoria Friend*, 10 Sept. 1914.
22. *Cape Times*, 5 Aug. 1914.
23. Ibid., 16 Sept. 1914.
24. *Rand Daily Mail*, 12 Sept. 1914.
25. *Cape Times*, 11, 13, 19, 24 August 1914; *Cape Argus*, 20 August 1914; *Diamond Fields Advertiser*, 16 August 1914.
26. *Cape Times*, 20 August 1914.
27. *Cape Argus*, 13 August 1914.
28. *Cape Times*, 1 Sept. 1914; *Cape Argus*, 11 Sept. 1914.

29. *Natal Witness*, 13 August 1914; *Cape Times*, 8, 13 August 1914.
30. C. Villa-Vicencio, *Between Christ and Caesar: Classic and Contemporary Texts on Church and State in South Africa* (Cape Town, 1986), 48.
31. *Rand Daily Mail*, 14 Sept. 1914.
32. *Natal Witness*, 16 Sept. 1914.
33. *Robertson and Montagu News*, 15 Sept. 1914.
34. For instance, *South African News*, 21 August 1914; *Cape Times*, 7, 12 August 1914.
35. *Rand Daily Mail*, 11 August 1914.
36. *Natal Witness*, 25 August 1914.
37. See P. Randall, *Little England on the Veld: The English Private School System in South Africa* (Johannesburg, 1982), 111.
38. *Diocesan College Magazine*, 19, 2 (1914), 3.
39. See Nasson, 'Potchefstroom to Passchendaele', *Southern African Review of Books*, May/June (1994), 23.
40. *South African College Magazine*, 16, 1 (1915), 4; I. Uys, *Rollcall; The Delville Wood Story* (Johannesburg, 1991), 6.
41. F. Meli, *South Africa Belongs to Us: A History of the ANC* (London, 1988), 46.
42. S.T. Plaatje, *Native Life in South Africa* (London, 1916), 301.
43. J. Pampallis, *Foundations of the New South Africa* (London, 1991), 101.
44. See, *South African News*, 11 August 1914; *Cape Times*, 3, 7, 19 Sept. 1914; *Izwi la Kiti*, 12 August 1914; *Imvo Zabantsundu*, 1 Sept., 13 Oct. 1914.
45. *Cape Times*, 12 August 1914.
46. M. Adhikari, 'Protest and Accommodation, Assimilation and Separatism: Ambiguities in the Racial Politics of the APO, 1909–1923', unpublished seminar paper, History Department, University of Cape Town, 1992.
47. *APO*, 22 August 1914.
48. Ibid., 5 Sept. 1914.
49. Ibid., 3 Oct. 1914.
50. Ibid., 7 August 1914.
51. Ibid., 22 August 1914; *South African News*, 11 August 1914.
52. G. Lewis, *Between the Wire and the Wall: A History of South African 'Coloured' Politics* (Cape Town, 1987), 85.
53. *APO*, 19 Sept. 1914; similarly, *Ilanga lase Natal*, 27 Sept. 1914.
54. *Izwi la Kiti*, 27 August 1914. My thanks to Dr. Patricia Hayes for drawing my attention to this theme.
55. Barker, *King and Country Call*, 211.
56. *Izwi la Kiti*, 12 August 1914.
57. *APO*, 4 Sept. 1914.
58. *Tsala ea Batho*, 8 Sept. 1914.
59. *APO*, 7 August 1914.
60. See, Nasson, 'Great Divide', 57.
61. Cited in Grundlingh, *Own War*, 14.
62. See J.J. Lee, *Ireland 1912–1985; Politics and Society* (Cambridge, 1989), 20–1.
63. *Het Volk*, 28 Sept. 1914.
64. C.M. van den Heever, *General J.B.M. Hertzog* (Johannesburg, 1946), 183. In 1899, Bourassa had resigned his parliamentary seat over Canadian participation in the South African War.
65. *Colesberg Advertiser*, 16 Oct. 1914; *De Zwartlander*, 19 Oct. 1914; *Robertson and Montagu News*, 7 Nov. 1914; *De Zuid Afrikaan Verenigd met Ons Land*, 4 Nov. 1914.
66. *De Zwartlander*, 19 Dec. 1914.
67. Cape Archives (CA), Carnarvon magistracy records, 1/CAR 5/1/5, J.N. Botha to Special Justice of the Peace, 28 Oct. 1914; *Colesberg Advertiser*, 18 Nov. 1914.
68. *De Zwartlander*, 17 August 1914; *De Zuid-Afrikaan*, 19 August 1914.
69. P.K.A. Digby, *Pyramids and Poppies: The 1st SA Infantry Brigade in Libya, France and Flanders 1915–1919* (Johannesburg, 1993), 11.
70. Garson, 'South Africa', 78.

71. P. van der Byl, *From Playgrounds to Battlefields* (Cape Town, 1971), 108; for personal flavour, M. Maritz, *My Lewe en Strewe* (Pretoria, 1935), Ch. 3.
72. Cited in P.H. Molotsi, 'The Decline of British Influence on South African Native Policies, 1855–1925', Ph.D. Thesis, New York University, 1979, 195.
73. Schreuder, 'Tribal Nationalism', 220.
74. J.C. Smuts to D. Reitz, 22 Sept 1914, in W.K. Hancock and J. van der Poel (eds), *Selections from the Smuts Papers*, 3 (Cambridge, 1966), 198.
75. K. Ingham, *Jan Christian Smuts: The Conscience of a South African* (London, 1986), 79; R. Kraus, *Old Master: The Life of Jan Smuts* (New York, 1944), 210.
76. L-M. Kruger. 'Gender, Community, and Identity: Women and Afrikaner Nationalism in the Volksmoeder Discourse of *Die Boerevrou*, 1919–1931', M.Soc.Sci. Thesis, Cape Town, 1991, 172.
77. *Ons Land*, 12 Oct 1914.
78. I. Hofmeyr, 'Popularising History: The Case of Gustav Preller', in S. Clingman (ed.), *Regions and Repertoires: Topics in South African Politics and Culture* (Johannesburg, 1991), 70.
79. For the latter, see D.W. Miller, *Church, State, and Nation in Ireland, 1898–1921* (Pittsburgh, 1973), 308–14.
80. C.F.A. Borchardt, 'Die Afrikaner Kerke en die Rebellie', in A. Eybers *et al.* (eds), *Teologie en Vernuwing* (Pretoria, 1975).
81. A. Ehlers en D.J. van Zyl, 'Die Invloed van die Helpmekaarbeweging in Suid-Afrika, 1915–1920', *Historia*, 35, 1 (1990), 73; Ehlers, 'Die Helpmekaar-beweging in Suid-Afrika: Die Storm en Drangjare, 1915–1920', *Argiefjaar-boek vir Suidafrikaanse Geskiedenis* (Pretoria, 1991), 8–9, 149.
82. M. Lacey, ' "Platskiet–Politiek": The Union Defence Force (UDF) 1910–1924', in J. Cock and L. Nathan (eds), *War and Society: The Militarisation of South Africa* (Cape Town, 1989), 35.
83. J. Bottomley. 'The Orange Free State and the Rebellion of 1914: The Influence of Industrialisation, Poverty and Poor Whiteism', 29–39; R. Morrell, 'The Poor Whites of Middelburg, Transvaal, 1900–1930: Resistance, Accommodation and Class Struggle', 11–15, in Morrell (ed.), *White But Poor: Essays on the History of Poor Whites in Southern Africa, 1880–1940* (Pretoria, 1992).
84. Hofmeyr, ' "Building a Nation from Words": Afrikaans Language, Literature, and Ethnic Identity, 1902–1924', in S. Marks and S. Trapido (eds), *The Politics of Race, Class and Nationalism in Twentieth Century South Africa* (London, 1987), 107.
85. *Zululand Times*, 24 Sept 1914.
86. Garson, 'The Boer Rebellion of 1914', *History Today*, 12, 2 (1962), 139; T.R.H. Davenport, 'The South African Rebellion of 1914', *English Historical Review*, 78 (1963), 93–4.
87. D. Yudelman, *The Emergence of Modern South Africa* (Cape Town, 1983), 133.
88. D. Ticktin, 'The War Issue and the Collapse of the South African Labour Party, 1914–15', *South African Historical Journal*, I (1969), 63.
89. For this, see W.D. Rubinstein, *Elites and the Wealthy in Modern British History* (Brighton, 1987), 348–9.
90. Cited in S. Forman and A. Odendaal (eds), *Lion Forman-A Trumpet from the Rooftops: Selected Writings* (London, 1992), 47.
91. The maverick W.B. Madeley, who later repented and supported the war effort.
92. *Cape Times*, 1 August 1914.
93. Ticktin, 'War Issue', 59, 62.
94. *War on War Gazette*, 19 Sept. 1914.
95. CA, Uitenhage magistracy records, 1/UIT 670/14, C. Bletherwick to Special Justice of the Peace, 25 Nov. 1914; *De Zwartlander*, 21 Nov. 1914; *Robertson and Montagu News*, 28 Nov. 1914.
96. *International*, 10 Sept. 1915; 8 Oct. 1915.
97. Forman and Odendaal, *Trumpet*, 47.
98. *International*, 15 Sept. 1915.
99. Quoted in Grundlingh, *Own War*, 15.

100. *Imvo Zabantsundu*, 15 Sept. 1914.
101. A.J. Hunter, 'Anti-German Riots in Cape Town, 1915', BA Hons. Dissertation, University of Cape Town, 1980, 12–28.
102. Dare, 'Bells and Bands'. My thanks to Dr. Robert Dare for permission to quote from his unpublished paper.
103. F.Z.S. Peregrino, *His Majesty's Black Labourers: A Treatise on the Camp Life of the South African Native Labour Corps* (Cape Town, 1917), 3, 40.
104. *South African News*, 17 August 1914.
105. B. Willan, *Sol Plaatje: A Biography* (London, 1984), 11, 181.
106. Equally, to one careful to hedge his bets, a second son (1918) was named George.
107. Section based generally on Grundlingh, *Own War*.
108. W. Beinart and C. Bundy, *Hidden Struggles in Rural South Africa: Politics and Popular Movements in the Transkei and Eastern Cape 1890–1930* (Johannesburg, 1987), 201.
109. *Christian Express*, 10 Oct. 1914.
110. See P.S. O'Connor, 'The Recruitment of Maori Soldiers, 1914–18', *Political Science*, 19, 2 (1967), 54; P.J. Gibbons, 'The Climate of Opinion', in W.H. Oliver (ed.), *The Oxford History of New Zealand* (Wellington, 1981), 212.
111. M. Shain, *The Roots of Anti-Semitism in South Africa* (Johannesburg, (1994), 80–1; cf. similar Canadian experience: D. Saunders, 'Aliens in Britain and the Empire during the First World War', in F. Swyripa and J.H. Thompson (eds), *Loyalties in Conflict: Ukrainians in Canada during the Great War* (Edmonton, 1983), 107.
112. P. Brock, *Freedom from War: Nonsectarian Pacifism 1814–1914* (Toronto, 1991), 276. Gandhi was, however, later to change his mind and to accept British ambulance duties.

The War Munitions Supply Company of Western Australia and the Popular Movement to Manufacture Artillery Ammunition in the British Empire in the First World War

John S. Connor

Among the nations that comprised the British Empire, the First World War has generally either been forgotten, as in India, as irrelevant to the achievement of political independence, or remembered, as in Canada, as the catalyst for developing a separate national identity. This article argues that both these historical interpretations ignore the extent to which the First World War was a shared British Empire experience. The article examines the establishment of the War Munitions Supply Company of Western Australia as an example of the popular movement to make artillery ammunition that swept many parts of the British Empire in 1915. The munitions movement provided an outlet for the patriotic surge that occurred in April–May 1915 in reaction to the German use of poison gas and the sinking of the Lusitania. It was also an attempt to overcome wartime economic disruption by creating a new local industry. The practicalities of cost and shipping meant that by 1917 artillery ammunition production was continued only in Britain, Ireland, and Canada, but in 1915 the Western Australian company was part of an Empire-wide movement to make munitions and support the war.

It was, according to a senior trade union official, 'a Patriotic Industrial Enterprise'.[1] In 1915, a wide range of the Western Australian community, from the ladies of Perth society to the mine workers of Kalgoorlie, bought shares and created a company to make ammunition for the British Empire's armies. This article investigates the establishment and demise of the 'Patriotic' and 'Industrial' Munitions Supply Company of Western Australia[2] in order to propose three arguments about the broader British Empire's experience of the First World War. The first is that the surge in British popular patriotism identified by Adrian Gregory in *The Last Great War: British Society and the First World War* as occurring in the second half of April and first half of May of 1915 (in reaction to German acts including the use of poison gas and sinking of the *Lusitania*) was also experienced in the rest of the British Empire. When the British Army's artillery ammunition shortage became public in the second half of May 1915, this surge of loyalty found expression in the popular movement to aid the Empire by making munitions. Of course this response was not found to the same extent in all parts of the Empire. As Robert Holland has written more generally about the idea of Imperial solidarity during the Great War, the munitions movement was found most strongly in Canada, Australia, and New Zealand and 'replicated elsewhere only in cantonal miniatures'.[3] Nonetheless citizens formed munitions committees in Waterford in Ireland just as they did in Wellington in New Zealand. In India, Sir Dorabji Tata's company provided the steel for munitions factories in which Indians made up the majority of the workers. The second point is that ammunition production was also advocated as an opportunity to increase local industrial capacity at a time when the wartime dislocation of shipping and other factors had badly affected economies in many parts of the Empire. The third is that the popular movement to make ammunition was a shared Imperial experience. Communities in the Empire looked to Britain for guidance, but they were also keenly aware of the munitions movements in other parts of the Empire. Australians looked to Canada for inspiration and to India for technical advice; Canadian conservatives viewed their manufacturing achievement as evidence of the superiority of Canadian private enterprise over the Australian Labor Government's socialism; Rhodesians sought links with South Africa, as did New Zealanders with Australia. Although this was so apparent to the people at the time, more recent historians of the nations that once formed the British Empire have generally seen the First World War in terms of gaining political independence or developing national identity, and this shared historical episode was forgotten.[4]

On 10 May 1915, the Perth *West Australian* described the torpedoing of the *Lusitania* as 'the latest and deepest crime of the Germans against humanity'.[5] The news of the sinking of a passenger liner and the drowning of over a thousand civilians would have particularly affected the people of Western Australia. As the transcontinental railway was still under construction, any travel outside the state, whether to the rest of Australia, the UK—almost one in five of Western Australia's 350,000 non-Aboriginal population was British or Irish-born—or elsewhere, had to be by sea. Adrian Gregory convincingly argues in *The Last Great War* that the British did not, as has generally been assumed, greet the outbreak of war in August 1914 with mass enthusiasm.[6] Instead, he finds that the rise in 'anti-Germanism and popular patriotism' in Britain can be linked to four events in the last two weeks of April and the first two weeks of May in 1915: the *Lusitania* attack, the use of poison gas at the Second Battle of Ypres, the Zeppelin bombing raids on Britain, and the release of the British Government report into German atrocities in Belgium.[7] As the *West Australian*'s reaction to the *Lusitania* sinking suggests, Western Australian society experienced a similar surge in patriotic support for the war. This was a reaction both to the incidents that had outraged British opinion,[8] as well to the news that the soldiers of the Australian Imperial Force were now in combat, having landed at Gallipoli on 25 April.

This fervour in Western Australia and elsewhere in the Empire[9] found an outlet in trying to overcome what became known as the 'shell crisis'. This crisis was partially an actual shortage of artillery shells resulting from the unprecedented use of heavy guns on the Western Front. As the *West Australian* told its readers in late April, in a few days in March at the Battle of Neuve Chapelle, the British Army had used more artillery ammunition than it had during four years of war in South Africa.[10] The 'shell crisis' was also the means by which some British politicians and generals expressed their dissatisfaction with Lord Kitchener as War Secretary and H. H. Asquith as Prime Minister, eventually leading to the Conservatives joining the Liberals in a coalition government, the responsibility for ammunition production being stripped from the War Office and given to a new Ministry of Munitions, and David Lloyd George taking the role of Minister for Munitions and then Prime Minister.[11]

From the beginning of May, Western Australian men offered to go to Britain to work in munitions factories,[12] but on 18 May Colonial Secretary Lord Harcourt publicly declined a New Zealand offer to provide workers.[13] In June, as newspapers reported British businessmen forming local munitions committees, volunteer workers increasing the output of Woolwich Arsenal, and the conversion of factories to shell production throughout the UK,[14] Western Australians began to ask, as one letter writer wrote in the Perth *Daily News*: 'Is it not possible for us to offer to make munitions for the British Government?' This correspondent answered his or her own question by proposing 'let us at least put one factory in activity in W.A., thus doing our share, and lessening the tension at home'.[15]

Perth businessman Hugh Plaistowe determined to turn this talk about producing artillery ammunition into reality. At a meeting of the Perth Chamber of Commerce on 22 June 1915, he moved that the Chamber begin discussions with the Ironmasters' Association and the Chemical Society of Western Australia about making munitions. The motion was carried unanimously, and the following week representatives of these three organisations met with members of the Chamber of Manufactures and established the Western Australian Munitions Committee.[16] The most significant decision to come out of the committee's inaugural meeting was to send a delegation to Melbourne, then Australia's federal capital, to meet with their Victorian equivalents and the Defence Department to obtain the specifications and other information required to manufacture shells. The delegation consisted of Ernest Tomlinson, co-owner of Western Australia's largest engineering firm, Tomlinson Brothers—who, with Plaistowe, had decided to step back from his business to concentrate full time on the munitions committee, fellow engineer W. Monteath, E. A. Mann of the Chemical Society, who was also the state's Chief Inspector of Explosives, and E. S. Hume, Chief Mechanical Engineer of the Western Australian Government Railways. The committee received donations to cover Tomlinson and Monteath's fares, while the state government paid for the civil servants. The four men embarked on 3 July.[17]

The Western Australian delegation's voyage to Melbourne was merely one part of the wider Imperial movement to make munitions. The *Windsor Magazine*'s pronouncement that 'Britain's reply' to Germany's 'uniquely dreadful' attacks was 'to transform her Empire into an arsenal and divert every available lathe and wheel, every brain and hand of her peoples, into purposes of war' was written as propaganda, but it also had an element of truth.[18] Canada, which before the war had an established steel industry in Ontario and factories making rifle ammunition and the locally-designed (but ultimately unsuitable) Ross rifle in Quebec, was already making munitions for Britain. In August 1914, the War Office had asked Sam Hughes, the Canadian Minister of Militia and Defence, to help place artillery ammunition orders with American manufacturers. Hughes did this, but also gained British contracts for a number of Ontario businessmen, who were formed into an *ad hoc* Shell Committee. Canada would become a major source of ammunition for the Empire's armies on the Western Front, but delays in fulfilling contracts in the first half of 1915 would lead the British Government to sidestep the Shell Committee and Hughes (who would be forced to resign in 1916 after a royal commission found evidence of profiteering on the initial contracts) to establish in November a more efficient administration in the form of the Imperial Munitions Board that answered directly to London and was chaired by Canadian businessman James Flavelle.[19]

On 6 July 1915, while the Western Australians were still in transit, India created the Railway Boards Munitions Branch. This was the culmination of meetings on the production of artillery ammunition that had commenced in May in London between the War Office and the India Office and in India between private manufacturers and government railway engineers.[20] Before the war, India had an extensive system of government armament factories aimed at equipping the Indian Army for colonial warfare and the Tata Iron and Steel Company making steel in Bombay (now Mumbai). This company's chairman, Sir Dorabji Tata, agreed in August 1915 to the Government of India taking control of Tata's entire steel output.[21] Lathe owners offered their machinery 'as a patriotic contribution' for the establishment of munitions factories. By September 16 railway workshops and 9 private companies were making 18-pounder artillery shell cases. These included the Albion and Hastings Mill factories in Calcutta (now Kolkata) and the Chora factory in the nearby Raniganj coal mining district.[22]

The 'very large number of patriotic offers of assistance' from the Empire to the British Government led the Ministry of Munitions to call a meeting in London on 12 August with representatives of the India Office, Tata Iron and Steel, Australia, South Africa, New Zealand, and Colonial Office civil servants representing Ceylon, the Federated Malay States, Nigeria, and Singapore to determine to what extent the enthusiasm to make munitions in these portions of the Empire could be matched by the actual capability to do so. The conference found that India, with a local steel supplier and a pre-existing system of government armament factories and inspectors, could produce and export ammunition, but the ability of the other attending colonies and dominions to do the same was not as certain. Nigeria, Ceylon, Malaya, and Singapore all had substantial engineering workshops associated with their ports and railways which could be converted to produce munitions, but none made the steel needed for the shells.[23]

Of the three dominions attending, only Australia had a steel industry, and this had commenced production only in April 1915. New Zealand, where there had been a rifle ammunition factory since 1885, was the scene of enthusiastic discussion about making munitions, but they would need Australian steel to do so.[24] South African Unionist Party leader Sir Thomas Smartt had advocated local munitions production a few days before the London meeting, but this issue's interest for minority of White English-speakers in South Africa and neighbouring Rhodesia was not necessarily shared by the more numerous Africans or Afrikaners.[25] South Africa's industrial heartland was based in the inland Witwatersrand goldfields, and, as H. F. Marriott, one of the South African delegates at the London conference asked: 'Was it worth while shipping the steel 5,000 or 6,000 miles by sea and 1,000 by railway, to make it into shell, and then re-ship it?'[26]

The Irish experience of the First World War, as Catriona Pennell has written, reflected the island's 'complicated politics of national and imperial unity', but it also had more in common with the wider wartime experience of Britain and the Empire than has generally been acknowledged.[27] In 1915, many Irish people shared the enthusiasm for making munitions. In August, Waterford became one of several Irish cities to form a munitions committee. Though the Waterford committee was disbanded in September, by the end of the year, local engineer Frank Thompson was producing shell cases at the Neptune Works at a rate of 500 a week.[28]

When the Western Australian Munitions Committee delegation disembarked in Melbourne, their first important meeting was on 9 July 1915 with the Federal Munitions Committee.[29] This body had been created to provide technical advice to the Labor Government's defence minister, Senator George Pearce of Western Australia. As defence minister from 1910 to 1913, Pearce had established five state-owned factories to provide the Australian military with uniforms, horse saddles, and accoutrements, cordite, Lee–Enfield rifles and rifle ammunition.[30] On returning to the portfolio following the short-lived Liberal Government's defeat in the September 1914 election, Pearce asked the War Office to provide details of the 18-pounder gun, the British Army's main artillery piece, and its ammunition to enable both to be produced in Australia. Given the amount of detailed specifications involved in answering this request and its arrival at the commencement of a major war, it is not surprising that the War Office replied—two months later—that the current pressure of work meant it was unable to provide this information. Undeterred, Pearce continued to pursue his idea of making 18-pounder ammunition in Australia, approving a plan in March 1915 to construct a government arsenal in the new Federal capital of Canberra.[31] After the Ministry of Munitions was established, Pearce repeated his request in June for the 18-pounder shell specifications, but again the information was slow in coming, owing to what the replying telegram described as 'great pressure of war incidental to organization of new department and exceptional pressure of current business in England'.[32]

The Labor senator was so fixed on his vision of producing artillery ammunition in a new state-owned arsenal that he did not anticipate the community movement to make munitions. As Pearce later admitted, he initially did not even consider the possibility of converting existing privately owned factories to manufacture shells.[33] The minister's preference for an arsenal, and his apparent inability to gain the necessary details to start making munitions immediately, put him at odds with many, particularly conservatives, in the munitions movement. The Melbourne *Argus*, which described Pearce as a 'humiliating contrast' to his Canadian counterpart, Sam Hughes,[34] complained in late June:

> The weeks have been slipping by since first the desire that Australia should bear its share in the production of munitions developed into an insistent public demand, and still the record is of very little attempted, and nothing substantial done.[35]

The Western Australian delegation left their meeting with the Federal Munitions Committee with 'a feeling of discouragement' after they learned that the specifications for the 18-pounder shell, necessary to start production, still had not arrived from the UK. The next day, 10 July, they met with Herbert Brookes, President of the Victorian Chamber of Manufactures, and a prominent member of the Victorian Munitions Committee. Brookes, who in June had publicly called for a national munitions conference, took advantage of the Western Australians' presence to immediately send telegrams to the other state munitions committees in New South Wales, Queensland, South Australia, and Tasmania, inviting them to meet in Melbourne the following week.[36]

On the afternoon of 14 July 1915, at the Chamber of Manufactures rooms in the appropriately named Empire Building, representatives of all the state munitions committees, except South Australia, met together for the first time.[37] By a remarkable coincidence, the arrival of the Western Australians in Melbourne, which had made the interstate conference possible, had coincided with the arrival at last of a telegram from London, which gave the meeting purpose. This stated that 'Australia can help best by producing eighteen pounder shell bodies' and offered a price of one pound and two shillings each for the first 20,000 shell cases produced.[38]

Brookes opened the conference by stating that, when he had called for this meeting only a few days previously, he did so because the position regarding ammunition production in Australia 'had become intolerable and the reasons for inaction inexplicable'. His intent had been to establish a united position among the state munitions committees and demand that Pearce ask the British Government 'to give a definite answer whether Australia was to be permitted to make munitions or not'. But this changed when the minister told the businessman on 12 July, 2 days before the conference was due to commence, that the Ministry of Munitions had sent him the necessary information. According to Brookes, this 'transformed' the situation. He withdrew from the position of conference president, and asked Pearce to chair the meeting. On rising to speak, the senator received a spontaneous ovation.[39]

The Western Australian delegation later reported that the meeting generally evoked 'an enthusiasm and national spirit which was in every respect encouraging and inspiring'.[40] Pearce proposed a national organisation in which state munitions committees (which in some states would need to be created by amalgamating several existing committees) would be linked to the Federal Munitions Committee. The state committees would submit the tenders to make shell cases from manufacturers in their state to the national body. In return, the Federal Munitions Committee would provide the state committees with the detailed shell specifications (which, along with a sample 18-

pounder shell, were still to arrive from London by sea mail),[41] the steel, produced by Broken Hill Proprietary (BHP), to make the munitions, and the gauges to ensure they had been properly produced.[42]

There was some opposition to Pearce's proposal. After the meeting, some manufacturers argued that they had 'higher technical knowledge' than the Federal Munitions Committee, 'and that to subject [their] firms to departmental control would limit their usefulness and considerably hamper their operations'.[43] At a subsequent interstate munitions conference in August, a South Australian delegate complained that the minister's organisation would leave the state munitions committees 'merely in existence, without having any power to do anything'.[44] But the majority of the munitions movement, including the Western Australian delegation, supported Pearce's plan.[45]

Following the meeting, the defence minister assisted the men from his own state to visit railway workshops and factories around Melbourne, as well as travelling to New South Wales to see the BHP steelmaking plant in Newcastle and the government small arms factory in Lithgow. After this, and brimming with enthusiasm for the possibility of establishing a munitions industry, the Western Australian delegation set sail for home, arriving in Perth on 27 July.[46]

The Western Australian Munitions Committee, however, would have to overcome a major difficulty to commence ammunition production in the state. Unlike the English Midlands, Western Australia did not possess any large metalworking establishment that could be easily converted into a munitions factory. The state's manufacturing sector was small, consisting mostly of small companies involving in food processing, sawmills, and brickworks. Western Australia owed its recent economic development to the 1892 discovery of gold in the region around Coolgardie and Kalgoorlie. The wealth of the mines had attracted the attention of British investors who eagerly purchased state government bonds. These funds allowed governments, both Liberal and Labor, to invest heavily in constructing railways in agricultural districts in the decade leading up to the outbreak of war in order to develop a wheat export industry. The state government played a significant role in the local economy. It owned railways and tramways, a bank and a small agricultural machinery factory, dairies and butcheries to provide fresh milk to hospitals and fresh meat in mining towns, and, in 1911, had founded the University of Western Australia as a fee-free institution.[47]

When the munitions debate commenced in Western Australia in June 1915, many immediately thought of converting the government's Midland Junction railway workshops on the outskirts of Perth into an ammunition factory.[48] But others pointed out that that if the workshops stopped repairing trains, the railway network and the state would grind to a halt.[49] The lack of a single obvious site or manufacturer held the attention of the munitions committee during August as they searched for a solution. On 20 August, the committee announced that it had decided to establish a limited liability company and make munitions itself. It called on engineering firms to sell or hire lathes, with Adam Baird of the engineering sub-committee asking lathe owners to 'give your very best terms in the interest of a movement which is a purely national and patriotic one'. Within a week, 20 were donated free of charge for making shell cases at the Perth Central Markets.[50]

On 3 September the Mayor chaired a packed meeting in the Perth Town Hall. Tomlinson's company had already made a few sample shell cases, and these were on display on the chairman's table. The Western Australian Governor, Sir Harry Barron, moved a resolution in support of making munitions in the state, and acknowledged the large number of women in the audience by suggesting that female munitions workers might take the same role in Western Australia that they were already playing in Britain.[51] The speakers described the company's formation as a patriotic act that should unify the community. Frank Wilson, leader of the Liberal Party opposition in the Western Australian Parliament, stated that 'we could not do too much to assist the British Empire'. Alexander McCallum, secretary of the local trade union organisation, the Australian Labor Federation, noted 'the fact that every class in the community was supporting the movement showed that it had been lifted altogether above sectional strife or party feeling'. The next day, the *West Australian* published an advertisement announcing the formation of the War Munitions Supply Company of Western Australia Limited.[52]

Nonetheless, the idea of making munitions in Western Australia initiated a heated state-wide debate. The issue was not whether the war should be supported. As Bobbie Oliver has written in her study of wartime dissent in Western Australia, the majority of the population was conservative and 'fiercely loyal to the British Empire'.[53] These conservative and patriotic tendencies were reflected in the Western Australian labour movement as they were in the wider community. The lack of large-scale manufacturing in Western Australia meant that organised labour was made up of small craft unions of skilled tradesmen rather than big industrial unions of generally more militant unskilled workers.[54] When the Chamber of Commerce established the state munitions committee and omitted to invite the workers who would be expected to make the munitions, the local Australian Labor Federation strongly demanded their inclusion, and a labour sub-committee was soon added to the organisation's structure.[55]

The state-wide discussion was instead about whether it would be more helpful to the Empire to establish a factory and make munitions in Western Australia or to send skilled workers to the already existing factories in Britain. As one correspondent suggested in the *West Australian*, the latter option would be 'both cheaper and quicker' in increasing ammunition output.[56] The munitions committee and its supporters considered the departure of capable tradesmen from the state as short-sighted,[57] and countered this idea by bringing a new argument to their cause. This was, as a *Kalgoorlie Miner* editorial asserted, that munitions should be made in Western Australia 'not necessarily with the one sole object of giving immediate help to Britain and her partners in the present strife, but also in order to further her own general development'.[58]

This economic argument had strong appeal. A combination of drought, described by the *West Australian* as 'the formidable enemy within our gates', and the wartime disruption in shipping had resulted in unemployment and recession.[59] It is no wonder that McCallum looked to shell production to enable the 'permanent extension' of local industries.[60] Similar financial problems and ideas of opportunity were found in other parts of the Empire. In Ireland, the Waterford *Evening News*, reporting on the latest departure of workers bound for the munitions factories in England, commented: 'One could not help feeling what a pity it was that instead of sending these men to England we cannot find work for them on this island of ours.'[61] In Nigeria, the sudden and disastrous halt in the export of palm kernels and other cash crops to its largest customer, Germany,[62] may have led to the calls to make ammunition in the colony. The *Indian Patriot* saw making munitions as a solution to Indian poverty and stated: 'Let our emigration depots cease to be, and let ammunition depots rise everywhere.'[63] A recession in Canada encouraged manufacturers to take munitions contracts,[64] and the Toronto *Globe* saw the new industry as a way to pay off Canada's British debt.[65]

Despite these arguments, some in Western Australia still believed that the War Munitions Supply Company was impractical. On 23 August 1915, the chairman of the state munitions committee, W. W. Garner of the Chamber of Commerce, resigned from the committee in opposition to the company's formation. A further three Chamber of Commerce members would follow him in this action.[66] The most vocal critic of the company's formation was Arthur Lovekin, editor of the *Daily News*. After a pro-munitions advocate, Don Cameron of the Plumbers' Union, had attacked Perth's rich for not buying War Munitions Supply Company shares, Lovekin published an editorial on 18 October in which he described the venture as a 'mad-brained enterprise'. He claimed that Britain no longer needed the steel shell cases that the company was only now starting to make. Instead, it required shells complete with explosives and fuses, and the UK Government was continuing to accept plain shell cases merely 'as a matter of courtesy to Australia'. Lovekin followed this by publishing excerpts from Canadian newspapers and the *Australasian Engineering Journal* substantiating his assertion that Britain did not actually need expensive Australian-made shell cases. On 22 November Lovekin wrote 'to raise public funds and use them to supply heroes at the front with three shells instead of ten is a procedure unworthy of everyone connected with it'.[67]

The munitions committee had announced their decision to produce ammunition with an appeal to 'the patriotism of every loyal member of the community'. They had come to see the cause of the War Munitions Supply Company as being identical to the cause of the war itself.[68] Their response to the editor's critique was therefore to demand that defence minister Pearce prevent Lovekin 'seriously doing harm to the Munitions Company' by prosecuting him under the Australian equivalent of the *Defence of the Realm Act*, the *War Precautions Act*.[69] The Crown Solicitor, however, ruled that the legislation could not be made to apply to the 'financial criticism of a private company'.[70]

The Western Australian public's broad support for War Munitions Supply Company easily overwhelmed this opposition. When the company was established in September 1915 as a not-for-profit business, the labour movement agreed to waive overtime rates and work conditions in order to increase ammunition production.[71] The share price was set at five shillings so they would be 'within the reach of all'.[72] The prospectus was distributed to all union members, and committees were formed to enable workers to save a shilling out of each week's pay until they had accumulated enough to buy shares.[73] The number of women who purchased shares is not known, but their presence at the company's launch suggests strong female interest in the enterprise. The crowd at the Boxing Day race meeting in the small timber town of Greenbushes collected over seven pounds to invest in the company.[74] The new munitions committee chairman, A. C. Munro, had stated in August that the company would need £10,000 of capital to begin production. By the time the first shareholders' meeting was held on 22 December, 12,000 people had purchased over £14,000 worth of shares.[75]

The most significant feature of the War Munitions Supply Company of Western Australia was that it was consciously created as part of a wider Imperial effort. Munro explained the rationale for forming the company to the Western Australian Institute of Engineers by stating: 'It had been felt throughout the Empire that there was great need for something to be done.'[76] The establishment of munitions factories in Canada and India provided an inspiration for Western Australians to emulate. In July 1915, before he turned against the idea of local production, Lovekin had commented in the *Daily News*: 'It is reasonable to accept ... that what Canada can do is within the realms of possibility in Western Australia.'[77] Britain—regularly referred to as 'the old country',[78] as it was, either literally or emotionally, for much of the state's population—provided, with its volunteer workers of Woolwich Arsenal, the model for the Volunteer Munition League of Western Australia.[79] In November 1915, the munitions committee even dispatched Hubert Whitfeld and Norman Wilsmore, professors of engineering and chemistry, respectively, at the University of Western Australia, to the UK to collect steel, explosives, and artillery shell specifications.[80] In its turn, the non-profit aspect of the War Munitions Supply Munitions Company attracted the interest of both the New Zealand Government and the munitions committee in the New South Wales mining town of Broken Hill. The latter subsequently established the Barrier Munitions Company using the same financial model as Western Australia.[81]

These Imperial interconnections were found throughout the munitions movement. On 28 July 1915, the *Toronto Mail* praised Sam Hughes and his Shell Committee for 'grasp[ing] the opportunities presented our industry' in contrast to what it saw as the Australian Labor Government's lack of support for private companies interested in making munitions.[82] In the second half of the year, the New Zealand Government negotiated the purchase from Australia of five tons of steel and 250 copper bands for local manufacturers to produce shell cases.[83] Australia also provided copper to India to make munitions.[84] In return, India hosted an Australian committee in November and December 1915 that visited Indian factories to collect information for Pearce's (never to be completed) government arsenal project.[85] Also in November, the newly-formed Rhodesian Munitions Committee sought advice from its South African counterpart and compiled a list of all machinery in the colony that could be used for ammunition manufacture.[86]

The War Munitions Supply Company commenced operations in earnest in October 1915 with the arrival of 12 tons of steel and an Australian Government inspector who would approve the finished shell cases before shipment.[87] The company carried out production in four separate locations. Some of the initial drilling and rough turning was carried out in the Kalgoorlie mines and at the Millars Timber Company workshops in the south west town of Yarloop. At the latter, a vertical saw frame was ingeniously converted into a quadruple drill that could work on four steel billets at the same time. The Midland Junction railway workshops completed some of the shell cases and also fabricated some shell-making tools. The bulk of the finishing work was carried out in the company's main factory in the Perth Central Markets. Here, under Tomlinson's supervision, men—the company recruited no women as munitions workers—employed in two shifts served 27 lathes and other machinery, all donated by local firms. A shortage of gauges, used to measure shells and ensure they conformed exactly to the specifications, slowed production to a snail's pace. In two months' manufacturing to 21 December, the War Munitions Supply Company had completed only 800 shell cases.[88]

Unfortunately for the Western Australians, by the time they were able to help Britain by making munitions, Britain no longer needed it. By the beginning of 1916, ammunition production in the UK and Canada had already expanded to such an extent that the requirements for 18-pounder ammunition could be met without calling on Australian shells made in much smaller numbers, at much greater expense and with much longer distances of shipping. The British Government asked the Australian Government to cease making 18-pounder shell cases, but it was politically difficult for Pearce to tell companies to stop production when they had barely started. Instead, the defence minister delayed the halt in making 18-pounder shells for Britain until 30 June, and proposed continuing production by converting Australian factories to make the larger, and still required, 4.5 inch shell.[89]

In January 1916, Plaistowe, who had written to Lloyd George asking for advice, received the unofficial reply that the company would do better to shift from munitions to making equipment for the Australian Imperial Force.[90] On 16 May, the Perth Trades Hall asked Pearce 'whether patriotic people are justified in continuing to support local munitions works', and was informed of the 30 June end date for 18-pounder shell manufacture for British contracts. On 17 June, Plaistowe, who was in Melbourne on private business, passed on advice from the Federal Munitions Committee to continue making 18-pounders in small numbers until the company was able to produce larger calibre ammunition. It soon became obvious, however, that it would be too expensive to convert machinery to make 4.5 inch shells, and Baird of the engineering sub-committee sailed to Melbourne to join Plaistowe. After meeting with the Federal Munitions Committee, Baird told the War Munitions Supply Company on 30 June to cease production. The total number of 18-pounder shell cases that had produced in Australia was only 15,000. Tomlinson, who had taken leave from his engineering firm to establish munitions making in Western Australia, now devoted his time to winding up the business. The Defence Department reimbursed all Australian firms for the costs they had incurred in ammunition production. As part of this, the War Munitions Supply Company was paid just over £2,000.[91]

The patriotic and industrial impulses of the British Empire's munitions movement were brought to heel by the practicalities of economics and shipping availability. Ammunition production came to be concentrated in Britain, Ireland, where five state-owned munitions plants were established, including a rifle ammunition factory in Waterford,[92] and Canada, where production expanded to include 600 factories. In 1917, between a quarter and a third of all shells fired by the British Empire's armies on the Western Front were Canadian-made.[93]

India manufactured 1.3 million shells in factories and railway workshops between 1915 and 1917.[94] If, as Santanu Das has argued, the experience of Indian soldiers fighting for Empire in the First World War has been marginalised by both Indian historians who concentrate on the independence movement and by standard accounts of the war that concentrate on Europe,[95] then the experience of these Indian munitions workers remains almost entirely unknown.[96]

As it had with Australia, the British Government told India to stop making munitions because they were not needed and ships would not be made available to transport them. In the latter part of 1915, the British Government began making a concerted effort to systematically mobilise the resources of the Empire, including those parts that had not attempted ammunition production, to the war effort. India, the dominions and the colonies were all asked to increase local manufacture in order to minimise their needs for British imports. This request had the dual aims of enabling all available workers and machinery in the UK to be 'concentrated upon the difficult problem of producing complete rounds of ammunition', and reducing the shipping requirements for these non-essential items to the 'smallest possible amount'.[97]

In line with this request, the South African explosives factories serving the mining industry cut down their need for glycerine imports by developing substitutes. Rhodesia started manufacturing previously imported machinery. In New Zealand, a Department of Munitions and Supplies was created in August 1915 and it organised the local manufacture of boots and uniforms for the New Zealand Expeditionary Force.[98] In Australia, the wartime shipping shortage and the resulting scarcity of imports led to an estimated 400 items, ranging from sheep dip to aeroplane engines, being manufactured domestically for the first time.[99] The Indian Munitions Board was established in March 1917 with the aim of directing the Indian economy towards developing import replacement industries and supplying the British Empire armies operating in the Middle East and East Africa. The Tata factory's steel output still remained under the Government of India's control, but was re-directed from making munitions to producing almost a thousand miles of rail track. This was shipped to nearby Mesopotamia where it was used to build railways to supply the advancing Indian Army.[100]

At the same time, the British Government sought to encourage the import to the UK of a limited number of raw materials from with the Empire. This was because they were either vital for war production, or because the item had previously been exported to Germany and it was economically imperative to provide an alternative market. An example of the former was the Ministry of Munitions Empire-wide survey to identity deposits of mica, a mineral vital for the manufacture of electrical equipment. This led to the establishment of a mica mine in the Nysasaland Protectorate (now Malawi) in 1918.[101] An example of the latter was the successful publicity campaign in 1915 by the Board of Agriculture and Fisheries to encourage British farmers to accept crushed palm kernels from Nigeria as stock feed, and make up for the loss of this commodity's main German market.[102]

The main obstacle to the Munitions Supply Company of Western Australia providing ammunition to the British Empire armies on the Western Front was that it would have been an inefficient use of scarce wartime shipping. On the outbreak of war, the British Government gained the power to requisition merchant ships and sail them on routes with cargoes of the government's choosing. As the voyage between the UK and North America could be completed three times faster than the voyage between the UK and Australia, British authorities naturally transferred shipping away from the Australian route to concentrate on the Atlantic.[103] This dire lack of shipping for Australian exports and imports would lead the Australian Prime Minister, Billy Hughes, in June 1916 to purchase 15 merchant ships and establish the state-owned Australian Commonwealth Shipping Line.[104]

Ironically, the men involved in the Western Australian munitions movement would make their greatest contribution to the Empire's war effort by doing the thing they originally vehemently opposed: sending Western Australian workers to work in British munitions factories. In August 1916, the Australian Government began recruiting fillers and turners and other skilled workers to go the UK.[105] Tomlinson, who had played a major role in establishing the Western Australian Munitions Committee and had managed the Central Markets factory, worked on a selection panel that chose workers for the scheme. Baird, who had been a member of the engineering sub-committee, went to Britain to work in the munitions industry. Professor Whitfeld, who had gone to the UK in November 1915 on a fact-finding mission for the War Munitions Supply Company, was offered a position as a Ministry of Munitions inspector and stayed. His colleague, Professor Wilsmore, returned to Western Australia with the information they had acquired, and then went back to Britain where he worked in explosives production.[106] These Western Australians joined over 6,000 other Australian men and some women in munitions work in the UK, as well as 2,872 Canadians directly recruited by the Ministry of Munitions and 844 South African and 87 New Zealand skilled workers who travelled as individuals to join the British munitions industry.[107]

The War Munitions Supply Company of Western Australia was just one manifestation of the wider munitions movement that developed throughout the British Empire in 1915. The patriotic outrage that arose in April and May found a focus by June in making ammunition to help the soldiers in the front line and end the 'shell crisis'. Alongside this expression of Empire loyalty, there was also the hope, in Western Australia and elsewhere, that munitions production could develop local industry and overcome the serious economic problems that accompanied the outbreak of war. Both the proponents and opponents of the War Munitions Supply Company were aware that they were part of a wider Imperial conversation about making munitions. This debate was carried out in public at meetings and in newspapers, and almost certainly in private by engineers scattered throughout the Empire, but linked by social and professional networks that await investigation.[108] The Imperial world of the munitions movement was forgotten with the end of Empire, with most historians interpreting the events of the Great War according to national themes of developing cultural identity or gaining political independence. In Australia, a succession of what Jeffrey Grey terms 'traditional, populist' historians have seen the First World War purely in terms of the 'Anzac Legend' and the rise of Australian nationalism.[109] Examining the Western Australian munitions movement as part of a wider Imperial experience allows for a more nuanced account of Australia in the Great War. Realising the existence of this Imperial world offers a new key to understanding the First World War, not only in Australia, but in all the countries that once formed the British Empire. What have been previously seen as uniquely national experiences[110] may be found to share hitherto unrecognised interconnections.

Notes

[1] Cornell (assistant secretary Perth trades hall) to Ernest Tomlinson (secretary War Munitions Supply Company of WA), 19 July 1917, JS Battye Library of West Australian History (JSBL), MN300, ACC1688A, 112. The author wishes to thank the WA Branch of the Australian Labor Party for granting permission to consult its records.
[2] Great War and Western Australian historians have given little attention to the Munitions Supply Company. It receives one sentence in both Ernest Scott's home front volume of the Australian First World War official history and Frank Crowley's 1961 history of Western Australia, and is not mentioned in either Bobbie Oliver's study of wartime dissent in Western Australia or in Geoffrey Bolton's recent state history. Scott, *Australia During the War*, 245; Crowley, *Australia's Western Third*, 182–83; Oliver, *War and Peace in Western Australia*; Bolton, *Land of Vision and Mirage*.
[3] Holland, 'British Empire', 115.
[4] Connor, 'Empire's War Recalled', 1131–35. The concept of the 'British World' has been developed in part to counter these narrowly nationalistic historical interpretations. See Bridge and Fedorowich, 'Mapping the British World'; Dubow, 'How British Was the British World?'.
[5] *West Australian*, 10 May 1915.
[6] Gregory, *Last Great War*, 11. A similar reaction in New Zealand is suggested by Hucker, 'Great Wave of Enthusiasm', 71.
[7] Gregory, *Last Great War*, 39, 46. Similar points been made by Bourne, *Britain and the Great War*, 210; Wilson, *Myriad Faces of War*, 182.
[8] For pioneer feminist Bessie Rischbieth organising the shipping of clothing to the UK for Belgian refugees, Baptist Minister F. E. Harry's sermon regarding poison gas and Dr Trethowan's reference to 'treacherous' German behaviour in a speech at the Perth Dinghy Club 'smoke social', see *West Australian*, 21 and 27 April, 10 May 1915.
[9] For anti-German riots in South Africa following the *Lusitania* attack, see Garson 'South Africa and World War I', 70; for Zeppelin raids 'influenc[ing] public thought to a large extent' among Rhodesian White settlers, see Rhodesia Munitions and Resources Committee, *Interim Report*, 2.
[10] *West Australian*, 23 April 1915.
[11] Bourne, *Britain and the Great War*, 107–14, 185–90; Wilson, *Myriad Faces of War*, 215–38.
[12] *West Australian*, 13 and 18 May 1915. This followed a House of Commons statement that the UK Government had contacted the Dominion Governments about recruiting skilled munitions workers; *PD*, Vol. 71, 27 April, 550–51.
[13] *PD*, Vol. 71, 18 May 1915, 2158; *West Australian*, 20 May 1915. Harcourt had already privately refused a similar Australian offer. Lord Harcourt (Colonial Secretary) to Sir Ronald Munro Ferguson (Australian Governor-General), 15 May 1915, National Archives of Australia (NAA), A11803, 1914/89/79.

[14] *West Australian*, 8 and 14 June 1915; *Daily News*, 10 June 1915.
[15] *Daily News*, 10 June 1915.
[16] *West Australian*, 23 and 30 June, 22 December 1915; *Daily News*, 23 and 30 June 1915.
[17] *West Australian*, 1, 2 and 3 July 1915; Hugh Plaistowe (Munitions Supply Company of WA) to David Lloyd George (UK Munitions Minister), 5 October 1915, NAA, A11803, 1914/89/79.
[18] Fitzgerald, 'The Workshops of War', 350.
[19] Haycock, 'Done in our Own Country', 50–51, 56–57, 62; Haycock, 'Early Canadian Weapons Acquisition', 52, 54; Haycock, *Sam Hughes*, 119–23, 235–36, 241–52; Bliss, 'War Business as Usual', 45–8.
[20] Roy, 'Equipping Leviathan'; *Times of India*, 1 July 1915; T. L. Matthews, 'The Manufacture of Munitions of War in India', 5 September 1917, 14–6, British Library (BL), IOR/L/MIL/7/18978; Ministry of Munitions, *History*, Vol. II, Pt V, 5–7.
[21] Calcutta *Hindoo Patriot*, 28 June, 5 July 1915; *Times of India*, 18 November 1915; Government of India, *India's Contribution*, 128–29.
[22] 'Manufacture of Munitions of War in India', 18, BL, IOR/L/MIL/7/18978; Ministry of Munitions, *History*, Vol. II, Pt V, 10.
[23] 'Minutes of Proceedings of the Indian & Colonial Conference. Held at Armament Buildings, on Thursday, August 12th, 1915', 1–6, The National Archives (TNA), MUN5, 176/1144/1.
[24] McGibbon, *Oxford Companion*, 239; H. B. Barrett (secretary Auckland Harbour Board) to James Allen (NZ Defence Minister), 23 June 1915; Allen to Senator George Pearce (Australian Defence Minister), 9 September 1915, Archives New Zealand (ANZ), AD1, 6/114.
[25] *West Australian*, 6 August 1915; Rhodesia Munitions and Resources Committee, *Interim Report*, 3. For the varied South African attitudes to the Great War, see Nasson, *Springboks on the Somme*, 10–11.
[26] 'Minutes of Proceedings of the Indian & Colonial Conference', 5, TNA, MUN5, 176/1144/1.
[27] Pennell, 'Going to War', 47.
[28] Waterford *Evening News*, 4, 7, 12, 18 and 26 Aug., 8 Sept. 1915; Dooley, *Irishmen or English Soldiers?*, 122.
[29] [E. A. Mann], 'Report of the Delegation Sent by the W.A. Munitions Committee to Melbourne' ('Delegation Report'), [July 1915], JSBL, ACC5893, A/7.
[30] John Jensen, 'Defence Production in Australia', Chapter, 7, 223–25, 228, 236–37, 247–48, NAA, MP598/30, 7. There was also a privately-owned rifle ammunition factory established in 1890. Dennis, *Oxford Companion*, 276.
[31] *Commonwealth Parliamentary Debates* (CPD), Vol. 77, 17 June 1915, 4066–70.
[32] Munro Ferguson to Andrew Bonar Law (Colonial Secretary), 11 June 1915; Bonar Law to Munro Ferguson, 9 July 1915, NAA, A11803, 1914/89/79.
[33] *CPD*, Vol. 77, 17 June 1915, 4068.
[34] *Argus*, 24 June 1915.
[35] *Argus*, 21 June 1915.
[36] 'Delegation Report', JSBL, ACC5893, A/7; *Argus*, 15 June, 14 July 1915.
[37] *Argus*, 14 and 15 July 1915.
[38] Bonar Law to Munro Ferguson, 9 July 1915, NAA, A11803, 1914/89/79.
[39] *Argus*, 15 July 1915.
[40] 'Delegation Report', JSBL, ACC589, A/7.
[41] In fact, the Australian Government received the specifications from BHP, whose London office had gained them from the Ministry of Munitions, before it received a copy from the Ministry itself. Bonar Law to Munro Ferguson, 28 June 1915; H. Llewellyn Smith (Under-Secretary Ministry of Munitions) to John Anderson (Under-Secretary Colonial Office) 9 July 1915, NAA, A11803, 1914/89/79; *Argus*, 21 July 1915.
[42] *Argus*, 15 July 1915.
[43] *Argus*, 16 July 1915.

[44] 'Interstate Conference of Munitions Committees', 30 Aug. 1915, 4, NAA, A2023, B11/23/64.
[45] 'Delegation Report', JSBL, ACC589, A/7; *Argus*, 16 July 1915.
[46] 'Delegation Report', JSBL, ACC589, A/7; *West Australian*, 29 July 1915.
[47] For more on Western Australia in this period, see Crowley, *Australia's Western Third*; Bolton, *Land of Vision and Mirage*.
[48] *West Australian*, 12, 23 and 25 June 1915.
[49] *Daily News*, 17 June 1915; *West Australian*, 23 June 1915.
[50] *West Australian*, 16, 20, 26 and 30 Aug. 1915; 'Interstate Conference of Munitions Committees', 19, NAA, A2023, B11/23/64.
[51] For female British munitions workers, see Woollacott, *On her their Lives Depend*.
[52] *West Australian*, 4 and 5 Sept. 1915.
[53] Oliver, *War and Peace in Western Australia*, 31. Western Australia was the only Australian state to overwhelmingly support the introduction of conscription in both the 1916 and 1917 plebiscites. Scott, *Australia During the War*, 352, 427.
[54] Merritt, 'Pearce: Labour Leader', 39–47; Oliver, *War and Peace in Western Australia*, 52–3.
[55] *West Australian*, 2 and 23 July, 5 Aug. 1915; *Westralian Worker*, 6 and 13 Aug. 1915. The Australian Labor Federation was the name given to the local Western Australian trade union organisation.
[56] *West Australian*, 22 June 1915.
[57] 'Delegation Report', JSBL, ACC589, A/7.
[58] *Kalgoorlie Miner*, 17 Aug. 1915.
[59] *West Australian*, 19 April, 25 Aug., 2 Sept. 1915; Haig-Muir, 'Economy at War', 97.
[60] *Kalgoorlie Miner*, 16 Aug. 1915.
[61] *Evening News*, 30 Sept. 1915.
[62] Osuntokun, *Nigeria in the First World War*, 25–26.
[63] Quoted in *Times of India*, 5 July 1915.
[64] Bliss, 'War Business as Usual', 46.
[65] *Globe*, 8 May 1915. A similar argument was made by Pearce regarding the Australian trade deficit with the UK. *Argus*, 15 July 1915.
[66] *West Australian*, 23 and 25 Aug., 6 Oct. 1915; Plaistowe to Lloyd George, 5 Oct. 1915, NAA, A11803, 1914/89/79.
[67] *Daily News*, 18 and 22 Oct., 22 and 25 Nov. 1915.
[68] *West Australian*, 24 Aug., 25 Nov. 1915.
[69] Commandant 5th Military District, to Thomas Trumble (secretary Defence Department), 26 Nov. 1915, NAA, A2023, B11/18/690. The committee also publicly attacked Lovekin. *West Australian*, 24 Nov. 1915.
[70] Gordon Castle (Crown Solicitor), Opinion No. 571, 22 Nov. 1915; Opinion No. 29, 18 Jan. 1916, NAA, A2023, B11/18/690.
[71] *West Australian*, 4, 14 and 21 Sept. 1915; 'State Munitions Committee of Western Australia. Industrial Agreement' [Sept. 1915], JSBL, ACC589, A/1.
[72] *West Australian*, 30 Aug. 1915.
[73] *West Australian*, 10 Sept. 1915; Plaistowe to Lloyd George, 5 Oct. 1915, NAA, A11803, 1914/89/79.
[74] *West Australian*, 4 Sept. 1915, 20 Jan. 1916.
[75] *West Australian*, 24 Aug. 1915; *Kalgoorlie Miner*, 23 Dec. 1915.
[76] *West Australian*, 2 Sept. 1915.
[77] *Daily News*, 22 June 1915. See also *West Australian*, 14 Aug. 1915; *Kalgoorlie Miner*, 17 Aug. 1915.
[78] 'Joint Meeting of the Labour and Engineering Sub-Committees. Held on 19 Aug. 1915 at the University' ('Joint Meeting'), JSBL, ACC589, A/4.
[79] *West Australian*, 23 July, 9 Aug. 1915.
[80] *West Australian*, 27 Feb. 1917.

[81] *West Australian*, 30 Aug. 1915; Scott, *Australia During the War*, 245.
[82] Quoted in *West Australian*, 5 Oct. 1915.
[83] Victorian Munitions Committee meeting, 23 Nov. 1915, National Library of Australia, MS1924, 16/51; A. J. C. Bult (secretary Victorian Munitions Committee) to Arthur Myers (NZ Munitions & Supplies Minister), 7 Dec. 1915; Major General Alfred Robin (GOC NZ Military Forces) to Myers, 26 Jan. 1916, ANZ, AD1, 6/114.
[84] Ministry of Munitions, *History*, Vol. II, Pt V, 10.
[85] Lord Hardinge (Indian Viceroy) to Munro Ferguson, 8 July 1915, NAA, A11803, 1914/89/79; 'Report upon visit to India by Arsenal Committee' [Dec. 1915], NAA, MP891/7, Vol. 2; *Times of India*, 1 Dec. 1915.
[86] Rhodesia Munitions and Resources Committee, *Interim Report*, 1–3.
[87] *West Australian*, 9 Oct., 22 Dec. 1915. A single bar of steel for production trials had arrived on 20 Aug. 1915. 'Joint Meeting', JSBL, ACC589, A/4.
[88] *West Australian*, 22 Dec. 1915, 31 Jan., 30 June, 1 July 1916; Ministry of Munitions, *History*, Vol. II, Pt VI, 10.
[89] H. W. Just (Colonial Office) to Llewellyn Smith, 7 Feb. 1916, TNA, MUN5, 176/1144/2; Bonar Law to Munro Ferguson, 8 March, 31 March 1916, NAA, A11803, 1914/89/79; Scott, *Australia During the War*, 245–46.
[90] Plaistowe to Lloyd George, 5 Oct. 1915, Bonar Law to Munro Ferguson, 16 Dec. 1915, Prime Minister's Department memo, 26 Jan. 1916, NAA, A11803, 1914/89/79.
[91] Cornell to Pearce, 16 May 1916, Pearce to Cornell, 24 May 1916, JSBL, MN300, ACC1688A, 112; *West Australian*, 1 and 3 July 1916, 27 Feb. 1917; Scott, *Australia During the War*, 246; 'Expenditure in Connection with Shell Manufacture', 13 March 1919, NAA, MP392/10, 473/568/117.
[92] Puirséil, 'War, Work and Labour', 184–85; Dooley, *Irishmen or English soldiers?*, 123.
[93] This was the high point of Canadian production. From the middle of 1917 orders declined due to the British dollar shortage. Bliss, 'War Business as Usual', 49, 53.
[94] Younghusband, 'India', 195.
[95] Das, 'India and the First World War', 63.
[96] These workers included Chinese fitters and turners recruited in Hong Kong by the Albion Shell Factory. Ministry of Munitions, *History*, Vol. II, Pt V, 11.
[97] Bonar Law to Munro Ferguson, 25 Nov. 1915, 9 Sept. 1916, NAA, A11803, 1914/89/79.
[98] Rhodesia Munitions and Resources Committee, *Interim Report*, 3, 20; Drew, *War Effort of New Zealand*, xxi; McGibbon, *Oxford Companion*, 239–40.
[99] Scott, *Australian During the War*, 549.
[100] Ministry of Munitions, *History*, Vol. II, Pt V, 11–2; Younghusband, 'India', 196; Government of India, *India's Contribution*, 104–5.
[101] Circular letter to governors, 26 Feb. 1918, TNA, MUN4, 2056; 'Nyasaland Protectorate Local Purchases', 31 Jan. [1919], TNA, MUN4, 6350.
[102] Osuntokun, *Nigeria in the First World War*, 22–32.
[103] Salter, *Allied Shipping Control*, 12–13, 39, 49–50, 92; Scott, *Australia During the War*, 531–35.
[104] Scott, *Australia During the War*, 614–17. For a new analysis of Hughes and the shipping issue, see Bridge, *William Hughes*.
[105] Before this scheme began, Vickers had brought about a thousand Australians, including Western Australians, to the UK. Munro Ferguson to Bonar Law, 1 August 1916, NAA, A11803, 1914/89/79; 'Memorandum for Committee Invited to Select Munitions Workers for Duty in England', 5 Aug. 1916, NAA, A2023, E168/2/23; MacLeod, 'Industrial Invasion', 39; *West Australian*, 19 May 1916.
[106] See entries for Adam Baird, Ernest Tomlinson, Hubert Whitfeld, and Norman Wilsmore in the *Australian Dictionary of Biography*. Available at www.adbonline.anu.edu.au
[107] MacLeod, 'Industrial Invasion', 43, 45.
[108] Bridge and Fedorowich, 'Mapping the British World', 6.

[109] For the persistence of the 'Anzac Legend' in Australian military history, see Grey, 'Cuckoo in the Nest?', 456–59.
[110] One example could be the conscription debates in Ireland, Canada, and New Zealand. For national accounts of these debates, see Gregory, 'Recruit Germans'; Granatstein and Hitsman, *Broken Promises*; Baker, *King and Country*.

References

Baker, Paul. *King and Country Call: New Zealanders, Conscription and the Great War*. Auckland: Auckland University Press, 1988.

Bliss, Michael. 'War Business as Usual: Canadian Munitions Production, 1914-1918'. In *Mobilization for Total War: The Canadian, American and British Experience, 1914–1918, 1939–1945*, edited by N.F. Dreisziger, Waterloo: Wilfrid Laurier University Press, 1986, 43–55.

Bolton, Geoffrey. *Land of Vision and Mirage: Western Australia since 1826*. Perth: University of Western Australia Press, 2008.

Bourne, J. M. *Britain and the Great War 1914–1918*. London: Edward Arnold, 1989.

Bridge, Carl. *William Hughes: Australia. Makers of the Modern World: The Peace Conferences of 1919–1923 and their Aftermath*. London: Haus Press, 2011.

Bridge, Carl, and Kent Fedorowich. 'Mapping the British World'. *Journal of Imperial and Commonwealth History* 31, no. 2 (2003): 1–15.

Connor, John. 'The Empire's War Recalled: Recent Writing on the Western Front Experience of Britain, Ireland, Australia, Canada, India, New Zealand, South Africa and the West Indies'. *History Compass* 7, no. 4 (2009): 1123–145.

Crowley, F. K. *Australia's Western Third: A History of Western Australia from the First Settlements to Modern Times*. London: Heinemann, 1960.

Das, Santanu. 'India and the First World War'. In *A Part of History: Aspcts of the British Experience of the First Worl War*. introduced by Michael Howard, London: Continuum, 2008, 63–73.

Dennis, Peter, Jeffrey, Grey, Ewan, Morris, Robin, Prior, and Jean, Bou, eds. *The Oxford Companion to Australian Military History*. 2nd ed. Melbourne: Oxford University Press, 2008.

Drew, H. T. B., ed. *The War Effort of New Zealand. A Popular History of (a) Minor Campaigns in which New Zealanders Took Part; (b) Services Not Fully Dealt with in the Campaign Volumes; (c) The Work at the Bases*. Auckland: Whitcombe & Tombs, 1923.

Dooley, Thomas P. *Irishmen or English Soldiers? The Times and World of a Southern Catholic Irish Man (1876–1916) Enlisting in the British Army during the First World War*. Liverpool: Liverpool University Press, 1995.

Dubow, Saul. 'How British was the British World? The Case of South Africa'. *Journal of Imperial and Commonwealth History* 37, no. 1 (2009): 1–27.

Fitzgerald, W. G. 'The Workshops of War'. *Windsor Magazine* 42 (1915): 349–63.

Garson, N. G. 'South Africa and World War I'. *Journal of Imperial and Commonwealth History* 8, no. 1 (1979): 68–85.

Government of India. *India's Contribution to the Great War*. Calcutta: Superintendent Government Printing, 1923.

Granatstein, J. L., and J. M. Hitsman. *Broken Promises: A History of Conscription in Canada*. Toronto: Oxford University Press, 1977.

Gregory, Adrian. "You Might as well Recruit Germans': British Public Opinion and the Decision to Conscript the Irish in 1918'. In *Ireland and the Great War: 'A War to Unite Us All'?*, edited by Adrian Gregory and Senia Pašeta, Manchester: Manchester University Press, 2002, 113–32.

———. *The Last Great War: British Society and the First World War*. Cambridge: Cambridge University Press, 2008.

Grey, Jeffrey. 'Cuckoo in the Nest? Australia Military Historiography: The State of the Field'. *History Compass* 6, no. 2 (2008): 455–68.

Haig-Muir, Marnie. 'The Economy at War'. In *Australia's War 1914–1918.* edited by Joan Beaumont, Sydney: Allen & Unwin, 1995, 93–124.

Haycock, Ronald G. 'Early Canadian Weapons Acquisition: "— That Damned Ross Rifle"'. *Canadian Defence Quarterly* 14, no. 3 (1984/85): 48–57.

———. *Sam Hughes: The Public Career of a Controversial Canadian, 1885–1916*. Waterloo: Wilfrid Laurier University Press, 1986.

———. "Done in our Own Country': The Politics of Canadian Munitioning'. In *Canada's Defence: Perspectives on Policy in the Twentieth Century,* edited by B.D. Hunt and R.G. Haycock, Toronto: Copp Clark Pitman, 1993, 44–68.

Holland, Robert. 'The British Empire and the Great War, 1914-1918'. In *The Oxford History of the British Empire,* vol. 4, edited by Judith Brown and Wm. Louis Roger, Oxford: Oxford University Press, 1999, 114–137.

Hucker, Graham. "The Great Wave of Enthusiasm': New Zealand Reactions to the First World War in August 1914—A Reassessment'. *New Zealand Journal of History* 43, no. 1 (2009): 59–71.

MacLeod, Roy. "The Industrial Invasion of Britain': Mobilising Australian Munitions Workers, 1916–1919'. *Journal of the Australian War Memorial* 27 (1995): 37–46.

McGibbon, Ian, ed. *The Oxford Companion to New Zealand Military History.* Auckland: Oxford University Press, 2000.

Merritt, John. 'George Foster Pearce: Labour Leader'. M.A. diss., University of Western Australia, 1963.

Ministry of Munitions. *History of the Ministry of Munitions.* London: His Majesty's Stationery Office, 1923.

Nasson, Bill. *Springboks on the Somme: South Africa in the Great War 1914–1918.* Johannesburg: Penguin, 2007.

Oliver, Bobbie. *War and Peace in Western Australia: The Social and Political Impact of the Great War 1914-1926.* Perth: University of Western Australia Press, 1995.

Osuntokun, Akinjide. *Nigeria in the First World War.* London: Longman, 1979.

Pennell, Catriona. 'Going to War'. In *Our War: Ireland and the Great War,* edited by John Horne, Dublin: Royal Irish Academy, 2008, 37–48.

Puirséil, Niamh. 'War, Work and Labour'. In *Our War: Ireland and the Great War,* edited by John Horne, Dublin: Royal Irish Academy, 2008, 183–94.

Rhodesia Munitions and Resources Committee. *Interim Report for Period Ended 30 June, 1916.* Bulawayo: Argus Printing & Publishing Co Ltd, 1916.

Roy, Kaushik. 'Equipping Leviathan: Ordnance Factories of British India, 1859–1913'. *War in History* 10, no. 4 (2003): 398–423.

Salter, J. A. *Allied Shipping Control: An Experiment in International Administration.* London: Clarendon Press, 1921.

Scott, Ernest. *Australia During the War.* Sydney: Angus & Robertson, 1936.

United Kingdom. *Parliamentary Debates,* 5th ser., vol. 71 (1915).

Wilson, Trevor. *The Myriad Faces of War: Britain and the Great War, 1914–1918.* Cambridge: Polity Press, 1986.

Woollacott, Angela. *On her their Lives Depend: Munitions Workers in the Great War.* Berkeley, CA: University of California Press, 1994.

Younghusband, Francis. 'India'. In *The Empire at War,* edited by Charles Lucas, vol. 5. London: Oxford University Press, 1926, 151–352.

The Expatriate Firms and the Colonial Economy of Nigeria in the First World War

Peter J. Yearwood

The Great War has often been presented as a turning point in the economic and social development of Nigeria. For many writers this was when an oppressive and exploitative system was firmly established by the joint actions of the expatriate firms and the colonial government.[1] There is much to sustain this point of view.[2] For Nigeria the terms of trade had been quite favourable in the immediate pre-war years. In 1914 they shifted decisively, and remained adverse for the rest of the colonial period. The conversion of European economies to war production, the scarcity of shipping, and then the rapid post-war inflation drove up the costs of imports. Prices of palm produce, previously the staple export, sank as German markets, German firms, and German tonnage, so important before 1914, were eliminated. The emergence of cocoa, groundnuts, and tin as new staples did not adequately compensate for the decline of the older trade. Freed from German competition, the British firms which now dominated the export economy began at the end of the war to combine into great conglomerates, a process which, a decade later, would end with the formation of the United Africa Company and Unilever. During the war itself, African traders in Lagos complained loudly about the misuse of power by the British firms and the shipping company Elder Dempster. Their complaints have rightly attracted the attention of historians.

Occasionally cautions have been raised, notably by A.G. Hopkins, who warned of the dangers of over-simplistic analyses which employed loose terminology and were not sufficiently appreciative of differences of time and place and the possibly divergent interests of African entrepreneurs in the domestic and external sectors. In particular, he questioned the 'presumption that the newly established colonial governments served as the executive arm of expatriate business'.[3] Nevertheless, most historians, especially within Nigeria, still accept almost without question that 'the colonial state is known to have been generally pro-big business, in this case the Combine firms'.[4] Correctly, they insist that the colonial and metropolitan governments and the expatriate companies all wanted to promote trade, or integrate the colony into the world capitalist economy. But arguments of such generality may not illuminate the specific historical conjuncture of Nigeria in the First World War. How far, if at all, businessmen and officials agreed on what was to be done and how to do it needs to be discovered from empirical investigation rather than deduced from broad assumptions. Accordingly, this article will examine in some detail how expatriate firms in Nigeria responded to the new circumstances created by the war, and how in turn their actions were viewed by the authorities in Lagos and London.

I

By the outbreak of war the regional divisions which had previously been so important in the colonial economy of Nigeria were beginning to break down.[5] This process was restrained by a legally binding agreement creating a pool between two of the leading British firms, Miller Brothers and the African Association, which were restricted to the south of the colony, apart from the narrow band of territory bordering the Niger which was reserved to the third party, the once-sovereign Niger Company, along with the whole of northern Nigeria.[6] This reflected the old pattern in which commercial zones were defined by coasts and rivers. The extension of the railway to Zaria and Kano in 1912 created what was in effect a new coast and new ports,[7] which rapidly attracted the other large German and British firms, but from which Miller Bros. and the African Association were barred. Miller Brothers were especially keen to break into the newly established and rapidly expanding Kano groundnuts trade.[8] In the near future the development of Port Harcourt and the eastern railway looked likely to draw other firms into the eastern delta and its hinterland, threatening the position there of Millers and the Association.[9]

All this undermined the working agreement. As Robert Miller told Lord Scarbrough, the Chairman of the Niger Company, in 1914, if the arrangement 'were continued in its present form it will do more to hinder the development of the contracting parties than to advance their interests'.[10] Either it would break down, with potentially ruinous competition as the consequence, or the parties would move forward to an amalgamation which would largely control the export trade of Nigeria.

Negotiations for this were under way in 1914, but were not proceeding smoothly.[11] Personal rivalries were evidently important, especially as the Niger Company would dominate the new firm – the proposals envisaged it having seven out of fourteen directorships – and it would be more likely to streamline operations by closing stations in the south, where there was much duplication between the three other companies, than in the Niger territories and the north, where it was trading alone. Moreover, the southern firms were concerned almost exclusively with the produce trade, while the Niger Company had wider interests, especially in mining, which formed an increasingly significant element in the company's profits. This gave its shares a healthy premium, which it wanted reflected in the terms of the merger. The African Association demurred, stating that it was not willing in effect to invest £214,000 'in Mining ventures in West Africa, which is so apart from our ordinary business'.[12] Discussions continued for another month with Miller Bros., but, as no agreement was possible on the figures, the negotiations were suspended in mid-July 1914.[13]

The outbreak of the war some three weeks later presented the companies with dangers, but also with opportunities. It hit immediately at the most important single item in Nigeria's colonial economy, the export of palm kernels to Germany, worth £2,405,625 in 1913. Palm oil, which had gone mainly to Britain,[14] was less seriously affected, but in August 1914 kernels were simply unsaleable in Liverpool.[15] These conditions lasted for some three months,[16] but were clearly temporary. The long-term prospects for kernels were in fact favourable. While palm oil was used mainly in the production of soap, and had to be hardened for use in margarine, kernels were crushed for a different oil, rich in lauric acid, which could be used directly to make high quality margarine. After crushing, the kernels themselves could be treated to produce cattle cake. Glycerine, used in explosives, was a by-product. Crushing of kernels had been done mainly in Germany, as had the preparation of cattle cake, a process which the British were unable to copy. Much of the kernel oil had gone to the great Dutch producers of margarine, Anton Jurgens and Van Den Bergh. These in turn had supplied about half the British market. British crushers used mainly lighter seeds, cotton, rape, and linseed. They could not economically crush palm kernels, or copra, which gave an equivalent oil.[17] The one big British margarine maker, Maypole Dairy, did little of its own crushing, but relied rather on the purchase of oils on the market. It had few connections with the expatriate firms in Nigeria, which in 1915 failed to include it on their list of manufacturers of margarine. Instead its links were with the French buyers of Senegambian groundnuts.[18]

British consumption of margarine had been growing before 1914. During the war it expanded steadily. The government encouraged both the domestic manufacture of margarine and Dutch imports. The latter continued to increase both absolutely and relatively, reaching almost a 60 per cent market share by 1916. The Asquith administration tolerated this, partly because British production was clearly unable to meet the rising demand, partly, no doubt, to encourage the Dutch to ship to Britain rather than to Germany, but also because the Dutch product included raw materials brought to the Netherlands by foreign shipping, thus reducing the strain on British tonnage. Controls were established to ensure that the Dutch did not sell to Germany products made with raw materials from the British Empire.[19] Seeing better future markets in Britain, Jurgens and Van Den Bergh went far to cut their ties with Germany, while making moves to establish production in Britain itself.[20]

The increasing demand for margarine in Britain and the Netherlands, and the British government's pressing need for explosives, and therefore for glycerine, led to a quick revival of the kernels trade. By early 1915 J.E. Trigge, the Managing Director of the Niger Company, was exulting over 'wonderful markets'.[21] Liverpool prices of oil and kernels rose well above their pre-war levels, with a particularly sharp increase at the beginning of 1916. Despite this, Nigerian prices remained depressed. Before the war the difference between Lagos and Liverpool prices had been of the order of £5–£6 for oil and £4–£5 for kernels. By 1916 the differences were £22 and £13. In both cases the cost in Lagos was now less than half that in Liverpool.[22]

Lack of tonnage was certainly the main reason for this disparity. All of West Africa was affected, but the impact on Nigerian palm produce was particularly acute, as this was bulky compared to cocoa, the staple of the Gold Coast, while even after the costly improvements of 1907–13, Lagos was a poor port.[23] Above all, German shipping, which had provided almost forty percent of pre-war tonnage, had not been replaced.[24] The British company Elder Dempster now had an almost complete monopoly. It claimed to be shipping the same amount of kernels as had previously gone to Britain and Germany combined, but had had repeatedly to increase its rates. By October 1915 these were 41 per cent over pre-war for kernels and 25 per cent for oil.[25] Admiralty requisition of ships meant bleak prospects for 1916. The Lagos authorities complained bitterly. The Colonial Office looked into the matter, and concluded that West Africa had been badly treated over tonnage, but not over rates. No amelioration was likely. Trigge noted resignedly that to press the company over tonnage would simply encourage it to put up rates.[26] On paper these did not rise in 1916, but companies had to rely more on charter than on regular sailings. As a consequence, average rates for a ton of kernels rose from £1/9/6 to £2/4/9, a further 50 per cent. Elder Dempster continued to stress that it alone was shipping almost as many kernels as had been shipped pre-war. Independent shipping by Lever Brothers and John Holt should have made up the total. Nevertheless, by November the companies were complaining of a backlog of 100,000 tons of produce, almost a year's supply, rotting in Nigeria for lack of transport.[27]

External factors imposed low produce prices in Nigeria, but these were maintained by the deliberate policy of the expatriate firms. In August 1914, when kernels had been unsaleable in Britain, the major companies had entered into an agreement. In Lagos this was known as the 'Ring'. Its members were: John Holt, Miller Bros., MacIver, Lagos Stores, H.B.W. Russell, G.B. Ollivant, Paterson Zochonis, and C.F.A.O. Parties to the agreement elsewhere in Nigeria included: The African Association, Company of African Traders, Company of African Merchants, Holt Brothers, MacNeill Scott, Thomas Welsh, and the Niger Company. This wider grouping can be called the 'combine'.[28] When prices revived in Liverpool the combine did not dissolve itself. Instead, its activities became more co-ordinated. Its policy was simple. 'What you have to do now is to buy all the produce you can as cheaply as possible', was the instruction sent to Niger Company agents in January 1915.[29] The policy was justified on the grounds that higher local prices would lead only to greater accumulation of unshippable produce and an eventual cessation of trading. Uniform low prices would at least ensure a steady, if minimal, return for the local producers. On the other hand, high prices in Europe reflected scarcity and unreliability of shipping, not just from West Africa but also between Liverpool and Rotterdam, and sharp rises in rates for freight and insurance. Agents were told, 'we can only buy produce with any hope of profit by buying it cheaply and allowing a very wide margin'.[30] This was intended not just as a temporary response to war conditions. The immediate pre-war years were seen as having been abnormal ones in which competition had forced produce prices up to uneconomic levels. The Niger Company wanted a new approach to West African trade, and hoped that 'our competitors have learnt the lesson of the past and will in consequence certainly be as keen as any of our agents to keep down prices'.[31] For the firms in the combine the war years would be ones of rising profits and increasing dividends.[32]

Flimsies of the Niger Company's instructions to its agents in Nigeria are preserved up to April 1915. These shed considerable light on the early stages of the combine. Thereafter only an incomplete, impressionistic picture is available. Potential instability is revealed in one document from 1916, the minutes of the subcommittee of the Committee of Control of the pooling agreement. This shows vividly both the tensions in the combine and its ability to resolve them:

> it has now been finally arranged with the French Co. that they and the other firms at Port Harcourt should buy to limitswhich [sic] have now been agreed upon and cabled out. This has enabled firms in Opobo and New Calabar to reduce their prices to those which were current before the French Co's trade had become so marked. As a result of the reduction of prices in New Calabar the Niger Co. and Messrs. Holts have agreed to continue the arrangement as between themselves for the two months and to maintain a difference of –
> 15/- per puncheon Oil and
> 15/- per ton kernels
> between prices ruling in the New Calabar and the Oguta district and Messrs. Thos Welsh and Co. have agreed to the continuation of the New Calabar agreement for the two months after the end of June.[33]

Clearly the arrangements were short term and renegotiable, but in practice, for palm produce at least, they were renegotiated, proved durable, and covered not just prices, but also, as the Lagos authorities suspected, buying limits.[34] Attempts in the north to make similar arrangements for groundnuts, a new rather than an established trade, with firms like the rapidly expanding Tin Areas of Nigeria and the long-established London and Kano Trading which were otherwise strong critics of the combine, were much less successful, and proved ephemeral.[35]

In the south the combine was indeed substantial. Only in a few places was its monopsony challenged. One such was Onitsha, where Trigge repeatedly complained of the presence of 'small people', and Burrowes noted that kernels fetched £13, whereas in Abeokuta, where there was no competition, they sold for £8/10/-.[36] At Onitsha the small independents were G.W. Christian and J.M. Stuart-Young.[37] The latter, a proud palm oil ruffian and a prolific writer in prose and verse, was called the Kipling of West Africa, a title he had enough literary judgement to disclaim. Once securely established in Onitsha, he had proposed a pool, but no agreement had been possible. War with Germany removed markets rather than competitors. Between the British firms there was a 'sincere rivalry' which Stuart-Young considered almost suicidal. While attempts were made to avoid formal price wars, dashes were usual and often unscrupulous, and agents might be sent up to four miles out along the roads to intercept sellers, a process which Stuart-Young feared would destroy Onitsha's middleman role and turn it into a Deserted Village.[38] The ruin of the Onitsha trader was indeed often proclaimed, but never accomplished. If in fact villagers were now more likely to sell directly to the expatriate firms, they preferred to buy from indigenes in Onitsha. The great wealth of Omu Okwei, the famous 'Merchant Queen of Ossomari', dated from this period. Between 1916 and 1918 she would construct her main residence at a cost of £834/15/8.[39]

Competition at Onitsha would remain a problem for the Niger Company, but a relatively minor one. Eventually, in 1918, it bought out both Christian and Stuart-Young.[40] Far more worrying was the degree to which the Lagos Ring brought Miller Brothers into close co-operation with the firms which were now the rivals of the Niger Company in the north. This threatened the pooling agreement. The negotiations for amalgamation suspended in July 1914 were renewed in September 1915. Again they proved to be tortuous and prolonged.[41] Nevertheless, by August 1916 success seemed imminent. There had even been talk of bringing in John Holt.[42] Yet at the last minute they broke down, ostensibly on a technical point.[43] The details which feature so prominently in the papers of Lord Scarbrough provide few clues to the real reasons. Clearly personal factors, which cannot now be reconstructed, remained important.[44] As Sir George Goldie, chairman in the days of the 'crowned company' now recalled as a special adviser, noted:

> The question of organization and administration has, I think been the chief obstacle to completion throughout; and to my mind the best policy is the one which will fairly satisfy the aspiration of obstinate individuals who, if they do not get their way, will again wreck the scheme – not openly on this ground but on some other issue.[45]

Behind all this was the continuing divergence of approach between the Niger Company and the other firms. Trigge had ambitious plans for the company once fusion had been achieved. These were required to meet the demands of the rapidly expanding and much more integrated and sophisticated colonial economy which would emerge after the war. They were being held up by negotiations in which Trigge felt the other parties were concerned above all with preserving the goodwill of the existing businesses.[46]

Two issues in 1916 brought matters to a head. The first was the revival of the Kano groundnuts trade, which had virtually collapsed in 1915. Miller Bros., felt that the Niger Company was not effectively defending its position in the north and was incurring losses which the other firms had to meet through the pooling arrangement. More than ever they pressed to break into Kano and Zaria.[47] The second issue was the auction of German real property in Nigeria, which was held in London in November. The most important sites were those of G.L. Gaiser, which had been the leading firm in Lagos and the Niger Company's main competitor in Kano. The Ring particularly wanted to acquire these properties cheaply and keep competitors out. It considered several possibilities: it could buy up the sites at the sale and divide them among its members by ballot or by subsequent auction; or it could form a new company to acquire and run them.[48]

Here the interests of the Niger Company diverged sharply from those of its southern partners, especially Miller Bros. The company feared that if its competitors secured the German properties, either individually or as part of a new concern, they would be placed in so powerful a position along the railway that they might gain control of the groundnut trade. It wanted instead to complete the amalgamation so that the new company could buy most of the sites.[49] Millers preferred to work with the other Ring firms in forming what they called an all British company – the presence of C.F.A.O. in the Ring was invariably overlooked – to purchase the properties at a 'fair price' without an auction.[50] The Scarbrough papers are very scrappy for the period when the amalgamation discussions broke down, but this coincided precisely with the approach of the sale and the increasing urgency of a decision over the German sites.[51] Other factors were involved, especially Niger Company suspicions that its partners, Miller Bros. above all, were violating the agreement and infiltrating the north;[52] but the question of the German properties was likely to have been decisive. The combine could agree on the desirability of excluding neutral bidders. This was also supported by British firms outside of the combine, such as Tin Areas and the recently established African Oil Nuts.[53] But when the Association of West African Merchants, the pressure group recently established by the combine, put forward the idea of a new all-British company to buy the properties *en bloc*, the Niger Company promptly dissociated itself from the proposal, which was firmly rejected by the British government.[54]

II

The dispute over the German properties laid bare not only the degree to which Miller Brothers now preferred to co-operate with its new associates in the Lagos Ring rather than with the Niger Company, its old partner in the working agreement, but also the profound lack of sympathy between the firms of the combine and the authorities in Lagos and London. The Governor-General, Sir Frederick Lugard, considered it a cardinal point 'that the interests of a large native population shall not be subject to the will either of a small European merchant class or of a small minority of educated and Europeanized natives'.[55] Historians have rightly emphasized his hostility to the Lagos elite; in the early years of the war his suspicions of the Liverpool firms had a comparable influence on his policies. Following his Controller of Customs, T.F. Burrowes, Lugard quickly concluded that the elimination of the German commercial presence had been a disaster for Nigeria. The removal of this competition and the emergence of the combine had 'caused a large reduction in the prices paid for produce with a corresponding effect on the purchasing power of the community'. This in turn had led to a sharp drop in customs revenue, which was the government's main source of income. The revival of foreign competition was 'almost essential to preserve a healthy trade and secure to the producer a reasonable value for his produce'. Burrowes and Lugard were especially concerned to attract American capital into Nigeria. Therefore they advertised the sale of the German properties heavily in the United States and held it in London, rather than locally and quietly as in the other colonies. This was part of a broader economic policy which Lugard outlined in April 1916. This also included the elimination of the spirits trade, the introduction of export duties on cocoa and palm products, and the imposition of direct taxation in Southern Nigeria.[56]

Lugard was well placed to get his way. His relations with the officials in London had been poor, but the constant carping criticisms of the Niger department had led the colonial secretary to circulate a minute at the end of 1915 stating: 'I hope that in every department the C.O. will start with the assumption that the man on the spot is likely to be right and will not interfere with him unless there is a real necessity for doing so.'[57] When Lugard returned to England in the summer of 1916 he discussed his proposals with the Colonial Office, which largely accepted them. He was told that he would have to take full personal responsibility for the imposition of direct taxation. No similar reservation was made over the need to encourage competition and to prevent the combine from getting a stranglehold over the Nigerian economy.[58]

Officials in the Niger and West Africa departments were for the most part strong believers in free trade who abhorred the idea of running a colony for the exclusive benefit of British merchants. This was incompatible with the principle of trusteeship, indeed it was the mistaken policy which had led to the loss of America. Where non-native interests were involved, the Colonial Office preferred to look not to those of the traders but rather to those of British manufacturers, who would want high prices for their exports to Nigeria, and of British consumers, who expected low prices for imported raw materials. Both were injured by the combine's policy of low Nigerian and high British prices. The Liverpool firms were seen as an unenterprising lot who were doing very well out of the war. At the very least, new British and African firms should be given every opportunity of challenging their monopoly.

While the permanent under-secretary from 1916, Sir George Fiddes, was somewhat more attentive to the merchants' case,[59] the political leadership fully shared the distrust of the departmental officials. The colonial secretary since the formation of the first wartime coalition government in May 1915 was Andrew Bonar Law, the leader of the Conservative party. His appointment to a second-rate office had been a deliberate snub by Asquith, the Liberal prime minister, who preferred to work with Arthur Balfour, the former Conservative leader. As a member of the inner cabinet, Law gave only routine attention to departmental affairs,[60] which he left in the hands of his parliamentary under-secretary, Arthur Steel-Maitland. The latter, as chairman of the Conservative party, was himself a political figure of some importance. He took a close and keen interest especially in the commercial and economic issues confronting the Colonial Office, and he actively sought information from non-official sources. He was quite ready to initiate policy. For him the bottom line was that, whatever justifications they might give, the combine was making greatly increased profits.[61]

Such attitudes made the authorities in Lagos and London particularly receptive to the complaints against the Ring which rose to a crescendo in 1916. These came with particular force from African traders in Lagos and from British firms outside the combine. In Lagos the agitation centred on the allocation of shipping space. Given the enormous gap between Lagos and Liverpool prices, those who could ship at the regular rather than the charter rate were bound to make thumping profits. This tempted many newcomers into the produce trade. As the major existing exporters, the Ring tried to monopolize shipping, taking about three quarters of the produce brought across the lagoon from the ports of Epe, Ejinrin, and Ikorodu, and about sixty per cent of the shipments which came from the railway. Allocation was on the basis of the previous six months' shipments, a provision which obviously favoured the established firms.[62]

For the Ring such arrangements were almost self-evidently fair. Its constituent firms had warehouses full of produce awaiting shipment, but meanwhile incurring increasing costs of storage, insurance, spoilage, and rebagging. On the other hand, interlopers with small but guaranteed allocations of shipping space could buy cheaply on the local market (where the authorities noted that, in the abnormal conditions, the African trader was making the price by November 1916) and ship immediately, thus getting the full advantage of the price differential. Moreover, the Ring asserted, many of the local claims for shipping were being made by front men and dummy companies unconnected themselves with the produce trade.[63]

For local traders the Ring's policy was blatantly oppressive, an attempt to stop them taking over a share of the former German exports.[64] Despite some of their claims, there is little to suggest that they had previously been independent exporters of palm produce on any scale.[65] Before the war, profits had been made mainly on imports of goods into Nigeria, while export of produce had been seen by the expatriate firms mainly as a form of remittance.[66] Now the produce trade had itself become lucrative. The complaints of 1916 came from those who were trying to break in, not from those who were being squeezed out. Osuntokun's claim that Lagos firms went bankrupt at this point is not supported by instances, while the *Red Book of West Africa*, published in 1920, gives details of several African companies which went into produce in 1915–16 and flourished as a result.[67] The protests of the traders merged with the more general discontent in Lagos in 1916 against a colonial administration which was rightly seen as deeply prejudiced against the African educated elite.[68] In July 1916 several of the African traders issued a 'Manifesto' complaining that 'the Native Produce Shippers of Nigeria have been undergoing untold hardships', as the Ring was 'determined to prevent all exportation of local produce by the Native Shippers'.[69]

The signatories of the 'Manifesto' were by no means without allies. British firms like Tin Areas and Oil Nuts also tried to break into the produce trade, and complained strongly to the Colonial Office about the stranglehold of Elder Dempster and the Ring. The chocolate maker H.T. Van Laun was even more indignant.[70] Moreover, African traders had links with firms such as Dyer and Wintle which specialized in taking their business on commission and representing their interests in Britain. As the Lagos merchants imported British goods, especially Manchester textiles, British manufacturers were also willing to take up their case. After the 'Manifesto' was signed, Samuel Duncan of the British and African Produce Supply Company was sent to lobby in Britain. He secured the support of a Liverpool firm, Taylor and Co., of Dransfield and Price, commission agents who were now moving into produce, of Rose Hewitt, a Manchester cotton company which was beginning to act on commission for Lagos produce traders, and even of the British Cotton Growers' Association, which helped to secure an interview for him at the Colonial Office.[71]

Despite some reservations, for instance over the 'rather Babuish' wording of the 'Manifesto', the authorities in Lagos and London were largely sympathetic with the cause of the African exporters.[72] The Liverpool firms had fewer friends. Their most important was Alfred Bigland MP, a former produce broker with a romantic view of empire, who was now a senior adviser in the Ministry of Munitions, where he gloried in his role as a 'Vulture for Glycerine'.[73] The limits of his influence were well illustrated when the question of shipments of palm oil to France came up in August 1916. The amount involved was small, 3,000 tons a quarter (out of a total yearly export of over 67,000 tons), but the principle established would eventually constitute a major precedent. The Ministry of Munitions wanted to restrict participation to firms already established in the French trade, so that shipping arrangements could easily be made in Liverpool. It agreed to a request from Tin Areas, which had arranged shipping independently, but was disinclined to grant a licence to J.J. Fischer, a prominent expatriate firm on the Gold Coast, to ship on behalf of S. Thomas and Co., the leading African firm in Lagos, and one which conspicuously had not signed the 'Manifesto'. This decision was taken on the advice of Robert Miller, who considered that 'these native shippers are simply taking advantage of the present position'. Asked to approve, the Colonial Office was aghast. There would be 'a holy row if the non-combination firms find that they are not being given licences while the old gang are and that Miller Bros are the advisers of the M of M in assigning such privileges'. Fischer and Thomas were precisely the sort of people to assist against the Ring, or at least not to assist the Ring against. Discussions between the Colonial Office and the Ministry ended with an agreement that the Liverpool firms would divide 3,000 tons, but that an additional 1,000 tons would be provided, with 500 tons going to Nigeria, 200 to Sierra Leone, and 300 tons to the Gold Coast.[74]

This was part of a pattern of governmental decisions deliberately adverse to the interests of the combine. When Lugard imposed export duties on palm products in 1916, he was partly following advice from African Oil Nuts, which had argued that, producer prices being at a minimum, the incidence would fall instead on the companies in the combine, a reasoning which was accepted by A.J. Harding, the number two in the Niger department, though more senior officials were less convinced.[75] Relations between the Colonial Office and the firms deteriorated throughout 1916. When the Association of West African Merchants was established in August, the department noted that it was 'just the old mob in a new grouping', regretted that it could not decently be overlaid, and decided to 'turn a very cold shoulder to it'.[76] At the same time, Steel-Maitland began actively to investigate how far the firms might be abusing their position. His interest in that question was leaked by Bigland to Robert Miller.[77] A deputation on 10 October achieved few concrete results, leaving its members with the feeling that they 'did not appear to have altogether removed ... the impression that the Nigerian merchants had not, since the commencement of the War, paid a fair price to the natives for their produce'. Above all, it failed to shake the Colonial Office's resolve not to exclude neutrals from the auction of the German properties.[78]

Historians of British politics are well aware that the challenge to this decision, which led to the House of Commons 'Nigeria Debate' of 8 November 1916, precipitated the political crisis which ended with the overthrow of Asquith.[79] What was remarkable in this was not the ability of the Liverpool firms to wrap themselves in the Union Jack and to exploit 'those nationalist, anti-foreign, anti-neutral, sentiments which always predominate in time of war',[80] but rather the willingness of Bonar Law to make this a test of strength which he intended to win by showing how the patriotic rhetoric of his opponents concealed the sordid material interests of the Lagos Ring in its attempt to stifle competition and engorge itself with profits at the expense of the Nigerian producer and the British consumer. In the division, the crucial question was whether Law would retain the support of a majority of Conservative MPs which he did, though narrowly.[81] The Ring got as far as it did, not because parliamentarians, apart from Bigland, were eager to defend its interests, but partly because, over the exclusion of neutrals, it had the support of British firms outside of the combine, notably Tin Areas and African Oil Nuts, and partly because, by offering to commit itself to paying a fair price for produce, it had avoided attack from the Anti-Slavery and Aborigines' Protection Society,[82] but mainly because the most visible intending neutral purchaser was Jurgens, a company suspected of German sympathies which during the debate was revealed once to have been fined for trading with the enemy. The attack on Jurgens was a by-product of its marketing war with Maypole Dairy, and had little to do with the agitation got up by the combine.[83]

Just before the debate, the government reduced the maximum permissible enemy shareholding in a neutral bidder from fifty to ten per cent. Jurgens had to withdraw.[84] No neutral bidder was successful. In Lagos the main sites went either to Elder Dempster or to the Ring firms. The Cooperative Wholesale Society was the only significant newcomer. Nevertheless, the intense publicity given to the auction meant that prices were far higher than Burrowes, who had charge of it, had expected.[85] This would have been a heavy capital cost, which may have exacerbated the companies' problems after 1920.[86]

Some of the main Lagos sites purchased by Ring firms were later transferred to a new concern, the British Nigerian Company, in which they were partners. The Niger Company considered this a definitely hostile move.[87] It contributed greatly to the acrimony with which the working agreement began to break up in 1917. Looking back a year later, Trigge reflected that:

> the Enemy Properties fiasco in October 1916 demonstrated how impossible it is to get the West African Trade to work together in unity. The high prices paid for the Properties, the embittering of the wealthy Dutch Margarine Manufacturers against the West African Trade, the pooling of the purchases against Merchants and the formation of the British Nigeria Co. Ltd. are now matters to be remembered as object lessons of what not to do in the future.[88]

Now there were repeated accusations of poaching and other violations of the agreement. The Niger Company bought out the Company of African Merchants, which brought it into the sphere reserved for its partners.[89] They, in turn, proposed to amalgamate with John Holt, the main rival of the Niger Company in its own territories. This may mainly have been intended to put pressure on the Niger Company to allow them to 'assist' it in Kano and Zaria, a proposal which it still stoutly resisted.[90] While the agreement was not yet formally denounced, Miller Bros. and the African Association did move into Kano, and the Niger Company into Lagos.[91] Amalgamation negotiations were never resumed. By the end of the war the working agreement was clearly dead. Its breakdown was eventually backdated to 31 December 1916.[92]

III

The war had delayed the formation of a horizontal cartel of the main expatriate firms in Nigeria, and eventually destroyed its prospects of success. The post-war pattern would be significantly different, with vertical linkages at least as important as horizontal ones. Lever Brothers was now the main actor. Its subsidiary, MacIver, had become the largest exporter of palm oil by 1919.[93] From 1917 it was again on the prowl for merchant concerns to absorb.[94] This threatened all the trading firms. In response, Miller Bros. and the African Association merged with African Traders, Lagos Stores, MacNeill Scott, and Crombie Steadman to form the African and Eastern Trade Corporation. While this did establish some vertical links, most notably by acquiring the soap manufacturers T.H. Harris, it was essentially a horizontal amalgamation, and, as the Niger Company had predicted, a badly organized one at that. This would be a major element in bringing the Corporation to grief in 1928.[95] The Niger Company chose a more radical solution. Lacking the capital to carry out the 'bold forward policy' Trigge wished to pursue, it agreed to Lever Brothers' purchase of all its ordinary shares at a high price of £6/10/- in January 1920.[96]

This first major round of mergers, late in the war and immediately after it, was the product not of hard times but of economic revival and the expectation of rapid expansion. This also affected the African traders. The Colonial Office insisted on greater non-combine representation in the allocation of tonnage.[97] Elder Dempster changed its policy in 1917, and made its allocations dependent on goods awaiting shipment.[98] When London at last controlled produce prices in 1917, these were eventually set high enough to ensure good profits alike for expatriate firms and for the African merchant, though the biggest gainer was the new Ministry of Shipping, which now benefited directly from a massive increase in freight rates.[99] By the end of 1919 there were over 350 shippers from Lagos, almost all of them African. Of the railway traffic, the Ring had only a half.[100]

The complaints which had filled the Colonial Office files in 1916 died away, though the shipping monopoly remained a grievance to be raised at the first meeting of the National Conference of British West Africa in 1920.[101] As the *Red Book* shows, many who went into produce at this time were thriving in 1920. African Oil Nuts, established at Lagos, Port Harcourt, Kano, and seven other places, was an example on the European side. On the African side was T.B. Johnstone, who also had started in 1916, now had one of the largest indigenous enterprises in West Africa, and was one of the leading shippers of produce. He had just hired a Scots accountant as his chief of clerical staff, and was photographed with his racehorse. He was part of the Lagos elite so vividly displayed in the *Red Book* as it sought to present itself, confident, prosperous, cultured, with diverse interests: J.C. Thomas with his philanthropy and his model farm run by an American couple; Samuel Pearse with his F.R.G.S. and his palatial Elephant House, roof garden, and ballroom with the 'music of a full orchestra . . . supplied by a large orchestrion operated by electric power'; Karimu Koton, cotton importer, signatory of the 'Manifesto', and in 1907 president of the first Mohemmedan

Cricket Club in Lagos. The establishment of the National Conference of British West Africa, whose group photograph also appears in the *Red Book*,[102] was partly the work of this national bourgeoisie while it was still rising, and not, as Michael Crowder has suggested, of it as a frustrated and embittered group after the economic collapse of 1920.[103]

Economic revival was also shown by the entry of new expatriate firms into Nigeria after 1916. Some were British companies already established elsewhere on the West Coast; some were French. Jurgens came in, though on a much smaller scale than intended when it had hoped to purchase the German properties. The large American firm Grace Brothers arrived in 1917. It was expected to be the first of many. At the same time, companies like Tin Areas and T.B. Johnstone expanded from Nigeria to other parts of the Coast. The Colonial Bank, previously restricted to the West Indies, opened in Lagos in 1917.[104] The economic indicators seemed especially favourable in 1919. Prices of oil and kernels rose to almost twice 1913 levels. With the steady growth in the demand for margarine, the market for kernels and groundnuts seemed set to expand. The emergence of cocoa and tin along with groundnuts as major exports showed that the Nigerian colonial economy was diversifying as well as growing.[105]

It did not last. Early in 1920 produce prices crashed. Import prices remained high. Helleiner has attempted to construct an index of real producer prices. Whatever criticisms can be made about the details, and they are likely to be many, the catastrophe was unmistakable. For kernels the index had stood at 276.0 in 1913; by 1916 it had fallen to 93.3; the recovery took it to 145.2 by 1919; in 1921 it stood at 40.0. The figures for oil were similar: not so steep a fall to 1916, a better recovery by 1919, an even worse crash by 1921.[106] This was disaster on the grand scale. The Niger Company had invested heavily in produce. It almost went under, taking Lever Brothers with it. The combination was rescued, but Lord Leverhulme had to relinquish his unchallenged control over his company.[107] Tin Areas did go down.[108] The African trader, expecting to expand his business and now holding large stacks of unsaleable goods, was even more severely hit. Few survived.[109] The optimism of the *Red Book*, still to a degree reflected in Allan McPhee's *Economic Revolution in British West Africa* written in 1926,[110] would be mocked by the near stagnation of the colonial economy in the inter-war years.

Ten years ago, writing about the historiography of big business in Africa, Hopkins remarked that 'bad data sustain simple theories of a complex world; good data inhibit easy generalization'.[111] Clearly, one can no longer maintain that there was a special relationship between the colonial government and the expatriate firms in Nigeria. The Lagos authorities, backed by those in London, considered the growth of oligopsony to be a threat to the development of the colonial economy. They did what they could to thwart it. Far from encouraging the British firms, they looked to foreign capital to restore the degree of competition which they considered necessary. A more sophisticated view of the combine and its actions is also necessary. Menacing as it appeared to Burrowes and Lugard, to the African traders in Lagos, and to Stuart-Young in Onitsha, the participating companies were acutely aware of its fragility, and feared the dangers of the war more than they perceived its opportunities. Neither the elimination of German competition nor the emergence of the combine led directly to the mergers of the immediate post-war period. Rather they ensured that the existing working agreement would break down in bitter recrimination. At the end of the war the big firms, far from having squeezed out their competitors, were facing effective and vigorous challenges from newer and smaller concerns, both African and expatriate.

Any new work of major synthesis will have to take all this into account. But if it invalidates a simplistic semi-conspiratorial view of colonialism in Nigeria in this period, it does not automatically validate one of its beneficence. Critical analysis does not need conspiracy theories. Marx argued that capitalism was exploitative, not that capitalists were wicked. The Nigerian colonial economy did indeed come to be dominated by a very few large expatriate firms. This was despite, not because of, the conscious policy of the Lagos and London governments.

Radical historians in Nigeria are fond of quoting Walter Rodney that the African peasantry went into colonialism with the hoe and came out of it with the hoe. Obviously this makes an important point, but it is misleading to the extent that it suggests that all Africans were peasants before colonialism and remained peasants throughout. Many were or became traders, entrepreneurs, middlemen. Some of these competed against the European firms, others, like Omu Okwei, acted as their agents, many, perhaps most, did both. Their histories can only have been hinted at in a work of this scope. Even less has it been able to touch on how the events of this period affected the primary producer. Here again the need is for a carefully differentiated analysis. Insofar as Nigeria did remain technologically backward under colonialism, this was largely the consequence of the dominance of merchant rather than industrial capital, and a paternalistic government's increasing attachment to the preservation of peasant production.[112] The government which we have seen trying to save the producer from oligopsony also ended up shielding him from technical change.

Reading

Notes

I should like to thank the University of Jos for granting me the study leave in the rainy seasons of 1993–4 in which the bulk of the archival research for this article was done. For comments on earlier drafts I am grateful to my former colleagues Dr C.C. Jacobs and Dr M. Mangvwat of the Department of History, University of Jos.

1. See especially W. Ibekwe Ofonagoro, *Trade and Imperialism in Southern Nigeria 1881–1929* (New York, 1979); R.J. Gavin and Wale Oyemakinde, 'Economic Development in Nigeria since 1900', in Obaro Ikime (ed.), *Groundwork of Nigerian History* (Ibadan, 1980), 482–517; Akinjide Osuntokun, *Nigeria in the First World War* (London, 1979); Richard Rathbone, 'World War I and Africa: Introduction', *Journal of African History*, 19 (1978), 1–9.
2. In addition to the works already cited, the development of the Nigerian colonial economy is considered in general terms in A.G. Hopkins, *An Economic History of West Africa* (London, 1975), and Gerald K. Helleiner, *Peasant Agriculture, Government and Economic Growth in Nigeria* (Homewood, Illinois, 1966). For the wider context, Michael Havenden and David Meredith, *Colonialism and Development, Britain and its Tropical Colonies, 1890–1960* (London, 1993).
3. A.G. Hopkins, 'Big Business in African Studies', *JAH*, 28 (1987), 119–40, quotation on 129.
4. Ayodeji Olukoju, 'Elder Dempster and the Shipping Trade of Nigeria During the First World War', *JAH*, 33 (1992), 255–71, quotation on 264.
5. The pattern of the colonial economy in Nigeria is revealed in three contemporary sources. The 'First Schedule. Immovable Property vested in the Receiver under Section 3(2)', copy in CO 583/48/41329, Colonial Office (CO) archives, Public Record Office (PRO), Kew, England, lists the properties of the German commercial firms in Nigeria on the outbreak of

the war. 'Local Stations of European Firms', CO 583/54/53413, was drawn up by T.F. Burrowes, the Controller of Customs, who was also Receiver of Enemy Property, at the beginning of November 1916. Allister Macmillan, *The Red Book of West Africa* (London, 1968 [1920]), a volume produced with the assistance of the Chambers of Commerce, gives details of many of the expatriate and African firms operating in Nigeria in 1919–20.

6. There was also a small southern firm, the Company of African Merchants. For details see Frederick Pedler, *The Lion and the Unicorn in Africa, A History of the Origins of the United Africa Company 1707–1931* (London, 1974), 265–8; Ofonagoro, *Trade and Imperialism*, 339–42; Colin Newbury, 'Trade and Technology in West Africa: The Case of the Niger Company 1900–1920', *JAH*, 19 (1978), 557–8.
7. Gavin and Oyemakinde, 'Economic Development', 500. The challenge of the railway to the Niger Company's river based position is a major theme in Newbury, 'Trade and Technology'.
8. For the development of the groundnuts trade Jan Hogendorn, *Nigerian Groundnut Exports, Origins and Early Development* (Zaria, 1978).
9. J.E. Trigge (Managing Director, Niger Co.) to Lord Scarbrough (Chairman, N.C.), 21 May 1917, MSS Afr s.93, Scarbrough papers, Rhodes House, Oxford.
10. Miller to Scarbrough, 29 June 1914. A similar opinion had already been voiced by Harry Cotterell of the African Association, to Scarbrough, 23 June 1914, MSS Afr s.93, Scarbrough papers.
11. These can be followed in ibid.
12. Cotterell to Scarbrough, 15 June 1914, ibid.
13. Miller to Scarbrough, 7 and 9 July, Committee of Control minutes, 16 July 1914, ibid.
14. Tables of Nigerian exports can be found in *Red Book*, 45–46.
15. Addition to unsigned note, 15 Aug. 1914, MSS Afr s.99, Scarbrough papers.
16. Trigge to Scarbrough, 15 Sept. 1915, MSS Afr s. 86, Scarbrough papers.
17. Charles Wilson, *The History of Unilever, A Study in Economic Growth and Social Change* (London 1954), 2, 148–51, 155, 156; Osuntokun, *Nigeria in the First World War*, 30–31.
18. African Trade Section, Liverpool Chamber of Commerce, to Colonial Office, 3 Sept. 1915, CO 554/25/40937; Pedler, *Lion and Unicorn*, 196; Wilson, *Unilever*, 2, 156.
19. British Board of Trade, 'Policy in Licensing Exports', 13 March 1916, CO 323/721/12938; Wilson, *Unilever*, 2, 157.
20. Wilson, *Unilever*, 2, 158, 174–8.
21. Trigge to Agent General, Nigeria, 12 Jan., to Agent Upper Igarra, 18 Jan. 1915, flimsies, MSS Afr s.99 Scarbrough papers.
22. 'Nigeria Trade Statistical Abstract No. 8', 12, CO 660/4.
23. A.J. Harding (Acting First Class Clerk, Niger Dep't, CO) min., 1 Jan., W.D. Ellis (Principal Clerk, West Africa and Mediterranean Department) and Sir Charles Strachey (Principal Clerk, Niger Dep't) mins., 3 Jan., A. Steel-Maitland (Parliamentary Under Secretary, CO) min. 6 Jan. 1916, CO 583/38/5921; Elder Dempster to CO, 11 Dec., Ellis min., 20 Dec., Strachey min., 21 Dec. 1915, CO 583/43/57279.
24. Total shipping in Nigerian ports fell from 900,000 tons in 1913 to 500,000 tons in 1916, *Red Book*, 46.
25. P.H. Davies, *The Trade Makers, Elder Dempster and West Africa 1852–1972* (London, 1973), 198, 477 (table 79).
26. Steel-Maitland min., 6 Jan. 1916, CO 583/38/59211; Trigge to Scarbrough, 13 Dec. 1915, MSS Afr s.99, Scarbrough papers.
27. Association of West African Merchants (A.W.A.M.) to Steel-Maitland, 9 Nov. 1916, CO 583/53/37164; Owen Philipps (Chairman, Elder Dempster) to Steel-Maitland, 13 Nov. 1916, Steel-Maitland papers, GD/193/93/1, Scottish Record Office, Edinburgh.
28. T.F. Burrowes, 'Notes on the trade combine in Nigeria', 6 Nov. 1916, CO 583/54/53413. Burrowes omits Thomas Welsh, which was certainly a member. CO memorandum to Lagos, Accra, and Freetown, 24 Aug. 1916, CO 583/53/37164.
29. Niger Co. to Agent, Anambra, flimsy, 18 Jan. 1915, MSS Afr s.99, Scarbrough papers.
30. Niger Co. to Agent General, Nigeria, to Agent, Nassarawa (quotation), 26 Jan., to Agent General, 9 and 16 Feb. 1916, flimsies, ibid.; A.W.A.M. to Steel-Maitland, 'Produce Trade in Nigeria', 23 Oct. 1916, CO 583/53/50893.
31. Niger Co. to Agent, Upper Igarra, flimsy, 18 Jan. 1915, MSS Afr s.99 Scarbrough papers.

32. The African Association paid 12 per cent on ordinaries in each of the eight years up to and including 1914. In 1915 it paid 15 per cent, in 1916 and 1917, 20 per cent. *Red Book*, 64.
33. Subcommittee of Control Committee, 12 July 1916, MSS Afr s.93, Scarbrough papers.
34. Burrowes, 'Notes on the combine', 6 Nov. 1916, CO 583/54/53413.
35. Information on the groundnut combines is scanty and conflicting: Burrowes, 'Notes on the combine', 6 Nov. 1916, CO 583/54/53413; Harding to R.H. Wiseman (Ministry of Shipping), 20 June 1917, CO 554/35/31308; Hogendorn, *Groundnut Exports*, 126, 144, 270–1; Pedler, *Lion and Unicorn*, 169.
36. Trigge to Agent General, Nigeria, flimsy, 9 Feb. 1915, to Scarbrough, 1 Sept. 1916, MSS Afr s.99,86, Scarbrough papers; Burrowes, 'Notes on the combine', 6 Nov. 1916, CO 583/54/53413.
37. These are the names as given in Burrowes' list, CO 583/54/53413. In Felicia Ekejiuba, 'Omu Okwei, The Merchant Queen of Ossomari, A Biographical Sketch', *Journal of the Historical Society of Nigeria*, 3/4 (1967), 638, Christian is listed as G.W. Matter, and Stuart-Young as Jack Odoziaku. Odoziaku was in fact a local name given to Stuart-Young, *onye-ndozi-aku*, one who composes or arranges the wealth and property of the town. John Moray Stuart-Young, *The Iniquitous Coaster* (London, 1917), 157. The reason for the Christian/Matter discrepancy is not clear. In his lightly fictionalized account Stuart-Young refers to this firm as Matan. Stuart-Young, *The Coaster at Home, Being the Autobiography of Jack O'Dazi, Palm Oil Ruffian and Trader of the River Niger* (London, 1916), 91–92.
38. This account is mainly based on 'Typical Trading Conditions' in Stuart-Young, *Coaster at Home*, 89–92, and 'Trading Amenities: A Digression' in Stuart-Young, *Iniquitous Coaster*, 192–95. For the loss of the Hamburg market, and the prospects as seen in Onitsha on the outbreak of the war, *Iniquitous Coaster*, 68–69; for fierce competition, ibid., 387.
39. Ekejiuba, 'Omu Okwei', 637–40, 643. For a 1917 lament over the fall of Onitsha, Osuntokun, *Nigeria in the First World War*, 81.
40. Christian was purchased for £50,000, Stuart-Young for £12,200. Trigge noted that as a result of the elimination of competition at Onitsha the N.C. 'is buying produce there at relatively low prices'. Control Committee minutes, 21 Nov., 16 and 19 Dec. 1918, Trigge memo, 7 Oct. 1919, MSS Afr s. 93,86. The terms of the purchase prevented Stuart-Young from resuming in Nigeria, but by 1930 he was back in Onitsha and appealing to Winifried Tete-Ansa's West African Co-operative Producers Ltd to 'save the River from becoming the Cemetery of the Native Trader and the Garden of the Merger and the Merger's Fellow-Conspirators'. Circular of 11 March 1930, quoted in J. Ayodele Langley, *Pan-Africanism and Nationalism in West Africa 1900–1945, A Study in Ideology and Social Classes* (Oxford, 1973), 231.
41. As with the previous negotiations, these can be followed in MSS Afr s.93, Scarbrough papers.
42. Trigge to Scarbrough, 4 April 1916, ibid.
43. The disagreement concerned the rotation of directors. The draft under discussion provided that it should be arranged to the formula 7 Niger Co., 3 African Ass., 3 Miller Bros., 1 Co. of African Merchants with which the amalgamation would start. Millers wanted instead a provision that if a director died or vacated office within the first three years, 'his place shall be filled by the appointment of a successor to be made in like manner as the appointment of the Director so dying or vacating office'. R. Miller to Scarbrough, 14 Aug. 1916, ibid.
44. Trigge to Scarbrough, 4 April 1916, is both revealing and enigmatic on this point; also C.B. Edgar (Director, N.C.) to Scarbrough, 5 April 1916, ibid.
45. Goldie to Scarbrough, 23 Feb. 1916, ibid.
46. Trigge to Scarbrough, 21 May 1917, ibid.
47. Hogendorn, *Groundnut Exports*, 130–2; Pedler, *Lion and Unicorn*, 269; [Trigge] to T.S. Braithwaite (Solicitor to Niger Co.), 13 July 1918, flimsy, MSS Afr s.93, Scarbrough papers.
48. These alternatives were set out in a meeting of the subcommittee of the Control Committee, 12 July 1916, MSS Afr s.93, Scarbrough papers.
49. Edgar to Scarbrough, 14 July 1916, Trigge to Scarbrough, 21 May 1917, [Trigge] to Braithwaite, 13 July 1918, flimsy. When he first raised the question with the Niger Co., Robert Miller had argued: 'At first sight one would be inclined to say that in doing this we were creating a powerful opposition to ourselves, but I scarcely think this would be so as amongst us we would have a largely preponderating interest.' Miller to Scarbrough, 11 July 1916, MSS Afr s.93, Scarbrough papers.

50. R. Miller to Scarbrough, 11 July 1916, MSS Afr s.93, ibid. Leslie Scott (M.P., Liverpool, Exchange) parliamentary question for 24 Oct. 1916, CO 583/52/50160. A.W.A.M. to CO, 3 Nov. 1916, CO 583/53/52806. African Ass., Miller Bros., and John Holt to CO, 7 Nov. 1916, CO 583/53/53560. While the position of the C.F.A.O. was repeatedly raised during the debate, neither side pointed out that it was a member of the A.W.A.M. and of the Ring, Britain, H.C. Deb., 5 series, 87, 249–368.
51. For the urgency of the matter: R. Miller to Scarbrough, 11 July, subcommittee mins., 12 July 1916. Miller's letter to Scarbrough of 14 Aug. 1916 was the last significant document in which the fusion negotiations were treated as a matter of active concern. MSS Afr s.93, Scarbrough papers. Trigge's notes of 1 Sept. 1916 for the annual meeting of the Niger Co. hoped that complete agreement would be reached that month. MSS Afr. s.86, ibid. The N.C. Board closed the negotiations on 13 Sept. 1916, MSS Afr s.93, ibid.
52. [Trigge] to Braithwaite, 13 July 1918, flimsy, MSS Afr s.93, ibid.
53. Tin Areas to CO, 2 Nov. 1916, CO 583/53/53014; Britain H.C. Deb., 5 series, 87, 251–2, 8 Nov. 1916, speech of Leslie Scott.
54. Niger Co. to CO, 4 Nov. 1916, CO 583/53/52990.
55. Lugard to Sir Lewis Harcourt (Colonial Secretary), 24 Feb. 1914, quoted in Osuntokun, *Nigeria in the First World War*, 8.
56. Lugard to CO no. 1126, 4 Dec. 1915, CO 583/38/59211; Lugard to CO no. 282, 8 April 1916 (first quotation), and confidential, s.d. (second quotation), CO 583/45/20789,20906. For the advertisement of the sale of enemy property, Lugard to CO no. 643, 30 Aug. 1916, CO 583/48/41329, and Crown Agents to CO, 5 Dec. 1916, CO 583/51/58558. This was done without consulting the CO, Sir George Fiddes (Permanent Under Secretary, CO) min., 23 Oct. 1916, CO 583/52/50041.
57. Law min., 30 Nov., circulated to all departments, 2 Dec. 1915, CO 583/38/50522. For Lugard's relations with the CO generally, Margery Perham, *Lugard, The Years of Authority 1898–1945, The Second Part of the Life of Frederick Dealtry Lugard later Lord Lugard of Abinger P.C., G.C.M.G., C.B., D.S.O.* (London, 1960), 607–12, 628–33.
58. Harding and Strachey mins., 21 July, Fiddes min., 25 July, CO to Lugard, conf., 21 Aug 1916. The CO would have declined to support Lugard's proposal to promote American entry into Nigeria, but Law amended the despatch to give it qualified approval if encouragement were first given to British firms. CO 583/53/20906.
59. For attitudes within the CO, see the minutes in CO 583/45/20906; by Harding, 17 May 1916, CO 583/45/20789, by J.E. Flood (Second Class Clerk, West Africa and Mediterranean Dep't), 2 Sept. and Ellis, 4 Sept. 1916, CO 554/32/41764; by Harding, 25 Sept. 1916, with marginal note by Fiddes, CO 583/53/45223; by Strachey, 11 Nov. 1916, CO 583/53/54100.
60. Robert Blake, *The Unknown Prime Minister, The Life and Times of Andrew Bonar Law 1858–1923* (London, 1955), 251, 261; Roy Jenkins, *Asquith* (London, 1967 [1964]), 418–19; Perham, *Lugard*, 628.
61. Steel-Maitland min., 10 June 1916, CO 583/45/20906; Britain H.C. Deb., 5 series, 87, 270, 8 Nov. 1916.
62. A.G. Boyle (Lieutenant Governor, Southern Nigeria) to CO, 31 Oct., and memorandum by A.S. Cooper, General Manager, Nigeria Railways, 20 Oct. 1916, CO 583/49/55579.
63. The fullest statements of the Ring's case are: R. Miller, 'Produce Trade in Nigeria', 10 Oct.; A.W.A.M., 'Produce Trade in Nigeria', 23 Oct. 1916, CO 583/53/47412,50893; and Alfred Bigland's speech in the Nigeria Debate, Britain H.C. Deb., 5 series, 87, 315–17, 8 Nov. 1916. For the African trader making the price in Lagos, although 'the competition is not sufficiently strong to bring about a normal market', Burrowes, 'Notes on the combine', 6 Nov. 1916, CO 583/54/53413.
64. The fullest statement of the Lagos traders' case was their 'Manifesto' of 12 July 1916: 'The Shipping Difficulty or the Restrictions and Disadvantages Placed upon Native Shippers in the Export of Local Produce', CO 583/54/43145.
65. Olukoju, 'Elder Dempster', though highly critical of the Ring and sympathetic to the 'Manifesto', recognizes that its signatories were newly attracted into the trade by the abnormal wartime profits. His evidence suggests that some African traders may have exported cocoa before the war, 261. On the import side, they competed effectively in textiles, Newbury, 'Trade and Technology', 567.

66. Miller, 'Produce Trade', 10 Oct. 1916, CO 583/53/47412. Late in 1917 Trigge noted the 'possibility that after the War produce may *again* become merely a currency exchange and that profits be made only on the sale of goods for cash'. Trigge to Scarbrough, 18 Oct. 1917, MSS Afr s.86, Scarbrough papers, emphasis added.
67. Osuntokun, *Nigeria in the First World War*, 40, 292; *Red Book*: T.B. Johnstone, 105–06, E.S. Kester, 107, D.A. Taylor, 108, British and African Produce Supply Company, 109, S.O. Bamgbose and Bros., 110.
68. Osuntokun, *Nigeria in the First World War*, 68–84.
69. 'Shipping Difficulty', 12 July 1916, CO 583/54/43145.
70. For Tin Areas and Oil Nuts: *Red Book*, 72, 84; Tin Areas to CO, 2 Nov. 1916, CO 583/53/53014; Oil Nuts to Ministry of Munitions, 8 March, to Bonar Law, 7 Nov. 1916, CO 583/54/12460,53803. For Van Laun: *Red Book*, 197; Harding min., 20 Sept. 1916, CO 583/53/45500; Van Laun to CO, 20 Oct. 1916, CO 583/54/50359. Van Laun may have been the British merchant whose article 'The palm-kernel Trust – Crown Colonies that are "owned" by a combine – The "seven" ' appeared on the front page of the *Daily Express* on the day of the Nigeria Debate, and which is heavily used in Ofonagoro, *Trade and Imperialism*, 15–16, 398–99.
71. For Dyer and Wintle, *Red Book*, 90. For Taylor and Co., Dransfield and Price, and Rose Hewitt: Taylor and Co. to CO, 7 Aug., Dransfield and Price to CO, 1 and 9 Sept., Rose Hewitt to CO, 25 Sept. 1916, CO 583/54/37635,41989,43145,46053, and Cooper memo, 20 Oct. 1916, CO 583/49/55579. For the B.C.G.A.: B.C.G.A. to CO, 12 Sept. 1916, CO 583/53/43832. For the British and African Produce Supply Company: *Red Book*, 109.
72. Harding min., 13 Sept. 1916, CO 583/54/43145.
73. For Bigland: Osuntokun, *Nigeria in the First World War*, 62, n. 82, and his memoirs, *The Call of Empire* (London, 1926), from which the phrase 'Vulture for Glycerine' is taken, 66.
74. Strachey to Bigland, 3 Aug., Bird (Propellant Supplies Branch, Min. of Munitions) to Strachey, 4 Aug. (with copy Miller Bros. to Director, Propellant Supplies), Harding (quotation) and Strachey mins., 8 Aug., account of meeting between CO and Min. of Munitions, 17 Aug., CO memo to Lagos, Accra, and Freetown, 24 Aug. 1916, CO 583/53/36731,37164. For S. Thomas: Cooper memo, 20 Oct. 1916, CO 583/49/55579, Hogendorn, *Groundnut Exports*, 60, *Red Book*, 95–96. J.C. Thomas would become the first African President of the Lagos Chamber of Commerce in 1929. Olukoju, 'Elder Dempster', 262 n.38. For J.J. Fischer: *Red Book*, 196–7. For the decision as a precedent: Harding memos, 14 Sept. and 5 Oct., CO to colonies, 12 Oct. 1917, CO 554/34/47011.
75. Harding min., 17 May, Strachey min., 25 May, Fiddes min., 7 June 1916, CO 583/45/20905; Harding min., 10 Oct. 1916, CO 583/55/48013; Oil Nuts to Law, 7 Nov. 1916, CO 583/54/53803.
76. Flood min., 2 Sept. (first quotation), Ellis min., 4 Sept. 1916 (second quotation), CO 554/32/41764; Harding min., 25 Sept. 1916, CO 583/53/45276.
77. Miller to Bigland, 28 Sept., Bigland to Steel-Maitland, 29 Sept., Steel-Maitland to Bigland, 29 Sept. (carbon, sent 4 Oct.) 1916, Steel-Maitland papers, GD/193/93/1.
78. The documents relating to the delegation are in CO/583/53/45276,47412. The disappointment of the firms is expressed in A.W.A.M. to Steel-Maitland, 'Produce Trade', 23 Oct. 1916, CO 583/53/50893.
79. I am currently preparing an article on this in collaboration with Professor Cameron Hazlehurst.
80. Blake, *Unknown Prime Minister*, 298.
81. Law was supported by 73 Conservatives, opposed by 65. Ibid, 299.
82. For Tin Areas and Oil Nuts, see above n. 70; for the Aborigines' Protection Society, Britain, H.C. Deb., 5 series, 87, 257–58, (Leslie Scott), 8 Nov. 1916.
83. As Steel-Maitland noted, this was 'a long and complicated story', min., 15 Nov. 1916, CO 583/53/54400. It will be considered in the article which I am preparing with Professor Hazlehurst. There are brief accounts in Wilson, *Unilever*, 2, 158–60, 174, and Pedler, *Lion and Unicorn*, 196. The revelation about Jurgens' fine was made late in the debate by Sir H. Dalziel, Britain, H. C. Deb., 5 series, 87, 342–43, 8 Nov. 1916. The CO subsequently looked into this; for the main documents: CO 583/53/54126,54564,54595.
84. The documents on the redrafting and on Jurgens are in CO 583/53/53280,54126,54564.

85. Burrowes to Steel-Maitland, with 'Particulars of Sale', 18 Nov. 1916. There was one significant African purchaser: S. Thomas bought the Jackel site in Lagos for £5,000. CO 583/57/29427.
86. Sir Alfred Mond had pointed to this possibility in the Nigeria Debate, Britain, H.C. Deb., 5 series, 87, 286, 8 Nov. 1916.
87. Pedler, *Lion and Unicorn*, 194–5; *West Africa* clipping, 10 March 1917, CO 583/63/13125; Oldfields Solicitors to CO, 20 March 1917, CO 583/64/14824; Trigge to Scarbrough, 21 May 1917, MSS Afr s.93, Scarbrough papers.
88. Trigge to Scarbrough, 18 Oct. 1917, MSS Afr s.86, Scarbrough papers.
89. The main documents are in MSS Afr s.93, ibid. There are brief accounts in Ofonagoro, *Trade and Imperialism*, 342, and Pedler, *Lion and Unicorn*, 171.
90. 'Case for the Opinion of Counsel on behalf of African Association', n.d., and Opinion by F.H. Maugham (Solicitor, Hill Dickinson), 7 Nov. 1917, MSS Afr s.1525/5/2, John Holt Co. papers, Rhodes House.
91. For Miller Bros. and the African Assoc. in Kano, Hogendorn, *Groundnut Exports*, 140; for the Niger Co. in Lagos, Trigge to Scarbrough, 18 Oct. 1917, MSS Afr s.86, Scarbrough papers.
92. The documents on the termination of the agreement are in MSS Afr s.93, Scarbrough papers.
93. *Red Book*, 73.
94. Trigge to Scarbrough, 21 May 1917, MSS Afr s.93, Scarbrough papers; Pedler, *Lion and Unicorn*, 64, 181–82, 226.
95. Pedler, *Lion and Unicorn*, 226–8, 231–2, 235–9.
96. Ibid., 183–4; Wilson, *Unilever*, 1, 250–3; Trigge memos, 7 Oct. 1919, 19 March 1918, MSS Afr s. 86,100, Scarbrough papers. Only a few documents relating to the purchase of the Niger Company are preserved in MSS Afr s.100. These indicate that the first approach was made by Lord Leverhulme through the Niger Co.'s bankers, Glyn Mills, in October 1919. Hon. Algernon G. Mills to Scarbrough, 14 Oct. 1919.
97. CO to Lugard, no. 1672, 2 Dec. 1916, CO 583/49/55579.
98. Davies, *Trade Makers*, 202.
99. The Liverpool price for kernels was set at £26 per ton. CO to Lugard, no. 745, 3 July 1917, CO 554/35/33696. The average Liverpool price for kernels in 1916 had been £22/15/4, and had gone above £26 only in May and December, CO 554/33/6563. For traders' satisfaction, Harding min., 27 Oct. 1917, CO 583/60/52616. For a summary of material in Colonial Office files relating to the imposition of control: Osuntokun, *Nigeria in the First World War*, 44–52. For freight rates, see also, Olukoju, 'Elder Dempster', 270.
100. Olukoju, 'Elder Dempster', 269. Olukoju provides no evidence for his assertion that this was purely a post-war development. For a similar pattern in the Gold Coast, David Killingray, 'Repercussions of World War I in the Gold Coast', *JAH* 19 (1978), 42–43.
101. Langley, *Pan-Africanism*, 129.
102. *Red Book*: Oil Nuts, 84; Johnstone, 105–06; Pearse, 97–98; Thomas, 95–96; Koton, 113; N.C.B.W.A., 140.
103. Michael Crowder, *West Africa under Colonial Rule* (London, 1968), 293; cf. Langley, *Pan-Africanism*, 178–80.
104. *Red Book*: Crombie Steadman, 81; Stavely and Co., 86, 190–1, 214; W.H. Sassen, 87; Edwards Brothers, 87, Barker and Camoin, 89; S.C.I.A.O., 77; Compagnie bordelaise, 87; Jurgens Colonial Products, 75; Grace Bros., 69, 180; Tin Areas, 192; Johnstone, 105–06; Colonial Bank, 302–03; Trigge to Scarbrough, 21 May 1917, MSS Afr s.93, Scarbrough papers. The initial capital of Jurgens Colonial Products was to be £50,000 from Jurgens family funds. Jurgens to CO, 19 Jan. 1917, CO 583/64/3853. In November 1916 Jurgens had been contemplating a company with £500,000 capital (£250,000 paid up). Jurgens to Burrowes, 10 Nov. 1916, CO 583/53/54564.
105. Helleiner, *Peasant Agriculture*, tables II-B-2,3; Havinden and Meredith, *Colonialism*, 119 (table 6.5); *Red Book*, 43–46 (tables) and 305; Hogendorn, *Groundnut Exports*, 130.
106. Helleiner, *Peasant Agriculture*, tables II-6-2,3. Helleiner's base year is 1948. It is not clear how far he has taken into account possible shifts in the importance of items in the import index over a period of almost forty years. For the period to 1939 his producer prices were

in fact the average of monthly averages of Lagos prices. He has made no attempt to ascertain how closely these reflected prices actually paid to peasant producers in the villages. Using 1913 as a base Havinden and Meredith show a fall in the total Nigerian terms of trade from 80 in 1919 to 52 in 1921, *Colonialism*, 122 (table 6.7).
107. The story is well told in Wilson, *Unilever*, 1, 249–66; the Niger Company side can be followed from the documents in MSS Afr s.100, Scarbrough papers. Niger Company problems had been compounded by a disastrous fire at its main port Burutu in January 1918 and long delays in the payment of the insurance.
108. Hogendorn, *Groundnut Exports*, 140.
109. Crowder, *West Africa under Colonial Rule*, 286, 293; Gavin and Oyemakinde, 'Economic Development', 505; Langley, *Pan-Africanism*, 216–17; A.G. Hopkins, 'Economic aspects of political movements in Nigeria and in the Gold Coast, 1918–1939, *JAH*, 8 (1966), 135; Olukoju, 'Elder Dempster', 270. None of these writers provides details as to the firms which failed.
110. Allan McPhee, *The Economic Revolution in British West Africa* (London, 1971 [1926]), 99–100, 105. McPhee based himself on the *Red Book* without realising how much had changed in the intervening years.
111. Hopkins, 'Big Business', 130.
112. An excellent recent analysis of this is Anne Phillips, *The Enigma of Colonialism; British Policy in West Africa* (London, 1989).

The Influence of Racial Attitudes on British Policy Towards India during the First World War

by Gregory Martin

A picture is sometimes presented of the course of European or 'Western' history developing in a linear or near-inevitable fashion towards today's more-or-less liberal values. The selectivity this requires has been identified by Professor Mansergh in British colonial affairs as deriving from the 'progressive' or 'liberal interpretation of Imperial–Commonwealth history'. It fails to comprehend or take into account parts of the Commonwealth heritage derived from forces or visions antithetical to those current today. The danger of distortion in thus reading backwards from the present is 'not the less corrupting because it appeals to the heart and mind of a later generation'. This general historical warning is of especial application when assessing the intentions behind great progressive reforms, the spirit of which may be invoked to endorse 'the liberal interpretation'. A closer look at some of the less conspicuous attitudes held by involved people may reveal the eventual outcome or consequences of their actions to be not necessarily what their authors might have wished, nor what need have occurred. To attain a clearer picture of the past involves then, not only the inclusion of those views not selected in the progressive picture of the British Empire's development. It also requires an understanding of the qualifications or confusions which existed in the minds of those who did advocate 'liberal' policies. Such correctives are necessary, even if we remain satisfied that the liberal interpretation is not finally inadequate 'in terms of the broad themes of imperial policy'.[1] The subject matter of this article consists of three case studies during the First World War in which racial attitudes persisted in the official mind, despite the authorities being forced to act, or acquiesce in affairs, in a progressive manner. These cases are the establishment of Indian hospitals in England, a mixed marriage between an Indian Rajah and an Australian, and finally, official attitudes towards the grant of King's commissions to Indian soldiers.

The last two years of Lord Hardinge's viceroyalty in India (1914–16) during the First World War was an anxious time for the Indian government. The main reason for this was the despatch in 1914–15 of most of the war-ready part of the Indian army to the principal military theatres.[2] After August 1914 the Government of India was partly occupied with preparing proposals for its own reform, as it had been in peace. But it had also to fret continually about the sufficiency of its own resources to meet requirements for internal security, for the Mesopotamian campaign, and obligations elsewhere. Indian hospitals and mixed marriages were among the multitude of lesser worries it was called on to deal with. The details of the opposition which commissions for Indians aroused during the war appears to have gone relatively unnoticed. The same is true of the concern which existed at the presence of Indian troops in Europe.[3] Attitudes on these matters, it will be seen, shaped much of British policy towards

India's contribution to a common war effort. Those involved in mixed marriages give a concrete example of the body of practice established by the British in their overseas' possessions. It stood ready-made to be transferred and applied to the presence of Indians in the home country and Europe. Procedures in the United Kingdom to some extent had to be improvised, for it had never been contemplated that such a large-scale influx would occur, although measures had been evolved to meet previous limited instances, for example, jubilee and coronation contingents, and, it should be remembered, Indian students. The Rajah of Pudukota's case illustrates the empire-wide nature and extent of what concerned the authorities in Brighton. These beliefs were such that they could come into operation to limit official policy, either when it was a question of Indians appearing in Europe or when reforms were being debated which involved their fuller integration into the war-effort and the community of the empire.

I

Indian troops' hospitals in England and France

The object of the policy of the Viceroy of India from 1910 to 1916, Lord Hardinge of Penshurst, was to appease the clamour of advanced Indian opinion with progressive measures. He hoped thereby to strengthen Britain's hold on India. It was in these terms that he urged the Cabinet to send the first Indian expeditionary force (IEF) to the western front instead of keeping them as a reserve in Egypt. 'It will be the removal of a stigma and a colour bar upon the Indian troops', he explained to Lord Crewe, the Secretary of State for India on 20 August 1914.[4] On 27 August he repeated more strongly that if the troops were to land in Europe, he felt he could ask for almost anything as a contribution to pay for the expeditionary forces. It should be explained that India was officially debarred from paying for any operations of its troops outside its own frontiers, unless a resolution permitting it to do so was passed by both Houses of the British Parliament. This they were unlikely to do if the indications were that it did not comply with the wishes of the Indian taxpayers.

At the start of the war, moreover, the Viceroy was ready to take more risks in denuding India of its garrison, if it could be pointed out to the population that their troops were being employed in Europe. It would demonstrate a new British appreciation of their Indian fellow subjects' worth.[5] As he wrote to his friend Sir Valentine Chirol of *The Times*, the prospect of having 'raw Canadians, Australians & C. (*sic*), who have no military organization' in France instead, made him wild. 'How little the Cabinet know about India, and what an uphill game this is to fight!'[6] He was delighted when the 'colour bar' had been lifted and the Indian troops could thus associate equally with colonials and Europeans. It seemed certain an unofficial member of the Indian Legislative Council could be found to sponsor an offer from the empire to bear part of the cost of the IEF. (The task would rather be to restrain the givers. From early on Hardinge was anxious lest the war strain India's revenues unduly.) The Viceroy indeed was so confident that over the coming months he was to release all the troops at his disposal, except the three divisions reserved for use on the north-west frontier and for internal defence.[7] The King himself had come out in favour of the Indians fighting in contrast to the opposition of his secretary, Lord Stamfordham. The latter wondered whether Hardinge could really approve of using native troops against

Europeans. He was troubled by the consequences this might have on the questions of equal citizenship and the grant of King's commissions to Indians. Chirol likewise feared that what the 'fighting races' did for the British Empire on the battlefield, the politicians would claim the credit and payment for. But he was prepared to defer to his friend's judgement.[8]

In October 1914, the commander of the Indian troops in France, Lt. General Sir James Willcocks, in a despatch to the India Office strongly deprecated the employment of European women in any capacity in the Indian hospitals. Lord Crewe agreed. Sir Havelock Charles, of the St. John's Ambulance Brigade, while protesting that women were employed in civilian hospitals in India, did not attempt to contest the practice in military hospitals. But he stood firm on continuing it in his own as 'women can be employed without scandal & [sic] with great advantage to efficiency'. In St. John's establishments women supervised only cleanliness, sanitation, diets and medicine. The Secretary of the Military Department at the India Office reported to the War Office on 24 October that 'Lord Crewe supports this proposal on the distinct understanding that no woman will be employed on menial or nursing duties with Indian troops and followers'.[9]

Consequences like these of making a political gesture in India by 'breaking through the colour bar' in Europe had not been foreseen. In part this was because before the war the Indian soldier had still been treated in his own regimental hospital according to the standards deemed suitable in the nineteenth century. These were scantily equipped with trained staff and medical supplies. 'Punkahs and fans were generally not provided. On admission to the hospital the patient brought his own bedding and his own clothing. He subsisted generally on his rations.' The Indian troops in France sent to the battlefields had swiftly suffered heavy casualties. The Viceroy, still true to the spirit in which the men had been sent, defended their treatment on a scale superior to what had been customary before, on the grounds of gratitude and justice.[10]

But in England this presented problems, as Willcocks pointed out. Crewe regretted the whole necessity for action, as he explained to Hardinge:

> It's bad luck that we have been obliged to bring the Indian wounded to England at all, and I am vexed about it. But there was absolutely no help for it, as our intended stages of Southern France–Egypt–India were made impossible by French unwillingness or inability to help in their share of the transaction.[11]

Brighton had offered the Pavilion and Dome for the Indian hospitals. They were large, airy and easy to supervise, but

> ... in other respects Brighton seems to me a bad place, since even if 'Arry (sic) has to some extent enlisted, 'Arriet is all the more at a loose end and ready to take on the Indian warrior. I hope there may be some garden adjoining where the man can get exercise without being stared at or teased.[12]

Sir Walter Lawrence was appointed by Lord Kitchener, the Secretary of State for War, as his special commissioner for Indian hospitals in England and France on 19 November 1914. He was to report direct to Kitchener and Sir Alfred Keogh, head of the Medical Department at the War Office. Lawrence also wrote regularly to Hardinge. In a letter of 18 March 1915 he described the general running and establishment of his hospitals. On the main question involved he held that stories of trouble with women in Marseilles were grossly exaggerated:

> At any rate, whatever may have happened when the troops first landed there is nothing of the sort now ... At the time of the Coronation when the Indian troops came over to England, scandals arose from the perverted behaviour of English women; and when Brighton was selected as a centre for Indian hospitals I was attacked for running into the danger arising from women. You will be glad to hear that there have been no scandals in Brighton, and the Indians in hospital and the convalescents who are allowed out for exercise have behaved themselves like gentlemen. I have the most gratifying testimony from the Chief Constable at Brighton and from others to this effect.[13]

The position was unchanged on 10 May. Lawrence's one difficulty was with the Indian hospital personnel, who, unlike the patients, could not be confined within the institution's grounds. Inquiries were made to keep track of these individuals, however, and 'we have a very efficient plain clothes police system at Brighton'. Not much harm had been done but some people had spread untrue scandal.[14]

This referred to a communication to the Indian government by an official in the India Office's Medical Department, Bruce Seton. A worried telegram from India reported that in Seton's view special measures were necessary to prevent 'too frequent intercourse with Indian attendants and patients' by the civilian population of Brighton. He suggested arrangements similar to those taken at the last coronation which worked very well. 'We [the Indian Government] regard lessening of evil as most important.' Lawrence at the War Office responded by assuring Sir Edmund Barrow, the Military Secretary at the India Office, on 19 March, that:

> I have gone very fully into the matter with Bruce Seton & [sic] others & with the Chief Constable of Brighton, and the arrangements are ample & Bruce Seton is [now] confident that there will be no incidents. The Indians are behaving like gentlemen & it is a pity that Bruce Seton should have alarmed Lord Hardinge needlessly.

A telegram in these terms was sent to the Indian government on 24 March. As for the British and Indian coronation contingents in 1911, which Seton had referred to, it was pointed out that 'the large number of British and Indian officers present ... made it possible to make special regulations as to the men only leaving Camp in parties and in charge of an officer, moreover the camp was not in a town'.[15]

After Austen Chamberlain replaced the Liberal Lord Crewe in the first coalition government as the new Secretary for India in May 1915, he visited the Indian hospitals in Brighton over the weekend of 3–4 July. He was impressed by the arrangements which had been taken. At a dinner with the mayor of Brighton, Alderman Otter and his wife, he learnt from Colonel Gentle, the Chief Constable, that there had been no problem with the soldiers. The officers were allowed out freely, the men only in company with an officer. 'This is, of course, very necessary, but they feel it to be a hardship & it constitutes their one grievance as far as the hospital treatment is concerned.' In replying to the letter giving him the news, Hardinge remarked that Lawrence wrote to him constantly on the subject. Nevertheless he was especially interested to have confirmed 'that there had been no trouble of any kind with the soldiers at Brighton, since one hears out here such strange stories of the relations of Indian soldiers and women in England'.[16]

It was not only the Viceroy who had been alarmed. On 4 June 1915 the War Office wrote to the General Officer Commanding Southern Command that it had been deemed advisable to withdraw all members of the Queen Alexandra's Imperial Nursing Reserve from the Pavilion and York Place Hospitals at Brighton. It requested that the same be done with the nurses at the Lady Hardinge Hospital at Brockenhurst Park. Inquiries made in response led to a protest by P. Hewett, Chairman of the Indian Soldiers' Fund Committee. Writing to Keogh on 17 June he professed himself to be at a loss, 'for to the knowledge of the Committee no irregularity of any kind affecting the Nursing Staff has occurred at the Hospital'. Nurses had been selected in accordance with the requirements of the War Office, i.e. a knowledge of Indian languages and patients. The War Office had been satisfied as it had asked for these nurses to be employed at the Pavilion Hospital before the Lady Hardinge institution was completed. Their own representative, Colonel Sir Walter Lawrence, had inspected the facility several times and certified in writing that 'All the arrangements seem to me to be perfect'. In conclusion Hewett emphasized that the establishment at the Lady Hardinge Hospital (one matron, two assistant matrons and 17 nurses) was as low as possible. 'The menial staff has been imported from India.' If the nurses were forced to leave the hospital would have to close.[17]

Sir Havelock Charles seconded Hewett's stand. He pointed out that as the hospitals were on private property, and the nurses on monthly contracts, the authorities had no power to interfere with the existing arrangements. Keogh, however, was not the source of the trouble. He was still quite ready to accept the ruling of Chamberlain on the matter. Unable to get a clarification of the original measure, Charles insisted on further explanation. He pointed out the 'spirit and the letter' of the War Office's own instructions had been observed. 'Why has the order been issued? What advantage will be gained by carrying it out? Has any fault been imputed to the Hospl [sic]? Has any scandal arisen?' *The Proceedings of the Indian Soldiers Committee* of 10 June at which the matter had been discussed, may help to explain his peremptory tone. According to the minutes, Colonel Perry, in charge of the Lady Hardinge Hospital, had received the War Office instruction and shown it to Charles. The latter had told him to sit tight until he went to see Keogh. According to his own evidence to the committee.

> I asked him [Keogh] what was the reason of wishing to remove our nurses. He told me that a photograph of a nurse standing behind a wounded Sepoy had been published in the *Daily Mail* on May 24th, and that the Field Marshal, Commander in Chief abroad [Sir John French] had written complaining of this. The matter had also come to the notice of one of the officers connected with the Censor Department. The picture and its publication was then put before an officer who advises the War Office on Indian Hospitals. He condemned absolutely and totally the employment of nurses with Indian Troops and said, 'I told you so', and that anyone who knew anything about Indian customs would have prevented this scandal by forbidding the services of women nurses with Indian troops. Not knowing whether this unfortunate occurrence had been at Brockenhurst Park I could say nothing ... [in fact] in this case we are totally innocent. If this has

occurred at Brighton it is very hard that the Lady Hardinge Hospital should be made to suffer by it.

Charles summed up that it seemed 'this decision has been founded on the advice of an officer of no importance and little experience of Indian peoples'. The whole correspondence was forwarded to the President of the Medical Board on 24 June 1915. The matter was finally settled, not on any contest of the principles raised, but because of the lack of evidence to sustain the charges. The fact that the Lady Hardinge Hospital would have to close if the nurses did go, was also vital. Sir Thomas Holderness, the Permanent Under Secretary at the India Office, noted on 30 June 1915,

> The War Office give no reasons for the proposed withdrawal. The Indian Soldiers' Fund Committee give good reasons agt (*sic*) it. As the case is presented to us, we ought to recommend retention of the existing arrangements.

This was done.[18]

II

The Rajah with the Australian wife

Soon after this settlement, the Indian official world was exercised by the actual violation of the same taboo. This was the affair of the Rajah of Pudukota and his Australian wife. An irate letter from George V to Hardinge, on 11 May 1915, announced that the Queen had received a telegram from the Rajah, the ruler of one of the smaller Indian states which survived under British protection in India. It told of the Rajah's marriage to an Australian and asked for the Queen's blessing. The telegram would be ignored, the King wrote, 'as I strongly disapprove of such alliances and feel sure you will agree with me'. An explanation from the Governor General of Australia, Sir Ronald Munro Ferguson, in a letter to the Viceroy dated the twelfth, revealed that Pudukota's marriage had come as a surprise to him. It would not be popular in Australian society. The clubs, and society generally, following the advances made to women by the Rajah of Johore (who was from the Malay States) had already begun to refuse admission to 'distinguished visitors from India'. Only with letters from the Indian government had Pudukota been received. After this it would be difficult to receive such princes at all. 'This people is *au fond* [*sic*], a white labour aristocracy, not a democracy as we know it in Europe – and throughout society there is a fixed intention to keep the white race pure.'[19] The Viceroy's reply to Ferguson was that Pudukota's marriage had come as 'very unwelcome news' to him as well. He had tried to discourage such a move over the years and had warned the Rajah of what the official attitude would be if he took it. He had grave doubts as to the position if there were children. Hardinge wrote to the King that he shared his views on Pudukota, who had been informed that he would be treated as the Maharajas of Kapurthala and Jind had been in previous years.

Austen Chamberlain gave full vent to his feelings, writing to Hardinge on 14 October 1915. The Governor of Madras, Lord Pentland, had apparently ordered Pudukota, who was in his province, not to marry an European, but a woman from his own people. The Rajah had defied him and married a Miss Molly Fink in Melbourne. Chamberlain had learnt of this only in an 'impudent' telegram asking for his blessing.

He refused, but had heard that Pentland, while officially declining also, had sent his 'personal good wishes'. In addition, seemingly, Pentland had indicated to the Rajah in a final interview in May that it would be impossible for him to be received officially but he, the Governor, would be prepared to do so personally. 'It seems to me that Pentland has acted with singular weakness, and apparently he contemplates being as weak in the future.' The Secretary of State's view at this stage was that the government could not separate its private and public personalities. He was writing to inform Pentland. Hardinge might wish to as well, as they could not condone unofficially the defiance of the official wishes of both Governor and Viceroy.[20]

Initial outrage past, the question arose as to what measures could and should be taken. Ferguson, writing to Hardinge on 12 October, concurred in disapproving of mixed marriages. He admitted, though, that the ceremony which had taken place had to be treated as legal in Australia. The Viceroy reassured Chamberlain that he had always informed Pudukota that if he married an European there would be no possibility of his being received. He had also let him know that the Advocate General of Madras considered that any children of his union would be illegitimate under Hindu law and not recognised by the Indian government. Hardinge passed this news on to Ferguson too. One other objection to such alliances that occurred to him was that it was possible to have any number of wives under Hindu law in India. 'In any case, all these mixed marriages should be strongly discouraged since the result is only generations of Eurasians who generally are imbued with the worst characteristics of the two races.'[21]

With time to reflect, Chamberlain was ready to moderate his stance so as to leave the matter in the Viceroy's hands. He continued to wish the courts of the Viceroy and Governors to follow uniform practice in all such instances. Lord Islington, his Parliamentary Under Secretary, had brought to his attention the case of the Maharajah of Kapurthala 'and his Spanish lady ... it was a well established rule that that lady was not recognised officially and I know that the late King always refused to receive her'. The Secretary of State disclaimed any personal opinion, but he believed the Viceroy should act on similar lines. He wrote to Hardinge on 30 December 1915 that marriages of Indian princes with Europeans ought to be treated in the same way as morganatic marriages in Europe. No official recognition or title would be accorded to the consort, but officials who chose to do so could meet her unofficially. There would be no imputation of any 'moral slur upon her character'. (As a matter of fact it is interesting to note that not much more than a month after George V had recorded his initial displeasure at Pudukota's message, the King and Queen had received Kapurthala.) So in the end Chamberlain had effectively come round to the position he had found so reprehensible in Pentland.

Finally, Hardinge had another interview with an unhappy Pudukota in the New Year. He duly made it clear that the Indian government's decision was irrevocable and that if the Rajah tried to go to the United Kingdom he would meet with no sympathy. If he was not prepared to stay in his own state, which he said bored him, it would be better if he resigned and went to live in Europe. The Viceroy forwarded the notes of an interview of the Political Secretary of his government, J.B. Wood, with the Rajah, with the letter reporting this meeting. The former explained the Indian government's approach as being that the ruling chief was expected to follow his people's customs. The Rajah disputed this, as well as stressing the popularity of the marriage in his state. But it was pointed out to him that he did not have the same freedom of choice as a private individual. He could acquiesce or resign. The government intended to make no exceptions in this matter on the grounds of education and upbringing.[22] Chamberlain's only difference with this outcome was that he preferred a morganatic solution for Pudukota, whom he regarded as a 'great deal more trouble than he is worth'. He did not wish to see him living in Europe where he was likely to get into further mischief. The veteran Indian writer, Sir George Birdwood, thinking along parallel lines, commented to Hardinge on the alleged infection of India with disloyalty through the agency of visiting or resident Germans (including missionaries). He linked this with the liking of well-travelled Indians for Germany and Switzerland: 'I put it down to the greater freedom with lax women they enjoyed there.'[23]

III

King's commissions for Indian soldiers

At the same time India's rulers had to deal with the more intricate question of King's commissions for Indians. 'One of the most momentous decisions of the Great War, so far as the Indian Army is concerned, was that which rendered Indians eligible to hold a King's commission in the Army.'[24] Previously Indian soldiers had only been able to hold the Viceroy's commission. This bestowed a status and power of command limited by the regulations of the Indian Army Act. The opening of King's commissions to Indians, carrying equal professional status with the British army officer, had been a much sought after reform before the war and one always denied, not least, through the opposition of the British officer corps. Full consummation of this was not actually to be achieved until India's constitutional status had been transformed, along with much else, during the interwar period – and then only in a compromised form at first.[25] During the First World War, the proposal, forming part of a wider project of Indian reforms, was enough to arouse prolonged controversy amongst governing circles.

In September 1914 Crewe vaguely anticipated that the very favourable response in Britain to reports of the overwhelming demonstrations of Indian loyalty would revive the question of commission. If so, he thought 'surely the new temper created by the new events' would facilitate some solution to a problem that had always seemed so difficult in the past. On the other hand, the traditional objection – military efficiency – which was apparently only strengthened by war, was aired by Chirol in a letter of 5 December. He had read flamboyant stories in the press on the Indians' deeds in France, he told Hardinge, but 'on the whole I am afraid . . . [these] are like most other stories in the press'. From friends on the staff and at the front he had heard that Indian troops, having shown some initial dash, did not have the required stamina 'and under prolonged stress crumple up entirely'. They just did not understand the nature of the fighting and did not have the wit to adapt to it. The Indian army was not suffering heavier officer casualties than the British, but the crux was 'the Indians are certainly ten times more helpless without their officers than white troops are'. It was a point Sir George Birdwood had made a week earlier. This was the vital importance of keeping the IEF 'well white officered – and by officers who knew the men and race'.[26] Hardinge did not need to be told this in December 1914. One difficulty in the question of commissions, he wrote to Crewe, was that even if one could enforce a British sub-lieutenant's obedience to an Indian captain, you could 'never' get an English Tommy to obey an Indian officer. Indian troops by contrast 'are completely lost without their British officers'. They would not rely on their own Indian officers, but would rally behind even a strange British one.[27]

If the civilians spoke with such certainty it is not surprising that these were the even more emphatic and virtually unanimous views of British officers themselves. On 27 January 1915 the War Office, seeking to alleviate the British army's paucity of trained officers, wrote to Sir John French to enquire whether the maintenance of one British officer to 60 other ranks in the IEF was not unduly wasteful. This matter was referred to Willcocks, who may of course have been spurred on when making his reply by the heavy losses in Indian officers, already thinned by the needs of the British army when war broke out.[28] At any rate, on 28 January he explained that not only was the establishment not excessive, it was far below what was required. The Indian army could not carry out its difficult and dangerous trench-warfare duties without British officers. 'The knowledge, training and capacity of Indian officers is altogether insufficient to perform the tasks required in the trenches.' In open warfare the same proportion was required as in the British infantry. But for trench-war, with its special features such as sapping, grenades and trench mortars, even more were needed. The bravery alone of Indian officers in no way fitted them for such tasks. '. . . It has been conclusively proved that Indian Infantry Corps must have a large number of British officers if they are to meet with any prospect of success such troops as are now opposed to us.' Only one official reading this report underlined the importance of noting that it was not only superior British leadership but the lack of technically trained Indian officers which was vital.[29]

Hardinge does not seem to have reconciled these particular 'facts' with his general strategy of pursuing a liberal policy of granting gradual representation to the Indians and an amelioration in their conditions. He was determined overall to take a stand against what he saw as the 'exploded ideas' of Curzon, the Tories and 'well-known reactionaries'. In his view these had as a common aim keeping the Indians down as much as possible. King's commissions for Indians remained a politically desirable reform within a larger programme. It was his task to carry the Secretary of State with him in the matter. Shortly after taking office in 1915, Chamberlain learnt of a visit Islington had made to the western front. It revealed

> . . . what I have heard from other sources, that this war has confirmed the 'immense superiority' of white regiments over our Indian troops. Willcocks even went to the length of saying . . . that with the experience of this war before him we could hold India with 30,000 white troops. I give you this for what it is worth and without laying too much stress upon it. It has both its good and its bad sides. One cannot help wishing that the Indian troops could stand the strain of modern warfare better, and yet there is some compensation in the thought that British superiority is as marked as ever.[30]

Nevertheless Chamberlain reported that in principle everyone had come to agree to the concession of commissions except the Army Council. It believed the question should be considered for inclusion in the package of reforms to be introduced after the war. If it were brought up at all, the Army Council was against any method of appointing Indians to crack English regiments. So was Islington. Neither believed this could lead to happiness or success in the circumstances. Holderness, on the other hand, did not see how an Indian Sandhurst, maintained for the few Indians selected for admission as officers, could work. It could not prepare its graduates for life in the mess of an Indian regiment. 'And unless they can mix freely with the British regimental officers they will be a source of weakness.'[31] He therefore preferred to see the Indian cadets go to Sandhurst proper unless an Indian college were to train English cadets as well. Chamberlain favoured a college in India – but this was because he joined with Islington in opposition to any training in England. In a memorandum on the matter of July 1915 Islington's conclusion was that Indians would actually prefer training in India to Britain. He also wrote 'My own opinion is that the Sandhurst scheme presents grave objections and might jeopardize the future success of the movement'. Among his reasons were:

> (iv) There would be occasional instances of marriage with European girls which always creates a difficult problem and often would end in the Indians in question settling down in this country.
> (v) The control over Indian boys in this country is more difficult than it is in India.

Chamberlain, however, did see that it was only among those who had enjoyed an English education 'and learned to hold their own at an English public school and college that you will find men capable of taking their place in a mess and of sharing the regimental life'.[32]

Such considerations influenced Islington sufficiently to produce a second memorandum on commissions a few weeks later. He was ready to concede 'that solely from the point of view of military efficiency education in England would be better, especially if it were preceded by a training in an English public school'. But this was outweighed by 'obvious disadvantages'. The 'lads', it had to be remembered, would be removed from their 'natural environment'. It was a political question, however, and the military authorities should be prepared to face an initial sacrifice of military efficiency to meet Indian political difficulties. Experience had shown that the 'majority of the best families in India' would not be ready to let their sons go to England, as would be necessary at an age somewhere between 14 and 19. It came back to the fact that those who did go would lose touch with their own people 'especially with their own women'. They would create 'all kinds of social and religious difficulties' for themselves. Estranged both from the English around them and their home, the cadets would 'establish relations in this country which result only in unhappiness for themselves and others'. The best thing would still be for a dozen Indian candidates to be trained in India with British comrades. But 'I might mention that the "Chiefs Colleges" from which institutions the boys for the army would probably be selected, are very well regulated on British public school lines'.[33] Such compromises were not acceptable to the military authorities. 'As the war goes on,' Willcocks informed the Viceroy on 18 July 1915,

> so am I the more convinced that nothing in the Indian army can replace the British officer. If I cannot get a British officer give me a British non-commissioned officer or good private soldier, these will lead and the men will follow. No Indian (Native) officer I know can replace a British and the day they try to officer units with Indians, that day will see the end of efficient fighting units. The Native officer is very useful, and very necessary, for the interior economy could not get on without

him and he can, on occasions, take command temporarily, but *never* [sic] permanently or even for long. This, Sir, is the only way in which this great Indian army can take the field against an enemy worthy of the name.[34]

Hardinge himself was not innocent of such convictions. Like so many others he was inconsistent in his publicly expressed and publicly effective admiration for the Indians' prowess, his advocacy of reform and his own day-to-day operating assumptions. For instance, in the preamble to the memorandum he compiled as a political testament, *Questions Likely to Arise at the End of the War*, he urged the case for fundamental reforms in the Indian empire's constitution. Adopting the voice of Indian public opinion he found a conclusive argument for the recognition of the political activity stimulated by the war, in the performance of the Indian soldiers on the western front. This had 'proclaimed to all the world that they are worthy to fight side-by-side with British soldiers and has raised the self-esteem of India to a pitch never hitherto attained'. 'There was', he wrote later in the same document, 'no sound reason' why commissions should not be granted to Indians.[35] At the same time he himself confided, on 6 August:

> What I am particularly glad to hear is that the war has proved so clearly the superiority of our British over our Indian troops ... when the Government at first refused to allow Indian troops to go to the front in Europe and I pressed so hard that they should go, I did so not only because I saw the immense political advantages to be gained from such a step, but also because I knew in pitting the Indians against Europeans they would not be slow to recognise their own inferiority and their absolute dependence on their British officers, and that this could only be of the highest advantage to the British *raj* (sic) in India. The Indian is no fool and you may be quite sure that he will recognise, though he will never admit, the fact.[36]

But this could not bring him to support the Army Council and Willcocks in root and branch opposition to granting King's commissions to Indians. Rather, he thought the concessions should be granted at the end of the war, since he anticipated a good effect throughout India from the return of an Indian army which had learnt 'the real superiority of British troops'. These men would know just how indispensable was the British officer's leadership and the application of science in modern warfare. Hardinge wrote to Chamberlain fully endorsing the training of Indian cadets in India alongside their English peers, and reminded Holderness that it would ruin ordinary young men of good position in British India to go to the United Kingdom to serve in one of the best British regiments. The Viceroy foresaw that the Permanent Under Secretary might not like some of his views on future reforms. Holderness replied that he saw the futility of admitting Indians to English units if these places were reserved for just a few chiefs. But he was entirely behind Hardinge 'as regards the absolute necessity' for some means of admitting Indians to King's commissions. He had, however, his doubts about an Indian Sandhurst. If any young Englishmen were to be trained there also, it might have its attractions. 'On the other hand perfect equality between the two races & forgetfulness of the colour distinction are more easily practised here than in India.' Lest there be any confusion in Hardinge's mind, he added: 'That is an argument for the training being given here'.[37]

The prospect of the war not ending in the foreseeable future led to reconsideration of whether all reforms should be postponed until after its close. By the end of 1915

Hardinge and Chamberlain had decided that it would be well to grant a few commissions immediately to combat the suspicion that the concession had already been refused. The Military Committee of the Secretary of State's Council agreed that the denial could not be maintained indefinitely. In meeting their reservations Chamberlain had contended that

> It is the Indian *Army* [sic] which merits recognition in this war and the loyalty, contentment and good will of the Army are of more importance to us than those of any other classes or sections in the nation.

The difficulties were undeniable. Yet how could no hope of advancement be held out to such vital elements, when the 'talking classes' could expect to rise to the highest positions in civilian government? In fact, 'how can anyone think that the present position is maintainable in the face of all that is happening around us?'[38]

Hardinge agreed that the principle of offering King's commissions during the war had to be established. The actual scheme to be worked out could be left for peacetime. The Commander in Chief in India, Sir Beauchamp Duff, submitted a memorandum no less steadfastly opposed than Willcocks to this step. But Chamberlain did no more than pass his arguments on to the Army Council, where no doubt they had an impact: 'its effects on the military efficiency of the Indian Army will be wholly bad. That effect will be greater or lesser according to the number of Indians admitted'. If the principle was allowed, Duff feared that the Viceroy's assurances of successful safeguards against too large an influx would prove illusory. But faced with Hardinge's statement that the matter was practically decided, he had to acquiesce though under protest. The King at least was delighted to hear that Hardinge was pressing for commissions to be granted to Indians. This was the stage the question had reached by the time Hardinge ceased to be Viceroy, in the spring of 1916.

Despite agreement in principle, there was only a token acceptance of the new practice during the last 18 months of the war.[39] Duff, for one, fighting a rearguard action in 1916, for a time insisted that any action should await the necessary legislation. If the external pressures had not been continuous, the reform might indeed have been smothered. But in 1917 the Mesopotamia Commission's report, for instance, recommended that the British government 'immediately reconsider whether the old-fashioned prejudice against giving the King's commission to natives of India cannot be set aside during the war', if only in view of the deleterious effect dearth of officers was having on the Indian Army's fighting value.[40] In August the Cabinet agreed to the reform in principle, but very little had been done by 1918. The Adjutant General of the Indian Army, Lieutenant-General H. Hudson, in view of the decision to raise a further 500,000 Indian troops, had actually proposed granting commissions to Indians before the Imperial Conference of that year. This belated expansion in the Indian Army had been forced on the British authorities as one way to deal with their most serious shortage, that of manpower. To raise such large numbers would require the assistance of influential Indians of every rank. Therefore King's commissions should be granted to Indian officers and NCOs, and facilities provided for Indians 'of good family' to go to Sandhurst. Those selected should be eligible at once for temporary commissions. Some of these would qualify for permanent commissions after the war. Their example would encourage recruiting which was why the Indian government constantly urged its importance. But the measure still had to be canvassed when the

Indian Constitutional Conference sat in April 1918. Serious measures to grant large numbers of Indians commissions were in fact only taken during the 1930s under the mounting pressure of the developments leading to Indian self-government.

The irony of granting commissions in connection with the recruitment of 500,000 men to the Indian army was that it had been argued that the lack of officers, and the inability of Indians to be trained as officers proved yet again by the war, made it impossible to expand recruiting on such a large scale. The imperative need of the war machine for more men forced an increase in the recruiting of Indians willy nilly and the granting of commissions to Indians seemed to be a military, rather than political, necessity. Yet hand in hand with indispensability of the British officer had always marched the doctrine that only a tiny proportion of India's total population could be made into soldiers. The idea had been old when Lord Roberts had expressed it in the nineteenth century. The two were quite logically the opposite sides of the same coin. Hudson himself was a believer in the 'martial races' theory at the same time as he called for 500,000 new recruits. The fact that most of the 500,000 eventually raised before the war's end were drawn from the traditional sources was to enable the doctrine to live on into the 1930s.[41] A crack in the customary recruiting patterns during the war had been opened with the adoption of territorial recruiting in December 1916, after the failure of the old class-based system.[42] This was despite a minute written by Barrow on 19 June 1916, explaining why it was impossible to raise territorial units in India to the extent of ten or twelve divisions, as had been suggested by Winston Churchill and others.

Quite simply, Barrow had written, the war had proved that the Indian soldier from even the best regiments was helpless without British officers. Finding enough such officers for existing units was already quite difficult. But Barrow rejected the idea of commissioning Indian officers instead because they lacked the physical and moral energy to be leaders: 'I cannot conceive a corps of officers recruited from the *literati* [sic] of Bengal or Madras who would be anything but a worthless or dangerous element.' Moving beyond the incapacity of educated Indians, it was the caste system, the result of ages of conquest and oppression, which had to be borne in mind; 'centuries of close and restricted breeding have evolved types of human beings just as much as centuries of selection in animals have produced distinct types and characteristics . . .' Lest this strike too close to home perhaps, he added '. . . and there is not the corrective of our public school discipline to improve matters'. Barrow applied further crude social Darwinian arguments.

> . . . It is this great fact which is ignored by theorists in England and visionaries in India . . . who put forward impracticable schemes based on false premisses or occidental ideals. One of these false premisses is that India contains a vast population of potential soldiers capable of fighting on equal terms with European enemies . . . By bestowing liberty, justice and education in India we have done much to emancipate it from the shackles of caste and prejudice but it will take many generations yet to reach the ideals of philanthropists and philosophers and to satisfy the longings of an awakened India.

The only 'suitable' areas for recruiting soldiers in India were the North-West Frontier provinces, the Punjab, United Provinces and Maturalla district of Bombay. Together with the 'fighting races' of the Native States of the Punjab and Rajputana, these regions contained about 100 million people out of India's 315 million population. Of these only one-third were 'suitable' in turn, from whom at the outside only 10 per cent (about 3 million men) could be extracted as volunteers.

> The real basic fact is that we have already utilised all the best military material in India and that people who regard that continent as a vast breeding ground of potential soldiers are either ignorant or oblivious of elementary facts. Had the facts been otherwise we should never have been the masters of India. We owe our position to the fundamental and inherent superiority of the European as a fighting man over the Asiatic . . .'[43]

IV

The other side of the question

It would be misleading to leave these matters without a reference to at least one of the contemporary voices raised on the opposite side of the question. It has been mentioned that in the period intervening between 1915–16 when the principle was receiving favourable consideration in the India Office and 1918, when necessity imposed more determined moves towards implementation, little progress was discernible on commissions reform. This was certainly how matters appeared to those who bore the responsibility of administering the Indian troops in the field, but were not privy to high policy discussion. One such was Lord Ampthill, a lifelong campaigner for Indian constitutional reforms, with a distinguished record in the Indian government around the turn of the century. He was sent from the United Kingdom to France in June 1917 to act as Indian Labour Adviser, with the rank of Lieutenant-Colonel and the task of reorganizing the Indian labour companies on their arrival at Marseilles. He sent 12,500 men to the front, in companies of 500 under supervisors, in the early months of his tenure. Until he was replaced at the end of April 1918 he filled his position in a manner consistent with his background in Indian affairs.[44] On 25 July 1917 he complained to Barrow's successor as Military Secretary, General Sir Herbert V. Cox, that the establishment he had set up for his labour companies had been scrapped. It was the old problem of officer-men ratios. The Director of Labour insisted that there be five British officers to every labour company. Ampthill was forced to admit the necessity of this so that the field officers in the armies to which the companies were attached, could communicate with each labour party. But he regretted the step:

> . . . On broad grounds of Imperial policy . . . I wanted these Indian companies to be self-sufficient and self-reliant and to have the opportunity of what they could do with only their own resources. I also wanted Indians and Anglo-Indians to have a fair chance, at this unique and favourable opportunity of proving their capacity. These things are worth trying and ought to be tried and now is the only time to try them. I believe that with a little patience and a little consideration the experiment would have succeeded.[45]

Like other reformers he had come up against the rock of military necessity, but in more pressing and immediate circumstances. Drawing on his own experience of efforts to secure reforms favourable to Indians in the colonies before the war, he could not accept the military view at face value. 'Why should the Government of India be narrow, antiquated, ungenerous, and prejudiced at this stage of the world war?' he asked Cox rhetorically, on several occasions. A week later Ampthill came back to the point in one of the most outspoken pleas submitted on behalf of the grant of commissions to Indians. To function as officers and enforce discipline, his companies' supervisors needed the unquestionable authority of a commission, over men subject to the Indian Army Act. It is worth quoting at length from this letter. It began by referring to the reports that were coming in from the various armies on the contributions of Indian labourers.

> ... a distinct limit to their ability is imposed by their inferior physique and intelligence and by their exotic nature. The reports however, all say that ... they are making daily improvements which is satisfactory.
>
> I daresay, however, that these reports are somewhat coloured by the good-humoured tolerance and compassion which the Englishman entertains towards all uncivilized races under his protection and these Nagas, Khasis, Manipuris and Lushais are very engaging savages. Their ... [characteristics] and the stark nudity which they affect at every possible opportunity all combine to disarm professional military criticism and in its stead to excite ethnological interest ...

It was the attitude of the British army to his reorganization, though, that filled him with depression.

> I have taken it for granted that, whatever their colour, these supervisors are fit for the duty and responsibility for which the Government of India selected and appointed them and I have made them Company Commanders or Company Second in Command in the new organisation. No other course was possible as no other officers of any kind were available. And now of course I want these men to have the commissions without which they cannot possibly discharge their duties as officers in command of troops in the field. But the Authorities are sticking at giving commissions with the Labour Coys [sic] to any except pure Europeans, and it is this which fills me with anger and disappointment. Why should not the Anglo-Indians and Indians have commissions if they are performing their duties efficiently as we we [sic] know they are? What is a commission that it must be withheld from the coloured man if in every respect he is serving His Majesty as faithfully and efficiently as his English comrade in the Labour Coys? What possible harm or damage could result from giving *temporary* [sic] commissions for the duration of the war only for service in the Indian Labour Coys?

It constituted no precedent for there had been examples both before and during the war of commissioned Indians. 'No, the dangerous thing would be to withhold the grant of commissions for that might well prove to be a trail of powder which could set the whole of India ablaze.' If supervisors were not properly commissioned, they would have to be turned out, and who would replace them? 'All I know is ... that the Authorities are boggling over the matter which seems to me a simple one of common-sense and ordinary justice.' To illustrate this point he cited supervisors' letters. 'Some Anglo-Indian supervisors in the same position are just as much Englishmen as Lord Fisher of Kilverstone or others whom I could name.'[46]

He made the same points the following month:

> After all, commissions are dirt cheap nowadays and the Officers who used to be styled 'T.Gs' [Temporary Gentlemen] are now known as 'N.E.Ts' [Not even thats]. The brothers of our house-maids are Officers nowadays. We have to teach them ordinary manners and personal cleanliness and those are things which you do not have to teach to the educated Indian . . . There is no case against me except that which rests on absolute prejudice.[47]

Cox, a rather different proposition from Barrow in these matters, wrote back sympathizing on all points:

> Of course there can be no objection to these men having Hon or Tempy [*sic*] British Commissions, while serving with the Labour Corps. It will certainly create no awkward precedent for, strictly between ourselves, the Cabinet have just affirmed the principle of King's Commissions for selected Indian Officers.

He would get the Secretary of State, Edwin Montagu, to recommend that supervisors in France who were acting as Company Commanders should receive the honorary and temporary rank of lieutenant. Commissions did, in fact, begin to trickle through for supervisors, and not just those who were British, towards the year's close, though not fast enough for the Indian Labour Adviser. Since their commissions were for convenience in the exercise of their duties only, they continued to be paid as supervisors by the British government, which was financially responsible for the labour corps raised by India.[48]

V

Effects on India's contribution

The task remains to resume very briefly how far the attitudes that have been presented here affected India's contribution to the First World War. In the first place it is quite obvious they limited the use made of Indian manpower. The Indian empire's contribution to the war in manpower remained small compared with its total population.[49] Material difficulties limiting that contribution did exist, in terms of shipping, munitions and the strategic priorities of the western front: but there was also the quite independent and wholesale dismissal of Indian leadership and military potential. It could only deter the military authorities from seriously contemplating the task of overcoming the other difficulties. Ideas of the resources available to replace the Indian army's losses, or to meet expanded requirements in Mesopotamia or other pressing theatres, were thus prejudiced. The recruiting and reserve structure bequeathed by the 'martial races' doctrine was wholly unequal to the demands of world war. The Indian army faced severe difficulties as a result, especially in 1914–15, in maintaining its unit's strength. This in turn hampered it in giving a good impression of its capabilities in action. Together with the economies imposed by peacetime budgets, this left the Indian army not only ill-equipped, but with a structure barely fitted to its local role. These handicaps help explain some of the criticisms of its performance.

On another level, suppressing warlike traits in the majority of the population was in the interests of British security in India. So too was confining recruitment to a few areas and keeping the Indian army's identity distinct from the mass of the population. So far as recruiting was concerned, this shift to the north was conscious policy, grounded in the perceived lessons of the Mutiny. Though modified later by Roberts and Kitchener to meet an increased external threat, such considerations were by no means abandoned.[50] Insofar as the attitudes reviewed here limited military developments in the Indian population, they served as an ideology to buttress official policy.[51] The effect of the war was to generate sufficient pressures, both external and internal, to undermine this imperial logic and push towards wider utilization of Indian personnel.

This conclusion would seem to be in accord with the work of Arthur Marwick, suggesting that military participation in the war furthered change in the circumstances of underprivileged groups in Britain or even nations within the empire, to their advantage. The exigencies of the war had a general effect in exposing as inadequate institutions and received beliefs, if these conflicted with the maximum utilization of a nation's potential in war-making.[52] During the course of the war the British and Indian governments did begin to show a greater readiness to employ Indians and other 'Native' personnel, even in Europe. This recognition was the result of the imperative needs of the war-effort, and the wearing effect on the imperial bureaucracy of meeting these, during a four-and-a-half year struggle. In the end Britain was happy to make use of whatever resources it could, exhibiting a greater intolerance for any old-fashioned practices that stood in the way. To a degree this emerges in the controversy over commissions, and in the increasing desire to bring Native Labour Corps to France. Finally, it may be objected that the men dealt with here were formed in the late nineteenth-century heyday of imperialism. Their approach to empire was possibly more ideological than that of preceding generations, and more self-confident than that of later. But these attitudes cannot be dismissed as aberrations. There were continuities in their underlying attitudes which linked them with both the pre- and post-war values and convictions of the British in India. The First World War was a period when India's constitutional future was being discussed. Officially it was still not contemplated that India could have a wider existence outside the British Empire, nor that it could achieve dominion status for many generations. The widespread persistence of these underlying attitudes helps in part to explain the restrictions on policy-makers, faced with the challenge of dealing with India on a basis of equality.

Emmanuel College, Cambridge

Notes

I am indebted to Dr. Zara Steiner, of New Hall, Cambridge, for advice in the preparation of this article

1. Nicholas Mansergh, *The Commonwealth Experience* vol. 1, *The Durham Report to the Anglo-Irish Treaty* (London, 1982), pp.4–8ff.
2. For the Indian Expeditionary Force in France, see J. Greenhut, 'The Imperial Reserve: the Indian Corps on the Western Front 1914–15', *Journal of Imperial and Commonwealth History* xii, 1 (Oct. 1983).
3. See the treatment of King's commissions in Philip Mason, *A Matter of Honour. An Account of the Indian Army, its Officers and Men* (London, 1984), and Stephen P. Cohen, *The Indian Army: Its Contribution to the Development of a Nation* (London, 1971).

4. Hardinge to Crewe, 20 Aug. 1914, Hardinge MSS 120, 132. Kitchener also urged the Cabinet to bring the Indian troops to France.
5. Hardinge to Crewe, 27 Aug. 1914, Hardinge MSS 120, 135.
6. Hardinge to Chirol, 27 Aug. 1914, Hardinge MSS 93, 187.
7. 60,000 British troops, 80,000 Indians and 330 guns had been despatched overseas by June 1915, exclusive of drafts, out of a pre-war establishment of 250,000. *Imperial War Cabinet: Memorandum on the Military Assistance given by India in the Prosecution of the War*, India Office Library and Records L/MIL/17/5/2393, 3.
8. Hardinge to Crewe 3 and 9 Sept. 1914, Hardinge MSS 120, 38 and 141.
9. *Objections to the Employment of Ladies in Indian Hospitals* (File preceded by note 'Military Dept. Found among Medical Board papers 10.10.27') L/MIL/7/17316.
10. Superintendent, Government Printing, *The Army in India and its Evolution* (Calcutta, 1924), p. 121; and cf. Ch.XIII, Hardinge to Lawrence 14 April 1915, Hardinge MSS 93, 301.
11. Crewe to Hardinge, 19 Nov. 1914, Hardinge MSS 76, 156.
12. Crewe to Hardinge, 4 Dec. 1914, Hardinge MSS 76, 161.
13. Lawrence to Hardinge, 18 March 1915, Hardinge MSS 93, 500–1.
14. Lawrence to Hardinge, 10 May 1915, Hardinge MSS 94, 19.
15. *Objections;* Sir Walter Lawrence was an experienced Indian administrator, by whom George V 'was much guided' in matters relating to the 1911 Indian Durbar, see James Pope-Hennessy, *Lord Crewe 1858–1945. The Likeness of a Liberal* (London, 1955), p.94; and for brief reference to Crewe's responsibilities as Secretary for India on the war's outbreak, p. 145.
16. Chamberlain to Hardinge, 9 July 1915, Hardinge MSS 77, 143–4; Hardinge to Chamberlain, 6 Aug. 1915, Hardinge MSS 121, 187. Chamberlain confided this to Hardinge, as was his custom with personal or delicate matters, in a personally written final paragraph, of his otherwise normally dictated letter to the Viceroy.
17. *Objections*.
18. *Objections*. Cf. Corporation of Brighton, *A Short History in English, Gurmukhi and Urdu of the Royal Pavilion and a Description of it as a Hospital for Indian Soldiers 1914–15* (Brighton, 1915), for much interesting background and corroborative detail.
19. George V to Hardinge, 11 Aug. 1915, Hardinge MSS 105, 82; Munro Ferguson to Hardinge 12 Aug. 1915, Hardinge MSS 94, 166.
20. Hardinge to Munro Ferguson 17 Sept. 1915, Hardinge MSS 94, 128; Chamberlain to Hardinge, 14 Oct. 1915, Hardinge MSS 77, 255–7.
21. Munro Ferguson to Hardinge 22 Oct. 1915, Hardinge MSS 94, 311; Hardinge to Chamberlain, 12 Nov. 1915, Hardinge MSS 121, 258; Hardinge to Munro Ferguson, 29 Nov. 1915, Hardinge MSS 94, 188.
22. Hardinge to Chamberlain, 14 and 21 Jan. 1916, Hardinge MSS 122, 12–13, 16–17, 22.
23. Chamberlain to Hardinge, February 1916, Hardinge MSS 78, 99; Birdwood to Hardinge, 29 Sept. 1915, Hardinge MSS 94, 278.
24. *Army in India*, p.159.
25. For a discussion of the granting of King's commissions, as it finally evolved after the First World War, see Mason, Ch.XVIII, section 4, and index.
26. Chirol to Hardinge, 5 Dec, 1914; Birdwood to Hardinge, 27 Nov. 1914, Hardinge MSS 93, 410b and 393.
27. Hardinge to Crewe, 23 Dec. 1914, Hardinge MSS 120, 207. Cf. Mason, p.348. The Indian soldier had after all been trained to rely on his British officers.
28. 253 officers out of a total establishment of 2,586 were detained for work under the War Office. These were men who had been on leave when the war broke out. Superintendent, Government Printing, *India's Contribution to the Great War* (Calcutta, 1924), p.80.
29. *Officer Reinforcements for Indian Troops*, L/MIL/7/17671. The British Army had the highest officer-to-men ratio of any of the major European powers. In a normal infantry division of 1914 this was in the region of 1:28. Frederick Myatt, *The Soldier's Trade. Military Developments 1660–1914* (London, 1974), pp.267–8.
30. Chamberlain to Hardinge, 8 July 1915, Hardinge MSS 77, 125–6.
31. Chamberlain to Hardinge, 23 July 1915; Holderness to Hardinge, 5 July 1915, Hardinge MSS 77, 153 and 156.

32. Memos by Chamberlain and Islington, Chamberlain to Hardinge, 29 and 30 July 1915, Hardinge MSS 77, 160ff.
33. Chamberlain to Hardinge, 6 Aug. 1915, Hardinge MSS 77, 176–8.
34. Willcocks to Hardinge, 27 July 1915, Hardinge MSS 94, 155. Willcocks had passed this on to Crewe and George V too, as the verdict of all in the war. In 1913 Hardinge had hoped Willcocks might be promoted to Indian Commander-in-Chief, though he feared that being a 'very rough diamond' with middle-class connections, he would not be popular with the court. Hardinge to Chirol, 23 April 1913, Hardinge MSS 93, 16.
35. *Memorandum by His Excellency the Viceroy upon Questions Likely to Arise in India at the End of the War*, Hardinge MSS 121, 1, 26.
36. Hardinge to Chamberlain, 6 Aug. 1915, Hardinge MSS 121, 187.
37. Holderness to Hardinge, 28 Sept. 1915, Hardinge MSS 77, 238.
38. Chamberlain to Hardinge, 18 Nov. 1915, Hardinge MSS 77, 325–7. Hardinge to Chamberlain, 24 Dec. 1915, Hardinge MSS 121, 130.
39. Cf. Mason, pp.453–66; *India's Contribution*, p.371. Honorary commissions had been bestowed on Indians by 1 Jan. 1923. When Hardinge agreed that only the principle need be established during the war, full implementation waiting for the peace (above), he did not anticipate the war continuing two more years.
40. Chamberlain to Hardinge, 2 March 1916, Hardinge MSS 78, 119; *Mesopotamia Commission*, 'Report of the Commission Appointed by Act of Parliament to Enquire into the Operations of War in Mesopotamia', Cd. 8610, 1917, 132. This recommendation was actually contained in the dissenting report submitted by Commander Josiah C. Wedgwood.
41. Cf. Mason, pp.24, 314–15ff, 348–9 and index. The concept of martial races was embedded in pre-British Indian history.
42. *Memorandum for the Indian Representatives at the Forthcoming Imperial War Conference*, 31 Jan 1918, L/MIL/17/5/2306, 5–7.
43. E.G. Barrow, *Minute: Proposals for Raising Territorial Units in India*, L/MIL/17/5/2389. Cf. Willcocks in a memo of 14 June 1915. 'The Indian soldier is of course in no way equal to the British; were he so, we should not have been in India . . .' Willcocks to Hardinge, 22 Sept. 1915, Hardinge MSS 94, 201. Barrow had been Military Secretary at the India Office since 7 Feb. 1914. At the time of his appointment he was the senior general in the Indian Army with 45 years' service. He fought to clear his own name, following criticism by the Mesopotamia Commission, securing the following testimony from Chamberlain: 'I have nothing but satisfaction to express with the service of the late Military Secretary', 22 June 1917, *Mesopotamian Commission Report Military Dept. Previous Papers*, L/MIL/5/769 and *Papers Relating to the Mesopotamian Commission from Sir E. Barrow's Room*, L/MIL/5/768. He also had an important incidental role in the Curzon-Kitchener controversy. Field Marshal Lord Birdwood, *Khaki and Gown, An Autobiography* (London and Melbourne, 1941), p.163.
44. *Papers on Indian Labour Corps*, L/MIL/5/738, Hardinge to Ampthill, 1 Oct. 1913, 86–9, and 23 Dec. 1913, 108–9. Arthur Oliver Villiers Russell (1869–1935), 2nd Baron Ampthill; assistant secretary at the Colonial Office with J. Chamberlain, 1900, Governor of Madras; acting Viceroy to Curzon, 1904. 'Lack of sympathy with the reform proposals put forward by the Liberal government prevented his return as Viceroy.' L.G. Wickham Legg, *Dictionary of National Biography, 1931–40* (Oxford, 1970).
45. *Papers*, 25 July 1917.
46. *Papers*, 31 July 1917.
47. *Papers*, 20 Aug. 1917.
48. *Papers*, 4 and 27 Aug. 1917. The mixture of elements in Ampthill comes out very clearly in his stand on Corporal Punishment in the labour companies. 'The Indian, like a child or a dog, does not understand deferred punishment. He understands immediate chastisement and when it is just he takes it with as much good grace and as little resentment as an English schoolboy. But he will sulk under the shadow of a long deferred and less summary punishment.' *Memorandum on Discipline*, 31 Aug. 1917, 2.
49. India had a population of roughly 315 million. From the outbreak of war up to 31 Oct. 1918, 943,344 Indian personnel were despatched overseas (132,496 to France). 1,381,050

British and Indian personnel were sent from India (or the United Kingdom) on service overseas direct to various theatres up to 31 Dec. 1919. *India's Contribution*, pp.96–8.
50. *Recruiting in India Before and During the War of 1914–18*, L/MIL/5/2152; *Mason*, section 'Martial Races', pp.346–7, 359.
51. Cf. the objections of Duff to admitting Indians to the Volunteers and relaxing arms licensing and those of Sir Charles Bayley, Lt. Governor of Bihar and Orissa to the latter measure in *Memo by His Excellency*, pp.15–16 and 48.
52. See Arthur Marwick, *Britain in the Century of Total War: War, Peace and Social Change 1900–1967* (London, 1968), as well as his earlier work on the First World War, *The Deluge* (London, 1965).

William Morris Hughes, Empire and Nationalism: The Legacy of the First World War

JAMES COTTON

Despite the amplitude with which Prime Minister W. M. Hughes voiced Australian claims during the First World War, his conduct in the immediate postwar years shows that his nationalism remained consistent with an imperial and British standpoint. This proposition is illustrated with reference to Hughes' role in the 1921 imperial conference, the Chanak crisis, and his post-prime ministerial memoir. While obsessed with expedients to improve the speed and scope of intra-imperial communications and thus facilitate consultation, Hughes was concerned to ensure that Australia played a proper role in arriving at a consensus on the deep common interest that unified Britain and the Dominions. His lack of concern for extending the scope for independent action won by the Dominions during the war, his dismissive remarks regarding the British role in the League of Nations, and the vehemence of his communications with London in 1922, must all be seen within the context of an imperial loyalty that survived the war undiminished.

IN THE OPINION OF HIS BIOGRAPHER, William Morris Hughes' 'whole career was guided' by a 'dual loyalty' to Australia and to Empire.[1] According to Neville Meaney, it was Hughes' understanding of race that allowed him to affirm these loyalties simultaneously: 'Hughes, more than any other political leader, felt profoundly and articulated repeatedly the British race vision'.[2] He gloried in the claim that Australia had even a unique title to its British identity, not only through its deeds but because it had seen the merging of populations that were still to a great extent separate peoples in the home islands. His many speeches in Britain in 1916, which he delivered to widespread acclaim, were devoted largely to the theme that the unique commitment to the war effort seen right across the Empire demonstrated that the British 'race' had faced and met a challenge that would have overwhelmed a lesser breed. Yet Hughes' experience in the counsels of the Empire fell far short of his vision of an uplifted and unified people.

Hughes is notorious in diplomatic history for the stridency of his claims, especially at the Paris Peace Conference of 1919, on behalf of Australia's interests. The question thus arises as to how far his insistence on the rights of his country was consistent with his sense of Britishness. According to the contemporary encomium on his exploits written by Percy Deane (Hughes' personal

---

[1] L. F. Fitzhardinge, *William Morris Hughes: A Political Biography*, vol. 1 (Sydney: Angus and Robertson, 1964), 224. This judgement has recently been endorsed by Carl Bridge, *William Hughes: Australia. Makers of the Modern World* (London: Haus, 2011), 70, 131.

[2] Neville Meaney, *Australia and the World Crisis* (Sydney: Sydney University Press, 2009), 376. See also Kosmas Tsokhas, 'Tradition, Fantasy and Britishness: Four Australian Prime Ministers', *Journal of Contemporary Asia* 31, no. 1 (2001): 3–30.

secretary in Paris), Hughes had pursued, in a 'spirit of broad Nationalism ... the fight for Australia's right to make her own laws, live her own life, and develop this great heritage in her own way'.[3] Hughes certainly had no reservations in disputing, to these ends, the positions taken by such global figures as British Prime Minister David Lloyd George and US President Woodrow Wilson. After his portrayal of Hughes' single-handed combat with opponents of all kinds in Paris, Deane nevertheless concluded with the observation that he 'spoke not only for Australia but for the whole British Empire'.[4]

For later generations of historians, there has been some inclination to emphasise the nationalist aspect of Hughes' manoeuvres, and to neglect the British cast of his assumptions. Peter Edwards, in reviewing Hughes' record in London and Paris, concludes that his 'preparedness to assert Australia's separate interests brashly, openly and defiantly ... drew the world's attention to the existence of an Australian foreign policy', even, as his cabinet colleagues in Melbourne feared, to 'the brink of open rupture with the Mother Country'.[5] Eric Andrews, in his comprehensive review of Anglo-Australian relations in the war years, finds Hughes' principal aim was to achieve Australia's particular national and especially economic objectives while maintaining Australian autonomy. Powerful British interests were annoyed at Hughes' repeated insistence in his wartime speeches that the Empire should concentrate on intra-mural trade, and once hostilities were concluded were quick to pursue trading strategies that did not serve Australian interests.[6] While Hughes' attachment to Empire was undoubtedly strong, its basis was largely transactional, providing Australia with 'economic strength and military security'.[7] W. J. Hudson, while acknowledging the pervasive 'Britishness' of the Australian view of the world of that era, describes Hughes' fundamental attitude to world politics as 'ultra-realist' and thus mostly free of ideological content.[8] How did Hughes' Britishness and his nationalism co-exist?

This article explores the practice of Hughes' foreign policy in the aftermath of the First World War, arguing that, despite Hughes' many wartime tussles with the leaders of Empire, his nationalism remained consistent with an imperial and British standpoint. It concludes with a discussion of his most considered reflections on the imperial subject, his book *The Splendid Adventure*.

---

[3] P. E. Deane, *Australia's Rights: The Fight at the Peace Table* (Melbourne: Sands & McDougall, n.d. [1919]), 3–4.
[4] Ibid., 23.
[5] P. G. Edwards, *Prime Ministers and Diplomats: The Making of Australian Foreign Policy 1901–1949* (Melbourne: Oxford University Press/AIIA, 1983), 52.
[6] E. M. Andrews, *The ANZAC Illusion: Anglo-Australian Relations during World War I* (Cambridge: Cambridge University Press, 1993), 196–8.
[7] Ibid., 212.
[8] W. J. Hudson, *Billy Hughes in Paris: The Birth of Australian Diplomacy* (Melbourne: Nelson/AIIA, 1978), 43; cf. Malcolm Booker, *The Great Professional: A Study of W. M. Hughes* (Sydney: McGraw-Hill, 1980), 239.

Hughes and Empire war aims

In his first foray to Great Britain as prime minister, from March to July 1916, Hughes exercised vigorous liberties of expression. His fiery public speeches—urging the greatest exertions for the war effort as vindication of his beliefs regarding the British racial mission, against Germany as the implacable foe of British values and beliefs, and in support of Empire economic autarchy in the struggle with competitors—were encouraged by critics of British Prime Minister Herbert Asquith in their emerging campaign to oust him.[9] Though Hughes scored some victories over shipping and on the sale of Australian commodities, he was less successful in advancing his other war aims, especially relating to the Pacific. Returning home to be absorbed in the struggles occasioned by the first conscription referendum, he then missed the watershed Imperial War Conference of April 1917 which resolved to recommend the 'readjustment' after the war of relations between and among Britain and the Dominions, the latter of which were recognised as 'autonomous nations of an Imperial Commonwealth' and thus possessed of a right to 'an adequate voice in foreign policy and in foreign relations'.[10] By the time Hughes returned to London in mid-1918, Canadian Prime Minister Sir Robert Borden had further pressed the case for a full role for the Dominions in the management of the war and its aftermath.[11]

At the Paris Peace Conference, Hughes energetically sought three outcomes.[12] Fearful of Japan, he wanted Britain to give unqualified support to his pursuit of local hegemony in the South Pacific, especially through untrammelled control of former German New Guinea. With the establishment of the League of Nations an inextricable part of the peace arrangements, he also wanted to ensure that the conditions of membership would be such that Australia remained in charge of essential domestic policies, notably immigration and tariffs. And he was determined that Germany would pay reparations under terms that were favourable to Australian claims. Aware, however, that Australia would count for little in world politics without the Empire, and personally committed to what he held to be a British perspective, he also sought to maintain Australia's firm identification as a 'British' entity. During the peace negotiations, Hughes' dispute with Lloyd George regarding the extent of German reparations reduced their relations to mutual recriminations—in Welsh according to Hughes' later account.[13] His confrontation with Wilson over the disposition of Germany's former colonies, and in particular Hughes' leakage to the press of a distorted account of the proceedings, led to threats by the

---

[9] W. M. Hughes, "*The Day*"—*And After* (London: Cassell, 1916); Andrews, 74.
[10] Imperial War Conference 1917 Resolution IX; R. M. Dawson, ed., *The Development of Dominion Status 1900–1936* (London: Oxford University Press, 1937), 175.
[11] Joan Beaumont, '"Unitedly We Have Fought": Imperial Loyalty and the Australian War Effort', *International Affairs* 90, no. 2 (March 2014): 397–412.
[12] W. J. Hudson and M. P. Sharp, *Australian Independence: Colony to Reluctant Kingdom* (Melbourne: Melbourne University Press, 1988).
[13] W. M. Hughes, *Policies and Potentates* (Sydney: Halstead Press, 1950), 236–9.

American president to withdraw and generated immense resentment.[14] Hughes had also been outspoken in his implacable (and, given Wilson's covert support, ultimately successful) opposition to Japan's attempt to introduce a racial equality clause into the League Covenant, despite support from France and Italy for the proposal.

These events of 1919 have been exhaustively analysed, though commentators are not entirely agreed whether Hughes' notoriously obstreperous style helped or hindered his campaigns.[15] Hughes' relations with Lloyd George had never really recovered after he was excluded—despite warnings from cabinet secretary Maurice Hankey and others—from the crucial deliberations that led to the acceptance by the British in October 1918 of Wilson's Fourteen Points as a basis for peace negotiations with Germany. Yet in many respects peace making placed Hughes in a difficult position, given the marginal importance of Australia and the immense demands from every quarter placed upon Lloyd George and the British delegation in Paris. As the mostly European delegations and lobbyists struggled with the redrawing of the European map, making and un-making nations and peoples in committee proceedings, few could follow Hughes' fixation on one quarter of a remote Pacific island in the interior of which no European had ever stood.

Hughes and the Empire at peace

During the remainder of his tenure as prime minister (until February 1923), Hughes' relations with London, though not without strains, entailed the discussion of a much smaller range of issues. His interlocutors were restricted to members of the political leadership and senior officials in London or, in 1921, to other members of the Empire–Commonwealth. In those circumstances the logic of Hughes' diplomatic reasoning is easier to follow if not always to accept.

The convening of leaders of the Empire had begun with the Colonial Conference of 1887; the term 'Imperial Conference' was employed for meetings from 1907. The resumption of these conferences after the First World War involved many new dynamics. In 1921 there was some controversy as to whether the meeting was a conference or something more, especially in the context of the intention, as stated in the 1917 resolution of the Imperial War Conference, to convene a post-hostilities meeting to reassess the evolving and imprecise constitutional relations between Britain and its various territories beyond the British Isles.

---

[14] Hankey's Notes, Council of Ten, *Papers of Woodrow Wilson January 11–February 7 1919*, ed. Arthur S. Link, vol. 54 (Princeton: Princeton University Press, 1986), 363–4; Hughes, *Policies and Potentates*, 238–43. On this episode see Thomas J. Knock, *To End All Wars: Woodrow Wilson and the Quest for a New World Order* (Princeton: Princeton University Press, 1992), 210–14.

[15] Peter Spartalis, *The Diplomatic Battles of Billy Hughes* (Sydney: Hale and Iremonger, 1983); see in addition the works of Hudson, Fitzhardinge, Meaney, and Andrews cited above.

Intra-mural imperial relations had been transformed by the experience of coordinating the war, by the distinct voices accorded to the leaders of the Dominions at the peace conference, and then by the emergence of the international diplomatic personalities of the Dominions through membership of the League of Nations. The latter clearly imposed unaccustomed duties on the Dominions, and amongst some internationalists there were even those who argued that obligations to Geneva transcended duties to London. The fear of strains in intra-imperial coordination becoming apparent in the workings of the League was cited by the Secretary of State Lord Milner as the grounds for his suggestion, in early 1920, that a branch of the cabinet secretariat in London be charged with the coordination of British and Dominion external policies. Hughes was eager to grasp the possibilities of new mechanisms for cooperation though he was equally quick to point out that Australia's separate membership of the League should not be compromised.[16]

The rationale for the 1921 Imperial Conference lay particularly in the unsatisfactory experience of superintending the war effort. Hughes remained anxious to revisit the issue of the coordination of imperial policy, cabling to Lloyd George in October 1920 his concern that without a specific effort, matters would unsatisfactorily 'drift along'.[17] This prompt struck a responsive chord in London.[18] Hughes was also concerned with the role of Japan, as he had been through most of the war years. In the newly created League of Nations he perceived Japan to be obstructing unreasonably the transfer of New Guinea to Australian authority as a League mandate. In the terms of the 1919 peace settlement, the former German territory, which Australia had occupied in September 1914, had been promised to Australia—after a vigorous campaign by Hughes—as a 'C' class mandate. This arrangement was close to a form of annexation, though Australia could construct no fortifications and was obliged to report periodically to the League on the governance and welfare of the inhabitants. The Japanese government, however, had persistently raised concerns about the rights of their nationals and firms to trade and own property.[19] This was a sensitive issue in light of the fact that Hughes had been bitterly disappointed that the peace conference had not definitively settled these issues.

Japan was also of especial interest to the wider Empire given the status of the Anglo-Japanese alliance, which was due for renewal (or repudiation) according to the prevailing view in 1921, and was possibly inconsistent with some features of the new League covenant. In May 1920 London sought Australia's views on the alliance. While fear of Japan was an enduring feature of

---

[16] Sec of State to Dominions, 22 January 1920: National Archives of Australia (hereafter NAA), CP103/12 Bundle 8/8; 'Channel of Communication between the various British members of the League of Nations and the Secretariat-General', 22 September 1920: NAA, CP360/9 Bundle 1/NN.
[17] Hughes to Lloyd George, [7 October] 1920: NAA, CP360/9 Bundle 1/NN.
[18] L. F. Fitzhardinge, *William Morris Hughes: A Political Biography*, vol. 2 (Sydney: Angus and Robertson, 1979), 460.
[19] Hughes to Milner, 2 February, 29 April 1920: NAA, A3934 SC12/5 Part 1.

Hughes' world view, both he and his advisers considered Australian security would benefit from renewal of the alliance while the nation built strength and developed closer relations with the United States.[20] At this time policy making in foreign affairs, as in most other areas of government, was largely in the hands of Hughes (who also became Minister of External Affairs when the position was re-established in December 1921). While he had access to excellent advice, notably from E. L. Piesse in the 'Pacific Branch', Hughes was as reluctant to share information and debate alternative views as he was obsessed with the future threat from Japan.[21] Since there was little in the way of systematic cabinet review or even parliamentary debate on foreign policy, the beliefs and motivations of Hughes himself must be central to any account. On the eve of his departure to London in 1921, Hughes addressed parliament outlining the policies he would seek to effect. He declaimed at length on the inappropriateness of any fixed constitutional formula for the Empire, on the pressing need for imperial naval defence, and on the desirability of renewing the Anglo-Japanese alliance in a form acceptable to the United States.[22]

Further insight into Hughes' fundamental beliefs can be gained by considering his depiction on this occasion of the Australian position within the Empire. He referred to the status gained by Australia as a result of the war:

In the supreme hour of the Empire's trial the Dominions proved themselves worthy of their breeding. The whole world recognised that they had put on the toga of manhood and became nations. The nations of the world recognised us as their equals, and we were admitted into the League on a footing of equality.[23]

Taken in isolation, this passage suggests an assertive nationalism, not least because it carries the implication that Australia had become an equal with all nations, a class that self-evidently included Britain. Yet when he turned to review the changes that had occurred 'between Britain and ourselves' in the same period, Hughes was able to say, with no hint of inconsistency, that 'our relations remain the same'. Consequently, he reasoned, no revisions in constitutional arrangements were needed since 'the British Constitution is the supreme achievement of the genius of our race for self-government'. Hughes then described the ties of Empire with reference to the monarchy, race and sentiment, as well as acknowledging the 'material' role performed by the protection afforded by the British Navy. Australia is a nation 'by the grace of God and the power of the British Empire'. On the latter, he emphasised that though Australia had now entered the hall of nations, it was unrealistic to imagine that without membership of the Empire it would long survive. Hughes was evidently

---

[20] E. L. Piesse, 'The Anglo-Japanese Alliance—Secretary of State's Cable of 3rd May asking views of Commonwealth Government—Notes for use in preparing reply', 12 May 1920: NAA, A2219, External Relations Vol. 9.
[21] Neville Meaney, *Fears and Phobias: E. L. Piesse and the Problem of Japan 1909–39*, Occasional Paper no. 1 (Canberra: National Library of Australia, 1996).
[22] *Commonwealth Parliamentary Debates*, House of Representatives, vol. 14, 7 April 1921, 7262–70.
[23] Ibid.

quite capable of holding Manichean, imperial and nationalist sentiments in his head all at the same time.

The 1921 Imperial Conference, attended by the leaders of all the Dominions (save Newfoundland) as well as delegates speaking for India, and chaired by the British Prime Minister, opened on 20 June and ran until August. Unlike his colleagues, Hughes brought no ministers or advisers with him, though he was supported again by his secretary, Deane. The Canadian Prime Minister, Arthur Meighen, in contrast, brought not only Navy Minister C. C. Ballantyne, but also Loring Christie, whose international affairs expertise was exceptional.[24] Taken together, Hughes' many contributions to the proceedings—which occupied thirty-four plenary meetings—comprised an eloquent and powerful, if not always convincing, exposition of a consistent view of the Australian national interest. Opinion is divided, however, regarding whether Hughes was at the 'pinnacle' of his achievements or whether his manoeuvres resulted in 'failure'.[25]

In his opening speech, Hughes voiced his concerns regarding demands by those seeking a more codified approach to the rules governing relations between the various British realms, his anxieties over the naval defence of the Empire, and also his hopes for improved intra-mural imperial consultation. His most sustained remarks, however, were devoted to the Anglo-Japanese alliance.[26] In parliament in Melbourne his phrase for the alliance had been that it was to national survival 'as precious as rubies'.

The members of the conference had before them secret policy papers on a number of subjects, the most significant of which were on the Anglo-Japanese alliance and on 'A Common Imperial Policy in Foreign Affairs'.[27] On the alliance, the Foreign Office was in favour of renewal, despite strong reservations regarding Japan's methods and ultimate objectives, especially in relation to China. In Paris, Japan had insisted on retaining the German concession of Tsingtao (Qingdao), despite protests from China which had joined the Allied powers in 1917. The alternative to renewal was to maintain forces (especially naval) in the Far East quite beyond current British capabilities. Yet, the Foreign Office argued, in the years ahead the interests of the United States and of Japan in the Far East were bound to be opposed. Equally, British policy could never be permitted to lead to hostilities with the United States. The only longer-term solution was an agreement of the three powers, but as this outcome was as yet only a hope, renewal of the alliance was held to be the better option—especially in the light of the constraints on power now entailed by the requirements of the League charter which committed all member states to a prescribed procedure for dispute settlement.

---

[24] C. P. Stacey, *Canada in the Age of Conflict*, vol. 1: *1867–1921* (Toronto: Toronto University Press, 1977), 332–8.
[25] Spartalis, 229; Meaney, *Australia and the World Crisis*, 491–2.
[26] Imperial Conference, 2nd Meeting, 21 June 1921, 2–7. References to the 1921 Conference proceedings taken from printed *Stenographic Notes*, copy in Hughes Papers, National Library of Australia (hereafter NLA), MS 1538, Sub-series 25:2, Box 124.
[27] *Imperial Conference, Stenographic Notes*, E1 and E6: Hughes Papers, NLA.

The Colonial Office, for its part, assumed as axiomatic the common citizenship and the common interests of the inhabitants of Britain and the Dominions, while admitting the new uncertainties resulting from separate national memberships of the League and the possibility of separate diplomatic establishments foreshadowed by the Canadian intention to appoint a resident minister in Washington. The memorandum supplied by the Colonial Office suggested that some new machinery was required to retain and revivify the close cooperation of equals achieved during the latter stages of the war. Yet it conceded the practical difficulties in the way of any scheme, whether it involved a new secretariat, visiting or resident cabinet ministers in London, or a greater reliance upon modern means of communication. On his personal copy of the Colonial Office paper, where it stated the 'difficulty' in the way of continuous intra-imperial consultation under present circumstances, Hughes scored out that word and wrote in the margin, 'impossibility'.[28]

The issue of the Anglo-Japanese alliance, to which much attention was devoted at the conference, tested the easy assumption of common interests expressed in these memoranda. Meighen, with whom Hughes crossed swords repeatedly, was adamant on two points. The first was that the Anglo-Japanese alliance should not be renewed since it entailed the possibility—remote, but its plausibility notably conceded in the analysis offered by the Foreign Office—of a future conflict between Japan and the United States. The second was that the maintenance of Canada's interests was entirely dependent upon close and cordial relations with the United States. This position led him, in relation to the subsequent discussion of imperial coordination, to adopt the doctrine that where the particular and vital interests of a member of the Commonwealth were affected by an issue, the member in question should have the principal role in determining the means of its resolution (a view that originated with Loring Christie).[29]

In sometimes pungent language, Hughes vigorously contested both propositions. Regarding the latter he rejected it utterly, pointing out that thereby Canada would be accorded veto power in any new arrangement in Anglo-American relations, yet those relations touched not only many vital interests of Britain but even the future of world peace. Invoking arguments drawn from geography and from racial identity, Hughes also contended that Australia's security was completely dependent upon the naval power of the Empire which in the conditions of the Pacific required the maintenance of the Anglo-Japanese alliance. America would be a preferable security guarantor by far, and Canadians were fortunate in having America as a *de facto* guarantor, but no such guarantee was likely to be offered to Australia. Neither had the United States taken up offers to discuss disarmament, nor had it joined the League despite the scheme's joint American parentage.[30]

---

[28] 'A Common Imperial Policy in Foreign Affairs', 'E6', 3: Hughes Papers, NLA.
[29] Stacey, 337.
[30] *Imperial Conference, Stenographic Notes*, 9th Meeting, 29 June 1921, 12–15: Hughes Papers, NLA.

In the event, although Hughes rejected Meighen's contention that there was some prospect of a Pacific agreement in which Japan and the United States would both be parties—provocatively ridiculing his approach as 'the case for the United States of America'— this outcome came about within the year. A Pacific regional disarmament meeting of the major powers, initiated by President Warren Harding, resulted in the Washington naval arms limitation agreements of 1921–22.

Naval defence occupied an important part of the 1921 conference. Though the rationale for the Royal Navy was the defence of the Empire as a whole, given British naval weakness in the Far East—Hughes was aghast to learn of its extent—it would henceforth normally be concentrated in the waters of the British Isles. While units could be dispatched to the Pacific if adverse events so necessitated, successful deployment would require a first-class base to be established in Singapore. The Admiralty sought an undertaking from the Dominions to help finance this project. Again Meighen and Hughes differed; the Canadian was adamant that his country did not need such naval protection in the Pacific, the Australian argued in favour of a common imperial effort but was aware that his own legislature would not support such an undertaking if the other Dominions abstained.[31]

Hughes' sometimes acerbic style was evident on other issues. He took the British government to task for its recognition of the claims—extravagant and unwarranted in his view—to nationalist leadership of the Egyptian politician, Saad Zaghul.[32] His somewhat cynical interpretation of the remarks of the Foreign Secretary, Lord Curzon, on the effectiveness of the League of Nations underlined his conviction that the Empire was the only assemblage of states that was at all effective in international affairs. As Hughes observed:

> I have refrained from saying anything publicly to belittle the League ... But I confess that from its very inception I despaired of its being of use—indeed, that in some circumstances it might be a menace—to our Empire, but I had never been able to see that other side of the question presented by Lord Curzon this afternoon. Now I see the League in quite a different light. Lord Curzon has shown that the Assembly—and to a lesser extent the Council of the League—is a sort of appanage of the Foreign Office, enabling us to do things for the glory of the Empire which would not be done so well, if at all, in any other way, and, as Lord Curzon has shown us, the League is to be brushed aside whenever it is necessary for the benefit of the Empire that we should act directly through the Foreign Office. I must confess that, as a zealous supporter of the Empire, such an interpretation appeals to me ... It is the most complete scathing exposure of the League's futility deciding the destinies of the world that I have heard.[33]

Here Hughes' 1919 suspicions of those within the Empire leadership who were willing to embrace Wilson's prescription for a future rule-governed world

---

[31] Meaney, *Australia and the World Crisis*, 487.
[32] *Imperial Conference, Stenographic Notes*, 17th Meeting, 6 July 1921: Hughes Papers, NLA.
[33] *Imperial Conference, Stenographic Notes*, 20th Meeting, 8 July 1921, 14–15: Hughes Papers, NLA.

order—South African Prime Minister Jan Smuts being most notable among them—were re-stated. Hughes was adamant that the only sure foundation for the peace of the world was the Empire, and if the League served to advance the same objective of global peace, it would do so through depending upon intra-mural Empire cooperation. Curzon, of course, bridled at Hughes' facetious but cutting remarks.[34]

A further question that revealed deep intra-imperial differences was the disputed status of the King's Indian subjects in the rest of the Empire, particularly in South Africa where their social and political rights were restricted. As a known and vocal champion of White Australia, Hughes nevertheless showed some sympathy with the position of the Indian spokesmen at the conference, even proposing in a draft resolution subsequently accepted by the conference that the Empire had a clear duty to recognise the rights of Indians to citizenship.[35] Given Hughes' many triumphalist assertions regarding the British racial genius, and in light of his later published doubts about the capacity and preparedness of India for home rule, this episode would seem to show his imperial sentiments overriding his racial prejudices. Hughes even agreed to host the visit of a delegation to Australia, to be led by politician Srinivasa Sastri, which would allow the Indians to make their case for citizenship in Australia.[36] Following this visit, and Sastri's laudatory account of his warm public reception, the Australian federal electoral act was amended in 1925 to enfranchise Indian residents.[37]

The issue on which Hughes made least headway was intra-imperial communications. This was a period of transition. In 1918 Dominion prime ministers had been accorded the right to communicate direct with the British prime minister on matters of cabinet significance, rather than by way of the Colonial Office, as had previously been the case. However, Hughes' pleas for faster movement of people and information across the Empire—including by way of a fleet of airships and investment in long-range radio relay stations—were rebutted on technical grounds, though the real issue was expense. He was clearly exasperated that few around the conference table in London appreciated the crippling effects of distance on Australia's imperial ties.

On the constitutional issue, Hughes rigidly insisted that the 1921 conference could only discuss an agenda for a future gathering to review the question of intra-mural relations between the components of the Empire–Commonwealth; it could not itself articulate new principles. Nevertheless, his reaction to the foreign policy *tour d'horizon* contributed by Curzon was to point out that his remarks outlined policies 'already done or in the doing' and thus beyond the scope of any influence from the Dominions. Yet while embracing the new status of the Dominions as full partners in the imperial project, Hughes vehemently rejected any codification of this status, despite its evident neglect in practice. He

---

[34] Ibid.
[35] 'Amendment proposed by Mr Hughes' [typescript]: Hughes Papers, NLA, 25/107.
[36] Srinivasa Sastri to Hughes, 2 August 1921: Hughes Papers, NLA, 25/106.
[37] Srinivasa Sastri, *Report Regarding the Deputation to the Dominions of Australia, New Zealand and Canada* (Simla: Government Printer, 1923); 'Dr Sastri Visit to Australia': NAA, A1, 1923/7187.

took the position that rigid rules might actually serve to restrict and prevent further growth, and might meanwhile prove fertile field for argumentative legal minds. In insisting on this position, Hughes successfully frustrated the plans of Smuts who had come prepared with proposals (partly inspired by the ideas of Australian scholar H. Duncan Hall) for a definitive 'declaration of constitutional right' on Dominion status (a step eventually taken in 1926 in the Balfour Declaration).[38] Hughes contributed a text when the conference considered the final communiqué, the cautious tone of which—extolling the virtues of the status quo—was echoed in the joint statement released at its conclusion.[39]

Although Hughes later pronounced himself satisfied that in London he had frustrated the 'constitutional tinkers', he was unhappy not to have secured the future of the Anglo-Japanese alliance, not to have materially improved imperial communications, and not to have achieved any agreement on sharing the burdens of naval defence.[40] The issue of communications aside, Hughes firmly believed—as he had told parliament on the eve of his departure—that the naval and alliance questions were of the greatest possible gravity, and that without their satisfactory resolution Australia's fundamental interests would be at risk. Without the 'material' British naval guarantee, the 'banner of White Australia' would soon be torn down by the jealous and resentful denizens of teeming Asia.[41] Yet though he subjected the views of Meighen to a withering critique, Hughes was not disposed to contemplating hypotheticals beyond the imperial space that any consideration of purely material factors and interests might have recommended. He could hardly conceive of an Australia unprotected by the Royal Navy.

Hughes' insistence on closer intra-imperial consultation, coupled with his strict avoidance of any codification of the precise forms and limits of that consultation, might be regarded as somewhat paradoxical. In essence, his answer to the problem of 'drift' was technological rather than legal or formal, and in retrospect his resistance to constitutional change can be seen to have been already anachronistic. Even as the Imperial Conference was in session, a truce was declared in the conflict between the British government and the nationalist regime in Ireland, and before the end of that year a treaty was negotiated that brought the Irish Free State into existence (though not without internal dissension) as a self-governing entity and somewhat reluctant affiliate to the Empire–Commonwealth. In retrospect, the changes in the status of Ireland were the beginning of the end for the British world.

---

[38] H. Duncan Hall, *The British Commonwealth of Nations* (London: Methuen, 1920); H. Duncan Hall, 'The Genesis of the Balfour Declaration of 1926', *Journal of Commonwealth Political Studies* 1, no. 3 (1962): 169–93.

[39] 'Report of the Conference of Prime Ministers, 1921', [Cmd 1474], 'XIV The Proposed Conference on Constitutional Relations': Dawson, 208–9.

[40] Hughes to Hankey, [August 1921], quoted in Stephen Roskill, *Hankey Man of Secrets*, vol. 2: 1919–1931 (London: Collins, 1972), 232.

[41] *Commonwealth Parliamentary Debates*, House of Representatives, vol. 14, 7 April 1921, 7265.

From the Washington conference to Chanak

The origins of the Washington talks lay in the 1921 Imperial Conference. Faced in particular with Canadian objections to the Anglo-Japanese alliance, Hughes had embraced Curzon's suggestion that some way might be found to allay American suspicions that the alliance might bring it into conflict with Britain over Japan. Meanwhile American policy, under the direction of Secretary of State Charles Hughes, was moving to seek an accommodation with the British Empire and Japan in the Pacific. To explore this possibility, President Warren Harding extended an invitation to Japan, China, Britain and France (later other European powers with interests in the Pacific also became involved) for a conference to explore arms limitations, to constrain the building of new fortifications in the Pacific, and also to reach an accord on guaranteeing the territorial integrity of China while permitting free commercial access to the Chinese market. The four main agreements that were eventually negotiated in Washington came to be known as the Washington treaties.

After a period of confused diplomacy, during which the British pressed unsuccessfully for a preliminary gathering that, advantageously, would have involved the leaders of the Dominions, arrangements were negotiated for a single British delegation to proceed to Washington. In contrast to the 1919 Paris Peace Conference, the Dominions would not be represented as principals; neither did the original British plan provide for any Dominion presence as part of the British contingent. Hughes subsequently blamed the Americans, but the record shows that it was Curzon who assumed there would be a single delegation of personnel from Britain and it was the Americans who took a flexible position so as not to exclude some voice for the Dominions.[42]

Anxious to mollify Hughes, Lloyd George urged him to attend as part of an enlarged British delegation. (It is an indication of the assumptions of the times that Lloyd George suggested that if Hughes himself were not available, Lord Novar (formerly Australian governor-general, 1914–20) might be a suitable substitute.[43]) Having just been absent for a prolonged sojourn in London and facing a precarious parliamentary situation, Hughes was unable to go to Washington, nominating Minister for Defence Senator George Pearce for the role.

There then occurred an exchange of communications with Smuts which gives the strongest indication of Hughes' views on the relationship between London and the Dominions. The South African had contacted Hughes to urge him to extract an invitation to the conference directly from Washington. By underlining the status of the Dominions as distinct entities, a principle that had been disputed by some Americans at Paris and later in the US Congress, this would constitute a significant advance in the 'battle for International recognition

---

[42] Harvey to Sec of State, 26 August 1921, *Foreign Relations of the United States 1921*, vol. 1 (Washington: US Government Printing Office, 1936), 63–4; Michael G. Fry, 'The Pacific Dominions and the Washington Conference, 1921–22', *Diplomacy and Statecraft* 4, no. 3 (1993): 60–101.

[43] D. L. George to Hughes, 3 October 1921: NAA, A6661 1370A.

[of] our equal status'.⁴⁴ Rather than replying directly, Hughes cabled Lloyd George to urge no concessions to Smuts, lest 'in the desire to meet his views you may be creating precedent which may make impossible that unity of Empire which is the rock on which it rests'.⁴⁵ He then set out as strong a statement of his inherent Britishness as could be conceived:

> I venture to remind you that General Smuts' concept of Empire and mine do not coincide. Our origin and circumstances sufficiently explain this. If the circumstances of every Dominion and of every leader were the same as those of Australia and New Zealand and of for example Massey and myself it would be immaterial how far you went in the direction to which I referred, but they are not. And that being the case I hope you will go very slowly and give ground only when there is a clear indication that this is essential in the interests of the Empire and not merely the wish of one Dominion.⁴⁶

Hughes concluded by pointing to the looming prospect of Ireland as a Dominion exercising the right to free action at the League and on treaties, thus threatening Empire unity.

Nevertheless, after further exchanges between Smuts, Lloyd George and Hughes, Smuts secured agreement to his suggestion that the Dominion delegates be separately credentialled by the King, and to their joint and collective assent being required for any decision of the conference to be binding on the Empire as a whole. While this arcana would have to be suitably justified to the Americans, it would preserve at least the form of distinct Dominion status. Some trouble was then taken to supply Pearce, already at sea, with the necessary documents.⁴⁷ A polite veil was thus thrown over Pearce's lack of a distinct national role in Washington. At the conference Pearce was a careful defender of Australia's interests, seeking to ensure that there were no additional restrictions placed upon Australia's exercise of the 'C' class mandate over New Guinea, and that the definition of 'insular possessions' on which fortifications were to be prohibited did not include any part of the Australian colony of Papua.⁴⁸ On the crucial issue of naval arms limitations, however, though Pearce showed himself to be acutely aware in the internal deliberations of the British Empire Delegation of the Pacific implications of the decline in British naval power, he was forced to accept the directions of London. Anxious to take advantage of the American proposal for a ten years' holiday in capital ship construction, Lloyd George overrode his own naval experts to insist that this measure be accepted. Though Hughes cabled Pearce to 'follow Beatty's advice', even the First Sea Lord's return to London from Washington to fight against this proposal—which placed Britain with its

---

⁴⁴ Smuts to Hughes, 19 October 1921: NAA, A6661 1370A.
⁴⁵ Hughes to Prime Minister, UK, 25 October 1921: NAA, A6661 1370A.
⁴⁶ Ibid.
⁴⁷ Hughes to Pearce, 31 October 1921: NAA, A4603 WashConf1922, 161.
⁴⁸ Robert Thornton, 'The Semblance of Security: Australia and the Washington Conference, 1921–22', *Australian Outlook* 32, no. 1 (1978): 65–83; John Connor, *ANZAC and Empire: George Foster Pearce and the Foundations of Australian Defence* (Cambridge: Cambridge University Press, 2011), 139–42.

ageing fleet at a disadvantage—was in vain.[49] Anglo-American accord (not to mention the economies sought by the chancellor of the exchequer) was clearly a matter of much greater moment in the calculations of the British government, as Hughes was informed in Pearce's secret report submitted on his return.[50]

Speaking to parliament on the motion to ratify the Washington treaties, Hughes characterised them as a great advance in guaranteeing the peace of the Pacific, but was careful to point out that they did not impose any obligations to come to the assistance of a threatened party. Given the tenor of his 1921 remarks on the value of the Anglo-Japanese alliance, some of his listeners would have been justified in pondering the value of trading a material alliance formed in 1902 for an agreement founded upon 'world opinion', albeit 'the moral force at the disposal of [the] four great Powers'.[51] Notoriously dismissive of any security guarantee outside that offered by the imperial tie, Hughes was obliged to endorse the replacement of an alliance that acted to restrain Australia's only likely Pacific foe with a multilateral statement of good intentions. Yet he gave no voice to criticism of British strategy.

It remains to consider Hughes' splenetic reaction to the Chanak crisis. On 17 September 1922, he had learned, through the press rather than from the dispatch from London which reached him later that day, that Australia would be called upon to contribute a contingent to the Dardanelles. War with the Turks threatened at Chanak (Çanakkale), the nationalists led by Mustafa Kemal rejecting the provisions of the 1920 Treaty of Sèvres, concluded by the Sultan, under which Allied forces were in occupation to guarantee the neutrality of the straits.[52] Hughes responded with a public declaration of willingness to support Britain, but his secret communication to London restated his views in the most direct terms. Keeping the Dominions in ignorance and then expecting them to rally to the imperial cause if war threatened—as a result of policies crafted in London—was conduct that 'gravely imperils the unity of the Empire'.[53] For the next three months he was subject to a deluge of paper from London on the crisis, but the larger issues were not addressed.

The outcome confirmed Hughes' worst fears. He was informed that a conference of the interested parties was to be convened at Lausanne. Britain would be represented by the secretary of state and the ambassador in Constantinople; 'Dominion Governments will be kept informed from time to time of the general lines of policy on which British Plenipotentiaries propose to proceed ... and will of course be invited to sign a new treaty'.[54] Hughes was further informed that French objections to Dominion representation had

---

[49] Hughes to Pearce, 9 December 1921: NAA, A4603 WashConf1922, 559.
[50] Pearce to Hughes, 'Confidential Report': NAA, A2219 ExRel V22, 334ff.
[51] *Commonwealth Parliamentary Debates*, House of Representatives, vol. 30, 26 July 1922, 789–93.
[52] David Walder, *The Chanak Affair* (London: Hutchinson, 1969); Peter M. Sales, 'W. M. Hughes and the Chanak Crisis of 1922', *Australian Journal of Politics and History* 17, no. 3 (1971): 392–405; Paul R. Bartrop, *Bolt from the Blue: Australia, Britain and the Chanak Crisis* (Sydney: Halstead Press, 2002).
[53] Hughes to D. L. George, 20 September 1922: NAA, CP78/32, 1.
[54] Sec of State for Colonies, 27 October 1922: NAA, CP78/32, 1.

prevented the formation of a larger British delegation. The British account of the diplomatic exchanges that led to this outcome must have added insult to injury, since French Prime Minister Raymond Poincaré had apparently insisted that if the Dominions were invited to the proceedings, an invitation would also have to be extended to Tunis and Algiers.[55] Hughes gave vent to his feelings in a searing three-page telegram in which he observed that Chanak had taught the Empire's policy makers no lesson and consequently 'we are to go on in the same old way'.[56] Of Chanak, he pointed out: 'Australia was prepared to go to War—not because she had signed the Treaty of Sevres, but because she was part of the Empire and Britain had rightly or wrongly committed herself to a policy which might lead to war, and the interests of the Empire were involved'. Then came the bluntest of critiques:

> Plain speaking between friends and blood relations is best ... This habit of asking Australia to agree to things when they are done and cannot be undone, and when in practice there is only one course open to us—and that is to support Britain—is one which, if persisted in, will wreck the Empire.[57]

So little had been achieved despite the experience of the First World War. While all parties accepted that many common ties and interests bound them, there had been no advance in securing any satisfactory mechanism that would guarantee Australia's role in shaping the Empire's common policies. Yet there is no indication that this profound disappointment, as bitter as the language he used to describe it, led Hughes to question his fundamental belief that the Empire's interests at once contained and enlarged the national interests of Australia.

Hughes' retrospective view

Is there any evidence that Hughes in his later career reconsidered his views on the respective appeals of Empire and nationalism? Hughes lost the prime ministership in February 1923, his confrontational tactics with London in his last months in office contributing at least in a small measure to his lack of political support at home. Though he served years later in several portfolios including External Affairs, he never regained his former prominence. The backbench gave him time for reflection, and his most sustained treatment of the Empire and especially of Australia's place within it is found in his *The Splendid Adventure*, part memoir, part polemic, published in 1929. According to L. F. Fitzhardinge it was a paean to an imperial empire that was past.[58] It is certainly notable that Hughes' few references to the watershed Balfour Declaration of 1926 are dismissive, though to some minds it promised those very intra-mural arrangements for which he had long fought.

---

[55] Sec of State for Colonies to Hughes, 28 October 1922: NAA, CP78/32, 1.
[56] Hughes to Sec of State for Colonies, 2 November 1922: NAA, CP78/32, 1.
[57] Ibid.
[58] Fitzhardinge, *William Morris Hughes*, vol. 2, 566.

However, while some of its sentiments are clearly dated this publication also contained some quite novel and unconventional suggestions. Its central concern was the current and emerging challenges to the coordination of Empire policy. While a variable combination of 'sentiment, tradition, habit, common interests, mutual forbearance, wise restraint, are the lubricants that make the wheels of Empire machinery go round', these were apparently no longer sufficient for its effective operation.[59] Hughes was candid enough to state that, given the equality of the self-governing units of the Empire, 'to devise a policy that shall serve all equally well and in the making of which all shall have an equal share is a problem that no one has solved'.[60] Although, as could be expected, British policy on Egypt, the Chanak incident, and especially the pernicious doctrine implicit in Woodrow Wilson's Fourteen Points—which, to Hughes' exasperation, had 'a profound effect in all Oriental countries'— were subject to a withering critique, Hughes suggested that longer-term centrifugal trends were at work which should be confronted with new policies.[61]

There were a number of factors, in Hughes' view, that placed imperial unity under great strain. The advent of modern communications, the growth of commercial 'interdependence', and particularly the awakening of the social and economic forces of 'the East', all rendered foreign policy matters of immense moment.[62] Yet the populations of the Dominions had been slow to appreciate these forces, and British statesmen had often seen them only from the point of view of London. In particular, while developments in China were of the greatest importance from the Australian perspective, British policy there tended to focus only upon local British interests.[63]

Foreign policy had also become prey to the fundamental divisions between the two major political forces in Britain; its course was therefore likely to fluctuate widely as a result of their shifting electoral fortunes. Hughes cited as one example Labour leader Ramsay MacDonald's enthusiasm for the Protocol of the League, which threatened to serve as 'the thin edge of the wedge of internationalism' and thus 'was inconsistent with the concept of the British Empire and the relations which must continue to exist between the Parliaments of the Empire'.[64]

To an extent, these divisions were reflected in the differences of opinion to be found amongst political groups in Canada and in South Africa. Meanwhile, in pursuit of that distinct role promised by their new place in the Empire–Commonwealth, Canada and the Irish Free State had appointed ambassadors to foreign states, and Canada served on the Council of the League. As members of the Empire, Hughes observed that they 'have gone considerably farther than

---

[59] William Morris Hughes, *The Splendid Adventure: A Review of Empire Relations* (London: Ernest Benn, 1929), 258.
[60] Ibid., 228.
[61] Ibid., 174.
[62] Ibid., 226–7, 435–7.
[63] Ibid., 226–7.
[64] Ibid., 255.

we think desirable or safe'.[65] Hughes evidently believed that without renovation of the means for imperial coordination, these developments would challenge Empire unity.

Hughes further held that the expedients already suggested—that is, Dominion ministers resident in London and a permanent coordinating secretariat—would not be sufficient. Ministers would not be equals in any imperial cabinet, and with distance their links with their own local political bases would soon weaken. Nor would a greater reliance upon the professionals of the Foreign Office properly isolate foreign policy matters from inappropriate pressures. Hughes reserved his strongest strictures for the foreign and colonial bureaucracies in London who, according to his experience, conducted their affairs with little knowledge of the Dominions.

The solution lay in convincing the populations across the Empire of the importance to their lives and prospects of its continued vitality, which would only occur with the encouragement of a much greater intra-mural familiarity not only among the elites but especially among ordinary people. Though he did not articulate these views very clearly, Hughes was evidently hopeful that such an awareness would convince those populations that as a unified entity the Empire was immensely strong; a reliance upon the Empire would become a fundamental assumption of policy which would thus be insulated from domestic political dispute.

How was this familiarity to be attained? Hughes argued that 'communications are to States what the nervous and vascular systems are to living organisms'; the revolution underway in communications as well as in transport opened 'limitless' possibilities for the Empire, serving to 'bind the people of the Empire more closely together': 'Wireless is to the people of the Empire a veritable gift from the gods'.[66] Indeed, Hughes was prescient enough to remark that 'later television' would occupy this role. On the one hand, knowledge about the Empire would be disseminated easily and quickly; on the other, it would very soon be possible for Downing Street to speak directly to all the leaders of the Dominions. If face-to-face exchanges were necessary then aviation would permit the rapid assembly of leaders from across the world.

So far, Hughes was arguing that, provided these technologies were sensibly employed, a genuine 'Empire standpoint' was possible. However, there were still obstacles to the evolution of the Empire. In particular, Hughes was convinced that caste and religious differences were so profound in India that the country could not sustain self-rule, let alone independence.

Moreover, Hughes' keen interest in advances in technology and in ideas allowed him at least to glimpse a time when the Empire–Commonwealth, as a united entity and also as a major force in the world, might experience transformation or even eclipse. Signs of what he took to be decadence in the Britain of the 1920s were too reminiscent of Rome at a similar stage in its

---

[65] Ibid., 283.
[66] Ibid., 269, 272, 277.

imperial cycle. And Hughes was prepared to contemplate a future when the metropolis of the Empire might move, as populations grew, to Canada or even Australia. Without positing a strict technological determinism, he also suggested, however, that the impact of the rapid changes in communications would be nothing less than revolutionary.[67]

Remarkably, the views of the mature Hughes differed little from his earliest sustained writing on these questions. As part of his occasional pre-war newspaper series, *The Case for Labor*, Hughes had touched intermittently upon international questions, his views undoubtedly influenced by his 1907 return to Britain for a conference on shipping during which visit he had met Ramsay MacDonald and debated with members of the Fabian Society. In his articles he articulated a view of Australia's position little different from that of Alfred Deakin. The Empire was bound, he wrote in 1908, by 'ties of race, religion, political and social institutions, and glorious tradition'. Nevertheless the consequences of imperial policy had such a powerful impact on all constituents of the Empire that their opinions should be consulted directly: 'we cannot any longer go on as we have been doing ... we ought to have a voice on all Imperial questions, on matters of peace and war'.[68]

In 1911 he gave voice to the same fears of Japan that he expressed a decade later. British naval supremacy was the ultimate guarantor for Australia's continued existence as a free, 'white' nation. However, the naval exigencies of the mother country had forced a greater and greater reliance in the Pacific theatre upon the Anglo-Japanese alliance. From the Australian perspective, he was honest enough to admit, this was to seek support through 'a treaty with a nation whom we have openly humiliated by declining to admit its people on terms of equality with those of other civilised nations'.[69]

Conclusion

Despite the strains imposed by the First World War and its management, until the end of his term of office Hughes remained emphatic that the Empire should be so organised that it might achieve that 'unity' that he felt sure was its greatest strength. Prescient in regard to some questions, in other respects he held views that were already dated. By his own lights he was an imperialist and a race patriot and proud to be such. Yet he was unable to appreciate fully the likely impacts of those contemporary trends—many the consequence of the technological innovations achieved during the war—that otherwise attracted his acute interest. Commercial and trading interdependence, the advances in communications and especially wireless technology, and the ever more rapid movement of people across the globe, in his view did not pose any ready challenges to his assumption of Empire identity. Nor were they ever likely to invalidate his beliefs

---

[67] Ibid., 438–9, 327, 429.
[68] W. M. Hughes, *Daily Telegraph* (Sydney), 6 June 1908, 12.
[69] W. M. Hughes, *Daily Telegraph* (Sydney), 27 May 1911, 11.

regarding racial solidarity. While he acknowledged the centrifugal forces at work in Canada and South Africa that were accelerated by the war, and was present in London in the months immediately prior to the creation of Eire, he did not detect the emergence of a more diverse and less coherent Empire–Commonwealth. His later and dismissive remarks on the Balfour Declaration indicated that he saw nothing new in its expression. A redoubtable and implacable proponent of the Australian interest, Hughes scarcely doubted the enduring nesting of that interest in the imperial fold. Though tested in the aftermath of the First World War by the events of 1919–22, these beliefs were never undermined. For Hughes, the Australian interest included the endurance of its Britishness; his nationalism and his imperial sentiment were cut from the single cloth.

Professor James Cotton
University of New South Wales, ADFA, Canberra

'You will not be going to this war': the rejected volunteers of the First Contingent of the Canadian Expeditionary Force

Nic Clarke

University of Ottawa, Ontario, Canada

Between the start of the war in 1914 and commencement of conscription in 1918, tens of thousands of men who volunteered for service in the Canadian Expeditionary Force (CEF) were rejected as unfit for service. However, despite forming both a numerically and socially significant minority with Canada's wartime population, these men are, generally speaking, non-existent in most Canadians' public and academic memories of the Great War. This paper seeks to redress this lapse in public and academic memory by examining the files of over 3050 men rejected for service during the formation of the First Contingent of CEF at Valcartier mobilization camp in August–September 1914. In all, these 3050 individuals account for approximately 60% of the over 5000 men that were ejected from the camp.

Divided into two parts, the first part of this paper describes these files and the information that can be garnered from it. It indicates that as well as offering insight into the physical characteristics of these men, this source also presents a conduit through which to engage with the nature of the CEF medical examination, the ways families might endeavour to undermine their husbands', fathers', brothers' and sons' attempts to enlist, and a rejected volunteer's wider experiences – both during and after the war. The second half of the paper then employs this source material to paint a portrait of these men. In doing so, it demonstrates that there were often no visible indicators – other than the lack of a khaki uniform – that marked rejected men as different from those deemed fit to fight. In engaging with this topic, this section also explores some of the implications rejection had for these men.

MICHAEL DUNNE
Name?

DAVID MANN
David Mann.

DUNNE
What's your marital status, David?

MANN
Single.

DUNNE
And you're of legal age?

MANN
Look, I applied before.

DUNNE
Yeah, I see that and according to this file you were rejected because you have asthma. Do you now have medical clearance on that asthma?
...[Mann angrily indicates he does not, and stresses his patriotism]...

As long as I'm sitting at this desk, you will not be going to this war. Next.[1]

Just like the fictional David Mann, many Canadian men who volunteered for service during the Great War were turned away from recruiting stations for medical reasons. Between the start of the war in 1914 and commencement of conscription in 1917 (Granatstein and Hitsman 1977, 60–104), tens of thousands of men who volunteered for service in the Canadian Expeditionary Force (CEF) suffered this fate. Evidence suggests that between one-fifth and one-quarter of men who volunteered to serve were turned away as unfit.[2] Such numbers made rejected men a numerically significant, and noticeable, minority within Canada's wartime population.

Indeed, the significant position rejected men held in Canada's wartime society is also suggested by the central position that rejected volunteers held in the public consciousness during the Great War. An examination of primary source material from the Great War period reveals a plethora of sources relating to these men and the issues surrounding them. These sources include cartoons, private letters, diaries and memoirs, newspaper articles, military policy documents, and government debates and memoranda.

Despite being a significant minority within Canada's wartime population, rejected volunteers generally speaking are virtually non-existent in both Canada's public and academic memories of the Great War.[3] Paul Gross's *Passchendaele* excepted, dramatic and literary works about the Great War have largely ignored rejected volunteers. Likewise, when historians have mentioned individuals who were rejected for service due to being deemed medically unfit, they have generally done so in passing while exploring other issues such as recruiting or the post-war eugenics movement (see, for example, Morton and Granatstein 1989, 32; Morton 1993, 10; Cook 2007, 24–6; McLaren 1990, 43, 63).

That the history of rejected volunteers has not received more attention is unfortunate not only because these men made up a significant minority within Canada's wartime population, but also because these men present an important means through which to further augment our understanding of the Canadian experience of the Great War. For example, the conflicts between civilians, the medical profession, and the military authorities over what made an individual fit to fight highlight the differing concepts of military fitness held by these groups, many civilians' lack of understanding about the realities of trench warfare, and the often strained state of civil–military relations in Canada during the Great War (Clarke 2009, 144–68).

This paper seeks to rectify the historiographic imbalance by engaging directly with Canada's rejected volunteers. Divided into two parts, the first part of this paper describes one set of source material pertaining to men rejected for service during the Great War – the files of over 3000 men turned away as unfit to serve by the Canadian authorities during the formation of the First Contingent of the Canadian Expeditionary Force (CEF) at Valcartier mobilization camp in August–September 1914. The second half of the paper then employs these files to paint a portrait of these men. In doing so, it demonstrates that there were often no visible indicators – other than the lack of a khaki uniform – that marked rejected men as different from those deemed fit to fight. In engaging with this topic, this section also explores some of the implications that rejection engendered for these men.

Library and Archives Canada holds 3.3 metres of textual records pertaining to CEF volunteers who were not sent beyond Valcartier. Held in 11 volumes and entitled 'Files of CEF volunteers who were rejected' (FVR), this record group contains the personnel files of men whose offers to serve in CEF were rejected, usually because they were deemed to be medically unfit.[4] Although the dates ascribed to this collection run from 1914 through to 1919, the records relate almost exclusively to men who were rejected at Valcartier in August and September 1914. In fact, only 18 documents out of a total of 3068 deal with men who enlisted after 1914 or who had been rejected outside of Valcartier. In all, these 3050 individuals account for approximately 60% of the over 5000 men who were ejected from the camp (Fortescue Duguid 1938, 57).

Stored by surname in approximate alphabetical order, these personnel files contain information that varies widely. In the vast majority of cases, a file contains the rejected man's attestation paper, and, not uncommonly, his pay card (the card used to record the individual's pay details). Double-sided documents, attestation papers are, in the preponderance of cases, only completed on the front page of the document (hereafter referred to as AP1) (Figure 1). This side of the document pertained to a recruit's physical description and religious denomination. As well as providing information about a recruit's physical characteristics and his religious beliefs, the unit to which he belonged is often also recorded in the top left-hand corner of the AP1 (Figures 2 and 4). While the front page of a rejected recruit's attestation is completed, the back page (hereafter AP2) is blank (Figure 3). This side of the document recorded a recruit's personal information, including his marital status, civilian occupation, next of kin, previous military experience, and place of birth. In some cases, AP1 was also incomplete.

Several factors explain the levels of completeness found on these forms. A recruit could be failed at any time during a medical examination. In some instances, failure early in the examination could mean that the rest of the examination was not carried out, especially if medical examiners were faced with large numbers of recruits needing examination.[5] The limited number of medical examiners available and the sea of volunteers that washed across Valcartier in August–September 1914, along with the physical evidence of incomplete attestation papers, suggest that a similar policy was followed in Valcartier.[6] With this in mind, if a recruit failed one of the early tests in the medical examination, later categories on AP1 would not have been completed because the tests would not have taken place. Similarly, if a recruit was declared unfit to serve he would not proceed to the final stage of attestation. AP2, which recorded this final act of enlistment, would thus remain uncompleted.

Human factors can also be held responsible for the incomplete or sparse nature of some of the AP1s. Some Medical Officers (MOs) at Valcartier were far more

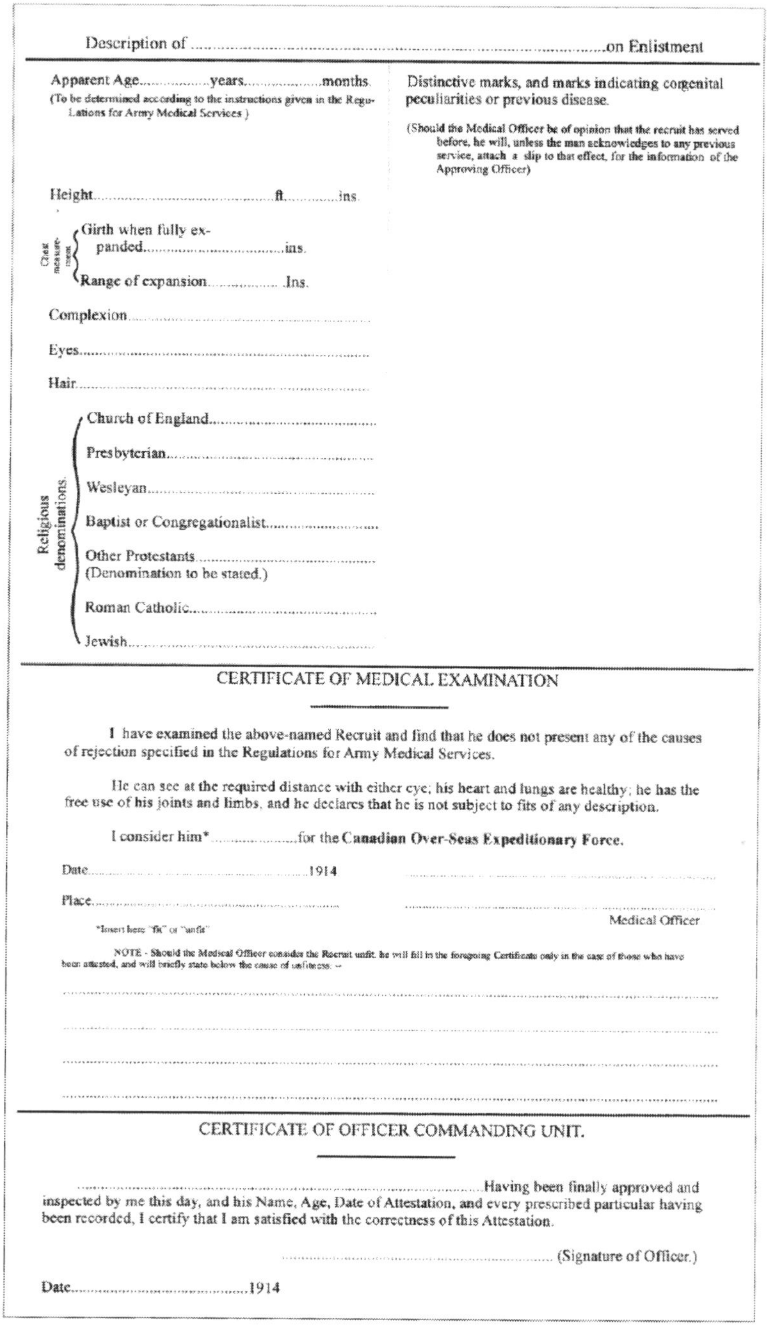

Figure 1. Front of a CEF Attestation paper, 1914 (AP1).

comprehensive than others when recording their observations on recruits' attestation papers. Indeed, in the case of noting distinctive characteristics, responses ranged from MOs recording nothing or writing 'none' to highly detailed descriptions that filled the space provided and flowed over into the surrounding margins.

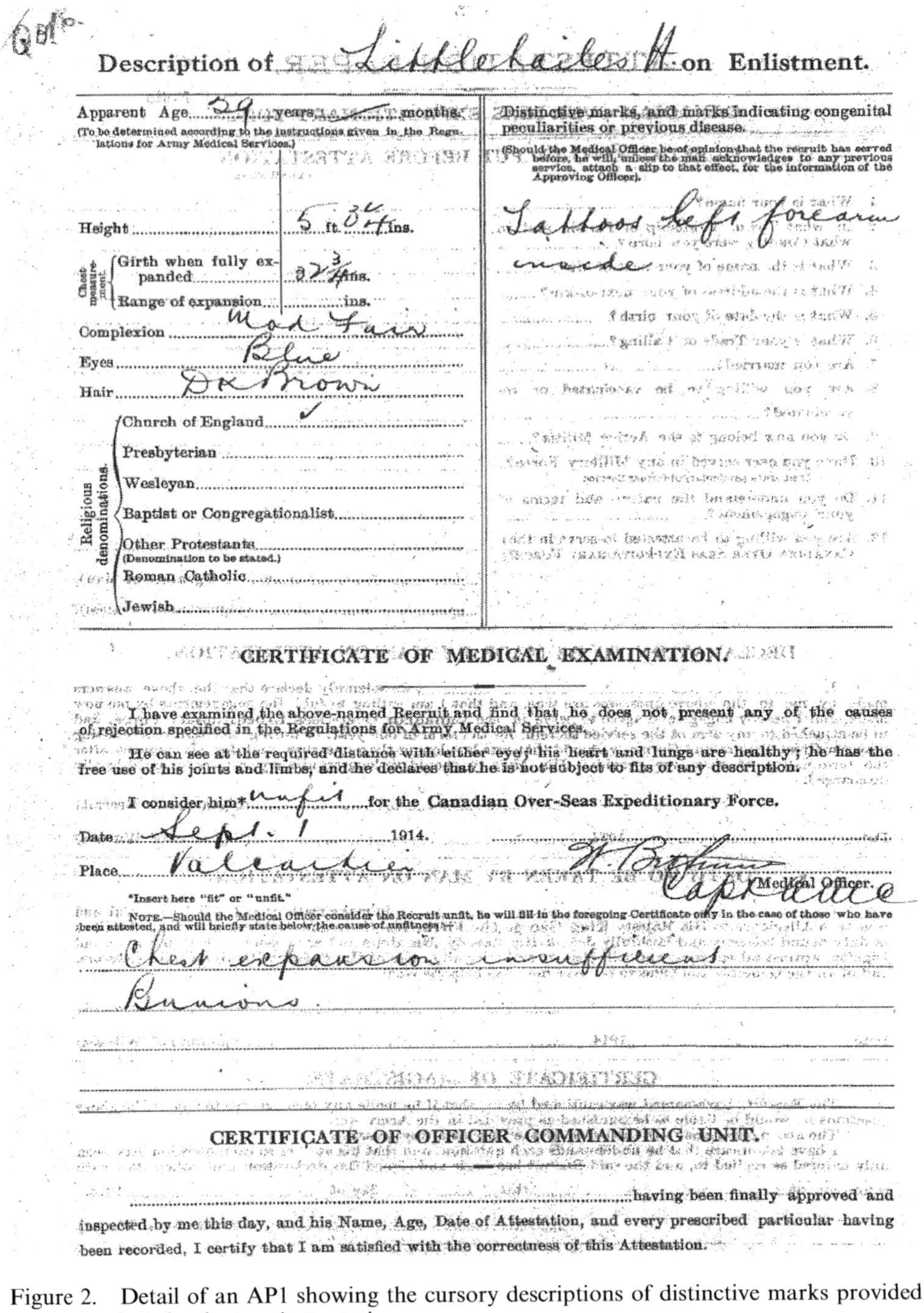

Description of Littlehailes H on Enlistment.

Apparent Age 29 years ... months.
(To be determined according to the instructions given in the Regulations for Army Medical Services.)

Height 5 ft. 8¾ ins.
Chest measurement: Girth when fully expanded 32¾ ins.
Range of expansion ..... ins.
Complexion Med Fair
Eyes Blue
Hair D Brown

Religious denominations:
- Church of England ✓
- Presbyterian
- Wesleyan
- Baptist or Congregationalist
- Other Protestants (Denomination to be stated.)
- Roman Catholic
- Jewish

Distinctive marks, and marks indicating congenital peculiarities or previous disease.
(Should the Medical Officer be of opinion that the recruit has served before, he will, unless the man acknowledges to any previous service, attach a slip to that effect, for the information of the Approving Officer.)

Tattoos left forearm inside

CERTIFICATE OF MEDICAL EXAMINATION.

I have examined the above-named Recruit and find that he does not present any of the causes of rejection specified in the Regulations for Army Medical Services.

He can see at the required distance with either eye; his heart and lungs are healthy; he has the free use of his joints and limbs, and he declares that he is not subject to fits of any description.

I consider him *unfit for the Canadian Over-Seas Expeditionary Force.

Date Sept 1 1914.
Place Valcartier   H. Brohim
                                    Capt ......
                                    Medical Officer.

*Insert here "fit" or "unfit."

NOTE.—Should the Medical Officer consider the Recruit unfit, he will fill in the foregoing Certificate only in the case of those who have been attested, and will briefly state below the cause of unfitness.

Chest expansion insufficient
Bunions

CERTIFICATE OF OFFICER COMMANDING UNIT.

.... having been finally approved and inspected by me this day, and his Name, Age, Date of Attestation, and every prescribed particular having been recorded, I certify that I am satisfied with the correctness of this Attestation.

Figure 2. Detail of an AP1 showing the cursory descriptions of distinctive marks provided on some rejected volunteers' attestation papers.

For example, while some doctors might note that a recruit was tattooed, others would take considerable time and effort to describe in considerable detail the position and nature of each tattoo (Figures 2 and 4).

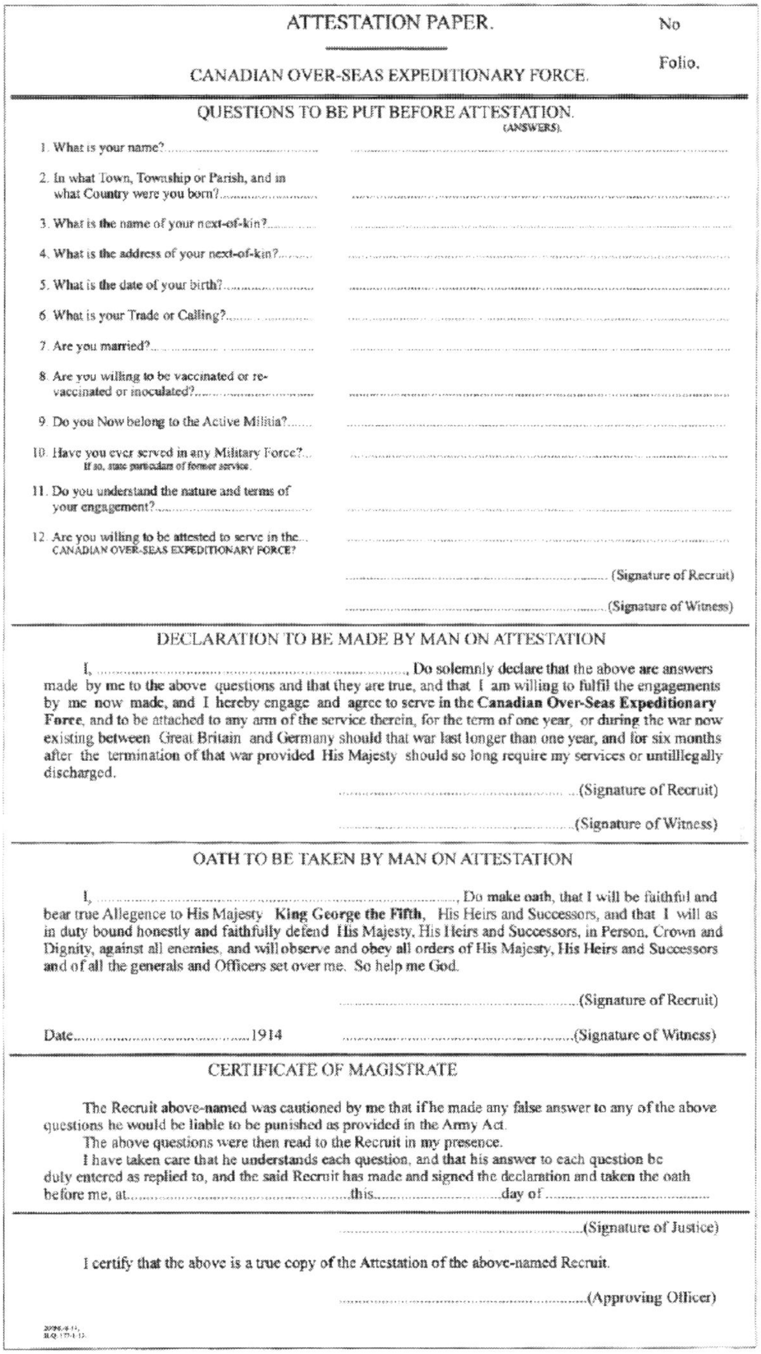

ATTESTATION PAPER. No

Folio.

CANADIAN OVER-SEAS EXPEDITIONARY FORCE.

QUESTIONS TO BE PUT BEFORE ATTESTATION.

(ANSWERS).

1. What is your name?..

2. In what Town, Township or Parish, and in what Country were you born?..

3. What is the name of your next-of-kin?..

4. What is the address of your next-of-kin?..

5. What is the date of your birth?..

6. What is your Trade or Calling?..

7. Are you married?..

8. Are you willing to be vaccinated or re-vaccinated or inoculated?..

9. Do you Now belong to the Active Militia?..

10. Have you ever served in any Military Force?..
If so, state particulars of former service.

11. Do you understand the nature and terms of your engagement?..

12. Are you willing to be attested to serve in the CANADIAN OVER-SEAS EXPEDITIONARY FORCE?..

.... (Signature of Recruit)

.... (Signature of Witness)

DECLARATION TO BE MADE BY MAN ON ATTESTATION

I, ..., Do solemnly declare that the above are answers made by me to the above questions and that they are true, and that I am willing to fulfil the engagements by me now made, and I hereby engage and agree to serve in the **Canadian Over-Seas Expeditionary Force**, and to be attached to any arm of the service therein, for the term of one year, or during the war now existing between Great Britain and Germany should that war last longer than one year, and for six months after the termination of that war provided His Majesty should so long require my services or untilllegally discharged.

....(Signature of Recruit)

....(Signature of Witness)

OATH TO BE TAKEN BY MAN ON ATTESTATION

I, ..., Do make oath, that I will be faithful and bear true Allegence to His Majesty **King George the Fifth**, His Heirs and Successors, and that I will as in duty bound honestly and faithfully defend His Majesty, His Heirs and Successors, in Person, Crown and Dignity, against all enemies, and will observe and obey all orders of His Majesty, His Heirs and Successors and of all the generals and Officers set over me. So help me God.

....(Signature of Recruit)

Date..1914 ....(Signature of Witness)

CERTIFICATE OF MAGISTRATE

The Recruit above-named was cautioned by me that if he made any false answer to any of the above questions he would be liable to be punished as provided in the Army Act.

The above questions were then read to the Recruit in my presence.

I have taken care that he understands each question, and that his answer to each question be duly entered as replied to, and the said Recruit has made and signed the declaration and taken the oath before me, at..this..day of ....

....(Signature of Justice)

I certify that the above is a true copy of the Attestation of the above-named Recruit.

....(Approving Officer)

Figure 3. Back of CEF Attestation paper, 1914 (AP2).

The level of detail provided by MOs when describing a recruit's reason(s) for rejection was also similarly wide-ranging. Some MOs only stated the reason, without providing any additional explanation or detail; others went much further. Capt.

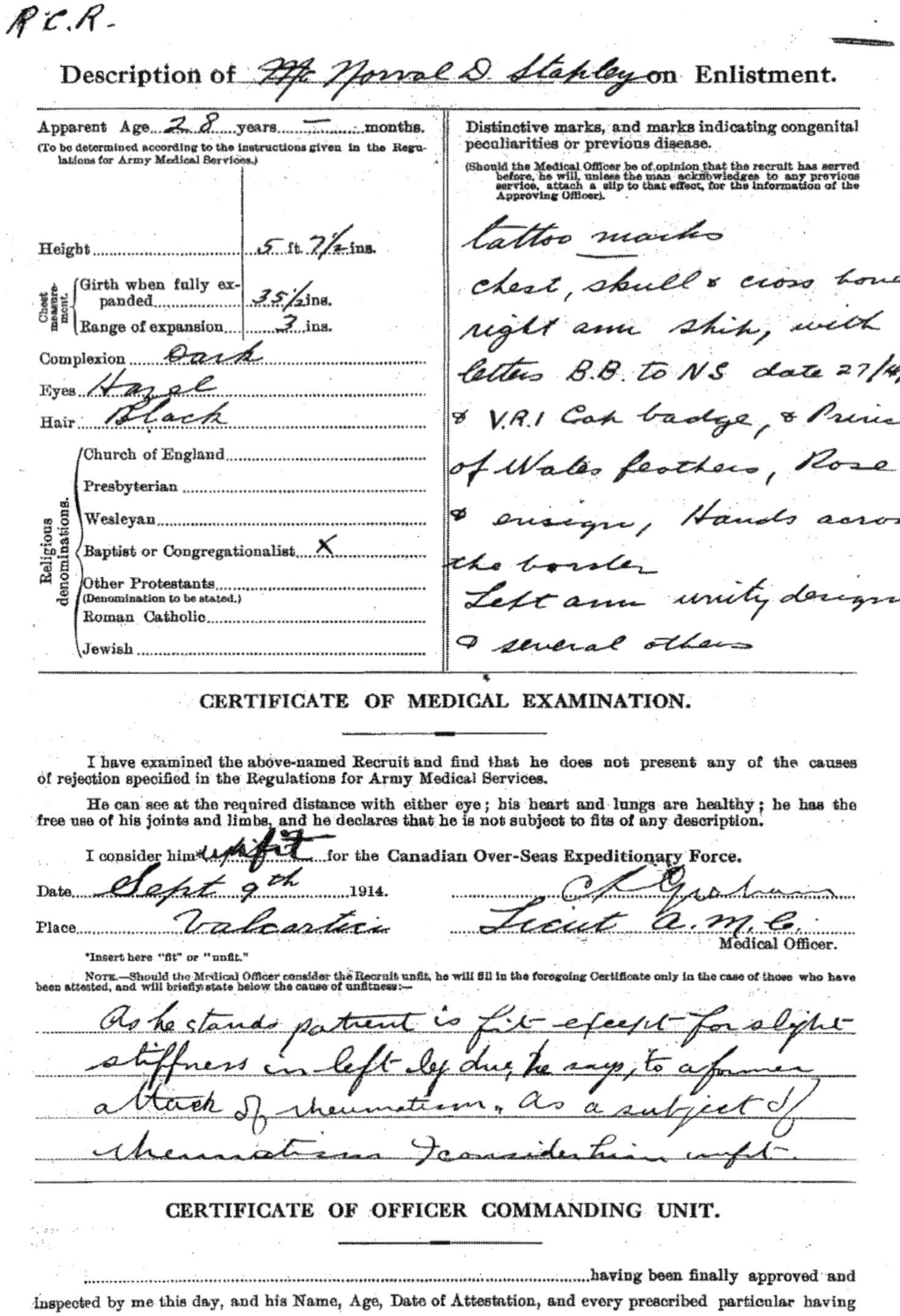

R.C.R.

Description of *Pte Norval D Stapley* on Enlistment.

Apparent Age 28 years ___ months.
(To be determined according to the instructions given in the Regulations for Army Medical Services.)

Height: 5 ft. 7½ ins.
Chest measurement: Girth when fully expanded 35½ ins. Range of expansion 3 ins.
Complexion: Dark
Eyes: Hazel
Hair: Black

Religious denominations:
- Church of England
- Presbyterian
- Wesleyan
- Baptist or Congregationalist X
- Other Protestants (Denomination to be stated.)
- Roman Catholic
- Jewish

Distinctive marks, and marks indicating congenital peculiarities or previous disease.
(Should the Medical Officer be of opinion that the recruit has served before, he will, unless the man acknowledges to any previous service, attach a slip to that effect, for the information of the Approving Officer.)

tattoo marks chest, skull & cross bones right arm ship, with letters B.B. to N.S. date 27/4/. & V.R.I. Cap badge, & Prince of Wales feathers, Rose & ensign, Hands across the border. Left arm unity design & several others

CERTIFICATE OF MEDICAL EXAMINATION.

I have examined the above-named Recruit and find that he does not present any of the causes of rejection specified in the Regulations for Army Medical Services.

He can see at the required distance with either eye; his heart and lungs are healthy; he has the free use of his joints and limbs, and he declares that he is not subject to fits of any description.

I consider him *unfit* for the Canadian Over-Seas Expeditionary Force.

Date: Sept 9th 1914.
Place: Valcartier
Lieut A.M.C.
Medical Officer.

*Insert here "fit" or "unfit."

NOTE.—Should the Medical Officer consider the Recruit unfit, he will fill in the foregoing Certificate only in the case of those who have been attested, and will briefly state below the cause of unfitness:—

As he stands patient is fit except for slight stiffness in left leg due, he says, to a former attack of rheumatism. As a subject of rheumatism I consider him unfit.

CERTIFICATE OF OFFICER COMMANDING UNIT.

....having been finally approved and inspected by me this day, and his Name, Age, Date of Attestation, and every prescribed particular having

Figure 4. Detail of AP1 showing a comprehensive description of a rejected volunteer's tattoos. This attestation paper is also of interest because of the detailed reasoning the medical examiner gives for declaring the recruit unfit. Also note the unit designation 'R.C.R.' (Royal Canadian Regiment) in the top left corner of the page.

Maynard, for example, generally provided only the most basic description of the impairment – 'eyes', 'weak heart', 'lungs bad' – that caused him to reject a recruit.[7] Other doctors provided the general reason for rejection while also describing the extent of the recruit's impairment. Capt. MacDermot, on the other hand, usually went into some detail when describing what ailed the men he rejected. For example, he wrote the following on the attestation paper of W. Ostarvet, 'Complains of intense pains in legs on marching. Is unable to walk on toes cannot raise himself hardly. Eyesight poor, especially left side. False teeth in upper jaw'.[8]

In the case of men rejected on account of their substandard eyesight, a number of doctors would include the unsuccessful recruit's visual acuity measurements. When rejecting C.A. McLuskey due to his eyesight, Capt. H.E. MacDermot recorded the 20-year-old's vision as 20/60 in his right eye and 20/120 in his left eye. Likewise, in the case of recruits with respiratory and/or circulatory problems, many doctors identified the exact nature of the illness. Capt. J.S. Nelson, for example, diagnosed 24-year-old William Keller's heart problems as endocarditis (inflammation of the endocardium).[9] It would appear that medical examiners also used detailed explanations when seeking to defend their decisions to rejected men who appeared to be fit for service. Lt. C. Graham, for instance, wrote the following on the 28-year-old Stanley Norval's attestation paper: '[a]s he stands patient is fit except for slight stiffness in left leg due, he says, to a former attack of rheumatism. As a subject of rheumatism I consider him unfit' (Figure 4).[10]

Some of the more meticulous MOs did not stop at giving detailed descriptions of a rejected volunteer's impairment, but went on to provide mini-case and personal histories of the men they examined. Capt. MacDermot wrote the following when explaining his decision to reject 41-year-old W. Chavis: 'Left eye almost sightless – had an iridectomy [removal of part of or the entire iris] two years ago. Has seen service in Boer War & seems a very good man. No other defects'. MacDermot also noted the following on the attestation paper of one E. Lesaux: 'Chest measurement only 31.5″. Right lung shows rather deficient expulsion. Had pneumonia of the right lung six months ago. Hearing on right side defective'.[11] While some medical examiners recorded their subjects' histories, others provided their opinions about a recruit's suitability for service despite his impairment. Capt. Cockburn, for example, noted that although 21-year-old Charles Holy's heart condition made him unfit for service overseas, he 'would be alright for home service'. Likewise, 27-year-old N. Thom's attestation paper stated 'defective eyesight, try him in cook house'.[12]

In a number of cases, more than one, and sometimes three or more, reason(s) were provided by a medical examiner when explaining why a recruit was unfit to serve. Timothy Devonport, for example, was rejected as unfit not only on the grounds of his (very) poor vision, but also because he had varicose veins and a heart condition. Similarly, Harold Newbery was rejected not only because his right forefinger (his trigger finger) had been amputated at the first joint, but also because he suffered from eczema and hemorrhoids.[13] Medical examiners' methods of recording multiple impairments – usually one after the other, with little in the way of explanation – makes it unclear if they considered any particular impairments they listed to be the pre-eminent reason for a recruit's rejection. What these lists do indicate, especially since the impairments included in them are not obviously connected, is that some medical examiners at Valcartier were conducting thorough examinations of the men who passed before them. Based on the list of Devonport's disqualifying impairments, for example, it is possible to ascertain that the 30-year-old experienced an eye test, had been examined naked, and had been subjected to a stethoscopic examination.

MOs' explanations offered hints about the nature of the tests conducted during the medical examination. Such information is of considerable importance, given that little direct evidence exists on how the medical examinations were carried out in the summer of 1914. Twenty-year-old H. Bowden's attestation paper, for example, stated that he was unfit because he was 'flat-footed, unable to hop across the room'.[14] The observation that Bowden was 'unable to hop across the room' is enlightening because it indicates that medical examiners at Valcartier were using a mobility test set down in the British medical examination. even though this test was not recorded in Canadian documentation at the start of the conflict.[15]

Less commonly, other documents would be enclosed in the file. These documents included letters or telegrams written by a recruit or his family, and correspondence between militia authorities regarding the recruit. On rare occasions, files would also include a recruit's full medical history or post-war correspondence between the individual and the Canadian government. When discovered, such sources often offer compelling insight into a volunteer's wider experiences and the ways his family might endeavour to subvert his attempts to enlist. For example, Mrs. J.K. Shinn wrote directly to Sam Hughes asking him to have her son, Max, discharged due to her belief that 'he was not strong enough', and because of an injury he had suffered to his toe. She further implied that Max had joined up in a fit of depression because he could not find any work. Not content to end her case for Max's discharge there, Mrs. Shinn sought to pull on Hughes' heart strings by stating 'I just lost a dear daughter June a year ago and it is pretty hard now to loose [sic] a son too'. Shinn was discharged soon after.[16] Examples such as this provide an invaluable means by which to explore the mechanisms through which the Canadian military interacted with civilian society.

In one heartrending case, J.W. Graham, Fire Chief of the City of Ottawa, wrote to Col. Victor A.S. Williams, Commandant of Valcartier, requesting the discharge of Ivan Thomas on compassionate grounds. Graham explained that Ivan's older brother, Bernard, had recently succumbed to injuries he had received while fighting a fire in the city. Bernard's death, Graham stated, had devastated his mother, leaving her on 'the verge of collapse and ... necessitat[ing] the constant care of her physician'. As a result, Mrs. Thomas's family and friends 'fear[ed] the result when Ivan [who had been granted compassionate leave] leaves her to return to camp'. Given such circumstances, Graham requested, '[a]t the earnest solicitation of his [Ivan's] mother', that Ivan be relieved of his military duties and be permitted to remain with his mother. Showing considerable empathy for Ivan's position, the Fire Chief noted 'the young man is in a very trying and unenviable position'. Ivan was 'keenly anxious to fight his country's battles at the front and took particular pride in being chosen for the First Canadian Expeditionary Force', yet Graham believed that Ivan 'would never forgive himself for not requesting permission to be allowed to remain at home on account of the subsequent occurrences and his mother's grave condition'. Ivan, like Max Shinn, was soon discharged.[17]

If some letters offered insight into rejected volunteers' personal experiences and family tragedies, post-war correspondence was especially enlightening since it indicated that the rejection for service in 1914 continued to affect men long after shot and shell had ceased to be fired in Europe. The files of Roy Coates and Charles Garner contained correspondence between the men and the Department of Veteran's

Affairs which took place in 1951. Both men were seeking proof that they had volunteered to serve, only to have been turned away at Valcartier.[18]

While some files contain extensive material, others are much more limited. Some only contain a statement noting that the individual had been struck off the unit's strength. Often handwritten, these struck-off-strength (SOS) statements followed a set formula, providing the date the recruit was struck off a unit's books and a general statement as to the reason he had been rejected for service. In some cases envelopes are empty, which it seems was a result of files not being replaced after having been removed for review, copying of files, or a recruit's later acceptance for service. In the case of files that had been removed for review, the most information that can be gleaned about the individual is his name, unit, and reason for rejection.[19] In the case of envelopes emptied because the individual had been later accepted for service, regimental numbers and the battalion in which the individual was enlisted were noted on the envelope. Recorded under the 'Rejected at Valcartier 1st Contingent', Thomas Francis Daly's empty file envelope is 'for C.E.F. Documents see [regimental number] 1048094 Pte [Private] Daly Thomas Francis 242 Bttn [Battalion]'.[20]

Indeed, belying the lack of material they contain, the envelopes of rejected men later accepted for service often provide information about the fate of the individual to which they are attached. Written under George R. Manning's regimental number and battalion is the stark comment 'Died 6-5-18'.[21] In another instance, J. Bramball's SOS statement was accompanied in his otherwise empty file envelope with a notice from the Canadian Convalescent Hospital Record Card for Toyleth Hill, Liverpool. The card stated that Bramball had been admitted to the hospital suffering from a gunshot wound to the back.[22] Likewise, C.E. Lamond's equally sparse file noted that his left leg had been amputated at Granville Canada Special Hospital on 12 July 1917, as the result of a gunshot wound he had received. This kind of data, limited as it may seem, is important, since it proves that rejection at Valcartier in 1914 did not necessarily close the door to service. Indeed, faced with an increasingly acute manpower crisis as the Great War continued, Canadian military authorities repeatedly lowered the minimum physical standards for service. This meant that many men rejected as unfit for service in August–September 1914 were later deemed fit to serve (Clarke 2009, 69–82, 326–31).

The historical record left behind by these documents makes it possible to sketch a picture of the physical characteristics, and reasons for rejection, of many men turned away at Valcartier in August–September 1914. The rest of this paper shall focus on just that.

So what characterized rejected volunteers in August–September 1914? In matters of faith, Anglicans predominated, making up 43.9% of 2294 rejected volunteers whose attestation papers recorded a faith.[23] Roman Catholics and Presbyterians followed, making up 22.7% and 18.3% of respondents, respectively, with the Methodist Church coming in a poor fourth, at 8%.[24] These proportions are in general agreement with those found in the CEF for the years 1914–18, except with regard to the numbers of Anglicans and Methodists in each dataset. Records indicate that 31% of CEF members were Anglican, 23% Roman Catholic, 21% Presbyterian, and 14% Methodists.[25] While difference in proportion of Anglicans and Methodists in each dataset might result from the differing sizes of the two samples, historical factors could also be involved. The heavy weighing of Anglicans in the rejected volunteer sample may reflect the flood of English-born recruits that swelled the ranks of the CEF's First Contingent (Brown and Loveridge 1996, 303; Morton 1993,

278–9). Equally, the relatively low number of Methodists found among rejected volunteers might reflect the strong support the members of this church demonstrated for liberal pacifism during the pre-war period.[26]

Altogether, 386 (21.2%) of the 1822 men whose attestation papers recorded distinctive characteristics were tattooed. The level of tattooing varied from individual to individual, ranging from dots or simple initials on hands and forearms through to heavy tattooing on arms, legs, and torso. The tattoos borne by these men offer some indication of their personal histories, social backgrounds, and individual affiliations. W. Hadden and M.H. McLeod's sectarian loyalties were, for example, proclaimed by the Orange Order scars they bore over their hearts.[27] James Scott Simmons, on the other hand, expressed his religious affiliations with the words 'Coronation Lodge' on his left forearm.[28] In what can only been seen as an expression of Canadian identity, four men – Ulysses Adlerard, Samuel Jones, Robert W. Wilson, and Ernest Williams – had maple leafs tattooed on their arms.[29] Another three men had the word 'Canada' etched on their bodies.[30] Nor were such national symbols limited to the Dominion of Canada or the countries that comprised the United Kingdom. Nine men bore either an American flag and/or eagle on their bodies, while one individual, Antonio Lapierre, had the French tricolour tattooed on his left arm.[31]

In addition to proclaiming sectarian and national loyalties, many men who had marked their bodies with tattoos were proclaiming their membership in specific and highly masculine groups that were often identified with strenuous physical labour and danger. The tattoos of a number of individuals, for instance, indicated that they had spent at least part of their lives in front of the mast. The heavily tattooed Stanley Norval commemorated his voyage from Barbados to Nova Scotia by having a ship with the letters 'BB to NS' underneath it on his right arm. Another 65 men wore other tattoos traditionally associated with sailors – such as ships, anchors, and depictions of sailors – on their bodies. In addition to demonstrating that a number of rejected volunteers had been seafarers, the tattoos worn by three men also directly identified them as having had prior military experience. Reginald Neor, for instance, wore, one assumes with great pride, the words 'Soldier South Africa 1899–1902' on his right forearm. Similarly, 53-year-old Joseph Clamondou bore 'Pensioners of Transval [Sic] War' on his right forearm.[32] The aforementioned Stanley Norval, on the other hand, had the cap badge of his regiment, the Royal Canadian Regiment, tattooed on his right forearm.

Evidence of prior military service extends beyond rejected volunteers' tattoos. Medical examiners noted on attestation papers of four rejected men that the individual in question had seen prior military service. William Chavis, Lawrence Eaves, and George Jobin's had served in the Anglo-Boer War, while the one-armed bugler Martin Wilson was listed as a veteran of the 1885 North-West campaign.[33] This type of information is highly useful, since the section regarding prior military experience was seldom completed on the attestation papers of men rejected at Valcartier.

The average age of men rejected for service at Valcartier during this period was 26.7 years, with a median age of 24 years (Figure 5). The majority (96.6%) of rejected volunteers in the sample fell well within the CEF's age limits of 18–45 years.[34] Of 2413 men whose age was recorded, only 37 individuals (1.5%) were listed being under age, while an equally paltry 46 (1.9%) were said to have been over 44. In fact, the average age of these men was within 0.4 years of the age (26.3 years) recorded for CEF members over the entire period of the Great War (Morton 1993, 279).

As well as resting comfortably within the CEF's age requirements, the majority of rejected volunteers were also well within the CEF's minimum physical standards. With an average chest expansion of 35.8 inches (median 36 inches) in diameter, most rejected volunteers were comfortably over the CEF's requirement that a recruit be able to puff out his chest to at least 33.5 inches. In fact, of the sample of 2202 individuals whose attestation papers recorded chest size, only 260 men (11.8%) had expanded chest sizes below the 33.5 inches. Of these 260 individuals, 130 (50%) failed to meet the minimum requirements by an inch or less (Figure 6). Importantly, preliminary data drawn attestation papers of over 50,000 men who served in the CEF between 1914 and 1918 indicates that the average chest measurement of those individuals who met the 1914 requirements for chest expansion was 36.6 inches (median 36.5 inches).[35] Thus, the difference in chest measurement between men rejected as unfit to serve in 1914 and their successful colleagues was less than one inch.[36]

Similar observations can be made with regard to rejected volunteers' heights. With an average height of 66.8 inches (5'7"/169.7 cm) (median 67 inches), the majority of these men were well above the CEF's 1914 minimum height requirement of 63 inches (5'3"/160 cm) (Figure 7). In fact, of the 2282 men whose attestation papers recorded a height measurement, only 135 (5.9%) stood below 63 inches. Of these 135 men, 85 (63%) measured an inch or less under the minimum. The shortest

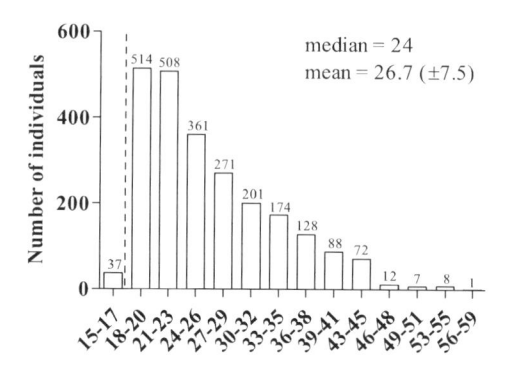

Figure 5. Age of Rejected Men (years).
Note: Measurements to the left of the dotted line are below CEF minimum.

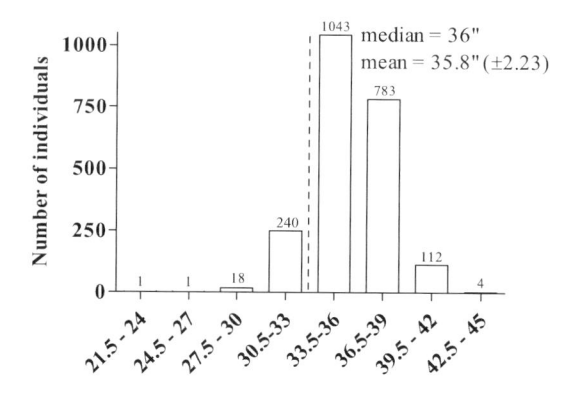

Figure 6. Diameter of Rejected Men's Expanded Chests (inches).
Note: Measurements to the left of the dotted line are below CEF minimum.

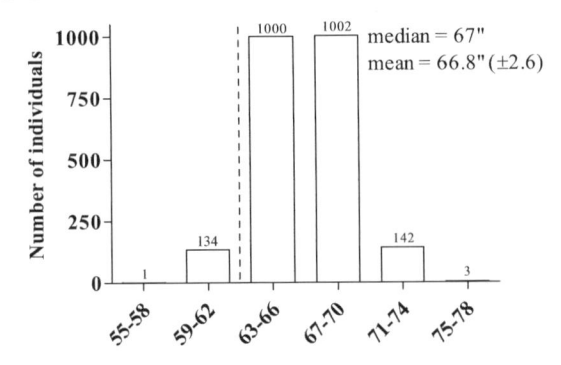

Figure 7. Recorded Height of Rejected Men (inches).
Note: Measurements to the left of the dotted line are below CEF minimum.

individual in the sample stood at 56 inches (4'8"/142.2 cm); however, he was 15 years old, and thus had yet to reach his full adult height.

If one removes the 135 men who stood below the CEF's minimum height requirements from the calculation of the average height of men rejected as unfit to serve at Valcartier in 1914, the average height of these men rises to 67.1 inches (170.4 cm).[37] This places the average height of rejected volunteers on a par with that of Canadian-born members of the CEF. A recent study has indicated that the average height for CEF members born in the 1870s and 1880s was 67.4 inches (5'7"/171.2 cm), an average that declines slightly to 67.2 inches (5'7"/170.7 cm) for those born in the 1890s (Cranfield and Inwood 2007). No systematic study of the height of British-born members of the CEF, or, indeed, the British Expeditionary Force, has been conducted. However, it is likely that the height of CEF's British-born recruits was similar to that of their Canadian-born comrades.[38] This observation is important when it is called to mind that approximately 60% of the CEF's First Contingent was British-born (Brown and Loveridge 1996, 303).

The lack of noticeable difference between rejected volunteers and those accepted as fit to serve can be further stressed by examining the reasons men were deemed unfit to serve at Valcartier in August–September 1914. Of the 3050 men examined, 2534 (83.1%) were rejected because they were deemed medically unfit. The balance of individuals had either been discharged for non-medical reasons such as misconduct or family protest, or had records that did not clearly indicate why they had been rejected.[39]

The four most common reasons for rejection recorded were substandard eyesight (24.4%), poor teeth (9.8%), varicose veins (6.5%), and varicocele (6%). Hernias (4.6%) and heart problems (4.5%) were also common reasons for rejection (Table 2).[40] Of these reasons for rejection, the two most common – substandard eyesight and poor teeth – would not have been immediately obvious to the casual observer. Not all men whose eyesight failed to meet the stringent requirements of the CEF in 1914 wore – or needed to wear – glasses. In fact, some of these men would have been unaware that they suffered from any visual deficiency.[41] Likewise, until he opened his mouth, the dental deficits of a man rejected on account of his bad, or lack of, teeth would have been all but invisible to those around him. This would have been especially true in the case of an individual who wore a well-fitted pair of dentures.

Table 1. Summary of the data on height, chest size and age of 3050 men rejected at Valcartier Mobilisation Camp, August to September 1914.

	N	N*	Median	Average (mean)	Standard deviation
Height (in)	2282	768	67	66.8	2.6
Expanded chest (in)	2202	848	36	35.8	2.23
Age (years)	2413	637	24	26.7	7.52

N = number of responses; N* = missing values.

Table 2. Reasons for rejection.[54]

Reason for Rejection	Number	Percentage
Appearance	45	1.25
Chest	156	4.33
Flat Feet	87	2.41
General Foot Problem	49	1.36
Height	75	2.08
Haemorrhoids	54	1.5
Hernia	166	4.6
Heart Condition	161	4.47
Injury	39	1.08
Medically Unfit, reason not specified	197	5.46
Protest	183	5.08
Request	40	1.11
Sexually Transmitted Disease	80	2.22
Teeth	354	9.82
Undesirable	96	2.66
Underage	42	1.17
Undersize	70	1.94
Varicose Veins	235	6.52
Varicocele	215	5.96
Vision	879	24.38
Other	278	7.71
Amputation	12	
Anaemia	2	
Arm problem, not elsewhere categorised	6	
Arthritis	4	
Back Problems	4	
Blackouts/convulsions	2	
Cancer	3	
Chest lesions	1	
Chronic ulcers	1	
Clinical history bad	1	
Commanding Officer's recommendation	5	
Deformity	16	
Does not read/speak English	3	
Does not want to go	7	
Duty complete	5	
Enlarged testicle/s	4	
Gall stones	2	
General debility	1	

(*continued*)

Table 2. (*Continued*).

Reason for Rejection	Number	Percentage
Genital problem, not elsewhere categorised	4	
Hearing	16	
Hydrocele	13	
Inflamed lymph node	1	
Inflamed vaccination scar	1	
Kidney problems	2	
Leg problem, not elsewhere categorised	8	
Lungs	23	
Malaria	1	
Mental Competency	9	
Not approved	1	
Ostesitis	1	
Overage	28	
Over plus	2	
Pain	3	
Paralysis, facial	1	
Physically unfit	3	
Post-operative pain/recent operation	7	
Poorly nourished	1	
Recent appendicitis	3	
Recovering from measles	1	
Refused examination	1	
Refused for family reasons	1	
Refused oath	5	
Rheumatism	12	
Sinus problems	2	
Skin Condition	16	
Thyroid	8	
Tuberculosis	11	
Typhoid phlebitis	1	
Under weight	1	
Undescended testicle	3	
Urethritis	8	
Illegible, unclear, or not recorded	104	2.89
Total	3605	100

Of the other four reasons for rejection mentioned, three – varicose veins, varicocele, and hernias – would have been hidden to all but the most intimate of observers by a man's clothing, while heart problems would have been, for all intents and purposes, invisible.[42] Those with such hidden or invisible impairments were not readily identifiable as physically unfit by members of the wider public. Advertising one's subjection to these medical conditions did not always help. Many civilians did not consider bad teeth, substandard eyesight, limited height, flat feet, varicose veins, or hernias to be valid reasons for keeping a man from serving his country.[43] Furthermore, echoing the above comments about eyesight, a 1915 report on men with disabilities examined by a medical board at Canadian Headquarters in Shorncliffe, England, noted that some men were unaware that they had varicose veins (Primrose 1915, 856).

While invisible impairments may have been common among the men rejected as unfit to serve by medical officers at Valcartier, more obvious impairments were not.

Potentially visible physical deformities (congenital and traumatic) only occurred 16 times (0.4%) in the records, while amputations were even rarer (0.3%). In the case of physical deformities, the most common condition recorded was spinal curvature (five instances), followed by deformities of the feet and legs (each with three instances), the knees (two instances), and finally the chest, hands, and toes (one instance). Of the 12 instances of amputations recorded as reasons for rejection, eight involved the removal, either wholly or partially, of a single digit, and one each the removal of an arm, a hand, a testicle, and the toes on one foot.

That many rejected volunteers were not visibly different from those deemed fit to fight is also evidenced by other factors. First, there was the employment of false claims of disability by fit men unwilling to experience the trenches in order to avoid facing public denigration for not enlisting.[44] Second, the provision of badges to legitimately rejected men that at once identified them has having offered their services, while concurrently acting as a tool to help recruiters identify those men who had not attempted to enlist.[45]

Coming in a variety of forms, the badges provided to rejected volunteers were originally supplied to rejected volunteers by municipal recruiting committees and individual regiments.[46] However, the resulting sea of badges that inundated Canada in the first two years of the war 'led to confusion and uncertainty as to whether a badge was genuine and opened the way for counterfeiting badges to avoid service' (Johnson 1995. 77). As a result, the provisioning of identifying badges to rejected volunteers was taken over by the Canadian government as part of its move to regulate war service badges in August 1916.[47]

In laying out the conditions surrounding the granting of badges to rejected men the Dominion government made the following statement regarding who were excluded:

> In no case will a badge be issued to persons who have been rejected on account of temporary disability, or who are obviously unfit for service in, and have not served with, the Expeditionary Forces, for example, men who are totally blind, crippled, paralytic etc.[48]

With this provision, which was included in all succeeding legislation relating to the issue of war badges, the Dominion government implicitly acknowledged that these badges were intended to shield those who looked fit to serve against any suggestion that they had shirked their obligations to King and Country. The *obviously* unfit – those with visible impairments that were recognized as disabling by the general population – did not need a badge that identified them as incapable of shouldering a rifle in defence of home and hearth. Rather, those who needed the protection of these badges were those who were not visibly different from their khaki clothed brethren. Indeed, this short 45-word proviso not only underlines the fact that the vast majority of Canadians' perception of martial (in)ability and disability more generally was founded on visual indicators, but also that there were many men rejected by the military authorities who were not instantly recognizable as unfit to serve by civilians and recruiting officers.

Importantly, the Dominion government's proviso also indicates why, generally speaking, the majority of men rejected at Valcartier in August–September 1914 were not visibly different from those men deemed fit to shoulder a rifle. When it came to recruiting, an informal weeding-out process began on the streets of Canadian towns and cities before men faced any type of formal medical examination. Recruiting officers did not approach men, whom they deemed, based on visual inspection, unfit to serve. Likewise, they turned away such individuals when they attempted to enlist. The same can be said with regard to informal recruiters. Civilians placed pressure to enlist on men who looked fit to fight, not those who were obviously unable to. The prime candidates for such filtering were the visibly different; those individuals whom civilians would have readily recognized as 'unfit': those afflicted with the paralysis, severe deformity, debilitating sensory impairments, or clear intellectual or psychological impairments.

To make such an observation is not to imply that men with noticeable physical impairments never made it to Valcartier in 1914, because some in fact did.[49] Rather, the observation offers some explanation as to why so many rejected men at Valcartier were not visibly different from those men accepted for combat. Generally speaking, the visibly impaired had already been removed from the sea of men that descended on the mobilization camp in the summer of 1914, leaving only those who looked fit to fight.

Men rejected for service on account of hidden or unrecognized impairments were often – those with identifying badges not withstanding – subjected to condemnation from people who believed that they were shirking their responsibilities to king and country. Those men who attempted to defend themselves by drawing attention to their infirmities were either not believed, or were told they had not tried hard enough. Martin Colby, for example, described his experiences on the streets of Toronto during the Great War as 'hell'. Constantly questioned by strangers as to why he was not in the khaki, Colby's explanations that he had been rejected on multiple occasions due to his limited hearing were countered with 'Go on, try again' (qtd. in Read 1978, 103). Many rejected men did try again, and more than a few were successful in their quest to enlist.

Such success was often born of equal parts of perseverance and skulduggery on the part of these would-be warriors. Rejected for service at a regimental recruiting station in Alberta on 22 August 1914 because the diameter of his expanded chest was one inch below the minimum required, Harold Peat visited the regimental MO at his home the following day. Falsely claiming to be a Belgian whose two brothers had been killed by Germans, Peat demanded that the medical officer pass him fit to serve so that he could exact revenge. The MO, although likely not fooled by Peat's claim, acquiesced to Peat's demand. Once at Valcartier, Peat took advantage of the general chaos that afflicted the camp to avoid his final medical examination.[50] Nor was Peat the only individual to use the chaos of Valcartier to his advantage. Initially rejected at on account of his poor eyesight, 18-year-old William Dix simply waited in camp for 22 days and then tried again. He was passed fit. However, both Dix and Peat's efforts pale in the light of the persistence of 23-year-old George Stanley Atkins. Suffering from injury-induced kyphosis (curvature of the spine), Atkins claimed to have attempted to enlist almost 200 times (!), crossing most of Western Canada in the process, before finally being accepted by the 1st Tunnelling Company on 12 November 1915.[51]

For those men with infirmities who were unable to join the ranks, the psychological toll exacted by accusing looks, derogatory comments, ostracism, and personal shame was often heavy. As a result, some rejected men cut themselves off from their communities in an attempt to escape their torments.[52] Others, broken by their experiences, choose to take their own lives. Twenty-four-year-old George Baker, for example, hanged himself in March 1917 after suffering repeated rejections for service.[53]

The majority of rejected volunteers at Valcartier in 1914 were virtually, if not completely, indistinguishable from their accepted colleagues. Generally speaking, they were of the same height, age and physical builds as those who boarded the troopships for England in October 1914. More importantly, the physical and medical characteristics that caused them to be rejected were often invisible or incomprehensible to the general public. As a result, they often faced considerable hostility on the streets of Canada's towns and cities from people who believed they should have been wearing the khaki.

Acknowledgement

The author wishes to express his thanks to Serge Durflinger, Galen Perras, Anthony Di Mascio, and the reviewers of *First World War Studies* for the insightful comments they made on various drafts of this article. Angela Crawley deserves special thanks for her help drafting Figures 5, 6, and 7. As always, thanks to my wife Marcia and daughters Nyah and Niobe.

Notes

1. *Passchendaele*, directed by Paul Gross. I am thankful to Mr. Gross and Whizbang Films for generously providing me with a copy of *Passchendaele's* script.
2. Department of Militia and Defence [Hereafter DMD], 'Memoranda (February 26, 1917 and April 27, 1917),' file HQ 1982-1-83, RG 24, Vol. 6600, Library and Archives Canada [hereafter LAC]; Kemp 1916, 2879–80. Also see Clarke 2009, 2.
3. In early 1917, a Department of Militia and Defence (DMD) report estimated that in 1916 (the first full year of reliable information) alone, over 50,000 men – almost 25% of those who had volunteered in that year – had been deemed unfit to serve. This estimate was rough at best. Rejection-rate data provided by Military District (MD) 13 (Alberta) to the DMD was so fragmented that it was not included in the department's final calculations. Likewise, other MDs stated that they were unable to provide information regarding men rejected by civilian practitioners conducting examinations outside of the military's purview. Moreover, the framers of the report were also careful to point out that the statistics only related to men who had failed the medical examination, and not to those individuals who had been had been turned away by recruiting sergeants before they even crossed the threshold of a recruiting station's door. No records were generally kept with regard to such rejections. On the opposite side of the ledger, it should also be noted that the report did not take into account the possibility of multiple enlistment attempts. Contemporary attempts to calculate rejection rates are also hindered by the fact that statistics relating to men discharged (as opposed to rejected outright) as medically unfit do not differentiate between those deemed unfit based on pre-war impairments and those who developed disqualifying impairments while on service.

    Following the formula used by David Silbey to calculate the possible numbers of medically rejected volunteers in the British population, this data suggests that one can estimate that between 100,000 and 200,000 men were deemed unfit to serve by the Canadian authorities between 1914 and 1918. To put this number in the context of twenty-first-century Canada, which, with a population of 32,000,000 people, has approximately four times the population than it did during the Great War, this equates to between 400,000 and 800,000 individuals. DMD, 'Memoranda (February 26, 1917 and April 27, 1917),' file HQ 1982-1-83, RG 24, Vol. 6600, LAC; Silbey 2004.
4. DMD, 'Files of CEF Volunteers who were rejected,' RG 150/Accession 1992-93/175, LAC [Hereafter FVR].
5. DMD, 'Officer Commanding Military District No. XI to The Secretary, Militia Council, March 7, 1917,' file HQ 593-3-7, RG 24, Vol.1312, LAC.
6. At Valcartier, some 30 medical examiners, supported by 100 clerical orderlies, were tasked with examining over 30,000 men (Adami 1918, 42).
7. This is not to imply that Maynard was derelict in his duty. Medical officers were not required to offer a detailed explanation as why they had rejected a volunteer as unfit, but rather only to note the reason for his rejection. E. Armstrong, FVR, Vol. 1; W.

Desjardins, FVR, Vol. 3; Anthony Mayers, FVR, Vol.7; Zac Randell, FVR, Vol. 8; Richard Rice, FVR, Vol. 8.
8. W. Ostarvet, FVR, Vol. 8.
9. William Keller, FVR, Vol. 6; C.A. McLuskey, FVR, Vol. 7.
10. Stanley Norval, FVR, Vol. 9.
11. W. Chavis, FVR, Vol. 3; E. Lesaux, FVR, Vol. 6.
12. Chas Holy, FVR, Vol. 5; N. Thom, FVR, Vol. 9.
13. Timothy Devonport, FVR, Vol. 3; Harold Newbery, FVR, Vol. 7.
14. H. Bowden, FVR, Vol. 1.
15. *Regulations for the Canadian Medical Service, 1910* (Ottawa: Government Printer, 1910): 48–9; *Instructions for the Physical Examination of Recruits* (London: King's Printer, 1914): 4; Clarke 2009, 41–55.
16. Max Shinn, FVR, Vol. 9.
17. Ivan Thomas, FVR, Vol. 10.
18. Roy Coates, FVR, Vol. 2; Charles Garner, FVR, Vol. 4. Also see Harold Delaney, FVR, Vol. 3.
19. In five cases, empty envelopes contained handwritten notes stating that the documents had been removed. All five envelopes had been removed during a two-day period in late September 1917, perhaps indicating that files of rejected volunteers were reviewed with the introduction of conscription after the passing of the *Military Services Act* into law on 29 August of the same year.
20. Thomas Francis Daly, FVR, Vol. 3.
21. George R. Manning, FVR, Vol. 7.
22. J. Bramball, FVR, Vol. 2; C.E. Lamond, FVR, Vol. 6.
23. Percentages in text are rounded to the closest whole number for ease of reading.
24. The Methodist count includes both men recorded as being Methodists (63) and those listed as Wesleyans (119). The Presbyterian count includes one individual who was recorded as being a member of the 'Scottish Church'.
25. It should be noted that these numbers were not reflective of the relative strength of the denominations within the Canadian population. Indeed, the *Fifth Census of Canada, 1911* recorded that the dominant religion (based on a numbers of adherents) within the Dominion was Roman Catholic, which accounted for 39.3% of the population. Despite making up the vast majority of men serving in the CEF, Anglicans, who made up 14.5% of the population, came in fourth after Presbyterians (15.5%) and Methodists (15%). This difference can best be explained by the underrepresentation of Francophone Canadians, who made up the majority of Canada's Roman Catholic population, and the overrepresentation of English-born/first-generation English Canadians in the CEF. Further explanations might be found in the fact that in a number of cases, the faith recorded on a man's attestation paper often expressed the enlisting officer's sensibilities rather than the individual's religious beliefs. Admittedly, such acts did not always favour the Anglican Church. Thomas Dinesen, an avowed atheist, had Presbyterian recorded in his attestation paper's religion column because his recruiters stated that all soldiers must have a religion. Presbyterian was chosen because Dinesen had enlisted in a kilted regiment (Canadian Black Watch). These acts of misrepresentation were not limited to Canada; Gervase Phillips has noted that British recruiting officers encouraging non-conformist Welsh recruits to give their religious denomination as Anglican. *Fifth Census of Canada, 1911: Religions, Origins, Birthplace, Citizenship, Literacy and Infirmities, by Provinces, Districts and Sub-Districts* (Ottawa: King's Printer, 1913): vi–vii; Morton 1993; Phillips 1993; Dinesen 1929, 31–2.
26. Admittedly, one should be careful not to push such an explanation too far. Although at the start of the conflict a number of influential Methodists condemned the war as 'foolish, costly, and unchristian,' by autumn 1914 many had thrown their full support behind the conflict. Moreover, as J. Michael Bliss has noted, 'the [Methodist] [C]hurch's tradition of pacifist statement has to be measured against it proclaimed support for every British war after and including the opium wars'. Nonetheless, government reports, supported by the Army and Navy Board's own research, argued that Methodists were under represented in the Canadian forces as late as 1918. See Socknat 1987, 49–52; Bliss 1968, 214; Shaw 2009, 111–4.

27. W. Hadden, FVR, Vol. 4; M.H. McLeod, FVR, Vol. 7.
28. James Scott Simmons, FVR, Vol. 9.
29. Ulysses Adlerard, FVR, Vol. 1; Samuel Jones, FVR, Vol. 5; Robert W. Wilson, FVR, Vol. 11; Ernest Williams, FVR, Vol.11.
30. J. Beech, FVR, Vol. 2; H. Ouelette, FVR, Vol. 8; Amede Sauve, FVR, Vol. 10.
31. Ulysses Adlerard, FVR, Vol. 1; James Cook, FVR, Vol. 2; Arthur Giles, FVR, Vol. 4; Antonio E. Lapierre, FVR, Vol. 6; Robert Orkney, FVR, Vol..7; Richard Quinn, FVR, Vol..8; John Robillard, FVR, Vol. 9; John Strain, FVR, Vol. 9; R. Warne, FVR, Vol. 11; Charley Woodman, FVR, Vol. 11.
32. Reginald Neor, FVR, Vol. 8; Joseph Clamondou, FVR, Vol..2. Also see H. Shaw, FVR, Vol. 10.
33. William Chavis, FVR, Vol. 2; Lawrence Eaves, FVR, Vol. 3; George Jobin, FVR, Vol. 5; Martin Wilson, FVR, Vol. 11. It is likely that Wilson had lost his arm as a result of the serious wound he received at the Battle of Fish Creek (1 May 1885), during the Riel Rebellion. See 'Report of the Department of Militia and Defence, upon the suppression of the rebellion in the North-West Territories and matters in connection therewith' *Sessional Papers of the Dominion of Canada*, Vol. 5 (Ottawa: MacLean, Roger and Co., 1886), 20.
34. 'Mobilization Order – Qualifications for Service,' 17 August 1914, cited in *General Orders, Militia Orders and Precis of Headquarters Letters Bearing Upon The Administration of the Canadian Army Medical Service Published Between August 6 1914 and December 31, 1916* (Ottawa: Militia Council, 1917), 14.
35. The minimum requirements for chest expansion declined as the war continued, reaching as little as 30 inches for some units (Clarke 2009, 76–7, 326–7).
36. The data on which this calculation was based comes from material generously provided by Professor Kris Inwood of the University of Guelph. It is drawn from his ongoing anthropometric research into the physical well-being of Canadians.
37. The median remains 67 inches.
38. An examination of a number of anthropometric studies suggests that the average height of British males in their early twenties during the late nineteenth and early twentieth centuries rested somewhere between 66.7 and 67.4 inches (Allison 1982, 55; Beggs 1915, 9; Boyne and Leitich 1954; Professor Sir Roderick Floud, correspondence with the author 29 August 2007; Floud, Wachter, and Gregory 1990, 154–63; Galton 1884).
39. This number encompasses all men, whose files listed one or more medical condition(s) in their reasons for rejection, including height and chest size. Rejection due to age (over or under) on its own was not included. Men struck off strength for both medical and non-medical conditions are included. It should be further noted that figure of 2534 medical rejections is contrary to the figure – 2164 – provided by Canada's official Great War historian, Col. A. Fortescue Duguid, in his *Official History of the Canadian Forces in the Great War, 1914–1919*. It is unclear why Duguid's count is low, although it is possible that when faced with an individual that was discharged on both medical and non-medical grounds Duguid favoured the non-medical explanation. It is more likely, however, the many men rejected on medical grounds rest in the second largest group – 1530 individuals – identified by Duguid: 'reason not stated' (Duguid 1938, 57).
40. The fifth most common reason for medical rejection was as 'medically unfit' at 5.5%. Given that this reason for rejection is a general description, it is impossible to comment on the visibility of the impairments of the men so classified.
41. This point was made in the 6 May 1916 issue of the *Lancet* by Drs. J.V. Paterson and H.M. Traquair, ophthalmic surgeons at the Edinburgh's Royal Infirmary (Paterson and Traquair 1916, 955).
42. For example, 23-year-old Herrick Duggan – whose four attempts to join the Princess Patricia's Canadian Light Infantry in August 1914 had been thwarted by a heart condition – told his mother in a letter he wrote from London, England, in October 1914 that few people believed that he was physically unfit to serve. Herrick S. Duggan Fonds, 'Herrick Duggan to Mildred Duggan, 4/11/14,' MG30-E303, LAC; Clarke 2008.
43. See, for example, 'Unfit for Military Service,' Toronto *Globe*, 27 January 1915; Alphonse Verville, 16 May 1916, *Debates of the House of Commons of the Dominion Canada, 6th session, 12th Parliament* (Ottawa: King's Printer, 1916), 4072; Bird 1930, 13–14.

44. Macphail 1925, 158, 283; DMD, 'Mrs. J.A. Johnston to Edward Kemp, May 23, 1917,' file HQ 593-3-7, RG 24, Vol. 1312, LAC; DMD, 'General Officer Commanding MD 5 to The Secretary, Militia Council, January 9, 1917,' RG24, Vol. 1144, LAC; 'Force Bogus Recruits To Keep Their Pledges,' Toronto *Star*, 26 October 1915.
45. 'Button or Badge for Rejected Ones', Toronto *Star*, 11 December 1915.
46. 'Certificate For Rejected Men,' Toronto *Globe*, 24 April 1916; 'Buttons for the Rejected,' *Ottawa Evening Citizen*, 1 March 1916; 'Winnipeggers Are to Sport Button On Which is the Magic Word 'Excused',' *Vancouver Sun*, 29 March 1916.
47. As part of its move to regulate the provision of war service badges, the Dominion government created penalties for their misuse. Providing a badge to some who was not entitled to one or wearing a badge without authorization would lead to the guilty party facing either a fine not exceeding Can$100 or imprisonment for no more than 30 days. In 1916, Can$100 had the equivalent value of Can$1574/€984 in 2008 (www.bankofcanada.ca/en/rates/inflation_calc.html). In early 1917, these penalties were increased to a maximum fine of Can$500 (Can$6825/€4268), or a term of imprisonment not exceeding six months. These penalties were far from minor. In 1917, for example, the average annual wage of a person working in Canada's manufacturing industries was approximately Can$760 (Can$10,374/€6487). See Noah M. Meltz, 'Wages and Working Conditions', http://www.statcan.ca/english/freepub/11-516-XIE/sectiona/toc.htm. Privy Council of Canada [Hereafter PC], 'Order in Council P.C. 1944, August 16, 1916, and Order in Council P.C. 275, February 27, 1917,' A-1-a, RG2, LAC; Johnson 1995, 4–16.
48. PC, 'Order in Council P.C. 1944, August 16, 1916,' A-1-a, RG2, LAC; 'Registration System Provided for Canada', Toronto *Globe*, August 17, 1916.
49. Thirty-three-year-old Lieutenant Archibald Grogan, for example, made it to Valcartier in spite of the fact he had had his left hand amputated (A. Grogan, FVR, Vol. 4).
50. In his memoir, Peat claimed that he managed '[t]hrough some very fine work ... [to] ... escape the examination' at Valcartier. The work was fine indeed. The Albertan's attestation paper not only indicates that he was examined on 4 September 1914, but also a records an expanded chest as measurement of 34 inches. While Peat provided no explanation how this came about, it is possible he had a friend take his place during the examination (Peat 1917, 2–3, 12). DMD #18535, Peat, Harold, RG 150, Accession 1992–93/166, Vol. 7692 – 11, LAC.
51. DMD, #301178, Atkins, George Stanley, RG 150, Accession 1992–93/166, Vol. 283–6, LAC; #501178 [sic] Atkins, George Stanley, *Appendix to the proceedings of the Board of Inquiry into the report on the Canadian Army Medical Service by Colonel Herbert A. Bruce and the interim report of Surgeon-General G.C. Jones*: M27–M28, William Babtie Fonds, MG30-E3, LAC; William J. Dix, FVR, Vol. 3; DMD, '#10981 Dix, William John,' RG 150, Accession 1992–93/166, Vol. 2534–25, LAC. Also see Cook 2007, 24–6.
52. 'War's Effect On Religion,' Toronto *Globe*, 20 October 1917.
53. Baker was not the only individual to take his own life after having been rejected for service. Eighteen-year-old Daniel Lane took strychnine after failing the CEF's medical examination in 1914. One year later, 28-year-old Joseph Coley drank carbolic acid because, so it was reported, he feared that a recently acquired disability would not only cause him to lose his job, but also cause him to be 'rejected by the military doctors' ('Disappointed Lad Attempts Suicide', Toronto *Globe*, 18 September 1914; 'Dragoon Ends His Life In Despondent Mood,' Toronto *Globe*, 18 October 1915; 'Rejected Three Times, Then Hangs Himself,' Toronto *Star*, 17 March 1917).
54. The greater number of reasons for rejection than rejected men (3605 vs. 3050) is due to the number of individuals having been rejected on multiple grounds (usually multiple impairments). All reasons for rejection were recorded and counted, because it was not possible to divine which impairment on a rejected volunteer's attestation paper was the most important factor in his rejection for service.

References

Adami, J.G. 1918. *The war story of the CAMC, 1914–1915*. Toronto: Musson.
Allison, Sidney. 1982. *The Bantams: The untold story of World War One*. Oakville: Mosaic Press.

Army Medical Corps Instructions. 1917. *General orders, militia orders and precis of headquarters letters bearing upon the administration of the Canadian Army Medical Service published between August 6th, 1914, and December 31st, 1916*. Ottawa: Militia Council.
Baldwin, Harold. 1918. *Holding the line*. Chicago: A.C. McClurg.
Beggs, S.T. 1915. *The selection of the recruit*. London: Baillière, Tindall and Cox.
Bird, Will, R. 1930. *And we go on*. Toronto: Hunter-Rose Ltd.
Bliss, J.M. 1968. The Methodist Church and World War 1. *Canadian Historical Review* 49, no. 3: 213–33.
Boyne, A.W., and I. Leitich. 1954. Secular change in the height of British adults. *Nutrition Abstracts and Reviews* 24, no. 2: 255–69.
Brown, Craig R., and Donald Loveridge. 1996. Unrequited faith: Recruiting the CEF, 1914–18. In *Reappraisals in Canadian history: Post Confederation*, 2nd ed., ed. C.M. Wallace, R.M. Bray, and A.D. Gilbert, 300–19. Toronto: Prentice Hall.
Clarke, Nic. 2008. 'He was my best subaltern': The life and death of Lieutenant Herrick S. Duggan, 70th Field Company, Royal Engineers. *Canadian Military History* 17, no. 2: 21–32.
Clarke, Nicholas. 2009. Unwanted warriors: The rejected volunteers of the Canadian Expeditionary Force. PhD diss., University of Ottawa.
Cook, Tim. 2007. *Canadians fighting the Great War, 1914–1916*. Vol. 1, *At the sharp end*. Toronto: Viking.
Cook, Tim. 2008. *Canadians fighting the Great War, 1917–1918*. Vol. 2, *Shock troops*. Toronto: Viking.
Cranfield, John, and Kris Inwood. 2007. The great transformation: A long-run perspective on physical well-being in Canada. *Economics and Human Biology* 5, no. 5: 204–28.
Dinesen, Thomas. 1929. *Merry Hell! A Dane with the Canadians*. London: Jarrolds.
Duguid, A. Fortescue. 1938. *Official history of the Canadian Forces in the Great War, 1914–1919*. Ottawa: King's Printer.
Fifth Census of Canada. 1913. *1911: Religions, origins, birthplace, citizenship, literacy and infirmities, by provinces, districts and sub-districts*. Ottawa: King's Printer.
Floud, Roderick, Kenneth Wachter, and Annabel Gregory. 1990. *Height, health and history: Nutritional status in the United Kingdom*. Cambridge: Cambridge University Press.
Floud, Roderick. 1973. *An introduction to quantitative methods for historians*. London: Methuen.
Floud, Roderick. 1997. *The people and the British economy, 1830–1914*. Oxford: Oxford University Press.
Galton, Francis. et al. 1884. Final report of the Anthropometric Committee. *Report of the British Association for the Advancement of Science*. London: John Murray.
Granatstein, J.L., and J.M. Hitsman. 1977. *Broken promises: A history of conscription in Canada*. Toronto: Oxford University Press.
Johnson, Robbie. 1995. *Canadian war service badges, 1914–1954*. Surrey, British Columbia: Johnson Books.
Kemp, Hon, A.E. 1916. *Debates of the House of Commons of the Dominion Canada, 6th Session, 12th Parliament*. Ottawa: King's Printer.
Macphail, Andrew. 1925. *Official history of the Canadian Forces in the Great War, 1914–19: The Medical Services*. Ottawa: King's Printer.
McLaren, Angus. 1990. *Our own master race: Eugenics in Canada, 1885–1945*. Toronto: McClelland & Stewart.
Meltz, Noah M. 1983. Wages and working conditions. In *Historical statistics of Canada*, ed. F.H. Leacy. http://www.statcan.ca/english/freepub/11-516-XIE/sectiona/toc.htm.
Morton, Desmond. 1993. *When your number's up: The Canadian soldier in the First World War*. Toronto: Random House.
Morton, Desmond, and J.L. Granatstein. 1989. *Marching to Armageddon: Canadians and the Great War 1914–1919*. Toronto: Lester & Orpen Dennys.
Passchendaele. Directed by Paul Gross. Toronto, Canada: Whizbang Films, 2008.
Paterson, V., and H.M. Traquair. 1916. The visual standards used in the medical examination of recruits in the British Army and continental armies. *Lancet* 187, no. 4836: 954–5.
Peat, Harold. 1917. *Private Peat*. Indianapolis: Bobbs-Merrill Co.
Phillips, Gervase. 1993. Dai bach y soldiwr: Welsh soldiers in the British Army, 1914–1918. *Llafur: The Journal of Welsh Labour History* 6, no. 2: 94–105.

Primrose, A. 1915. Disabilities, including injuries, caused by bullets, shrapnel, high explosives, etc., as illustrated by cases examined before a medical board at Canadian Headquarters, Shorncliffe, England. *Canadian Medical Association Journal* 5, no. 10: 853–66.

Read, Daphne, ed. 1978. *The Great War and Canadian society: An oral history*. Toronto: New Hogtown Press.

Shaw, Amy. 2009. *Crisis of conscience: Conscientious objection in Canada during the First World War*. Vancouver: University of British Columbia Press.

Silbey, David. 2004. Bodies and cultures collide: Enlistment, the medical exam, and the British working class, 1914–1916. *Social History of Medicine* 17, no. 1: 61–76.

Socknat, Thomas P. 1987. *Witness against war: Pacifism in Canada, 1900–1945*. Toronto: University of Toronto Press.

War Office. 1914. *Instructions for the physical examination of recruits*. London: King's Printer.

Dominion Cartoon Satire as Trench Culture Narratives: Complaints, Endurance and Stoicism

JANE CHAPMAN* AND DAN ELLIN**
*Lincoln University and Research Associate Wolfson College Cambridge, Cambridge, UK;
**Warwick University, Warwick, UK

ABSTRACT *Although Dominion soldiers' Great War field publications are relatively well known, the way troops created cartoon multi-panel formats in some of them has been neglected as a record of satirical social observation. Visual narrative humour provides a 'bottom-up' perspective for journalistic observations that in many cases capture the spirit of the army in terms of stoicism, buoyed by a culture of internal complaints. Troop concerns expressed in the early comic strips of Australians, Canadians, New Zealanders and British were similar. They shared a collective editorial purpose of morale boosting among the ranks through the use of everyday narratives that elevated the anti-heroism of the citizen soldier, portrayed as a transnational everyman in the service of empire. The regenerative value of disparagement humour provided a redefinition of courage as the very act of endurance on the Western Front.*

Introduction

The First World War represented the peak of soldier newspaper production, thus textual expressions by soldiers in their own trench and troopship newspapers are relatively well known (Fuller, 1990; Seal, 1990, 2013a, 2013b; Kent, 1999; Nelson, 2010, 2011), but the way the men created and used cartoon multi-panel format is not. Humorous visual self-expression represents a record of satirical social observation from a 'bottom-up' perspective, with potential to contribute to the trend towards use of a wider range of sources in First World War historiography.[1]

Why cartoon narratives? Today's protagonists turn to their mobile telephones for visual communication, but it is all too easy to forget that throughout the golden age of the press during the early 20th century, comic strip illustrations acted as a comparable tool for journalistic observation and comment on a regular basis. This ephemeral medium can tell us the attitudes of ordinary soldiers and aspects of collective First World War experience, concerns about daily life, complaints about officers, medical services, discomforts, food and drink, leave, military routines and soldiers' expectations versus emerging reality.

By the outbreak of war there were already some Dominion precedents for comic strips aimed at adults. *The International Socialist*, a Sydney-based weekly, ran a strip with a main character on its front page—'The Adventures of William Mug'—from July 1913 to September 1914.[2] During the war the satirical ordinary man in cartoon form was continued, not just by celebrity cartoonists at the front, such as Bruce Bairnsfather, but by the men themselves.

In troop publications, the central comic character was the citizen soldier—a volunteer recruit in the lower ranks. This was the ordinary soldier, the everyman as main actor, portrayed as a source of satire, entertainment and morale boosting. Although they were also popular, single panel cartoons have not been included in this study as it aims to explore contributions made by the neglected popular medium of multi-panel visual observation. These sequential narratives had a contribution to make towards the origins of the newspaper comic strip.[3] This article explores how the interaction between the picture and textual elements in this form of communication should be construed, focusing mainly, but not exclusively, on Canadian examples from the Western Front.

Shared Experiences

The two panel cartoon format provided an ideal way of presenting quick, simple contrasting narratives of shared experiences. Longer sequential storylines could add further sophistications to the format, such as a more complicated storyline with several events, episodes, or milestones. The comic strip genre as it appears in trench publications was not usually formalised by the symmetric panel framing and regular characters that are commonplace today. Text captions and balloon dialogue were more frequent than box borders.

In terms of content, complaints were central to the genre: these began even during initial training, and were not confined to any particular Dominion nationality, or to life at the front. For example, 'Where Life is Not Monotonous', a multi-panel narrative, very cleverly uses the same visual to illustrate a range of different training situations. Thus, a visual of two officers talking in front of a squad of very bored-looking soldiers is reproduced six times with different captions that include 'Bayonet Fighting', 'Squad Drill' and 'A Tale of Adventure' (*Chevrons to Stars*, October 1917, p. 52). Figure 1a, b also tackles military routines. Troops carried up to 60 lb of kit, often on route marches during training that intended to accustom the men to marching at the front. Marches of between four to eight miles with full kit were common (Bet-El, 1990, pp. 80–81).

The 'voice' of the ordinary soldier has often been articulated in a 'top-down' literary form by the better educated among them, as letters, diaries and memoirs. Whereas this cultural voice of the officer class and war poets has been hugely influential (Fussell, 1975), more recently scholars have adopted a more 'bottom-up' approach (Morton, 1993). In addition, much of the scholarship on *mentalités* during the war centres on psychological human resilience (Watson, 2008) and emotional survival (Roper, 2009), but by and large without resort to trench publications as a source, despite the fact that publications included parodies of news stories and of advertisements, snippets of gossip, jokes, poetry, anecdotes, cartoons as well as sequential illustrative narratives. Nevertheless, this large body of material (800 editions from a variety of countries held by Cambridge University library alone, but some without cartoons) is significant

Figure 1 a, b. Sling, the Salisbury Plain camp where reinforcements were trained and casualties rehabilitated (*Chronicles of the NZEF*, 1917, vol. 2, no. 5, pp. 180–181).

because it represents an increase in the number of participant voices using an accessible form of publishing.[4]

Some troop publications were supported officially and printed on the Western Front, either on abandoned French presses (as with *The Wipers Times*) or sent for printing to Paris or London. Official journals tended to have higher standards of production and more illustrative material, although this was not always the case, especially if the smaller, more makeshift publications, such as the Australian *Ca Ne Fait Rien* from the Western Front, could boast a talented caricaturist (Chapman and Ellin, 2012). However, there were usually more and better produced sequential cartoons in newspapers with greater resources, such as the Canadian *Listening Post*.

Many were produced, written and conceived by lower ranks for their peers, that is, by, with and for citizen soldiers. Scholars have recognised that journalism has traditionally also provided a service to, by and for 'imagined communities' (Anderson, 1991; Allan and Thorsen, 2009; Chapman and Nuttall, 2011). Yet citizens' journalism has not generally been historicised, overlooking previous precedents such as trench publications.

Cartoons as Imagined Communities of Identity

Using humorous content, soldiers' illustrative narratives drew on their own oral culture of songs, anecdotes and gossip to consolidate and communicate their own specific collective morality and outlook. Recruits, by definition, were positioned in a new community that needed to express an identity, and they used collective communication to cement cohesion. Trench publications were influenced by oral culture, with slang, humour, songs and music hall performance all acting as badges of identity, but also as a means of uniting otherwise disparate Empire nationalities (Ashworth, 1980, p. 48; Cook, 2009, p. 238; 2013, p. 344).

In fact, the language and in-jokes may well have been incomprehensible to those on the home front who read them (Seal, 2013b, p. 14). For example, a special edition of the Australian *The Yandoo* was entitled: 'Chatty Number: Printed in a Fritz Dugout' (Australian War Memorial, 1918, 1 September 1917, folder 5, vol. 3, part 4). As a running joke, the 'R and R' story of a night out in town that was featured as a front page in July 1918 with a heading 'Issued in No Man's Land' (Australian War Memorial, 1918, folder 10, vol. 111, part 11) depicted a routine referred to as 'Tummy and Tub'. 'Tub' shows the men's communal bathing, a big bath before they go out. One of the nine nude bathers in the middle of the huge water barrel asks 'Who says I'm chatty?' The reader can only understand the illustration with the shared knowledge that lice were known as 'chats'. 'Tummy' shows a French peasant woman who has rustled up the usual menu for soldiers, egg and chips. An Australian soldier sits at her table, happily brandishing a knife and fork. Her speech balloon asks 'Good Oh, Eh Monsieur?!!'. He replies 'Oofs and chips. Tray bon madarm'. Again, 'franglais' language formed part of daily conversation on the Western Front.

Similar knowledge is required to appreciate the humour of Figure 2. It refers to a shell known as a rum jar because of its likeness to the gallon SRD (Special Red Demerara) jars used to transport the rum ration (Cook, 2000, p. 7). The wordplay centres on 'S. R. D.' or 'seldom reaches destination' for rum, as opposed to the shell, which 'seldom fails to reach its destination'.

David Kent (1999, p. 8) points out that 'In a sense the field publications became the corporate diaries of tens of thousands of servicemen. These publications allowed them to recall and share experiences among themselves while also, in many cases, transmitting that experience to the people at home'. The *Listening Post*, for example, was sent home, along with other publications that included British journals—evidence that Canadians saw themselves as part of the British army. The last post-war editions of the newspaper were more like souvenir publications. This publication of the 7th Infantry Battalion, British Columbia Regiment, was published twice monthly ('Huns permitting') and was available from a military tailor in London's Strand, the canteens of most Canadian units and army, and YMCA canteens in Canadian areas. The editorial team

Figure 2. 'Rum Jar', *In and Out*, 1918, vol. 1 p. 18.

consisted of editors Captain W. F. Orr, Major D. Philpot and Major A. C. Nation. The news editor was a private, J. W. Campbell (later sergeant). In terms of its production style, it fell midway between the more modest publications and the semi-professional journals (Seal, 2013b, pp. 26–28).

    This article's sample of approximately 100 mainly Canadian multi-panel cartoons provides a sense of personal agency, manifesting a desire for control over their environment in order to encourage endurance and perseverance as a moral code. This, it will be argued, can be interpreted as a new definition of courage and loyalty. Feelings of geographic isolation prompted some Dominion troops to produce a record for friends and family back home, a motivation that was particularly relevant in the case of troopship publications on the return journey to Australia.[5] Despite the fact that Canadians were generally the most prolific producers of the Empire, especially on the Western Front, the authors found only two Canadian troopship examples. This is probably a reflection of their shorter sea voyage. There were differences in multi-panel cartoons between outgoing and returning journals, especially in how the Germans were depicted. Keshen (1996, p. 148) observes that the attitudes of trainees and combatants grew progressively more distant from those who remained in Canada, asserting a direct correlation between the levels of satirical content in Canadian trench journals and proximity to the Front (see Figure 3).

Certainly, on the home front cartoons focused more on heroism, jingoistic rhetoric and talk of glory,[6] although this remained prominent in papers printed for fresh recruits (Keshen, 1996, p. 135). By contrast, soldiers developed an ironic anti-heroism through their humour, epitomised by seasoned old soldiers, malingerers, and characters such as Bairnsfather's 'Old Bill', who always seemed to know the tricks for survival. Anti-heroism found its iconic representation in multi-panel narratives about the range of uses for the bayonet (other than the obvious, for killing). It could be used as a toasting fork, a hook or a corkscrew, for instance (*Chronicles of the NZEF*, 30 January 1918, vol. 3, no. 36).

Figure 3. 'Housie', *Listening Post*, March 1919, vol. 33—a reference to the infamous bingo call.

Once on the Western Front troops joked about each other and those 'back home'. Figure 4 provides an example of infantry satire about the cavalry, although both are Canadian. The Germans were not demonised: troops felt that the Germans shared the horror of trench warfare. This resulted in what Ashworth (1980, p. 135) refers to as 'live and let live', a mentality that 'was accompanied both by an increase in sentiments of linking among antagonists and a decrease in sentiments of enmity'. This point is supported by Eksteins (1989, pp. 232, 230, 229), who argues that soldiers could feel more disdain for civilians at home than for the enemy, because the 'spiritual bond' developed by men in the trenches led all nationalities to agree 'that the war experience, the experience of the "real war" in the trenches, marked men off from the rest of society'. This view is supported by Seal (2013a, p. 178): 'It was not uncommon to find references in trench journals to the feeling that Allied soldiers had more in common with their "enemies" suffering the same thing in German trenches than they did with their own military, press, and home front. Regardless of nationality, soldiers on active duty came to identify with the insular community of the trenches'.

Humour for Survival

As a form of social observation, narrative humour relies on recognition of absurdity and incongruity in familiar situations. Humour in multi-panel trench cartoons offers an insight into the general culture, self-image and preoccupations of the troops, by showing and not simply telling; implied criticism is combined with some visual exaggeration as satire, cynicism and shared experience. The comic strip format proved ideal for a snapshot story revealing absurdities through the interaction of dialogue and captions as narrative, and sequential drawings. These were typically based on the difference between civilian perceptions of warfare (influenced by propaganda and censorship) and the reality of experience. A significant number of cartoons reinforced trench culture by presenting affectionate jokes about the naïve misconceptions of new recruits, who needed to learn the slang as well as the outlook.[7] In cartoons the recruit corrected by the seasoned 'old soldier' provided a reality break which often highlighted a grumbling or anti-authoritarian message. In Figure 6, a new recruit thinks a machine gun is a

Figure 4. 'Western Canadians', *Listening Post*, August 1917, vol. 27—both the cavalry and the home front are 'other-ed'.

Figure 5. *Listening Post*, April 1918, vol. 30, p. 19.

woodpecker. In Figure 5, a new soldier thinks a mirror is for shaving rather than looking into no-man's-land. This example contains two examples of rudimentary comic strip style that are not found in today's more developed formats: in panel 3, the first speech balloon is positioned lower than the second, defying present-day conventions of reading from left to right and from top to bottom; in panel 4, dots indicating eye line are used to ensure that readers appreciate that the experienced soldier is looking directly at the trainee. Figures 6 and 8 (see later) use the same technique, almost as if the artist feels the need to emphasise the relatively new (for adults) format he is using.

Figure 6. *Listening Post*, July 1918, vol. 31, p. 11.

The self-mocking humour of anti-hero stories was an aspect of soldiers' culture that can be misinterpreted as evidence of disloyalty. Interestingly, in works by the popular artist Hugh Farmer in the *Listening Post* (circulation 20,000 by 1917; Cook, 2008, p. 174), Canadians were depicted as larger than other troops, while still manifesting the anti-hero audience appeal of Bairnsfather's more physically feeble characters. In cartoon humour the anti-hero is allowed to admit fear, fatigue, 'leadswinging' (malingering) and/or a search for 'Blighty wounds' (severe enough to be sent back to England); in fact, such an admission is part of the culture. 'While cheating one's mates, brawling, or malingering were serious military charges, these deviant actions appeared to be condoned in the cultural products, and seemingly accepted by the led and the leaders as good for morale' (Cook, 2008, p. 190).

Satire acted as a vent for grievances, thus officers often turned a blind eye to criticism of them in publications (compulsory if complaints were anonymous). They recognised that without this particular psychological escape valve, insubordination was likely at the front and there could even be a possibility of mutiny (Keshen, 1996, p. 135). This pragmatic approach is compatible with the ideas of theorists such as Mikhail Bakhtin (1984, chapter 1), who discusses the use of laughter in response to official seriousness. The regenerative value of humour that he signals is evidenced by illustrative narratives that frequently centred on complaints about everyday life: humour kept men going, against all the odds.[8]

The act of disparagement in soldiers' cartoons and early comic strips is likely to have had a cathartic effect as a substitute for more direct protest, thereby preventing internal conflict by providing a voice and a language that helped soldiers to make sense of their new, and painful, environment. Humour theory identifies this process as 'disparagement humour': 'Disparagement humor refers to remarks that (are intended to) elicit amusement through the denigration, derogation, or belittlement of a given target (e.g., individuals, social groups, political ideologies, material possessions) ... Because humor communicates that its message is to be interpreted in a non-serious manner, disparagement humor can uniquely denigrate its target while stifling challenge or criticism' (Ferguson and Ford, 2008, pp. 283–284).

Trench publications could offer a 'sounding-board in the uncertainties of front line or near front line existence' (Seal, 1990, p. 30) and alert officers to potential discontents. Humour held the potential to undermine the power of officers and to 'reassert the masculine independence of the rank-and-file soldier' (Wise, 2007, p. 241), even if cartoons tended to avoid more fundamental questions such as the justice of participation in the conflict. According to Mulkay (1988), the eventual serious content of humorous discourse can always be denied in the event of the speaker finding his/her assertions to be socially unacceptable. In other words, the retractability of humour allows for subaltern challenge, even facilitating embarrassing or aggressive interactions or the negotiation of dangerous topics such as death, which tended to be referred to via euphemisms such as 'becoming a landlord' (Seal, 2013b, p. 169). The 'paradigm of everyday courage that soldiers both respected in others and attempted to cultivate in themselves' demonstrates a 'defiant rejection of victimhood' (Madigan, 2013, p. 97). This approach amounts to a partial reshaping of identity, in contrast to images of war on the home front: it was a symbolic rebellion in cultural expression, articulated in communications. Soldiers rarely challenged orders more directly.

National versus Empire Identity

A total of 620,000 Canadians enlisted between 1914 and 1918, primarily civilian soldiers who signed up for King and country.[9] Among the first contingent of 33,000 men, more than 70% were British born, and of those on the Western Front more generally, 50% were born in Britain. Most saw themselves as both British and Canadian (Cook, 2008, p. 172; 2013, p. 327). Although linguistic differences can emerge from the colloquialism in dialogue (also a characteristic of comic strips), in Australian slang such as 'cobbers', 'dinkum' and 'bonzer', themes tended to be common to more than one nationality and front, with uniforms and backdrops changing, and differing geographical features acting as a variable.[10] Cook (2013, p. 344) points out that although many Canadians believed they had their own national slang, in fact it was empire-wide shared language. Similarly, most of the complaints about officers, commonly expressed through humour, seem to be common to the various nationalities of the Allied side.[11]

In some cases, the same topics appear in prisoner of war and internment camp cartoons, such as Changi in the Second World War (National Library of Singapore, 1942). In fact, repetition of themes could become an ongoing joke, the appreciation of which acted as a bond between men. Common topics included the mismatch between the reality of wartime life and the image held by the folks back home, cultural differences of local populations in battlefield countries, perceptions of officer weaknesses, and discomforts and bad food (Table 1).

Food and drink, so essential for physical and mental well-being, was a favourite. Both British and French armies operated similar rations and calorific value, but in practice most complaints emanated from supply problems that rendered ration scales meaningless, thus bully beef and hard biscuits became the target of much humour, also reflected in the fact that in 1917 the War Cabinet received reports that food was one of the main causes of troop discontent (The National Archives, 12 September 1917, War Cabinet Minute 231, CAB 23/4). Figure 7 focuses on the contrast between food and drink while Australian men were in 'Blighty', as opposed to sustenance among the bleak destruction of the front, whereas the Canadian Figure 8 concentrates on the desperate ruses that may be devised in order to cadge a drink.

Limitations in Scope and Self-censorship

Trench publications were a refraction not a reflection of culture in that they were primarily a source of entertainment aimed at encouraging a sense of community at unit level, or to use an officer term, an *'esprit de corps'*. The episodes and thoughts that

Table 1. Broad themes of cartoon content

Topics	Canadian	New Zealand	Australian
Civilian life and leave	8	4	4
Food and drink	5	2	5
Service life	17	4	9
Contrasts	2	0	10
Officers and discipline	2	0	2
Medics	2	2	2
Transport	3	3	0
Other	6	6	7
Totals	45	21	39
Total: 105 multi-panel cartoons			

HOW WE DO IT IN BLIGHTY—

AND IN FRANCE.

Figure 7. a, b. 'Blighty and France', *Aussie*, June 1918, no. 5, p. 1.

Figure 8. 'Beer mug', *Listening Post*, December 1918, vol. 32.

were visualised inevitably portray everyday situations rather than battle, death, or military observations on the progress and strategy of the war. Maybe because of the relative isolation of trench-based soldiers on the Western Front from the bigger picture of overall strategy, immediate social observation tended to provide instant narrative reactions through the interconnection of dialogue, captions and illustration, offering snapshots that reveal shared feelings and emotions as wartime experiences, but these have their limitations.

Officially backed trench journals were censored at both battalion and divisional levels, and all newspapers—including unofficial ones—were subject to self-censorship.

The editorial process restricted content and language. Condon (2011) asserts that New Zealand soldiers in their publications (mainly officially endorsed and carefully edited, but aimed at reflecting back to the men unit loyalty and identity) 'are identified closely with an Empire that represents strength, courage and liberation from an aggressor'. It is possible to argue that combat culture not only gave men a distinct short-term identity confined to the war years, but that this same culture also set boundaries and definitions of acceptability by readers themselves as well as the editor. Contributions were accepted not necessarily on aesthetic merits, but in order to create a voice for the shared mentality of the unit (Pegum, 2007, pp. 134–135).

Within their chosen parameters, newspapers 'attempted to use, rather than deny, the depressing discrepancies of this Great War, and compared with home front mainstream press, there was certainly more freedom of expression' (Keshen, 1996, p. 134). Illustrations were based on content themes that were common to all theatres of conflict. On the Western Front British, Dominion and French troops faced the same enemies: lice, rats, mud, cold, rain and shells. Illustrative narratives depict situations where endurance was tolerated with good humour, danger nonchalantly accepted, along with stoicism about the potential outcome. Editors had to be responsive to their readership, because they were among them and could not ignore 'their state of mind ... Censorship and self-censorship could not prevent the trench newspapers from responding little by little to the concerns, interest, grievances and hopes of their readers, and echoing them' (Audoin-Rouzeau, 1992, pp. 33–34).

In Figure 9, a soldier in his trench experiences 'that minnie', then machine gun noise and fire, followed by a 'wizz bang', then a mine, a '5 point 9', and finally a 'potato masher'. In the final panel, he sets about sending his family the news. Although he has escaped from shells, grenades and machine gun fire, when he writes home, the soldier does not know what to say. Once again, this demonstrates the break from the home front, the lack of civilian comprehension (as perceived by the troops) and self-censorship.

Newspaper reactions to medical issues exemplify the responsiveness alluded to by Audoin-Rouzeau. On the Western Front, soldiers stated that the medical corps were never seen within 500 yards of the firing line, and referred to Royal Army Medical Corps as the 'rob all my comrades brigands' (Fuller, 1990, p. 61). This is countered by publications by the medical corps themselves, who clearly saw the need to correct their image, given the fact that the regimental medical officer had the unenviable task of deciding whether a man should be sent from the firing line to the rear. This required him to differentiate between faked as opposed to real illnesses. In cases of the former, a common remedy was the 'No. 9 Pill', a laxative that became the butt of many cartoon jokes. However, any desire to 'shirk', despite the humour, was usually tempered by men's sense of duty and feelings of loyalty to their 'mates', as a collective identity that emerges in their publications.

For the Canadian Field Ambulance, the contrast depicted by Sergeant T. W. Whitefoot in *Now and Then* was the 'fiction' of fast, efficient stretcher bearers in a clear battlefield tending one or two wounded men on the field, whereas 'fact' involved carrying a heavy soldier on a stretcher through knee-high mud to a derelict-looking medical post, sweating, with a speech caption that says 'censored' (Cambridge University Library, 1918, WRA540, Reel 1,). Humour allowed for the communication of truth.

Figure 9. *Listening Post*, April 1918, vol. 30, p. 15.

Both editors and readers despised home front propaganda and the mainstream press as pedlars of unrealistic jingoism and heroism, yet by exercising their own editorial values—itself an attempt to gain control over their disastrous surroundings—they were simultaneously selective about content and tone, favouring contributions that encouraged entertainment and boosted morale. Trench journals presented issues and topics as 'disarmingly humourised and shorn of their more demotic dimension' (Seal, 2013b, p. 190).

Nevertheless, multi-panel cartoons still had a sharp edge: probably the most devastating comment on the subject of war followed by peace was entitled 'The Profiteer' (National Library of Australia (NLA), *Aussie*, 15 June 1920). The first panel is captioned 'France 1918' and shows a war-weary soldier walking through mud, burdened with kit and surrounded by desolation in a barren landscape. In the second panel, the landscape is also barren and desolate, but it is hot and sunny, and captioned 'Aussie, 1920'. The same man is now a hobo burdened with a backpack of bedding and a billy-can in his hand, this time sweating, but otherwise in an identical pose.

Conclusion

This article has sought to demonstrate how Canadian and Dominion use of humour aimed to encourage a collective identity and a specific culture of warfare, experienced by the 'everyman' anti-hero as pragmatic survival. Clearly newspapers at the time would not have survived if they did not articulate content that was more generally acceptable to their main readership of the lower ranks in a largely volunteer, citizens' force.

The regenerative value of 'disparagement humour' in the context of illustrative narratives by Canadian and Dominion soldiers meant that a new kind of courage was re-imagined. Trench publications provided an insight not only into morale, but also into the code of perseverance that helps account for Dominion long-term loyalty during what has been called the 'Great War of Endurance' (Hynes, 1998, p. 73). Sarcasm in drawings should not be confused with rebellion, for men were still prepared to play the game: as scholars such as Fuller have noted, desertion and mutiny were rare—indeed, his enquiry seeks to establish how far the existence of soldier publications (but not specifically their cartoons) helped to avoid these eventualities.

Multi-panel cartoons, however, were no panacea—they have their limitations as a representational source, but one of their strengths is that they demonstrate an attempt to use humour as a form of control over the environment. This served to enhance morale, encourage endurance and facilitate survival. Historians are generally agreed that Allied morale, defined by Bond (2002, pp. 2, 14) in terms of attitudes, cohesion and combat effectiveness of groups, held up, 'although brittle at times'. Given the Canadian reputation for bravery,[12] military expertise and concomitant prolific 'trench' publishing, these findings are probably the clearest example of Great War satire that encouraged, in the extremely dire circumstances of the Western Front, endurance and persistence, qualities that amounted to loyalty.

Acknowledgements

Reproduction of images with thanks to Cambridge University Library and the Canadian War Museum Military History Research Centre.

Funding

This work was supported by the Arts and Humanities Council (AHRC) collaborative research grant 'Comics and the World Wars, a Cultural Record', 2011–15 [grant number AH/I022120/1].

Notes

1. For more on First World War historiography, see Bond (2002).
2. For more on Australian multi-panel trench cartoons, see Chapman and Ellin (2012).
3. For more on this point, see Chapman *et al.* (forthcoming).
4. The only other event in modern history that prompted a similar self-publishing explosion was the French Revolution, when the number of publications mushroomed to 2,000 from only one official journal during the *Ancien Régime* (Chapman, 2005, pp. 15–22; 2008, pp. 131–132). Fuller (1990) selected 107 for the study of text (not illustrations) from Britain and the many Dominions, concentrating on 61 that were uniquely produced by and aimed at the infantry. The French had 400 trench publications, but only 200

have survived (Audoin-Rouzeau, 1986, p. 7). Nelson (2010, p. 175) argues that owing to larger print runs and professional distribution, the Germans had by far the largest number, with 1.1 million editions distributed per month on the Western Front, and even more on the Eastern Front. He correctly notes that the most prolific of the allies, the Australian and Canadians, were, like the Germans on the Eastern Front, far from home (Nelson, 2011, p. 53, note 127).

5. There are approximately 70 Australian troopship newspapers (Kent, 1999, p. 11), in fact almost every boat had one. Overall, a total of about 200 Australian journal editions have survived. Condon (2011) takes a sample of 41 New Zealander trench publications.
6. In terms of mainstream cartoons, there was a difference between those artists who had been to the front and those who had not. Hiley (2007) also maintains that the majority of early British home front cartoons poked fun at the Germans while European artists demonised them.
7. Trench journals regularly published dictionaries of slang for this educative purpose. See the *Listening Post*, 10 August 1917, with a list for the new Americans.
8. See also Obrdlik (1942), Freud (1905) and Le Naour (2001).
9. Approximately 60,000 died and a further 170,000 were wounded or maimed (Cook, 2000, p. 19).
10. Wise (2007, pp. 237–238) notes that a single panel cartoon produced by the British soldier-cartoonist Bruce Bairnsfather was reproduced to depict an Australian soldier at Gallipoli by changing the uniform and the backdrop—everything else remained the same.
11. For German trench publications, the most numerous, but frequently officially backed, see Nelson (2010, 2011).
12. Well-known episodes of bravery include: the initial experience of chlorine gas by the First Canadian Division at First Ypres, 1915; 'one of the war's slickest set-piece attacks' (Holmes, 2004, p. 52) by four divisions fighting side by side for the first time at Vimy Ridge; and the capture of 400 men and nearly 100 machine guns in one day by the Canadian Cavalry Division in 1916 (Holmes, 2004, p. 445).

References

Allan, S. and Thorsen, E. (Eds.) (2009) *Citizen Journalism: Global Perspectives*. New York: Peter Lang.
Anderson, B. (1991) *Imagined Communities: Reflections on the Origin and Spread of Nationalism*, revised edn. New York: Verso.
Ashworth, T. (1980) *Trench Warfare 1914–18: The Live and Let Live System*. London and Basingstoke: The Macmillan Press.
Audouin-Rouzeau, S. (1986) *1914–1918, Les Combattants des Tranchées*. Paris: A. Colin.
Audouin-Rouzeau, S. (1992) *National Sentiment and Trench Journalism in France during the First World War*, trans. H. McPhail. Providence, RI: Berg.
Australian War Memorial (1915–42) Troopships and unit serials, 1915–42, folders 5, 7, 8, 10, 11, 13, 71, 73, 102, 119, 178.
Bakhtin, M. (1984) *Rabelais and His World*. Bloomington: Indiana University Press.
Bet-El, I. R. (1990) *Conscripts: The Lost Legions of the Great War*. Stroud: Sutton Publishing.
Bond, B. (2002) *The Unquiet Western Front: Britain's Role in Literature and History*. Cambridge: Cambridge University Press.
Cambridge University Library (1918) *War Reserve Collection*, WRA–WRE, part 2 trench journals, personal narratives and reminiscences, Reels 1–15.
Chapman, J. L. (2005) *Comparative Media History: 1789 to the Present*. Cambridge: Polity Press.
Chapman, J. (2008) Republican citizenship, ethics and the French revolutionary press 1789-92, in R. Keeble (Ed.), *Communication Ethics Now*. Troubadour: Leicester, pp. 131–141.
Chapman, J. L. and Ellin, D. (2012) Multi-panel comic narratives in Australian First World war trench publications as citizen journalism, *Australian Journal of Communication*, 39(3), 1–22.
Chapman, J. L., Hoyles, A., Kerr, A. and Sherif, A. (forthcoming) *Comics and the World Wars: A Cultural Record*. Basingstoke: Palgrave.
Chapman, J. L. and Nuttall, N. (2011) *Journalism Today: A Themed History*. Malden, MA: Blackwell-Wiley.
Condon, J. (2011) 'Mainly about us': identity and marginality in the troop magazines and newspapers of the New Zealand expeditionary force, 1914–19, *NZLIMJ*, 52(3), www.linaza.org.nz/lianza-publications/nzlimj, accessed 11 July 2013.

Cook, T. (2000) More a medicine than a beverage: 'demon rum' and the Canadian trench soldier of the First World War, *Canadian Military History*, 9(1), 7–22.

Cook, T. (2008) Anti-heroes of the Canadian expeditionary force, *Journal of the Canadian Historical Association*, 19(1), 171–193.

Cook, T. (2009) The singing war: Canadian soldiers' songs of the Great War, *American Review of Canadian Studies*, 39(3), 224–241.

Cook, T. (2013) Fighting words: Canadian soldiers' slang and swearing in the Great War, *War in History*, 20 (3), 323–344.

Eksteins, M. (1989) *Rites of Spring: The Great War and the Birth of the Modern Age*. Boston: Houghton Mifflin Company.

Ferguson, M. A. and Ford, T. E. (2008) Disparagement humor: a theoretical and empirical review of psychoanalytic, superiority, and social identity theories, *Humor: International Journal of Humor Research*, 21(3), 283–312.

Freud, S. (1905) *The Joke and its Relation to the Unconscious*. New York: McGraw-Hill, 1966.

Fuller, J. G. (1990) *Troop Morale and Popular Culture in the British and Dominion Armies 1914–1918*. Oxford: Clarendon Press.

Fussell, P. (1975) *The Great War and Modern Memory*. Oxford: Oxford University Press.

Hiley, N. (2007) A new and vital morale factor: cartoon book publishing during the First World War, in M. Hammond and S. Towheed (Eds.), *Publishing in the First World War*. Basingstoke: Palgrave Macmillan, pp. 148–177.

Holmes, R. (2004) *Tommy: The British Soldier on the Western Front, 1914–18*. London: Harper Collins.

Hynes, S. (1998) *The Soldiers' Tale: Bearing Witness to Modern War*. London: Pimlico Press.

Kent, D. A. (1999) *From Trench and Troopship: The Newspapers and Magazines of the AIF 1914–1918*. Alexandria, NSW: Hale and Iremonger.

Keshen, J. A. (1996) *Propaganda and Censorship during Canada's Great War*. Edmonton: University of Alberta Press.

Le Naour, J.-Y. (2001) Laughter and tears in the Great War: the need for laughter, the guilt of humour, *Journal of European Studies*, XXXI, 265–275.

Madigan, E. (2013) 'Sticking to a hateful task': resilience, humour, and British understandings of combatant courage, 1914–18, *War in History*, 20(1), 76–98.

Morton, D. (1993) *When Your Number's Up: The Canadian Soldier in the First World War*. Toronto: Random House of Canada.

Mulkay, M. (1988) *On Humour: Its Nature and Its Place in Modern Society*. London: Polity Press.

National Library of Australia (NLA) RNB world war one series, *The Aussie*, 1918–1937.

National Library of Singapore (1942) Bed bugs. William Haxworth Exhibition: Images of Internment.

Nelson, R. L. (2010) Soldier newspapers: a useful source in the social and cultural history of the First World War and beyond, *War in History*, 17(2), 167–191.

Nelson, R. L. (2011) *German Soldier Newspapers of the First World War*. Cambridge: Cambridge University Press.

Obrdlik, A. J. (1942) Gallows humour: a sociological phenomenon, *American Journal of Sociology*, 47, 709–712.

Pegum, J. (2007) British army trench journals and a geography of identity, in M. Hammond and S. Towheed (Eds.), *Publishing in the First World War*. Basingstoke: Palgrave Macmillan, pp. 129–147.

Roper, M. (2009) *The Secret Battle: Emotional Survival in the Great War*. ManchesterNH: Manchester University Press.

Seal, G. (1990) Written in the trenches: trench newspapers of the First World War, *Journal of Australian War Memorial*, 16, 30–38.

Seal, G. (2013a) 'We're here because we're here': trench culture of the Great War, *Folklore*, 124(2), 178–199.

Seal, G. (2013b) *The Soldiers' Press: Trench Journals in the First World War*. Basingstoke: Palgrave Macmillan.

The National Archives (1917) *War Cabinet and Cabinet Minutes, 1914–1918*.

Watson, A. (2008) *Enduring the Great War: Combat, Morale and Collapse in the German and British Armies, 1914–1918*. Cambridge: Cambridge University Press.

Wise, N. (2007) Fighting a different enemy: social protests against authority in the Australian imperial force during World War 1, in M. Hart and D. Bos (Eds.), Humour and Social Protest, *International Review of Social History*, supplement 15, pp. 225–242.

'Accurate to the Point of Mania': Eyewitness Testimony and Memory Making in Australia's Official Paintings of the First World War

MARGARET HUTCHISON

The collection of official war art housed in the Australian War Memorial has played an important role in shaping a memory of the First World War for almost a century. This article explores the importance of eyewitness testimony in the production of war paintings for the Memorial's collection during the interwar years. Focusing on the repainting of official artist Harold Septimus Power's canvas Saving the Guns of Robecq, *it explores the reasons why—in the inevitably contested construction of memory—Charles Bean and John Treloar privileged veterans' memories over artists' interpretations of the conflict. It argues that in the process of memory making aesthetics mattered less than portraying the war in a way acceptable to the men who had experienced it.*

THE AUSTRALIAN WAR MEMORIAL (AWM), Canberra, has a vast collection of paintings of the First World War. Produced under Australia's first, official war art programme, these canvases played an important role over the years in articulating and shaping collective memories of this conflict. Despite this, there has been little analysis of *whose* memories were articulated or *how* they came to be portrayed in official war paintings.[1] Scholarly interest in the memory and commemoration of the First World War has boomed since the 1980s and has gone beyond examining the traditional forms of Western memorialisation, such as monuments and cemetery inscriptions, to explore the diversity of artistic responses to conflict as 'sites of memory'.[2] War paintings have received special attention from scholars, such as Laura Brandon, who argue that as sites of social remembering the aesthetic qualities of a canvas matter less in the process of memory making than the particular meanings that are imposed on or derived

---

I would like to thank Alex Torrens of the AWM's Art Section for her untiring assistance with my research of the paintings, and Joan Beaumont, Pat Jalland and Richard White for their invaluable comments on drafts of this article.

[1] Scholars of Australia's official war paintings focus on the artists and an analysis of their work. See, for example, Anne Gray, *A. Henry Fullwood: War Paintings* (Canberra: Australian War Memorial, 1983); Catherine Speck, *Painting Ghosts: Australian Women Artists in Wartime* (Melbourne: Craftsman House, 2004); and Gavin Fry and Anne Gray, *Masterpieces of the Australian War Memorial* (Adelaide: Rigby, 1982). Anne-Marie Condé has begun to shift the focus away from the artists to those individuals commissioning the official paintings. See Anne-Marie Condé, 'John Treloar, Official War Art and the Australian War Memorial', *Australian Journal of Politics and History* 53, no. 3 (2007): 451–64.

[2] The first of these studies to consider the commemoration of the war in a range of cultural forms was Jay Winter, *Sites of Memory, Sites of Mourning: The Great War in European Cultural History* (Cambridge: Cambridge University Press, 1998). There have since been a number of histories published that explore the variety of forms which commemorate the First World War.

from it.[3] Central to this process is the dynamic interaction and exchange between individuals, or 'agents of memory', who determine what is remembered, shaping or reshaping the memory of the collective to suit changing contemporary needs.[4]

During the interwar years, Charles Bean, Australia's official war historian and a leading figure in the development of the AWM, and John L. Treloar, director of the AWM (1920–52), were key figures in constructing a memory of the First World War through amassing a collection of artefacts, textual documents, photographs, film and art. In the case of the official war art, they not only selected artists but also guided the choice of subjects for commissions. This article focuses on an unexplored aspect of their role and criteria: the significance that they attached to eyewitness testimony. Acting not only as agents but also as arbiters of memory, Bean and Treloar assumed responsibility for the translation of veterans' recollections of the war into publicly displayed paintings, mediating between former soldiers' desires for the art to capture what they recalled as being accurate and authentic and the artists' sense of professional integrity. Examining the case of one official artist, Harold Septimus Power, and focusing particularly on his repainting of *Saving the Guns at Robecq* (1920), this article explores the constant interventions in the creation of this canvas and in doing so provides new insights into Bean and Treloar's role in constructing memories of the First World War in Australia.

Factual accuracy versus artistic quality

Following Canada's and Britain's lead, the Australian government established an official art scheme in May 1917. Ideas for such a programme had emerged in the previous year, when in August 1916 Will Dyson, an expatriate cartoonist, approached the High Commissioner in London, Andrew Fisher, with a proposal to 'sketch the special Australian characteristics' of the soldiers in France.[5] Concurrently, Bean, spurred on by his role as editor of the *The Anzac Book*, a collection of satiric sketches and writings from soldiers at Gallipoli, lobbied the government to employ artists serving within the Australian Imperial Force (AIF) to sketch the war.[6] Despite competing proposals, such as the one submitted to Fisher by Baldwin Spencer, eminent anthropologist and art connoisseur, and Bertram Mackennal, renowned Australian sculptor, it was Dyson's and Bean's ideas that formed the basis of the scheme established in 1917.[7] This was

---

[3] Laura Brandon, 'The Canadian War Museum's Art Collection as a Site of Meaning, Memory and Identity in the Twentieth Century' (PhD thesis, Carleton University, 2002), 24; see also Laura Brandon, *Art or Memorial? The Forgotten History of Canada's War Art*, illustrated edn (Calgary: University of Calgary Press, 2006).
[4] Joan Beaumont, *Broken Nation: Australians in the Great War* (Sydney: Allen & Unwin, 2013), xix.
[5] Will Dyson to the Official Secretary of the Commonwealth of Australia, 23 August 1916, AWM93 18/7/5 Part 1, Australian War Memorial, Canberra (hereafter AWM).
[6] Bean to Minister of Defence George Pearce, 16 September 1916, AWM93 12/12/1 Part 2; Betty Churcher, *The Art of War* (Melbourne: Miegunyah Press, 2004), 23.
[7] Fisher to Prime Minister William Morris Hughes, 31 January 1917, AWM93 12/12/1 Part 2.

managed under two separate sections: the first was overseen by the Australian High Commission in London, and employed expatriate artists; the second, managed by the Australian War Records Section (AWRS), and also based in London, came under the Department of Defence and employed artists who were already serving in the AIF. Despite their lack of any professional artistic training, Henry Smart, Publicity Officer at the High Commission, managed the first section, while Treloar, at that time Officer-in-Charge of the AWRS, supervised the artists under the second. Bean acted in an advisory role as the AIF representative to both sections of the scheme.[8]

These men, Bean especially, were convinced that paintings and sketches 'actually made at the front' would form an 'invaluable' part of the larger collection of unit diaries, battlefield artefacts, photographs and film being amassed for a future national museum.[9] To this end, artists under the scheme were employed essentially as eyewitnesses to war, and were instructed to capture what they observed of the conflict in their work, while enjoying the freedom to paint whatever they liked, as long as it portrayed what they saw. Artists drawn from the expatriate art community in London, such as George Bell, Charles Bryant, Henry Fullwood, George Lambert, Fred Leist, John Longstaff, Septimus Power, James Quinn and Arthur Streeton, were sent to the front to live alongside Australian soldiers for periods of up to three months. Each was charged with creating twenty-five images of scenes he witnessed there. In addition, artists already serving as soldiers in the AIF, such as George Benson, Frank Crozier, Will Longstaff, Louis McCubbin and James Scott, were employed to sketch what they saw of the front when they could be spared from military duties.[10]

Although there were a range of Australian artists working in various styles in Britain and France during this period, only expatriate painters who were trained in an academic tradition—a tradition concerned with 'harmonious composition', attention to the 'arrangement of colour and tone' and creating visually realistic images—and who eschewed modernism were chosen for the art scheme.[11] Bean and Treloar considered such a style appropriate for the paintings they were amassing for a future museum—particularly in the context of the institution's commemoration of those who had fought and died. Treloar would later argue during debates about the choice of official artists for the Second World War that '[a]rtists of the Contemporary School cannot provide as accurate or enduring [a] record of war as others who adhere to academic methods'.[12] As Jay Winter has put it: 'Traditional modes of seeing the war ... provided a way of

---

[8] Bean, 'Australia's Records: Preserved as Sacred Things', 29 September 1917, AWM93 12/12/1 Part 2; Lieutenant-General William Birdwood to Robert Henry Muirhead Collins, 21 April 1917, AWM93 12/12/1 Part 2.
[9] Charles Bean, The Australian Records, c.1917, AWM93 12/12/1 Part 1.
[10] Fry and Gray, 9–13.
[11] Ibid., 11.
[12] Treloar cited in Michael McKernan, *Here Is Their Spirit: A History of the Australian War Memorial 1917–1990* (Brisbane: University of Queensland Press in association with the Australian War Memorial, 1991), 183.

remembering which enabled the bereaved to live with their losses'.[13] Australian official art was imbued with a memorialising purpose and, as Anne-Marie Condé writes, Bean and Treloar assumed that veterans and relatives of those who had died would visit the AWM 'looking for inspiration and consolation'. Hence, such 'a memorial to the war dead could not possibly represent the war experience as formless and meaningless'.[14] Bean's attitude to modern art also reflected that of many Australian critics who saw it as an 'alien disease'.[15] Believing that modern styles of painting were not a fitting mode of expression and would be 'insulting' to the veterans and relatives visiting the AWM, Bean declared that other national war art collections, such as Canada's, had been 'relegated to obscurity' after the war because they embraced 'freak art'.[16] However, Bean claimed that the emphasis of the Australian scheme on collecting 'sketches and small pictures of what the artists *actually saw* at the front', captured in the more conventional style of academically trained artists, made the collection a more 'suitable memorial'.[17]

By the time of the armistice in November 1918, the art collection consisted of an eclectic array of genres. Artists, though restricted in the subjects they could sketch by Bean and Treloar's insistence that they depict only what they observed of the conflict, produced images that ranged across a wide spectrum of genres, from intimate sketches in pencil of Australian troops in the trenches, to sweeping landscapes in oils, to numerous portraits of soldiers. This work represented only a small aspect of the Australian war experience and other significant events involving Australian troops went unrecorded since artists were often not present or were unable to observe specific military operations. It was only on their return from the front that they were commissioned with larger works that, as Treloar later argued, would supplement the smaller sketches by 'representing the more important events, on land and sea, in which the Australians took part'.[18]

Commissioning larger canvases of significant events, at which artists had often not been present, made it difficult for Bean and Treloar to maintain the precision of detail they believed artists had attained in their work at the front.[19] Consequently, during the war they directed artists to compose their larger images from the sketches they had created on the battlefield and provided them with photographs and equipment on which to base their commissions. Furthermore, artists were instructed to consult with soldiers who had taken part in the action and were also often sent back to the front for shorter periods so that they

---

[13] Winter, 5.
[14] Condé, 'John Treloar', 457.
[15] John Frank Williams, *The Quarantined Culture: Australian Reactions to Modernism 1913–1939* (Cambridge: Cambridge University Press, 1995), 24.
[16] Bean cited in Parliamentary Standing Committee on Public Works, *Report Together with Minutes of Evidence Relating to the Proposed Australian War Memorial, Canberra* (Canberra, 1928), 4.
[17] Bean to Edwin and Lucy Bean, 19 January 1919, AWM38 3DRL 7447/7. Emphasis added.
[18] John Treloar, *Australian Chivalry: Reproductions in Colour and Duo-Tone of Official War Paintings* (Canberra: Australian War Memorial, 1933).
[19] Streeton's Agreement, 3 May 1918, AWM93 18/7/12.

could capture the terrain of the battlefield.[20] These finished canvases were then inspected by members of the scheme's Art Committee in London, including Bean, Treloar, Smart, and prominent British painters Algernon Talmage and Luke Fildes. They were tasked not only with judging the quality of the art but also with checking for any factual errors against the official record before accepting the canvas.[21]

Witnessing war

This emphasis on the accuracy of Australian artists' work reflected Bean's own passion for reportage. Bean himself was an eyewitness, living alongside the Australian troops both at Gallipoli and on the Western Front, and his writing was infused with his personal observations of the war.[22] Bean's official histories, with their narrative focus on tactics rather than strategy and celebration of the common soldier, drew heavily not only on what he witnessed of the Australian troops at the front but also on interviews with soldiers after battle. As he later claimed, 'accuracy is found only in the narratives of eyewitnesses'.[23] Dyson, who worked closely with Bean during his time at the front, commented that although Bean's approach made him something of 'a dull writer', he was 'accurate to the point of mania'.[24]

Bean's mania applied not only to his own writing but also to his ideas about the collection of war records for Australia. Both he and Treloar were determined to amass a collection that represented the soldiers' exact experience, seeing this as being the only fitting memorial to these men.[25] They especially prized soldiers' personal accounts of the war and from the mid-1920s began to collect soldiers' diaries and letters from next-of-kin as well as surviving members of the AIF.[26] In 1928 Bean claimed that this material supplemented the 'frigid records' of official documents 'with the warm, personal narratives of the men actually engaged in the fighting'.[27] As Tanja Luckins argues, Bean used these sources 'to considerable effect in his official histories'.[28]

Although Bean and Treloar did not clearly define what they understood to be authentic, Bean's now infamous arguments with official war photographer

---

[20] Bean to Edwin and Lucy Bean, 19 January 1919, AWM38 3DL 7447/7.
[21] Minutes of Meeting of AWM Art Committee, May 1917, AWM38 3DRL 6673/286.
[22] Dudley McCarthy, *Gallipoli to the Somme: The Story of C.E.W. Bean* (Sydney: J. Ferguson, 1983), 7.
[23] Charles Bean, 'The Technique of a Contemporary War Historian', *Historical Studies Australia and New Zealand* 2, no. 6 (November 1942); Charles Bean, 'The Writing of the Australian Official History of the Great War: Sources, Methods and Some Conclusions', *Royal Australian Historical Society* 24 (1938): 110.
[24] Will Dyson to Edward Dyson, May 1918, Edward Dyson Papers, MS 10617 Box 269, State Library of Victoria.
[25] McKernan, 34–49.
[26] Anne-Marie Condé, 'Capturing the Records of War: Collecting at the Mitchell Library and the Australian War Memorial', *Australian Historical Studies* 37, no. 125 (April 2005): 142.
[27] Parliamentary Standing Committee, *Report Together with Minutes*, 6.
[28] Tanja Luckins, *The Gates of Memory: Australian People's Experiences of Memories of Loss and the Great War* (Fremantle: Curtin University Books, 2004), 212.

Frank Hurley over composite photography indicate what he believed was not. For Bean, the role of photography was to capture 'the plain and simple truth' of the war.[29] Hurley's assertion that the chaos and drama of what he witnessed at the front could not be caught 'on a single negative', and his resorting to 'combination pictures' to show 'what modern battle looks like', was unacceptable to Bean.[30] As Robert Dixon argues, Bean saw Hurley's composite images as a 'falsification of reality' which he would not consent to including in Australia's war record collection at 'any price'.[31] In 1922 he stopped production on the twelfth volume of the official history, *Photographic Record of the War*, because he was determined that the images published should be 'free from faking'. Claiming that he would be 'the only judge' on issues of accuracy, Bean, with the help of his assistant Arthur Bazley, ensured that Hurley's images were rigidly accurate, going as far as to crop the sky in Hurley's image entitled *The First Battle of Passchendaele* to make certain that any trace of Hurley's composite methods were eliminated.[32]

Bean and Treloar took a similar approach to accuracy in official war paintings. Between 1919 and 1923 the two sections of the art scheme in London were amalgamated under the newly established AWM's Art Committee and the collection transferred to Australia. Bean and Treloar were central members of the committee, acting in their roles as official historian and director respectively. The other members included Henry Gullet, author of the seventh volume of the official history, Tasman Heyes, veteran and secretary of the Art Committee, and Bernard Hall, director of the National Gallery of Victoria.[33] Notably, Hall was the only art expert on the committee, but his opinion was, as Treloar confessed, often ignored if a painting was considered by the other members to be factually accurate. As Treloar declared in 1921, 'art is not necessarily the predominant note we aim at in our collections'.[34] This was because, as he later explained, while '[m]ost of the former diggers who inspect our collection may not know much about art ... they are very quick to detect mistakes in colour patches, equipment, etc!'.[35]

Hence, while other institutions, such as the Imperial War Museum, made a distinction in their official collections between, as Sue Malvern argues, smaller images 'intended as records to supplement the collection of artefacts' and large-scale canvases of commemorative significance primarily aimed at fulfilling 'criteria relevant to "art"', there was no such distinction made in the case of

---

[29] Bean, 'Australia's Records'.
[30] Hurley cited in Robert Dixon, 'Spotting the Fake: C. E. W. Bean, Frank Hurley and the Making of the 1923 Photographic Record of the War', *History of Photography* 31, no. 2 (2007): 166; Hurley cited in Martyn Jolly, 'Australian First World War Photography', *History of Photography* 23, no. 2 (Summer 1999): 142.
[31] Dixon, 'Spotting the Fake', 166; Bean cited in ibid., 166.
[32] Dixon, 'Spotting the Fake', 165–6, 175.
[33] Minutes of AWM Art Committee, February 1921–July 1927 and February 1941, AWM170 4/1.
[34] Treloar to Bean, 5 May 1921, AWM38 3DRL 6673/314.
[35] Treloar to Adams, 6 April 1936, AWM93 18/1/42.

the Australian paintings.[36] Bean and Treloar conceived of all Australian official war art as preserving for posterity 'truthful portrayals of the subjects depicted' and believed it was the responsibility of the AWM as the newly emerging national memorial to 'guarantee' that the canvases were both a 'truthful record as well as a work of art'.[37]

Yet as the war faded into memory, Bean and Treloar believed that artists' physical and temporal distance from the front reduced their ability to depict the details of the war. This coincided with wider debates during this period over, as Janet Watson argues, 'who was best qualified to recapture the "experience" of the war'.[38] Progressively there was a narrowing in what were deemed to be legitimate experiences of war and a limiting of those who could claim, as Jay Winter and Antoine Prost argue, 'the authority of direct experience': veterans' memories of the conflict became more valued than artists' interpretations.[39] In Australia, this shift resulted in returned soldiers becoming more directly involved in the production of official paintings during the interwar years. Artists' work was not only scrutinised by members of the AWM's Art Committee but also by veterans who, at the request of Bean and Treloar, were encouraged to point out any errors or elements they thought might be improved in the artists' representation.

Fragile memories

It is axiomatic that any single eyewitness account is partial and, hence, this privileging of veterans' accounts was not without its difficulties. As Alistair Thomson's work on Australian soldiers and their memory of the First World War has shown, veterans often edit recollections of their war experience to accord with a public narrative, remaking or repressing memories in an attempt to match the past with their present and future lives.[40] To add to this, the AWM's reliance during the interwar years on eyewitness testimony meant veterans were being asked to recall events that had occurred sometimes over two decades previously. As Tim Cook writes, although veterans' memories were an important source, caution was required when using them, particularly 'when the passing of time could dull accuracy'.[41] Some veterans were themselves aware of the fragile nature of their memories. As one of four veterans to inspect Power's *Zizа* (1935) canvas, Major Claude Cadman

---

[36] Sue Malvern, 'War, Memory and Museums: Art and Artefact in the Imperial War Museum', *History Workshop Journal* 49 (January 2000): 188–9.
[37] Treloar to Power, 11 December 1925, AWM93 18/4/40.
[38] Janet Watson, *Fighting Different Wars: Experience, Memory, and the First World War in Britain* (New York: Cambridge University Press, 2004), 200.
[39] Jay Winter and Antoine Prost, *The Great War in History: Debates and Controversies, 1914 to the Present* (Cambridge: Cambridge University Press, 2005), 174.
[40] Alistair Thomson, 'Anzac Memories: Putting Popular Memory Theory into Practice in Australia', *Oral History* 18, no. 1 (Spring 1990): 25.
[41] Tim Cook, *Clio's Warriors: Canadian Historians and the Writing of the World Wars* (Vancouver: UBC Press, 2006), 51.

Easterbrook remarked that 'After such a lapse of time everybody seems to have different ideas on matters'.[42]

Artists who had served as soldiers in the war were aware that their experience on the battlefield did not necessarily make them reliable witnesses. Charles Wheeler, who had worked as a professional artist in Australia before the war and who had fought with the 22nd Battalion, Royal Fusiliers in the British Expeditionary Force, had not initially been permitted to paint for the Australian scheme during the conflict—though Bean had lobbied hard for permission from the War Office. However, when approached by Bean and Treloar in 1918 with a commission for the AWM, Wheeler stated that, as he had not made accurate sketches while serving at the front, any painting he produced would be drawn from memory. He therefore 'declined ... on the grounds that it would necessarily be a fake': he had 'never faked a picture ... and never will'.[43] After the war Wheeler did accept several commissions, producing portraits as well as battle scenes. Yet, despite having fought in the conflict, he constantly requested eyewitness accounts as well as other material about the specific details of the scenes he was to paint.[44] With regard to one commission, he claimed that 'he did not feel justified in attempting to paint the picture without ... [this material] as it would necessitate a certain amount of faking', and only after having received these sources was he satisfied that he could complete the canvas.[45]

Official artists who could not claim any direct combat experience responded in various ways to the importance being placed on eyewitness testimony. Some were granted access to veterans while working on their commissions. In 1925 George Bell, a well-known painter and official artist with the High Commission section who only reached the front in the final days of the war, 'had the assistance of General Foott' to get the facts correct in his painting of the construction of the Eterpigny Bridge. The resulting painting satisfied both the demands of accuracy as well as those of art.[46] In contrast, other artists found it restricting when they were asked to alter their work if it did not accord with veterans' memories of the war. Power, for example, became deeply frustrated in 1925 when two of his canvases, *The Incident for Which Lieutenant F.H. McNamara Was Awarded the VC* (1924) and *Camel Corps at Magdhaba* (1925), did not meet with veterans' approval, despite his having consulted them about the scenes.[47]

Power was a well-respected artist whose specialty was painting animals. He had trained in Melbourne and Paris and found success in London during the

---

[42] Easterbrook to Treloar, 26 May 1937, AWM93 18/4/40 Part 3.
[43] Letter from Treloar to Bean, 17 April 1918, AWM38 3DRL 6673/323.
[44] Letters between Treloar and Bean about Wheeler, 1920–29, AWM38 3DRL 6673/323.
[45] Treloar's notes on Wheeler, 29 December 1919, AWM38 3DRL 6673/323.
[46] Treloar to Bean, 7 October 1925, AWM38 3DRL 6673/292; George Bell, *Australian Engineers Constructing a Bridge at Eterpigny*, 1925, oil on canvas, 76.2 x 101.8 cm, ART11416, AWM. This painting had several titles and is also known as *The Bridge Builders* or *Battle Scene, France 1918*.
[47] Septimus Power, *The Incident for Which Lieutenant F.H. McNamara Was Awarded the VC*, 1924, oil on canvas, 143 x 234.7 cm, ART08007, AWM; Septimus Power, *Camel Corps at Magdhaba*, 1925, oil on canvas, 178.5 x 268.5 cm, ART09230, AWM.

1920s painting the stag hunt, landscapes and his beloved horses. Although rejected from enlisting in the army, he had been employed by the High Commission as one of the original official war artists in September 1917 and continued to receive commissions from the Memorial throughout the 1920s.[48] Power's paintings were consistently exhibited on the line—the most coveted space—at the Royal Academy in London and his art was admired for its 'vivid realism' and appeal to both 'the critical gaze of the artist' and 'the lay and unskilled eye'.[49] His war works, in particular, had received wide acclaim in Britain, praised as masterpieces 'full of dash and spontaneity'.[50]

However, despite their critical reception in art circles, several of Power's paintings did not meet with approval from veterans in Australia. Frank McNamara, the subject of Power's *The Incident for Which Lieutenant F.H. McNamara Was Awarded the VC*, claimed that the painting 'was incorrect in a number of details', particularly in the way it showed 'the ground ... rougher than it actually was, and the cavalry more massed and closer to the machine [aeroplane] than the Turks got'.[51] Only a month after this letter, Treloar asked Power to alter his canvas of the battle at Magdhaba, a painting Power believed was 'one of the best pictures' he had produced for the AWM and which had been exhibited in the Royal Academy to wide acclaim.[52] The special correspondent for *The Argus* had also noted that it was 'excellent' and showed 'much ability'.[53] Yet, George Langley, who had been present during the Magdhaba operation, claimed that 'the scene is very clear in my own mind' and complained to Treloar about the many inaccuracies he saw in Power's representation of the event.[54] Although Treloar and other members of the Art Committee were aware that the canvas was 'artistically ... up to your [Power's] high standard', there was 'a certain amount of disappointment that the picture lacks the element of action'. Treloar advised Power that he would need 'to revise the picture to introduce this element'.[55]

In terms of McNamara's criticisms, it became apparent that there were competing memories at play. Power had initially 'carried out what Capt. McNamara said' but had 'started a new picture' after having received complaints about the canvas from another veteran, Colonel Williams. Hoping to avoid any further discrepancies Power had asked Williams to inspect the repainted canvas to 'make absolutely certain it was correct in every detail'.[56] There were also inconsistencies and variations over time apparent in individual veterans'

---

[48] Harold Septimus Power, Service Record, B2455, National Archives of Australia, Canberra (hereafter NAA).
[49] 'Display of Paintings: Mr. H. Septimus Power's Work', *The Advertiser*, 10 July 1928.
[50] 'Septimus Power: Famous War-Artist', *The Sydney Morning Herald*, 29 April 1922; 'Picture of the Year, Royal Academy Exhibition: Australian Artists', *The Argus*, 28 June 1919.
[51] Treloar to Power, 26 June 1925, AWM93 18/4/40.
[52] Tasman Heyes to Treloar, 4 November 1925, AWM93 18/4/40.
[53] 'Royal Academy Exhibition', *The Argus*, 6 June 1925.
[54] George Langley to Treloar, 13 July 1925, AWM93 18/4/40.
[55] Treloar to Power, 20 August 1925, AWM93 18/4/40.
[56] Power to Treloar, 30 September 1925, AWM93 18/4/40.

Figure 1. Septimus Power, *The Incident for Which Lieutenant F.H. McNamara Was Awarded the VC*, England, 1924, oil on canvas, 143 x 234.7 cm (Australian War Memorial, ART08007).

memories. Power was 'considerably' concerned at Langley's criticism of the scene at Magdhaba, given he had 'painted the picture entirely from information give [sic] me by Col Langley', and from this information had, in his role as artist, 'depicted the best outlook ... that allowed of that subject to be painted'. He declared that it would be 'impossible' to revise the canvas, as any changes would 'mean entirely painting a new picture'.[57]

Power was not a confrontational man. Bean described him as 'loveable' though 'a very shy gauche chap' and 'intensely nervous'.[58] He took his work for the war art scheme seriously: 'I have always tried to give my best services to the War Museum'. However, when asked to repaint the McNamara canvas for a *third* time despite his having taken measures to avoid the necessity for doing so, and considering the criticism levelled at his prized *Magdhaba*, Power stated: 'I'm sure you will understand me when I say I can't keep on under these conditions'.[59] He was so disillusioned that he was no longer interested in completing his next commission, *Leaders of the Australian Light Horse in Palestine, 1918* (1926), which he had begun working on. The requests to alter his other canvases had made 'the conditions so unsatisfactory that I am obliged to turn it down'.[60] Treloar assured Power that he understood the 'burden upon artists' in meeting veterans' expectations and that it was only with 'the best motives' that the AWM suggested

---

[57] Heyes to Treloar, 4 November 1925, and Power to Treloar, 30 September 1925, AWM93 18/4/40.
[58] Bean, Diary, 3 September 1917, AWM38 3DRL606/88/1.
[59] Power and Treloar, 30 September 1925, AWM93 18/4/40.
[60] Heyes to Treloar, 4 November 1925, and Power and Treloar, 30 September 1925, AWM93 18/4/40.

revisions and with the aim of obtaining a canvas that was accurate and artistic.[61] Eventually, through some deft and delicate letter writing, Treloar persuaded Power to continue with his work and Power eventually altered both canvases.

Septimus Power's *Saving the Guns at Robecq*

However, worse was to come for Power. While it was commonplace for Bean and Treloar to ask artists to alter their work before the AWM acquired the final painting, they rarely requested that a canvas be repainted after they had accepted it. Yet, this was the fate of Power's *Saving the Guns at Robecq* (1920), which depicted the 45th and 47th Batteries of the 12th Field Artillery Brigade withdrawing from the line during the battle of the Lys in April 1918 and saving all the guns in the face of approaching German troops.[62] Power had visited the Western Front several times during the war as an official artist and had been attached to the 1st Division. Although he had not been present at this specific event, Bean and Treloar had supplied him with written material about the incident at Robecq when commissioning the canvas in 1919. They had also directed Power to consult with officers of the 12th Field Artillery Brigade on the particulars of the incident.[63] When completed by Power in 1920, the painting had been inspected for any factual inaccuracies by the AWM's representatives in London who, finding none, had accepted the canvas.[64] The painting had been displayed on and off during the 1920s. It had also been published in a book of colour and duo-tone reproductions of the AWM's official paintings, edited by Treloar, *Australian Chivalry*, without its drawing censure from veterans.[65]

Yet, in 1933, thirteen years after the painting had been completed, Bean received a letter from Lieutenant-Colonel George Hill Adams challenging the accuracy of Power's interpretation of the scene. Adams had been an officer with the 47th Field Artillery Battery, had received the Military Cross in 1917 and had made a successful career in the army on returning to Australia.[66] After seeing Power's painting he wrote:

The picture is certainly very good, but as a representation of what occurred on that occasion it is ridiculous ... it seemed to me that if this were a matter worthy of being recorded in paint it would be a pity that it should be a source of amusement to anyone who was there.

---

[61] Treloar to Power, 11 December 1925, AWM93 18/4/40.
[62] Septimus Power, *Saving the Guns at Robecq*, 1920, oil on canvas, 152.3 x 244 cm, ART03332, AWM.
[63] Treloar to Bean, 24 August 1933, AWM93 18/1/42.
[64] Charles Bean, 'Australian War Memorial Pictures Commissioned', 1919, AWM38 3DRL 6673/286; Treloar to Adams, 4 September 1933, AWM93 18/1/42.
[65] *Saving the Guns at Robecq* was displayed in the first exhibition of the AWM in Melbourne, 1922. Charles Bean, *Australian War Museum: The Relics and Records of Australia's Effort in the Defence of the Empire, 1914–1918* (Melbourne: AWM, 1922), 27. Treloar, *Australian Chivalry*.
[66] Adams George Hill, Service Record, 1914 – 1920, B2455, NAA; letters between Treloar and Adams, 1929, AWM93 12/11/2109; *The Army List of the Australian Military Forces* (Melbourne: Govt. Printer, 1940), 1003.

Figure 2. Original version of Septimus Power's *Saving the Guns at Robecq*, England, 1920, oil on canvas, 152.3 × 244 cm. Reproduced in John Treloar, *Australian Chivalry: Reproductions in Colour and Duo-tone of Official War Paintings* (Canberra: Australian War Memorial, 1933).

Despite having no professional artistic training, Adams supplied his own small sketch 'of what actually occurred'.[67]

Bean and Treloar were greatly troubled by Adams' comments, particularly because they were unable to understand how the painting, which had followed the process of production prescribed for larger commissions, could be so inaccurate. Consequently, Treloar suggested that the official records of the incident be consulted before any action was taken and that Power should be contacted to ascertain 'from whom he obtained data for the picture'.[68] Although he never questioned that, 'As one who took part in the incident Colonel Adams must … know what he is talking about', Treloar did note that Power's painting was 'not inconsistent' with what he believed to be an 'authoritative' account written by Frederic Cutlack, an intelligence officer in the British Expeditionary Force attached to the AIF during the war and later an official war correspondent and author of the eighth volume of the official history, *Australian Flying Corps*.[69]

---

[67] Lieutenant-Colonel G. H. Adams to Charles Bean, 4 August 1933, AWM93 18/1/42. Unfortunately, the sketch has not survived.
[68] Treloar to Bean, 24 August 1933, and Treloar to Bean, 30 August 1933, AWM93 18/1/42.
[69] Treloar to Bean, 24 August 1933, and Treloar to Adams, 4 October 1933, AWM93 18/1/42; A. J. Sweeting, 'Cutlack, Frederic Morley (1886–1967)', in *Australian Dictionary of Biography* (Canberra: National Centre of Biography, Australian National University), http://adb.anu.edu.au/biography/cutlack-frederic-morley-5859 (accessed 25 August 2014); Frederic Cutlack, *The Australians: Their Final Campaign, 1918. An Account of the Concluding Operations of the Australian Divisions in France* (London: Sampson Low, Marston, 1918).

However, after considering Treloar's material, as well as his own records, amongst which were 'two excellent accounts' of the incident from Colonel Lloyd, commander of the 12th Field Artillery Brigade and Lieutenant Waterhouse of the 47th Battery that described 'many of the details required to be known', Bean was convinced that Power's representation was flawed.[70] Unable to discover where Power had obtained his information or if he had consulted veterans as instructed, Treloar officially concluded that the material supplied by the AWM to Power had been insufficient and the details 'necessary for the painting of a picture' omitted.[71] Treloar pointed out that ultimately the AWM was at fault since the inaccuracies should have been caught at the time the commission was produced, and it seemed that 'the precautions usually adopted to ensure the factual accuracy of a painting appear to have been relaxed in this case'.[72]

What followed illustrates the extent to which Bean and Treloar privileged the lived experience of combatants over a professional artist's interpretation of the war. Initially Bean raised the idea that the canvas might be sold, or be given back to Power as part payment for another commission. Drawing on his own authority as historian and eyewitness, Bean also proposed two different scenes if the AWM ever decided to recommission an artist with the Robecq scene: such a painting, he suggested, should focus on 'the batteries beginning to limber up' or 'a couple of guns racing along the Robecq road'.[73] Both of these, as it happened, aligned closely with his own description of the incident in the official history.[74] However, Bean also claimed that 'perhaps the best solution might be to withdraw the picture and say nothing about it until he [Power] approaches us, as he probably will some day, with an inquiry as to whether we have any more work for him'. Alternatively, Bean suggested that the AWM might keep Power's work and consider it an 'imaginative' piece depicting the Australian artillery in action, and that another canvas of the Robecq incident be painted if the opportunity arose later.[75] Treloar, in turn, agreed that the Art Committee should 'regard it as an imaginative work', and suggested that the AWM 'exhibit it under the more generic title "Bringing Up the Guns"', discarding its links with a specific incident in the war and thereby bypassing Adams' criticisms about its accuracy. In suggesting this Treloar appeared to overlook the fact that there was already a painting by Power entitled *Bringing Up the Guns* which had been completed in 1921.[76] As a further option, there was some discussion between Bean and Treloar about altering the painting and its title to show an incident Bean himself witnessed

---

[70] Bean to Treloar, 4 September 1933, AWM93 18/1/42.
[71] Treloar to Bean, 7 September 1933, AWM93 18/1/42.
[72] Treloar to Adams, 4 October 1933, AWM93 18/1/42; extract from 21st Meeting of Finance Committee, 11 December 1933, AWM93 18/4/40.
[73] Bean to Treloar, 4 September 1933, AWM93 18/1/42.
[74] Charles Bean, *The Australian Imperial Force in France: During the Main German Offensive 1918*, Official History of Australia in the War of 1914–1918, vol. 5 (Sydney: Angus & Robertson, 1941), 438–42.
[75] Bean to Treloar, 4 September 1933, AWM93 18/1/42.
[76] Treloar to Bean, 7 September 1933, AWM93 18/1/42; Septimus Power, *Bringing Up the Guns*, oil on canvas, 147.3 x 233.7 cm, 1921, ART03334, AWM.

near Lihons in 1918, which he claimed the painting fairly closely resembled.[77]

Given Power's reaction to criticism of his work in 1925, Bean and Treloar were faced with a delicate task. Bean asked Adams as to how the painting might be altered to make it 'more truly representative [of] any phase of this incident'.[78] At the same time he wrote to Treloar noting that 'Power's pride in his work must be considered'.[79] Bean then met with Power to discuss Adams' criticisms and ascertain if anything could be done to 'fix' the painting. Together they concluded that Adams' suggestions were so extreme that they could not be carried out without the scene being painted anew.[80] However, this did not satisfy Adams who insisted that 'it would be comparatively easy to alter the picture in question'. He added that 'apart from the fact that the picture is incorrect as regards the terrain it would be a great pity if such an excellent painting were withdrawn permanently'. Adams even offered to 'assist' the AWM with the details and went on to explain that alterations were necessary only to eliminate the team in the background on the left of the painting.[81] Power found that these suggestions were not as drastic as he and Bean had initially anticipated and, after speaking with Adams in person at the urging of Treloar, decided he would be able alter the canvas to accommodate Adams' memory of the incident.[82]

In late 1934 Power sent a photograph of the revised painting to Treloar with an express wish that it also be forwarded to Adams. Treloar, in turn, invited Adams to 'criticize it so that [Power] may know if it is now satisfactory or requires further alteration'.[83] In response, Adams replied that the 'picture gives a very faithful idea of what happened', adding that he could find 'nothing to criticize in the general surroundings' and thought 'the picture excellent'.[84] The reworked painting differed significantly from the first version. For example, there was no sign of the team on the left who have been replaced by several guns. However, Adams was most impressed with the striking change in the landscape, declaring that Power's representation of his own description of the surroundings was 'extraordinarily good', especially since 'he could only paint them from his own imagination'.[85]

The reasons why Power deferred to those with less artistic authority than himself remain elusive in the archives. Possibly, he did not want to jeopardise his chances of obtaining further commissions from the AWM. As Treloar commented, he had 'been having a rather thin time in London' and he

---

[77] Bean to Treloar, 4 September 1933, AWM93 18/1/42.
[78] Bean to Adams, c.18 August 1933, AWM93 18/1/42.
[79] Bean to Treloar, 4 September 1933, AWM93 18/1/42.
[80] Note from Treloar, 2 October 1933, AWM93 18/1/42.
[81] Adams to Bean, 7 October 1933, AWM93 18/1/42.
[82] Treloar to Adams, 11 October 1933, and Treloar to Heyes, 30 November 1933, AWM93 18/1/42.
[83] Treloar to Adams, 18 December 1934, AWM93 18/1/42.
[84] Adams to Treloar, 3 January 1935, AWM93 18/1/42.
[85] Adams to Treloar, 8 April 1936, AWM93 18/1/42.

Figure 3. Photograph of the altered painting, c.1934 (Australian War Memorial Registry File, AWM93 18/1/42).

appeared keen to talk with Adams in late 1933.[86] Further, though many of the state galleries had acquired war paintings from official artists in the years immediately after the conflict, as Treloar acknowledged, in the 1930s 'war pictures are not popular with galleries' and it was unlikely that Power could have sold the canvas to another institution.[87] He was paid one hundred pounds to alter the canvas, and although only roughly a third of what he was paid for the original commission, this may have appeared to him the best option for a painting unlikely to be popular elsewhere.[88]

Unsurprisingly, there were details about the Robecq incident that Adams remembered incorrectly, as well as ones that he missed. For example, in reference to a key component of the gun, he emphatically stated that 'In the case of the air recuperator the buffer was below the gun instead of being on top as in the case of the spring buffer'.[89] Treloar checked this detail with Robert Peacock, librarian at the Department of Defence, only to learn that the 18 pounder Mark II had the air recuperator on top of the gun and not below as Adams claimed.[90] When Treloar then asked Adams if the first gun, the Mark II, was the gun he had in mind and supplied him with photographs, he replied that 'It is quite clear from the photographs that my memory was at

[86] Treloar to Bean, 13 February 1933, AWM38 3 DRL 6673/314; Treloar to Adams, 2 November 1933, AWM93 18/1/42.
[87] Treloar to Bean, 7 September 1933, AWM93 18/1/42.
[88] Extract from 21st Meeting of Finance Committee, 11 December 1933, AWM93 18/4/40.
[89] Adams to Treloar, 9 May 1936, AWM93 18/1/42.
[90] Treloar to Peacock, 6 June 1936, AWM93 18/1/42.

fault in this matter'.[91] Treloar claimed to have shown the repainted image to several other former AIF artillerymen who allegedly pointed out some minor inaccuracies that still existed in the painting. However, whether this occurred remains uncertain.[92] Regardless, it became evident that there were other details Adams missed, such as whether, as Treloar asked, Power had 'erred in placing a saddle on the off-side horse'.[93] Adams took another, and closer, look at the photograph of the repainted canvas and declared that it was not a saddle but a rolled blanket which in itself was wrong as it should be laid flat against the horse. He also commented that there was a small error in the depiction of the team on the right, where a brake seemed to be showing on the off wheel of the gun instead of on the gun.[94]

Treloar relayed these remaining inaccurate details to the long-suffering Power, leaving him to decide on 'whatever action they may suggest'.[95] Power in fact chose to ignore several of Adams' comments, as became apparent when the repainted canvas arrived at the AWM's premises in Melbourne in 1936. Adams pointed out these details, particularly noting that the gun limber was *still* shown with a brake.[96] As a result, Power returned to the Exhibition Building to make

Figure 4. Final version of Septimus Power's *Saving the Guns at Robecq*, England, oil on canvas, 152.3 x 244 cm (Australian War Memorial, ART03332).

---

[91] Treloar to Adams, 8 July 1936, AWM93 18/1/42; Adams to Treloar, 20 July 1936, AWM93 18/1/42.
[92] Treloar to Power, 3 May 1935, AWM93 18/1/42
[93] Treloar to Adams, 5 February 1935, AWM93 18/1/42.
[94] Adams to Treloar, 8 February 1935, AWM93 18/1/42.
[95] Ibid.
[96] Adams to Treloar, 8 April 1936, and Treloar to Power, 22 July 1936, AWM93 18/1/42.

these final corrections. Overall, though, Adams was very pleased with the picture and wrote to Treloar that it 'generally gives a very true idea of what actually happened' and 'the general spirit of the thing is just right'.[97]

Conclusion

Accuracy came at a price. In this case, it was the artistic quality of the painting which was lost in the process of translating eyewitness testimony into paint. Power's original canvas was a vivid and arresting representation of a scene that evoked the chaotic atmosphere of battle. The final painting lacked this intensity. The scene is stiff, the dash and spontaneity Power was famous for in his war work having disappeared in the attempt to impose factual accuracy. The landscape in which the men fight is almost serene, the menacing clouds, planes and towering smoke from the distant artillery have vanished, replaced by more tranquil surroundings—a featureless sky, an empty horizon, a few willow trees, a bridge over a stream. While there remain some traces of the energy captured in the original, such as the rushing momentum of the central team of horses in the foreground, the painting as a whole has lost its vitality and the repainted section on the left is particularly stilted.

Adams was aware of the painting's loss of drama, noting when he viewed the final alterations to the canvas that 'it is probably a good deal less dramatic than the original painting'.[98] However, in a statement that candidly articulated Bean and Treloar's aims for the war art, Treloar assured Adams of their gratitude for his assistance and satisfaction with the repainted image:

> We have always endeavoured to ensure the accuracy of paintings so that they can be handed down to posterity with the assurance that their veracity is vouched for by men with first-hand knowledge of the subjects depicted. Unfortunately we 'slipped' with regard to the Robecq painting and are, therefore, grateful that you not only drew attention to its shortcomings but furnished the information which enabled the artist to achieve the historical accuracy for which we have always striven.[99]

For Treloar, aesthetics mattered less than the accuracy of the painting and its depiction of a scene drawn from the testimony of an eyewitness who could claim the authority of lived experience.

After the pedantry of this process, the question arises, was the repainted canvas an effective site of memory? Certainly it conformed to Bean's idea that meaning was found in the narrative of the eyewitness. The process of altering the canvas mirrored Bean's own aims for the official histories, which he explained were to 'right many wrongs' and 'bring to thousands of actions recognition'.[100] Consequently, by imposing or embedding Adams' recollections of the Robecq

---

[97] Adams to Treloar, 8 April 1936, AWM93 18/1/42.
[98] Ibid.
[99] Treloar to Adams, 2 May 1936, AWM93 18/1/42.
[100] Bean, 'The Technique of a Contemporary War Historian', 79.

incident in Power's painting, Bean and Treloar saw themselves according to the veterans the status of the privileged eyewitness. However, by insisting on changes that had the effect of divesting the painting of its aesthetic and emotive intensity, Bean's and Treloar's dogged pursuit of accuracy compromised the canvas as a site of memory. The consolation and inspiration which Bean and Treloar hoped visitors would discover in the AWM's collections was found not in canvases which strove to capture 'accuracy' through the flawed memory of veterans, but in evocative images such as Will Longstaff's *Menin Gate at Midnight* (1927). This canvas was, significantly, painted outside of the official scheme and acquired by the AWM in 1927.[101] Depicting the ghostly forms of soldiers moving toward the moonlit monument at Ypres, Longstaff sentimentalised the war. Yet this entirely fictional scene, imbued with a spiritualism popular in the years following the conflict, captured the imagination of grieving Australians who were attempting to come to terms with the consequences of the conflict—thousands of reproductions were sold during this era.[102]

It is not certain whether Power's original canvas would have enjoyed greater popularity than the repainted image. Although there is evidence to suggest that the altered painting was exhibited in the AWM until the late 1960s, it is no longer on display and is housed in the AWM storage facility at Mitchell, Canberra.[103] What is evident is that Bean and Treloar's pursuit of accuracy in the official art and intervention in the production of the paintings—reflecting a wider trend of the AWM's collecting practices of the period—meant that veterans' personal recollections profoundly shaped the art commissioned during this era and, thereby, the broader and more public memory of the First World War.

Margaret Hutchison
Australian National University

---

[101] Will Longstaff, *Menin Gate at Midnight*, 1927, oil on canvas, 137 x 270 cm, ART09807, AWM; Anne Gray, exhibition catalogue, 'Will Longstaff: Art and Remembrance', November 2001–February 2002, Australian War Memorial.

[102] John Stephens, '"The Ghosts of Menin Gate": Art, Architecture and Commemoration', *Journal of Contemporary History* 44, no. 1 (January 2009): 23.

[103] *Guide to the Australian War Memorial* (Canberra: Government Printing Office, 1968). The painting was loaned to Museum Victoria briefly in 2001 before returning to storage until 2008 when it was temporarily on display in the AWM's First World War Gallery until 2009: correspondence between author and AWM Art Section, 25 September and 7 October 2014.

Informing the enemy: Australian prisoners and German intelligence on the Western Front, 1916–1918

Aaron Pegram

Research School of Humanities and Arts, Australian National University, Canberra, Australia

This article considers the intelligence value of prisoners captured during the First World War. 3848 troops of the Australian Imperial Force (AIF) were taken prisoner by the German Army on the Western Front between the years 1916 and 1918. Because their capture was at odds with a heroic representation of the Australian war experience in the post-war period, little has been written about their war in captivity. But historians who have written about captivity tend to dwell on the personal, subjective nature of captivity and rarely consider the benefit prisoners are to the armies that capture them. This study addresses both omissions, and looks at prisoners of war as intelligence sources through the experience of Australian troops captured by the German Army on the Western Front. This paper uses prisoner testimony and German intelligence records to demonstrate that most Australian prisoners were 'sturdily determined' not to reveal any information of value to the enemy, yet the German Army still managed to obtain 'very important information' from them. It looks at AIF counter-intelligence methods, German procedures for handling prisoners for intelligence purposes, interrogation methods, prisoner experiences, what the German Army learned from Australian prisoners, as well as examples of how the German Army used information obtained from prisoners. It also looks at two cases of Australian troops who willingly disclosed information about the AIF and its operations having deserted to the enemy.

Captain Charles Mills was captured at Fromelles on the morning of 20 July 1916. At first light, German troops showered his position with 'potato masher' grenades and rushed it on foot, firing their rifles from the hip. A German sergeant stopped his men on the parapet, jumped into the waterlogged ditch and seized Mills by his wounded hand. 'Why did you not put up your hands, officer?' he demanded in English, 'Come with me.' As the battle drew to a close, Mills and the surviving members of his company were escorted along a communication trench to a farmhouse which the Germans called *Neuhof*. There in the courtyard they joined three officers and 200 other ranks – all Australians – in what was evidently a collecting station for prisoners of war. A German surgeon took care of the walking wounded, and Mills had his hand cleaned and bandaged. But what happened next altered German knowledge of British intentions in the Fromelles area.

At the request of a German intelligence officer, Mills turned out the contents of his pockets, producing a photograph and a diary. The photograph was of Mills – a studio portrait taken in Melbourne – which the German officer kept to assist in the visual recognition of Australian troops. The diary was of interest because it provided a daily account of the 31st Battalion since its departure from Egypt just a few weeks before, and activities since arriving in France. Also, inside the diary was a copy of the orders issued to the Australian 5th Division by the British XI Corps commander, General Sir Richard Haking. They revealed that the intention of the Fromelles attack was to pin the Germans in the Lille area and prevent their reinforcements from being drawn into the British offensive on the Somme. The Germans confirmed through Mills that the attack was nothing more than a diversion, so by taking the orders into battle, Mills had inadvertently revealed sensitive information that undermined the very purpose of the operation. Mills made no mention of the incident after his release from captivity, but to his interrogators at the 6th (Bavarian) Reserve Division headquarters that morning he confessed it was 'a serious error of judgement' to allow such an important document to fall into their hands.[1]

Mills' indiscretion illustrates why armies take prisoners of war. Since ancient times, those who take them have denied their enemy the manpower to fight on the battlefield, and have used prisoners as hostages and forced labourers. Above all, prisoners of war have been a very valuable source of military intelligence on the enemy's morale, strength, disposition and activities. Historians demonstrate how prisoners were sometimes killed in the First World War in flagrant disregard of international law, yet these were usually isolated incidents carried out on the initiative of individuals rather than on the order of higher authority.[2] As far as Allied prisoners captured on the Western Front were concerned, there was a very important reason why the German Army took prisoners, and that lay in their value as sources of intelligence. Armies fighting on the Western Front obtained this information from a host of other sources, such as aerial photography, signals intelligence and espionage.[3] But in the routine of trench fighting on the Western Front, prisoners were considered an essential means by which British, French and German armies obtained tactical-level information on the enemy and his intentions. For *Oberst* Walter Nicolai, the first senior intelligence officer of the German Army and head of its military secret service, prisoners were the 'most valuable source of news in the western theatre of war'.[4]

Historians who write about captivity tend to concentrate on the subjective, personal nature of the prisoner experience, and neglect the value they are to the armies that capture them.[5] Niall Ferguson acknowledged that prisoners are 'especially important' as sources of intelligence, yet the most recent scholarly literature on captivity during the First World War overlooks this aspect of the prisoner experience in favour of dwelling on how the enemy treated them.[6] The recent work of Heather Jones examines the neglected issue of violence against British, French and German prisoners captured on the Western Front, but makes no mention of their value other than a source of forced labour.[7] Similarly, little is written in Australia about the 4044 members of the Australian Imperial Force (AIF) captured during the First World War, of which 3848 were taken by the German Army on the Western Front.[8] In Australia, as in Britain, France and Germany, captivity remains a 'missing paradigm' in First World War studies.[9]

This omission is perhaps due to the heroic theme in Australian war writing that emerged in the post-war period.[10] The most intense criticisms of this tradition have been levelled at the Australian official historian Charles Bean, who is said to have been the creator of the 'Anzac Legend'. Alistair Thomson argues that Bean's 12-volume *Official History of Australia in the War of 1914–1918* depicted an idealized version of the Australian war experience which neglected and understated aspects such as cowardice, desertion, self-inflicted wounds and ill-discipline. Thomson writes that 'Bean was a brilliant myth-maker, not because he denied or ignored evidence which contradicted his ideal, but because he admitted and then reworked that evidence in terms of his own preconceptions so that it was less challenging'.[11] There were few places in the *Official History* where Australian prisoners were dealt with in any great detail, but Bean acknowledged that men of the AIF 'were usually under intense strain and suffering from shock' after falling into the hands of the German Army. Bean recognized that Australian prisoners were 'sturdily determined' not to give away intelligence of any value, but 'comparatively seldom' did they refuse to answer questions under enemy interrogation.[12]

There are examples in Australian records showing that Australian prisoners made 'a good military impression' on their captors by refusing to respond to questions other than to give their name and rank, as they were required to do.[13] But a study of German intelligence records show that the enemy still managed to obtain valuable military information from Australian prisoners of war. First World War scholars have been hindered by a lack of German sources since a single bombing raid by the Royal Air Force in April 1945 destroyed 90% of operational records of the Imperial German Army. The significance of this loss cannot be understated, but copies of some Prussian material survive in archives at Dresden, Munich, Stuttgart, Karlsruhe and Freiburg im Breisgau.[14] Fortunately, the operational records of German formations from Bavaria, Saxony, Baden and Württemberg survive, including intelligence files from several German divisions that captured Australian troops. Because most Australians were captured by units from Bavarian or Württemberg divisions, it has been possible to locate German Army intelligence reports based on their interrogation. It has also been possible to compare these reports with individual statements made by Australian prisoners that document the circumstances of their capture and treatment in captivity.

An example of how this methodology is applied involves a trench raid that took place on the night of 27–28 September 1916, when 14 men of the 13th Battalion raided the German trenches at Piccadilly Farm in the St Eloi sector in Belgium. The intention of the raid was to inflict 'loss on the enemy, establishing identification of units opposed to us, and maintaining the offensive spirit'.[15] The officer leading the raiding party, Lieutenant Frank Fitzpatrick, had studied the ground by telescope over the preceding days and was confident he could bring his men close to the German wire while artillery and trench mortars sealed off the selected point of entry with a 'box barrage'. That night, Fitzpatrick led his men off-course to a position next to where the raiders had intended to enter the German trenches. Australian records document how British artillery fell on the raiding party: Fitzpatrick was killed and four others were seriously wounded.[16] The raiding party returned to Australian lines without Fitzpatrick or Private Donald Muir, an experienced soldier who had recently been awarded the Military Medal. The 'box barrage' separated Muir from the raiding party, but rather than retire, he continued to attack the German trenches on his own. According to German records, 'a soldier from this patrol managed to get through our wire defences and approach our position ... from behind with a sack of hand grenades. By the determined and clever intervention of *Gefreiter* Kieselbert of the 12th *Komp. Inf. Regt.* 127., the enemy was forced to throw away his hand grenades and was then taken prisoner'.[17]

Muir was wounded in the leg during his encounter with *Gefreiter* Kieselbert, and was searched and interrogated by an intelligence officer at a dressing station behind German lines. Muir, according to his examiner, was considered 'very stubborn'. It is likely that Muir did not verbally disclose any information of military value, but his uniform, colour patches and national insignia identified him as a member of the Australian 4th Division which the German Army's *Oberste Heeresleitung* (Supreme Army Command, or OHL) believed was still fighting on the Somme. The examining officer at XIII (Württemberg) Army Corps headquarters considered this 'very important information' for the Allied order of battle, because 'it has become very likely that an Australian division has replaced the Canadian division which had been there before'.[18] To encourage German troops in the St Eloi sector to continue capturing prisoners, XIII Army Corps rewarded *Gefreiter* Kieselbert with 300 Marks (approximately US$15 in 1916), while *Grenadiers* Schock, Ebhard, Kübler and Huβ from Grenadier Regiment 123 shared a modest reward of 100 Marks (US$5 in 1916) for retrieving the body of Lieutenant Fitzpatrick.[18] Muir did not have to reveal anything for the Germans to acquire information from him, but because he could be interrogated and elicit a meaningful response, his capture demonstrates that the Germans considered live prisoners far more valuable for the purposes of intelligence than the bodies of dead enemy soldiers.

Counter-intelligence training and the AIF

How prisoners responded to interrogation was partly informed by the counter-intelligence training they received before capture, although little or no training on interrogation was provided before the first Australians were captured in France in May 1916. Neither the *Field Service Regulations* nor *Notes for infantry officers in trench warfare* said what to do should a man fall into the hands of the enemy, even though the former gave clear instructions on the handling and treatment of enemy prisoners of war.[19] The problem was not just limited to the AIF. The British Second Army, for example, repeatedly stressed the importance of ciphers in all forms of telecommunications and informed troops of counter-espionage measures, yet failed to cover what was expected of them in the event they were interrogated by German intelligence staff.[20] As soon as the AIF arrived in France in 1916, battalions did what they could to ensure the German Army did not acquire intelligence from captured sources. In June, as the 7th Brigade prepared for the AIF's first trench raid on the Western Front, raiding party members were instructed that 'neither officers or men [should be] carrying anything likely to be of value to the enemy, such as letters, identity discs, badges, pay-books etc.'.[21] Rifles, revolvers and other items of field equipment had identifying markings obliterated, and raiders were instructed to wear generic British Army tunics with sandshoes and puttees instead of their distinctive Australian pattern uniform.[22] Such steps made it difficult to identify the nationality of those killed in enemy trenches, but they were of little help when raiding party members were captured alive.

It was not apparent until the end of the 1916 Somme campaign that prisoners could sometimes be an operational liability. In September, Allied intelligence received reports that the German Army had obtained Haking's order for the Fromelles attack from a captured Australian officer. Lieutenant Colonel Cyril Wagstaff, General James McCay's chief of staff, issued a memorandum informing battalions of the 5th Division 'that they are betraying their duty by giving any information other than their name and rank if they shall fall into the hands of the enemy'.[23] The memorandum made three key points:

(1) Prisoners taken by the Germans carried on them copies of our battalion orders;
(2) A German posing as an American interrogates all prisoners who arrive in prisoners of war camps;
(3) The colonial troops in particular are found to give information very readily. The attention of this Division is specifically directed to (3).

The message was clear: the enemy took prisoners as sources for military intelligence. Wagstaff directed that 'No documents of use to the enemy are to be forward of Battalion Headquarters in an attack', and he made platoon commanders submit signed certificates that guaranteed the memorandum had been read to all men under their command.[24] Wagstaff's memorandum marked the beginning of counter-intelligence training throughout the AIF that told men what was expected of them should they be taken prisoner. According to Article IX of the Hague Convention, 'a prisoner of war is bound to give, if he is questioned on the subject, his true name and rank, and if he infringes this rule, he is liable to have the advantages given to prisoners of his class curtailed'. The rules and customs of war on land became the subject of lectures in rear-area billets. The most important elements were distilled into simple instructions, such as 'DON'T refuse to give your name and regiment; it doesn't do any good, and your people won't know what has become of you'.[25] The training coincided with a wider effort across the British Army to inform and remind troops of their obligations if they had the misfortune of falling into the hands of the enemy. After the Somme, General Headquarters notified formations that a captured man 'is not to give any information beyond his name and rank. The enemy cannot and will not compel him to say more – though he may threaten to do so – on the contrary he will respect a man whose courage and patriotism do not fail even though wounded or a prisoner'.[26]

Training received by the airmen of the Australian Flying Corps (AFC) was far more rigorous. Unlike the infantry, who always fought from static positions and had infrequent face-to-face contact with the enemy, pilots from the two Australian scout squadrons, No. 2 and No. 4 Squadrons AFC, flew deep into German territory fulfilling the Royal flying corps (RFC) 'air offensive' policy. Australian scout pilots ran the risk of being shot down and captured everyday. In German skies, Nos. 2 and 4 Squadrons conducted patrols and ground attack sorties, sought combat with enemy fighters and escorted the slower bombers and photo-reconnaissance machines. They did this to ensure the twin-seaters from corps squadrons could go about artillery spotting and performing reconnaissance duties above enemy trenches unmolested by German fighters. But taking the air war into enemy territory was extremely hazardous, and 21 AFC scout pilots were forced to land their damaged machines on the German side of no man's land.[27]

Aircrew were highly skilled, were sound in operational knowledge, had a good sense of geography and navigation, and were equipped with some of the most advanced technology of the period. These qualities made them extremely valuable for intelligence purposes, and as such, airmen were informed and reminded of the techniques German intelligence staff used to extract information from prisoners. To prevent their machines from being captured, studied, salvaged or pressed into service by the German Air Service, Australian pilots flew with a flare pistol in their cockpits so that a disabled aircraft and any maps, letters or operational documents could be set alight after a forced landing.[28] Airmen were also instructed to keep the enemy guessing as to the identity of their squadron and the names their commanders and other pilots, and at the event of being captured, 'no communications must be sent direct to their squadrons'. Instead, captured airmen were instructed to address all communication from captivity to 'Major — C/o Cox & Co.', the financial military agents in London, who then passed all incoming correspondence to the War Office and confirmed with the Red Cross and the RFC that the missing airman was alive as a prisoner of war in the hands of the Germans.[29]

Prisoners and German intelligence procedures

The experience of prisoners in the hours after capture was determined by the procedures the German Army had in place for handling and processing captives for intelligence purposes. Line regiments of the 6th Bavarian Reserve Division received new instructions on how to handle and process large groups of prisoners several days after capturing 470 Australians in the attack at Fromelles in July 1916. After patrols, raids or major defensive actions, regiments were instructed to report to III (Bavarian) Army Corps headquarters stating the number of prisoners they had captured. They also reported the prisoners' units from division down to company level, the time and place of their capture, and brief details on how they were captured. This report, communicated by telephone or telegraph, made its way to the intelligence officer attached to 6th Army Headquarters. This officer was responsible for conducting interrogations and evaluating captured material either at brigade or divisional headquarters when large numbers of prisoners were captured, and interrogated smaller groups of prisoners as they passed through corps headquarters.[30]

Prisoners were stripped of their weapons and equipment before being escorted to the German rear. They retained personal items such as their identity discs, pay books, photographs of family members, money and uniform insignia, but forfeited official documents, letters, maps, newspapers, diaries and any other papers for examination. Officers were separated from non commissioned officers (NCO) and other ranks men as soon as possible so that the chain of command would be disrupted and the prisoners' state of uncertainty heightened. All talk was forbidden, and to prevent compromising interrogations, German soldiers were warned not to converse with captives before prisoners had been examined by intelligence staff.[31] Looting was common in rear areas, so German troops were often reminded about the importance of colour patches and national insignia on prisoner uniforms for positively identifying enemy units and establishing an accurate order of battle.[32]

Interrogations had to be conducted as soon as possible so that the information could be distributed to German line regiments and used immediately. Examining officers often asked seemingly innocuous questions, such as identity of the prisoner's battalion, its place in the order of battle, where it had previously fought and how long it had been in the line. To help German defences prepare for further attacks, they asked prisoners captured during patrols, raids and major offensive actions about their objectives, casualties and when their battalions were last reinforced. Examining officers also asked about the location of troop billets, artillery batteries and march routes so they could be shelled. Finally, examining officers often asked about the possibility and locations of any further attacks, as these were considered 'extremely important' in the long-term defence of the corps sector.[33]

Australian prisoners were interrogated in accord with these procedures, often within hours of their capture. Non-wounded prisoners were questioned once they had made their way to the rear, while the wounded were examined days later, if their state allowed. Ernest Gaunt, an Australian Army Medical Corps stretcher-bearer, was captured at Mouquet Farm in August 1916. The awkward exchange Gaunt recalls with his examiner was typical of the conversations Australian prisoners shared with German intelligence staff:

> 'Have you been very busy, had many wounded?'
> 'No.'
> 'How many patients have you carried today?'
> 'Five or six.'
> 'How many are there in your section?'
> 'Only fifteen.'
> 'Any casualties among your officers?'
> 'No.'
> 'Any wounded officers?'
> 'No.'
> 'What did you join for?'
> 'I am a Britisher.'
> ...

'Were you on Gallipoli?'
'Yes.'
'You had a lot of casualties there?'
'Yes, but the Turks had more.'[34]

Reports of verbal abuse and acts of violence were infrequent. Instead, prisoners were often subjected to attempts by intelligence staff to try to lull them into a false sense of security through offers of cigarettes, alcohol and displays of sympathy. Captured at Bullecourt on 11 April 1917, Claude Benson was taken to the village of Écourt-Saint-Quentin, where about 150 of the 1170 Australian troops of the 4th Division captured that morning were singled out and interrogated at the headquarters of the Württemberg 27th Division:

> On our arrival some German officers questioned us separately about our battalion. The treatment we received from these polite officers was good as they offered us cigarettes and told us to light up ... I thought it better not to smoke as I had been taught to take no risks if taken prisoner, really doubting what the cigarettes might contain.[35]

Most prisoners interrogated at Écourt-Saint-Quentin were officers and NCOs, who by virtue of their rank and experience, knew more about the AIF and its operations than the 900 other ranks men detained in the chateau yard. Captain Joseph Honeysett was the first officer from the 47th Battalion to fall into German hands and 'was not surprised' when he was taken to the chateau for questioning. He was 'ushered into a comfortably furnished bedroom' where he met his examiner:

> Lying on the bed there was a most affable looking man of middle age, who in perfect English, promptly apologised for any discourtesy he appeared to show in receiving me in that manner! At the bedside, notebook in hand, was seated a very aristocratic looking young Lieutenant ... In French, he asked me to accept a cigarette and a glass of cognac.[36]

Honeysett was 'certainly not prepared ... for the extraordinary interview which followed' as he was fully expecting to be subjected to a running fire of 'bulling cross-examination by several typical Prussian officers of the "English newspaper" type'.[37] German intelligence staff found kind treatment elicited good results because prisoners expected 'beatings and other ordeals' from their captors. They found British troops 'spoke more willingly even than the deserters' when they were kindly treated.[38] In much the same way, an intelligence officer examining Australians captured on the Somme found it was 'generally believed [among Australians that] prisoners were shot on capture'.[39] Kind treatment worked particularly well within the first few hours of capture when prisoners were still suffering from the fear and shock of trench fighting.[40] In February 1917, a German intelligence officer wrote how four Australians of the 22nd Battalion captured near Warlencourt were 'quite shocked that they are being treated so well ... particularly as they had been gripped by rumours of barbarism and rough treatment'. Because of their treatment, the prisoners expressed joy they felt towards the outcome of the first conscription referendum in Australia, and made it known 'they are all particularly happy to have landed in captivity, through which they have escaped a heavy workload on frugal provisions'.[41]

Captured airmen were certainly better prepared for interrogations than infantrymen. In October 1917, Lieutenant Ivo Agnew of No. 2 Squadron became the first Australian airman captured by the Germans after the AFC started flying operations on the Western Front. Agnew was separated from his patrol during an encounter with a German twin-seater, got lost, developed engine trouble and mistakenly landed his DH.5 scout on a German airfield outside Valenciennes. That night he wrote in his diary how he 'was treated well', 'had dinner with the officers of the 42nd Squadron' and was afterwards 'taken down to the Aerodrome to see some of their machines, mostly Albatross scouts, though there were 4 of ours among them resplendent in black iron crosses etc.'.[42] Despite attempts by German pilots to alleviate Agnew's anxiety and prepare him for questioning, their chivalrous hospitality was to no avail. When questioned at Le Cateau the following morning, Agnew revealed his nationality and civil employment but refused to answer questions about the identity of his squadron or the names of his commanders. He managed to make 'a good military impression' on his examiner, who considered him to be 'considerably better educated than the average soldiers who stem from the English colonies'.[43]

Airmen also were subjected to more subtle forms of cross-examination. Australian pilots were often detained with British airmen before being transported to Germany, the idea being that prisoners would compare stories, discuss aircraft or operational matters, much to the benefit of listening intelligence staff. Lieutenant Wentworth Randell of No. 4 Squadron, for example, 'found two megaphones hidden in the wall' of the locked room he shared with two other airmen at Lille.[44] Most AFC and AIF officers were sent from France to Karlsruhe, where they spent several nights locked in a room at the Hotel Europäischer Hof before being moved to the main processing and distribution camp in the centre of town. Knowing a 'Dictaphone' was 'cunningly concealed in the walls', Archie Rackett of No. 2 Squadron found the situation quite amusing: 'I was placed in with a French officer who spoke no English. We managed to purchase a pack of cards and thus we amused ourselves without hardly speaking.'[45] Captain William Cull from the 22nd Battalion had been there some months earlier. He was unaware that a recording device was being used, but was conscious that a 'quiet listener outside the door might hear something to his advantage'.[46] A similar technique was sometimes used at prisoner collecting stations behind German lines, where enemy soldiers dressed in British uniforms would sit and listen-in on prisoners' conversations. Percy Cook remembers 'a German who claimed to be a New Zealander' who attempted to befriend him at Cambrai. 'He may have been "dinkum", but I had my suspicions and I "sang dumb"'.[47] Another man recalls seeing a German soldier at a prisoner cage at Sailly-le-Sec in April 1918 wearing 'a "Tommy" tunic beneath his own, which he wore unbuttoned'.[48]

There were exceptions to the rule that prisoners were treated well. Some were beaten and insulted by German troops before being formally interrogated. Whereas troops of the 10th and 11th Battalions were 'almost happy' to have been captured at Mouquet Farm on 22 August 1916, men of the 51st Battalion captured there on 3 September were treated with disdain after what Bean described as 'one of the bitterest fights in the history of the A.I.F.'[49] The two vastly different experiences reflected the increased intensity of the fighting and the temperament of the Prussian 5th Guard Division that occupied the Mouquet Farm defences in the latter attack. One man was 'knocked about the head with German stick bombs' for refusing to reveal the location of artillery batteries and 'was told that I would be forced to give this information' through further threats of violence.[50] A German officer told another man at Cambrai, 'You are obliged to answer' all forms of questioning. When the man refused to tell the officer anything more than his name and rank, the officer 'kicked me and threatened to shoot me. I tried to sleep, but they worried me all the time'.[51] A wounded Australian was questioned by a German Medical Officer:

'Are you an Englander?'
'No, I'm an Australian.'
'You're a liar! – Australians are black!'[52]

Notwithstanding the significance of colour patches, national insignia, uniforms, captured orders and other documents in piecing together an accurate picture on the AIF and its intentions, German intelligence staff were more likely to treat captured men with courtesy and respect, as it was found to be one of the most effective means of eliciting a meaningful response. 'Whether their statements are pretence or truth there is no means of proving', wrote one German officer after examining Australians in August 1918. 'All were reticent and only after a lot of talking did their tongues become loose.'[53]

What the German Army learned from Australian prisoners

The first examination of Australian prisoners on the Western Front took place at Douai on 6 May 1916, the morning after two companies of the Reserve Infantry Regiment 230 raided the 20th Battalion in the Bridoux Salient near Armentières. *Hauptmann* Fritz Lübcke, the intelligence officer for 6th Army, interrogated the 11 men seized during the raid, and later examined Australians captured at Fromelles. From the prisoners, Lübcke was able to piece together an accurate picture of the 2nd Division in its first few weeks in France. This included the location of its headquarters, the effectiveness of German artillery, and the strength, disposition and arrangement of the 5th Brigade defences. Just as important for the visual recognition of Australian troops were the uniforms and insignia worn by the prisoners: 'The Australians wear floppy hats as headgear', Lübcke wrote. 'The left brim is rolled up and fixed with the badge ... the "badge" consists of a crown with rising sun and the inscription "Australian Commonwealth Military Forces".'[54]

The most useful informant among the captives was Lieutenant Norman Blanchard, who was recovering from gunshot and shrapnel wounds in the field hospital at Douai. Lübcke's report details how Blanchard confirmed the 2nd Division's order of battle, which included the 13th Light Horse Regiment as divisional cavalry, the use of a 'detectaphone' to intercept German telephone messages from the Australian front-line positions and the names of several officers at brigade and battalion headquarters. Blanchard also stated that 'a comprehensive English attack is planned for the foreseeable future'.[55] Lübcke did not document how this information was interpreted or put to use, but it would have been passed on to OHL's intelligence branch IIIb for further analysis and action. In the following days, Lübcke circulated a drawing throughout 6th Army based on a captured photograph from the Bridoux Salient raid that depicted two Australian soldiers to illustrate how Australian uniforms and equipment differed to those of other British formations.[56]

As well as factual information, German intelligence staff often included 'mood pictures' in their reports as snapshots of the war and its effects behind Allied lines. For individual prisoners, this included accounts of their service before capture, comments on their state of mind, thoughts, opinions and grievances, observations on the relationships between Allied troops, and remarks on the political and domestic situation at home.[57] The summaries allowed intelligence staff to make assessments of the character of the Australian troops in France. Ernest Fitch of the 5th Battalion, for example, was one of the few men captured during the 1st Division's attack at Pozières on 26 July 1916. Fitch conveyed a 'first-rate impression as a soldier' on *Hauptmann* Friedrich Weber, the intelligence officer of 1st Army: 'He already has considerable experience under his belt, having participated in all battles in the Dardanelles, and is extremely intelligent.' Lübcke and Weber went to great lengths to determine how many *Gallipolikämpfer* were among captured Australian troops, and often concluded that those who had seen service on Gallipoli made better soldiers than the reinforcements who had little or no combat experience.[58] Weber considered men of the 1st Division to be:

a completely different calibre to the average English soldier ... Each and every man knows how to fend for himself in an emergency and even if the leadership completely disintegrated, they would still constitute an excellent unit, which is not the case for the English.[59]

In the following days Weber examined troops from the 1st and 2nd Australian Divisions, and was able to make tentative conclusions about the fighting ability of I ANZAC Corps.

In comparison with the average units of the English battalions ... the Australian troops are without doubt of a completely different calibre ... Where something special has to be accomplished, the English leadership deploys Australian troops, amongst whom there is fierce competition for success at the battalion level.[60]

In August, he examined Australians from the 4th Division, a formation raised after the Gallipoli campaign in February 1916:

One cannot avoid the impression that the quality of the men of the 4th Australian Division is below that of the 1st and 2nd Divisions. Their officers are decidedly below the average English officer; they differentiate themselves only slightly from their troops, and in personal interactions pay no attention to the difference in rank.[61]

Indiscipline was what struck Lübcke of prisoners from the 5th Division, another formation raised after Gallipoli:

The officers ... despite repeated protestations that their conscience as officers would not allow them to disclose military secrets, cheerfully dictated to us complete details of the planning and execution of the attack, and the dispositions of the units involved.[62]

In spite of the reminders and official warnings, Australian troops were frequently captured with letters, diaries and important documents that the German Army was able to use for intelligence purposes. Weber, for example, learned of the effectiveness of a German bombardment near Messines on 1 July 1916 from the diary of an unknown Australian, either killed or captured at Mouquet Farm. The diarist recorded:

We went forward through an old sap, crawling over the parapet and into a shell hole. Here we remained when I suddenly saw rising gas from our trench, whereupon I called my friends to put on their gas masks ... Then the real show began. They set up a hellish barrage of shells and flares on us. I had never seen such a magnificent sight before.[63]

Private accounts indicated the effectiveness of bombardments and raids against Allied positions, but were also good indications of morale. A letter from a 37th Battalion man captured at Houplines in February 1917 read:

A terrible and mighty push will be made during the Spring, and this will probably end the war. Then we will go home forever and [I will] never leave Australia again. I have had enough of it. How often do I long to be with you all at home. I am sorry that I did not listen to your words and left you. Now I am paying for it. I wish it was all over ... I send you some tears with this letter.[64]

Other intelligence disclosures had greater operational significance. After the Battle of Menin Road on 20 September 1917, a German prisoner spoke of a 'British' officer who had been taken by a patrol the night before who had revealed an attack on their front was imminent. Among the 2nd Division's missing was Lieutenant Harold Ferguson of the 7th Machine Gun Company, whose disappearance was the subject of a court of enquiry that determined he had 'lost direction' and was captured hours before the attack. Ferguson was later confirmed as a prisoner of war in Germany, and after his return from captivity in December 1918, was placed under arrest for 'scandalous conduct' on suspicion of having deserted to the enemy.[65] It was not until Ferguson's repatriated prisoner statement was reviewed at AIF Headquarters some weeks later was he absolved of any wrongdoing. He told clerks from AIF administrative headquarters at Ripon in Yorkshire how he mistakenly stumbled out into no man's land the night before the attack where he encountered three enemy soldiers: 'I immediately dropped to my knee and drew my revolver and rushed at the patrol, killing two of them.' Ferguson tripped and fell into a shell hole, where he was rushed by a second party and captured. 'They then conducted me to a pill box. On my way there I destroyed all papers ... they took my Sam Brown belt and private papers.'[66]

Despite Ferguson's attempts to destroy the orders, it was clear that the patrol was able to recover them which resulted in a bombardment along the I ANZAC Corps front. Aware that an attack was imminent, staff from the Prussian 121st Division ordered 'annihilation fire' to be brought down on the Australian positions, striking at all known approaches, rear lines, battery nests and strong points as indicated in the recovered documents.[67] Neighbouring units were warned by telephone, and special counter-attack divisions further to the German rear were prepared for fighting. The Australian trenches were packed with infantrymen preparing for their assault, but the news arrived far too late for the German response to be effective in any way. The 'annihilation fire' failed to stall the attack, and within hours of the orders being recovered from Ferguson, the 1st and 2nd Divisions captured the German positions they set out to take. Ferguson's disclosure did not stop I ANZAC Corps from attacking at Menin Road, but he spent a month imprisoned at Warwick Square in London after returning from Germany before being permitted to return to Australia.[68] It was clear that Ferguson had unintentionally disclosed intelligence to the enemy, although not all prisoners were so reluctant. Two Australian soldiers intentionally deserted to the enemy to use their limited knowledge of the AIF and its operations to improve their chances of having their lives spared from any further fighting on the Western Front.

Private Allan Yeo of the 14th Battalion deserted to the Germans on the evening of 1 December 1916, and is the young soldier referred to by Bean in the *Official History* as having 'walked over to the enemy'. Bean writes that

> [a] captured German officer told of a youngster of the 4th Australian Division who had come across saying that he could no longer bear the cold and mud and want of sunlight; the officer had taken him into his own dugout and talked to him for half-an-hour – 'quite a nice chap,' he said.[69]

Yeo was carrying orders and a barrage map for a brigade attack on the position known to the British as Fritz's Folly in the Flers–Gueudecourt sector when he was captured. Due to the poor weather, the fighting by this stage had come almost to a standstill, but Fritz's Folly was a small salient that protruded into the I ANZAC Corps front. Previous attempts to take it had been hindered by mud, poor weather and well-placed enemy machine-guns. In the attack proposed by 4th Division staff, guns of six siege batteries with almost unlimited supplies of high-explosive shells were allocated the task of shelling the salient for three hours, so there was 'nothing living in the area' when the infantry began its assault.[70]

Zero hour was fixed for the evening of 4 December, with 14th Battalion receiving orders to capture Fritz's Folly and two nearby positions, Hilt and Lard Trenches. The commanding officer of the 14th Battalion sent Yeo 100 yards into the forward positions with the orders and barrage map for one of his company commanders on the far side of the battalion front to examine and comment on.[71] Yeo was returning the orders to his battalion commander when he deserted to the Germans. Instead of making his way through the trenches which were waterlogged and congested with mud, he returned down the length of the sunken road that constituted no man's land in full view of both Australian and German sentries. Despite warnings from Australian sentries, Yeo turned towards the enemy positions as he reached the end of the road and was taken in by Saxon troops of the

Reserve Infantry Regiment 101. With the enemy aware of the forthcoming operation, 4th Division headquarters cancelled the attack on Fritz's Folly.[72]

Nothing more of Yeo's capture is documented in Australian records; he was not interrogated, so he does not appear in Saxon records either. What is known is that the information Yeo disclosed to the enemy did not influence their activities in the area. A German runner with documents and map stumbled into the Australian positions just hours after Yeo's desertion. His captured documents revealed that, because of the inherent dangers of holding such a sharp salient, staff at XII Reserve Corps headquarters were planning to abandon Fritz's Folly as soon as construction on a fall-back position had been completed. The prisoner told how troops of 23rd Reserve Division favoured the salient because its close proximity to the 'British' lines meant that it got little attention from Allied artillery. Saxon troops were apprehensive about abandoning the salient, because their new position would be under direct observation from the Australian lines and would be under constant trench mortar fire. As a precaution against the proposed attack on 4 December, German artillery kept the sunken road and the ground in front of Fritz's Folly under heavy fire, and on 6 December, the salient was abandoned in accordance with XIII Reserve Corps plans.[73] Yeo informed the Saxons that a renewed attempt to capture the position was coming, but this had no bearing on their activities and spared the lives of the 14th Battalion men set to attack it. It was a mutually beneficial outcome for I ANZAC Corps who ended up occupying Fritz's Folly without incurring any losses.

The information willingly disclosed by Private Charles Christiansen was not so innocuous. Twenty-three-year-old Christiansen from the 44th Battalion was a first-generation Australian whose father had emigrated from Flensburg on the German border with Denmark in the 1870s.[74] Christiansen had enlisted in the AIF in 1914 against his parents' wishes, was among the first ashore at Gallipoli with the 11th Battalion on 25 April 1915 and was twice wounded by Turkish shrapnel later in the campaign. He repatriated to Australia and was discharged owing to the severity of his wounds, but re-enlisted as soon as he returned to civilian life. He evidently had a change of heart by the time his battalion arrived on the Western Front to fight the German Army, because in France, he was 'always complaining' and 'seemed to think that as a result of his wound received at Gallipoli he was titled to a position well in the rear of the line'.[75] Christiansen's eccentric behaviour came to a head a few days after participating in a trench raid on the German positions opposite Port Egal Farm in the Houplines sector on the night of 13 March – an enterprise that cost the battalion nine men killed and 54 wounded and missing.[76]

Christiansen abandoned his sentry post on the morning of 17 March 1917. German documents record how he drew rifle and machine-gun fire until troops of 23rd Royal Bavarian Regiment understood his intention to desert. He was interrogated by *Major* Hermann Hagen, the intelligence officer at II (Bavarian) Army Corps headquarters, to whom he said 'he did not particularly want to be part of the war in France' on account of his German heritage. Christiansen made a series of frank statements about what he knew about II ANZAC Corps in the Lille–Armentières sector. Hagen reported:

> he is obviously anxious to get across that he has important information. He states to have been particularly encouraged in his decision when he learned that undertakings against our positions will be made on the nights of 17/18th and 18/19th March. He had wanted to warn us about those.[77]

No raids were planned nor conducted in the days after Christiansen's desertion, indicating that he either fed misinformation to the enemy believing it to be true or manufactured the story to curry favour with the enemy.[78] Christiansen went on to reveal how the 11th Brigade defences were arranged and held, the location of artillery and mortar batteries in Ploegsteert Wood and mentioned 'a rumour that Ypres will be attacked in approximately eight weeks'. Discontented with his platoon commander and the Regimental Medical Officer who both rejected his requests for a base job well behind the front line, Christiansen commented how 'the officers are supposed to have a compassionate attitude but they do not really understand anything'. In spite of these admissions, Hagen found Christiansen to be a very unreliable intelligence source: he commented that 'upon interrogation, the statements that had been uttered with high certainty became more insecure. He makes contradictory statements that undermine his credibility'.[79]

How the Bavarians used the information Christiansen disclosed is not documented in Hagen's intelligence report, but as Christopher Duffy writes, deserters were not looked upon favourably by German intelligence staff: 'The German officers, as upholders of military virtue, regarded the deserters with suspicion and distaste. They prized honest prisoners of war more highly in every respect.'[80] Desertion to the enemy was comparatively seldom in the British Army, but OHL was naturally weary of men like Christiansen on suspicion they were really spying on behalf of their own command, and would return to their own lines at the first opportunity.[81]

The information obtained from Yeo and Christiansen did not drastically alter the AIF's operations in France and Belgium, but their deliberate revelations had the potential of harming their comrades still fighting in the trenches. The dangers of talking to the enemy were made clear on the night of 30 May 1918, when several high-explosive rounds from a German rail gun were fired at the chateau at Allonville, several kilometres behind the Somme front, which was occupied by 4th Division headquarters. Two shells hit an adjacent barn in which two companies of the 14th Battalion were resting: 18 men were killed and 68 wounded. Only the day before the shelling, 7th Brigade headquarters circulated a translated German intelligence document stating that captured Australians had revealed the location of the 3rd Division headquarters then at Allonville.[82] As the official Australian war correspondent, Charles Bean, was at Allonville the morning after the shelling, and wrote of the incident in his diary:

> The Germans were really shooting for the chateau. They were told some time ago, apparently, probably by a man of ours who they captured, that this was 3rd Division headquarters ... If any man of ours gave this news to them he himself killed those 18 comrades as directly as if he clubbed them.[83]

Bean later referred to the incident in the *Official History* as 'the Allonville disaster' and described as a 'warning to all captured men against giving away information, or even talking of such things among themselves'.[84]

Conclusion

It is hard to contest Bean's assessment that most Australian troops were 'sturdily determined' not to give away intelligence of any value. Scared, frightened and anxious men needed little encouragement to talk during interrogations after the ordeal of trench fighting, so 'comparatively seldom' did they refuse to respond to questions. In instances where captured Australians refused to talk, German intelligence officers still managed to obtain important intelligence from their uniforms, the documents they carried into battle and their thoughts of home and petty grievances. From these, German officers were able to maintain an accurate order of battle of Allied forces, observe the activities on Australian units and formations, and make assessments on morale of Allied troops beyond the front line. Prisoners of war were important for the German Army's intelligence network, but the disclosures made by individual prisoners during interrogations, such as the two Australian deserters Yeo and Christiansen, did little to undermine the ability of the AIF to carry out its operations against the German Army.

As for Captain Charles Mills, the Australian officer captured at Fromelles, he was moved to Germany, then later Switzerland, where he located the whereabouts of Australian prisoners in Germany on behalf of the Wounded and Missing Bureau of the Australian Red Cross Society – a task that earned him an OBE after the war. The copy of Haking's orders Mills took into battle revealed to the Germans that the attack at Fromelles was a feint designed to prevent German reserves from being transferred to the Somme. But despite this, and in spite of heavy casualties on both the Verdun and Somme fronts, German commanders decided to retain troops in the Fromelles area.[85] Mills' 'serious error of judgement' in revealing the purpose behind the Fromelles attack was thus annulled, but his transgression shows that divulging operational information to the enemy, either willingly or unintentionally, was a reality of captivity during the First World War.

Acknowledgements

The author expresses his gratitude to his supervisors Bill Gammage and Peter Stanley, as well as, Karl James, Lachlan Grant, Robert Nichols and Ashley Ekins. He also thanks Peter Barton, Amelia Hartney, Andrew Arthy, Barbara Schäfer, Immanuel Voigt and Annerose Scholz for their assistance.

Notes

1. Australian War Memorial (AWM) AWM30 B16.7, repatriated prisoner statement by Capt Charles Mills, 31 Bn; Solleder, *Vier Jahre Westfront*, 229–31; Bayerisches Hauptstaatsarchiv Abteilung IV (BayHStA/Abt.IV), RIR21, Bü 7, *Ergebnis der Unterhaltung mit den gefangenen australischen Offizieren*, 22 July 1916. Bean refers to the incident but makes no mention of Mills. Bean, *The A.I.F. in France, 1916*, 442. Excerpts from Mills' captured diary are held at BayHStA/Abt.IV, 6BRD, Bü 23, *Auszüge aus Briefen an Angehörige der 5. austral. Division*, 5 August 1916.
2. Kramer, *Dynamics of Destruction*, 63–64; Cook, 'The Politics of Surrender'; and Blair, *No Quarter: Unlawful Killing*.
3. Pöhlmann, 'German Intelligence at War'.
4. Nicolai, *The German Secret Service*, 182.
5. van Emden, *Prisoners of the Kaiser*; Morton, *Silent Battle: Canadian Prisoners*; Jackson, *The Prisoners, 1914–18*; Noble, 'Raising the White Flag'; and Moynihan, *Black Bread and Barbed Wire*.
6. Ferguson, *The Pity of War*, 371; Speed, *Prisoners, Diplomats and the Great War*; Rachamimov, *POWs and the Great War*; Connes, *A POW's Memoir*; and Heinz, *Gefangen in Großen Krieg*.
7. Jones, *Violence against Prisoners of War*.
8. Coombes, *Crossing the Wire*.
9. Jones, 'A Missing Paradigm?'
10. Gerster, *Big-Noting: The Heroic Theme*, 2, 20, 230; and Gerster, 'Hors de combat', 222.
11. Thomson, 'Steadfast Until Death?', 477.
12. Bean, *The A.I.F. in France, 1916*, 442.
13. AWM27 312/12, 'Example Set by an Officer and Man of Our Forces after Capture (March 1918)'.
14. Sheldon, *The German Army on the Somme*, 40.
15. AWM4 23/4/12, war diary, 4th Bde, September 1916, 13 Bn raid order, 25 September 1916.
16. AWM4 23/30/23, war diary, 13 Bn, entry for 27–28 September 1916, 'Appendix B4'; 'Appendix 19'.
17. B-WürHStA M33/2, XIIIAK, Bü588, untitled handwritten intelligence document, 30 September 1916.

18. AWM30 B13.1, statement by Pte Donald Muir, 13 Bn; Baden-Württemberg Hauptstaatsarchiv (B-WürHStA) M33/2, XIIIAK, Bü 578, *Aussagen des am 28. 9. morgens im Diependaal Grund am Taleck vom J. R. 127 gemachten Gefangenen*, 28 September 1916; B-WürHStA M33/2, XIIIAK, Bü 588, untitled handwritten intelligence document, 30 September 1916.
19. War Office, *Field Service Regulations 1909*, 148–55.
20. AWM25 423/4, 'Instructions for Intelligence Duties, Second Army, revised 23 March and 10 June 1916'; AWM27 491/4, 'Notes on the Prevention of Espionage and Leakage of Information', 21 October 1915.
21. AWM4 23/7/10, war diary 7th Bde, June 1916, 'Operation order No. 14'.
22. AWM4 23/7/10, war diary, 7th Bde, June 1916, 'Operation order No. 14'.
23. AWM4 1/50/7, war diary, 5th Div, September 1916, Part II, 'Memorandum No. 27'.
24. AWM4 1/50/7, war diary, 5th Div, September 1916, Part II, 'Memorandum No. 27'.
25. Hague IV (1907), Chapter II, Article IX; AWM27 474/7, 'The soldier's DONT'S of international law', c.1917.
26. AWM27 491/1, 'Notes on the Prevention of Espionage and Leakage of Information', 17 December 1916.
27. An additional 11 Australian pilots were captured flying in RFC and Royal Naval Air Service squadrons, but have not been included in this figure. Roberts, *Wingless*: 20–38.
28. Royal Air Force, *Instructions Regarding Precautions*, 2–5.
29. Untitled extract published in the newsletter of the Society of Australian World War 1 Aero Historians, April 1971.
30. BayHStA/Abt.IV, 6BRD, Bü 23, *Nachrichtengewinnung durch Gefangenenvernehmungen*, 29 July 1916.
31. Ibid.; B-WürHStA M33/2, XIIIAK, Bü 588, *Eintreffen von Gefangenen*, undated, c.1917.
32. B-WürHStA M33/2, XIIIAK, Bü 588, *Auszug aus Armeebefehl Nr. 3.*, 30 July 1916.
33. Ibid.
34. AWM30 B11.10, statement by LCpl Ernest Gaunt, 13 Fld Amb.
35. State Library of New South Wales (SLNSW) ML MSS885, LCpl Claude Benson, 13 Bn, manuscript: 2.
36. AWM 3DRL/4043, Capt Joseph Honeysett, 47 Bn, manuscript: 17.
37. AWM 3DRL/4043, Capt Joseph Honeysett, 47 Bn, manuscript: 17.
38. Duffy, *Through German Eyes*, 41.
39. AWM47 111.05/01, 'Note on Prisoners Statements', 71.
40. See Bean, *The A.I.F. in France, 1916*, fn 641.
41. B-WürHStA M33/2, XIIIAK, Bü 581, *Vernehmung von 4. Gef. vom 22. austr. Batl. 6. austr. Brig. 2. austr. Div. gef. gen. am Morgen des 26. II. im Warlencourtriegel (Abschnitt E) auf Höhe 124*, 26 February 1917.
42. AWM PR0112, 2 Lieut Ivo Agnew, No. 2 Sqn AFC, diary entry for 2 October 1917.
43. B-WürHStA M33/2, XIIIAK, Bü 582, *Vernehmung eines am 2.10. mittags südöstlich Valenciennes notgelandeten englischen Fliegeroffizieres*, 5 October 1917.
44. AWM30 B3.12, statement by Lieut Wentworth Randell, No. 4 Sqn AFC.
45. Private collection, Lieut Archibald Rackett, No. 2 Sqn AFC, manuscript: 35–6.
46. Cull, *At All Costs*, 143.
47. AWM30 B13.14, statement by Pte Percy Cook, 51 Bn. Cook could be referring to Pte William Nimot, 1st Bn Wellington Regiment NZEF, who deserted to German troops at Houplines in June 1916. See Puglsey, *On the Fringe of Hell*, 77–90.
48. AWM30 B6.7, statement by Cpl Thomas Grosvenor, 30 Bn. Official memoranda after the Somme warned of such practises. See AWM27 491/1, 'Prevention of Espionage and Leakage of Information', 27 December 1916.
49. Bean, *The A.I.F. in France, 1916*, 858.
50. AWM30 B11.3, statement by Pte Hugh West, 51 Bn.
51. AWM30 B13.14, statement by Pte Percy Cook, 51 Bn.
52. AWM30 B11.3, statement by Sgt Luke Ramshaw, 51 Bn.
53. AWM4 23/13/31, war diary, 13 Bde, 18 August, 'Interpretation of a Captured German Document'.
54. BayHStA/Abt.IV, 6BRD, Bü 23, *Aussagen von 1 Offizier und 10 Mann vom XX/Bat New South Wales "B" und "C" Comp, 5. Brig., 2nd austral. Div. (Australian Imperial Exp. Force)*, 6 May 1916.

55. AWM30 B6.14(1), statement by Lieut Norman Blanchard, 20 Bn; BayHStA/Abt.IV, 6BRD, Bü 23, *Aussagen von 1 Offizier und 10 Mann vom XX/Bat New South Wales "B" und "C" Comp, 5. Brig., 2nd austral. Div. (Australian Imperial Exp. Force)*, 6 May 1916.
56. Ibid.; *Hauptmann* Karl Tettenborn, intelligence officer of AOK6, circulated a diagram of 9 Bde colour patches after the first 3 Div prisoners were captured in December 1916. BayHStA/Abt.IV, 6BRD, Bü 35, *Aussagen von 2 Mann vom 33. Jnf. Batl. (a-Komp.) 9. austr. Brig., 3. austr. Div. gefangen genommenen am 12.12. abends hart nördlich der Strasse Armentières-Lomme*, 14 December 1916.
57. B-WürHStA M33/2, XIIIAK, Bü 588, *Bericht ueber Dienst im Gefangenen-Lager der 1. Armee getrennt nach Vernehmungs-und Lager-Dienst*, no date.
58. Duffy, *Through German Eyes*, 41, 55.
59. B-WürHStA M33/2, XIIIAK, Bü 579, *Vernehmung eines Sergeanten des V. Jnf Batl. (2 austr. Brig. 1. Austr. J.D.), gefangenen genommen 26.7. 3° früh nördlich Pozières*, 27 July 1916.
60. B-WürHStA M33/2, XIIIAK, Bü 579, *Nachtichten über den Gegner vor der Front der Armeegruppe Böhn (25.-28.7.16)*, 29 July 1916.
61. B-WürHStA M33/2, XIIIAK, Bü 579, *Vernehmung von in der Nacht vom 14. zum 15. VIII. 16. gef. gen. Offizieren und Mannschaften des XIII. Batl., 4.Brig., 4. austr. Div.*, 21 August 1916.
62. BayHStA/Abt.IV, 6BRD, Bü 23, *Der Angriff auf die 6.bayer.Res-Div. in der Gegend nordwestlich von Fromelles am 19. 7. wie von Gefangenen beschrieben (hauptsäschlich Offizieren)*, 30 July 1916.
63. B-WürHStA M33/2, XIIIAK, Bü 579, *Auszüge aus dem Tagebuch eines Unteroffiziers vom XXV. austr. Batl. (2. austr. Div.)*, 10 August 1916.
64. B-WürHStA M33/2, XIIIAK, Bü 581, *Aus australischen Papieren*, 30.3.17; AWM38 3DRL 8042/86, 'Broadcasts, 1917; comprise abstracts from German broadcasts relating to Australian POWs'.
65. National Archives of Australia (NAA) B2455, Lieut Harold Ferguson, 'Court of Enquiry Proceedings'; 'Service and Casualty Form'.
66. AWM30 B6.11(2), statement by Lieut Harold Ferguson, 7MGC.
67. The orders were those issued to 7 Bde on 17.9.17. AWM4 23/7/25, war diary, 7th Bde, September 1917, 'Order no. 127'.
68. AWM38 3DRL606/88/1, diary entry for 21 Septmeber 1917; Bean, *The A.I.F in France*, 1917, 758–9; AWM47 111.05/01, 'Did the Germans Capture an Officer with Plans and Maps on His Person?'; and NAA B2455, Lieut Harold Ferguson, 'Return of Officers of the AIF under Arrest in the London Area during Week Eending 8.2.19'.
69. Bean, *The A.I.F. in France*, 1916, 940–1. According to Australian Red Cross records, Yeo was one of just two 4th Division men captured by the German Army in the winter of 1916.
70. Bean, *The A.I.F. in France*, 1916, 951–2.
71. AWM4 23/4/14, war diary, 4 Bde, November 1916, 'Fourth Australian Infantry Brigade Order No. 94'.
72. AWM4 1/48/9, war diary, 4 Div, December 1916, entry for 1 December 1916; AWM38 3DRL606/245: 115.
73. AWM4 1/20/11, I ANZAC Corps Intel HQ, December 1916, 'Intelligence Summary No. 126'; 'Information Obtained from Prisoner (Wounded) Belonging to the Ist Co., I Bn., 101 R.I.R. Captured in N.20.I. on 1 December 1916'; and Bean, *The A.I.F in France*, 1916, 951–2.
74. NAA A1 1914/2454, Peter Christian Christiansen Petersen, 'Certificate of Naturalisation'.
75. NAA B2455, personal service dossier, 161 Pte Charles Christiansen, 'Court of Enquiry', 21 March 1917.
76. AWM4 23/61/6, war diary, 44 Bn, entry for 13 March 1917.
77. BayHStA/Abt.IV, 23. Inf. Regt., Bü 9, *Aussagen eines Überläufers der A - Komp. des XXXXIV. Btl., der 11. Brig. der 3. austr. Div.*, 18 March 1917.
78. AWM4 23/61/6, 11 Bde, March 1917.
79. BayHStA/Abt.IV, 23. Inf. Regt., Bü 9, *Aussagen eines Überläufers der A = -Komp. des XXXXIV. Btl., der 11. Brig. der 3. austr. Div.*, 18 March 1917.
80. Duffy, *Through German Eyes*, 38.
81. Nicolai, *The German Secret Service*, 184.

82. AWM27 312/12, '7th Australian Infantry Brigade Circular – Extracts from German Intelligence Summary Indicating Information Passed by Captured Men (May 1918)'; see also Bean, *The A.I.F. in France during the Allied Offensive*, fn 90–1; AWM30 B7.2, statements by officers and men, 33 and 34 Bn.
83. AWM38 3DRL606/113, diary entry for 31 May 1918.
84. Bean, *The A.I.F. in France during the Allied Offensive*, fn 109.
85. Bean, *The A.I.F. in France, 1916*.

References

Bean, C. E. W. *The A.I.F. in France, 1916*. Vol. 3 of *Official History of Australia in the War of 1914–1918*. Sydney: Angus & Robertson, 1929.

Bean, C. E. W. *The A.I.F in France, 1917*. Vol. 4 of *Official History of Australia in the War of 1914–1918*. Sydney: Angus & Robertson, 1933.

Bean, C. E. W. *The A.I.F. in France during the Main German Offensive, 1918*. Vol. 5 of *Official History of Australia in the War of 1914–1918*. Sydney: Angus & Robertson, 1937.

Bean, C. E. W. *The A.I.F. in France during the Allied Offensive, 1918*. Vol. 6 of *Official History of Australia in the War of 1914–1918*. Sydney: Angus & Robertson, 1942.

Blair, Dale. *No Quarter: Unlawful Killing and Surrender in the Australian War Experience 1915–1918*. Canberra: Ginninderra Press, 2006.

Connes, Georges. *A POW's Memoir of the First World War: The Other Ordeal*, edited by Lois Davis Vines. Oxford: Berg, 2004.

Cook, Tim. 'The Politics of Surrender: Canadian Soldiers and the Killing of Prisoners in the Great War.' *Journal of Military History* 70 (July 2006): 637–655.

Coombes, David. *Crossing the Wire: The Untold Stories of Australian POWs in Battle and Captivity in WWI*. Newport: Big Sky Publishing, 2011.

Cull, William. *At All Costs*, Melbourne: Australasian Authors Agency, 1919.

Duffy, Christopher, *Through German eyes: the British & the Somme, 1916*, London: Weidenfeld & Nicholson, 2006.

Ferguson, Niall. *The Pity of War: 1914–1918*. London: Penguin Books, 1998.

Gerster, Robin. *Big-Noting: The Heroic Theme in Australian War Writing*. Carlton: Melbourne University Press, 1988.

Gerster, Robin. 'Hors de combat: The Problems and Postures of Australian Prisoner of War Literature.' *Meanjin* 42 (1983): 221–229.

Jackson, Robert. *The Prisoners, 1914–18*. London: Routledge, 1989.

Jones, Heather. 'A Missing Paradigm? Military Captivity and the Prisoner of War, 1914–1920.' *Immigrants and Minorities* 26 (March–July 2008): 19–48.

Jones, Heather. *Violence against Prisoners of War in the First World War: Britain, France and Germany, 1914–1920*. Cambridge: Cambridge University Press, 2011.

Heinz, Uta. *Gefangen in Großen Krieg: Kriegsgefangenenschaft in Deutschland, 1914–1921*. Stuttgart: Klartext, 2006.

Kramer, Alon. *Dynamics of Destruction: Culture and Mass Killing in the First World War*. Oxford: Oxford University Press, 2007.

Morton, Desmond. *Silent Battle: Canadian Prisoners of War in Germany 1914–1919*. Toronto: Lester, 1992.

Moynihan, Michael, ed. *Black Bread and Barbed Wire*. London: Leo Cooper, 1978.

Nicolai, Walter. *The German Secret Service*. London: Stanley Paul, 1924.

Noble, Roger. 'Raising the White Flag: The Surrender of Australian Soldiers on the Western Front.' *Revue Internationale d'Histoire Militaire* 72 (June 1990): 48–79.

Pöhlmann, Markus. 'German Intelligence at War, 1914–1918.' *Journal of Intelligence History* 5 (Winter 2005): 25–54.

Puglsey, Christopher. *On the Fringe of Hell: New Zealanders and Military Discipline in the First World War*. Auckland: Hodder & Stoughton, 1991.

Rachamimov, Alon. *POWs and the Great War: Captivity on the Eastern Front*. Oxford: Berg, 2002.

Roberts, Tom. *Wingless: A Biographical Index of Australian Airmen Detained in Wartime*. Ballarat: T.V. Roberts, 2011.

Royal Air Force. *Instructions Regarding Precautions to be Taken in the Event of Falling into the Hands of the Enemy*. London: F.S. Publication, 1918.

Sheldon, Jack. *The German Army on the Somme*. Barnsley: Pen & Sword, 2005.
Solleder, Fridolin. *Vier Jahre Westfront: Geschichte des Regiments List R.I.R. 16*. München: Verlag Max Schick, 1932.
Speed, Richard B. *Prisoners, Diplomats and the Great War: A Study on the Diplomacy of Captivity*. New York: Greenwood Press, 1990.
Thomson, Alistair. '"Steadfast Until Death?" C.E.W. Bean and the Representation of Australian Military Manhood.' *Australian Historical Studies* 23 (1989): 462–478.
van Emden, Richard. *Prisoners of the Kaiser: The Last POWs of the Great War*. Barnsley: Pen & Sword Military, 2009.
War Office. *Field Service Regulations 1909* (Part II). London: HMSO, 1914.

The Prisoner Dilemma: Britain, Germany, and the Repatriation of Indian Prisoners of War

ANDREW TAIT JARBOE
Berklee College of Music, Jamaica Plain, USA

ABSTRACT *Between October 1914 and December 1915, nearly 135,000 Indian riflemen—known as sepoys—fought in the trenches of France and Belgium at the battles of Ypres, Festubert, Givenchy, Neuve Chapelle, Second Ypres and Loos, suffering some 34,252 casualties. At a prisoner of war camp outside Berlin, Indian revolutionaries and emissaries from the Ottoman Empire attempted to convert the allegiances of the sepoys in their custody with a combination of pan-Islamic and nationalist appeals. Although this campaign ultimately failed, it profoundly shaped British repatriation policy at the end of the war when, cautioned Secretary of State for India Austen Chamberlain, the British could not allow men who had been exposed to 'strongly hostile influences' to return home unmonitored. The 1918 armistice and British repatriation policy therefore presented a host of new challenges to Britain's colonial subjects from South Asia as they navigated the post-war imperial landscape and secured what was most important to them—safe transportation home.*

Introduction

Between October 1914 and December 1915, nearly 135,000 Indian riflemen—known as sepoys—fought in the trenches of France and Belgium at the battles of Ypres, Festubert, Givenchy, Neuve Chapelle, Second Ypres and Loos, suffering some 34,252 casualties.[1] *The Times* rejoiced at the time of their arrival in Europe, assuring readers that the men were 'determined to help with their Emperor's battles or die'.[2] But few could overlook the fact that Britain's decision to deploy colonial subjects to European battlefields could undermine the stability of imperial rule. It would be much more difficult after the war, for example, for the British to enforce racist policies. As the sepoys took up positions in the trenches in late October 1914, the Punjabi newspaper *Zamindar* chimed that the soldiers in Europe 'will see Europe with their own eyes … and will see that there is no difference—except in colour—between Indians and Europeans'.[3] German wartime policy also presented a challenge to the future stability of British rule in India (this was assuming, of course, that the British and French armies won the war on the

Western Front). Propagandists, believing that the sepoys 'nourish and cherish the hope of national liberation as a religious ideal', distributed pamphlets over the Indian trenches, imploring the men to mutiny and kill their British officers.[4] At a prisoner of war camp outside Berlin, Indian revolutionaries and emissaries from the Ottoman Empire attempted to convert the allegiances of the sepoys in their custody with a combination of pan-Islamic and nationalist appeals. Although this campaign ultimately failed, it profoundly shaped British repatriation policy at the end of the war when, as Secretary of State for India Austen Chamberlain cautioned, the British could not allow men who had been exposed to 'strongly hostile influences' to return home unmonitored. The 1918 armistice and British repatriation policy therefore presented a host of new challenges to Britain's colonial subjects from South Asia as they navigated the post-war imperial landscape and secured what was most important to them—safe transportation home.

British Subjects and Germany's Holy War

Captivity was a central part of the war experience for millions of human beings during the First World War. The decentralised nature of Germany's network of prison camps, combined with poor record keeping, make it nearly impossible to pin down the exact number of Indian soldiers taken prisoner during the war. In all likelihood, the Germans never really knew the actual number.[5] In August 1915, Field Marshal French complained that the Germans never furnished him with an accurate list of Indian prisoners. The lists he did receive were 'so incomplete in details that hitherto it has been impossible to identify more than sixty per cent of the individuals mentioned'.[6] One list, for example, identified an Indian prisoner only as 'Thapa'. A beleaguered secretary at the Prisoners of War Department in London circled the name and scribbled in the margins 'In one Gurkha regt alone there are over 100 "Thapas" missing'.[7] By November 1915, the Indian Soldiers' Fund had the names of nearly 500 Indian prisoners in Germany to whom it sent care parcels.[8] At that time, 3,247 Indian soldiers were still categorised on its rolls as 'missing'.[9]

Germany's strategy for world war involved hitting its British, French and Russian enemies where they were presumed weakest—Africa and Asia. Its Foreign Office did this by instituting a far-reaching propaganda campaign calling alternatively for nationalist revolution and pan-Islamic *jihad*. On 30 July 1914 when it became apparent that 'perfidious Albion' would intervene, the Kaiser furiously scribbled a note in the margins of a telegram from the German ambassador in St Petersburg:

> England must ... have the mask of Christian peaceableness torn publicly off her face ... Our consuls in Turkey and India, agents etc., must fire the whole Mohammedan world to fierce rebellion against this hated, lying, conscienceless people of hagglers; for if we are to be bled to death, at least England shall lose India.[10]

On 2 August, the Kaiser's ministers secured Turkey's allegiance and three months later, on 14 November, the Sheikh-ul-Islam in Constantinople gave the German government what it really wanted: the declaration of an Islamic holy war against Britain, France and Russia. Britain was the world's foremost 'Muslim Power', ruling over nearly 100 million Muslim subjects. In India alone, where British officials had long feared the appeal of pan-Islam, the Muslim population exceeded 60 million.[11] Even before the formal call to *jihad*, the German Foreign Office in Berlin began laying the groundwork, recalling the services of the errant orientalist and one-time diplomat Baron Max von Oppenheim on 2 August. Oppenheim fronted his own fortune and created the *Nachrichtenstelle für den Orient* (Intelligence Office for the East), which quickly became a pan-Islamic clearing house responsible for distributing anti-entente pamphlets in every conceivable language. He urged the German government to send an expedition to Afghanistan to incite its Emir, Habibullah Khan, to invade British India at the head of an Islamic army. This, he believed, would inspire India's Muslim population to a revolt that would, he assured Chancellor Bethmann Hollweg, 'force England to [agree] to peace terms favorable to us'.[12]

Germany's plans for India also incorporated the revolutionary elements of nationalism. As the German army slogged it out in a two-front war, a ready-made batch of expatriate Indian revolutionaries flocked to the services of Oppenheim's Intelligence Office and formed the Indian Independence Committee. This group of radicals included Har Dayal, the most outspoken early theorist and propagandist of Ghadar—a loose confederation of activists committed to the violent overthrow of the British Empire in India. Founded in California in 1913, Ghadar wanted much more than just a handover of the existing governmental institutions. Its activists demanded 'a revolution in social ideals so that humanity and liberty would be valued over property, special privilege would not overshadow equal opportunity, and women would not be kept under subjection'.[13] The outbreak of war in 1914 represented a moment when Ghadar activists believed the interests of Germany aligned enough with their own to warrant an alliance.

At a prisoner of war camp in Zossen, outside Berlin, Ghadar revolutionaries and Ottoman officials persuaded Indian prisoners of war to betray their allegiance to the British Empire, combining the appeals of nationalism and pan-Islamic *jihad* interchangeably. 'Everything should be done to impress upon the prisoners that we are not their enemies', Oppenheim wrote, 'and that it is only because of circumstance that we find ourselves opposite one another'.[14] The Kaiser provided the 45,000 marks required for the construction of a small mosque for the camp's Muslim inhabitants.[15] Ottoman officials and religious leaders delivered frequent lectures focused on the glory of the former Islamic Empire, the history of various Islamic peoples, exchange and interaction between the Orient and the Occident, the political, economic and intellectual strength of Germany, and wartime relationships between Germany and Muslim territories.[16] In November 1915, a member of the Indian Committee delivered a lecture at Zossen for the Indian troops on the 'political geography' of India, concluding on the subject of: 'The people of India, their essential unity in spite of apparent diversity of races and creeds'.[17]

The propaganda campaign was relentless. Captured in November 1914, Sepoy Mahomed Arifan later recalled that 'the camp [Zossen] was overrun with Mahommedan propagandists, Turks, Fakirs, and what not, who tried by every means to influence the Indian soldiers to break their allegiance to the British Empire'.[18] By the end of 1915, Germany's efforts yielded 44 'converts', who were rearmed, re-equipped and redeployed to Constantinople and the Middle East.[19] Other sepoys collaborated with the Germans, securing favourable treatment and jobs. Most Indian soldiers maintained their allegiance to the British and 'as a result the Germans systematically persecuted them by every means, withdrew the sanction hitherto accorded to caste feeling, and finally sent away from Zossen those who stood out firmest', Arifan remembered.[20]

Repatriation and Collaboration

From the very first months of the war, British authorities considered the eventual repatriation of Indian prisoners of war a politically sensitive matter. They questioned the loyalty of prisoners of war who received special treatment behind German lines and suspected that some sepoys, upon their release, might become revolutionary catalysts. A 7 May 1915 telegram from the Government of India to the Foreign Office read:

> Reliable information has been received by Criminal Intelligence Department that German newspaper invited some Indians in Europe to go to Germany where they will be well paid for talking to captured Indian soldiers. Those prisoners most amenable to the talk will be the first selected for exchange if and when exchange of prisoners with England begins. Germans intend that after exchange these men should do their best to persuade other soldiers to revolt against the British. It is known for a fact that some Indians are employed by [the] German Government. In the event of exchange becoming [a] practical question or of Indian prisoners being permitted to escape, [the] mental attitude of such Indians will require consideration.[21]

Concern for the 'mental attitude' of Indian prisoners of war only intensified as the war dragged on. In August 1916 the Secretary of State for India, Austen Chamberlain, estimated that there were about 700 Indian soldiers in German hands. The Secretary warned that these soldiers, in addition to those interned in Turkey, had been exposed to 'strongly hostile influences'.[22] If the British did not safeguard against the influence of these men after the war, the soldiers might contribute to growing unrest in India.

> There would seem to be a risk that some of these men when they return to their homes may become the willing tools of extremist and anarchist factions in India; and the possible influence in Nepal of men whose minds may have been poisoned against the British connection will not be overlooked.[23]

Indian soldiers played a prominent role in helping the British determine who, among the internees, would enjoy an expedited return home and who would serve additional time in prison after the war. Some Indian prisoners of war had collaborated with the British during their time in Germany, smuggling information out of the prison camps through various channels. While an internee at Zossen in 1916, Subedar-Major Mala Khan compiled a list of 35 Indian prisoners of war from the 129th Baluchis, the 127th Baluchis and the 58th Rifles who had 'gone over to the enemy'. His list also included the names of Indians who were working for the Germans in the camps, trying to spread sedition. He managed to sneak this list out of the camp to British authorities by hiding it in the clothes of a sick Indian who German authorities had agreed to repatriate to England.[24] Other sepoys, repatriated to Britain prior to the end of the war, collaborated with British authorities from the comfort of hospital beds. By drawing on the testimony of repatriated Indians and lists smuggled out of Zossen, in October 1918 the British finalised a master list of 92 Indian prisoners of war who had deserted to the enemy or given information or assistance to the enemy after their capture in France.[25]

Guided by a deep-seated concern for the political stability of the British Empire in India, the India Office devised a policy in late 1918 for handling repatriated Indian soldiers.[26] All Indian prisoners of war released on the Western Front congregated at Marseilles. Those released by way of ports on the North Sea (such as from Holland) passed first through London before rejoining their compatriots in southern France. At both sites, the British sifted the soldiers into four categories: (a) genuine prisoners of war; (b) declared deserters to the enemy; (c) those among (a) who were known to have taken up arms against the British or to have accepted service with the enemy; and (d) those among (a) who were believed to have been armed and equipped by propaganda and required watching in India. Protocol stipulated the following: for (a) and (d), repatriation to India where on arrival special arrangements would be made for (d); for (b), returned to unit for trial or to India in custody to await trial on return of unit from overseas, or dispatched to unit overseas if more convenient and evidence unobtainable in India; and (c) returned to India in custody pending collection of evidence against them.[27] In effect, the British plan assumed that every Indian soldier belonged in one of two groups: loyal or disloyal. While the India Office expedited loyal soldiers' return home, military authorities and the Government of India placed every obstacle in the way of disloyal soldiers.

The Long Road Home

After the war, former Indian prisoners of war (POWs) who had collaborated with the Germans faced further internment if they fell back into the custody of the British. But remaining in Germany proved to be a no-less frightening prospect. Guli Jan, who deserted to the German trenches in March 1915, told members of the Indian Independence Committee that he would need their help after the war because he could not speak a word of German. One member of Oppenheim's Intelligence Office for the East collaborated with Guli Jan and nine other sepoy POWs, drawing on a fund to cover the initial expenses required to secure housing and work in Berlin at the end of hostilities.[28] This small community of Afghans settled in Charlottenburg, amidst the chaos of the German Revolution. Two years later, some of these men tried to secure amnesty from the British government. In June 1920, Mir Baz Khan and Mir Zamir, both deserters, walked into the offices of the British Passport Control Officer in Berlin and applied for papers to proceed to India. The Passport Control Officer offered the men tickets to travel to Allied-occupied Cologne to report to the army authorities, but they refused to leave unoccupied Germany until granted a written pardon. The Passport Officer was not sure what to do and wrote to the India Office asking for guidance. 'May I be informed whether any special pardon is granted to Indian soldiers who deserted on religious grounds, and if so whether I should be authorized to give them a written guarantee that they would not be Court Martialed.' The Officer continued: 'It is thought that under proper treatment they might be of use to Indian Intelligence, but in the hands of unscrupulous people in Berlin they might become a possible danger to the Empire'.[29] The Passport Control Officer included the soldiers' letter.

Berlin 15 May 1920

Sir

We have the honour to beg you that we are Afghan Afridis of Khyber. We were since a long time in British India Army 57th Regiment. At the beginning of the Great War we were sent with other Indian troops to West Front France to fight against Germany. We were engaged for about 2 years in the West Front & fought faithfully for our King Emperor against the enemy, but unfortunately again we were sent to Egypt to fight against our Religious fellows, the Turks, & our Khalifa. It was impossible according to our religion to fight against our religion. Our religion forbids us to fight against a Muslim. In the meantime our Khalifa declared a Holy War (Jihad) against the Allies & we must have fought for our Khalifate. As we were [all] English loyal soldiers, we might not fight against England but we thought it better to go over to the Turks our Muslim fellows. There they treated us like their brothers, but sent us with other war prisoners to imprisonment, there we remained for some time but afterwards the Turks told us that we were sending you to your brother country & brought us here in Germany. They wanted to use us for their purpose in sending us to the Oriental countries to serve them, we however refused to serve them & did not go to our country under our undesirable conditions for that they let us in imprisonment in the Lager and treated us severely like the others. Now we are willing to go to our country if we will be benefitted by the King's Clemency Order & Amnesty issued before the last few months for the Indians. We should be satisfied by the King's Amnesty. We have done nothing against our Govt only that we did not fight against our Khalifa & it was our religious duty to do so. During this long time we remained neutral & did not serve the British enemy. We have served our Govt & our nations the Afridis also helped the British Govt during the Great War. Now we are starving we have nothing to live with. We hope you would be kindly enough to send for our Amnesty & feed us till we leave for our country. For this act of kindness we should pray for your long & prosperity.

> We are your most obedient servants Mir Baz Khan
> & Mir Zamir Afridis Afghans. Charlottenburg

The soldiers, so long as they remained in Berlin, were beyond the reach of British military authorities. The most the India Office could do was deny the soldiers' request. An internal memo from the India Office noted 'The suggestion that the men who deserted to the enemy in the war should be pardoned, because of "the possible danger to the Empire" involved in their stay in Germany, seems thoroughly unsound from the point of view of the effect produced on the men who did not desert'.[30] The War Office verified that in no case had any pardon been given for Indian deserters.[31] The India Office denied the pardon, and, as best we can tell, Mir Baz Khan and Mir Zamir remained in Berlin.

Without the support of the British government, other sepoys found their own way home. Guli Jan, with a German wife and their infant in tow, navigated the landscape of civil war-torn Russia and central Asia, reaching Afghanistan safely in 1921. We know his story because in October 1923 his wife walked into the British Legation in Kabul and asked for a permit to visit India. She recounted that the couple met shortly after the war and lived together in Danzig until November 1920. They travelled to Afghanistan by way of Riga, Moscow, Tashkent, Kushk, Herat and Kandahar, reaching Kabul in March 1921. In July 1923, the German woman—who we only know by the name Rabinski—left her husband. She appealed to the British government to allow her to stay in Delhi until she could prevail upon her husband to give up their daughter, aged two-and-a-half, at which time she promised to return with the child to her parents in Danzig.[32]

Other soldiers appealed to British friends and acquaintances in order to secure safe transport home. One of these was Havildar Abdul Aziz Khan, an Afghan from Peshawar, who enlisted in the Indian army at the outbreak of the war and served with 9th Hodson's Horse in France. He was taken prisoner sometime in 1914 or 1915 by the Germans and spent the remainder of the war as a prisoner of war in Germany. Repatriated at the end of hostilities and shipped to London, he lived in a YMCA with other former Indian POWs until April 1919 when the authorities placed him on a boat for India. On arriving in Bombay, he was arrested by the local authorities, suspected of feeding information to the Germans while in captivity. A confidential memo from the Government of India to the India Office read: 'The Government of India had been warned in regard to the possibility that the Germans had taken steps to tutor Indian prisoners of war for propaganda purposes' and that 'they could not afford to run the risk of setting suspects at liberty, particularly at a time of internal disturbance and with trouble on the frontier of India'. The Chief Commissioner and Agent to the Governor General of the North-West Province, within whose jurisdiction Abdul Aziz Khan's home was situated, 'was unwilling to allow men suspected of contamination to return to the North-West Frontier Province at [this] juncture'.[33]

Confined with four other Indians 'in a small room of 4 sq. yards' after having already 'suffered for four years in France and Germany',[34] Khan utilised the contacts and friendships he made during his short stay in Britain to secure his release from jail in India. He wrote a letter to a Miss Fisher in England. 'You must be very sorry to know that these pages are written by me in utter sadness', he began. 'On 3rd May I landed in Bombay. Immediately I and another man, who also has come with me from England and is my countryman were put under arrest. I tried to know the reason of the sudden calamity and failed. Even till today nothing can I know but what I have gathered is that the government suspect me, why and how rests with the government.'[35] Miss Fisher handed the soldier's letter to a friend, Mrs Mary Cruikshank, who also knew the man and must have known somebody in the War Office, because her August 1919 letter found its way through the hands of various government offices.

> I beg to invite your attention to the enclosed true copy of a letter just received by a friend of mine from an Indian non-commissioned officer of the 9th Hodson's Horse. This man, Abdul Aziz Khan, who is of good family (his brother being Khan of Zaida near Peshawar) is an Afghan. He enlisted in the Indian Army for the war, & was for some time a prisoner of war in Germany. He was released & came to England in December or January of the last winter, & remained in London staying at a Y.M.C.A. hostel with other released Indian soldiers until April 1st when he left England with two other Indian soldiers & proceeded overland to Taranto, whence he sailed for India. During his stay in England, he was not, to my

knowledge, under any suspicion, he appeared free to go anywhere he wished in London. He also paid a short visit to my friend in Leicestershire. Some weeks ago I saw a letter from him dated about June 25th in which he said he had been arrested on arrival at Bombay: the officer who arrested him refused to give any reason.[36]

Not long after Mrs Cruikshank appealed to the War Office on the behalf of the soldier and Miss Fisher, authorities in India released the havildar. 'It has now been decided that it would not be in the interests of the service to retain Dafadar Abdul Aziz Khan and he has accordingly been discharged', noted a secret memo from the Government of India.[37]

Conclusion

The repatriation of Indian prisoners of war was fraught with imperial concerns. The assurances of metropolitan propaganda trumpeting the loyalty of India notwithstanding, the war left the political situation in India more volatile than it had been prior to the war. Soldiers who had collaborated with the enemy during the war, the British believed, might become the catalysts for revolution after the war. In this way, German wartime policy and imperial anxieties profoundly shaped British post-war policy vis-à-vis former Indian prisoners of war. Indian soldiers, however, did not simply allow British policy to dictate their fates after the war. Some soldiers chose to remain in Berlin, beyond the reach of British military authorities. Still others appealed to friends and acquaintances in Britain to secure safe passage home. A small number managed to secure what they could from the German government before the end of the war in order best to ensure their chances of returning home. Guli Jan, along with his wife and child, safely returned to Afghanistan across a landscape torn apart by civil war.

Notes

1. Jack (2006, p. 329); Merewether and Smith (1918, p. 459).
2. 'The Indian troops at Marseilles', *The Times*, 2 October 1914.
3. India Office Records (IOR) L/R/5/195, *Zamindar*, 16 October 1914.
4. Political Archives of the Foreign Office, Berlin (PAAA) R21070, Paul Walter, 'Indien und der Weltkrieg', n.d.
5. Doegen (1921). Doegen made no distinction between British and Indian soldiers in his tables showing the total number of prisoners captured by the Germans, lumping both together under the category 'Engländer'.
6. IOR L/MIL/7/13561, dispatch from Field Marshal French to the War Office, 31 August 1915.
7. IOR L/MIL/7/13561, list of Indian prisoners of war, received 15 December 1915.
8. Merewether and Smith (1918, p. 503).
9. Merewether and Smith (1918, p. 459). A century has elapsed and the frustrations of the war's contemporaries have not been settled. Historian Gerhard Höpp counted anywhere between 500 and 600 Indian prisoners of war in Germany. The estimates of other historians are higher, in the range of 1,000.
10. Fischer (1967, p. 121).
11. Lüdke (2001, p. 63).
12. McMeekin (2010, p. 91).
13. Ramnath (2011, p. 8).
14. PAAA R21245, plan for the handling of Muslim and Indian prisoners, 27 February 1915.

15. PAAA R21245, Nadolny to the Foreign Office, 27 March 1915.
16. PAAA R21245, plan for the handling of Muslim and Indian prisoners, 27 February 1915.
17. PAAA R21252, outline of the first lecture by Mr Dutt, 17 November 1915.
18. The National Archives, Kew (TNA) FO 383/390, treatment of Indian prisoners at Zossen and Goerlitz, statement of Sergeant J. P. Walsh, 1/Gloucester Regiment, obtained by Major M. Wylie, 1/4 Gurkha Rifles, 6 March 1918.
19. PAAA R21254, list of Indians sent to Turkey on 3 March 1916.
20. TNA FO 383/390, treatment of Indian prisoners at Zossen and Goerlitz, statement of Sergeant J. P. Walsh, 1/Gloucester Regiment, obtained by Major M. Wylie, 1/4 Gurkha Rifles, 6 March 1918.
21. TNA FO 383/62, telegram from the Government of India to the Foreign Office, 7 May 1915.
22. IOR L/MIL/7/18501, secret memo from Austen Chamberlain to the Governor General of India, 11 August 1916.
23. Ibid.
24. IOR L/MIL/7/18501, statements of repatriated Indian prisoners of war, 16 December 1918.
25. IOR L/MIL/17/5/2403, nominal roll of Indian prisoners of war, suspected of having deserted to the enemy or of having given information to or otherwise assisted the enemy after capture (revised to 24 October 1918), Indian Expeditionary Force 'A'.
26. The India Office had been content to table the matter earlier in the war, acknowledging that the method of dealing with prisoners would depend to a great extent on the conditions under which peace was declared. See IOR/L/MIL/7/18501, secret dispatch from the Government of India to Sir Austen Chamberlain, 16 March 1917.
27. IOR L/MIL/7/18501, paraphrase of a cipher telegram from War Section, AHQ, Simla, India to the DAG, 3rd Echelon, GHQ, Indian Section, Rouen, France, 15 November 1918.
28. PAAA R21262, letter from Graetsch to (Foreign Office?), 11 December 1918.
29. IOR L/MIL/7/18899, letter from Passport Control Officer, Berlin, 25 June 1920.
30. IOR L/MIL/7/18899, India Office, internal memo, 1920.
31. IOR L/MIL/7/18899, note from the War Office, 22 July 1920.
32. IOR L/PS/11/237, P4421/1923. The Government of India refused her request.
33. IOR L/MIL/7/18501, confidential memo from the Government of India to the Secretary, Military Department, India Office, 23 October 1919.
34. IOR L/MIL/7/18501, extract of a letter from Havildar Abdul Aziz Khan, 24 May 1919.
35. IOR L/MIL/7/18501, letter from Havildar Khan to Ms Fisher.
36. IOR L/MIL/7/18501, letter from Mrs Mary Cruikshank to the War Office, 10 August 1919.
37. IOR L/MIL/7/18501, confidential memo from the Government of India to the Secretary, Military Department, India Office, 23 October 1919.

References

Doegen, W. (1921) *Kriegsgefangene Völker*, Vol. I. Berlin: Verlag fuer Politik und Wirtschaft.
Fischer, F. (1967) *Germany's Aims in the First World War*. New York: W.W. Norton.
Jack, G. M. (2006) The Indian army on the Western Front, 1914–1914: a portrait of collaboration, *War in History*, 13(3), 329–62.
Lüdke, T. (2001) *Jihad made in Germany: Ottoman and German Propaganda and Intelligence Operations in the First World War*. Munich: Lit Verlag.
McMeekin, S. (2010) *The Berlin-Baghdad Express: The Ottoman Empire and Germany's Bid for World Power*. Cambridge, MA: Harvard University Press.
Merewether, J. W. B. and Smith, F. (1918) *The Indian Corps in France*. London: John Murray.
Ramnath, M. (2011) *Haj to Utopia: How the Ghadar Movement Charted Global Radicalism and Attempted to Overthrow the British Empire*. Berkeley, CA: University of California Press.

Archives

The National Archives, Kew
India Office Records, London
Political Archives of the Foreign Office, Berlin

Newspaper

The Times

'All in the Same Uniform'?[1] The Participation of Black Colonial Residents in the British Armed Forces in the First World War

Jacqueline Jenkinson

Black colonial people volunteered for the British Army and Royal Navy during the First World War because they regarded themselves as Britons. However, many, including those white crowds which attacked black colonial war veterans during the seaport riots of 1919, did not. Similar racist attitudes were also demonstrated in the wartime deliberations and policy making of government and the military hierarchy. Historians writing about the Second World War have demonstrated that 'British identity' became more sharply defined in the period 1939–45. This article suggests that the constructed hierarchy of 'Britishness' in which black Britons from the empire were ascribed a lesser identity was also evident in the period during and just after the First World War; as demonstrated by the outbreak of the 1919 riots and the subsequent government decision to repatriate black people to the colonies.

By drawing upon detailed individual profiles of hundreds of black colonial Britons included in local Liverpool police records submitted to the Home Office to aid the process of repatriation, this article examines the role of black colonial people who enlisted in the home British armed forces during the First World War. Little has hitherto been written about black colonial people who joined the ranks of the regular British armed forces; as opposed to involvement in native regiments and labour battalions. This article redresses this imbalance using detailed Liverpool police authority information to show that more than 1 in 7 of the many hundreds of male black colonial British residents in that city served in Britain s regular armed forces in the First World War.

I

This article will examine black colonial participation in the British military during the First World War using detailed information from Liverpool. While the involvement of 'native' regiments and labour battalions in the Great War has been discussed by historians, lack of information hitherto has meant that little has been written about black colonial people who joined the ranks of the regular British armed forces.[2] Another reason for the limited analysis of black colonial military involvement is that, at the time and since, the narrow view prevailed that black British residents from colonies in Africa and the Caribbean who arrived around the time of the First World War were civilians employed as merchant sailors and, as a part of a peripatetic workforce, had few domestic ties to metropolitan Britain. This article re-evaluates this portrayal by demonstrating that a sizeable proportion of long-term residents and wartime arrivals from these areas joined Britain's armed forces. By looking at detailed occupational and personal information uniquely available for black colonial workers in Liverpool it will show that many such workers, including war veterans, moved into occupations other than the merchant marine and often married, becoming settled residents in Britain.

The black population of Liverpool by the early twentieth century has been variously estimated at between a few hundred and 5,000.[3] Many black people were locally born, while Liverpool's trade with West Africa meant that hundreds of African sailors had settled in the port for life.[4] Others, particularly African-Caribbeans, arrived during the First World War in their hundreds for work purposes and for military service. Following the Armistice, mass demobilisation caused unemployment, displacement and housing shortages which provoked outbreaks of social unrest, strikes and rioting across Britain. As part of this wave of unrest, Liverpool employers were put under pressure to favour returning (white) veterans over established black colonial workers.[5] In June 1919, rioting broke out in areas of black residence in the port when large crowds of white people focused wider frustrations over unemployment and resettlement issues on the black population. The Liverpool riots were the most sustained of nine seaport riots around Britain in 1919.

Following the riots and under central government instruction, the local police authority produced detailed lists of the names and a broad range of personal details of hundreds of colonial West African and African Caribbean residents. These lists were submitted to the Home Office to aid the process of repatriation which the government believed was the best way to solve the mass unrest around the seaports.[6] Although Liverpool's black colonial population has attracted attention from several writers since the 1970s, only Frost has utilised the local police records of *c.* 300 black colonial individuals in her work on West African residential patterns in the city.[7] This resource, including its detail on war service, makes the black colonial population of Liverpool, relatively speaking, one of the best documented of such settlements in early twentieth century Britain.

II

The data which form the basis of this article derive mainly from a Liverpool police authority report to the Home Office compiled in June 1919. The transcripts record information extracted from personal interviews with 285 male black colonial residents.

In the course of this information gathering, personal details on five wives (one Jamaican and four white British) of the interviewees were recorded. Thirty-five other wives were referred to in the police return but not named. Information recorded on name, gender, age, address, birthplace, occupational history, degree of solvency, in addition to information on military service, provides an exceptional insight into a black colonial population living in the metropole at the end of the First World War. The comprehensive police enquiries into this group of Liverpool residents were prompted by the seaport riots which peaked in June 1919.

The seaport riots were part of a wave of global unrest that affected Britain, parts of its empire, continental Europe and North America during and in the wake of the First World War. The trigger for the violence in many of Britain's seaports was dissatisfaction among sections of Britain's working class at a range of unsatisfactory peacetime circumstances, the chief of which were severe post-war competition for jobs and local housing shortages. The riots were a product of general post-war circumstances and the poor employment situation following demobilisation. As argued by Castles and Kosack, the relative economic status of overseas guest workers was a crucial aspect to understanding their position in society. The basic determinant of guest-worker status in any host society was the function immigrants played in the socio-economic structure of that society.[8] The violent events of 1919 were determined by the pressing economic and social motivations of those involved, yet minority ethnic workers were targeted and racist views were apparent among white rioters.

Racist views were common (but not pervasive) among all sections of British society from the second half of the nineteenth century onwards. Darwin's mid-nineteenth-century discoveries on the descent of humankind gave fresh impetus to racist anthropologists.[9] Anthropological research had led to the establishment of a 'scale of humanity' which supported the theory of the natural 'superiority' of the white 'race'. This was based on such findings as variations in the size of skulls between the 'races' and the alleged lack of development in the so-called 'darker races' after puberty.[10] A further element in the growth of popular racist thought was the vindication that the belief in the innate inferiority of the 'darker races' gave to Britain's growing imperial conquests.[11] In this way, as Curtin and others have argued, autocratic rule was portrayed as not only a necessity, but also a blessing to peoples who were unfit to govern themselves.[12] Black people in the empire and the metropole were subjected to a growing sense of white superiority which, as Lorimer has shown, spread across social class, as many working-class white people shared in a jingoistic disdain for foreigners, with black people often regarded as the most alien of all.[13] This view was exacerbated at a time of war when all those regarded as outsiders came under suspicion. Rose has made the point that 'British identity' became more sharply defined in times of war.[14] Paul has similarly written about constructed British national identity following increased immigration to Britain after the Second World War. According to Paul, a hierarchy of 'Britishness' was created in which white Britons enjoyed superior status, with black Britons from the empire/Commonwealth possessing a lesser British identity.[15] These feelings were also evident in the period immediately after the First World War, as demonstrated by the attacks on those perceived to be outsiders during the seaport riots of 1919.

In the course of these riots crowds of white working-class people thousands strong targeted minority ethnic workers, including African, African Caribbean, Arab, south Asian and Chinese, and their businesses and property. The riots broke out in Glasgow and further rioting took place in South Shields, Salford, Hull, London, Liverpool, Newport, Cardiff and Barry, between January and August. Liverpool witnessed some of the worst rioting: one of the five people killed was in the city: black Bermudan Royal Navy sailor Charles Wootton. Sixty-five of the more than 250 arrests during the riots were in Liverpool (29 black and 36 white).[16]

This major episode of rioting led the Home Office to send out letters to the police forces of several of the riot locations requesting the 'particulars of the unemployed coloured population' with a view to inducing black colonial residents 'to return to their own countries as quickly as possible', even though it was conceded that it was 'not possible to deport compulsorily any coloured men who are British subjects'. In these cases, the Home Office requested information on 'how many are definitely prepared to avail themselves of the opportunity of being repatriated and give particulars of the countries to which they should be sent'.[17] Following inter-departmental discussions in June 1919 the government had reached the decision that a repatriation policy was the best solution to the issues raised by the seaport rioting. On 23 June 1919, four days after the initial inter-departmental meeting, the colonial secretary, Lord Milner, issued a 'Memorandum on the Repatriation of Coloured Men'. This amounted to an 'official' response to the riots and indicated that paid repatriation would be introduced as an incentive to encourage black people to return to their home colonies:

> I am seriously concerned at the continued disturbances due to racial ill feeling against coloured men in our large sea ports. These riots are serious enough from the point of view of the maintenance of order in this country, but they are even more serious in regard to their possible effect in the colonies ... I have every reason to fear that when these men get back to their own colonies they might be tempted to revenge themselves on the white minorities there, unless we can do something to show that His Majesty's Government is not insensible to their complaints ... I am convinced that if we wish to get rid of the coloured population whose presence here is causing so much trouble we must pay the expense of doing so ourselves. It will not be great.[18]

Liverpool's assistant head constable, Lionel Everett, reported back to the Home Office within ten days of the request for details of those willing to be repatriated. The typed report denoted those willing to accept repatriation by underlining their name in red ink. The individuals recorded overwhelmingly hailed from Britain's West African and Caribbean colonies. Of the 285 males in the return, 117 (41.1 per cent) were Sierra Leoneans, 34 (11.9 per cent) were from Nigeria and 33 (11.6 per cent) from territories now part of Ghana. Solitary individuals came from Guinea, Senegal and one was identified only as from West Africa. Ninety-four males hailed from the Caribbean, 38 (12.9 per cent of the total) were Jamaicans, 17 (6 per cent) were Barbadians, 13 (4.6 per cent) were British Guianans (now Guyana) and seven

(2.5 per cent) were Trinidadians. There were a further five who were identified only as 'West Indian'. Four others came from St. Lucia and two each came from Antigua and Turks Island. Several British Caribbean territories were represented by single individuals; these came from Bermuda, Dominica, Grenada, St. Kitts, St. Vincent and British Honduras (Belize). One man gave only 'Bow' (presumably the east London district) as his birthplace. Of the women four were British-born and one Jamaican.

The Liverpool police return includes information on only three residents from outside British territory: one each from Brazil, Puerto Rico and Mauritius. It is possible that information on other people identified as 'coloured aliens' was extracted and used by a different section of the department. An internal Home Office memorandum from mid-July reinforced the idea that monitoring of aliens was part of this exercise: the request was 'for a return of the numbers of unemployed coloured aliens and British subjects in their areas, giving notes to show whether the aliens should be deported and stating whether the British subjects were willing to be repatriated'.[19] The recording and monitoring of aliens in Britain had begun following the passage of the Aliens Act of 1905, but had become more systematic at the outbreak of the war after the speedy introduction of the Aliens Restriction Act and the Nationality and Status of Aliens Act in August 1914. The Liverpool police return and Home Office file on the information it contained gave no indication of whether the three aliens should be deported. In fact, only the Liverpool police return was evident in this large Home Office file series. This may be because the information from the other seaports was submitted to the Ministry of Shipping following the creation of individual repatriation committees in the nine riot ports in July 1919.[20]

The information derived from the Liverpool police return has been combined with details obtained from a range of other primary sources regarding a further 50 black people (including three locally born females) who were linked in some respect to the Liverpool rioting of June 1919. However, since this second group includes 29 people charged with riot offences (many of whom were remanded in custody until their cases were concluded in November and, therefore, were absent from Liverpool at this time), there are only two instances of overlap in these sets of data. The first is Jamaican Thomas Archer who was recorded in the police return as a resident of 16 Great George Square and who later featured in Colonial Office files following his repatriation from Liverpool.[21] The other is Tommy McCauley from Sierra Leone who served in the British Army in late 1918. He was also mentioned in Ernest Marke's autobiography as the older friend from Freetown, Sierra Leone, with whom the under-age Marke volunteered.[22]

III

Black people had a long history of service on the British armed forces. Killingray has noted that black musicians were employed in regimental bands in the eighteenth century.[23] At the end of that century, freed black slaves fought as British loyalists in the American Wars of Independence. As Britain's imperial possessions grew in the nineteenth century a bar on black service became formalised in the British Army.

Yet, throughout this time black sailors joined the Royal Navy, often as craftsmen on ships.[24]

Black people volunteered for the British military forces because they perceived themselves as integral members of the empire and loyal subjects of the crown.[25] These sentiments continued during the First World War; for example, Marke commented on the fellow feeling among all soldiers pulling together for the war effort when recalling his brief time in the British Army.[26] This mood was short-lived. The unemployment and rioting in the seaports which followed the Armistice led to emotions of betrayal and unrewarded wartime 'blood sacrifice' among Britain's black colonial population.[27] The London-based black political organisation the Society of Peoples of African Origin (SPAO) and its newspaper, the *African Telegraph*, strongly voiced such sentiments. Anger peaked when the government decided not to include black colonial troops in London's victory celebrations: the victory march for dominion troops of 3 May and the peace march of 19 July 1919. These slights prompted the *African Telegraph* to remark: 'we can only conclude that it is the policy of His Majesty's Ministers to ignore the services of the black subjects of the Empire.'[28] Troops representing Australia, Canada (with a separate force from Newfoundland), New Zealand and South Africa participated in the dominion troops' victory march. At the peace march in July, described as part of the 'Empire Peace Celebrations' by *The Times*, all branches of the British armed forces were represented, as was the merchant navy. They were joined by dominion troops, supplemented by representatives from the allied forces from America, Belgium, France, Italy and Japan. In addition, Indian troops came especially 'from the Indian Empire for the occasion'.[29] There was no black colonial representation.

In spite of this failure to acknowledge publicly the wartime contributions of black colonial troops, there was a clear identification with 'Britishness' which went beyond military service. For example, at the funeral of Mohamed Abdullah, an east African victim of the Cardiff riots in June 1919, a Union flag was draped over the coffin.[30] In August 1919 a petition to the acting governor from 44 Jamaican repatriated workers included a plea for fair play: 'We feel aggrieved at our ill-treatment by the white people of Great Britain, they like ourselves being British and we forming an integral part of the British empire...this being so our constitutional rights and privileges were attacked.'[31] Such loyalty to the empire was subjected to ridicule among the British press: 'The negro is almost pathetically loyal to the British Empire and he is always proud to proclaim himself a Briton.'[32]

Killingray has written that the role of black people in the British Army and Royal Navy in the First World War is a 'footnote in British history but an important issue in the history of black people in Britain and its empire'.[33] Although recognising the importance of the topic, limitations of sources meant he was unable to determine how many of his estimated black British population of 20,000 people had served in the military in the First World War. Instead, he recounted specific examples of the service of black people born in Britain and the empire who had come to wider public attention generally through reports in the British and colonial press. Killingray referred to a Colonial Office file which estimated that '80 or so' of the 700 black people lodged in protective custody by the Liverpool police during the June rioting were army or navy veterans.[34] This estimate, based on personal observations by a Ministry of Labour official during a visit to the city, is not far removed from the proportion of war veterans recorded in the police return to the Home Office. Of the 285 males there recorded, 43 (15.1 per cent) had been or remained in the British Army or Royal Navy. Twenty-seven had served in the British Army and 16 in the Royal Navy (one individual, Thomas Williams from Sierra Leone, had served in both but is counted only once among the 43 who had seen military service). Ten sailors in the Royal Navy were either on leave or had just been demobilised at time of interview; one soldier was just demobilised and awaiting back pay; a further 32 were army and navy veterans.

These recruitment levels—albeit for a sample population—show black colonial residents' war participation levels (at 15.1%) to have exceeded those witnessed among the total male population around Britain during the First World War. In Wales, 13.8 per cent of the population joined the armed forces. The figure was only slightly less in England, at 13.3 per cent; meanwhile in Scotland, 13 per cent of the population joined up. The recruitment rates were significantly lower in Ireland, at 3.8 per cent.[35] This is explained by the ongoing political and armed conflicts and the inability of the government to introduce conscription to Ireland. Conscription was effected elsewhere in Britain on 2 March 1916 and this factor must be considered when accounting for the high participation levels in the war. For many millions of British males aged between 18 and 41 after this point military service was compulsory rather than a matter of personal choice.[36]

The high level of black colonial recruitment, although based on a small sample of Liverpool residents, is striking since throughout the war black people born in Britain or coming to Britain from the colonies were officially discouraged from serving in the regular armed forces and encouraged to enlist in colonial battalions or 'native' labour units. During late 1914 and early 1915, a stream of volunteers from Britain's Caribbean colonies was rejected at metropolitan recruiting offices, some having paid their own way to get to Britain. Colonial Office concerns that this situation would play badly in the Caribbean encouraged the setting up of the British West Indies Regiment (BWIR) as a separate infantry unit within the British Army in mid-1915. The 1st and 2nd battalions of the BWIR fought in Egypt and Palestine.[37] However, in continental Europe, the BWIR was kept segregated from white British troops and was restricted to labour battalion duties.[38] The two-tier system in the British armed forces underlined the fact that there was no inclusive notion of British 'national identity' even in war. In official eyes, to be British meant to be white. This understanding prevailed despite the passage of the British Nationality and Status of Aliens Act on 7 August 1914 (effective from 1 January 1915) which stated: 'The following persons shall be deemed to be natural-born British subjects…Any person born within His Majesty's dominions and allegiance.'[39]

During the war years contrasting guidelines were issued regarding black British enlistment in the regular armed forces. According to the 1914 *Manual of Military Law*: 'any inhabitant of any British protectorate and any negro or person of colour, may voluntarily enlist...and when so enlisted, shall while serving in His Majesty's regular forces, be deemed to be entitled to all the privileges of a natural born British subject'.[40] Yet both the Army Council (the military executive) and the War Office ruled that both the professional army and the army raised by conscription should exclude black people.[41] However, there is evidence of both British-born and black colonial volunteers successfully enlisting in the armed forces throughout the war. Individuals from the Caribbean including future Jamaican Prime Minister Norman Manley and his brother Roy, enlisted in the Field Artillery in 1915, both serving in France where Roy was killed. The *Manual of Military Law* further limited 'aliens' and 'negroes' to a ratio of no more than one in 50 in any corps of regular forces and stated that only those of 'pure European descent' could be granted a commission in the British Army.[42] Again, there were exceptions: the best-known was Walter Tull, second lieutenant in the Middlesex Regiment and professional footballer. Born in Folkestone in 1888, the son of a white local woman and a Barbadian carpenter father, Tull was a Northampton Town player when he enlisted in December 1914. He was given a commission in May 1917. He was killed at the second battle of the Somme in March 1918.[43]

Following the 1916 Military Service Act all male black colonial British residents of service age were liable for conscription. However, call-ups for black people in Britain were by no means a guarantee that the individual would be admitted into the ranks. Killingray has discussed the confusion over both black British-born and colonial residents receiving call-up papers but finding it impossible to gain admission at recruiting offices.[44] It was not until mid-1918 that War Office policy softened and the Army Council officially sanctioned the admission of 'British subjects of colour' into combatant units of the British Army providing they met language and dietary requirements. Even then unofficial guidelines sought to undermine this ruling.

The practicalities of recruitment meant that the prohibition on black enlistment was never absolute. Marke recalled in his autobiography that he and his fellow Sierra Leonean chum Tommy McCauley went to the 'nearest recruiting office' in Liverpool in 1918 and were admitted into the ranks of the British Army without difficulty. Although, according to Marke's account, McCauley was then aged 18, his age in June 1919 is recorded as 23 in the Liverpool police return. It is possible that McCauley lied about his age as had Marke in order to enlist. He was smaller in stature than Marke who was aged just 15 in 1918. Despite his lack of years Marke enlisted without difficulty: 'I was only asked my age, which I lied about and was never asked for any proof. That was it: we were in the army.'[45] Marke and McCauley were taken to Seaforth Barracks and then transferred to Preaseth camp in Whitchurch, Shropshire, and initially enlisted into 159th Recruitment Distribution Battalion for training. The Armistice followed shortly after and Marke spent only two months in the Army.

The Liverpool police return demonstrates that, although black colonial British residents enlisted throughout the war years, conscription may have further opened up the British Army to black recruits. Eighteen of the 28 black colonial army veterans gave recruitment dates in 1916. The Liverpool police return makes no reference as to how the men enlisted: whether they volunteered or were conscripted. Of the ten soldiers recorded who did not enlist in 1916, one joined in 1914, two in 1915, three in 1918 and three others gave no specific dates for military service beyond the detail that two had served for one year and one for eight months. The remaining recruit, Tom John (20) from Nigeria joined the British Army in West Africa at some unknown date and was discharged in 1917.

Information on regiments was supplied in only five cases in the police return: for Joseph Anoah (28) from the Gold Coast (Ghana) and Isaac Ennes, described only as from the West Indies, who both served in the Cheshire Regiment (an infantry regiment of the regular army which recruited in Birkenhead). It is safe to assume Ennes and Anoah were friends since, in addition to serving in the Cheshire Regiment, both were employed at the time of the police interviews on SS *Chamah*: Anoah as a steward and Ennes as a seaman.[46] Samuel Nichols (26) from Sierra Leone and Gold Coaster Thomas K. Ward (27) served in the Royal Engineers. Richard Roberts (25) from Sierra Leone served in the 'KL' which is very likely to have been the King's Liverpool infantry regiment, from April 1918 to March 1919.

According to Smith, the recruitment of black colonial workers into the Royal Navy was less contentious than their service in the ranks of the British Army. He noted a picture published in Jamaican newspaper the *Daily Gleaner* in July 1915 of three 'Sons of Jamaica in Britain's Royal Navy' on board HMS *Bristol*. Smith stated that enlistment, particularly for service as stokers and firemen, continued as it had done before the war years.[47] Smith's findings support Killingray's assertion that the Royal Navy was more open to the recruitment of black people over a longer period than was the case in the British Army.[48] The Liverpool police return provides further evidence to support this view. Thomas Williams (26) from Sierra Leone, who was on shore leave at the time of his police interview and was attached to HMS *Eaglet*, had first joined the Royal Navy in 1907 until discharged in 1911. He joined the army in September 1916 and was discharged in August 1918 at which time he rejoined the Royal Navy.

For the twenty-one soldiers for whom both enlistment and discharge dates were recorded length of service varied from one to 36 months. The average length of service was seventeen months. Twenty-three of the soldiers had discharge dates recorded, which indicates that police officers examined their army papers. In three cases where no specific dates of service were listed the comment 'no discharge papers' was included in the police return. Among the sixteen Royal Navy sailors, eight each were African Caribbean and West African. None had joined before 1917, although all but one had enlisted in the course of that year. Ten of the sixteen were either still in the Royal Navy, on demobilisation leave or had been discharged between March and June 1919. Specific enlistment and discharge dates were recorded for only six of the sixteen sailors. Length of service varied between 13 and 23 months. The average time spent in the navy was nineteen months, two months longer than the army service average for those included in the police return.

No members of the Royal Flying Corps (RFC) were recorded in the Liverpool police return; however, black colonial people served in the newest service of Britain's military forces (founded in 1912). Two Jamaicans in the RFC, Sergeant L. McIntosh, an aerial observer, and W. 'Robbie' Clarke who was an aerial photographer, appeared in articles in Jamaica's *Daily Gleaner* newspaper in the course of 1916–17.[49]

The Liverpool police return information, although exceptional in its detail on hundreds of black colonial residents, was not out of step with information derived from alternative sources which provide additional evidence of black colonial wartime service. For example, in May 1919 Jamaican John Martin, a Royal Navy fireman on four weeks' shore leave, was confronted by a large white crowd which attacked his boarding house in London's Limehouse district. Martin, who received head and facial injuries, was later charged with wounding a white man. Martin explained he had fired his gun in self-defence. Evidence of his war service was used by his lawyer. This and his stable family background (he had a wife and two children living in Jamaica) may have assisted in the not guilty verdict returned on him.[50] In Glasgow, three African Caribbean war veterans called into the offices of a local evening newspaper in June 1919 to protest about pressure being but on them to repatriate. One man stated that he had served for more than four years in the Army Service Corps[51] in both France and Salonika. Another, Cornelius Johnstone, had served in the army for three and a half years during the war, including time in the King's Own Yorkshire Light Infantry. He questioned 'why aliens who had done nothing for the country remain here and peaceable British subjects be forced to go'.[52] Percy Samuel White, a soldier serving with the local Monmouthshire Regiment, was among the black people charged with riot offences at Newport, south Wales. The unusual aspect to White's conviction was that his actions were directed against black colonial workers' boarding houses in the town's George Street. White argued he had just followed the white crowd, but evidence that he had been seen throwing himself at a door in George Street was sufficient for his conviction on a charge of riotous assembly and he was sentenced to three months' hard labour.[53]

Black colonial war veterans were also caught up in the June rioting in Liverpool. Royal Navy sailor Benjamin Bennett was one of a group of people charged with attempted murder of a police officer and riotous assembly on 6 June. He was released two weeks later when no evidence was offered against him and all charges were dropped. Royal Navy veteran Charles Wootton was turned out of his lodging by police officers sweeping the area for black trouble makers on 5 June, the first night of severe rioting. Wootton, aged 24, was from Bermuda. He had come to Britain as a youth and originally worked as a ship's fireman.[54] He was one of a number of people the police attempted to take into custody from 18 Upper Pitt Street—six black people were arrested at this house. Four of the black colonial people recorded in the police files to the Home Office also resided at this address, which was a lodging house run by Mrs Gibson, a black Liverpudlian whose black sailor husband had been killed in the war. Wootton evaded the police by escaping by the back door. He was chased by a large crowd of white locals, driven down to the dockside and somehow forced into the water, where he drowned. An inquest later failed to determine how Wootton entered the water, whether he was pushed in or dived in to avoid the crowd at his heels. The inquest verdict of death by drowning left many unanswered questions, particularly as to the role played in his death by the hail of stones with which he was attacked while in the dock. The *Liverpool Echo* described Wootton's death as murder: 'It is reported that a detective climbed down a ship's rope and was about to pull the man out of the water when a stone thrown from the middle of the crowd struck Wootton on the head and he sank. His body was later recovered by means of grappling irons.'[55] Jamaican Thomas Archer claimed to have witnessed Wootton's final minutes and he recounted this event in a subsequent interview for the Colonial Office.

> One coloured man who was only an eye witness of what was going on was chased by the police. He was grabbed from the police by the dock workers who threw him into the sea and started to stone him whenever he came to the surface of the water until he was killed ... I was occupying an upstairs building and was able to see everything that was going on.[56]

Archer was recorded as living at 16 Great George Square in the police return to the Home Office. The location of Great George Square in relation to Upper Pitt Street makes his account feasible. Recently demobilised army veteran Ernest Marke was also attacked during the Liverpool rioting: 'a young West Indian friend and I went up to Brownlow Hill on a visit. We saw a mob about a dozen strong. They started chasing us the moment we were spotted.' Marke himself escaped by boarding a passing tram, but his friend was badly beaten. A few days later Marke, too, was attacked and beaten up.[57] The veterans' protest in Glasgow, the attacks on Marke, the false arrests of Martin and Bennett and, most vividly, the killing of Wootton provide evidence of the harsh reality of post-war existence for black colonial military veterans.

IV

Black ex-service personnel and war workers faced unemployment difficulties soon after demobilisation. In May 1919 around 600 West Africans were reported as unemployed in Liverpool: 'some have been in the Army, some in the Navy and others in civil employment, but are at present receiving out of work pay.'[58] There were also thousands of white locals recently demobilised and out of work. Following a meeting with a deputation representing unemployed veterans, Liverpool Lord Mayor John Ritchie contacted the Colonial Office, voicing his concerns regarding the hostility among white war veterans to the presence of black workers in the city. 'Recently, I had a deputation of about five thousand discharged soldiers and sailors residing in Liverpool, and those out of employment. One of the strong points made by this deputation was the presence of black labour in our midst, a sentiment with which I thoroughly agree.'[59]

Ernest Marke recalled how attitudes towards black colonial people changed after the war: 'things became different with the demobilisation of thousands of men from the armed forces and the closing down of munitions factories. It now became scarcity of jobs, not men, with the demobbed men wanting their old jobs back and Negroes being sacked to make room for them.'[60] Many members of Liverpool's black colonial workforce were made unemployed or faced unemployment on demobilisation. The manager of the Liverpool employment exchange reported that 'farmers will not employ Chinese and Negroes on account of the bitter feeling that at present exists, and in the Ormskirk District, Irishmen are also unacceptable'.[61] In June 1919, 120 black workers in Liverpool were sacked in the space of a week.[62] The companies that employed them were put under pressure from white workers who refused to work with black people any longer and by ex-service organisations which complained that blacks should not be employed where whites could fill the positions. The involvement of veterans' associations in pressing for the restoration of the pre-war workforce was apparent in many industries at the end of the war. Trades unions also campaigned for the removal of black workers.[63] Organised union opposition to black people in the workforce was most evident in the continuing campaign, initiated in the late nineteenth century, by the white-dominated sailors' unions for a 'colour bar' on British ships.[64]

Black colonial people organised their own protests as a result of this exclusion from the workforce. A deputation, including representatives of Liverpool's Ethiopian Association, met with the lord mayor, to discuss unemployment issues in May 1919.[65] The deputation suggested introducing paid repatriation as a solution to the unemployment situation. The sum suggested, perhaps symbolically, was £5—the same level as the basic government payment or 'war gratuity' given a private soldier. Following the meeting Mayor Ritchie put forward the paid repatriation proposal in a letter to the Colonial Office. The suggestion was rejected on the grounds that the government was unwilling to 'bribe those unwilling to be repatriated' to go with £5.[66] This indifferent response was revised with the outbreak of rioting and at the beginning of July the government initiated a £5 resettlement allowance with the addition of a £1 voyage allowance for those agreeing to be repatriated.

Severe job competition triggered the rioting which began on 4 June 1919, when black sailor John Johnston was badly injured by a white gang identified in the press as Scandinavian and Russian sailors. Despite the many episodes where black people and their homes and properties were attacked, the Liverpool police authority blamed the mass violence on black people. Head Constable Francis Caldwell reported his view to the local council: 'For some time there has existed a feeling of animosity between the white and coloured population in this city ... Since the Armistice the demobilisation of so many negroes into Liverpool has caused this feeling to develop more rapidly.'[67] His assistant, Everett made the same point more bluntly in a letter to the Home Office at the height of the rioting: 'the trouble has been caused between the citizens and the blacks, mainly on account of the blacks interfering with white women, capturing a portion of the labour market and West Indians having been demobilized here with plenty of cash assuming an aggressive attitude.'[68]

Despite the references to war service by the police hierarchy, a view gained currency among Liverpool police that black people had not taken the same risks as white in the war. This was re-iterated in a 1920 report by Everett to the Ministry of Labour. 'The plight of the coloured men is no worse; in fact it is better than that of the ordinary white seamen of whom there are a large number out of work. These latter men have a higher standard of living and more family ties than the coloured men. Besides they took greater risks during the war than most of the coloured men.'[69] Black colonial residents reacted to the assumption that they shirked war duty by wearing their military service ribbons to prove that they had 'done their bit' for the empire. Another reason for sporting military insignia was the mistaken belief that this would protect them from white crowds during the rioting.

The Liverpool police authority continued its discrimination against black people in its arrest procedure during the riots: 'Detective Inspector Burgess said that with one exception in every case the coloured men were the aggressors.'[70] However, among 29 black people arrested as a result of the rioting in June 1919, 12 were later found not guilty, or freed without trial, while 17 were subsequently found guilty. On the other hand, of the 36 whites charged, 33 were found guilty and 31 were imprisoned.[71]

The close police monitoring of the black colonial population evident in biased police reports and arrest procedure was further demonstrated in the removal of black people from their homes. The initiative to accommodate hundreds of black families temporarily in the bridewell (central police holding prison) in Great George Street, a few streets away from Upper Pitt Street where the riot began, amounted to an admission of police failure to protect Liverpool's black population.[72] Black families were removed from their homes and marched through the streets in the middle of the night to avoid white crowds. The police report to Liverpool council on the riots recorded that 720 black people were for a time lodged in the bridewell.[73]

Jamaican Thomas Archer's account of his riot experience stated that he and others sharing his accommodation were taken to the nearby bridewell with little advance notice. Their compliance with this instruction indicates that both sides recognised that the forces of law and order could not adequately protect black people in their homes. Contemporary newspaper accounts suggested that the detention measures were voluntary: 'there were between 600 and 700 black men safely housed at their own request in the main bridewell in Cheapside. 400 were marched through the streets by the police between 1 and 2 o'clock yesterday morning when all was quiet.'[74] Despite newspaper references to the removal of black men, families were displaced from their homes. Nine-year-old Liverpool-born Katie Aynsu was one of a family group taken to the bridewell. The jail was very overcrowded and there was little food offered, except for those who could afford to buy from enterprising street vendors who pitched up outside. After a week of cramped conditions the family requested their return home. Ignoring warnings from a female warden that it remained dangerous in their area, they walked home (since black people were banned from the trams to avoid flash points). The family were met with abusive shouts as they walked, but returned to find their home largely intact with only one window broken.[75]

This episode was an indication of how police were 'squeezing' Liverpool's black population. The fact that the police authority's records of the personal family, employment, past military career, outstanding debt and residency details of 290 people were passed on to the Home Office days after the mass detention raises the possibility that the interviews were carried out during this enforced stay in the bridewell. Involuntary detention unsurprisingly resulted in a hostile response among those being held, leading Everett to inform the Home Office: 'the negroes are again beginning to assume an aggressive attitude to white people and unless something is done very soon, there may be further trouble.'[76]

V

The Liverpool police record passed on to the Home Office reveals that, although the majority of black colonial people were employed in the merchant navy, around one in five did other jobs. Shipboard occupations accounted for 234 of the 285 (82.1 per cent) last recorded positions held by the males in the police return; this total was composed of 109 firemen, 64 seamen, 27 stewards, 11 cooks, eight greasers (semi-skilled engine room crew), two laundry workers, one deck hand, one donkeyman (crew member who cleaned and lubricated the donkey boiler) and one sculleryman. There were also ten current Royal Navy crew whose range of employment included sailor, fireman, cook, greaser and one, 27-year-old Jamaican Colin McKenzie, who held the responsible position of boatswain.[77]

Of the remaining 51 men, three had no occupation listed in very brief entries in the police return, while the occupations for 48 (16.8 per cent of the sample) were recorded. Some of these were employed on the dockside: there were 12 dock workers (nine in the employ of Elder Dempster); eight trimmers (who prepared and arranged a ship's cargo), together accounting for 20 of the land-based workers in the police return. Among the outstanding 28 there were eight oil cake mills and cattle food production workers;[78] seven sugar refinery workers (including two who worked at Tate's sugar refinery); four general labourers; and single workers in gas, rubber, and tar works. Other single entries were a canal worker, a crane driver and one soldier: Jamaican Arthur Jones.

There were also three individuals who, judged by occupation, could be described as middle or skilled working class. The first was motor mechanic 22-year-old Joe Cole who came from the Gold Coast in 1916. Reuben Robinson (23), also from the Gold Coast, was a student who stated he was moving to London to continue his studies. George King (28) from Sierra Leone, who came to Britain in 1903, was a boarding-house keeper at 49 Mill Street. King appeared to have a thriving business, since nine other people in the police return gave this address as their place of residence.

Further information on the range of employment among black colonial people in Liverpool came via an approach by black workers, mainly Africans, to a delegation visiting Britain in September 1919 seeking settlers for British Guiana (Guyana). Skilled workers were among those who contacted the leader of the delegation, Sir W. Collet, who thought they 'ought to be able to earn good wages anywhere' and he questioned 'whether they would be happy with the dollar a day pay'.[79] Many of those looking to move were from Liverpool and had their names put forward for the scheme by the Reverend E. A. Ejesa Osora, chaplain to the Elder Dempster African Sailors' Hostel.[80]

Irrespective of skill level, black colonial workers, including war veterans, faced long-term unemployment. The range of occupations recorded notwithstanding, over three-quarters of the 285 males in the police return to the Home Office were jobless at the time of interview: 218 were idle and only 67 were in work. Duration of unemployment ranged from one person who had been out of work for a day to two who had been unemployed for a year. One hundred and eighty-six of the 218 jobless had their length of unemployment listed; of these 109 had been out of work for three months or more. Seventy-two of the unemployed had been in receipt of out of work payment, but the longest period of such benefit recorded was for six months; generally payments ranged from a few weeks to up to three months. A hundred and one of the interviewees owed money to landladies, landlords and boarding-house keepers; all but two of these debtors were out of work. Some owed substantial amounts, with three owing £30 or more. Fifty of these men had also pawned their belongings for a few pounds. Six owed £15 for pawned clothing; one had also pawned his watch and two others pawned their boots for a few additional shillings. The scale of debt can be highlighted by comparison with the wage levels recorded for some of the employed black colonial workers. All but five whose wages were noted received a weekly income of 29 shillings (£1.45). This sum was only one shilling above the level of out of work benefit at that time. In contrast, the average weekly wage for an agricultural labourer in May 1919 was just under 38 shillings.[81] Defaulting on rent and pawning clothing was a frequent occurrence, particularly for merchant sailors whose work was irregular; however, paying off debt and redeeming belongings was dependent on obtaining work within a few months, or destitution followed.

The Liverpool police return compiled in mid-1919 indicated that many black colonial people were facing financial hardship. This situation did not improve and throughout 1920 the Colonial Office dealt with applications for repatriation from black colonial workers who were destitute following prolonged periods without work. Seventy-three such unemployed workers from Liverpool submitted a petition requesting urgent assistance in April 1920; many of the signatories were not sailors, but included engineers, waiters, a blacksmith, a tailor, a French polisher, a druggist and a chauffeur.[82] The Colonial Office took no new initiative for the group, and merely replied that they would be repatriated when suitable shipping was available.[83] There had been no improvement six months later in November 1920 when CID Chief Inspector Burgess reported on the poor condition of 150 unemployed black colonial workers in the city: 'Nearly all of these men came to the country as seamen but some drifted into work ashore in sugar refineries and other factories ... most of the West Indians who were thrown out of jobs are receiving out of work donation'.[84] Burgess displayed little sympathy for unemployed black colonial workers, contrasting their situation favourably with the much larger number of local white British workers who were unemployed.

In the years after the war and the seaport rioting, the police built on the detailed investigations they had undertaken into the composition of the black colonial settlement in the city. The superintending officer at the port of Liverpool introduced a special registration card with photograph and fingerprinting required as proof of identity before West African sailors could be paid off or signed on for a ship. This system was part of a package of police and government measures designed to control the movements of black colonial people. Soon all black sailors classified as aliens under the 1920 Aliens Order were required to contact the police on arrival at Liverpool and carry documentary proof of identity, even though many of these workers were British subjects. The scheme was later extended to all black overseas workers and eventually implemented around Britain's ports following the passage of the Special Restriction (Coloured Alien Seamen) Order of 1925. This included a requirement for a registration card to be shown to immigration officers before taking up or leaving employment. If a passport or valid alien card was not produced on demand imprisonment, followed by deportation, was a real possibility.[85] Deportation under alien status was a simpler procedure to execute than the arrangements required for voluntary repatriation to the colonies. Chronic underemployment remained a feature of black experience in Liverpool in later years, with the exception of the Second World War, when once again the black colonial contribution was welcomed. However, in 1948 further rioting broke out in Liverpool as large white crowds attacked individual black residents. Black people barricaded themselves into a social club following two days of mass white attacks on black African and African Caribbean people in restaurants and sailors' homes. The police reacted vigorously to the bottle-throwing used to keep out white crowds, by baton-charging the black inhabitants of the social club and lodging houses. The police arrested 60 black and ten white people following the riots. The police actions and imbalance in arrest procedure were similar to those in the June 1919 rioting mentioned earlier in this article.[86]

VI

The Liverpool police return reinforced the view that many of Liverpool's black colonial residents arrived during the war, often to join the armed forces. The group was a young one: the ages of 279 of the 285 males were recorded. The average age was 26.5. The youngest were two aged 16 and the oldest was 51. This was a community dominated by those in their 20s and 30s, since only ten of the 279 were aged below 20 and a further eight were over 45. Hence, the vast majority of people recorded were of an age to enlist. Recorded year of arrival available for 275 of the 285 black colonial males shows that 184, almost two-thirds, had come in 1914 or after. Conversely, ninety-one men had come to live in Britain before the war: 67 West Africans and 24 African Caribbeans. Twenty-eight of the pre-war arrivals had been in Britain between 11 and 29 years and 63 had been in Britain between five and ten years. Three men had been in Britain more than 20 years: the longest resident of the sample was 48-year-old Joseph Jones from Bermuda. He came to Britain in 1890 and initially worked as a merchant seaman. At the time of the police report he was employed as a crane driver by Mersey docks. He had four children with his unidentified black British wife.

Eight of the 28 who had been in Britain more than a decade were married; 11 of the 61 who had been in Britain between five and ten years were also married. Eighteen of the 181 wartime arrivals were married. A further three of the 40 married men in the police return to the Home Office had no recorded year of arrival. West Africans were less likely to be married than African Caribbean males: 21 of 187 West Africans were married, compared to 19 of 94 African Caribbeans. Five army veterans were married:

four to white British women and one Barbadian, Alonza Downes (41), was married to a Canadian resident in Halifax. He expressed a desire to return there rather than to Barbados. Three of the navy veterans were married. These included Nigerian Benjamin Leno Pratt (23) a former ship's greaser who arrived in Britain in 1909, who was married to a white Briton; together they had one child. Pratt served in the Royal Navy between December 1917 and June 1919.

These figures provide firm evidence of stable marital relationships both among those who arrived during the war and, more particularly, for those long domiciled in Britain. This evidence is in contrast to the disparaging portrayal of ethnically diverse relationships by white working-class rioters in 1919. Press reports on the riots echoed these sentiments. For example, a *Times* report, while acknowledging that many ethnically diverse marriages had been successful, focused on the hostile response to them among sections of Liverpool's local white population. 'Many have married Liverpool women, and while it is admitted that some have made good husbands, the inter-marriage of black men and white women, not to mention other relationships, has excited much feeling.'[87] Similar racist attitudes were displayed in 'colonial circles' during the 1919 riots. Sir Ralph Williams, former governor of the Windward Islands, informed *The Times*: 'It is an undeniable fact that to almost every white man and woman who has lived a life among coloured races, intimate associations between black or coloured men, and white women is a thing of horror. And yet this feeling in no sense springs from hatred between the races.'[88] Moreover, the reputation of white women who married black colonial men was often the subject of disparaging comment. Self-confessed Liverpool slummy, Pat O'Mara (born in 1901), depicted such women as 'half-starved illiterates, desperately anxious to secure economic independence'.[89]

In the main, women remained an 'unidentified other' in contrast to the detailed information supplied in the police return on black colonial males. The ages of only three of the five named females were supplied. All were in their 20s; 29-year-old Jamaican Claudina Sterling was the oldest. Although of working age, no occupational information was given on any of the wives in the police return. Yet other sources confirm black female residents of Liverpool were employed. Maisie Yaro, who was born in 1904 to a white British mother and a black Portuguese father, recollected that black females played their part in the war effort by moving from other employment and into war industries alongside many white women.[90] Black Liverpudlian lodging-house keeper Mrs Gibson had been married to a black sailor killed in the war 'and to make ends meet for her and her children, let the top half of the house to lodgers'.[91]

Thirty-five of the 40 women whose presence is recorded appear tangentially as 'wife of' a black British colonial male. The nationality and current country of residence for these wives was generally noted in the police return but little additional information given. Twenty-three of the anonymous wives recorded were white British and two were black British, four were Africans resident in Sierra Leone, three were Canadian, one was American, one was African Caribbean living in Barbados and one was a white female living in Sierra Leone. The five women identified by name who lived in

Liverpool with their husbands were Jamaican Claudina Sterling and white British women Mary Kenny, Vera Jones, Levinia Maud Benoni and Ellen Morgan. The police return noted that Jones had no children, Benoni one child and Kenny two children (aged 3 and 5). More pertinently for the purposes of the police return, 28 of the 40 wives were recorded as wishing to accompany their husbands should they be repatriated.[92] Repatriation of married black colonial workers with their families took place from September 1919 into at least 1921. Repatriation was dependent on when suitable passenger accommodation could be found for families.[93]

VII

This article has demonstrated that the image portrayed by police, press and government agencies of black colonial workers from Africa and the Caribbean in the early twentieth century as a transient group in metropolitan Britain with few commitments, who made little tangible contribution to the British cause in the First World War, is one-dimensional and inaccurate. Examination of the detailed Liverpool police authority information supplied to the Home Office in 1919 reveals that black colonial workers followed varied occupational paths, changing jobs from sea- to land-based occupations, while also enduring periods of unemployment. Rather than accepting government inducements to accept repatriation, many settled in Britain, marrying and having children. Crucially, judging by the Liverpool sample, which, of course, does not include wartime fatalities, more than one in seven served in Britain's regular armed forces in the First World War. By drawing upon the detailed individual profiles of hundreds of black colonial Britons included in the Liverpool police records submitted to the Home Office, this article has contributed to filling the gap in knowledge identified by Killingray regarding the role of black colonial service personnel enlisted in the home armed forces during the First World War.

Black colonial people volunteered for the British Army and Royal Navy because they regarded themselves as loyal imperial Britons. However, many thousands of members of the host population did not, including those who attacked black colonial war veterans—some still in uniform or wearing service ribbons—during the 1919 seaport riots.[94] The work of Rose and Paul has suggested that, during the Second World War and immediately after it, colonial Britons were regarded as having an inferior form of British identity. This article has shown that such an attitude was also in evidence during and after the First World War and was demonstrated in broadly negative public perceptions and the racist wartime deliberations and decisions of government and the military.

The contribution of black colonial service personnel in the home armed forces may have been recognised by those white troops who served alongside them, as is claimed by black colonial Briton, one-time Liverpool resident and former soldier Ernest Marke in his autobiography. However, that service was under-valued, over-looked and misinterpreted by the police and by sections of the white population during and after the war. Similar views were also demonstrated by central government which, far from including black war veterans in peace celebrations in 1919, took initiatives to repatriate and, ultimately, to challenge the British identity of black colonial subjects living in the heart of empire. Yet, as this article has demonstrated, many black colonial Britons followed up their war service by maintaining their residential and family commitments in Britain, in spite of universally difficult post-war employment conditions.

Notes

[1] This phrase is part of a quote taken from west African Ernest Marke recalling his time in the British Army in 1918: 'The two months I spent in the army were very happy times. I encountered no colour prejudice of any kind and the feeling that we were all in the same uniform was a strong one.' Marke, *Old Man Trouble*, 25.

[2] For example, David Killingray has noted: 'little is known about the part played by Blacks who enlisted in the United Kingdom for service with home regiments and corps'. Killingray, 'All the King's Men', 164. Detailed general histories of black people in Britain have limited coverage of black colonial involvement in Britain's regular armed forces in the Great War. See, for example, Fryer, *Staying Power*.

[3] Liverpool police estimates were of around 3,000, while contemporary press accounts quoted the higher figure of 5,000. See *The Times*, 10 June 1919, 9. Recent research has also produced contrasting assessments. Murphy has suggested that police estimates of black population numbers were inflated to serve the interests of law and order: 'it is difficult to avoid the conclusion that the numbers of transient and resident Black people in Liverpool in 1919 was very much exaggerated.' Murphy, *From the Empire to the Rialto*, 39. However, in a *History of Race and Racism in Liverpool*, 26, fn. 29 on 39), Law and Henfrey suggested a black population of 'about 5,000' in 1919. They arrived at this figure using data from the 1911 Lancashire census which show that 3,015 people from the British colonies, dominions and protectorates, of whom 693 were born in the Caribbean and Africa, were resident in Liverpool on census day. They then factored in the unknown variable of a growing British-born black population, plus an influx of hundreds of black colonial people in the war years. Since place of birth as recorded in the census is not an indication of ethnicity it is difficult to come to a precise figure on the size of the black population at 1919. However, from the information on individuals provided in the Liverpool police return it is evident that at least 720 black people were then resident in the city. This number, of course, omits those who did not report to the police for shelter during the riots and those residents who had fled the city during the violence.

[4] Diane Frost has shown that from the late nineteenth century Kru sailors came increasingly to Liverpool as a result of the burgeoning trade. See, for example, Frost, 'Racism and Social Segregation', 85–95, *Work and Community*, 197–98, and, ed., *Ethnic Labour and British Imperial Trade*.

[5] The demobilisation of Britain's combined armed forces, which totalled 6.6 million at the end of the war, caused massive displacement of workers.

[6] Records of unemployed west Africans and West Indians, 18 July 1919, Home Office (HO) 45/11017/377969, The National Archives (TNA).

[7] See Frost, 'Racism and Social Segregation', 87–90, *Work and Community*, 197–98. Other works on Liverpool's black population at this time include: Julienne, 'Charles Wootton; Law and Henfrey, 'A History of Race and Racism in Liverpool'; May and Cohen, 'Interaction between Race and Colonialism', 111–26; Murphy, *From the Empire to the Rialto*. See also Rowe, *Racialisation of Disorder*, 51–73, 'Sex, "Race" and Riot in Liverpool', 53–70. More general studies on black history in Britain also describe the main events of the Liverpool and other seaport riots and suggest some of the reasons behind them. See, for example, Fryer, *Staying Power*; Holmes, *John Bull's Island*; Joshua et al., *To Ride the Storm*; Walvin, *Black and White*. For a comprehensive survey of the causes and events of the 1919 seaport riots, see Jenkinson, *Black 1919*.

[8] Castles and Kosack, *Immigrant Workers and Class Structure*, 6–7.
[9] Bolt, 'Race and the Victorians', 129–30.
[10] Fryer, *Staying Power*, 165–81.
[11] Hall, 'Lords of Humankind Re-Visited', 474.
[12] Curtin, *The Image of Africa*, 364–79; Bolt, *Victorian Attitudes to Race*, 17.
[13] Lorimer, *Colour, Class and the Victorians*, 12–14.
[14] Rose, *Which People's War?*, 9.
[15] Paul, *Whitewashing Britain*, xii.
[16] Jenkinson, *Black 1919*, 1, 81.
[17] Letter from Home Office to Francis Caldwell, 17 June 1919, HO 45/11017/377969.
[18] Lord Milner, 'Memorandum on the Repatriation of Coloured Men', 23 June 1919, Colonial Office (CO) 323/814 282-283, TNA.
[19] HO Internal Memorandum, 18 July 1919, HO 45/11017/377969.
[20] The Home Office memorandum of 18 July 1919 stated: 'As the Ministry of Shipping are now asking the local committee for returns, the Home Office is only concerned with aliens.' A search of relevant Ministry of Shipping files for this period uncovered no similar statistical returns of black workers from the other ports. HO Internal Memorandum, 18 July 1919, HO 45/11017/377969.
[21] This group of black rioters and riot victims was considered in some detail alongside similar individuals involved in the riots (in whatever respect) in the port rioting in Jenkinson, *Black 1919*, 103–54.
[22] Ernest Marke, who came to the metropole as a teenager for work, served in the army during the First World War and spent his adult life in Britain. Marke, *Old Man Trouble*, 25.
[23] Killingray, ed., *Africans in Britain*, 10.
[24] Ibid., 11.
[25] There is a great deal of secondary literature on this topic as part of a wider debate on the 'Black Atlantic' and imperial inter-connectedness. See, for some examples, Hall *et al.*, *Defining the Victorian Nation*, ed., *Civilising Subjects*; Evans, 'Across the Universe'; Jenkinson, *Black 1919*; Killingray, 'A Good West Indian', 370–73.
[26] Marke, *Old Man Trouble*, 25.
[27] The notion of a 'blood sacrifice' among colonial peoples fighting imperial battles was well known at the time and also featured in the writing on the martyrdom of Irish nationalist leaders, including James Connolly and, after the 1916 Easter Rising, Padraig Pearse. For more on this topic see http://www.bbc.co.uk/history/british/easterrising/insurrection/in05.shtml (accessed 5 July 2011).
[28] *African Telegraph* 3 (July–Aug. 1919): 243.
[29] *The Times*, 8 July 1919, 12. See also *The Times*, 30 April, 13, for more information on the victory march.
[30] Evans, 'The South Wales Race Riots of 1919', 20.
[31] Enclosure in government despatch, 1 Oct. 1919: petition by 44 signatories to Colonel Bryan, 29 Aug. 1919, CO 318/349.
[32] *The Times*, 13 June 1919, 5.
[33] Killingray, 'All the King's Men?', 180.
[34] Ibid., 181. The estimate was given by Mr Hackney, Ministry of Labour representative at the Inter Departmental Conference on Repatriation, 19 June 1919, CO 323/814.
[35] Colley, 'Britishness and Otherness', 326.
[36] The Military Service Act of 2 January 1916 specified that single men aged between 18 and 41 were liable to be called up for military service unless they were widowed with children or ministers of religion. Conscription started on 2 March 1916. The act was extended to married men on 25 May 1916. The law went through several changes before the war's end, including

eventually raising the age limit to 51. For more on this legislation see http://www.spartacus.schoolnet.co.uk/FWWconscription.htm (accessed 9 March 2010).

[37] Details from 'The Long, Long Trail: The British Army in the Great War', http://www.1914-1918.net/britishwestindiesregiment.html (accessed on 22 June 2011).

[38] For more on colonial military units, see Garson, 'South Africa and World War One'; Willan, 'The South Native African Labour Contingent'; Joseph, 'The British West Indies Regiment'; Smith, *Jamaican Volunteers in the First World War*. For other wartime black British colonial activity, see also *Journal of African History* special edition 'World War One and Africa'; Killingray, 'Race and Rank', Killingray, 'Labour Exploitation for Military Campaigns'; Killingray and Matthews, 'Beasts of Burden'; Killingray and Omissi, *Guardians of Empire*; Matthews, 'World War One'; Stovall, 'Colour Blind France?'; Tabili, *'We Ask for British Justice'*.

[39] British Nationality and Status of Aliens Act, 1914, ch. 17, 4 and 5, Geo 5, Part I.

[40] *Manual of Military Law*, 471.

[41] Killingray, 'All the King's Men?', 169.

[42] *Manual of Military Law*, 471.

[43] For more on Tull, see Vasili, *Colouring over the White Line* and *Walter Tull, 1888–1918*. Other black officers included Leicester-born James Albert Gordon Smyth, 2nd lieutenant in the 5th Battalion Machine Gun Corps, whose Sierra Leonean father was the Reverend Henry Armstrong Smyth. He was killed in action on 29 June 1918 and was buried at a military cemetery in Merville, France. His death notice appears at http://www.thisisannouncements.co.uk/5845612?s_source=clna_zzzz (accessed 22 June 2011). In addition, London-based Guyanese Doctor James Samuel Risien Russell served as a captain in the Royal Army Medical Corps from 1908 to 1918. Additional biographical information on Dr Russell is available at http://www.jeffreygreen.co.uk/dr-james-samuel-risien-russell-1863-1939 (accessed on 22 June 2011). Jamaican Reginald Collins served as a second lieutenant in the BWIR, details available at http://www.jeffreygreen.co.uk/066-lieutenant-reginald-collins-of-jamaica (accessed 22 June 2011).

[44] Killingray, 'All the King's Men?', 177–78.

[45] Marke, *Old Man Trouble*, 25.

[46] SS *Chamah* was named after a place in the Gold Coast (Ghana), Anoah's homeland.

[47] Smith, *Jamaican Volunteers*, 60.

[48] Killingray, *Africans in Britain*, 11.

[49] Smith, *Jamaican Volunteers*, 65.

[50] *The Times*, 1 July 1919, 4.

[51] The Army Service Corps was the British Army's transport and logistical division which included thousands of 'native' labourers under ASC orders as carriers and stores suppliers to front line troops.

[52] *Evening Times* (Glasgow), 19 June 1919, 1.

[53] *South Wales Argus*, 5 July 1919, 4.

[54] Law and Henfrey, *History of Race and Racism*, 155.

[55] *Liverpool Echo*, 6 June 1919, 5.

[56] Enclosure in Jamaica despatch no. 515, 1 Oct. 1919, CO 318/349. Thomas Archer had been employed as a greaser on merchant ships plying the route from New Orleans to Liverpool since 1916. He was signed off in Liverpool in April 1919 and had been unemployed since then. He was detained at the police bridewell and was then repatriated to Jamaica aboard the SS *Santille* in July 1919. The vessel was the subject of much unrest on the voyage to the West Indies. The Colonial Office later conducted an enquiry (including the interview with Archer) into the grievances of those on board who were being returned 'home'.

[57] Marke, *Old Man Trouble*, 30.

[58] Letter from Lord Mayor Ritchie to Colonial Office, 13 May 1919, CO 323/819.

[59] Letter from Ritchie to CO, 13 May 1919.

[60] Marke, *Old Man Trouble*, 32.

[61] Letter from 'E.N.C.', Superintending Aliens Officer to Home Office, 11 June 1919, HO 45/11017/377969.

[62] 'Last week there were under 120 black men employed in Liverpool and today the coloured men say that they are all out of work. Some are existing on the 28/- per week unemployment allowance, and others are going from day to day on credit.' *Liverpool Courier*, 11 June 1919, 5.

[63] 'The attitudes of unions and white workers rather than the management, appear to have been decisive'. May and Cohen, 'Interaction between Race and Colonialism', 118.

[64] See Jenkinson, *Black 1919*, 50–57, for a discussion of the sailors unions' stance on black colonial workers.

[65] The Liverpool Ethiopian Association was a black student organisation set up in 1904.

[66] Internal Colonial Office minute, May 1919, CO 323/819.

[67] Head Constable Caldwell's Report, Liverpool Watch Committee Minute Book, 17 June 1919, No. 56, 251–62, 352, Min/Wat 1/56, Liverpool Record Office, Central Library, Liverpool.

[68] Letter from L. Everett to Mr Scott, 10 June 1919, HO 45/11017/377969.

[69] L. Everett, 'unemployment of coloured men in Liverpool', enclosed in report from Ministry of Labour to CO, 7 Nov. 1920, CO 323/848.

[70] *Liverpool Echo*, 10 Nov. 1919, 8.

[71] Jenkinson, *Black 1919*, 132.

[72] Caldwell reported: 'many of the negroes had to be removed under police escort to Great George Street Fire station for their own safety.' Liverpool Head Constable's Report on 1919 riots sent to Colonial Office by Director of Intelligence, Scotland House, 15 Nov. 1919, CO 318/352.

[73] Caldwell's Report to Liverpool Corporation Watch Committee, 17 June 1919.

[74] *Liverpool Courier* 12 June 1919, 5.

[75] Wilson, 'Hidden History', 159.

[76] Letter from L. Everett to Mr Scott, 27 June 1919, HO 11017/377969.

[77] A boatswain or 'bossun' operates and maintains shipboard equipment associated with cargo handling and inter-ship transfer of cargo or personnel.

[78] In these mills, linseed and cotton seed were crushed, heated and then pressed to extract the oil, and the residual slabs of cake were sold as cattle food.

[79] Letter from Sir W. Collet to Lieut. Col. Leo Amery, 8 Sept. 1919, CO 111/627.

[80] Anglican priest the Reverend Ejesa Osora was born in Sierra Leone and educated at the African Institute, Colwyn Bay in Wales and at Oxford University. He worked in Liverpool from 1916 to 1919, when he returned to Sierra Leone accompanied by his white British wife Maisie to take up church and teaching appointments. Information on Ejesa Osora gathered from the following sources: http://www.jeffreygreen.co.uk/colwyn-bays-african-institute-1889-1912; http://books.google.co.uk/books?id=Vg9yAie74vEC&pg=PA56&dq=ejesa+osora&hl=en&ei=m80BTrLpHpSo8AOikvWyDQ&sa=X&oi=book_result&ct=result&resnum=1&ved=0CCsQ6AEwAA#v=onepage&q=ejesa%20osora&f=false; http://books.google.co.uk/books?id=YMgWAQAAIAAJ&q=ejesa+osora&dq=ejesa+osora&hl=en&ei=m80BTrLpHpSo8AOikvWyDQ&sa=X&oi=book_result&ct=result&resnum=8&ved=0CEkQ6AEwBw (all accessed 22 June 2011).

[81] Information on agricultural labourers' wages taken from http://privatewww.essex.ac.uk/~alan/family/N-Money.html (accessed 7 July 2011).

[82] CO Internal Memorandum 'Distressed Coloured Colonial workers in Liverpool', 29 April 1920, CO 323/849.

[83] Memorandum from Ministry of Labour to CO, 1 Nov. 1920, CO 323/848.

[84] H. Burgess, Chief Inspector C.I.D. Report, 1 Nov. 1920, enclosed in report from L. Everett to CO re: 'unemployment of coloured men in Liverpool', 7 Nov. 1920, CO 323/848.

[85] Law and Henfrey 'History of Race and Racism in Liverpool', 27.

[86] For more discussion of the 1948 Liverpool riot, see Fryer, *Staying Power*, 367–71.

[87] *The Times*, 10 June 1919, 9.

[88] Sir Ralph Williams, letter to *The Times*, 14 June 1919, 8.

[89] O'Mara, *Autobiography of a Liverpool Slummy*, 8.
[90] Wilson, 'Hidden History', 145.
[91] Julienne, 'Charles Wootton', 3.
[92] Letter from L. Everett, Assistant Head Constable, Liverpool to Mr Scott, Home Office, 27 June 1919, HO 11017/377969.
[93] See repatriation chapter of Jenkinson, *Black 1919*, 155–89.
[94] Ibid., 8.

References

Bolt, Christine. *Victorian Attitudes to Race*. London: Routledge & Kegan Paul, 1971.

———. 'Race and the Victorians'. In *British Imperialism in the Nineteenth Century*, edited by C. C. Eldridge. Basingstoke: Macmillan, 1984.

Castles, Stephen and G. Kosack. *Immigrant Workers and Class Structure in Western Europe*. Oxford: Oxford University Press, 1973.

Colley, Linda. 'Britishness and Otherness: An Argument'. *Journal of British Studies* 31, no. 4 (1992): 302–29.

Curtin, Philip D. *The Image of Africa: British Ideas and Action 1780–1850*. Madison, WI: University of Wisconsin, 1973.

Evans, Neil. 'The South Wales Race Riots of 1919'. *Llafur* 3 No. 1 (1980): 5–29.

———. 'Across the Universe: Racial Violence in the Post-War Crisis in Imperial Britain 1919–1925'. In *Ethnic Labour and British Imperial Trade: A History of Ethnic Seafarers in the United Kingdom*, edited by D. Frost. Ilford, Essex: Frank Cass, 1995.

Frost, Diane, ed. *Ethnic Labour and British Imperial Trade: A History of Ethnic Seafarers in the United Kingdom*. Ilford, Essex: Frank Cass, 1995.

———. 'Racism and Social Segregation: Settlement Patterns of West African Seamen in Liverpool since the Nineteenth Century'. *New Community* 22, no. 1 (1996): 85–95.

———. *Work and Community among West African Migrant Workers since the Nineteenth Century*. Liverpool: Liverpool University Press, 1999.

Fryer, Peter. *Staying Power: The History of Black People in Britain*. London: Pluto Press, 1984.

Garson, N. G. 'South Africa and World War One'. *Journal of Imperial and Commonwealth History* 8, no.1 (1979): 68–85.

Hall, Catherine, ed. *Civilising Subjects: Metropole and Colony in the English Imagination 1830–1867*. Cambridge: Polity Press, 2002.

———. 'The Lords of Humankind Re-Visited'. *Bulletin of the School of Oriental and African Studies* 66, no. 3 (2003): 472–85.

Hall, Catherine, Keith McClelland and Jane Rendal. *Defining the Victorian Nation: Class, Race, Gender and the British Reform Act of 1867*. Cambridge: Cambridge University Press, 2000.

Holmes, Colin. *John Bull's Island: Immigration and British Society 1871–1971*. Basingstoke: Macmillan, 1988.

Jenkinson, Jacqueline. *Black 1919: Riots, Racism and Resistance in Imperial Britain*. Liverpool: Liverpool University Press, 2009.

Joseph, C. L. 'The British West Indies Regiment, 1914–18'. *Journal of Contemporary History* 1, no. 2 (1971): 94–124.

Joshua, Harris and Tina Wallace with Heather Booth. *To Ride the Storm: The 1980 Bristol 'Riot' and the State*. London: Heinemann, 1983.

Journal of African History special edition 'World War One and Africa' 19, no. 1 (1978): 1–9, 35–39, 61–86, 101–16.

Julienne, Louis. 'Charles Wootton: 1919 Race Riots in Liverpool'. Liverpool: Charles Wootton Centre for Adult and Further Education, June 1979.

Killingray, David. 'Race and Rank in the British Army in the 20th Century'. *Ethnic and Racial Relations* 10, no. 3 (1987): 276–90.

———. 'All the King's Men: Blacks in the British Army in the First World War'. In *Under the Imperial Carpet: Essays in Black History 1780–1950*, edited by Jeffrey Green. Crawley: Rabbit Press, 1987.

———. 'Labour Exploitation for Military Campaigns in British Colonial Africa 1870–1945'. *Journal of Contemporary History* 24, no. 3 (1989): 483–501.

———, ed. *Africans in Britain*. Ilford, Essex: Frank Cass, 1994.

———. 'A Good West Indian, a Good African, and in Short, a Good Britisher: Black and British in a Colour-Conscious Empire, 1760–1950'. *Journal of Imperial and Commonwealth History* 36, no. 3 (2008): 363–81.

Killingray, David and J. K. Matthews. 'Beasts of Burden: British West African Carriers in the First World War'. *Canadian Journal of African Studies* 13, nos. 1–2 (1979): 5–23.

Killingray, David and D. Omissi. *Guardians of Empire: The Armed Forces of the Colonial Powers*. Manchester: Manchester University Press, 1999.

Law, Ian and J. Henfrey. *A History of Race and Racism in Liverpool*. Liverpool: Merseyside Community Relations Council, 1981.

Lorimer, Douglas. *Colour, Class and the Victorians: English Attitudes to the Negro in the Mid-nineteenth Century*. Leicester: Leicester University Press, 1978.

Manual of Military Law. London: HMSO, 1914.

Marke, Ernest. *Old Man Trouble*. London: Weidenfeld & Nicolson, 1975.

Matthews, James K. 'World War One and the Rise of African Nationalism'. *Journal of Modern African Studies* 20, no. 3 (1982): 493–502.

May, Roy and R. Cohen. 'The Interaction between Race and Colonialism: A Case Study of the Liverpool Race Riots of 1919'. *Race and Class* 16, no. 2 (1974): 111–26.

Military Service Act, 2 Jan. 1916, discussed in http://www.spartacus.schoolnet.co.uk/FWWconscription.htm (accessed 9 March 2010).

Murphy, Andrea. *From the Empire to the Rialto: Racism and Reaction in Liverpool 1919–1958*. Birkenhead: Liver Press, 1995.

O'Mara, Pat. *Autobiography of a Liverpool Slummy*. Liverpool: Bluecoat Press, 1994 [1934].

Paul, Kathleen. *Whitewashing Britain: Race and Citizenship in the Postwar Era*. Ithaca, NY: Cornell University Press, 1997.

Rose, Sonya O. *Which People's War? National Identity and Citizenship in Britain 1939–1945*. Oxford: Oxford University Press, 2003.

Rowe, Michael. *The Racialisation of Disorder in Twentieth Century Britain*. Aldershot: Ashgate, 1998.

———. 'Sex, "Race" and Riot in Liverpool, 1919'. *Immigrants and Minorities* 19, no. 2 (2000): 53–70.

Smith, Richard. *Jamaican Volunteers in the First World War: Race, Masculinity, and the Development of National Consciousness*. Manchester: Manchester University Press, 2004.

Stovall, Tyler. 'Colour Blind France? Colonial Workers during the First World War'. *Race and Class* 35, no. 2 (1993): 35–55.

Tabili, Laura. *'We Ask for British Justice': Workers and Racial Difference in Late Imperial Britain*. Ithaca, NY: Cornell University Press, 1994.

Vasili, Phil. *Colouring over the White Line: The History of Black Footballers in Britain*. London: Mainstream Publishing, 2000.

———. *Walter Tull, 1888–1918 Officer, Footballer: All the Guns in France Couldn't Wake Me*. London: Raw Press, 2009.

Walvin, James. *Black and White: The Negro and English Society, 1555–1945*. London: Allen Lane, 1973.

Willan, Brian. 'The South Native African Labour Contingent 1916–1918'. *Journal of African History* 19, no. 1 (1978): 61–86.

Wilson, Carlton E. 'A Hidden History: The Black Experience in Liverpool, England, 1919–1945'. PhD diss., University of North Carolina, 1992.

Australian and New Zealand fathers and sons during the Great War: expanding the histories of families at war

Kathryn M. Hunter

Department of History, Victoria University of Wellington, Wellington, NewZealand

Fathers with sons of eligible military age have not figured in social and cultural histories of the Great War. The focus of these histories has emphasized bonds between mothers and sons and has been based largely on soldiers' letters home. Widening the range of sources beyond soldiers' personal correspondence, this article demonstrates the array of emotional and material support offered by fathers in Australia and New Zealand to their sons during the war. This article relies largely on the military archive, rather than the personal archives in public repositories, for its evidence thereby using the military archive to illuminate civilian experience. Fathers' tenacious connection with their sons, and advocacy on their behalf, was an attempt to mitigate the extreme physical separation experienced by families in Australasia and the disruption of their roles as protectors of and providers for their children. Evidence from sons' requests for early repatriation as well as from sources revealing fathers' grief demonstrates the strong bonds of affection as well as duty between fathers and their adult sons during this period. A persistent theme in the evidence is the tension between duty to one's family and that to the empire, illuminating men's complex and often ambivalent feelings about war and their role in it.

Recalling the chaos of the first few days of the Gallipoli landing in his diary, New Zealander Lieutenant Colonel William Malone wrote of the wounded being brought back and laid along the track to the beach in preparation for evacuation. He framed this tragedy in ways that would support historians' assertions of his Edwardian stoicism, commenting that the soldiers were all 'very brave. No cries or even groans ... Many greeted me cheerfully ... The world never saw better men or braver'.[1] Both the men's evident resilience and Malone's recounting of the episode represent the stereotype of 'the most extreme form of manliness as self-control' that permeated much of the early published accounts of the Great War.[2] At the end of this insistently rosy recounting of a terrible afternoon in which fully one-third of Malone's men were wounded and over 10% killed, one line stands out: 'One man,' he wrote, 'kept saying "Oh Daddy", "Oh Daddy" in a low voice'. Malone could not ignore the distress of this man because it pulled at him at a fundamental level: Malone was not at Gallipoli only as a soldier, but as a father. Two of Malone's own sons were with him on the Gallipoli peninsula and so the pain of another man's son and his raw need for the comforting hand of his father penetrated even Malone's considerable psychological defences.

Malone was unusual in being a father at war alongside his sons, yet this aspect of his war service has been little remarked upon. Great War historians have generally not examined fathers as figures within the family, or as affected by anxiety, bereavement or stress during the war. The absence of soldier-fathers of young children has been more important in the historiography, as well as in newspapers of the time, than the presence and experiences of older men.[3] Where they do appear, fathers tend to have been made visible as men denied military experience because of their age, living vicariously through their sons and responding to the emotional challenges the Great War presented by channelling 'the pain into affirming the values of heroic sacrifice and pride'.[4] This reinforces, or, indeed, is derived from, broader arguments about middle-class masculinity in the late nineteenth century: that men's relationship with their children was increasingly distant, being 'recoded as "influence" instead of "authority"', and that the rise of 'imperial manhood' saw a flight from domesticity more generally.[5] At the other extreme of virtual neglect has been the focus on 'ultra-bereavement'. It is telling that the few Australian studies of bereavement that examine specifically – or even briefly touch on – fathers' responses have relied on the papers of Garry Roberts, father of Frank Roberts who was killed, along with most of his platoon, at the Battle of Mont St Quentin on 1 September 1918. The extraordinary character of the Roberts' collection – its letters, scrapbooks and mementos compulsively collected over years – speaks to an all-consuming grief that, as historian Peter Stanley has observed, cast a shadow over the entire family for decades after the war.[6] It is Roberts' very un-representativeness that has made him the central figure in these studies. It is precisely his response to Frank's death, with its overwhelming rejection of the notion of the distant or stoic father, that acts to confirm the 'stiff upper lip' of fathers who did not leave this kind of record. In addition, authors note that Roberts was obsessed, implying that his grief over Frank pushed Garry to the edge of rational behaviour. Stanley refers to Roberts as 'wrapping himself up in [his grief]' rather than denying it or repressing it; Bruce Scates 'cannot help but feel for a father whose every waking hour was devoted to honouring a "cherished" son'.[7] Garry may have been profoundly connected to his son, but the depth of that connection is presented as certainly unusual and possibly unbalanced. It is also, as Scates suspects, 'a comment on power and privilege', with Roberts having access to key figures including General Monash and official war historian, Charles Bean.[8]

This article seeks to fill the gap between these two historiographical extremes of neglect and Garry Roberts' case by exploring a wider range of wartime records of men in their roles of fathers and sons. In the case of Australians and New Zealanders, families could be separated by vast distances for years at a time but, as Bart Ziino has argued, civilians in these countries were deeply connected to the war despite their remoteness from its key sites. Distance refracted their experiences but did not lessen their intensity. Ziino asserts that civilians 'deliberately and insistently spoke into that perceived gulf, showing the boundaries between fronts to be … "porous"'.[9] The few other historians who have attempted to reduce the distance between the home front and the battlefront – a distance that is so stark in Australia's and New Zealand's cases – have used emotional connectedness as the main instrument, and especially the role of women in bridging this distance.[10] I argue here that, far from aloof or tentative figures, fathers too used a range of means to maintain emotional proximity to their combatant-children.

Focusing on wartime fathers whose sons were of eligible military age, this article expands, both in substance and in geographical focus, Michael Roper's assertion that 'wartime correspondence highlights the different roles which fathers of this period could occupy'.[11] Using a range of sources beyond soldiers' correspondence to their families, I argue that Australian and New Zealand fathers were intensely concerned with the physical and emotional well-being of their sons, and that they used a variety of methods to maintain their paternal roles as providers for and protectors of their sons. In addition, I suggest that pursuing fathers and sons through the archive in this way, especially through letters from fathers to military authorities, reveals the tensions men experienced between their duty and loyalty to family and that to their empire. The complexity of soldiers' feelings about the war, both during it and in the aftermath, has been well established by Australasian historians who have examined ambivalence and dissent, as well as the wide range of men's motivations for enlisting.[12] The reluctance of men to enlist because of their duty to their families, as well as fathers' varying responses to sons' enlistment, is less well understood, however, and yet are persistent themes in sources written by fathers and sons.

In part, the relationship between fathers and sons has been overshadowed by the prominence of mothers as the dominant civilian figures in the literature of the past two decades. Feminist historians' endeavours to break the nexus of masculinity and war, as well as the increasing interest in the history of emotions, have resulted in an emphasis on affective bonds between soldiers and their mothers. The place of mothers in the various rituals of mourning and bereavement has also figured largely.[13] This focus on mothers has been made possible by the survival of soldiers' letters in public repositories, and by collection policies and judgements about which personal papers are historically interesting.[14] In Australian and New Zealand repositories, letters *from* soldiers vastly outnumber letters from civilians *to* soldiers, and dutiful sons wrote to their mothers. This mirrors other collections around the world with, for example, Michael Roper estimating that in British repositories for every letter to a soldier's father, there are five to mothers.[15] Another important factor has been the emphasis placed on mothers in public discourse during the Great War, especially surrounding enlistment and memorializing the dead.[16] Australian historians of commemoration found, for example, that while soldiers were the main focus and participants in early Anzac Day commemorations, mothers were central to unveiling ceremonies for war memorials. Fathers, on the other hand, were less significant in public rhetoric and are simply less well-represented correspondence in Australian and New Zealand repositories.

More fathers become visible, however, if the focus is shifted away from soldiers' letters home in archives of personal papers to civilians' letters to the army that survive in the military record. This article takes as its main source letters and official requests that survive in the archives of the Australian and New Zealand armies, the Australian Imperial Force (AIF) and the New Zealand Expeditionary Force (NZEF). Very briefly, 330,000 men enlisted in the AIF, 60,000 of whom were killed and 150,000 wounded. The NZEF was made up of 110,000 recruits, approximately one-third of whom were conscripted and 18,000 of whom died. Overwhelmingly, members of the AIF and NZEF were single upon enlistment. Thousands of Australian and New Zealand-born men also served with other imperial forces. Significant in the lives of families during the war, the 1918 influenza pandemic caused a further 8500 deaths in New Zealand, while its impact was much more localized in Australia resulting in 12,000 deaths in a population four times that of New Zealand.

In the armies' archives – the records of Army headquarters and of Base Records[17] – thousands of letters from family members survive. As studies of mothers during the First World War have revealed, fathers did not have a monopoly on public correspondence or on speaking for the family during the war. Soldiers' relatives of all sorts, as well as their friends, wrote to 'the Army' for news of their kin, as well as on financial matters, medal distribution and the return of soldiers' effects.[18] Fathers are better represented in official correspondence however, than in other archives. Large-scale analysis has not been completed on soldiers' choice of next-of-kin, but a small sample of 430 soldiers who enlisted in the New Zealand town of Invercargill reveals that just under half of them (48%) nominated their fathers as next-of-kin, with a further 32% nominating their mothers. The remainder nominated a sibling, other relative or friend.[19] Regardless of whether fathers were nominated next-of-kin or not, they become visible through public correspondence in a range of ways. Their role as advocates is particularly strong in the Army archive: letters about post-war opportunities, changes in healthcare, pensions and requests for early repatriation survive in AIF and NZEF records, as do fathers' protests against their sons going to war. Other sources in combination with military records also reveal the strains of war on older men and the tensions they experienced between their roles as fathers and as loyal supporters of the empire. Sons too negotiated the sometimes-opposing calls of duty towards their families, especially ageing fathers, and military service. Strong bonds of interdependence and affection between fathers and sons are evident in the thousands of requests from soldiers to be repatriated. It is through sources such as these that a range of fathers' responses to war, separation and bereavement can be revealed, bringing fathers more fully into the picture of civilians at war.

It is important to note that fathers and sons occasionally served together blurring the binary image of civilian fathers and soldier sons. The *Kalgoorlie Western Argus,* for example, reported the return to Australia of Sergeant McCraig who had been wounded, noting that his son Private Charles McCraig was still on active service.[20] The *British Australasian (BA)* reported that 'Dr Thomas, who has for nearly 25 years lived in Manly [Sydney], is going to join the Australian Hospital in France. His son, Mr H. Thomas, is going with him'.[21] Australian Wilhelm Muller's father and brothers all enlisted, perhaps for reasons related to their German ancestry and the need to demonstrate their loyalty. Muller's father was 47 years of age when he enlisted in February 1916. He did not leave Australia in the end and was discharged to Home Service in Adelaide because of his age. Wilhelm wrote in his application for early repatriation:

> My mother has expressed a wish that I should return to Australia with my brother 3903 Pte LJ Muller ... who is now stationed at Codford ... Our father ... left Adelaide with the remounts, was returned and is still in the Military doing Home Service. Our other brother left with the 10th Battalion and has been returned since the Armistice. The above is 100% of our family inclusive of the father and I am proud to state the whole of us still retain clean records ...[22]

In New Zealand, the most famous father serving alongside his sons was Colonel William Malone. Malone was 55 years of age when he was commissioned in 1914, and was a veteran of the 1880s New Zealand Wars in Taranaki as well as a long-serving reservist. His reputation was one of 'conservatism and determination to master anything he attempted' and as an officer both hard on his men and fiercely protective of them.[23] Malone's three elder sons, Terence, Edmund and Brian, all enlisted with him at the outbreak of war. Malone wrote in his diary from the troopship on which he was embarking, 'Edmund and Terry are [also] on the *Arawa* in A Squadron 2nd Mounted Rifles. I am glad that three of my boys volunteered without hesitation to serve and fight for their country. Maurice will come too next May when he is twenty ... '.[24] These siblings – including their sister Norah Malone who served with the British Red Cross – were the children of Malone and his first wife Elinor who died in 1904 when the youngest, Maurice, was only nine years old and the eldest, Edmund, was 16 years old. While Malone remarried in the following year, to Ida Withers, it is clear from the fact that all four sons and his eldest daughter enlisted in the war that the children's emotional world was firmly tied to their father, his values and beliefs. When Malone was killed at Gallipoli in August 1915, his family's service and his age (57 when he was killed) were emphasized in newspaper reports as models of commitment to the Empire.

Less publicly, Robert Gilkison and his son Rob served overseas at the same time, Robert with the YMCA and Rob with the New Zealand Rifle Brigade. They both departed on the same troopship in November 1917 and returned within a week of each other in January 1919. When Rob was 'dangerously wounded in the chest' and was in hospital in France, then transferred to New Zealand General Hospital at Brockenhurst, Robert managed to get transferred within the YMCA to each place so he could be near his son.[25] In October 1918, he wrote to his daughter Norah from a British Red Cross hostel in France, 'It is really a great thing that we parents are allowed to come over and stay like this. Poor old Rob still has his ups and downs, and I was warned at the first it would take a long time to effect a cure'. Even after four weeks, Rob was still bedridden. By late November, he had been transferred to Brockenhurst and Robert wrote to Norah, 'I am down here to see Rob who is progressing very rapidly.'[26] These slim notes are given some flesh by Robert's other comments that indicate he was an affectionate and dutiful father. In a letter before he embarked to 17-year-old Norah, he wondered how his children 'will get on without Daddy to put eucky [eucalyptus oil] on your pillow when you catch cold', and noted that he wrote 'every week to Mother and also to one of you'.[27] It is likely his presence by Rob's bedside would have been comforting and caring.

Paternal relationships also developed between older and younger servicemen, and older enlisted men sometimes found themselves standing in for fathers. Roper has described the care of men by their officers – the procurement of clothing, food and warm water where possible – as a position 'not unlike that of the middle-class housewife', but these actions could also be interpreted as paternal provisioning and protecting.[28] Importantly, this role, like that of Robert Gilkison, saw a convergence of paternal and military needs, which did not always occur. The desire on the part of older men to protect soldiers could be stronger and at odds with military needs when older men knew younger men from their towns back home. For example, Dr Samuel Richards had been in practice in Mt Morgan (Queensland) before the war and enlisted in late 1914 at the age of 50 years. He wrote regularly to his own wife and children from Egypt and then Gallipoli. Richards' care of his community continued even though he was away at war, and he wrote to his wife that he was trying to keep up with all the boys at the front from their area. He treated them leniently – possibly more leniently than men he did not know – and often sent them away from the front for a rest. In June 1915 he wrote from Gallipoli, 'Murray Swain was sent away about two weeks ago with slight injuries. I saw him. He was more frightened than hurt ... I sent Jessie von Bibra's boy off for a bit with some slight ailment.'[29] The Mt Morgan men would come to see Richards at the casualty clearing station, just to chat, and he wrote in his penultimate letter to his wife, 'I am a sort of "father" to them all.'[30]

Most fathers of servicemen were not in Europe or the Middle East with their sons and were reliant on the relatively efficient but not infallible systems of military communication for news. All but the worst news, which came by telegram, was slow to arrive in Australia and New Zealand with mail typically taking 50 days to arrive from the Western Front. As a result, the most common letter written to the Army by fathers was the letter seeking information. Ziino has identified many fathers seeking details of a son's death, fulfilling their role, perhaps as a family's official correspondent. Fathers also wrote when communication lines had broken down.[31] W.J. Rees, for example, wrote to New Zealand Base Records:

> I see by today's 'Herald' [newspaper] that the British losses at La Boiselle are very heavy, the East Lancashires suffering especially. My third son Joe is in the 7th King's Lancashire Regiment and has been in the advanced trenches for months. I feel very anxious regarding him.

Rees's worries were compounded by the fact that his son had married since going to England and Rees was no longer Joe's nominated next-of-kin. He asked, 'Can the Defence people here get information for me, or arrange that I be communicated with in the event of him being wounded or killed?'[32] Other sources reinforce fathers' search for information about their sons. For example, the 'Missing: News Wanted' column of the *BA* newspaper revealed a great many fathers, such as George Sanders, looking for news of their sons.[33] Private Tom Sanders had not been heard since April 1915 and his father placed an advertisement in September seeking any information from *BA* readers.

A second reason fathers wrote to the Army was to advocate on behalf of their soldier-sons, particularly to press for better healthcare for the wounded. Marina Larsson has detailed the persistence with which Australian families advocated on behalf of their sons after they were repatriated, but fathers also intervened in their sons' healthcare from a distance.[34] For example, Robert O'Brien was severely wounded on the Somme and his father wrote to AIF headquarters requesting his transfer to St David's hospital, Ealing:

> My son Dvr RG O'Brien 105 Howitzer Battery Australian Imperial Force now a paraplegia patient in Ward A3 King George Hospital Stamford St SW has been offered a vacant bed in St David's Hospital at Ealing which is [*sic*] was very pleased to accept. I also would be glad if he could be sent there as it is a Roman Catholic Hospital – is specially set apart for Paraplegia patients, and is near the few relations the boy has in England.[35]

O'Brien was concerned that Robert get the best care and be in a hospital catering more fully to his physical and religious needs, and that was close to his extended family even if that was not in an Australian hospital. It was clear from his file that Robert was extremely ill, and was probably transferred to St David's because his doctors thought he would die, which he did on 1 January 1919.

Many letters demonstrate active concerns about sons' emotional and mental well-being especially after long stays in hospital. The father of Machine Gunner Kershaw approached the Agent-General for New South Wales who then wrote to the Director of Medical Services on his behalf. Kershaw was in Napsbury Hospital 'recovering from some mental trouble and his father, who you may remember at Wahroonga in days gone by, is very anxious for his return'.[36] Bert King's father, Thomas, wrote directly to the Defence Department with concerns about his son's health and morale. Bert had lost his left leg at the thigh, his right thumb and had sustained other injuries to his other limbs in July 1917. By the time King's father wrote in December 1918, King had been in hospital for 15 months. Thomas wrote:

> Of course, I fully appreciate that with the injuries sustained my son would need to spend considerable time in England. He was very bright during the first few months in hospital due to the fact that he would so[o]n be back home again, but the months that have elapsed have had a very depressing effect on him, and his letters indicate that he is [in] an extremely unhappy state of mind, which naturally is a source of great anxiety to his mother and me.

Thomas suggested that the conditions in England were not conducive to improving Bert's morale, and that 'I feel sure he would soon be returned to robust health if we could only get him home again.'[37]

Military service, while held up as the epitome of adult masculine fulfilment, did not free or eject young men from their families especially when military service resulted in disability. Indeed, military service often increased men's dependence on their families, and strengthened paternal ties. As Larsson has demonstrated in the Australian case, the majority of invalided soldiers returned to the care of their parents and sisters.[38] It is not surprising, then, that when sons had been invalided home, fathers continued to advocate on their behalf. David Gray wrote to the New Zealand Defence Department complaining that his son had received three medical reports declaring he was entitled to a pension for at least three years, yet his pension had 'dwindled' to 15 shillings per week. Gray reported that his son 'is so anxious to do all he can [. H]e spends many a sleepless night with pains in that leg so if he could get a spell he might recouperate [*sic*] or get his original pension [of 30 shillings] he could take things easier.'[39] AA Gower demanded some recognition – perhaps a small medal – for his son who, even though being invalided home himself, had voluntarily nursed smallpox cases on the hospital ship *Willochra*. Gower wrote,

> there are not many men who would have done the work my son did ... and that while a semi invalid himself. Unfortunately he has not yet recovered from the severe nerve strain – of this he has had a very bad attack.[40]

Advocacy of this sort demonstrates fathers' enmeshment in their sons' lives, especially where their sons continued to need their protection and support.

Fathers also advocated for their sons over civilian professional matters, sometimes in combination with concerns over health. Captain Alwyn Nisbet's father, Walter, was anxious for his son's health as well as his future career prospects when he wrote requesting that his son be released from service with the Australian Army Medical Corps. Alwyn Nisbet had contracted appendicitis on active service and after being operated on in London, his father wrote, 'he appears to have made a lingering recovery during which time he also developed subacute rheumatism to which he is subject.' Alwyn had remained in England working as a radiographer at No.2 Australian Auxiliary Hospital at Southall. Walter was concerned that 'being a native of North Queensland and subject to rheumatic fever his health is likely to be permanently affected by the English climate'.[41] In spite of Walter's wishes, Alwyn remained on active service, marrying in England in June 1919 before being repatriated and discharged in July 1919. Of concern was also that Walter had built up a large medical practice that he was now ready to share with his son: he wrote, 'what should be an excellent opening for my son is gradually slipping away. New comers also who have failed to be stimulated by patriotic motives are finding the chances opportune to enter the field.'[42] Future careers were also on the minds of fathers such as that of New Zealander RFT Grace who had served as a medical orderly with the Royal Army Medical Corps. His father applied to the New Zealand government for a bursary for him to continue his studies in Britain when he was demobilized, but it was denied because he had not served with the New Zealanders.[43]

Fathers' concern for their sons' future careers is an example of the less-direct expression of paternal love at which Roper hints in his discussion of fathers' correspondence, or lack of it. Roper suggests that the emphasis on mothers in correspondence could be explained by sons and fathers sharing interests that were difficult to sustain through letters. In one example, he argues that the '*Architect* magazines that [Arnold Hooper's] father sent him in Mesopotamia were probably a more poignant reminder of paternal love than his letters'.[44] The preoccupation with their sons' careers that fathers exhibited was, indeed, significantly linked to emotional welfare. Gainful employment was the foundation of what New Zealand and Australian historians have called 'breadwinner masculinity' with an emphasis on ideas of 'manly independence' and its corollary of unmanly or feminine dependence.[45] Much more than this, however, gainful employment made possible young men's marriage and the support of families of their own, what John Tosh refers to as 'the qualifications for full masculine status'.[46] For New Zealand returned soldiers, employment was the crucial catalyst for the emotional intimacy and domestic futures that they had focused on during the war. While soldiers' personal papers were full of longings for reunion with kin and lovers, and of dreams of a golden peaceful future, men's preoccupations as war ended were with the practicalities of employment.[47] Les Harris, for example, met his future wife while he was in Britain during the war but they did not marry until 1926: 'If I'd had the money we'd have married [at the end of the war]'. Les borrowed money to buy a farm in order to establish himself more securely. As an engaged man, he felt, 'you want to have something to go on with, so I borrowed the money for the farm'.[48] Economic prosperity and marriage rates were clearly linked with marriage rates in New Zealand surging in 1918 and 1919, but slowing with the economic slump of 1920–1921.[49] Similarly in Australia, crude marriage rates spiked in 1919 before falling in the early 1920s and then plummeting with the depression of 1929–1932.[50] In addition to families' view that employment provided a foundation for a satisfying emotional life and social success, post-war employment was seen by authorities as crucial to successful repatriation. Men's idleness was seen as allowing men to dwell on their war experiences and giving them time to drink and gamble, while work and occupation were regarded as giving men focus and direction. Employment also reintegrated men into their communities: it gave them opportunities to re-establish their civilian lives.[51] Employment, then, was more than a financial need; it was central to the attainment of the emotional and social goals of marriage and fatherhood. The empire's need of young men's service at precisely the time they were establishing themselves in the world of work was of deep concern to both soldiers and their fathers, especially as the war dragged on. Fathers' concerns about soldier-sons' post-war careers were part of an ongoing civilian set of concerns that were ultimately about emotional well-being and masculine fulfilment.

Material support has featured in scholars' investigations of affective bonds between home and battlefronts, but the focus on women's patriotic work has subsumed evidence that fathers regularly supported sons materially. Particularly important in the antipodean context has been the work of patriotic organizations, especially the Red Cross. Bruce Scates details the labour of the New South Wales Red Cross during the war, including the 'endless stream' of comfort parcels. For Christmas 1916, they dispatched 36,000 parcels packed with 'chocolates and tobacco, pickles and powders, "thrillers of the best kind", "Bibles and improving literature"'.[52] The parcels sent by private individuals are far less visible in the historical record; however, records of the New Zealand Postal Service show that 329,235 parcels were sent to the NZEF in 1917 alone.[53] The inventories of dead men's effects sometimes contained clues to Christmas cakes, toiletries and small presents sent to them, but the senders remain anonymous.[54] It is clear from Red Cross magazines that men participated in large numbers in work such as bandage rolling, but the specifics of men's material support of their own sons are sparse. The New Zealand *Observer* newspaper quipped, 'It is unusual to find men of large wealth and distinction performing menial tasks, but war induces new views on these matters.' The report went on to detail the activities of 'Father of Takapuna' who 'engages in the growth of sweet peas, which are sold for patriotic purposes' who was seen shovelling horse manure for fertilizer on the streets of Auckland.[55] Indoors, scientist and New Zealand Member of Parliament George Thomson packed parcels for his son John. John's letters from Gallipoli provoked what has been characterized as a 'maternal' response. John was well, but found the vermin 'very hard to bear', so George packed parcels for John containing a fine tooth comb, a tin of 'Keating's insect powder' for the lice, soap, chocolates and 'a woollen comforter' knitted by a woman friend.[56] John's mother had died when he was four years old and it had been his father who, after a brief period where John lived with his aunt and uncle, reclaimed his son and raised him. George's emotional and material support of John extended throughout the war. The same was true for Private Robert Roper of the AIF whose mother had deserted the family home when he was young. His father was the provider of comfort and comforts.[57] While these fathers were solo parents, their provision of 'maternal' care was in no way a given. Tosh details the options open to widower-fathers including remarrying and, as epitomized in the case of Lord Kitchener's upbringing, sending the children to boarding school or the military.[58] In contemporary New Zealand newspapers, it was also understood that 'sometimes spinsters have had more to do in the bringing up of families than the fathers or mothers themselves'.[59] It had been a conscious choice for George Thomson to reclaim John from his relatives, and one driven by paternal love.

Care was not all one-way, however. Interdependent and affectionate relationships between fathers and sons in a range of social classes and occupations are revealed both in Military Service Board hearings and in soldiers' requests for early repatriation. These relationships were also often the cause of conflicting forms of duty for men. In the exemption hearings of the Military Service Board in New Zealand (where conscription was enacted in November 1916), relationships between fathers and sons, and their struggles over decisions to enlist, were often publicly laid out. While Boards were not likely to be sympathetic to an appellant's claim that his business or farm would suffer if he was conscripted, 'family responsibilities' – usually the reliance of ageing parents on sons – were slightly more likely to evoke at least a delay in encampment if not an exemption. In David Littlewood's study of Military Service Board hearings in the lower North Island, over 40% of men cited financial or physical dependence of family members on them as grounds for appeal.[60] Ernest Napier, for example, initially appealed his call-up on the grounds that it would cause undue hardship to his parents whom he supported: he contributed 32 shillings to the family each week, far more than he would earn in the Army. The Board was not satisfied and only granted Napier exemption when the most intimate details of his domestic situation became clear (and were subsequently published in the newspaper) that his mother was an amputee and his father 'suffered from such severe rheumatism that he was unable to dress himself'.[61] In a different vein, but illustrating the lengths fathers might go to in order to protect their families, Thomas Brocas did all that he could to prevent his sons from being balloted. He appealed on their behalf at board hearings, defended their actions in court when they failed to present themselves at all to the boards and even moved his family out of the district for a time in an attempt to confuse the bureaucracy. He could not prevent one of his sons, Harold, from voluntarily enlisting, however, and resented greatly the 'break-up of our happy circle'.[62]

The separation of fathers and sons who enlisted did not diminish the strength of emotional responsibility and bonds. The majority of applications for early repatriation were for 'family reasons' although these were not always detailed. Where details were forthcoming, the health of fathers was an important consideration. Australian medical student Angus Murray requested early repatriation in order to take care of his father. He wrote in his application that the Army's original plan for medical students to remain in England to carry on with their training would have 'suited me very well',

> but last month I had very bad news from home which altered everything for me. My mother died in October, and as you may remember I told you my Father suffers from a heart ailment, he has had to bear the loss of both my brothers and a sister in recent years, and I dread the effects of this crowning sorrow for him. I do not therefore feel inclined to forego any rights to

demobilisation I may have, but in duty to my Father and sister feel that I must get back as soon as possible ... I feel that I cannot do anything else but try to get back there as soon as possible ...[63]

Alfred Osborn, too, was anxious about his parents when he wrote from hospital in England where he was awaiting the fitting of an artificial leg,

I most respectfully beg to be allowed to return to Australia by the next boat. I have received news that my parents who are both old, are failing fast in health, and I wish to see them once again before they pass away, which latter is expected at any time ...[64]

Captain Sydney O'Riordan was also anxious to get home to see his father. In August 1918, he applied to the Surgeon General for a position on a transport or hospital ship:

The reason is the state of my father's health: He has been dying since April of last year from Heart Failure, Arterio Sclerosis and all its complications. He is only 57 years old and when I left Australia he had never had a day's sickness. I have been anxious of returning to him for a long time now, but I did not apply as I felt I could not be spared, and I was anxious to do a good spell of front-line service before making application.[65]

In this case, the Surgeon General acknowledged 'your anxiety with regard your father's health but the call of the Empire at the present time is so great that family considerations, however pressing, must take second place.'[66]

Fathers too wrote to the Army requesting the early repatriation of their sons. Age and poor health prompted the father of George Eccles to write to Base Records in March 1919 to request his son's early repatriation. Three men in the Eccles family had served in various capacities: one had been relieved of Military Service because he was working in an essential industry and had died of influenza in November 1918; George was serving with the Motor Boat Patrol with the Royal Navy; the third son was also in the navy and had been repatriated 'wrecked in health as a result of being gas shelled by a submarine'.[67] Mr Eccles went on to detail that he and his wife were in poor health and 'in losing our eldest son we lost our mainstay'. He continued, 'It is my desire and that of his mother that [George] ... be relieved from further service now that the great need of his service is over.'[68]

It was a cruel reality for fathers and their sons that the call of the Empire could take precedence over the dutiful and loving bonds between them. When soldiers were killed and those connections broken, the diaries and letters of fathers revealed the anguish they suffered. Bereavement affected fathers deeply but their avenues for emotional expression were curtailed in wartime society. As I have argued elsewhere, New Zealand families clung more tightly to available pre-war expressions of mourning in the absence of a body, details and the exclusivity of peace-time bereavement; Ziino argues that Australian families also engaged in a 'more diligent search for connection with familiar patterns of bereavement'.[69] Fathers noted often that they were part of a community of bereaved and that they were suffering 'what scores of thousands of other Australian homes will suffer'.[70] This awareness in addition to public discourses urging restrained grieving encouraged brave faces in public. Alongside many articles and editorials urging women to shorten their mourning period and to dispense with pre-war rituals of changing their clothing, the occasional advice dispensed to fathers encouraged them to repress their 'true' feelings. For example, well-known Presbyterian minister John Flynn urged fathers of enlisted men to be an 'approving, encouraging father [who] wished the boy Godspeed and safe keeping at the front. What matter if afterwards he again lay weak.' Even if a father was 'practically prostrated' with grief in private he should endeavour to be cheerful in public.[71]

George Thomson attempted to hide his feelings in public but his diary revealed a great deal of personal suffering. He had never been enthusiastic about his son's enlistment.

John Thomson was George's youngest child born only two years before Emma, John's mother, died of tuberculosis in 1894. Father and son were close and John's enlistment followed two tragedies in the preceding years: the death of George's daughter Annie from tuberculosis in 1909 and the death of his second wife Alice from cancer in 1911. John enlisted as a stretcher bearer in November 1914 and George wrote in his diary, 'I felt inexpressibly sad all day but I managed to hide my feelings ... I feel terribly upset at parting with my boy, but must make an effort to do my work without flinching. But it is awfully hard to be left alone.'[72] George was continually anxious throughout the war for John's safety. In March 1918, he wrote in his diary that a telegram had arrived: 'I went downstairs with my heart in my mouth, thinking some bad news had come, and was greatly relieved to find it was only a confidential message from Mr Massey [the Prime Minister] asking me if I would accept nomination to the Legislative Council.'[73] In May, George was not so fortunate:

> Just after tea Agnes and William came in with a telegram which had been sent to Sheen St ... '3/453 JH Thomson died of sickness on April 5th'. The news knocked me over. I thought from my dear boy's last letter dated 2nd March that he was in a safe occupation ... I can't realize the terrible news yet. I had hoped to be spared further bereavement in my family but it was not to be.[74]

George later described 1918 as 'the most ghastly year of losses in my experience of seventy years' and admitted that he was 'Feeling terribly depressed ... the strain is telling on me.'[75] By the end of the war, he had lost one of his sons and three nephews in the war, two more nephews returned wounded and a beloved niece died of influenza. For years after the war, anniversaries and public events to do with the war were exhausting and upsetting as they were for other bereaved fathers in his circle. In 1920, he commented in his diary that 'Any public reference to the losses we suffered in the war tries me very much.'[76]

Similarly, Australian Arthur Fry dreaded going to the church service marking the armistice. He had lost both of his sons, Alan and Dene by the middle of 1917. His sister Katie had written to him when the armistice was declared knowing it would be a difficult time for him, and indeed it was 'the saddest day I have passed for a long time'.[77] Arthur wrote,

> It required some effort yesterday to go to the service – I felt it was up to me to do it – but fortunately the preacher was not personal and we pulled through without sniffling, sitting there right under the maple board and crossed flags where Alan's name heads the list of church boys who went. Five of them will not come back.[78]

The grief of fathers over deaths of soldier-sons was also apparent in various obituaries and death notices during the war years and shortly afterwards. A report of the death of Dr William Warren in 1915 revealed some of the devastating emotional consequences of a son's death. Dr Warren,

> aged 62, who was formerly in practice in Australia, was found severely injured on the pavement immediately below his bedroom window in Marylebone, and died soon afterwards. It was stated at the inquest on Monday that he was greatly depressed owing to the death of a son at the Dardanelles and the fact that another son had been invalided home from the front. The jury returned a verdict of suicide while of unsound mind.[79]

In less extreme cases, there was often a link made between a man's death and that of his son, indicating the physical toll that emotional distress could have. The obituary of William Lowe in 1926 noted that his son had died as a result of wounds in 1918, and more directly, in noting the death of Gustav Diehl, the reporter offered the opinion that his death was 'hastened by news of his son's death'.[80] Ralph Diehl had been killed in action on 23 October 1915 and Gustav died suddenly on 27 November. Similarly, the proximity of the death of William Lewis in late April 1916 with that of two of his sons on one day, 9 August 1915 at Gallipoli, was also raised in Lewis's obituary.[81]

A wide range of sources reveal Australian and New Zealand fathers to be enmeshed in the care and well-being of their sons during the Great War despite their distance from the battlefront. Perhaps expectedly, many fathers acted as the public face of their families in correspondence with officials, but they also provided intimate material and emotional support for their sons. Symbiotically, sons were 'mainstays', dutiful and affectionate in their filial roles. From military records alone it is clear that they remained bound to their families and that absence, wounding or death brought suffering to their kin. Private papers and obituaries go some way to revealing the devastating effects of grief on fathers as well as their often ambivalent attitudes towards their sons' service. Their advocacy for their sons ranged across the gamut of opinions on the war and included attempts to prevent the state conscripting them. Fathers could be reluctant and resentful about sons' enlistment or they could adhere to definitions of loyalty that demanded their own enlistment. At home, fathers packed parcels and raised money; they wrote letters and brooded. The wartime experience of most fathers discussed in this article was shaped by distance: they lived in societies remote from the theatres of war and their sons were absent for the entire duration of the war or were repatriated wounded. All but the worst kind of communication – the dreaded telegrams – were slow and material support was expensive and difficult to provide. Neither distance nor the military's role in their sons' lives discouraged fathers from persistently attempting to protect and provide for their sons. Remoteness was physical: emotionally, fathers and sons remained powerfully bound to each other.

Notes

1. William George Malone, Diary, 27 April 1915 and Phillips, Boyack, and Malone, *Great Adventure*, 36.
2. Tosh, *Man's Place*, 184.
3. See, for example, Damousi, *Labour of Loss*, 47; McQuilton, *Rural Australia and the Great War* and Donson, *Youth in the Fatherless Land*.
4. Damousi, *Labour of Loss*, 49.
5. Francis's discussion of the literature on Victorian fathers in 'Domestication of the Male?,' 640; Tosh, *Man's Place*, 170–94; Broughton and Rogers, *Gender and Fatherhood*; see also, for example, MacKenzie, 'Imperial Pioneer' and in the white settler context Loo, 'Of Moose and Men.'
6. Stanley, *Men of Mont St Quentin*, 191 ff. See also Damousi, *Labour of Loss*; Luckins, *Gates of Memory* and Jalland, *Changing Ways of Death*.
7. Stanley, *Men of Mont St Quentin*, 163 and Scates, *Return to Gallipoli*, 17.
8. Scates, *Return to Gallipoli*, 17.
9. Ziino, *A Distant Grief*, 9.
10. For example Ziino, *A Distant Grief*; Larsson, *Shattered Anzacs* and Hunter, 'More than an Archive of War.'
11. Roper, *Secret Battle*, 62.
12. See, for example, Dawes and Robson, *Citizen to Soldier*; Thomson, *Anzac Memories*; Gammage, *Broken Years*; White, 'Europe and the Six-Bob-a-Day Tourist.' This is less well researched in New Zealand but some examples are Boyack and Tolerton, *In the Shadow of War* and Hucker, 'Great Wave of Enthusiasm.'
13. See particularly Damousi, *Labour of Loss*; Roper, *Secret Battle*; Roper, 'Maternal Relations' and Inglis, *Sacred Places*.
14. Some historians have recently discussed the role of the archive and of historians in shaping national war narratives: see, for example, Cook, *Clio's Warriors* and Luckins, 'Collecting Women's Memories.'
15. Roper, 'Maternal Relations,' 300.

16. See, for example, Grayzel, *Women's Identities at War*; Gullace, *Blood of our Sons* and Inglis, *Sacred Places*.
17. In Australia, the records of AIF Headquarters in London are lodged in the Australian War Memorial. AIF Headquarters was responsible for the mobilization of all medical personnel (who were mobilized as individuals, not units), requests for transfer and requests for early repatriation after 11 November 1918. Correspondence to Base Records – the department responsible for monitoring the movement of all personnel – was transferred to individual personnel files, or in many cases lost, except in the case in which the Australian served for a 'foreign' force. In New Zealand, the majority of Base Records files were microfilmed in the 1960s by the Defence Department, and then the paper record destroyed. The microfilms are now being digitized-on-demand by Archives New Zealand. Few have been digitized to date because the main demand for digitization of files has been of the First World War personnel files. Paper files do exist, however, for several hundred New Zealanders who served for forces other than the NZEF, particularly the AIF, the Royal Navy and the Royal Flying Corps.
18. 'The Army' will be used for ease of expression in this article reflecting families' understandings and terminology during the war, rather than the actual names of the departments.
19. Hunter, '"Sleep On Dear Ernie"', 41.
20. *Kalgoorlie Western Argus*, 29 August 1916, 5.
21. *British Australasian*, 3 June 1915, 26.
22. Wilhelm Muller (63957 AIF), Application for early repatriation, 5172–5178, AWM12, AWM.
23. See Pugsley, *Malone, William George*.
24. William George Malone, 25 September 1914 and Phillips, Boyack, and Malone *Great Adventure*, 21.
25. Norah Parr (nee Gilkison), covering letter about her family, MS-Papers-10282, ATL.
26. Robert Gilkison to his daughter Norah, 18 October 1918, 24 November 1918, MS-Papers-10282, ATL.
27. Gilkison to Norah, 2 December 1917, 10 July 1918.
28. Roper, 'Slipping Out of View,' 68. For a discussion of fathers as protectors and provisioners see Frank, 'About Our Fathers' Business.'
29. Samuel Jabez Richards letter to his wife Jessie, 6 June 1915, MLMSS2908, Mitchell Library, Sydney.
30. S.J. Richards to his wife Jessie, 27 June 1915. Richards died of pneumonia on the hospital ship Sicilia, 30 July 1915.
31. See Ziino, *A Distant Grief*, 12–18.
32. W.J. Rees to Base Records, 8 July 1916, BR37/68, AABK W5614, 22525, Box 94, Archives New Zealand.
33. *British Australasian*, 9 September 1915, 11. A court of enquiry in April 1916 found that he had been killed in action in the first days of May 1915.
34. See Larsson, *Shattered Anzacs*.
35. William O'Brien to AIF headquarters, 22 October 1918, file of Driver Robert George O'Brien (27963 AIF), 5184/2, AWM12, AWM.
36. Sir Charles Wade to Director Medical Services, 31 December 1918, 5130, AWM12, AWM.
37. Thomas King to Department of Defence, Melbourne, 11 December 1918, 5132, AWM12, AWM.
38. Larsson, *Shattered Anzacs*. See for example Chapters 2 and 4.
39. David Gray to Defence Department, 22 August 1923, 'Travel-Passages – Indulgence – Relatives with Soldiers buried in France', AD1 1024 58/218, Archives New Zealand.
40. AA Gower to Defence Department, 12 June 1917, 'Medical-Sick and wounded returning "Wilochra" 1916', AD1 942 49/70/28, Archives New Zealand.
41. Walter Nisbet to AIF headquarters, 3 November 1917, CT Nisbet (AAMC), 5180/4, AWM12, AWM.
42. Walter Nisbet to AIF headquarters, 3 November 1917.
43. Note in the file 'The father of this NCO...', 16 July 1919, file of RTF Grace, BR37/2880, AABK, W5614, 22525, Box 100, Archives New Zealand.
44. Roper, *Secret Battle*, 61.
45. See, for example, Frank, 'About Our Father's Business' Nolan, *Breadwinning* and Lake, 'Politics of Respectability.'

46. Tosh, *A Man's Place*, 79.
47. On men's longings for home see Hunter, 'More than an Archive of War.'
48. Les Harris interview with Jane Tolerton and Nicholas Boyack, 7 August 1988, World War One Oral History Archive, OHInt-0006/34, National Library of New Zealand.
49. Clarkson, 'Realities of Return,' 42–43.
50. Australian Bureau of Statistics, www.abs.gov.au and see also Vamplew, *Australians: Historical Statistics*, 45.
51. See Clarkson, 'Realities of Return'; Walker, '"Living Death"' and Larsson, *Shattered Anzacs*.
52. Scates, 'Unknown Sock Knitter,' 33.
53. Report of the Postal & Telegraph Department, *Appendices to the Journal*.
54. See, for example, Register of NZEF Buried in England, ACGO8398 IA76/2/2, Archives New Zealand.
55. *Observer*, 8 September 1917, 4.
56. Thomson in Galbreath, *Scholars and Gentlemen Both*, 207–208.
57. Roper, 'Slipping Out of View,' 64.
58. Tosh, *Man's Place*, 99, 165–66, 185–86.
59. "Correspondence" (*Wairarapa Daily Times*, 5 November 1917, 5).
60. Littlewood, 'Should He Serve?,' 64–66.
61. Littlewood, 'Should He Serve?,' 49.
62. Thomas Brocas, Diary, 25 February 1915, MS1199, volume 12, Auckland Museum Library.
63. Angus Murray (28102 AIF) application for early repatriation, December 1918, 5174, AWM12, AWM.
64. Alfred Osborn to AIF headquarters, 22 January 1917, file of CSM Osborn (258 AIF), 5187/2, AWM12, AWM.
65. Captain SM O'Riordan to Surgeon General, 28 August 1918, 5187/2, AWM12, AWM.
66. Surgeon General to Captain O'Riordan, 5 September 1918, 5187/2, AWM12, AWM.
67. Letter to Base Records from George Eccles' father, 25 March 1919, BR37/73A, ANZ.
68. Letter to Base Records from George Eccles' father, 25 March 1919.
69. Hunter, '"Sleep On Dear Ernie"' and Ziino, 18.
70. Arthur Fry to his sister Katie, 14 November 1918, MLMSS1159, ADD-ON2076, Box 1, Mitchell Library, Sydney. See also Henry Bournes Higgins cited in Ziino, 17.
71. John Flynn, *Inlander* (magazine of the Australian Inland Mission), vol. 2, 1915, 19.
72. GM Thomson Diary cited in Galbreath, *Scholars and Gentlemen Both*, 204.
73. Thomson in Galbreath, *Scholars and Gentlemen Both*, 211.
74. Thomson in Galbreath, *Scholars and Gentlemen Both*, 211–12.
75. Thomson in Galbreath, *Scholars and Gentlemen Both*, 213, 212.
76. Thomson in Galbreath, *Scholars and Gentlemen Both*, 213.
77. Arthur Fry to Katie, 14 November 1918, MLMSS1159, ADD-ON2076, Box 1, Mitchell Library, Sydney.
78. Fry, 14 November 1914.
79. *British Australasian*, 12 August 1915, 20.
80. *Poverty Bay Herald*, 16 December 1915, 6.
81. *Feilding Star*, 2 May 1916, 3.

References

Boyack, Nicholas, and Jane Tolerton, eds. *In the Shadow of War: New Zealand Soldiers Talk about World War One and their Lives*. Auckland: Penguin Books, 1990.

Broughton, Trev Lynn, and Helen Rogers, eds. *Gender and Fatherhood in the Nineteenth Century*. London: Palgrave Macmillan, 2007.

Clarkson, Coralie. 'The Realities of Return: The Experiences of World War One Soldiers After Their Return to New Zealand.' MA Thesis, Victoria University of Wellington, 2012.

Cook, Tim. *Clio's Warriors: Canadian Historians and the Writing of the World Wars*. Vancouver, BC: UBC Press, 2007.

Damousi, Joy. *The Labour of Loss: Mourning, Memory and Wartime Bereavement in Australia*. Melbourne: Cambridge University Press, 1999.

Dawes, J. N. I., and L. L. Robson. *Citizen to Soldier: Australia before the Great War. Recollections of Members of the First AIF*. Carlton: Melbourne University Press, 1977.

Donson, Andrew. *Youth in the Fatherless Land: War Pedagogy, Nationalism and Authority in Germany 1914–1918*. Cambridge, MA: Harvard University Press, 2010.
Francis, Martin. 'The Domestication of the Male? Recent Research on Nineteenth- and Twentieth-Century British Masculinity.' *The Historical Journal* 45, no. 3 (2002): 637–652.
Frank, Timothy. 'About Our Fathers' Business: Fatherhood in New Zealand, 1900–1940.' PhD Thesis, University of Auckland, 2004.
Galbreath, Ross. *Scholars and Gentlemen Both: GM and Allan Thomson in New Zealand Science and Education*. Wellington: Royal Society of New Zealand, 2002.
Gammage, Bill. *The Broken Years: Australian Soldiers in the Great War*. Canberra: Australian National University Press, 1974.
Grayzel, Susan. *Women's Identities at War: Gender, Motherhood, and Politics in Britain and France During the First World War*. Chapel Hill: University of North Carolina Press, 1999.
Gullace, Nicoletta. *The Blood of our Sons: Men, Women and the Renegotiation of British Citizenship during the Great War*. New York: Palgrave, 2002.
Hucker, Graham. '"The Great Wave of Enthusiasm": New Zealand Reactions to the First World War in August 1914 – A Reassessment.' *New Zealand Journal of History* 43, no. 1 (2009): 59–71.
Hunter, K. M. '"Sleep On Dear Ernie, Your Battles are Over": A Glimpse of a Mourning Community, Invercargill, New Zealand, 1914–1925.' *War in History* 14 (2007): 36–62.
Hunter, K. M. 'More than an Archive of War: Intimacy and Manliness in the Letters of a Great War Soldier to the Woman He Loved, 1915–1919.' *Gender and History* 25 (August 2013): 339–354.
Inglis, Ken. *Sacred Places: War Memorials in the Australian Landscape*. Melbourne: Miegunyah Press, 1998.
Jalland, Pat. *Changing Ways of Death in Twentieth-Century Australia*. Melbourne: Oxford University Press, 2002.
Lake, Marilyn. 'The Politics of Respectability: Identifying the Masculinist Context.' *Debutante Nation: Feminism Contests the 1890s*, edited by Susan Magarey, Sue Rowley, and Susan Sheridan, 1–15. Sydney: Allen and Unwin, 1993.
Larsson, Marina. *Shattered Anzacs: Living with the Scars of War*. Sydney: UNSW Press, 2009.
Littlewood, David. '"Should he serve?": The Military Service Board Operations in the Wellington District 1916–1918.' MA Thesis, Massey University, 2010.
Loo, Tina. 'Of Moose and Men: Hunting for Masculinities in British Columbia, 1880–1939.' *Western Historical Quarterly* 32 (Autumn 2001): 297–319.
Luckins, Tanja. 'Collecting Women's Memories: The Australian War Memorial, the Next of Kin and Great War Soldiers' Letter and Diaries as Objects of Memory in the 1920s and 1930s.' *Women's History Review* 19 (February 2010): 21–37.
Luckins, Tanja. *The Gates of Memory: Australian People's Experience and Memories of Loss and the Great War*. Perth: Curtin University Books, 2004.
MacKenzie, John. 'The Imperial Pioneer and Hunter and the British Masculine Stereotype in Late Victorian and Edwardian times.' In *Manliness and Morality: Middle-Class Masculinity in Britain and America, 1800–1940*, edited by J. A. Mangan, and James Walvin, 176–198. Manchester: Manchester University Press, 1987.
McQuilton, John. *Rural Australia and the Great War*. Carlton: Melbourne University Press, 2001.
Nolan, Melanie. *Breadwinning: New Zealand Women and the State*. Christchurch: Canterbury University Press, 2000.
Phillips, Jock, Nicholas Boyack, and E. P. Malone, eds. *The Great Adventure: New Zealand Soldiers Describe the First World War*. Wellington: Allen and Unwin, 1988.
Pugsley, Chris. *Malone, William George – Malone, William George, from the Dictionary of New Zealand Biography*. The Encyclopedia of New Zealand: Te Ara, www.teara.govt.nz updated 30 October 2012.
Report of the Postal & Telegraph Department, 1919. *Appendices to the Journal of the House of Representatives*. Wellington: Government Printer, 1919.
Roper, Michael. 'Maternal Relations: Moral Manliness and Emotional Survival in Letters Home During the First World War.' In *Masculinities in Politics and War: Gendering Modern History*, edited by Stefan Dudink, Karen Hagemann, and John Tosh, 295–316. Manchester: Manchester University Press, 2004.
Roper, Michael. 'Slipping Out of View: Subjectivity and Emotion in Gender History.' *History Workshop Journal* 59 (2005): 57–72.

Roper, Michael. *The Secret Battle: Emotional Survival in the Great War.* Manchester: Manchester University Press, 2009.
Scates, Bruce. 'The Unknown Sock Knitter: Voluntary Work, Emotional Labour, Bereavement and the Great War.' *Labour History*, no. 81 (2001): 29–49.
Stanley, Peter. *The Men of Mont St Quentin: Between Victory and Death.* Melbourne: Scribe, 2009.
Scates, Bruce. *Return to Gallipoli: Walking the Battlefields of the Great War.* Melbourne: Cambridge University Press, 2006.
Thomson, Alistair. *Anzac Memories: Living with the Legend.* Melbourne: Oxford University Press, 1994.
Tosh, John. *A Man's Place: Masculinity and the Middle-Class Home in Victorian England.*, 2nd ed. (1999) New Haven: Yale University Press, 2007.
Vamplew, Wray. *Australians: Historical Statistics.* Sydney: Fairfax, Weldon & Syme, 1988.
Walker, Elizabeth. '"The Living Death": The Repatriation Experience of New Zealand's Disabled Great War servicemen.' MA Thesis, Victoria University of Wellington, 2011.
White, Richard. 'Europe and the Six-Bob-a-Day Tourist: The Great War as a Grand Tour, or Getting Civilized.' *Australian Studies* 5 (1991): 122–139.

Contemporary newspapers

British Australasian

Evening Post

Feilding Star

Inlander

Kalgoorlie Western Argus

Observer (New Zealand)

Poverty Bay Herald

Wairarapa Daily Times

Loss and Longing: Emotional Responses to West Indian Soldiers during the First World War

RICHARD SMITH
Goldsmiths University of London, London, UK

ABSTRACT *This article traces the place of black soldiers within British military history from the 18th century to the eve of the First World War. It shows how during the war, attitudes to and representations of West Indian volunteers reflected anxieties surrounding white male efficiency.*

Introduction

As 'slaves in red coats',[1] and then as enlisted free men, the black West Indian soldier exercised the white imagination from the late 18th century. In the accounts of travel writers, statesmen and military officers, the West Indian soldier served as a justification for the imperial mission. His civility, character and discipline were all assumed to have been acquired through contact with British civilisation. Any perceived deficiencies were passed off as atavistic remnants of the African past. This paper explores how these representations of black military service were transformed as West Indians came forward as volunteers during the First World War.

Slavery and the Origins of Black Military Service in the West Indies

The place of black soldiers within British military history cannot be fully understood without addressing the impact of transatlantic slavery and the growth of plantation societies in the Caribbean. As well as providing workers for the sugar estates and the planters' households, slavery could also serve as a vehicle for pressed military labour. After abolition in 1807, British policing of the slave trade routes continued to produce a ready supply of military recruits from confiscated slave cargoes. Plantation slavery created a deeply embedded association between the black body and physical exertion exacted under coercion and discipline. The connection between slave and soldier was underlined further by the disciplinary regime of 18th and 19th century military life.

Flogging was permitted in the British army on Home Service until 1868, on active service until 1881 and in military prisons until 1907.[2]

The increasing association of military service with citizenship, evident in European revolutions from the late 18th century, created idealistic distinctions between slave and soldier. Furthermore, as the European settlers had been outnumbered by their slaves since the early days of colonisation, there was a tension between short-term pragmatism and long-term term effects whenever the decision was taken to arm slaves. In 1802, during the Napoleonic wars, the British government proposed a garrison of slave troops to prevent Jamaica falling into French hands. The planter class in the island's House of Assembly protested:

> Having ... armed slaves to defend and protect the rights, the liberties, and properties, not only of free men, but of British subjects ... [was] a measure not only considered to proceed from ignorance of our local circumstances, of our laws, and of our constitution, [but was] viewed with that abhorrence and indignation which it could not fail to excite.[3]

The planters reluctantly accepted the scheme when presented with the alternative of raising a local militia from their own funds. Following the outbreak of war with republican France in 1793, the British army established a systematic scheme of military slavery to defend its Caribbean territories.

After 1796, the British procured slaves directly from the transatlantic trade as plantation owners were often reluctant to sell their prized human possessions. Until the abolition of the slave trade in 1807, 12 regiments of black troops, the West India Regiments (WIR), were raised in this manner, supplemented by slaves captured from the French or handed over by royalist deserters. Some 13,400 slaves were purchased for military service, accounting for around 7% of slave exports to the British West Indies during the 12 years before abolition. Post-abolition, many Africans freed by British navy patrols were used to replenish the ranks of the WIR, a practice that continued until 1844.[4] Although only two West India Regiments were retained after 1815, they continued to play a pivotal role in the maintenance of British rule in both the Caribbean and later West Africa during the 19th century.

The Transition from Slavery and the West Indian Soldier as Mimic Man

Slavery was rationalised through the insistence that Africans were racially inferior. In pre-Darwinian terms Africans were regarded as the lowest human link on the 'great chain of being'.[5] Following the outlawing of the trade by the British in 1807, and the phasing out of slave labour between 1834 and 1838, the abolitionist movement questioned some of the most negative stereotypes perpetuated by the pro-slavery lobby, encapsulated by the supplicant African beseeching, 'Am I not a man and a brother?'. For the abolitionists, the black body carried the hallowed promise of human industry and effort within a free economy. However, they believed moral, intellectual and industrial progress could be achieved only with the guiding hand of white civilisation. Empire henceforth became a moral project to reform the racialised other; to enlighten those characterised as primitive and heathen. Model villages, established by non-conformist missionaries, inculcated the work ethic of the new free labour economy.[6] The central task of the civilising mission was to recreate the racialised other as a recognisable, domesticated figure who, while bodily different, was anglicised 'in tastes, in opinions, in morals, and in intellect';[7] as Homi Bhabha puts it, 'almost the same, but not quite'.[8]

The recruitment of black soldiers reached its pinnacle during the transition between slavery and free labour in the British West Indies. By this period a distinct West Indian creole identity could clearly be discerned.[9] The black West Indian was increasingly regarded as closer in terms of character, personality and religion to the English than the African and thus more suitable as a soldier. In the 1880s, Alfred Burdon Ellis, officer and historian of the first West India Regiment and writer on West African societies, advocated more vigorous recruitment in the West Indies. These additional battalions, Ellis argued, would be more suited to tropical service and more economical than garrison troops sent from the British Isles.

> Civilising influences have made this contrast between the Africans and their West India descendants ... striking. The latter have, since the abolition of slavery, been living independent lives, in close contact with civilisation, and enjoying all the rights of manhood under British laws. From their earliest infancy they have known no language but English, and no religion but Christianity; while the former are still barbarians, grovelling in fetishism, cursed with slavery, ignorant, debased, and wantonly cruel.[10]

Ellis suggested that the West Indian soldier regarded Africans with contempt and considered 'himself in every respect an Englishman'.[11] Regardless of how the West Indian soldier and his champions regarded his proximity to Englishness, notions of difference had to be preserved in order to uphold the hierarchy of empire.

The emergence of a distinctive uniform for the WIR illustrates how a sense of 'almost ... but not quite' was engineered by the imperial establishment. This process rendered the West Indian soldier into a familiar, domestic subject who might appear in prints of forgotten colonial outposts or cigarette cards. Previously, the WIR had worn uniforms similar to those of the other line regiments of the British army. During the Crimean War, the uniforms of French Zouave troops caught the eye of many observers, partly due to the heroism, ferocity and élan associated with these crack light infantry regiments.

Zouaves were originally recruited by the French colonial army from the hill tribes of Algeria and Morocco during the 1830s. When the French army was restructured shortly before the Crimean War, the Zouave regiments were henceforth composed of native Frenchmen. Algerian and Moroccan recruits, whose traditional attire influenced the Zouave uniform, were redesignated *Turcos* or *Tirailleurs Algériens*. In 1868, proposals were made to dress 'native' regiments in uniforms more suitable to the climates they served in. At the suggestion of Queen Victoria, who had 'an eye for the exotic' and who had seen the French Zouaves on parade, the adoption of a Zouave-style uniform by the WIR was agreed.[12]

The new uniforms also served to distinguish the WIR as 'native' units, rather than cementing an association with the Zouave military tradition. Significantly, white officers remained kitted out in more traditional military attire. The WIR's prescribed status as

British army regiments of the line was undermined with long-standing negative repercussions for pay and conditions. These persisted into the years of the First World War, affecting the West Indian men who volunteered to serve the Empire. In 1888, the remaining two West India Regiments were merged into a single regiment with two battalions. The Orientalist vision embodied in the Zouave uniform supported this diminishing process. A respected component of the colonial armed forces was gradually reduced to a ceremonial symbol of imperial subjecthood, despite continuing to play a key strategic role in the West African campaigns between the 1870s and 1890s. Thus, at her Diamond Jubilee of 1897, Queen Victoria regarded Sergeant James Gordon, who had received the Victoria Cross for bravery, in racially diminutive terms as her 'Zouave Boy'.[13]

The Character of the Black West Indian Soldier and the Scramble for Africa

Two accounts from officers who served with the West India Regiments during the Asante Wars of 1873–74 are notable for mixing admiration alongside deeply ingrained stereotypical beliefs about black physical and mental capacity. Alfred Burdon Ellis believed black West Indian troops were superior to whites in the West African climate, suggesting, however, that they became 'languid and inert' in cooler climes. He claimed black troops could march two to three times the distance of white comrades and could match European troops even when on half rations.[14] According to Ellis, 'The English-speaking negro of the West Indies is most excellent material for a soldier. He is docile, patient, brave, and faithful',[15] and even when treated harshly maintained passive obedience, rather than insubordination. For Ellis, white leadership was essential to ensure this state of affairs and to curb impetuous behaviour. 'The bravery of the West India soldier in action has often been tested, and as long as an officer remains alive to lead not a man will flinch. His favourite weapon is the bayonet; and the principal difficulty with him in action is to hold him back, so anxious is he to close with his enemy'.[16]

By contrast, Viscount Wolseley, who led the Asante campaign, argued for the greater use of African troops, particularly in frontier and bush-fighting campaigns. Wolseley believed the West Indian soldier was hampered by his relative proximity to white civilisation, which had not improved his physical strength or capacity for bravery. Men said to comprise the African martial races, such as the Asante or Zulu, however, possessed the 'intuitive knowledge of wild animals … which gives them … an immense advantage over the ordinary town-bred soldier'.[17] Wolseley argued that martial Africans possessed 'some hereditary bias in their brain, in their very blood, which fits them for the easy acquisition of a soldier's duties', but which could only be fully realised due to a 'childlike affection for, and implicit reliance upon, the officers'.[18]

The black West Indian soldier's apparent fondness for his white officer is a sentiment also remarked upon by Alfred Burdon Ellis.[19] There is more than a sense of self-flattery in such observations. More fundamental is a belief the black soldier lacked the independence of thought necessary for the self-actualising man of the Enlightenment. Following Kant's dictum *Sapere Aude!* [Dare to know!], the ability to use one's understanding without guidance from another was a mark of both courage and maturity. The affection towards his white officer purportedly demonstrated by the black West Indian soldier ultimately suggested inferiority and lack.

Charles William Day, a visitor to the West Indies in the late 1840s, captured attitudes regarding the discipline of the black soldier held by the colonial and military establishment. This was a position largely informed by the punitive practices fostered by the champions of plantation labour:

> The black troops are as courageous as the white ... but once fairly excited, they are beyond control. They are willing to obey an order, so far as they can be made to comprehend it, but their intellect is so limited, and their powers of reflection are so slight, that we can trust little or nothing to the non-commissioned officers ... Their ideas on discipline, rest and neatness, are extremely lax, so that we have great trouble in keeping them in anything like military order. They have furious animal passions, and were we to restrain them too far, they would mutiny.[20]

On the other hand there were observers, such as Charles Kingsley, who suggested that the rigours of military life inculcated a sense of propriety and appropriate behaviour in keeping with the project to produce anglicised colonial subjects in the West Indies:

> These Negro yeoman-veterans ... are among the ablest and steadiest of the coloured population. Military service has given them just enough of those habits of obedience of which slavery gives too much.[21]

The First World War and the Crisis of White Masculinity

Captain J. C. Dunn, a medical officer who had observed the British infantry at close hand during the Battle of the Somme, later remarked on the 'astonishing number of men whose narrow and misshapen chests, and other deformities or defects, unfitted them to stay the more exacting requirements of service in the field'.[22] This dismal depiction of the British soldier was not without foundation. The army revised its medical inspection system in 1917 and, in the remaining months of the war, 10% of those examined were rejected outright, while 41% were deemed unfit to serve either overseas or in home garrisons.[23] Throughout the war, concern about the physical fitness of recruits echoed doubts about the state of British manhood expressed during the South African War (1899–1902).[24]

Earlier imperial crises had also dented white masculine confidence. In an article for the *Daily Chronicle*, the eugenicist Francis Galton raised the question 'whether or no the British race as a whole is, or is not, equal to its Imperial responsibilities'. Shortly after the South African War, Galton unfavourably compared the physique of bathers in Hyde Park, London, with that of the black labourers he had seen on his visits to the colonies.[25] Charles Kingsley reported his sense of relief at finding 'everywhere health, strength, and goodly stature' among the West Indian peasantry, whom he compared most favourably with the 'short and stunted figures' of the Old World. Perhaps most significant was his observation that 'they seem to enjoy, they do enjoy, the mere act of living'.[26]

For many eugenicists, the war raised the prospect of national malaise, rather than prowess. The conflict threatened to overturn processes of natural selection, compounding the effects of the declining birth rate among the middle, upper and respectable working classes, renewing concern about male infant mortality rates. By the middle years of the war, broken and shattered ex-soldiers were a routine sight on Britain's streets, serving to underline the physical decline of white British masculinity, despite efforts to present the mutilated veteran as 'more of a man'.[27]

Anxieties about the physical condition of white manhood were compounded by apparent shortcomings in character. From the 1880s it had often been asserted that the fruits of empire and industry had produced indolence and moral torpor to the detriment of the imperial effort. In the words of Viscount Wolseley, 'Over-cultivation is calculated to convert manliness to effeminacy; it is conducive of luxury and love of ease, the same precursor of those indolent habits which kill all virile energy, and when that dies, not only the greatness of the nation but its independent existence are buried in the same grave'.[28]

More significantly, however, the psychological conditions displayed by thousands of soldiers undermined claims of white masculine superiority founded on rationality, stoicism and self-control.[29] Around 200,000 soldiers were discharged from the army on psychiatric grounds; many more were treated and sent back to the front line. By the end of the war, 20 specialist army hospitals dealt with shell-shock cases (from one in 1915), as well as numerous clinics and outpatient facilities.[30] Subsequent scholars have suggested that the wartime 'crisis of masculinity' identified by Elaine Showalter is not evident in contemporary accounts. Stryker argues that wartime psychiatrists did not equate the prevalence of shell shock with a decline in masculine ideals. Underlying manliness was often perceived among even the most intractable patients. For Meyer, ideals of white masculinity were not undermined during the war, but redefined through a culture of suffering.[31]

Although both these critiques highlight the shortcomings of Showalter's over-reliance on literary accounts of the war, neither considers the implications of changing representations of white masculinity within a politics of representation; either in terms of gender on the home front, or in terms of race and masculinity within the Empire. In the imperial context, the apparent waning of white British masculine ideals and character brought British authority and ascendancy into question. Dominion troops, for example, insisted it was they, rather than the British Tommy, who carried the decisive engagements on the Western Front through greater tenacity and physical robustness. In these circumstances, blackness could be rearticulated as a signifier of uninhibited sexual and emotional expression and renewed masculine vigour.

Black Soldiers and the White Imagination during the First World War

Black soldiers first came to British public prominence when a small detachment of the newly formed British West Indies Regiment (BWIR) marched in the Lord Mayor's show in November 1915. Formed in October 1915 for the duration of the war only, the British West Indies Regiment eventually comprised 12 battalions, enlisting around 15,200 men from Jamaica, Trinidad and Tobago, Barbados, British Guiana, British Honduras, Grenada, The Bahamas, St Lucia, St Vincent and the Leeward Islands. Accounts of the black West Indian contingents were preoccupied with the men's physique. The *Belfast Evening Telegraph* pictured 'sturdy West Indian troops' and the *Daily News* 'huge and mighty men of valour'.[32] A local newspaper reported on the 'splendid impression' made by the BWIR volunteers, stationed in the south coast town of Seaford between October 1915 and March 1916, declaring that 'Some of them are magnificently proportioned'.[33] Shortly after the war, Alfred Horner, padre to the 6th and 9th battalions of the British West Indies Regiment, provided an account of a regimental boxing match during which 'several officers ... were absolutely astounded at the fine figure and splendid outlines of our men'. Horner himself remarked how 'They look sometimes a little heavy and ill-built in their heavy kit, but remove that and ... it makes all the difference'.[34]

Horner, an enthusiastic 'muscular' Christian, trained by the Church Missionary Society, began to question his faith in masculine ideals when faced with the consequences of modern war. His homoerotic imagining of the black soldier represented a desire for spiritual and bodily vigour; for the natural, the innocent and unspoilt. Through such a lens, the black imperial subject could also be imagined as a child of nature, innately spiritual and untroubled by the cares of civilisation. But this regime of representation was paradoxical for it was underpinned by the association of the black body with plantation labour; an experience of modernity like industrial warfare itself. Indeed, Horner's vision of semi-clothed black men on the parade ground evokes the slave market, with soldiers, rather than slaves, performing for the benefit of white men, a vision that could provide comfort *and* the reassertion of white masculine authority.

It is also important to recognise that these imaginings were precisely that, although this does not detract from the symbolic significance of the black body in wartime. The rejection rate among Jamaican volunteers during the war was about 60%, a rate similar to the levels in Britain during the South African War. Twenty-six thousand six hundred and sixty-seven Jamaicans volunteered for service in the BWIR, medical rejections amounted to 13,940 and another 2,082 men were discharged or died before they could depart for overseas service.[35] Brigadier-General Blackden, the commander of the Jamaican local forces, complained that many volunteers were 'an undersized, ragged, barefooted set of fellows, who came forward probably to get a meal'.[36]

Furthermore, on racial grounds recruiters in Jamaica encouraged enlistment among the educated working and middle classes, who tended to be lighter skinned than the black peasantry and landless labourers. Brigadier-General Blackden asserted that 'Intelligence is required, and a certain amount of education ... although there is plenty of room for the muscle that drives the bayonet home, there is still more room for the brain that can use the complicated weapons of modern warfare'.[37]

With many black soldiers barred from front-line service, displays of physical strength could provide the opportunity to contest the marks of racial inferiority. Sport had become a metaphor for white racial dominance within the Empire, embodying the ideals of Social Darwinism and the team spirit, fair play and stamina identified with the imperial project. Therefore, the imperial authorities went to great lengths to ensure that contests between black and white competitors did not become public spectacles, an increasingly difficult task with the emergence of cinema, for 'the black man's victory' would be 'hailed as a proof that the hegemony of the white race is approaching the end'.[38] Black sportsmen could also be caricatured as naturalistic, raw and untutored; their achievements explained away as the outcome of brute force, rather than skill.

For white audiences, a more comfortable figure was the black soldier as entertainer or object of entertainment, who could serve as a repository for feelings and urges circumscribed by the demands of military masculinity. Apparently untouched by worldly cares, the black soldier-entertainer could be imagined as an authentic bearer of a universal human spirit able to transcend the upheavals and horrors of war. This way of viewing, which echoed Charles Kingsley's sentiments expressed some 40 years previously, framed the black soldier as both exotic and knowable; a discourse that while suggesting familiarity and connection, was never disentangled from imperial hierarchies of race. Alfred Horner described the men of his battalion as *le soldat noir aimable* (the friendly black soldier) and eagerly reported that the West Indians had 'a considerably larger emotional capacity than the English'.[39]

In these circumstances, the white British soldier found the black soldier-performer endearing, rather than viewing him with hostility, and, as Horner reported, 'If a canteen full of Tommies can only get our boys singing or dancing they are contented, and many a time and oft the role of society entertainer has fallen upon BWI boys'.[40] In the military hospitals, the black soldier provided a diversion from the harsh realities of war as 'the pet and plaything of both inmates and staff';[41] while for newspapers espousing the imperial war effort, images of smiling black soldiers 'Dancing the Rag' provided the ideal image of a united empire in which the racial order remained undisturbed by wartime upheaval.

The process of reimagining the black soldier as joyful and naïve is not without irony. As Sara Ahmed has so persuasively argued, philanthropic and benevolent gestures within the civilising mission of empire aimed to bestow happiness through utilitarian principles on peoples regarded as benighted and miserable; the heathen African, Hindu or obeah-practising Jamaican. The Empire gifted happiness by apparently instilling the good taste, character and civility observers perceived in the West Indian soldier. Happiness could also be guaranteed if colonised people adhered to imperial institutions and knowledge such as the rule of law, education and freedom of opinion.[42] These were the professed imperial values West Indians often eagerly enlisted to defend during the First World War. As European civilisation apparently reached its nadir, the white observer looked to the black West Indian soldier for emotional renewal. The black soldier also symbolised the tropics, where many soldiers in the mud and cold of France and Flanders dreamed of seeking sanctuary after the war.[43] But by focusing on exterior manifestations of happiness and vigour, the innermost elements of the black man's psyche were perhaps overlooked. As W. E. B. du Bois suggested, songs and performances that superficially signified that the black performer was 'careless and happy' disguised the 'music of an unhappy people', which 'tell of death and suffering and unvoiced longing toward a truer world';[44] of a people striving to be happy, rather than actually happy. Or perhaps the experiences of war and suffering allowed the white observer truly to empathise with this striving towards joy, rather than perceiving joy where there was little.

Conclusion

Within 19th century British imperial ideology, the black West Indian soldier provided evidence of the civilising potential of empire, although increasingly reduced to a ceremonial cipher. During the First World War, the West Indian volunteer became the focus of anxieties surrounding white male efficiency. He was simultaneously enlisted as an emotional repository by writers, observers and audiences for whom the notion of European rationality and progress could no longer be upheld.

THE BRITISH EMPIRE AND THE FIRST WORLD WAR

Notes

1. Roger Norman Buckley (1979) *Slaves in Red Coats: The British West India Regiments, 1795–1815*. New Haven: Yale University Press.
2. Richard Holmes (2006) *Sahib: The British Soldier in India 1750–1914*. London: Harper Perennial, p. 430.
3. *Cobbett's Weekly Political Register*, Vol. II, No. 11, 18 September 1802, p. 329.
4. Brian Dyde (1997) *The Empty Sleeve: The Story of the West India Regiments of the British Army*. St Johns, Antigua: Hansib, pp. 29–32, 136; Buckley (1979).
5. David Brion Davis (1988) *The Problem of Slavery in Western Culture*. Oxford: Oxford University Press, pp. 68–70.
6. Thomas C. Holt (1992) *The Problem of Freedom: Race, Labor, and Politics in Jamaica and Britain, 1832–1938*. Baltimore, MA: Johns Hopkins University Press.
7. Thomas Babington Macauley (1972) Minute on Indian education, in John Clive and Thomas Pinney (Eds.), *Selected Writings: Thomas Babington Macaulay*. Chicago, IL: University of Chicago Press, p. 241.
8. Homi Bhabha (1994) *The Location of Culture*. London: Routledge, p. 90.
9. Edward Kamau Brathwaite (1971) *The Development of Creole Society in Jamaica 1770–1820*. Oxford: Oxford University Press.
10. Alfred Burdon Ellis (1885) *The History of the First West India Regiment*. London: Chapman & Hall, pp. 11–12.
11. Ellis (1885, p. 12).
12. Dyde (1997, pp. 148–150).
13. Clinton Vane De Bross Black (1946) *Living Names in Jamaica's History*. Kingston: Jamaica Welfare, p. 19.
14. Ellis (1885, pp. 8, 21, 23).
15. Ellis (1885, p. 13).
16. Ellis (1885, pp. 14–15).
17. Viscount Wolseley (1888) The Negro as a soldier, *The Fortnightly Review*, 44, CCLXIV, 1 December, p. 689.
18. Viscount Wolseley (1888, p. 690).
19. Ellis (1885, p. 13).
20. Charles William Day (1852) *Five Years' Residence in the West Indies*. London: Colburn & Co., p. 219.
21. Charles Kingsley (1871) *At Last: A Christmas in the West Indies*, Vol. II. London: Palgrave Macmillan, p. 228.
22. J. C. Dunn (1938) *The War the Infantry Knew, 1914–1919*. London: P. S. King & Son, p. 245.
23. J. M. Winter (1985) *The Great War and the British People*. London: Palgrave Macmillan, pp. 50–59.
24. Richard A. Soloway (1990) *Degeneracy and Degeneration: Eugenics and the Declining Birthrate in Twentieth Century Britain*. Chapel Hill: University of North Carolina Press, p. 41.
25. Francis Galton (1903) Our national physique–prospects of the British race—are we degenerating?, *Daily Chronicle*, 29 July.
26. Charles Kingsley (1871) *At Last: A Christmas in the West Indies*, Vol. I. London: Palgrave Macmillan, p. 57.
27. Joanna Bourke (1996) *Dismembering the Male: Men's Bodies, Britain and the Great War*. London: Reaktion, p. 58.
28. Viscount Wolseley (1888, p. 692).
29. Elaine Showalter (1987) *The Female Malady: Women, Madness and English Culture, 1800–1980*. London: Virago, pp. 167–168.
30. Martin Stone (1985) Shellshock and the psychologists, in W. F. Bynum, R. Porter and M. Shepherd (Eds.), *The Anatomy of Madness: Essays in the History of Psychiatry*, Vol. II. London: Tavistock.
31. Linda Stryker (2003) Mental cases: British shellshock—politics of interpretation, in Gail Braybon (Ed.), *Evidence, History and the Great War: Historians and the Impact of 1914–18*. Oxford: Berghahn, pp. 154–171; Jessica Meyer (2004) "Not Septimus Now": wives of disabled veterans and cultural memory of the First World War in Britain, *Women's History Review*, 13(1), 117–138.
32. *Belfast Evening Telegraph*, 14 October 1915, p. 6; *Times History of the War* (1919), Vol. XIX. London, p. 86.

33. *Newhaven Chronicle*, 14 October 1915, p. 6. By this stage 'bantam battalions' were being formed to accommodate men who did not meet the minimum height requirement of five feet three inches (Winter, 1985, p. 32).
34. Alfred Egbert Horner (1919) *From the Islands of the Sea: Glimpses of a West Indian Battalion in France*. Nassau: *The Guardian*, pp. 7–8.
35. Stephen A. Hill (Ed.) (1920) *Who's Who in Jamaica, 1919–1920*. Kingston: *Daily Gleaner*, p. 247.
36. *Daily Gleaner*, 20 October 1915, p. 14.
37. *Daily Gleaner*, 12 October 1915, p. 13.
38. *The Times*, 25 May 1914, p. 40.
39. Horner (1919, p. 67).
40. Horner (1919, p. 50).
41. Horner (1919, p. 51).
42. Sara Ahmed (2010) *The Promise of Happiness*. Durham, NC: Duke University Press, pp. 124–125.
43. Paul Fussell (1982) *Abroad: British Literary Traveling Between the Wars*. New York: Oxford University Press, pp. 3–8.
44. W. E. B. Du Bois (1999/1903) *The Souls of Black Folk*. New York: W. W. Norton, pp. 156–157.

The First World War Centenary in the UK: 'A Truly National Commemoration'?

ANDREW MYCOCK
University of Huddersfield, Huddersfield, UK

ABSTRACT *Prime Minister David Cameron has called for 'a truly national commemoration of the First World War'. This article shows this to be problematic, politicised and contested. This is in part due to the elision of English and British histories. Scottish, Welsh and Irish responses are noted, and the role and commemorations of 'our friends in the Commonwealth'. There are tensions around interpretations of empire and race. There has been a failure to appreciate that the debates about the legacies of the First World War are deeply entangled with those of colonialism.*

Introduction

After a period of considerable anxiety in some sections of the British press about an apparent absence, Prime Minister David Cameron unveiled the UK government's plans to mark the centenary of the First World War in a speech at the Imperial War Museum in London in October 2012. He argued that it was crucial to commemorate the 'Great War' due to 'the extraordinary sacrifice of a generation' and the considerable impact of a conflict that 'changed our nation' and the world more widely. His ambition was, he claimed, to recognise the durable emotional connection of the conflict through the development of 'a truly national commemoration' while also seeking to acknowledge the sacrifice of 'friends in the Commonwealth' and from across all of Ireland.[1]

Centenary commemorations have, however, proved increasingly open to public contention, revealing tensions and divergence between politicians, academics and other commentators with regards to the thematic justification, coherence and purpose of the UK government's plans. This article seeks to explore some of these tensions, particularly the extent to which a 'politics of war commemoration' is founded on ideologically driven disputes regarding how the First World War is remembered. It will also assess the historical and contemporary challenges to establishing 'national' narratives and memory cultures to mark the First World War centenary that are inclusive and yet recognise diversity in how the conflict is remembered across Britain and across its former empire. This will be realised by considering how multinationality and transnationality have problematised the UK government's aspirations, as asserted by Cameron, for the centenary of the First World War to capture 'our national spirit'.

The Politics of War Commemoration

The deaths of the last surviving British combatants and the centenary of the First World War have initiated considerable political, academic and public deliberation about the causes, conduct and legacies of the conflict, and the potential lessons to be learnt. Intense debate has highlighted the complex and ever-increasing interactions between and interdependencies of history and memory. According to Jay Winter (2006), since the end of the First World War the position of historians as the primary mediators of nationhood through the articulation of national history has been gradually superseded by at least two 'memory booms' widely embraced by nation-states and their citizens alike. Emergent memory cultures have stimulated public discourse and transformed how past events are remembered, interpreted and articulated. Winter argues that the initial 'memory boom' was a response to the trauma of the First World War and sought to fortify and elevate national identities in an imperial age through war commemoration projects. However, he believes that a second 'memory boom' emerged in late 1960s, founded on revisionist approaches that fractured national ideological and cultural frameworks of collective war remembrance.

Winter's 'memory boom' thesis is important in developing understanding of the centrality of the First World War in shaping contemporary approaches to war commemoration. As 'collective' national forms of memory are intimately connected with the present, they are susceptible to instrumentalisation, manipulation and politicisation. This is, according to Pierre Nora (2011), increasingly realised through ongoing public debate about the content and purpose of history in which historians have been peripheralised. While history was once a *political* activity that supported the nation, it has become *politicised* in sustaining divergent ideological constructions of the present. These so-called 'history' or 'memory' wars have become a persistent feature of public discourse in many states, including the UK, and are typically linked to broader politicised debates about political, social, economic and cultural citizenship and identity. They reveal a shared belief among protagonists that states have the potential to articulate and inculcate homogenous collective identities founded on particularistic interpretations of the national past.

How past conflicts are interpreted and commemorated is a significant element of these emotionally charged debates, providing reference points for complementary or contradictory forms of memory and identity that underline political and cultural tensions between individuals and groups within and among nation-states. War commemoration is therefore primarily a political project whereby the state and its institutions mediate and order formal and informal collective memories and histories. The promotion of a homogenous national identity that references important conflicts is seen to establish symbolic continuity between the past, present and future of a nation-state (Ashplant *et al.*, 2004). This process is inherently multilateral, and is thus both contentious and contested. Politicised disputes over the interpretation, framing and articulation of past conflicts and their commemoration by public institutions such as museums, universities and schools are often febrile and also counter-intuitive as they enhance division rather than solidarity. This is, in part, because 'official' forms of war are typically founded on dominant or hegemonic state-approved historical narratives that seek to preserve and reinforce particular elites and ideologies. Consequently, they are seen by opponents as reflecting and reproducing unequal power relations shaped by phenomena such as race, ethnicity, class, gender and other social hierarchies (Graff-McRae, 2010).

Such debates therefore often hinge on the extent to which protagonists believe state-led war commemoration should be founded on 'orthodox' or revisionist reinterpretations of past conflicts. Such challenges reveal schisms about whether war commemoration should seek to inculcate positive collective forms of patriotism or more critical and pluralist interpretations. For example, popular responses to how past conflicts are remembered can often be allied with expressions of grief and mourning of traumatic loss that challenge attempts by states to promote more celebratory approaches to war commemoration (Marshall, 2004). War commemoration of past conflicts is also contextual and liable to reinterpretation by subsequent generations.

Historical Approaches to Commemorating the First World War

Complexities relating to history, memory and war commemoration raise significant challenges with regards to the stated aims of the UK government centenary plans. One of the most pressing questions relates to what is actually being commemorated during the centenary and why. As the conflict came to an end, the British state was proactive in seeking to mediate the 'official' and 'unofficial' collective memories to shape the commemoration of the First World War. This involved the 'invention' of national forms of commemoration including repetitive mass public participation in rituals, ceremonies and memorials, together with the dissemination of state-sponsored narratives concerning the conflict in museums and mass education programmes. But official and unofficial forms of commemoration of the First World War have proved to be neither static nor universal in terms of participation or meaning. While the inter-war and immediate period following the Second World War saw significant numbers involved in acts of war commemoration, public participation slowly declined in the latter half of the 20th century. However, the gradual dying out of the First World War generation, a series of significant conflict anniversaries, and the engagement of the UK in a series of conflicts have encouraged greater public recognition and participation in war commemoration (Shaw, 1997).

Participation in British First World War commemoration has been motivated by diverse narratives emphasising an (appropriately respectful) patriotic acknowledgement of the positive contribution of military action, a futile and terrible warning of the dangers of war, or even a call for world peace. Mosse notes that concerted efforts undertaken by the British state after the war sought to justify the fighting and sacrifice through the promotion of patriotic national myths and commemorative acts and rituals 'to make an inherently unpalatable past acceptable' (Mosse, 1990, p. 6). This was driven by a need to justify the scale of losses in the war in the name of the British nation *and* Empire, not least so that others might risk their lives in future wars. While the sense of shock regarding the scale of loss of life has proved durable, the precise nature of the cause for which combatants died has proved open to reinterpretation (Todman, 2005). More positive conceptions of the First World War that celebrated victory, prominent in the inter-war period, have largely dissipated in the wake of the Second World War. Since the 1960s, many Britons have been strongly influenced by revisionist accounts that construe the 1914–18 war as a largely futile conflict in which the huge loss of life was the result of political and military elite incompetence. State forms of war commemoration have reflected this more sombre revisionist tone.

The First World 'History' Wars

Tensions between state and popular perceptions of how the First World War is now understood and remembered have been evident in UK government pronouncements regarding its centenary plans and the ensuing debate. The special representative for the Centenary Commemoration of the First World War, Andrew Murrison MP, stated that commemorations would focus on remembrance, thus 'making no judgment about fault, right or wrong, or indulging in any jingoistic sentiment'. He acknowledged 'there are bound to be differences of opinion about how the Great War is remembered', but argued that 'it would be wrong for the government to insist on a particular narrative'.[2] The dominant themes underpinning contributions of politicians of differing ideological hues have often reiterated established revisionist themes regarding poor political and military leadership and the scale of human loss. This has been linked to a perceived need to avoid celebratory or jingoistic overtones in remembering the conflict.[3]

But heated debates between politicians, historians and the media more widely have highlighted that political ideology is an instrumental factor in framing the history, memory and commemoration of the conflict; for some on the political right have sought actively to counter revisionist themes disseminated by 'Marxist' historians since the 1960s that have skewed public perceptions of the conflict. UK Secretary of State for Education Michael Gove claimed that the 'existing left-wing version of the past' had strongly influenced British popular culture but was founded on myths deliberately designed to 'belittle Britain and its leaders'.[4] Others from the political right, such as UK Independence Party leader Nigel Farage and Conservative London Mayor Boris Johnson, concurred with Gove's analysis, with the latter denouncing the 'intellectual dishonesty of the left'.[5]

Such comments provoked a furious response from politicians and historians alike. Richard Evans, Regius Professor of History at the University of Cambridge, forcefully drew attention to the work of a number of 'right-wing' historians who were also critical of British military leadership.[6] Martin Pugh argued that the centenary commemoration plans were a product of 'a selected bunch of conservative historians and generals', offering a 'blinkered' focus of the Western Front without recognising the radical impact of the First World War on British society.[7] The Labour MP, Shadow Secretary of State for Education and historian, Tristram Hunt, agreed, noting the significant social and political implications of the war in terms of class, gender and British global power. He also declared Gove sought to 'sow political division' by rewriting the history of the war and to shift focus for its complex causes on to Germany alone.[8]

Boris Johnson responded by demanding Hunt's resignation, accusing him of denying that German militarism 'was at the root of the First World War'.[9] His comments revealed a wider tension about the extent to which the British victory should be commemorated or actively celebrated, particularly in relation to Germany. A leading member of the UK government's centenary advisory committee, Professor Sir Hew Strachan, argued that the avoidance of a more stridently positive tone to the commemorations revealed 'intent in government not to upset the Germans'.[10] This view has been supported by some sections of the British media. For example, an editorial in *The Times* suggested the UK government policy would appear to be 'don't mention we won the First World War'. It noted that Britain's role in the war was 'essentially just', being 'a necessary military response that stopped aggression by an expansionist power' that was 'xenophobic and anti-democratic'.[11] One commentator even made a case for 'why we SHOULD upset the Germans', arguing there was a 'politically correct' notion to 'suit contemporary sympathies' that it was 'somehow insulting to the millions who died to suggest that it wasn't all a monstrous waste of blood'. He concluded, 'give it long enough and we may find that we actually lost the Great War after all'.[12]

Uncertainties about the 'justness' of Britain's cause in the First World War have also permeated debate about how it has shaped contemporary society. Some, such as Hew Strachan, argue that the motivations of those who fought were of another age, suggesting they sought to defend the patriotic values of a 'strongly religious society', which was deeply hierarchical, and whose 'collective loyalties' were shaped by monarchy, empire and nation.[13] Politicians have, however, sought to relate the conflict to contemporary forms of patriotism and citizenship. For example, David Cameron has claimed that those who fought and died were defending 'the values we hold dear', though he struggled to articulate what these were beyond 'friendship, loyalty, what the Australians would call "mateship"'.[14] Michael Gove proposed that those fighting in the First World War were driven by a desire to defend Britain's 'special tradition of liberty' and 'the western liberal order'.[15] Richard Evans responded that such claims were compromised by the British preparedness to form an alliance with authoritarian Tsarist Russia.[16] *Guardian* columnist Seamus Milne went further, noting 'the idea that the war was some kind of crusade for democracy when most of Britain's population—including many men—were still denied the vote, and democracy and dissent were savagely crushed among most of those Britain ruled, is laughable'.[17]

Some commentators have sought to link the First World War with contemporary political issues. For example, British right-wing Eurosceptics have identified the genesis of the European Union as a political 'deception' by elites who fought in the First World War and then sought to build a 'United States of Europe' in the wake of the Second World War (Booker, 2014).[18] Influential right-wing polemicist Charles Moore (2014) has argued that opportunist socialists took advantage of the necessities of 'total war' to expand the power and influence of the state through nationalisation and welfarism.[19] This, he insisted, had led to long-term economic and social decline, initiating a moral collapse by making the poorest reliant on the state. On the left of the political spectrum, historian John Newsinger argued that the centenary commemorations were an attempt by the 'ruling class' to foster 'the spirit of Britishness' to supress the working class 'by mythologising a conflict of unimaginable horror'.[20] For some commentators, the lessons of the 'savage industrial slaughter' pursued by 'predatory imperial powers' have not been learnt, indicating there is a significant threat of another global conflict between great powers of the 21st century.[21] This is, according to Frank Furedi (2014), due to the divisive legacies of the First World War that have fragmented the potential for a universal liberal framework of political, economic and cultural values and ideologies that might negate conflict within and between states.

'A Truly National Commemoration'?

Debates about the centenary are complicated further in multinational states such as the UK where war commemoration can simultaneously draw on shared experiences of past conflicts involving all nations within the overarching state and also highlight distinctive or divergent sub-state national forms of remembrance founded on contradictory constructions of official and unofficial history and memory. British war commemoration has been predominantly framed on mutually inclusive narratives, rituals and symbols of remembrance involving all of the nations of the UK.[22] However, the conflation of British and English narratives informing state war commemoration reveal ethno-national hierarchies that have often marginalised or overlooked non-English official and unofficial histories and memory cultures. Such 'Anglo-myopia' appears to have influenced the UK government's approach to the centenary. For example, David Cameron has claimed the commemorations will draw on 'our national spirit in every corner of the country'. However, the vast majority of UK government funding for 'national' events and projects has been allocated to England. For example, a programme involving battlefront visits for schoolchildren was claimed by one government minister to have the potential to 'bind us together as a nation', although funding was made available only to English schools.[23]

The proposition of a universal 'British' experience of the First World War thus conceals multinational asymmetries in 'national' forms of history, identity and memory informing war commemorations that are layered and interdependent but not necessarily homogenous. Scholars have explored the distinctive impact and legacy of the First World War in Scottish and Welsh national terms, drawing attention to distinctive frontline and domestic experiences and, in the case of Scotland, the disproportionate human cost.[24] But the changing political climate in the non-English nations of the UK, particularly since the creation of devolved parliaments in 1998, is clearly having an impact of the tone and focus of centenary commemoration plans.

In Scotland, the election of the Scottish National Party (SNP) in 2011 to take sole control of the Scottish Parliament has encouraged a distinctive approach to the centenary, emphasising the Scottish nation rather than the UK more widely. In March 2013, the Scottish government announced the formation of a Scottish advisory panel under the leadership of Norman Drummond, who noted 'it is important that Scotland remembers the sacrifice of those who served during the First World War and the wider impact that the war has had on our country and upon Scots across the world'.[25] This being noted, the Scottish government has drawn on a similar centenary narrative as the UK government, declaring it was in 'no sense a celebration of the centenary of this devastating conflict'.[26]

The forthcoming independence referendum in Scotland has provided a further dimension to debates about the centenary, although both pro- and anti-independence campaigns have formally signalled a 'political armistice'.[27] Supporters of Scottish independence have raised concerns about UK government's 'jingoistic celebrations' of the 'Great Slaughter' of Scotland's young who died because of 'misplaced loyalty'.[28] The greater ratio of Scots mortality rates on the Western Front when compared with other parts of the UK has been emphasised by Scottish nationalists, with one suggesting 'British military commanders have always viewed Scottish forces as expendable'. A vote for independence would, he argued, ensure future generations of Scots could not be 'sent like lambs to the slaughter for a monarch or a crusading Westminster zealot'.[29] Historian Michael Fry concluded the centenary was part of a UK government-orchestrated and politicised 'Britfest' that began with the Diamond Jubilee and Olympics celebrations in 2012.[30]

Conversely, those supporting the Union have argued the centenary provides 'ample opportunity to remind the Scottish people how they stood together with the English, Welsh and Northern Irish'.[31] Unionist politicians in both the Scottish and UK parliaments have accused the Scottish government of investing more funding in marking the 700th anniversary of the Battle of Bannockburn, at which the Scots defeated the English, while deliberately overlooking the centenary.[32] Such an approach has been interpreted by one commentator as an attempt by the Scottish government to appeal to the 'inner nationalist' of Scots rather than their 'outer Brit'.[33]

In Wales, commemoration plans for the centenary have similarly focused on Welsh national as well as British experiences, but have proved less politicised than in Scotland. First Minister Carwyn Jones has noted 'it is extremely important that we remember those who died and reflect on how it changed Wales'.[34] But Welsh nationalists have suggested that the centenary commemorations are 'reminiscent of the jingoistic nonsense we saw from the British state elite to drum up support for the war in the first place'.[35] One leading Plaid Cymru member has claimed that the origins of the Welsh independence movement can be located in the First World War as a response to 'British imperialism' within the UK.[36]

Commemoration of the First World War in Northern Ireland highlights most clearly the politically contentious and culturally divisive legacies of the conflict. The centenary is part of a wider series of high-profile commemorations between 2012 and 2021 that mark events such as the Home Rule disputes, the Battle of Somme, the Easter Rising and the Irish civil war, which all draw attention to the contemporary resonances of historical events surrounding Ireland's partition. The UK government has sought to extend established narratives underpinning the centenary to Northern Ireland that emphasise shared focus on British participation in the war—a theme that Unionist politicians have keenly supported. For example, Theresa Villiers, the Secretary of State for Northern Ireland, has stated 'World War One profoundly affected the whole community across Northern Ireland and involved terrible sacrifice … it is important that a century on, this generation recognises and pays tribute to those who gave so much for our country'.[37] It has also indicated that centenary commemorations offer further opportunities for reconciliation with the Republic of Ireland, with UK government representatives stating they will reflect Irish involvement.[38] However, the potential for 'poppy wars' to highlight enduring divisions across Ireland is significant.[39] While representatives of Sinn Fein have recently taken part in Remembrance Day services in Northern Ireland for the first time, dissident Republican groups have denounced the centenary of 'a war of imperial conquest'.[40]

The First World War and the Legacies of Empire

The role of Ireland in British centenary commemorations draws attention to the transnational dynamics of the First World War. The contribution of its Empire ensured British forms of war commemoration extended beyond the boundaries of the state to include former colonies that contributed soldiers and resources to previous conflicts. UK government representatives have sought to stress enduring Commonwealth ties, with David Cameron noting it was vital to recognise the 'extraordinary sacrifice' and 'catastrophic' death toll of 'our friends in the Commonwealth'.[41] This would appear to confirm Jay Winter's (2006) proposition that, in the wake of the conflict, the 'shadow of empire mattered' in encouraging a sense of shared loss and trauma underpinning transnational networks of memory. Such networks were particularly resonant for the large numbers of Australians, Canadians, South Africans and New Zealanders in the so-called 'White Dominions', many of whom were British-born or who had British ancestry, thus indicating that imperial war commemoration was strongly defined by shared bonds that were often racially determined.

The centenary of the First World War has, however, revealed the extent to which post-colonial revisionism in the wake of empire compromises dominant British national narratives and collective memories informing war commemoration. Although shared transnational modes of war commemoration across the 'White Dominions' have endured, the sacrifices of the First World War have become increasingly understood in terms of post-British nation-building and progression towards self-determination. Historical narratives and memory cultures have thus drawn on post-colonial interpretations of the perceived British military incompetence and scepticism of the British political leaders who took the Empire to war. For example, the 'legend' or 'myths' of the Australian and New Zealand Army Corps (ANZAC), particularly those troops involved in the Gallipoli landings of 1915, often emphasise perceived shared personal and group attributes and characteristics, such as courage, humour and ingenuity, and egalitarian values associated with ANZAC soldiers when compared with their British commanding officers and the 'mother country' more widely. Such mythology has been exposed to critical analysis (Connor, 2012; Wilson, 2012), but has proved powerful in shaping public perceptions of the war in Australia and government plans for the centenary.[42]

Suggestions by UK government ministers that the centenary offers opportunities to reflect on why 'Britain and her family' went to war reveal further tensions of empire.[43] Many troops did enlist voluntarily, their actions underpinned by a confluence of domestic and broader imperial motives (Omissi, 2007). However, a considerable number were conscripted and many lacked a comprehensive understanding of the cause for which they were expected to fight.[44] Many more imperial subjects supported the British war effort by providing resources and commodities—a contribution that is rarely acknowledged. Unlike their 'White Dominion' counterparts, transnational 'collective memories' informing the content of British war commemoration often overlooked the sacrifices of troops from the colonies and they were not afforded equal recognition in remembrance on war memorials.[45]

Although such 'memory gaps' were of particular resonance to those 'new Commonwealth' migrants who settled in the UK from the late 1940s, the contribution of troops from the Indian subcontinent, Africa and the Caribbean has proved a growing dimension of war commemoration and the wider historiography of the First World War (Das, 2011). Indeed, the UK government has sought to recognise explicitly the contribution of ethnic minority communities and the impact of the war on multicultural Britain. The First World War, according to David Cameron, marked 'the beginnings of ethnic minorities getting the recognition, respect and equality they deserve'.[46] As UK Faith and Communities Minister Baroness Sayeeda Warsi has noted, 'our boys weren't just Tommies; they were Tariqs and Tajinders too'. She argued that the centenary offered opportunities to acknowledge that 'so many men from so far away came to Europe to fight for the freedoms we enjoy today. Their legacy is our liberty, and every single one of us owes them a debt of gratitude'.[47]

The proposition that subjects from across the Empire sought to defend British domestic liberties is highly questionable though, particularly when considering the exploitative and hierarchical nature of British colonial rule. The post-war rewards for those from the colonies who fought were also scant and British rule remained largely unreformed in the inter-war period. Such claims also overlook the pervasive influence of racial categorisation and discrimination of troops from British colonies and others who supported the war effort. The experiences of those who served from the British dominions and colonies were profoundly different. For example, while two Indian divisions fought on the Western Front, West Indian troops were not trusted and instead were allocated dangerous but menial manual labour.[48]

There has been a failure to appreciate that debates about the legacies of the First World War are deeply entangled with those of British colonialism. Such an approach often overlooks the complex transnational dynamics of First World War commemoration or that the resonance and meaning of the conflict differ considerably across its former Empire. For example, the history of the 1.3 million Indian soldiers who fought in the conflict has been largely forgotten in India, lost in the pursuit of independence after the war and the subsequent framing of post-colonial Indian nationalism.[49] How the First World War is commemorated across the Commonwealth is also not centripetal in its relation to the experiences of the UK. The Australian government's plans for the centenary commemoration focus on the strength of post-conflict ties with New Zealand and Turkey, highlighting shared sacrifice between them, rather than ties with the UK.

Conclusions

This article has argued that a 'politics of war commemoration', underpinned by tensions between official and unofficial collective memories and histories, has shaped public debate about the centenary of the First World War. The UK government has claimed its role in the centenary was merely to provide leadership and encouragement in organising commemorative acts while not dictating the themes of commemoration itself. This position, though understandable, is naïve and overlooks its own role in stimulating ideologically founded divisions concerning how the conflict should be commemorated and what the legacies are for contemporary British society. The UK government also appears unaware of the implications of seeking to realise its aspirations to host a 'truly national commemoration'. By framing the First World War centenary in 'national' terms, it has failed to acknowledge fully the extent to which the multinational framework of the British state has and continues to layer and fragment war commemoration. Moreover, there appears to be a lack of recognition regarding the complex legacies of empire and how they affect transnational forms of British war commemoration. The centenary has the power to (re)ignite a diverse range of post-colonial responses that impair the UK government's proposition for a shared approach to the centenary across the Commonwealth. Therefore, the UK government's plans for the commemoration of the First World War centenary have failed to recognise fully and to accommodate sufficiently the complex and entangled memories and histories of the citizens and nations of the UK and its former Empire.

Notes

1. D. Cameron, 'World war centenary plans', speech at the Imperial War Museum, London, 11 October 2012.
2. Quoted in *The Guardian*, 8 February 2013.
3. See, for example, A. Murrison, 'A great tribute to the Great War', *Daily Telegraph*, 4 November 2011, or T. Hunt, 'We must strike a solemn tone to mark centenary of catastrophe', *The Sentinel*, 12 November 2012.
4. M. Gove, 'Why does the Left insist on belittling true British heroes?', *Daily Mail*, 2 January 2014.
5. N. Farage, 'British incompetence in World War One has been overestimated. It's politicians, not the military, who deserve censure', *Daily Express*, 5 January 2014; B. Johnson, 'Germany started the Great War but the Left can't bear to say so', *Daily Telegraph*, 6 January 2014.
6. R. J. Evans, 'Michael Gove shows his ignorance of history again', *The Guardian*, 6 January 2014.
7. *The Guardian*, 'Blinkered view of the First World War', 13 February 2013.
8. T. Hunt, 'Michael Gove using history for politicking is tawdry', *The Observer*, 4 January 2014.
9. B. Johnson, 'Germany started the Great War but the Left can't bear to say so', *Daily Telegraph*, 6 January 2014.
10. Nicholas Hellen and Richard Brooks, 'Don't mention that we won the First World War', *The Sunday Times*, 13 January 2013.
11. *The Times*, 'Remembrance aright', 12 October 2012.
12. Robert Hardman, 'Why we SHOULD upset the Germans—by reminding them of their Great War atrocities', *Daily Mail*, 14 January 2013.
13. Andrew Frayn, 'Armistice Day and a mythologised distant version of the First World War', *The Guardian*, 12 November 2011.
14. D. Cameron, speech at the Imperial War Museum, London, 11 October 2012.
15. M. Gove, *Daily Mail*, 2 January 2014.
16. R. J. Evans, *The Guardian*, 6 January 2014.
17. Seamus Milne, 'The First World War: the real lessons of this savage imperial bloodbath', *The Guardian*, 16 October 2012.
18. C. Booker, 'How the First World War inspired the EU', *The Spectator*, 8 February 2014.
19. C. Moore, 'How socialism created a moral no mans land', *Daily Telegraph*, 2 February 2014.
20. J. Newsinger, 'A history soaked in blood the British Empire's crimes are nothing to celebrate', *Socialist Worker*, 7 January 2014.
21. S. Milne, *The Guardian*, 16 October 2012.
22. See, for example, A. King (1998) *Memorials of the Great War in Britain: Symbolism and Politics of Remembrance*. London: Berg; D. Todman (2009) 'Representing the First World War in Britain: the 90th anniversary of the Somme', in H. Herwig and M. Keren (Eds.), *War Memory and Popular Culture*. Ottawa: McFarland.
23. E. Pickles, 'We all have a duty to remember the millions who lost their lives during the First World War', *Daily Telegraph*, 10 June 2013.
24. See, for example, T. Royle (2006) *The Flowers of the Forest: Scotland and the First World War* Edinburgh: Birlinn; D. Young (2006) *Scottish Voices from the Great War*. Stroud: Tempus; C. Williams (2007) 'Taffs in the trenches: Welsh national identity and military service, 1914–1918', in M. Cragoe and C. Williams (Eds.), *Wales and War: Religion, Society and Politics in the Nineteenth and Twentieth Centuries*. Cardiff: University of Wales Press, pp. 126–164.
25. Scottish Government, 'Former military chaplain to lead WW1 commemorations', 24 January 2013.
26. Scottish Government, 'WW1 commemorations in Scotland', 25 May 2013.
27. D. Maddox, 'Political armistice promised as Britain marks WWI centenary', *The Scotsman*, 12 October 2012.
28. J. McAlpine, 'Slaughter of Great War cast a shadow over Scotland that took decades to lift... there's nothing to celebrate', *Daily Record*, 5 November 2013.
29. M. MacLachlan, 'Why Ypres matters more than Bannockburn in the independence vote', *Caledonian Mercury*, 16 April 2012. The loss ratio of Scots was 26.4% compared with an average death rate of 11.8% for the rest of the British army.
30. M. Fry, 'Time to reflect, not celebrate', *The Scotsman*, 19 October 2012.

31. S. Johnson, 'Why war anniversaries will influence the battle over Scottish independence', *Daily Telegraph*, 8 November 2011.
32. D. Maddox, 'Clash between WWI and Bannockburn memorials feared', *The Scotsman*, 28 April 2013.
33. A. Cochrane, 'What we should unite behind in 2014 inner nat or not', *Daily Telegraph*, 11 October 2012.
34. National Library for Wales (2012) 'Expert advisor appointed to help Wales remember the First World War', 2 March 2012.
35. J. Edwards, 'Why we shouldn't commemorate the start of WWI', *Morning Star*, 31 October 2012.
36. A. Stevenson, 'MPs fight back against WW1 commemoration', Politics.co.uk, 24 October 2012.
37. A. Maguire, 'Northern Ireland schools will play a part in WWI centenary', *Belfast Telegraph*, 15 October 2012.
38. Andrew Murrison, quoted in *The Irish Times*, 27 January 2014.
39. See, for example, D. Horspool, 'The poppy wars', *The Times Literary Supplement*, 9 November 2011.
40. Republican Sinn Fein, 'The only fitting way to honour 1916 is to build a New Ireland', 3 January 2014.
41. Cameron, speech at the Imperial War Museum.
42. See, for example, Australian Government (2013) *Government Response to the Report of the Anzac Centenary Advisory Board on a Program of Initiatives to Commemorate the Anzac Centenary*.
43. Andrew Murrison, quoted in *The Guardian*, 8 February 2013.
44. See, for example, A. Grundlingh (1987) *Fighting their Own War: South African Blacks and the First World War*. Johannesburg: Ravan Press; G. D. Howe (2002) *Race, War and Nationalism: A Social History of West Indians in the First World War*. Kingston: Ian Randle; D. Omissi (1994) *The Sepoy and the Raj: The Indian Army, 1860–1940*. Basingstoke: Palgrave MacMillan.
45. M. Barrett (2011) 'Death and the afterlife: Britain's colonies and dominions', in S. Das (Ed.), *Race, Empire and First World War Writing*. Cambridge: Cambridge University Press, pp. 301–320.
46. Cameron, speech at the Imperial War Museum.
47. Department for Communities and Local Government, 'Baroness Warsi kick-starts campaign to remember Commonwealth servicemen of the First World War', 16 April 2013.
48. Arthur Torrington, 'West Indian soldiers in the First World War', Imperial War Museum, 11 March 2013.
49. M. S. Sharma, 'World War One: the India story retold', *The Times of India*, 9 February 2014.

References

Ashplant, T., Dawson, G. and Roper, M. (2004) The politics of war memory and commemoration: contexts, structures and dynamics, in T. Ashplant, G. Dawson and M. Roper (Eds.), *The Politics of War Memory: Commemorating War*. London: Routledge, p. 22.

Connor, J. (2012) The 'superior', all-volunteer AIF, in C. Stockings (Ed.), *Anzac's Dirty Dozen: 12 Myths of Australian Military History*. Sydney: University of New South Wales Press, pp. 35–50.

Das, S. (2011) Introduction, in S. Das (Ed.), *Race, Empire and First World War Writing*. Cambridge: Cambridge University Press.

Furedi, F. (2014). *First World War: Still No End in Sight*. London: Bloomsbury Continuum.

Graff-McRae, R. (2010) *Remembering and Forgetting 1916: Commemoration and Conflict in Post-Peace Process Ireland*. Dublin: Irish Academic Press, pp. 6–10.

Marshall, D. (2004) Making sense of remembrance, *Social and Cultural Geography*, 5(1), pp. 37–54.

Mosse, G. L. (1990) *Fallen Soldiers: Reshaping the Memory of the World Wars*. Oxford: Oxford University Press, p. 6.

Nora, P. (2011) 'Recent history and the new dangers of politicization', *Eurozine*, 24 November, http://www.eurozine.com/articles/2011-11-24-nora-en.html.

Omissi, D. (2007) Through Indian eyes: Indian soldiers encounter England and France, 1914–1918, *English Historical Review*, 122(496), 371–396.

Shaw, M. (1997) Past wars and present conflicts: from the Second World War to the Gulf, in M. Evans and K. Lunn (Eds.), *War and Memory in the Twentieth Century*. Oxford: Berghahn Books, pp. 191–205.

Todman, D. (2005) *The Great War: Myth and Memory*. London: Hambledon Continuum.

Wilson, G. (2012) *Bully Beef and Balderdash*. Newport, NSW: Big Sky Publishing.

Winter, J. (2006) *Remembering War: The Great War between Memory and History in the Twentieth Century*. New Haven: Yale University Press, pp. 170–179.

Index

Entries in **bold** denote tables; entries in *italics* denote figures.

1/5th Northamptonshires 79
2/15th London Regiment 86
4th Cavalry Division 75, 83
4.5 inch shells 225
5th Light Infantry 7
6th Pune Division, Indian Army 97–8
12th Field Artillery Brigade 343, 345
16th Indian Infantry Brigade 97
18-pounder gun 219–20, 225, 347
54th Division 86

Abadan 94, 102
Abdullah, Mohamed 384
Abeokuta 238
Abercorn 1
abolitionist movement 420
Abura 157, 163, 167
Accra 158, 169n7
Adams, George Hill 343–4, 346–9
AE2 (submarine) 131
AFC (Australian Flying Corps) 133, 344, 355, 357–8
Afghanistan 26, 371, 373–6
Afghan War of 1919 27
Africa: in *The Empire at War* 34; resistance to recruitment in 7–8, 164–5; as theatre of war 1, 40–1; *see also* East Africa; South Africa; West Africa
African agency 150–2, 155, 159, 164, 168
African and Eastern Trade Corporation 244
African Association 235, 237, 244, 248n32,43
African-Caribbeans 380, 382, 387–8, 394–5; *see also* black colonial people; West Indians
African intelligentsia: administrative prejudice against 241; Clifford's opposition to 169n9; definitions of 169n2; marginalization of 153; and marriage customs 159–61; promoting recruitment 150–1, 154–9, 167–8; in South Africa 199–201, 207

African Oil Nuts 239, 241–4
African Political Organisation 45
Africans: discrimination against 13; recruitment of 16n17
The African Telegraph 384
African Times and Orient Review 156
African traders 234, 237, 241, 244–5, 249nn64–5
Afrikaans language 44, 51
Afrikaans-speaking Christians 197–8, 204, 210
Afrikaner Nationalism 9, 13, 43–4, 203–4
Afrikaner Rebellion 8, 13, 41–2, 49, 58, 203–5, 209
Afrikaners: non-white criticism of 200; opposition to war 8, 42–4, 47, 194–6, 201–5, 208; reconciliation between *see hereniging*; in South West Africa 57
Agnew, Ivo 357–8
AIF (Australian Imperial Force): artists serving in 334–5; as 'cannon fodder' 132n50; counter-intelligence training in 354–5; deserters from 361–3; in Egypt 91n44; as elite formation 141; at Gallipoli 9, 131–2, 217; letters from parents to 408; letters to parents from 405; manpower strain on 7; naming 129; POWs from 14, 351–3, 356–60, 364; RAN convoy of 130; records of 415n17; on Western Front 136–7, 139
airships 36, 282
Akyem Abuakwa 151, 159, 162, 166, 168, 169nn11–13
Algeria 26, 120, 421
The All-Australian Memorial 125–6
Allenby, Edmund 74–9, 81, 90n3, 134
Allonville 363
All our Yesterdays (Tomlinson) 19–20
ALP (Australian Labor Party) 206, 216, 224
Alsace 208
Amanfi II of Asebu 167

INDEX

American Wars of Independence 383
Amiens 137
ammunition, in Mesopotamia 97
Amoy 31
Ampthill, Lord 266–7, 271n48
amputations 305, 307
Angaur 57
Anglican Church 81–3, 197, 301, 310n25
Anglo–Boer War *see* South African War (1899–1902)
Anglo-Italian blockade in Egypt 115–17
Anglo-Japanese alliance 27, 128, 277–80, 283–4, 286, 290
Anglo-myopia 434
Anglo-Persian Oil Company 94, 102
Angola 27
animals: from Cyprus 143, 147; feeding 96, 100, 108, 111, 227; rations for **101**; transport by 109–11
Anoah, Joseph 387, 399n46
Anomabu 162–3, 167
anti-German propaganda 14, 151, 154, 156
Antigua 383
anti-heroism 315, 320, 323–4
Anti-Slavery and Aborigines' Protection Society 243
Antwerp, diamond sales in 62, 69
ANZAC (Australian and New Zealand Army Corps): at Gallipoli 3, 131–2; and South African uprising 13, 41–2, 204
The Anzac Book 334
ANZAC legend 228, 436
APO (African People's Organisation) 45, 54n19, 199–201, 204
Arab nationalism 11
Archer, Thomas 399n56
Arifan, Mahomed 371
Armenian refugees 146
Armentières 359, 362
Army Service Corps 35, 388, 399n51
ARPS (Aborigines' Rights Protection Society) 151, 157–8, 161, 164, 169n3
artillery, technological developments in 139
asafo companies 157–8, 163–4, 166–7, 169n6
Asante 152–3, 162, 164–5, 167, 169n1
Asante Wars 422
Asianization, of Germans in propaganda 14, 172–3
Asians, Australian fears of 13, 69, 172–4, 180–1
Asquith, Herbert: dissatisfaction with 217; entering war 23, 196; and European theatre 11; and Ireland 8; and Nigeria Debate 240, 243; and William Hughes 275
Assin Apinimim 163
Assin Attandanso 163

Association of West African Merchants 239, 242
atheists 310n25
Atkins, George Stanley 308
atrocity propaganda 69, 172–3, 183–5, 191n6, 208
atta 96
Australia: commemoration of First World War 3, 405, 437; constructing memories of war in 228, 334, 339; employment for returned soldiers 410; enlistment in 6, 31; enthusiasm for war in 193; entry into war 128–9; food supplies from 98–9, 104; foreign policy of 56–7; heroic theme in war writing 352; Hughes' loyalty to 273–4, 278; importance of war effort 125–7, 139–41; Indian residents of 282; munitions movement in 219–21, 226; official art scheme in 15, 334–8; patterns of bereavement 412; racist discourse in 172–4, 179; 'Recruiting Kit' 185–7, 189–90, 191n15; rejection of conscription in 7–8; role in Imperial decision-making 287; steel industry in 218–19; trade policy of 60; war record collection of 337–8; *see also* Western Australia
Australian Aborigines 10
Australian and New Zealand Mounted Division 2, 88, 133
Australian Chivalry 343
Australian Commonwealth Shipping Line 227
Australian Labor Federation 222, 230n55
Australian light horse brigades 132–3
Australian Mounted Division 134
Australian-ness 9
Austria–Hungary 13, 22, 26–7
Austro-Hungarians, in South Africa 197
AWM (Australian War Memorial): AIF records at 415n17; art collection of 333, 336, 338–41, 350; commissions from Power 341–3, 345–6, 348; and eyewitness testimony 339; research on First World War 127
AWRS (Australian War Records Section) 335
Aylmer, F. J. 98, 100, 102–4
Aynsu, Katie 391

Baghdad, Indian Army at 7
Bahamas 36, 424
Baird, Adam 221
Bairnsfather, Bruce 316, 320, 323, 331n10
Baker, George 308, 312n53
'bakshish' 83
Balfour, Arthur 240
Balfour Declaration 283, 287, 291
Balkan wars 21, 26
BA newspaper 408

INDEX

Bank of England 22
Banque de France 22
bantam battalions 428n33
Barbados 36, 302, 382, 395, 424
barbarism 172–3, 181, 183–4, 186, 357
barley 35, 147
Barrier Munitions Company 224
Barron, Harry 222
Barrow, Edmund 256, 265, 268, 271
Bar-Yosef, Eitan 76, 82
Basra: flooding in 102, 105; river transport from 106; shipping supplies to and from 98, 100–2, 105, **106**, 108; strategic importance of 94
Basra, capture of 14, 95
Basra, Chinese Labour Corps in 31
Basra War Memorial 3
Battle of Jutland 130
Bazley, Arthur 338
Bean, Charles: at Allonville 363; on AWM Art Committee 338–40; and Garry Roberts 404; and official art programme 333–7; and photography 337–8; and Power's paintings 342–6, 350; war writing of 9, 337, 352–3
Bechuanaland 6; *see also* Botswana
Bedouin 117, 120
Beersheba 77–8, 134–5
BEF (British Expeditionary Force): Australians in 135, 138–9; Dominion and colonial forces in 4, 6, 137; purchasing munitions for 9
Belgium: as colonial power 4; German atrocity stories from 183, 202, 216
Bell, George 335, 340
Bennett, Benjamin 388
Benoni, Levinia 396
Benson, Claude 357
Benson, George 335
bereavement 404–6, 412–13
Bermuda 36, 383, 388, 394
Bethlehem 78, 83
Bethmann Hollweg, Theodor von 21
Beyers, C. F. 41, 43, 203–4
bhoosa 101, 108
BHP (Broken Hill Proprietary) 221, 229n41
biblical vernacular tradition 82
Bigland, Alfred 242
Birdwood, George 260
biscuits 98–9, 117, 325
bittereinders 203
Black and Tans 9
black bodies 419–20, 425
black colonial people: civilizing mission towards 420–1; discrimination against 381, 389–94; marriage among 394–5; rioting against *see* rioting, anti-black

black entertainers 425–6
black sailors 384, 390, 393–5
black soldiers: discrimination against 386; as entertainers 425–6; in Liverpool rioting 385, 387, 396–7; reasons for enlistment 379–80, 384; and slavery 419, 421; white attitudes to 14, 422–5, 437
black workers: Galton on 423; in Liverpool 380, 387–90, 392–4, 396; in South Africa 45–6, 209
Blanchard, Norman 359
blood sacrifice 9–10, 384, 398n27
Board of Trade 59, 61, 65, 68, 71, 72n19
boatswain 392, 400n77
Boer rebellion of 1914 *see* Afrikaner Rebellion
Boer War *see* South African War (1899–1902)
Bogazi 146
Bolsheviks 9, 11, 37
Bonar Law, Andrew: and diamond sales 62; and Nigeria 240, 243; and South African overseas pay question 47
Borden, Robert 10, 275
Botha, Louis: and Afrikaner rebellion 8, 41–3, 203–4; and Imperial conduct of war 10, 44; invasion of GSWA 202, 209; non-white support for 198–9; and Unionist Party 52–3; war policy of 41, 45–9, 57, 195–6
Botswana 3
Bottomley, Horatio 180
Bou, Jean 129, 132–5
Bougainville 59
Bourassa, Henri 201–2, 212n64
box barrage 353
Brandon, Laura 333
Bridges, William Throsby 129
Bridoux Salient 359
Brighton, Indian troops in 254–8
Bringing Up the Guns (Power) 345
Britain: enlistment in 6, 193; entry into First World War 22–3; First World War commemorations in 431–7; global strategy of 4–5; importing skilled workers from Empire 227; monitoring of aliens in 383; physical stature in 423–4, 428n33; physical stature in 311n38; religious traditions in 76; war spending in United States 23
British Army: black service in 383–6; flogging in 420; medical inspections in 423; native units of 421–2; officer-to-men ratio 270n29
British Empire: civilizing mission of 426; cultural commonalities of 318; declaration of war 40, 128; delegation to Versailles 38; Hughes' vision for 274, 288–9; indigenous attachment to 168; manpower mobilization

from 6–8; official view of 38; origins of troops *140*; in post-war period 8–9, 32–4, 276–83; racial ideology of 174, 182, 184, 190n1, 253, 381; remembrance of First World War 1–2; resource mobilization of 111, 125; role in First World War 3–4, 11–12, 15, 31–2; shared war experience of 215–16, 435–7; South African loyalty to 45, 53; sub-imperialism within 56–7
British Guiana 382, 392, 424
British Honduras 36, 383, 424
British identity 273, 379, 381
British Indian Army 111n2; *see also* Indian Army
British League (South Africa) 49, 51, 208
Britishness: and centenary commemorations 433; hierarchy of 379, 381, 385, 396–7; William Hughes' sense of 273–4, 285, 291
British Nigerian Company 243
British race theory 273, 275, 280, 282, 423
British settler Dominions *see* Dominions
British shell crisis 111
British soldiers: diet of 96, **98**; in Jerusalem 76, 80; in Mesopotamia 110–11
British War Cabinet 40
British West Indies *see* West Indies
British World 228n4
Brocas, Thomas 411
Brockenhurst 257, 407
Broken Hill 224
Broodseinde 136
Brookes, Herbert 220
Brothers, Grace 245
Bryant, Charles 335
Bulgaria 26–7, 147
Bullecourt 136, 357
The Bulletin: cartoons and illustrations from 173, *179*, *180*, *182*, 185, *186*; as white supremacist journal 174
bully beef 117, 325
Bülow, Bernhard von 21
Burns, James 63, 70
Burns Philp and Co 59, 64
Burrowes, T. F. 238, 240, 243, 245, 247n5, 248n37
Buxton, Lord: on Afrikaners 50; as Governor-General of South Africa 41; in South West Africa 66; support for Botha 44, 52–3
BWIR (British West Indies Regiment): creation of 37, 385; as entertainers 426; impression on British 424–5; and national identity 9–10
bye-laws, special 150–1, 159, 169nn10–11

Cairo, EFF in 85, 88
Calcutta: Black Hole of 172, 184, 191n10; munitions factories in 218

Caliphate 25, 89, 96, 119, 374
Camel Corps at Magdhaba (Power) 340–2
camels 36, 101, 103, 110
Camel Transport Corps 36
Cameron, David 429–30, 433–4, 436
Cameron, Don 223
Cameroons 1, 21, 31, 70, 152, 155
Canada: conscription in 7–8; conscription in 310n19; in *The Empire at War* 33; field publications of troops 318–20, 323; Christian denominations in 310n25; French-Canadian opposition to war 201–2; lending to Britain 9; market for Caribbean goods 36; munitions movement in 216, 218, 223–4, 226; position of rejected volunteers in 15, 293–4, 307–9; recruitment in 6, 31, 307–8; and United States 280; war memorials of 3; war service badges in 307, 312n47
Canadian Corps 138–9
Canadian Field Ambulance 328
Canadian First Nations (Indians) 10
Candler, Edmund 97
Canterbury Mounted Rifles 81
Cape Coast 152–3, 155–7, 159–64, 167–8
Cape Corps 199–201
Cape South African Native Congress 199
Caribbean *see* West Indies
carob beans 147
cartoons: in field publications 320–1, **325**, 329–30; on home front 320, 331n6; of 'the Hun' 172; and Palestine campaign *78*, *79*, *80*, *84*; in pre-war Dominion periodicals 316; racist imagery in 174–7
Casely Hayford, J. E. 154, 158
cattle cake 235–6
Caucasus 25–6, 122
Cawnpore 184
CEF (Canadian Expeditionary Force): Attestation papers *295*–8; English-born members of 301, 310n25, 324–5; rejected volunteers for 292–4, 300–4, 307, 30n39, 312n53 (age *303*; physical data of *303*–4, 305–6)
Central Province, Gold Coast 150–2, 157–9, 162–4, 167–8
Ceylon 31, 33, 218
Ceylon Sanitary Company 32
C.F.A.O. 237, 239, 249n50
Chamberlain, Austen 256–62, 264, 270n16, 369–70, 372
Chamberlain, Joseph 32, 174
Chanak incident 9, 273, 286–8
chaplains 81, 392
Charles, Havelock 255, 257–8
Charlottenburg 373
Chauvel, Henry 133–5

INDEX

Cheshire Regiment 387
chest expansion *303*, 311n35
children, in atrocity propaganda 183–5
Chilembwe, John 8
China: Australian interest in 288; entry into war 27; Japanese ambitions in 28; at Washington Conference 284
Chinese Labour Corps 31–2
Chinese people: Australian demonization of 172–3; Germans compared to 182
Chirol, Valentine 254–5, 260
chivalric ideology 81
Choiseul Plantation Company 59
Christian, G. W. 238, 248nn37–40
Christianity: muscular 425; and recruitment on Gold Coast 150, 161–2
Christiansen, Charles 362–4
Christie, Loring 279–80
Christmas cards 86, *87*, *88*
Churchill, Winston 9, 265
Church of the Holy Sepulchre 80–1, 83
Church of the Nativity 83
cigarettes 147–8, 357
ciphers 354
citizenship: of Indians 282; and military service 420; modern concepts of 433; in South Africa 200
citizens' journalism 318
citizen-soldier 315–16, 318
Clarke, F. S. A. 81
Clauson, John Eugene 143–4, 146–7
Clayton, Gilbert 118–19, 121
Clifford, Hugh 153, 167,169n9
CO (Colonial Office): and black workers in Britain 393; and Cyprus 145; and Lucas' history 1, 32; on Melanesia and Micronesia 57, 59, 63; and Nigerian trading 236, 240–2, 244; and relations with Dominions 280; and seized German assets 68; and South West African diamonds 62, 65, 73n37; and war histories 33; and West African recruitment 155
Coates, Roy 300
Cochin 109
cocoa 36, 166, 234, 236, 240, 245, 249n65
Cocos Island 37
Colby, Martin 308
Cold War 19, 22, 28
Cole, Joe 392
collaboration, and imperialism 69–71, 71n1
Colombo cenotaph 3
Colonial Bank 245
Colonial Conferences 276
colonial labour 31–2; *see also* black workers
colour bar 46, 254–5, 390
combat culture 328

the 'combine' (Nigeria) 237, 239, 241, 245
comfort parcels 410
comic strips 315–16, 321–2, 324
Committee of Imperial Defence 24, 33, 57, 143
commodities, strategic 61, 69
Commonwealth Bank 59, 65
Company of African Merchants 237, 243, 247n6, 248n43
Company of African Traders 237
Conrad von Hötzendorff, Franz 21, 25
conscription: Australian referendums on 186, 230n53, 275, 357; in Britain 385–6; and commemoration 436; Dominion resistance to 7–8, 70, 232n110
Consolidated Diamond Mines of South West Africa Ltd 67
Consolidated Mines Selection 65–7
conspiracy theories 246
convalescent homes 14, 145
Cook, Joseph 128
Cook, Percy 358
Cooker, Chief 152, 157, 162, 165
Cooperative Wholesale Society 243
copper 61, 224
copra 59–60, 64–5, 69
Cork 8
Coronel 24
corporal punishment 60, 271n48, 420
Cox, Herbert 266–8
Creswell, F. H. P. 206
Crewe, Lord 98, 254–6, 260, 271n34
Crimea 146
Crombie Steadman 244
Crozier, Frank 335
Cruikshank, Mary 375–6
Crusades 75
Ctesiphon 97
Cull, William 358
Currie, Arthur 138
Curzon, Nathaniel 9, 261, 281–2, 284
Cutlack, Frederic 344
Cypriot Mule Corps 144
Cyprus: annexation of 142; convalescent homes in 145; in *The Empire at War* 33, 35; enlistment from 144–5; espionage in 146–7; home front in 14, 148; refugees in 143, 146–7; supplies from 147; wartime measures in 143
Cyprus Convention 142, 148n1
Cyprus Military Police 35
Cyrenaica 118–19

Daily Gleaner 387–8
Dallas, Lieutenant-Colonel 103
Damascus 135

INDEX

Dardanelles campaign 115–16, 121, 131, 145; *see also* Gallipoli
Darwinism, racist misapplication of 265, 381, 425
Davis, Edmund 65
Day, Charles William 423
Dayal, Har 371
Deakin, Alfred 128, 174, 290
Deane, Percy 65, 273–4, 279
death, euphemisms for 324
De Beers 62–3
debtor prisoners 164, 170n15
De Burger 44
Defence Act 1903 (Australia) 129
dehumanisation 183
de la Rey, Koos 41, 43, 49, 203–4
The Deliverance of Jerusalem 80
Delville Wood 3, 42
Dernancourt 136
Der Weltkrieg 2, 21
Desert Column 133–4
desertion: historical silence on 352; by Indian soldiers 373–4; from Ottoman Army 97; on Western Front 330, 351, 360–2
Desert Mounted Corps 133–5
Desmore, Abe 201
Deutsche Afrika Bank 61
Deutsche Kolonial Gesellschaft 66–7
de Wet, Christiaan 41–2, 203–4
Diamanten Regie 62, 69
diamonds, from South West Africa 57, 61–3, 66, 69–70
diaries: Bean and Treloar collecting 337; as officer-class form 316; Orientalism in 74, 89; of POWs 352, 360
Diehl, Gustav 413
Discontogesellschaft 65
disparagement humour 14, 315, 324, 330
Dix, William 308
domesticity, flight from 404
dominion nationalism 56
Dominions: aspiration for status 40; enthusiasm for war in 193, 330; field publications of soldiers 315; independent foreign policy of 277, 284–5, 287–9; nation-making in 5, 43, 278; relations with British government 10, 70–1, 275–6, 281–2, 286; victory march of 384; war commemoration in 3, 436; war effort of 1–2; on Western Front 24, 424
donkeys 100–1, 105, 110, 147
'Doppers' 203, 205, 210
Downes, Alonza 395
Dresden (ship) 36
Drummond, Norman 434
Dube, John 200, 207
du Bois, W. E. B. 426

Duff, Beauchamp 264
Duggan, Herrick 311n42
Duguid, A. Fortescue 311n39
Duncan, Samuel 242
Dunkwa 158–9
Dunn, J. C. 423
dysentery 96, 100, 110
Dyson, Will 334, 337

East Africa: Chinese labour in 31; enlistment in 6; German tactics in 25; Gold Coast soldiers in 152, 161–3; historiography of First World War in 12; South African intervention in 42
Easter, in Jerusalem 80
Easterbrook, Claude Cadman 339–40
Eastern Christianity 82–3
Eastern Front 25, 331n4, 367
Eastern Province, Gold Coast 150–1, 155, 158, 162, 166–8
Easter Rising, Dublin 1916 8, 398n27, 435
East Prussia 25–6
Écourt-Saint-Quentin 357
Edmonds, James 2
EEF (Egyptian Expeditionary Force): Anzac Mounted Division in 133–5; and crusading rhetoric 74–7, 80–2, 84–5; education for 88–9; Indianization of 84; official history of 90n1; and orientalism 85–7, 90; religious attitudes among 14, 82–3; in war histories 2, 36
eggs 35, 147
Egypt: AIF in 132; in British official war history 21; desertion of Indian soldiers in 374; EEF's cultural experience of 85, 87–8; in *The Empire at War* 34, 36–7; expanding campaign out of 11; Ottoman interests in 26; Sanussiyya jihad against 14, 115–17, 122; strategic importance of 121; West Indian troops in 37, 385
Egyptian Labour Corps 85, 133
Egyptian Revolution 8, 27
Ejesa Osora, E. A. 392, 400n80
Ekumfi 163, 167
Elder Dempster 234, 236, 241, 243–4
Elder Dempster African Sailors' Hostel 392
electric light 108, 146
Ellis, Alfred Burdon 421–2
Elmina 162–3, 167
emotional survival 316
emotions, history of 327, 405
empire, crisis of 9
The Empire at War (Lucas) 1, 31, 33–8
EMSIB (Eastern Mediterranean Special Intelligence Bureau) 142, 146–7
Enemy Trading Bill 1915 (South Africa) 49, 208

446

INDEX

England: recruitment in 385; UK commemoration funding in 434; *see also* Britain
English public schools 20, 262
English sickness 195
Ennes, Isaac 387
Enver Pasha 118–20
espionage 142, 146, 352
esprit de corps 325
Eterpigny Bridge 340
eugenics 423–4
Euphrates, River 97, 100–2, 105, 108
Europe, global centrality of 22
European colonies in Africa 151
European Union 433
Evans, Richard 432–3
Everett, Lionel 382, 390–2
expatriate firms 234, 236–8, 241, 244–6
eyesight, substandard 299, 304, 306, 308
Ezra's Tomb 108

Falkland Islands 3, 20, 24, 130
Falls, Cyril 2, 20, 75
Famagusta 35, 143–4, 146–8
Fante people 157–8, 160–1
Fao 95, 97
Farage, Nigel 432
Farmer, Hugh 323
fathers of soldiers: bereaved 412–14; letters to 404–6; serving alongside sons 403–4, 406–7; sons' support for 411–12; support for sons 409–11; writing to sons 407–8
Federal Munitions Committee (Australia) 219–21, 225
Federal Reserve Board 23
Federated Malay States *see* Malaya
Ferguson, Harold 360–1
Ferguson, Ronald Munro 258–9
Fezzan 118
Fiddes, George 240
field publications 315–21, 324–5, 327–30, 330–1n4, 331n7; cartoons from *317, 319–23*, **325**, *326–7*
Fiji 6, 32
Fildes, Luke 337
financial crisis of 1907 22
financial liabilities 161
Fink, Molly 258
First Contingent of CEF 292, 294, 301, 304
First World War: British experience of 434; centenary commemorations of 15, 429–31, 436–7; colonial legacies of 12, 437; exposure of received beliefs by 269; as global war 10–11, 16n10, 19–20; as imperial conflict 4–5, 23–4; imperial narratives of 5–6, 12–13; motivations for entering 26–7; national births during 9–10, 228; official British history of *see Official History of the Great War*; use of term 21–2; veterans' recollections of 91n36, 334, 339, 345, 349; wave of unrest following 381
Fischer, J. J. 242
Fisher, Andrew 63, 128, 334
Fitch, Ernest 359
Fitzpatrick, Frank 353–4
Flavelle, James 218
Foch, Ferdinand 136
food shortages 32, 117, 147
forced recruitment 166
Forrest, John 174
Fourie, Josef 204
Fourteen Points 276, 288
Fowle, W. H. 65, 68
France: African colonies of 24, 26, 165–6; Armenian volunteer legion of 146; centrality in First World War 126–7; Labour Corps in 31; enlistment from colonies 24, 421; historiography of empire 5; Indian troops in 255, 260
'franglais' 318
Franz Josef, Emperor of Austria-Hungary 21–2
French, John 257, 261, 370
French-Canadians 202, 310n25
French Revolution 330n4
Fritz's Folly 361–2
Fromelles, battle of 136, 351–2, 354–5, 359, 364
fruits, fresh 99–100, 424
Fullwood, Henry 335
funerals 150–1, 159–60, 168–9, 384
Furedi, Frank 433
FVR (files on volunteers who were rejected) 294

Gaiser, G. L. 239
Gallipoli: Australian and New Zealand commemoration of 3, 9, 127, 436; bravery at 403; in British official war history 21; Cypriots at 145; Entente forces at 131–2; and European theatre 11–12; Maltese at 35; POWs having served at 357, 359–60, 362
Gallipoli (film by Weir) 4
Gandhi, Mohandas 8, 15, 195, 210, 214n112
Garner, Charles 300
Garner, W. W. 223
Gaunt, Ernest 356
Gaza: EEF defeats at 80, 134; Rarotongans at 2; and Suez campaign 11
gender, in recruitment propaganda 187
Genghis Khan 189–90

INDEX

George V, King 258–9, 270n15, 271n34
German Army, field publications from 331n4
German assets: in Nigeria 239–40, 242–3; in occupied territories 56, 63–7, 69–71
German colonies: Dominion capture of 13, 42, 56, 63–4, 71; pre-war relations with Dominions 57
German East Africa 25, 37, 42
German East Asiatic Squadron 129
German New Guinea 57–9, 129
Germans: cartoon depiction of 321, 331n6; in India 260; in South Africa 197, 200, 208–9; in South West Africa 66
Germany: African sympathy for 209–10; Afrikaner support for 49; atrocity stories about 156, 172–3, 183–4; Australian attitudes to 180; colonial practices of 154–6, 158, 208; and First World War commemorations 432–3; former POWs settling in 373; global strategy of 10, 13, 20–1, 24–5, 370–1; and Indian nationalism 369–70; and Nigerian economy 15, 223, 227, 234–6, 238, 240; racial caricature of 174, 178–82, 187, 189–90 (*see also* 'the Hun'); reparations imposed on 275; and Sanussiyya jihad 118–19, 122; shipping blockade of 5, 23; surrender of 19, 27
Ghadrite movement 7, 371
Gibraltar 33–5, 147
Gilbert, Vivian 76–7
Gilbert, Web 2
Gilkison, Robert 407
Gillard, Julia 127
Gillett, Arthur 193
Glasgow 108, 382, 388–9
glycerine 226, 235–6, 242
goats 35, 147
Gold Coast (later Ghana): chieftaincy in 153–4, 157–8, 167; conditions of service of recruits **156**, 157; enlistment from 382, 387; gratuities for disablement **157**; migrant workers from 392; newspapers in 152, 154–6, 164, 168; normative culture in 151, 159–60; palm oil from 242; protest migration to 170n16; recruitment in 14, 150–3, 158–9, 162–4, 166–8; use of firearms in 165–6
Gold Coast Leader 150, 153–6, 158, 161, 163–7
Gold Coast Nation 150, 154–6, 162–3
Gold Coast Regiment 152
Gold Coast Volunteer Force 155
Goldie, George 238
gold mining *see* mining
gold standard 4, 22
Gomoa 163, 167

Gool, A. H. 199, 201
Goold-Adams, Hamilton 142–3, 145
Gordon, James 422
Gorges, E. H. L. 61, 67
gorillas, symbolism of 178–9, 181, 185
Gove, Michael 432–3
Government of India: colonial nature of 104–5; and Indian Army deployment 6; and Mesopotamian campaign 94–5, 98, 104, 109–11, 253; and munitions 218; and repatriating prisoners 372; and South Africa 46
Gower, A. A. 409
Graaff, David de Villiers 66–7, 70
Grace, R. F. T. 409
Graham, J. W. 300
Grainger, John 75, 90n3
Gray, David 409
Great Eastern Hotel Company 98
Greater Britain 128, 141
The Great Illusion 4
Great War, Entente use of term 19, 21–2, 24
Greece 26, 144, 147
Grenada 383, 424
Grey, Edward 22–3, 121
grief 403–4, 412–14, 431
Grobler, Piet 196
Grogan, Archibald 312n49
groundnuts 234–6, 238–9, 245, 248n35
Grunshi, Alhaji 1
GSWA (German South West Africa): Afrikaner resistance to intervention 8, 41–2, 49–50, 68, 196, 202–3, 205; Cape migrant workers in 200; commandeered forces used in 42–3; costs of campaign 46, 60–1; fear of invasion from 208;), German assets and residents in 65–8, 70; labour movement backing for invasion 206; memorials to intervention in 3; non-white support for intervention 199; occupation of 58, 61; pre-war relations with South Africa 57; South African retention of 56, 63
guest workers 381
Gulf of Paria 36
Guli Jan 373–6
Gullet, Henry 338
gur 99, 101, 103
Gurkhas 20, 96, 183, 370
Gwalior, Maharaja of 9

Habibullah, Emir of Afghanistan 27, 371
Hagen, Hermann 362–3
Hague Convention 355
Haking, Richard 352, 354, 364
Hall, Bernard 338
Harcourt, Lewis 50, 63, 153, 202

INDEX

Harcourt Papers 52
Harding, A. J. 242
Harding, Warren G. 281, 284
Hardinge, Lord: Chamberlain's communication with 270n16; dispatching Indian Army 253–4; and Indian hospitals 255–6; and Indian officers 261, 263–4; and Mesopotamian campaign 6, 95; and Rajah of Pudukota 258–60; on Willcocks 271n34
Hare, Steuart 81
Harris, Les 410
Harris, T. H. 244
Hatton, S. F. 84–5
Haywood, A. H. W. 155
hereniging 50, 52–3
hernias 304–6
Hertzog, J. B. M. 43–4, 47, 51–3, 195–6, 202–4
Het Volk 196
Heyes, Tasman 338
Hindenburg Line 125
Hindu Biscuit Factory 98
Hindu soldiers 96
Hinton, James 195
history wars 430, 432
Holderness, Thomas 258, 261–3, 270
Holland: diamond sales via 61–2; in First World War 5; margarine production in 236, 243
Holmes, Brigadier 57–60, 63
home front: historiography of 12; propaganda for 321, 324, 328–9; reducing distance from 404
Honeysett, Joseph 357
Hong Kong 6, 231n96
Hong Kong and Singapore Mountain Battery 31
Hopkins, Livingston 174, *175*, 176–7
Horner, Alfred 425–6
horses: from Cyprus 143, 147; in Mesopotamian campaign 96, 100, 103, 109–10
Houplines 360, 362
Hudson, H. 264–5
Hughes, Charles 284
Hughes, R. H. W. 108
Hughes, Sam 218, 220, 224, 300
Hughes, William: at 1921 Imperial Conference 279–83; on Australian nationhood 277–8; and British conduct of the war 10, 275; and Chanak crisis 286–7; and conscription referenda 7; on intra-imperial communications 273, 282, 289–90; and occupation of New Guinea 63–5, 71; at Paris Peace Conference 273–6; and shipping 227; and trade policy 60; and Washington Conference 284–6

Hull, Henry 66–7, 72n32
humour, in trench publications 318, 320–1, 324–5, 328, 330
'the Hun': and atrocity propaganda 183–5, 190; Australian version of 180–1; demonization of 14, 172–4; use of stereotype in South Africa 208
Hunt, Atlee 64
Hunt, Tristram 432
Hurley, Frank 338
hybridity 174–6, 179, 182, 184–5
Hyderabad 109

iconophobia 83
ICU (Industrial and Commercial Workers Union) 46
identity, collective 328, 330
IEF (Indian Expeditionary Force): officers in 260–1; sent to Western Front 254
IEF D 95–8, 100, 104, 110–11
imagined communities 318
Imperial Camel Corps 133
Imperial Conferences: 1909 128; 1917–8 46; 1918 264; 1921 273, 277, 279–84; first 276
Imperial Diamond Taxation Ordinance 63
Imperial Fleet 128, 131
Imperial Mounted Division 134
Imperial Munitions Board 218
Imperial War Cabinet 10, 40, 64
Imperial War Conference 40, 275–6
Imperial War Museum 338, 429
Imvo Zabantsundu 207–8
The Incident for Which Lieutenant F.H. McNamara Was Awarded the VC (Power) 340–1, *342*
India: British racial attitudes towards 253–4; constitutional reform in 9; contribution to war effort 46, 268; in *The Empire at War* 33, 37–8; enlistment in 6, 24, 31, 265, 268–9, 271–2n49; extraction of resources from 105; Hughes on 282, 289; munitions movement in 216, 218, 223–4, 226; Muslim population of 371; representatives at Imperial Conference 279; *see also* Government of India
Indian Army: commissions in 260; components of 111n2; German appeals to POWs from 14, 371–2; impact of racial ideology on 268; recruitment to 96–7; relations between British and Indians in 99, 261–3, 265; unrest in 7; war contribution of 6–7, 34
Indian Bearer Companies 46
Indian Constitutional Conference 265
Indian followers 99, 103, 110
Indian hospitals 253, 255–8

449

Indian Independence Committee 371, 373
Indian labour companies 266–9
Indian Legislative Council 254
Indian military hospitals in Britain 14
Indian Mutiny 173, 184, *185*, 269
Indian National Congress 46
Indian nationalists, German support for 369–71
Indian Ocean 105–6, 121, 131
Indian princes 9, 259
Indian Relief Act 46
Indians, in South Africa 46
Indian soldiers: commemoration of 436–7; diet of 96, 98–100, *99*, 103–4, 147; in Dominion victory march 384; King's commissions for 260–8, 271n39; mutiny in Singapore 20; as POWs 369–73, 375–6, 376n9; use against Europeans 254–5, 369; *see also* sepoys
Indian Soldiers' Fund 257–8, 370
India Office: and commissions for Indian soldiers 266; and munitions movement 218; and POWs 373–5, 377n26; and war histories 16n5; and women in Indian hospitals 255–6, 258
indigenous populations 10
indirect rule 153
Indo-China 24
industrialisation, in South Africa 45
Inland Water Transport Fleet 106, 108
International Socialist (weekly) 316
internment, in South Africa 58, 65, 197, 208
Invercargill 406
Ireland: in British centenary commemorations 435; munitions movement in 216, 219, 223, 225–6; nationalist insurgency in 8–9, 37, 283; opposition to war in 201; recruitment in 385; *see also* Northern Ireland
Irish Free State 283, 285, 288, 291, 435
Irish people: discrimination against 390; racial caricature of 181
irrigation canals 103, 108
Islam: al-Senussi's defence of 119–20; crusading against 74; and European imperialism 116; *see also* Muslims
Islamic culture, EFF encounter with 85–6
Islamic revolution 13, 25–6
Islington, Lord 259, 261–2
Italy: entry into war 27; fund raising in United States 23
Ivory Coast 166, 170n16

Jabavu, D. D. T. 207
Jaffa Gate 77
Jamaica: conscription in 36; enlistment from 1, 6, 387–8, 424–5; ex-serviceman settlement schemes 10; repatriated workers from 384; slave troops in 420; workers in Liverpool from 382–3, 389, 391
Japan: admired by African Americans 190n3; Australian distrust of 59, 63, 276–81, 290; British communities in 37; Chinese interests of 279; entry into war 27–8
Japanese people, racial caricatures of 14, 172, 174, 177
Jaurès, Jean 207
Jebel Hamrin 110
Jerusalem: Anglican bishop in 81–2; capture of 11, 74–5, 77–8, 135; EFF attitudes to 80, 82–3, 85
Jewish refugees in Cyprus 146
Jewish South Africans 208, 210
jihad: British interpretation of 119–21; Caliphate declaration of 370–1, 374; of Sanussiyya order 115–16, 118
John Holt 237–8, 243
Johnston, John 390
Johnstone, Cornelius 388
Johnstone, T. B. 244–5
Johore, Rajah of 258
Jolley, F. R. 57, 65
Jones, Arthur 392
Jones, Carwyn 435
Jones, David Ivon 206
Jones, Joseph 394
Jones, Vera 396
Jordan Valley 1, 37
Judas Maccabeus 74–5, 80
July crisis 25
Jurgens and Van Den Bergh 236, 243, 245, 250n83, 251n104
Just War defence 173, 183

Kalgoorlie 215, 221, 225
Kano 235, 239, 243–4
Kapurthala, Maharajah of 258–9
Karaolos 146
Karlsruhe (ship) 36
Kenny, Mary 396
Keogh, Alfred 255, 257
Khalifa *see* Caliphate
Khalil Pasha 104
Khan, Abdul Aziz 375–6
Khan, Mala 372
Kieselbert, Gefreiter 353–4
King, George 392
King, Thomas 408
King's African Rifles 16n17
Kingsley, Charles 423, 426
King's Own Malta Regiment of Militia 35
King's Royal Rifle Corps 32
Kipling, Rudyard 183–4
Kitchener, Lord 5, 128, 217, 255, 269, 411

INDEX

Koton, Karimu 244–5
Kriegsmarine 10
Krobo 162
Kultur 26, 189
Kumasi 158, 165–6, 169n7
Kut disaster 7, 94–8, 102–5, 108, 110–11

Labour Legions 206
labour movement: in Australia 205–6; in South Africa 44–6, 195, 205–7 (*see also* SALP)
Ladybrand 202
Lady Hardinge Hospital 257–8
Lagos 234, 236–9, 241–6
Lagos Stores 237, 244
Lajj 97
Lake, Percy 102–3
Lambert, George 335
Langley, George 341–2
Larnaca 143, 146
'The Last Crusade' (cartoon) 78
Latin America, British communities in 37
Lawrence, T. E. 74–5
Lawrence, Walter 255–7, 270n15
Lawrence of Arabia (film) 4
laxatives 328
Leaders of the Australian Light Horse in Palestine, 1918 (Power) 342
League of Nations: Britain in 273; as constraint on power 279; Dominion membership of 40, 275, 277–8, 280; hopes for 28; Hughes' criticism of 281–2, 285, 288; US staying outside 280
League of Nations mandates 11, 56, 277
Lee-Enfield rifles 219
Le Hamel 137
Leist, Fred 335
Lenin, Vladimir 27
Le Queux, William 185
Les Armées Françaises dans la Grande Guerre 21
Lesotho 32
letters: from Australia and New Zealand 407–8; in AWM collection 337; from Canadian rejectees 293, 300, 311n42; from Egypt 117; from Palestine 74, 81, 83, 86, 88–9; prisoners in possession of 354–6, 360; from soldiers to parents 403, 405–6; as top-down form 316
Lettow Vorbeck, Paul von 1, 25, 42
Lever Brothers 237, 244–5; *see also* Unilever
Leverhulme, Lord 245
Lewis, William 414
liberal values 253
Libya, Italian invasion of 4, 116, 120
lice 318, 328, 411

lieux de mémoire 1, 3, 15n3; *see also* memory, sites of
Limassol 35, 143–6
Lindsay, Norman 172–4, 178–82, 184–5, 187, 190, 191n5; cartoons by *176*, *178*, *179*, *180*, *182*, *186–8*
The Listening Post 317–19, 323, 331n7; cartoons from *320–3*, *327*, *329*
'live and let live' 321
Liverpool: black colonial residents in 380–3, 385–94, 396, 397n3; black sailors at 393–4; palm products dealers in 235–7, 242; wives of black residents 395–6
Lloyd George, David: and global theatres 11; as Munitions Minister 217, 225; and Palestine campaign 77–8; and self-determination 51–2; and William Hughes 274–7, 284–5
logistics: and Allied victory 139; at Gallipoli 132; revolution in 111; use of term 95–6
London, as financial centre 4, 22–3
London and Kano Trading 238
Long, Walter 48
Longstaff, John 335
Longstaff, Will 335, 350
looting 58, 356
Lovekin, Arthur 223
Lowe, William 413
Lubbert, Erich 66–7
Lübcke, Fritz 359–60
Lucas, Charles: biography of 32–3; on Gold Coast recruitment 162; writings on the war 1, 33–4
Lucas, W. H. 59, 64–5
Ludendorff, Erich 136–7
Luderitzbucht 41, 57–8, 61, 63, 66
Lugard, Frederick 239–40, 242, 245
Lusitania 42, 49, 189, 207–8, 215–16, 228n9
Luxor 85, 87

MacDonald, Ramsay 288, 290
Macedonian front 27, 144
Macedonian Mule Corps 144–5
MacInnes, Rennie 81–2
MacIver 237, 244
Mackennal, Bertram 2, 334
MacMunn, George 2
MacNeill Scott 237, 244
Magasis 104
Magil 101, 105
*mahaila*s 102
Malan, D. F. 204
Malan, F. S. 42, 63, 67, 201
malaria 100, 144, 306
Malaya 31, 218, 258
Malay Ambulance Corps 199

INDEX

Malay Ford Van Motor Company 31
malingering 324, 328
Malone, Norah 406
Malone, William 403–4, 406–7
Malta 6, 33, 35, 143, 147
Maltese Labour Corps 35
Maltese refugees 146
Mangin, Charles 24
Manifesto (of Lagos traders) 241–2, 244, 249nn64–5
Manley, Norman 386
Mann, Tom 206
Manual of Military Law 385–6
Maori 10, 200, 210
maple leafs 302
margarine 235–6, 245
Maritz, Manie 41, 49, 204
Marke, Ernest 383–4, 386, 389, 397n1, 398n12
marriage: in African normative culture 159–61, 168; and masculine status 410; mixed-race 253–4, 259–60, 262, 395
Marseilles 32, 98, 256, 266, 373
Marshall, W. R. 104, 110
martial law 41, 43, 58, 143, 165, 204
martial races theory 265–6, 268, 422
Martin, John 388
Martinique 36
Marwick, Arthur 269
Marx, Karl 246
masculinity 403–5, 409, 423–6
*mashhuf*s 108
Massey, William 285, 413
Materialschlacht 95
Maude, Stanley 104, 111
Mauritius 6, 32, 41, 383
Maxwell, John 8, 119–20
Maypole Dairy 236, 243
McCallum, Alexander 222
McCauley, Tommy 383, 386
McCraig, Charles 406
McCubbin, Louis 335
McIntosh, L. 387
McKenzie, Colin 392
McMahon, Henry 121
McNamara, Frank 341
meat, preserved 98–9, 104
medical examinations 294–300, 302, 307–8, 309nn3,6, 423
medical examinations
Megiddo 7, 75–6, 83–4
Meighen, Arthur 279–81, 283
Melanesia: European ruling minorities in 69; German possessions in 57, 59; Japanese and Australian spheres of occupation 63
Memorial Gates on Constitution Hill in London 3

memory: arbiters of 334; sites of 2, 333, 349–50
memory cultures 429–30, 434, 436
Menin Gate at Midnight (Longstaff) 350
Menin Road 136, 360–1
merchant capital 246
merchant navy 35, 380, 384, 392
Mesopotamia: in British official war history 21; building of infrastructure in 105–6, 108–9, 226; colonial forces in 31–2; historiography of First World War in 12; logistics of campaign 14, 94–8, 102–5, 110–11; medical facilities in 100, 110; river traffic in 107; transport animals in 109–10; war memorials in 3
Mesopotamia Command 97–8, 101–6, 108, 110
Mesopotamia Commission 104, 264, 271n43
Messines 136, 360
Methodist Church 162, 301–2, 310nn24–6
Mhlolo Myuso Matanzima Mtirara 209
mica 226
Middle East, British expansionism in 11
militarism 31, 33
military efficiency 260, 262, 264
military service, motivations for 405, 420
Military Service Act 1916 386, 398n36
Military Service Board in New Zealand 411
Millars Timber Company 225
Miller, Robert 235, 242, 248n49
Miller Brothers 235, 237–9, 242, 244, 248n43
Mills, Charles 351–2, 364
Milne, Seamus 433
Milner, Alfred 9
Milner, Lord 277, 382
mining: in Gold Coast 154; in Nigeria 235; in South Africa 45; in South West Africa 61; in Western Australia 221
Ministry of Munitions 218–20, 226–7, 229n41, 242
Mir Baz Khan 373–4
Mir Zamir 373–4
miscegenation 175–7
Moberly, F. J. 95
Moltke, Helmuth von (the younger) 25–6
Monarga 35, 146
Monash, John 127, 137–9, 404
monopsony 238
Montagu, Edwin 268
Montagu-Chelmsford reforms 38
Mont St Quentin 404
mood pictures 359
Moore, Charles 433
Morgan, Ellen 396

INDEX

Morgan, J. P. 23
Morlancourt 136
Morley–Minto Reforms 105
Morocco 26, 421
Mosely, Alfred 61–2, 72n19
mosques 81, 85–6, 88, 146, 371
mosquito nets 100
mothers of soldiers 403, 405, 409
Mount Troodos Guards Base Hospital 145
Mouquet Farm 136, 356, 358, 360
mourning: available expressions of 412; mothers and 405; ritual 160
Mozambique 27
Mt Morgan 407
Muir, Donald 353–4
mules: from Cyprus 14, 142–4, 147; in Mesopotamia 96, 100, 103, 110
Muller, Wilhelm 406
multinationality 429, 434
munitions movement 215–18, 220–1, 224, 227
Munro, A. C. 224
Murray, Angus 411
Murray, Archibald 77, 122, 133–4, 146
Murray, J. H. P. 64
Murrison, Andrew 432
music hall 318
Muslims: in British Army 83, 96; of Gold Coast 157; under British rule 121, 370–1
Muslim world: European encroachment on 117; German agitation in 25–6, 370; and Ottoman Empire 37–8; postcards home from 86; Sufism in 120
Mustafa Kemal (Atatürk) 286
mutiny, humour as safety valve for 324, 330
Mysore 109

Nachrichtenstelle für den Orient 371, 373
Nana Sahib 184
Napier, Ernest 411
Napoleonic wars 420
narrative humour 315, 321
Nasiriya 3, 97, 100
Nasrullah 27
Natal 193–4, 197, 209–10
National Conference of British West Africa 244–5
national identity: in Australia 9, 173, 215–16; British 381, 385; in South Africa 198; and war commemoration 430–1
nationalism, German support for 370–1
National Party (South Africa) 44, 47–8, 50–2, 54, 195–6, 202–4
Native Labour Contingents (South Africa) 45
Natives Land Act 1913 (South Africa) 45
Nauen 24
Nauru 57

Navigation Act 1913 (Australia) 64, 69
Netherlands *see* Holland
Neuve Chapelle 217, 369
New Britain 57
New Calabar 237
Newfoundland: in *The Empire at War* 33; enlistment in 6, 31; in victory march 384
New Guinea: Australian conquest of 20, 25, 56–8, 69, 71, 129; Australian retention of 275, 277, 285; economy of 59–60, 64–5; German annexation of 180; as German colony *see* German New Guinea; German residents and assets in 69–70
New Jagersfontein 62–3
newspapers: indigenous African 150–1; of troops *see* field publications
New Zealand: Base Records files 415n17; casualties from 140; conscription in 7, 411; employment for returned soldiers 410; enlistment in 6, 31; enthusiasm for war in 193; fathers of soldiers from 406, 409, 411; munitions movement in 216, 218–19, 224, 226
New Zealand Mounted Rifles 77, 85–6, 133
New Zealand Rifle Brigade 407
New Zealand Social Democratic Party 206
New Zealand Wars 406
NGK (Nederduitse Gereformeerde Kerk) 197–8, 203–5
Nichols, Samuel 387
Nicolai, Walter 352
Niger Company 235–9, 243–5, 247n7, 248n43, 251n96, 252n107
Nigeria: animal feed from 226–7; colonial economy of 246n5; enlistment from 387; , German properties in 239; and munitions movement 218, 223; post-war economy of 244–6; terms of trade in 15, 234, 236–7, 252n106; trading cartel in 235, 237–44; workers in Liverpool from 382
Nigeria Debate in House of Commons 243
Nixon, John E. 95, 102, 104, 106
Nkrumah, Kwesi 164
Nkusukum 157, 163, 167
Nonconformist church 197, 310n25
Northampton Independent 79, 80
North China, British communities in 37
Northern Ireland, war commemoration in 435
Northern Territories, Gold Coast 152, 165, 169nn1,4
Norval, Stanley 302
Nuri Bey 119–20
Nur-ud-din 104
Nyasaland 8, 226
NZEF (New Zealand Expeditionary Force) 226, 405, 410, 415n17

INDEX

O'Brien, Robert 408
Official History of Australia in the War of 1914–1918 (Bean) 352–3, 361
Official History of the Great War 2, 19, 21
Ofori Atta, Nana 159
OHL (Oberste Heeresleitung) 353, 359, 363
oil: discovery in Persia 94; in Mesopotamia 14; from Trinidad 36
oligopsony 245–6
Omu Okwei 238, 246
onions 35, 100, 147
Onitsha 238, 245, 248n40
Operation Michael 136
Operations in Persia, 1914–1919 (Moreby) 16n5
opium 104
Oppenheim, Max von 27, 371, 373
Oppenheimer, Ernest 65–7, 70
oral culture 318
Orange Free State 41, 51, 194–6, 202–3
Orange Order 302
orientalism: in British Army 422; vernacular 74, 85, 89–90
Orientalism (Said) 89, 92n53
Oriental tropes 173–5, 184, 190, 190n2
O'Riordan, Sydney 412
Osborn, Alfred 412
ostrich farmers 202
Othering 172–3, 175, 185, 187
Ottoman Army, manpower problems of 97
Ottoman Empire: Britain undermining 11; dismantling of 9; and Indian nationalism 369–71; joining Central Powers 25–6, 28; railways in 108–9; as representing Islam 7, 74, 370; rhetoric of Britain against 14; and Sanussiyya jihad 115–19, 122
Ovambo people 58, 61
overseas pay question 46–7, 52

pacifists 19, 182, 197, 205–7, 302
painting, academic tradition of 335–6
Palestine: AIF in 133–4; in British official war history 21; disputes between Christians in 83; EEF's cultural experience of 88–9; in *The Empire at War* 34; end of war in 27; expanding campaign into 11; former churches in 81–2; historiography of First World War in 12; Indianization of campaign 6; mythic context of campaign 74–8; propaganda value of 78–80; West Indian troops in 10, 385
Palestine Exploration Fund 80, 89
Palestine News 88
palm kernels 223, 227, 235–8, 245, 251n99
palm oil 235–6, 238, 242, 244–5
palm tree plantings 60
Pan-Africanism 10

Panama Canal Zone 36–7
Pan-Islamic party in Constantinople 118
Papua 57, 59, 64, 69, 285
Paris Peace Conference 52, 66, 71, 273, 275–6, 284
Partridge, Bernard, cartoons by 78–9
pass laws 46
patriotic organizations 410
patriotism, popular 198, 208, 216
peaceful penetration 139
Peacock, Robert 347
Pearce, George 125–6, 219–21, 223–5, 230n65, 284–6
Pearse, Samuel 244
peasants: in Africa 194, 210, 246; in Cyprus 147
Peat, Harold 308
Pentland, Lord 258–9
Persia 31, 94
Perth Central Markets 221, 225, 227
Pethebridge, Colonel 59–60
photography, authenticity of 338
physical deformities 307
Piccadilly Farm 353
pickelhaube helmet 14
Piesse, E. L. 278
Pike, B. E. 174, *177*
Plaatje, Solomon 198, 209
Plaid Cymru 435
Plaistowe, Hugh 217, 225
plantation labour 423, 425
Poincaré, Raymond 287
poison gas 215–16, 228n8, 331n12
Polygon Wood 136
poppy wars 435
Port Harcourt 235, 237, 244
Port Said 2
Portugal 27
Portuguese East Africa 63
postcards 86
potatoes 35, 100, 147
Potiorek, Oskar 21
pound sterling 22, 160
POW camps: cartoons from 325; cross-cultural interactions in 12; in Cyprus 146; in Germany 369–72
Power, Harold Septimus 333–5, 339–50
POWs (prisoners of war): Australians as 351–3; in Cyprus 35, 143, 146; German interrogation of 354–9; German processing of 355–6; information gained from 359–60, 362–4; information value of 351–2; from Mesopotamia 97; Ottoman 146, 148; repatriation of 369–70, 372–6; violence and abuse against 357–8
Pozières 136, 139, 359
Pratt, Benjamin 395

INDEX

Premier (Transvaal) Diamond Mining Company 62–3, 69
princely states of India 105, 109, 111n2
Protestantism 82–3
puberty rites 160–1
Pudukota, Rajah of 254, 258–60
Punch 78
Punjab: home front in 12; unrest in 8
Punjab Canal Colonies scheme 105

Quakers 193, 197
Quebec 8, 201, 218
Questions Likely to Arise at the End of the War (Hardinge) 263
Quinn, James 335
Qur'an 85
Qurna 97, 101–2, 108

Rabaul 63, 65, 69–70, 129–30
race, in recruitment propaganda 187, 190
racial difference 190n3
racial discrimination 200
racial identity 9, 12, 280
racial stereotypes 14, 172, 179, 181–4, 190, 420
racism: and black volunteers 379, 381; and Indian soldiers 111; in South Africa 200
Rackett, Archie 358
Raemaekers, Louis 84
'railpolitik' 14
Railway Boards Munitions Branch 218
railways: German plans for 94; in Mesopotamia 108, **109**, 226; in Nigeria 235, 239
raisins 35, 147
Rajputana 109, 265
Rand Club 195
Randell, Wentworth 358
rape 160, 166, 191, 236
Rarotongan boat people 2
Ras el Ain 81
recording devices 358
Red Book of West Africa 241, 244–5, 247n5, 252n110
Red Cross 355, 364, 410
Redmond, John 201
Rees, W. J. 408
regimental literature 16n6
Rehoboth Bastards 58
Reichsbank 22
reparations 56, 68, 70–1, 275
repatriation: of black colonial workers 379–80, 382–3, 393, 396–7; of GSWA colonists 58; of Indian POWs 372–3, 376
Repington, Charles à Court 21–2
Republic of Ireland *see* Irish Free State
resilience 316, 403

'The Return from the Crusade' (cartoon) 79
revolution, Germany promoting 28
RFC (Royal Flying Corps) 104, 133, 135, 355, 365n27, 387–8
Rhodesia 1, 216, 219, 224, 226
Richard I, King of England 76, 78, 80–1, 84
Richards, Samuel 407
the 'Ring' (Nigeria) 237–9, 241–4, 249n50
rioting: anti-black 14, 379–82, 384, 388, 390–1, 394, 396–7, 397n7; anti-German 49, 208, 228n9
Rischbieth, Bessie 228n8
Ritchie, John 389–90
road construction 110
Roberts, Garry 404
Robinson, Reuben 392
Rodney, Walter 246
The Romance of the Last Crusade 76–7
Romani 90n2
Romania 26–7
Roos, Tielman 51
Roper, Robert 411
Ross rifle 218
Royal Army Medical Corps 328, 399n43, 409
Royal Army Service Corps 143
Royal Australian Navy (RAN) 125, 129–31, 141
Royal Canadian Garrison Artillery 36
Royal Canadian Regiment 298, 302
Royal Colonial Institute 33, 37
Royal Engineers Militia 35
Royal Malta Artillery 35
Royal Marines Artillery 36
Royal Marines Light Infantry 36
Royal Naval Air Service 104, 365n27
Royal Navy: black service in 384–5, 387–8, 395; and Empire contribution to war 4–5; Far Eastern power of 278, 281, 283, 285; at Gallipoli 131; in Indian Ocean 105; Maltese in 35; RAN assisting 130; in South Pacific 24; and West Indies 36
Rubusana, Walter 198–9, 201
rum jar 318, *319*
Russell, James 399n43
Russia: enlistment in 24; exiting war 22
Russian Civil War 27
Russian Jews, in South Africa 15
Russian Revolution, February 1917 28

Sackey, Chief 157, 161
Salonika 35–6, 79, 143–5, 147–8, 388
SALP (South African Labour Party) 50, 52, 54, 205–7
Samoa: German residents and assets in 69; New Zealand conquest of 25, 57, 129

INDEX

Sanders, George 408
Sandhurst 262–4
SANNC (South African Native National Congress) 45–6, 54n19, 195, 198–201
Sanussiyya Sufi Order 14, 115–22, 123n3, 124n42
Sarawak 37
sarcasm 330
Sastri, Srinivasa 282
satire 82, 315–16, 320–1, 324, 334
Saving the Guns at Robecq 333, 343, *344*, 345–6, *347*, *348*, *349*–50
Scarbrough, Lord 235, 238
Schlieffen, Alfred von 25
school patriotism 194, 198, 208
Scotland: commemoration of First World War in 434–5; recruitment in 385
Scott, James 335
scurvy 96, 100, 103–4, 110
Seaford Camp 37
Sea Island 36
Sea of Marmara 131
Second International 205
Second World War: becoming global 22; lack of official history 38n14; origins of 28
Sefwi district 164, 166
Seitz diamonds 63
Seitz notes 60–1
Sekhukhune II 201
self-censorship 325, 327–8
self-determination 11, 38, 51, 436
al-Senussi, Ahmed 117–19
al-Senussi, Idris 120, 122
al-Senussi, Muhammad 115
sepoys: collaboration with Germans 371; in First World War 6, 9; relationships with civilians 12; returning home 374–5; on Western Front 369–70; *see also* Indian soldiers
Serbia 21–2, 130, 143, 145
Seton, Bruce 256
Seychelles 6, 32
Shaiba Bund 105
Shantung 20
Shatt-el-Arab 101–2
Sheikh Ajlin 86
Shell Committee 218, 224
shell crisis 217, 227
shell shock 424
Shinn, Max 300
shipping: allocation in Nigeria 241–2, 244; requisitioning 227, 236
Sierra Leone: migrant workers from 382–3, 392; shipping allocations to 242; soldiers from 385–7; wives from 395
Sikhs 7, 20, 96, 183
Sinai 11, 31, 132–3

Singapore: Chinese Labour Corps in 31; and munitions movement 218; mutiny of 5th Light Infantry at 7, 20
Sinn Féin 8, 203, 435
Siwa oasis 117–18
slang 318, 325, 331n7
Slater, A. R. 155, 157, 165, 169n8
slavery: and black bodies 425; and black military service 419–20
Sling camp *317*
Slovenia 27
small nations, rights of 26,191n7
Smart, Henry 335, 337
Smartt, Thomas 48, 52, 55n27, 219
Smith, George Adam 77, 89
SMS *Emden* 105, 130–1
Smuts, Jan: and Afrikaner Rebellion 8, 41–2, 203, 208–9; Afrikaner support for 49; and Botha government 52–3; and East African campaign 42, 48; opposition to British conduct of war 10; and South African identity 44; and South West Africa 68, 70–1; support for war 195–6; in War Cabinet 40; and William Hughes 282–5
Smuts-Gandhi agreement 46
Smyrna 146
Smyth, James 399n43
SNP (Scottish National Party) 434
soap 235, 244, 411
socialists: in South Africa 49, 206–8; and 'total war' 433
soldier-fathers 404
soldier newspapers *see* field publications
soldiers: dependence on families 408–9; future gainful employment of 409–10; as substitute fathers 407
soldier settlement schemes 32, 70
Sollum 115–17
Solomon Islands 59
Somme, physical state of British soldiers at 423
Somme, South African troops at 3, 42
Sommers, Cecil 84–5
South Africa: in African theatre 40–1; commandeering in 42–3; enlistment in 6, 31; entry into war 196; foreign policy of 56; impact of war on 13, 15, 40, 44–5; Indian subjects in 282; munitions movement in 219, 226; national identity in 43–4; non-white communities in 45–6, 198–201, 209; party politics in 46–8, 50–4; popular opinion on war in 193–8, 207–8, 210; seizure of German assets 65–8; war memorials of 3; white population of 49–50, 53, 198

INDEX

South African College School 194, 198
South African Industrial Federation 206
South African Native Labour Contingent 32
South African Party 47, 49–51, 54, 195–6, 198
South African War (1899–1902): Canadian participation in 212n64, 302; former British soldiers from 197; former rebels in GSWA 49, 203; Galton's comments on 423; histories of 34; memories of 193, 195, 203
South West Africa *see* GSWA
South West Africa Company 57, 65
South West Diamond Company 66
South West Finance Corporation 67
SPAO (Society of Peoples of African Origin) 384
Spee, Maximillian von 3, 130
Spencer, Baldwin 334
spiritualism 350
The Splendid Adventure (Hughes) 274, 287–9
sport, and race 425
SS *Chamah* 387, 399n46
SS *Mendi* 32
Statute of Westminster 10
Stauch, A. 66–7
Steel-Maitland, Arthur 240–2
St Eloi 353–4
Sterling, Claudina 395–6
sterling–dollar exchange rate 23
St. John's Ambulance Brigade 255
St Kitts 36, 383
St Lucia 36, 383, 424
Strachan, Hew 433
Streeton, Arthur 335
struck-off-strength (SOS) 301, 311n39
Stuart-Young, J. M. 238, 245, 248nn37, 40
Stubbs, Reginald 33
Sturdee, Admiral 3
St Vincent 36, 383, 424
sub-imperialism 24–5, 71, 211
submarine warfare 36, 152
Suez Canal 2, 6, 11, 116, 118, 121, 133
suffering, culture of 424
Sufism 115, 117, 120–1
suicide 312n53, 413
sun helmets 100
Swakopmund 41, 58
Swaziland 6

Talmage, Algernon 337
Tamils 96
Taranto, mutiny at 10
Tarkwa 154, 158
Tata, Dorabji 216, 218
Tata Iron and Steel Company 109, 218, 226

tattoos 296, 298, 302
teakwood 109
teeth, poor 304–6
telegrams 407, 413–14
Telegu soldiers 96
Tel el Jemme 81
telephones 147
Tenniel, John *181*, 187, 189, 191n5
Thomas, Ivan 300
Thomas, J. C. 244
Thomas, S. 242
Thompson, Frank 219
Thomson, George 410–13
Tigris Corps 98, 102
timber 35, 109, 142, 147–8
tin 234, 245
Tin Areas of Nigeria 238–9, 241–3, 245
Tirpitz, Alfred von 21
tobacco: from Cyprus 142, 147–8; rations of 98; in Red Cross parcels 410
Togoland 1, 152, 154, 156, 162
Tomlinson, Ernest 217, 222
Tomlinson, H. M. 19–20, 22–3
total war: and empire-wide mobilization 6, 8; and imperial unity 9, 12; and socialism 433
tourism, glorified 14, 86, 89–90
Townshend, Charles 9, 95, 97–9, 102–4
Transkei 45, 199, 209
transnationality 429
Transvaal: Afrikaner rebellion in 41; Indians in 46; urbanisation in 44–5
Treaty of Lausanne 4
Treaty of Sèvres 286–7
Treaty of Versailles 28, 56
Treloar, John: on AWM Art Committee 338–40; and official art programme 333–7; and Power's paintings 341–9
trench publications *see* field publications
Trigge, J. E. 236, 238–9, 243, 248n40, 249n51, 250n66
Trinidad 36–7, 383, 424
Tripolitania 118
Troodos Mountains 35, 142, 145
troop-ship publications 320, 331n5
Trumper, Victor 89
Tsingtao 31, 279
Tull, Walter 386
Tunisia, German agitation in 26
Turkey: at Chanak 9, 286; post-conflict ties with Australia and New Zealand 437; *see also* Ottoman Empire
Turkish-Cypriots 144, 146

Ulster loyalists 199
ultra-bereavement 404
Unilever 15, 234

INDEX

Union Defence Force Act 1912 (South Africa) 200
Unionist Party (South Africa) 44, 47, 49–54, 195, 198
United Africa Company 234
United States: Australian relations with 278; entry into war 22, 27; and European finance 22–3; investment in South African mining 66; and Japan 279–81, 284; market for Caribbean goods 36; racial difference in 190n3
urbanisation 13, 44–5

Valcartier mobilization camp 292, 294, 299–302, 304–9, 309n6, 312n49
Van Laun, H. T. 241
van Rensburg, Niklaas 203–4
varicocele 304–6
varicose veins 299, 304–6
Versailles Conference *see* Paris Peace Conference
Viceroy's commission 260
Victoria, Queen 421–2
Victorian Munitions Committee 220
Vierkleur flag 202
Villers-Bretonneux 127, 136–7
Villiers, Theresa 435
Vimy Ridge 331n12
Vincent-Bingley Commission 104
violence, pro-war 208
Volunteer Munition League of Western Australia 224

Wade, Colin 206
WAFF (West African Frontier Force) 1, 156
Wagstaff, Cyril 354
Wales: recruitment in 385; war commemoration in 435
walking-sticks 37
The War and the Empire (Lucas) 33
war commemoration 429–32, 434–7
war experience: artistic recapturing of 339; as common to both sides 321; of labour contingents 32; of POWs 351; universal British 434
war memorials 2–3, 405, 417, 436
War Munitions Supply Company of Western Australia 15, 215, 222–5, 227, 228n2
War on War League 206–7
war relief funds 35
Warren, William 413
warrior tradition 156
Warsi, Sayeeda 436
War Trade Department 61–2, 69
war writing, diction of 84–5
Washington conference 284–6
Waterford 216, 219, 226

water transport units 31–2
Watt, W. A. 64
Wazza 88
weapons systems, integrated 139
Weber, Friedrich 359–60
Wei-Hai-Wei 37
Weltkrieg 20–1, 29
Weltpolitik 21
West Africa: British enlistment in 6; French enlistment in 24; Liverpool's trade with 380; pre-war emigration to Britain 394; sailors from 393, 397n4; shipping from 236–7; West Indian soldiers in 421–2; workers in Liverpool from 382
Western Australia: economy of 221–2; munitions movement in 15, 217, 219–25, 227–8; patriotism in 216–17
Western Desert of Egypt 115–22
Western Front: Allied prisoners from 351–2, 359; Australian divisions on 125, 135–8; historical focus on 2–4; and imperial manpower 6, 9–10; medical services on 328; Scottish deaths on 434; troop publications on 317–18, 321, 327–8, 331n4; West Indian soldiers on 385
Western Province, Gold Coast 154, 158, 165–6
West Indians: attitudes to 14, 426; physique of 424–5; recruitment among 2, 6–7, 9–10, 386–7, 419, 421–2; workers in Liverpool from 382–3
West Indies: communications with Britain 36; in *The Empire at War* 36–7; slavery in 419–21
West Indies Motor Launch Flotilla 36
Wheeler, Charles 340
White, Percy 388
White Australia policy 172–4, 176–7, 282–3
white masculinity 14, 419, 423–4, 426
whiteness 174, 183–4, 190n3
white officers 260, 421–2
white paternalism 184
white supremacy 192, 196
widow rituals 160–1
Wilhelm II, Kaiser of Germany 25, 77–8, 190, 370–1
Willcocks, James 6, 255, 261–4, 271nn34,43
Williams, Colonel 341
Williams, Ralph 395
Williams, Thomas 385, 387
Wilsmore, Norman 224
Wilson, Frank 222
Wilson, Henry 27
Wilson, Martin 311n33
Wilson, Trevor 126
Wilson, Woodrow 11, 28, 51, 274–6, 281, 288

INDEX

Windhoek 41, 58, 61, 69–70
Wingate, Reginald 81, 118–19, 121
Winneba 162, 167
WIR (West India Regiments) 36–7, 420–2
Witwatersrand 45–6, 195, 209, 219
Wolseley, Viscount 422, 424
women: and anti-black racism 390, 395; and Indian men 255–8, 260; married to black colonial workers 381; as munitions workers 222; violence against in propaganda 184–5, 187; and War Munitions Supply Company 215, 224
Woodward, David 75, 90n2
wool question 46, 48
Woolwich Arsenal 217, 224

Wootton, Charles 382, 388–9
world war, German use of term 19–21
Wrangel army 146

Yaro, Maisie 395
Yeo, Allan 361–4
YMCA 88, 375, 407
Younghusband, Francis 33, 37–8
Ypres 32, 184, 216, 350, 363, 369

Zaria 235, 239, 243
Zikr dance 85
Ziza (Power) 339
Zossen 369, 371–3
Zouaves 419, 421–2
Zulu communities 201, 209, 422

Printed in Great Britain
by Amazon